The Natural history of Juan Fernandez and Easter Island Volume v.1

Skottsberg, Carl, 1880-1963

Nabu Public Domain Reprints:

You are holding a reproduction of an original work published before 1923 that is in the public domain in the United States of America, and possibly other countries. You may freely copy and distribute this work as no entity (individual or corporate) has a copyright on the body of the work. This book may contain prior copyright references, and library stamps (as most of these works were scanned from library copies). These have been scanned and retained as part of the historical artifact.

This book may have occasional imperfections such as missing or blurred pages, poor pictures, errant marks, etc. that were either part of the original artifact, or were introduced by the scanning process. We believe this work is culturally important, and despite the imperfections, have elected to bring it back into print as part of our continuing commitment to the preservation of printed works worldwide. We appreciate your understanding of the imperfections in the preservation process, and hope you enjoy this valuable book.

THE NATURAL HISTORY OF JUAN FERNANDEZ AND EASTER ISLAND

EDITED BY DR CARL SKOTTSBERG

VOL I
GEOGRAPHY, GEOLOGY,
ORIGIN OF ISLAND LIFE

WITH 14 PLATES

UPPSALA 1920–1956
ALMQVIST & WIKSELLS BOKTRYCKERI AB

Table of Contents.

1	SKOTTSBERG, CARL Notes on a visit to Easter Island	3
2	HAGERMAN, T. H. Beiträge zur Geologie der Juan Fernandez Inseln	21
3	QUENSEL, P. Additional Comments on the Geology of the Juan Fernandez Islands	37
4	SKOTTSBERG, C. A Geographical Sketch of the Juan Fernandez Islands	89
5	——. Derivation of the Flora and Fauna of Juan Fernandez and Easter Island	193

THE NATURAL HISTORY OF JUAN FERNANDEZ AND EASTER ISLAND

EDITED BY DR. CARL SKOTTSBERG

VOL. I
GEOGRAPHY, GEOLOGY, ORIGIN OF ISLAND LIFE

PART I

1. C. SKOTTSBERG: Notes on a visit to Easter Island.

UPPSALA 1920
ALMQVIST & WIKSELLS BOKTRYCKERI-A.-B.

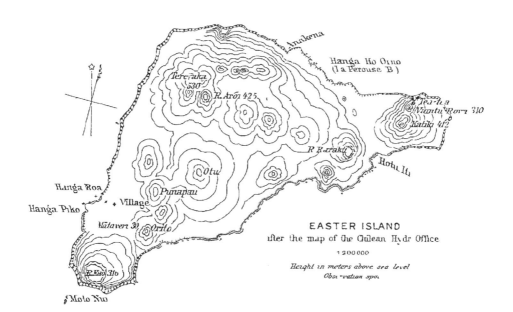

1. Notes on a visit to Easter Island.

By

CARL SKOTTSBERG

With 14 plates, 1 map, and 3 text figures

While working on the Juan Fernandez Islands, our party obtained permission to accompany the Chilean corvette »General Baquedano» on her cruise to Easter Island, in 1917. A short and very popular account of our visit appears in my book »Till Robinson-ön och världens ände» (1918). Although the purpose of our survey was purely biological, no scientist visiting the famous island can help taking a vivid interest in the archaeological remains, and we occasionally made a few observations. However, I have refrained from writing anything on the subject, as I had to wait for the publication of the results obtained by Mr and Mrs SCORESBY ROUTLEDGE of the British »Mana» Expedition. Last year Mrs ROUTLEDGE published a most interesting account of their work on the island (The Mystery of Easter Island), where the ancient monuments of all kinds are amply described and illustrated. A second volume will follow containing the detailed descriptions of the prehistoric remains.

I willingly admit that this little paper will appear rather unnecessary since the British Expedition has explored the place with such a wonderful accuracy. But it is Mrs ROUTLEDGE's excellent narrative which has induced me to collect a few notes and to use them as a basis for a discussion of some interesting points. I have also found it worth while to add a number of my photographs, which may be of some value.

The »General Baquedano» sailed from Iquique on May 27th, 1917. She carried a Government commission presided over by Bishop RAFAEL EDWARDS, a prominent Chilean ecclesiastic, who went to continue his studies on native conditions and to distribute a large amount of materials, clothing etc. among the members of the little island colony. Capitán de fragata J. T. MERINO was in command of the vessel, and he as well as the bishop and the officers of the ship did all in their power to assist us in our undertaking.

After a rather uneventful cruise our vessel anchored in La Perouse Bay on June 15th, and the same day we made our first excursion along the north coast. We were bound for Hanga Roa (Cook's Bay) but were detained in La Perouse on account of adverse winds; finally we resolved to cross the island on horseback, and arrived at Mataveri, the seat of the farm house, on the 19th. In the meantime we had made some excursions in the northeastern part, where Mt Katiki was ascended. At Mataveri we were cordially received by Mr PERCY EDMUNDS, the manager, and were invited to to take up our quarters in his house. Quite naturally, the natives were in a state of great excitement over the arrival of the vessel with their much beloved bishop, the missionaries (two Capuchin Brethren) and the many useful articles reported to be onboard, and consequently they were rather unwilling to render us any assistance. It was only through the kind intervention of the bishop that we were able to get an important part of our scientific baggage, which had been left on the beach at La Pérouse, transported to Mataveri. From our headquarters the district round Hanga Roa and Hanga Piko etc was visited and several trips undertaken to Rano Kao and Orongo, the famous stone village. Further, our work was extendend to Rano Aroi and Mt Terevaka, the highest mountain, and also to the south coast and to Rano Raraku, the image mountain.

We had expected to remain at least three weeks on the island, and greatly regretted that we were ordered onboard already after a fortnight's stay, especially as my capacity for hard work had become reduced on account of illness. The »Baquedano» left Easter Island on July 1st.

GENERAL NOTES ON THE GEOGRAPHY OF EASTER ISLAND

The topographical features of the island are fairly well illustrated on the accompanying map, the result of Chilean Navy surveys of later years. The position of the observation spot in Hanga Roa is given as Lat 27° 08' 06" S, Long 109° 25' 54" W. Mrs ROUTLEDGE's map is based on U S Hydrographic Office chart no 1119, from which it differs in the position of some of the mountains and in the geographical names. There are certain discrepancies between this map and the Chilean one and the difference between the latter and the U S chart are still more considerable, especially in the configuration of the northwestern part of the island. There has been some confusion in the placing of the names, but I take it for granted that all the names used by Mrs R are properly spelt and rightly placed.

The island is known to be wholly volcanic. There are no signs of recent action, save for a couple of tepid springs below high water mark reported to, but never seen by us. It is rather curious that both THOMSON (Smiths Inst Ann Rep 1889, Washington 1891) and AGASSIZ (Mem Mus Comp Zool Cambridge 33, 1906) should discuss volcanic eruptions and great earthquakes as a possible reason for the destruction of the megalithic monuments and for the disappearance of the greater part of the population, as all signs of recent catastrophes are entirely absent. On the other hand, not a few craters are well preserved, sometimes they are arranged on distinct lines suggesting lines of less resistance in the older, more or less horisontal basaltic beds, which form the bulk of the island. The tufas and ashes of the numerous cones present a great variation of colour contributing to lessen the monotony of the scenery. The attention of the visitor is especially drawn to the three great *Rano* Rano is the native name for a mountain which contains water. R. Kao forms the broad southwestern promontory. The greatest height of the rim was found by the writer to be 316 m., as the result of three aneroid observations (differences in temperature duly considered) at different occasions. AGASSIZ has 1 327 feet or 403 m., the Chilean map, 400 m. The crater lake measures, according to COOKE, 2 085 feet across (634 m.), this figure may be the result of a careful observation, but seems too small. Its surface was found by me to be 120 m. above sea level, THOMSON and COOKE (Smiths Inst Ann Rep 1897, Washington 1899), say respectively, that it is 700 and 600 feet below the crater rim, thus according to their figures for the latter corresponding to a height of 190 or 160 m., taking 316 m. as the starting point we get 106 or 134 m. I am sorry that we were unable to examine the thickness of the peat that covers the sheet of water save for some irregular pools, which do not appear to have decreased much in size since the photographs of the Albatross Expedition were taken. No reliable figure for the depth of the lake has been obtained, according to COOKE, Mr SALMON tried to sound, but at a depth of 300 feet the line broke without having reached the bottom. I need not tell that according to the belief of the islanders, the pool in Rano Kao belongs to the category of famous lakes without a bottom.

The lake is partly surrounded by stands of a very robust bullrush, an endemic variety of the wide spread *Scirpus riparius*, called *paschalis* by Dr KUKENTHAL.

The country NE of Rano Kao is hilly, one of the cones being known as Punapau (Plate 1), the seat of the hat quarry. The northwestern corner of the island is occupied by the highest mountain, the Terevaka (Plate 2), non seldom veiled by a bank of clouds. This name is not mentioned in Mrs ROUTLEDGE's book, where the entire high land in question is called Rano Aroi. But the latter name only applies to the crater on the southeast slope of the mountain. On the Chilean map appears Cerro Terevaka, separated from Rano Aroi (or Roi) by a shallow depression, and both names were recognized by the native JUAN TEPANO, who accompanied us to this place. The top of Terevaka did not present any marked signs of being a crater, the height was found to be 530 m., which I believe is nearer to the truth that the figure 770 put down on the Chilean map. I had expected to find some notable difference in the flora of the highland, but was rather disappointed. The cryptogams, mosses and lichens, however, played a much greater part here than in the lowlands, where they are of a very slight importance. Rano Aroi is a very modest and shallow rano and cannot at all be compared with the grand R. Kao. The height was found to be 425 m. The lake is overgrown with vegetation. There is a gap in the east wall through which, after prolonged rains, the water flows down to another pool, which empties itself into a long, narrow fissure, crossed by the track from La Perouse Bay to Hanga Roa. This fissure does not seem to have been eroded by water but suggests a volcanic origin.

The land along the north coast, from the hills backing Anakena Cove to Katiki, is a rather flat basaltic plain, with occasional outcrops of hard rock and strewn with innumerable sharp edged stones, partly hidden by the coarse grass and making walking disagreeable, more so for a person in a state of ill-health. The slope of Katiki (another name not found on Mrs ROUTLEDGE's map, but frequently used) is comparatively gentle. The top was found to be 412 m high (300 m on the Chilean map must be wrong), it presents a rather striking appearance, forming a shallow circular basin, perfectly dry and with a flat bottom 5—6 m below the rim, which is 75—80 m across. On the north slope is a succession of three cones, of which the northernmost is gradually eaten away through the action of the sea. The one nearest Katiki, Vaintu Rova, is of a light yellowish colour, the hight is 310 m. On the south slope we came across a deep fissure, containing rain water and surrounded by a fine growth of ferns. The natives, of course, all know this rare watering place, and I guess this is the well spoken of by Captain COOK in his second voyage »Towards the eastern end of the island they met with a well whose water was perfectly fresh, being considerably above the level of the sea, but it was dirty, owing to the filthiness or cleanliness (call it what you will) of the natives, who never go to drink without washing themselves all over as soon as they have done.« (the edition in Everyman's Library, p. 163). North of Vaintu Rova stands the somewhat lower Tea tea, the »white mountain».

SW of Katiki the famous image mountain, Rano Raraku, is situated, so ably described and illustrated by Mrs ROUTLEDGE, who gained an intimate knowledge of this unique place. It is shown on Plate 5. Between this rano and the hills east of Hanga Roa there is an extensive plain, only broken by a few higher eminences.

The visitor, even if he be not a geographer, cannot fail to notice the absence of every trace of valley or ravine caused by the action of running water. It is almost with surprise that one learns the figure for rainfall, 1 218 mm., the average of 8 years' observations. This is, indeed, no small amount, surpassing that of Juan Fernandez, where erosion has modelled the entire island into a system of deep valleys and sharp ridges. But in Easter Island there is no stream, no brook, only in the crater lakes water is always found. The great scarcity of water makes the high development of the ancient culture quite astonishing. The climate is warmer in Easter Island than in Juan Fernandez, the evaporation undoubtedly much greater, the winds at least equally frequent. Anybody will note the rapid disappearance of the water, after a heavy rain, the ground may become soaking wet, nevertheless, some hours later it is perfectly dry, the result of the combined forces of the burning sun, the strong winds, and the extreme porosity of the soil. Occasionally, water is encountered by digging deep holes, but to dig through the hard rocks must have been too difficult a matter for the natives. Subterraneous streams are reported, and are, of course, to be expected, and running water has played an important part in the formation of the numerous caves round the coast.

The vegetation is extremely poor, if one comes from Juan Fernandez, the contrast is very striking. The island is destitute not only of wood, but of trees, except for a few specimens in the crater of Rano Kao, where the last stunted dwarfs of the famous toromiro *(Sophora toromiro)* still linger, in company with mahute *(Broussonetia papyrifera)*, hau hau (or jau jau, spanish j), called *Triumfetta?* by FUENTES [I believe that it is *T. semitriloba*] and ti *(Cor-*

dylium terminalis f a).[1] From the earliest descriptions is seen that the island was never wooded, planted Eucalypts, Melia azedarach and other subtropical trees do pretty well, however.

In his »Informe» (Memorias del Ministerio de Relaciones esteriores, culto i colonizacion, Santiago 1892), P P TORO says »En otro tiempo formó (i e the toromiro) sin duda bosques pues en diversas partes de la isla se ven todavia innumerables i tupidos troncos secos de dos a tres metros de alto Parece indudable que esos bosques naturales han desaparecido, secandose la mayor parte de los árboles a consecuencia principalmente de la introduccion de animales vacunos i ovejunos que han quebrado las plantas o les han comido la corteza.»

THOMSON and especially COOKE also speak of the numerous groups of trees of small dimensions »In other parts of the island may be seen, in places in considerable numbers, a hardwood tree, more properly bush or brush, called by the natives toromiro, all or nearly all dead and decaying by reason of being stripped of their bark by the flocks of sheep which roam at will all over the island»

When COOK visited the place in 1774, he certainly did not come across anything like a forest, for he expresses himself thus »the country appeared quite barren and without wood» Both ROGGEVEEN and FORSTER (A voyage round the world London 1777, Vol I) assert that there was nothing like a forest on the island FORSTER gives a good description of the general appearance of the place, he mentions about ten species of plants, among them paper mulberry, Hibiscus populneus and Mimosa whether Hibiscus still occurs, I cannot tell, but the Mimosa is certainly Sophora, this was the largest tree, and a very small one »there was not a tree upon the island, which exceeded the height of ten feet» In some places, on the hills, Sophora seems to have formed small shrubberies FORSTER did not estimate the flora to comprise more than twenty species, including the cultivated plants On board the »Baquedano», Bishop EDWARDS showed me a letter from Brother EUGENIO EYRAUD, the missionary of the island, to his Superior General in Valparaiso, dated December, 1864 He writes »la vegetacion toda de yerbas y arbustos, faltando los árboles y plantas elevadas» It is possible that Brother EUGENIO includes the toromiro within his »arbustos» They cannot have been of any considerable size, or he would not have pointed out that trees were missing A toromiro of 3 m. decidedly has the look of a small tree, not of a shrub, especially in a place where there are no larger plants to compare it with TORO must be mistaken when he believes that there had grown forests on the island not long before his arrival Mr COOKE does not tell if he saw the numerous trunks himself or if he was only told of their existence

---

[1] In Anuario Hidrogr de la Mar de Chile (30) 1916, p 5, C DE LA MAZA mentions a small indigenous tree which he calls »tumahtu» »La madera del tumahtu es bastante dura y mas o menos flexible Lo utilizan los indios para construir yugos, arados etc Es el unico arbol que crece libremente en toda la isla» The fruit is described as oval-shaped, yellow, 1 cm long, with a stone within, and of bitter taste There is, however no tree growing freely over the island The description of the fruit suggests *Melia*, but this is called *miotaiji* (vide I FUENTES, Reseña botanica de la Isla de Pascua Inst Centr Meteor y geofis de Chile No 4 Santiago 1913) Tumahtu sounds like a corruption for te mahute, the paper mulberry, which certainly cannot supply materials for the implements mentioned

The dwarf trees now existing are, as has already been stated, almost wholly confined to the crater of Rano Kao and are on the verge of extinction. They grow not far from the lake, where the steep slope is covered with very large blocks, which prevent the sheep from reaching them. Mr EDMUNDS told me about some trees which grow along the steep bluff of the eastern headland, unfortunately, we were prevented from visiting the place, what I hope some future naturalist will do.

The greatest part of the island is covered with grass, wide spread species, either Polynesian or introduced from the old world via Chile, Tahiti or other places. Occasionally ferns are found, also outside the rano, *Microlepia strigosa* being the most common. We discovered two species of *Ophioglossum* to which the natives attribute medicinal qualities. Among the cryptogams are some endemic species. A detailed account of the Flora will appear in the volume dedicated to the Botany of the expedition.

The terrestrial Fauna is very poor, no indigenous mammals or land birds are known. There are two species of lizards, both of wide range. The insect fauna is remarkably poor, some species have been introduced by man, e. g. cockroaches and flies, which have increased enormously.

ARCHAEOLOGICAL REMAINS. THE AHU

These structures, the burial-places — but not the only ones — of the islanders, have been called »terraces» by most authors. Such a word tells us very little, while the word *ahu* is a proper technical term, strongly and justly recommended by Mrs ROUTLEDGE for regular use.

There are several kinds of ahu. The most striking is the image-ahu, which carried the now fallen statues of stone. We know that all the images were purposely upset as a result of internal warfare. During our stay in La Perouse Bay we devoted some time to the inspection of the ahu. One not far from the landing-place, close to the beach, was said to be one of the best preserved, although not one of the largest and having supported one statue only. This ahu was measured and described (see Plates 3—4 and text fig. 1). The central part is 23,5 m long and protrudes 4 m in front of the wings, as it stands on somewhat higher ground, it rises above the wings, in spite of the front wall being rather low or about 1,25 m. The front wall has a foundation of small stones and flat slabs, followed by large, very well wrought blocks, one of these was 2,3 m long, 0,9 high, and 0,45 broad, another 2,45 long and 1 m high. They are closely fitted. The space behind this wall was filled with boulders, the surface paved with larger, flat stones, making a level platform.

The wings are larger than the centre, the east 31,2, the west 32 m, giving as total length of the ahu 86,7 m. Their front wall is as high as or even higher (about 2 m) than that of the centre and is similar in construction, without being so neatly finished. The central part of the ahu, behind the platform, had been disturbed, a stone wall of 7,6 m stretching obliquely along the fallen image. The ahu slopes gently inwards. This slope, which could be traced inland about 12 m (measured from the front wall), is divided by a wall (not visible above the surface), as described and figured by Mrs R. The seaward part has a surface of boulders almost free from vegetation, while behind the dividing line it looks like an old pavement with grass between the stones. According to Mrs R., the vaults for bones are found in this part. In the case in question an open vault was to be seen in the seaward part of the west wing, it measured 1,9 × 0,7 m with a depth of 1 m. Two slabs had covered it. We do not know if the ahu were built with many vaults or if accomodations for the bones of the deceased were arranged on each occasion.

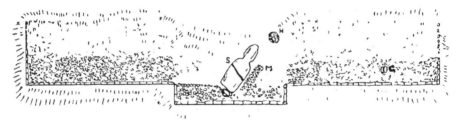

Fig. 1. Diagrammatic sketch of an ahu west of the landing place in La Perouse Bay. Scale 1:750. s fallen image, h hat, m stone wall, g vault.

In the centre of the front platform one large image or *moai* had stood (Plate 4). It had been brought down by undermining the foundation stone. This moai was the only one carefully measured.

Total length 10,27 m	Width across shoulders 3,2 m
Length of body 6,55 m	» » head 2,6 m
» » head 2,5 m	» » neck 1,9 m
» » neck 1,2 m	Circumference round shoulders 7,9 m
Width of body at base 2,7 m	» » neck 5,2 m
Thickness of body at base 1,6 m	Length of ear 2,4 m

Close by, the hat or crown rested flat upon the ground, its height was 1,85, its circumference 7, the greatest and smallest diameters 2,3 and 1,85 m, respectively. It is of the usual red stone from Punapau, but not finished. The finished hat had a knob on top and an oval depression below, this one showed neither on the exposed side. According to Mrs R. the hats were finished after having arrived at the ahu, I suppose this one never adorned the image. Could it not be possible that the stone wall spoken of above was part of a construction on which the hat was to be rolled up to the top of the image?

Naturally, I have tried to identify the ahu described here with one of those mentioned by Mrs R. Its position at once suggested the Paro, of which a sketch is communicated by Mrs R. As far as I can see, this must be the same (if so, it will undoubtedly be recognized by Mrs R. from my photographs), but there are some differences that I am unable to account for. In the sketch, there is no trace of the stone wall alongside the image, the two parts of this latter are far too much apart, and the hat seems to rest on its cylindrical side. Then, there is the size of the image. Mrs R. gives 32 feet, adding that it is the largest one ever found on an ahu and the last one to be upset. Are there two exactly similar ahu close to each other, each with an unusually large image? I think not. The measurements were taken by my wife and myself with a tape 25 m. long and the figures committed to paper on the spot.

It could possibly also be the same ahu as no 34 Punahoa of THOMSON l. c., p. 505. He also gives the total length of the single moai as 32 feet. However, the entire structure is said to have a length of 175 feet and a width of 8 feet, which figures must be entirely incorrect if ahu Paro is meant.

By what kind of apparatus or devices the statues were transported from Rano Raraku to the coast, in some cases to rather inaccessible places, remains a mystery. The natives possessed strong cordage, and Mrs R. has made out that long lines were used occasionally, but veritable hawsers would have been needed to drag the statues along over the ground in the manner imagined by THOMSON. We have seen that there is evidence against the island ever having produced good sized timber suitable for rollers. THOMSON thinks that, after a smooth road had been constructed, »the images were dragged by means of ropes made of indigenous hemp», »seaweed and grass made excellent lubricants» He could »clearly see how it was accomplished with a large force of able bodied men» (p. 498). I must confess that I find it less easy to understand how the work was done, for the least obstacle would become a serious one, and the roads must have been made as smooth as a floor in order to serve the purpose, the images being rather fragile. Mrs R. has traced the few highways leading from Rano Raraku to the coast, but if really the images were dragged up to the numerous ahu all round the island, these roads cannot have sufficed, but an elaborate network of very smooth paths was required, of which all traces would have disappeared. It is true that seaweeds are plentiful, but there is no species of any considerable size and I fail to see how the quantities required could have been brought together. It is astonishing that no tradition on the means of transport survives. According to Mrs R. the natives invariably offered one explanation: that the images were transported by the aid of supernatural forces.

On p. 486 THOMSON discusses the possibility of a transport by sea. Near a group of ahu he discovered a fine landing place made by art, »admirably adapted to the landing of heavy weights». From old drawings we know what the aboriginal canoes were like — not a single one, as far as I know, has been preserved to our days — but they were not strong enough to support any very heavy weight. One might suggest that large rafts were built but, on the other hand, there are several ahu which are unaccessible from the shore.

Still, there is another method to be reckoned with, although further speculation on this matter may appear pretty useless. Some sort of a sledge-like apparatus could have been constructed without the need of timber of any considerable size. A sledge would slide quite well over the grass, provided that the load was cleared from stones. A great number of people could be simultaneously engaged in pulling, while, if rollers were used, the image must have been more difficult to handle. Once arrived at the ahu, a sloping causeway could have been built, from which the image was lowered down in position, or, the same method could have been used that was applied when raising the images on Rano Raraku. Still, this was easier, as the statue was steadied by the hole in the ground. For details, see Mrs. R., p. 189. Also compare what is said above on ahu Paro. If a slope was built for the image, the same one might have been used for bringing the crown to the top, and perhaps the wall mentioned above will have to be explained in another and more natural manner than the one indicated. Anyhow, to erect the statues on the platform in the precise position required, turning their backs to the sea, must have demanded not only great skill but also perseverance, a quality not very characteristic of the present native population.

It is the merit of Mr. and Mrs. R. to have made out the various types of ahu and to have pointed out that not a few have been rebuilt. Some structures of this kind were noted by us. A »poe poe», not far from the western slope of Mt. Katiki, was even sketched (another by Mrs. R., fig. 95), a stone pillar stands on the surface, which is covered by grass.

THE IMAGE MOUNTAIN

Rano Raraku has been called the most interesting spot in the island. Truly, the sight of this wonderful mountain with its quarries and statues is one not likely to be forgotten. The place has been admirably well surveyed by Mr. and Mrs. R., making it quite unnecessary for the present writer to say anything on the subject, but he thinks that the reproduction of some of his photographs will be found pardonable. Plate 5 gives a total view of the mountain from the SW, plate 6 is a familiar sight from the outer slope. On plate 7 is shown one of the very largest statues in the quarries, no 41 in Mrs R's diagram, also figured by her, Fig. 49, and by AGASSIZ, Plate 39. Neither of these shows more than the left part of the image. It must be about 16 m long, while the largest statue is just over 20[1]. Mrs R finds it difficult to believe that the latter was ever made to be launched, the same, then, can be said of no 41. It is hard to see where the limit for the capacity of the ancient islanders should be drawn. Surely there are images in the quarries that are little more than rock carvings, but I am not prepared to include the two just mentioned under such a heading.

The two prostrate statues on Plate 8 are nos 64—65 in Mrs R's diagram, they show the narrowed base. Plate 9 is also from the inside of the crater, a quarry high up in the gap. It represents the heads of two images (possibly nos 15—16 of the diagram), one but roughly modelled, one finished. The first has a large »wart» on its cheek, perhaps this applies to the case mentioned by Mrs R on p. 181, where it is stated that the unexpected occurrence of large and hard nodules in the rock could cause the whole work to be abandoned.

It is the great triumph of Mrs R to have unveiled the mystery of the scattered statues outside the mountain, which were formerly believed to have been dropped on their way to the coast and left lying. We know now that

---

[1] GEISELER (resp. WEISSER) describes a statue of 25 m length (Die Oster-Insel. Berlin 1883, p. 9).

neither the images standing on the mountain nor those found scattered over the island were ever intended for the ahu, but that the latter lined the roads leading from the mountain to the coast. I cannot add anything to the explanation of the standing statues. If they were put up to celebrate »birdmen», it seems quaint that not the names of these heroes but those of the workers should have become attached to them, but such is the tradition, as told by Mrs R.

The rude stone implements (toki) used by the sculptors are often found. In Hanga Roa we came across a large and very well wrought stone adze of a rather international type, but not found in any of the accounts on the island. It had been picked up on the seashore at low water and is quite incrustated with the shells of animals. It measures 20 cm (Plate 14, fig 1) A few stone chisels were also obtained, two are figured on Plate 14, fig 2, 3.

REMAINS OF HOUSES AND PLANTATIONS

Foundations of old houses are seen in many places, and several were noted on our excursion to Mt Katiki. Of one a sketch was made, also showing the paved area in front, but without foundation-stones for a porch. None of these dwelling houses are left. Between Mataveri and Hanga Roa are a couple of grass huts (Plate 10) which give us a faint idea of what the old houses were like. They are small, lack the stone foundation, and have the entrance at one end.

There is another kind of structure in the shape of low, very strongly built towers of stone which cannot fail to arouse the curiosity of the visitor. The present people do not seem to be sure as to their former use. A fine tower at the landing place in Hanga Ho Orno (La Pérouse) is shown on Plate 11, another is figured and described by Mrs R (p 218, fig 87), a third one, in a ruined state, by THOMSON (p 484). The first-mentioned has a height of 3,4 m and is 6,5—7 m. across at the base. The only entrance is 0,65 m high and 0,9 wide. The roof is vaulted inside, outside, the wall ends in a girdle of stones. The size of the stones bears witness of the prehistoric era and of the makers of the great ahu. Mrs R , on the authority of some resident, explains these structures as »look-out towers whence watchers on land communicated the whereabouts of the fish to those at sea, these contained a small chamber below which was used as a sleeping apartment» (p 218)

It sounds strange that these solid towers should have had no other purpose than to serve as look out stations for fishermen. In order to keep a good look out, presumably to follow the movements of shoals — it has not been proved that there is any fish here of the social type, and Mrs R states that »fish are not plentiful» — an observer must seek an eminence dominating a considerable space of water. THOMSON tells us that from the towers the movements of the turtles were watched. The observer must keep outside the tower or on the top of it, not a very comfortable place. Really, the tower itself would have been little more than a refuge in bad weather and during the night, but for such a purpose a much simpler structure would indeed suffice. Thus the importance of the tower with its lower apartment appears to stand in no reasonable proportion to the vast amount of labour required to build it. We should perhaps remember that the permanent dwelling-houses were much more fragile. The tower suggests some kind of fortress, with a chamber for stores or treasures: it would be easy to defend the entrance. Speaking of the narrow entrances to the Orongo houses, THOMSON remarks (p. 483): »The low contracted entrances were used here as well as elsewhere for defence. Factional fights were common, and it was necessary that every house should be guarded against surprise and easily defended». He adds: »Another reason might be found for making the openings as small as possible, in the absence of doors to shut out the storms». But, at least at Orongo, there were plenty of slabs suitable for doors if wanted.

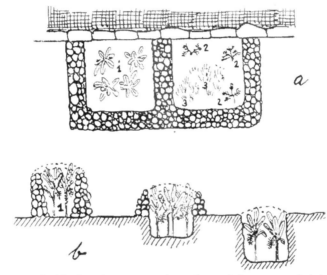

Fig. 2. Diagrams of old plantations; *a* seen from above; *b* three types of shelter, in section. 1 = bananas, 2 = Melia azedarach, 3 = Andropogon halepensis. Scale 1 : 250.

On the other hand, an enemy could pull down the roof over the occupants. Also, we should expect to find a communication between the tower and the underground chamber, which we have not found. So, after all, this theory may not hold good. Perhaps prisoners were locked up in the towers, where they could be easily guarded till the hour arrived to put them to death. But it is also necessary to consider whether these buildings may not have had some relation to unkown rites. Did they have a ritual purpose, we do not need to wonder about their elaborate structure, as natives may invest any amount of labour in connection with religious or other ritual buildings.

There is a description and figure of a similar building in La PÉROUSE's Voyage, reproduced by STOLPE in Ymer, 1883. He states that they are only found on the top of Rano Raraku, which is, of course, a mistake. They were oval in shape; close by was the underground chamber with its separate entrance. In several respects, especially concerning the ahu, there are great discrepancies between the statements and illustrations of the old navigators and the results obtained by modern explorers. A critical examination of the old stones would be welcome, and it is to be expected that Mrs ROUTLEDGE will undertake to scrutinize the entire literature. There are, e. g., in La PÉROUSE's and PINART's narratives designs of ahu which do not at all correspond to modern descriptions or photographs.

In the vicinity of Hanga Ho Ono we saw many remains of native plantations. They are of several types. One, seen in fig. 2 *a,* is probably of a later date, as the material has been taken from an ahu, the front wall of

Fig. 3. *a* Two »bird men» on rock at Orongo (height of the rock 1,6—1.7 m.) *b* Incised marks on door poost at Orongo

which forms the back wall of the garden. Circular miniature gardens are represented in fig. 2 *b.* The need of shelter and moisture is well understood. *Melia* was said to be grown for the sake of the timber. Probably it is of recent introduction.

ORONGO AND THE BIRD CULT

Mrs ROUTLEDGE devoted much time to the survey of the Orongo village, and as a detailed plan was made and every house measured and described, I shall content myself with a few short remarks.

The last house (if I remember right) towards the gap of the crater rim, close to the sculptured rocks, had one door-post with incised carvings left, vide fig. 3 b. This house was pointed out to us as the house of Ariki. The ariki was the chief of the Miru clan, the authority on the script (i. e. the »ariki mau», vide R. p. 241, all Miru were also called ariki). Now, the same design was found on a skull in the possession of the schoolmaster, Mr I. VIVES, and this skull was attributed to an ariki. Unfortunately, the owner did not want to part with his treasure. The design is unlike the one figured by Mrs R. (fig. 96) of another Miru skull.

The Bird Cult is described, with full details, by Mrs R. Special attention is paid to the rock carvings. I sketched a couple of the »bird men» (fig. 3 a). Their meaning is not known with certainty. Mrs R. believes them either to represent one of the egg-gods (they were spoken of as »Make-make») or made to immortalize the bird-men, the winners of the egg race; she finds the latter explanation more probable. I have not been able to form an independent opinion. The same carvings are seen on a flat stone opposite Orongo, marking the place where the path descends into the crater of Rano Kao.

All that is left of prehistoric remains, at least of the large ones, will remain on the island. Shortly before our visit a law was passed prohibiting the removal of statues etc., so that we had to abandon our idea of bringing home a small image presented to us by one of the residents. The »Mana» was just in time to rescue the small but unique statue from Motu Nui.

WOOD CARVINGS

The famous wooden statues as well as other pieces of carving are gone from the island for ever. What is offered to passing visitors is not worth mentioning. The art is gone. One old moai-miro, in a very much decayed state, had been discovered in a cave after the departure of the »Mana». It was presented to Bishop EDWARDS. In 1908, while staying at Valparaiso, a Swedish captain, Mr G. KARSTROM, who had been shipwrecked on Easter Island many years before, presented me with two beautiful wooden images, one of which is in the Etnographical Museum in Stockholm, the other is owned by a private person.

HOUSEHOLD GOODS, WEAPONS, ETC.

Very little of this kind is now to be encountered. Sticks used for net-knitting are available, and so are baskets or rather bags made of bullrushes (figured by THOMSON on Plate 51). There are still some people skilled in the preparation of tapa cloth from the mahute and of strings from the hau-hau, and we had samples made for the collection. Curiously enough, GEISELER does not mention the latter plant, but states that all the cordage, fishing-nets etc. were made from the bullrushes.

It is generally stated that the islanders never possessed any earthen ware. Contrary to this, RUTLAND (Transactions New Zeal. Inst. 29, 1896) says that the earliest discoverers had seen »rude earthen ware» on the island, a statement due to some misinterpretation. Of stone implements, besides the toki, and the stone adze and chisels, we got one fish hook, very neatly wrought but unfortunately not complete, as the point is missing (Plate 14, fig 4). There is a drawing of one of these hooks in THOMSON's report (Plate 58). Another curious article is the spherical stone ball, Fig 5 on Plate 14. It shows two holes which communicate so that a string can be passed through, and may have been worn as an ornament. No explanation was offered. Perhaps it is a »fetish stone». THOMSON has described and figured many such stones, but none of them present any likeness to this one.

The object on Plate 14, Fig 6 is not, as might be suspected, a broken spear head or *mataa* but has been given its present shape on purpose. It fits well into the hand and may have been used as a knife or scrape. But if it was used with a handle, my explanation may not be satisfactory. Spear-heads are commonly found in the soil and also manufactured to satisfy the demand of visitors. Two, of an ordinary type and apparently old, are seen on Plate 14, Figs 7, 8. According to THOMSON there were at least nine kinds, all with different names, a statement well needing the corroboration of Mrs R.

ORIGIN OF THE PEOPLE

The history of Easter Island is full of mystery, but I think that Mrs R has come pretty near the solution of some of the problems. She has drawn some important conclusions from the legendary traditions still alive. A tale of two different races and two successive colonizations runs through the old legends. The anthropological evidence seems to be in favour of a double origin, Melanesian and Polynesian. The comparative studies of the Bird Cult in the Solomon Islands and Easter Island (by H. BALFOUR, *vide* Mrs R.) seem nothing less than convincing. The bird represented in the numerous carvings, paintings etc of Easter Island is not the holy bird of this place, but the frigate bird, worshipped in the Solomon Islands. The bird figures were called penguins by LEHMANN (Essai d'une bibliographie, Anthropos, 1907), which undoubtedly must be a mistake, especially as penguins hardly ever visit these waters.

If we sum up the results obtained, there is evidence that the Easter Islanders are of a twofold origin and that, after the Melanesian immigration, a Polynesian immigration followed. The population now tends to assume a multicoloured aspect, there has been a late influence from Tahiti (so we were told) and various white men have contributed towards the »amelioration» of the race. The young girl figured on Plates 12—13 was said to be of »pure Easter Island race», but whether representing a Melanesian or Polynesian type I am unable to tell.

A critical examination of the language would be of interest. Many words are the same as in the Maori or other Polynesian tongues, such as *maunga* (mountain), *mahute* (paper mulberry), *ti* (Cordyline), *cumara* (sweet potato) a o A large vocabulary, collected by Padre ROUSSEL, was published in Santiago,

1917, but it must be used with much criticism, as it contains many Tahitian words and also corrupted English, French or Spanish, good examples are *ario* (agneau) and *mutoni* = sheep, *himene* (hymn) = to sing, *teperanate* = serpent, *tokini* = stockings, *traporo* (diablo) = devil, *viretute* = virtue, given without reservation. A closer look reveals that the material is not at all so rich as the number of words would indicate, for the author has invented hundreds of expressions for ideas wholly unfamiliar to the aboriginal soul, by combining the words and extending their meaning in a most improper manner, e. g. expressions for cabin, desert, doctrine, palace, river, saint, W. C. etc etc to quote a few obvious examples, of which scores could be given. This is, I believe, a common missionary method to enrich the language with ideas and expressions necessary for the translation of religious and other books, but otherwise never used by the natives.

Concerning the name of the sweet potato, see below. It has been advanced as indicating an American influence previous to the Columbian era. RUILAND (l. c.) thinks that the ancient monuments bear witness of a constant communication between the island and Peru and Mexico »from hence architects of Easter Island may have been derived».

CULTIVATED PLANTS

If we knew the history of the cultivated plants, many a mystery related to the history of mankind would be solved. But, unfortunately, discussion often begins with the original home of the wild parents of these plants, and there it also ends.

The first record of domesticated plants in Easter Island is that of ROGGIVEEN, the discoverer of the island or, at least, the first white man to set his foot upon it. He makes the following statement on p. 120 (De Reis van JACOB ROGGEVEEN Worken uitgeven door de Linschoten-Vereenigung 4 1911) »en toegebragt worden alles wat sy hadden, bestaende en boomvrugten, aardgewasch en hoenderen», that is, tree fruits, soil-fruits (rootcrops) and hens, and, farther down »want na verloop van een kleynen tijd bragten sy eene menigte van suykerriet, hoenderen, ubaswortelen en bananas», that is sugarcane, bananas and ubas roots. But what is *ubas*? Most likely the same word as the Malesian ubi (uwi, huwi), yams *(Dioscorea alata)*, now called *ufi* in the island. All these plants are of Old World origin and have spread from the Indo-malayan region over the Pacific. According to FRIDERICI, the same word, in a corrupted form, is current in South America »Dieses Wort schlagt eine Brucke uber den grossen Ozean es gehort als öp unter der Bezeichnung 'susse Kartoffel' zum Sprachschatz der Chimu, des kustenbewohnenden Kulturvolkes westlichen Sudamerikas» (Wiss Ergebn seiner amtl Forschungsreise nach dem Bismarck Archipel im Jahre 1908). But the bridge in question seems to be weak.

The word *cumara* is used for sweet potato *(Ipomaea batatas* or *Batatas edulis)* from New Zealand through Polynesia to Easter Island. According to CHEESEMAN (Manual of the New Zealand Flora) the Maori introduced the plant from Polynesia when they colonized the country (supposingly 1350—1400), and it was described by SOLANDER as Convolvulus chrysorhizus, now reduced to a synonym of I. batatas. This plant is universally considered to be of Central American origin, although wild plants are not found nowadays, nor is the more precise locality known where they grew. We must consider whether the same species was not originally a native both in America and in the Polynesian region or, whether the cultivated forms were not derived from more than one wild species, so that it is unnecessary to suppose that the sweet potato was introduced to Polynesia from the American coast. Yams is obtained from forms of several wild species characteristic of different continents.

If this theory holds good, we should expect to find different names for the sweet potato on the two sides of the Pacific. But according to R. LENZ (Diccionario etimolójico. Santiago 1910), the word *cumara* is found in the Quichua language; it is not indicated as the principal name of the sweet potato, which is *apichu* but nevertheless used, according to this author, for a »clase parecida» of the camote, thus for some form of the same plant. From this fact some people would conclude that, as the plant is American and called cumara by the Quichua, it was introduced to Polynesia under the same name long before the Columbian era. It is useless to discuss this matter any further till we know more of the history of the camote and also whether the word cumara in Quichua really applies to the true sweet potato and, if such be the case, belongs to the original Quichua language or has been introduced through the Europeans. If old communications existed between America and Polynesia, many other proofs must be found. Much has been written about old land bridges across the ocean, considered by some naturalists to be indispensable for the explanation of the distribution of animals and plants. But generally their existence was supposed to have ceased long before the age of Man. Only HALLIER (Über fruhere Landbrucken, Pflanzen- und Volkerwanderungen zwischen Australasien und Amerika. Mededeel's Rijks Herb. Leiden 13, 1912) gives them a longevity sufficient to let people march across. I am afraid that such bridges rest on a very unstable foundation.

To return to the sweet potato, we have seen that it is not mentioned by ROGGEVEEN as existing in Easter Island in 1722. COOK and FORSTER found it in cultivation. At that time also Broussonetia, Thespesia (also Triumfetta?) and toromiro were cultivated in addition to taro, bananas and sugar cane. According to tradition all of them were brought by Hotu Matua's party, the first settlers. The barahu mentioned by F. VIDAL GORMAZ, Jeografia nautica, p. 177 (Anuario Hidrogr. de la Marina de Chile, 7) is, to judge from the descripton, the same as the hau hau. The calabash mentioned by THOMSON, p. 535 is Lagenaria vulgaris. At present, the following food-plants are cultivated: sugar, wheat, Indian corn, taro, pineapple, yams, bananas, white mulberry, figs, maniok, oranges, lemons, grapes, peaches, quince, plums, beans, sweet potatoes, tomatoes, melons, artichokes and lettuce but several of these only on a very small scale and exclusively in the garden of Mataveri. Some tobacco is also grown. I do not know what THOMSON means by the »two varieties of indigenous hemp», as there is no plant of this kind either in a cultivated or abandoned state. The cordage has always been prepared from the hau-hau, as far as I have been able to ascertain. Nor does Mrs R. refer to any such plant, nor to the hau hau.

THE FUTURE OF THE ISLAND

The power of resistance of the Easter Island people was definitely crushed through the Peruvian slave raids, and through missionaries and farmers they lost the strength which lies in the possession of an aboriginal culture. Their removal to Hanga Roa, where a village was formed, was very unlucky, as it meant giving up many small plantations and induced the people to lead a parasitic life, expecting everything from their new rulers. Although they have left so many wonderful monuments to bear witness of earlier busy days and of a people of warriors, they are now, with few exceptions, lazy beggars. In part this may be due to their pronounced feelings of animosity against the intruders, as they regard themselves as the true possessors of the island. It appears that ever since the establishment of a farming company the state of affairs has never been lucky, and Mrs R has an interesting tale to tell of an anxious time. I do not at all believe that the present manager is to blame, for we got the impression that he is as well liked as any white man in his position can expect to be. In Chile, nobody seems to have taken much notice of the distant colony till Bishop EDWARDS entered the field. During his first visit in 1916, he informed himself of the state of things, and he returned in 1917 invested with powers to put everything right if he could. Among other things he wanted to take up war against the leprosy.[1] Not quite 5 ‰ of the population suffer from this disease, they are confined to a colony some distance from Hanga Roa. Apparently it is not very contagious, for the isolation is not quite effective. The surgeon of the »Baquedano», Dr G LONGO examined almost every soul, but only one or two new cases were discovered. As accomodations for the most advanced cases had been wanting, the vessel this time brought materials for the construction of a small hospital which was to be erected by the new »subdelegado» or governor. Captain MERINO carried instructions to examine the claims against the company, and a meeting was held where the natives put forth their demands. I understood that the Company was said to have taken possession of more land than it was entitled to and that the natives wanted it to be restored. Officers went round with natives who indicated the seats of their former homes and fields, and parts of the land were measured. The scheme was, I think, that certain parts should be restored to the old owners, that the village should be abandoned, and that the natives should move into »the camp» in order to become selfsustaining. A certain amount of native labour should be granted to the manager at a fixed rate of pay. I have had no chance to learn how far the realisation of this humanitary scheme has advanced, nor would I venture to foretell if it is likely to meet with success.

EASTER ISLAND AS A FIELD OF PSEUDOGEOGRAPHICAL SPECULATION

Finally, I shall make a few remarks in addition to what Mrs R tells us (p. 290) of the theosophists' views of Easter Island, which are based on errors

---

[1] The surgeon of the »Mohican», Dr COOKE, does not mention this malady as existing in the island in the year 1886. It was imported from Tahiti.

regarding the existing monuments. Last year a small book appeared, entitled »Det sunkne kontinent (Atlantis)», by a Norwegian, C. SUND (Copenhagen 1919) where also the supposed Pacific continent is spoken of. As might be expected, Easter Island forms an important item. With my permission, two of my photographs were reproduced. No doubt Mr. SUND regards himself as excused for his mistakes, for he has quoted various obscure authors, but it must be regretted that he should not happen to draw from a single reliable source, not even from my popular description which was known to him. Mr. SUND tells us of the Egyptian influence in Easter Island, of the enormous foundation walls and ruins of temples, almost every mountain had sculptured designs of goods, fishes and pyramids, the cave paintings were in the Toltec or Egyptian style, etc. There are 300 tablets with script on the island (if it were but true!), waiting to be deciphered. On the mountain terraces are fortresses with walls up to 80 feet high. The pyramid is the architectonical principle, built as the Egyptian one, even with the same kind of cement. All materials, bricks, glass, porcelain, everything was known in Easter Island, religion, symbols and habits were the same as in Egypt, only, the culture of the island was older. There are fantastic groups of statues roundabout, gods of hard stone with faces up to 25 feet high, in the highlands there are images on high stone pillars or staircase-like foundations, and with square hats of stone, most of them covered with script in a probably forgotten language. Round them are the remains of large walls and buildings, so they probably stood in vast temple-yards. And so forth. No wonder that Mr. SUND draws the most surprising conclusions. Now, this must not be taken too seriously and will do no harm in scientific circles. The general reader, however, will get a rather curious idea of Easter Island. I dare say the place is remarkable enough in itself and need not be glorified by such fantastic inventions.

Finally, I wish to express my sincere gratitude for kind assistance to the Commander and Officers of the »General Baquedano», to Bishop RAFAEL EDWARDS, Mr PERCY EDMUNDS, Mr J VIVES and Baron ERLAND NORDENSKIOLD.

Explanation of Plate 14

1. Stone adze, no 19 I 307, not quite $1/2$
2. Stone chisel, no 19 I 320, almost $3/4$
3. » » no 19 I 321, » $3/4$
4. Fish hook of stone, no 19 I 325, almost $3/4$
5. Stone ball, no 19 I 309, not quite nat. size
6. Knife or scraper no 19 I 315, not quite nat. size
7. Spearhead, no 19 I 313, $2/3$
8. » , no 19 I 311, $2/3$

The originals in the Museum Gothenburg

Photo by C. Skottsberg. View of Hanga Roa village from the sea, with Punapau in the background.

Nat. Hist. Juan Fernandez and Easter Isl. Vol. I. PLATE 2.

The northwest highland, seen from Rano Kao. Hanga Roa village in the centre.

Photo by C. Skottsberg.

Ahu near La Perouse Bay, seaward side, centre and part of wings. Eminence in centre, base of fallen image.

Photo by C. Skottsberg.

Photo by C. Skottsberg.

Same ahu as in Plate 3, landward side with fallen image. To the right, the hat Mrs. S. on the back of the image.

Rano Raraku, from the SW.

Statues on outer wall of Rano Raraku.

Very large image in quarry. Mrs. S. sitting on its throat.

PLATE 8.

Photo by C. Skottsberg.   Two images lying on their backs, inside of crater.

Heads of two images in quarry, inside of crater. The native is Juan Tepano.

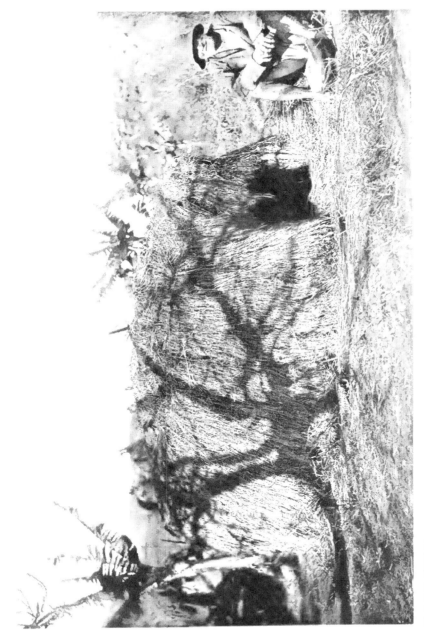

Grass hut with its old native owner, near Hanga Roa.

Photo by C. Skottsberg. So called watch-tower, La Perouse Bay. Mrs. S. in front.

Young native girl.

Photo by K. Bäckström. Same girl as in Plate 12.

Nat. Hist. Juan Fernandez and Easter Isl. Vol. I. PLATE 14.

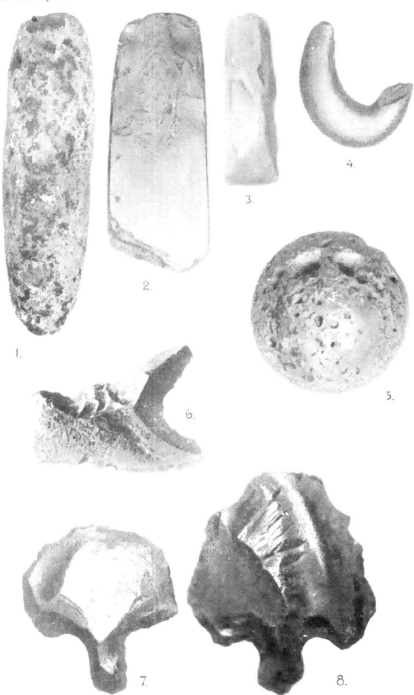

Photo by O. Thulin.
Stone implements. For explanation, see last page of text.

THE NATURAL HISTORY OF JUAN FERNANDEZ AND EASTER ISLAND

EDITED BY DR. CARL SKOTTSBERG

VOL. I
GEOGRAPHY, GEOLOGY, ORIGIN OF ISLAND LIFE

PART II

2. T. H. HAGERMAN: Beiträge zur Geologie der Juan Fernandez-Inseln.
3. P. QUENSEL: Additional Comments on the Geology of the Juan Fernandez Islands.
4. C. SKOTTSBERG: A Geographical Sketch of the Juan Fernandez Islands.

UPPSALA 1954
ALMQVIST & WIKSELLS BOKTRYCKERI AB

2 Beiträge zur Geologie der Juan Fernandez-Inseln.

Von

TOR H. HAGERMAN

Mit 12 Textfiguren

Die Schwedische Pazifik Expedition 1916—1917 unter der Leitung von Professor C. SKOTTSBERG brachte unter anderem eine Gesteinsammlung von den Juan Fernandez- und Oster-Inseln zurück, die dem Mineralogischen Institut der Hochschule zu Stockholm zu Bearbeitung übergeben wurde. Bei der von mir vorgenommenen Untersuchung von etwa 50 Handstücken von den Juan Fernandez Inseln stand mir ausserdem QUENSEL's Material von einer früheren Beschreibung[1] desselben geologischen Gebietes zur Verfügung.

Die Juan Fernandez Inseln liegen zwischen 33 und 34° S. Br., 660 km W. von Valparaiso. Die Inselgruppe besteht aus zwei grösseren Inseln, Masatierra, Flächeninhalt ca 95 qkm und W. von derselben Masafuera, 85 qkm. Nahe der erstgenannten liegt eine kleine Insel St. Clara, 5 qkm.

Der Gebirgsgrund dieser Inseln besteht ausschliesslich aus Effusivgesteinen. Eine exakte Altersbestimmung derselben kann kaum gemacht werden, da keine Sedimentgesteine vorhanden sind. QUENSEL[2] nimmt an dass die vulkanischen Gesteine kaum älter als jungtertiär sein dürften, und es ist seitdem nichts bekannt geworden, was für eine veränderte Auffassung spräche.

Die Inselgruppe ist einer kräftigen Erosion ausgesetzt gewesen, sodass die ursprünglichen Vulkankegel nicht mehr zu erkennen sind. Besonders auf Masafuera, wo die Wasserscheide weit nach W. verschoben liegt, hat sich eine ausgesprochene Cañon Landschaft gebildet. Die wilden Terrainformen sind deutlich aus den zahlreichen Photographien zu erkennen, von denen viele in SKOTTSBERG's Reisebeschreibung[3], wie auch in Vol. I und II dieses Werkes veröffentlicht worden sind.

Masatierra.

Die Untersuchung des Materials von Masatierra hat erneut bestätigt, was QUENSEL bereits hervorhebt, nämlich, dass die Gesteine untereinander chemisch und mineralogisch nahe verwandt sind, und sich im wesentlichen nur strukturell voneinander unterscheiden. Sie können als verschiedene Erstarrungsformen ein

---

[1] P. D. QUENSEL. Die Geologie der Juan Fernandez Inseln. Bull. Geol. Ups., Vol. XI, p. 253—290.
[2] L. c. p. 256.
[3] C. SKOTTSBERG, Till Robinsonön och världens ände. Stockholm 1918.

und desselben Magmas betrachtet werden; späterhin sind allenthalben stellenweise sekundäre Veränderungen infolge hydrothermaler Prozesse entstanden, die abweichende Ausbildungen hervorgerufen haben.

Die Gesteine sind im primären Zustande durchwegs mehr oder weniger olivinreiche Basalte mit der Zusammensetzung: Olivin, Pyroxen, Plagioklas, Magnetit, Ilmenit und oft ein wenig Glasbasis.

Charakteristisch für alle diese verschiedenen Teilen der Insel entnommenen Proben ist besonders die Zusammensetzung des Pyroxens. Dieser besteht aus einem Titanaugit, sofort erkennbar an seiner schwach rotvioletten Farbe und starken Dispersion der optischen Achsen. Doch ist zu bemerken, dass derselbe nicht zu den extremsten Typen gehört.

Auch die Feldspate weisen eine konstante Zusammensetzung auf. Sie sind fast alle zwillingsgebildet nach dem Albit- oder Karlsbader Gesetz. In Schnitten senkrecht zu M zeigen die Albitlamellen eine max.-Auslösung von 32—33°, in einigen Einzelfällen diese Werte mit höchst 2° variierend. Der Feldspat ist also ein Labrador von einer Durchschnittzusammensetzung $Ab_{42}An_{58}$.

Da die Basalte also mineralogisch einander nahe verwandt sind, wurden sie hauptsächlich nach der Struktur in folgende Typen eingeteilt:

basaltische Laven (teils dichte, teils grobkörnig doleritische, teils schlackige)
Tuffe, hydrothermale Umwandlungsprodukte.

Basaltische Laven

Diese Gesteine bilden, wie frühere Verfasser bereits betont haben, den Hauptbestandteil der Insel. Auf Grund des vorliegenden Materials konnte man den Verlauf der verschiedenen Lavaströme und deren Neigungsverhältnisse nicht bestimmen und so auch keine Klarheit über die Eruptionsstellen erlangen.

Die Fundstätten der dem Verfasser zur Untersuchung vorliegenden Handstücke sind ziemlich gleichmässig über die Insel verteilt. Von den zu den Laven gehörenden Gesteinsproben sind ungefähr $^2/_3$ sehr poröse und schlackige Typen, während $^1/_3$ (6 Stck.) dichte, dabei gleichmässigere und feinkörnige Gesteine darstellen.

Die Struktur dieser Gesteine ist im allgemeinen hypokristallin porphyrisch. In einigen Fällen, besonders bei den dichten Typen, kommt es vor, dass Glasbasis ganz fehlt.

Mit Bezug auf die mineralogische Zusammensetzung der basaltischen Laven sind folgende Mineralien beobachtet worden: Olivin nebst dessen Umwandlungsprodukten, die vorgenannten Pyroxene und Plagioklase sowie Erzmineralien (Magnetit und Ilmenit).

Die Einsprenglinge sind Olivine und ihre Umwandlungsprodukte sowie Feldspat. Die Augitkörner können sich zuweilen der Grösse der Einsprenglinge nähern.

Die Olivineinsprenglinge erreichen ihre grösste durchschnittliche Ausdehnung, ca 2 mm, in Proben, die von dem nördlichen Ufer der Padrebucht stammen. Gerade diese Einsprenglinge zeigen meistens in einer scharf begrenzten Zone die von QUENSEL[1] früher beschriebene Iddingsitumwandlung. Aus Dünnschliffen der genannten Gesteine ist klar ersichtlich, wie die Umwandlung von den Rän-

---
[1] L. c. p. 260.

dern nach der Mitte zu ausgegangen ist und sich 0,02—0,03 mm in den Olivin hineinerstreckt hat. An manchen Stellen ist die Umwandlung längs der Spaltrisse vor sich gegangen, während anderweitig die Durchgänge merkwurdigerweise vollkommen unveränderte Teile der Olivinkerne durchqueren. (Vergl. Fig. 1.) In der Gesamterscheinung des obengenannten Präparates möchte der Verfasser die Iddingsitbildung als das Resultat einer von aussen kommenden chemischen Beeinflussung ansehen. WASHINGTON[1] verweist die Iddingsitbildung bis auf magmatischen Ursprung zurück. Man braucht vielleicht nicht so weit zu gehen, da dieselbe ebensogut einer hydrothermalen Umwandlungsperiode zugeschrieben werden kann.

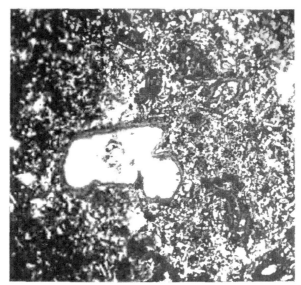

Fig. 1. An den Rändern iddingsitumwandelte Olivine. Olivinbasalt von der Padrebucht.— Vergr. 56×. Photo Hj. OLSSON.

In einem anderen Gestein von der Padrebucht, das etwas feinkörniger entwickelt ist, treten auch Feldspateinsprenglinge von 0,5—1 mm Länge auf, neben Resten von Olivinen. Der Olivinumwandlungsprozess hat hier ein anderes Produkt hervorgebracht, nämlich gewöhnlichen Serpentin. Dies ist auch bei den der Grundmasse angehörenden Olivinkörnern der Fall. Dieselben sind vollkommen als Serpentin ausgeflossen. Auch der Augit scheint an den Rändern etwas angegriffen zu sein. Beinahe identisch entwickelt sind zwei andere feinkörnige Basalte, der eine von der Mitte des südlichen Ufers, am Fuss des Yunque, der andere von einem Gebirgsrücken (385 m ü. M.) SW. von Tres Puntas, W. von der Villagra-Bucht, herstammend. Iddingsit- und Serpentinumwandlungen der Olivine sind, wie ich besonders hervorheben möchte, niemals in ein und demselben Gestein gleichzeitig angetroffen worden.

Die beiden erwähnten Gesteine von der Padrebucht und an beiden Seiten von Villagra zeigen eine eigentümliche primäre Struktur der gleichkörnig entwickelten Grundmasse, indem die Plagioklase mit einer mittleren Ausdehnung

---

[1] Italian petrogr. sketches. Journ. Geology. 4 1896, p. 835—836.

von 0,2 mm sich vielfach radialstrahlig mit den Augitindividuen geordnet haben. Ist man erst einmal auf diese sphärolitähnlichen Bildungen aufmerksam geworden, so findet man sie häufig hauptsächlich in den feinkörnigsten Proben dieser Gesteine ausgebildet. Besonders schöne Beispiele hiervon zeigt ein Handstück, das der »Pyramide», einem Berggipfel ungefähr in der Mitte der Insel unweit des SELKIRK-Denkmals, entnommen wurde. (Fig. 2.)

Eine sehr ähnliche Erscheinung ist von REITER[1] beschrieben worden. Er schmolz 45 % Albit, 45 % Augit und 10 % Magnetit zusammen. »Der Schliff

Fig. 2. Plagioklas-Augit-Sphärolit. Basalt von der »Pyramide». — Vergr. 250×. Zeichnung vom Verf.

einer durch 7 Stunden abgekühlten Schmelze zeigt eine sphäriodale Anordnung der Kristalle, in dem magnetitreiche Kerne von Glaspartien mit einzelnen ausgeschiedenen Augit- und Plagioklasleisten und Kristalliten umgeben sind. Die Wiederholung des Versuches bei 30-stündiger Abkühlung ergab eine Schmelze mit körnig-porphyrischer Struktur.» Zweifelsohne ist dies auch in dem vorliegenden Falle zutreffend, indem die sphärolitführenden Laven einer raschen und ungestörten Abkühlung ausgesetzt gewesen sein dürften.

In Anschluss an diese Sphärolite seien hier die in Fig. 3 abgebildeten kreuzförmig liegenden Olivinkristalle erwähnt. Der Dünnschliff entstammt einem etwas grobkörnigen Gestein von Bahia Cumberland. Wie aus der Figur deutlich her-

---

[1] H. H. REITER, Experimentelle Studien an Silikatschmelzen. Neues Jahrbuch. Beil. Bd. 22 (1906), p. 197.

vorgeht, handelt es sich um eine skelettartige Ausbildung der Kristallindividuen. Eine gesetzmässige Verwachsung der verschiedenen Individuen habe ich nicht nachweisen können.

*   *   *

Im Vaqueriatal tritt, wie aus der untenstehenden Photographie (Fig. 4) ersichtlich, ein fast horizontal liegendes Gestein auf. Nach ihrer grobkristallinischen Struktur zu urteilen, sind diese Basalte möglicherweise als intrusiv aufzufassen.[1] Das nur an zwei Seiten zugeschlagene Handstück ist vorzüglich durch Schrumpfung unter rechtem Winkel zerklüftet. (Fig. 5.) U. d. M. zeigt dasselbe ein unverändertes hochkristallinisches Aussehen. Reichlich albitlamellierte Feldspatleisten, durchschnittlich ca. 2 mm lang, bedingen mit Olivin- und Titanaugitkristallen eine ophitische Struktur. Ausser diesen Mineralien habe ich nebst Magnetit hier und da ein Biotitkorn gefunden. Möglicherweise erstreckt sich dieser Basalt bis zur Cumberland Bay, wo eine ähnliche Ausbildung von QUENSEL[2] beschrieben wurde. Auch das Material SKOTTSBERG's enthält eine ähnliche Probe von dort, in losem Block gefunden. Der Mineralbestand der beiden letztgenannten Handstücke ist derselbe wie jener der Vaqueriaprobe nur mit dem Unterschied, dass kein Biotit vorhanden ist. Auf Grund seiner grobkristallinischen Struktur muss das obenerwähnte Gestein zu den doleritischen Basalten gerechnet werden.

Fig. 3 a. Zentrisch angeordnete Olivine. — Vergr. 56×. Verf. phot.

Feinkörniger, aber im übrigen dem vorgenannten Gestein völlig gleich, ist der bei »Tres Puntas» genommene Basalt. Die Handstücke bestehen aus langen, schmalen, dreiseitigen Prismen.

*   *   *

Unter den schlackigen Laven weisen einige eine auffallende Analogie zu rezenter Oberflächenbildung auf. Besonders ist dies der Fall bei einem sehr porösen glasreichen Gestein vom Ufer s. von Yunque. Der vorerwähnte, auf dem Gipfel der »Pyramide» befindliche dichte Basalt hat ein schlackiges und glasiges Lavabett als Unterlage.

In einigen anderen der schlackigen Gesteine sind die Löcher mehr oder weniger mit Opal, Chlorit, Serpentin und Calcit ausgefüllt.

---

[1] Vergl. jedoch QUENSEL p. 263—264.
[2] L. c. p. 263.

Tuffe.

Unter dem mitgebrachten Material befinden sich zwei Proben von ausgesprochenen Tuffen. Der eine, ein poröses, dichtes Gestein, stammt von El Puente, dem Istmus zwischen der Padrebucht und Carbajal und ist ein Palagonittuff mit einigen sporadischen Augit- und Magnetitkörnern. Der andere Tuff stammt von dem nördlichen Ufer der Padrebucht, von wo einige umgewandelte Olivinbasalte (s. S. 23) herrühren. Ausser Augit und Magnetit enthält derselbe einige grössere vollkommen reine Olivinkörner in einem teilweise kryptokristallinisch aussehenden Glase. Stellt man diese verschiedenen Bildungen aus der Nähe der

Fig. 3 b. Detail von Fig. 3 a. — Vergr. 170×. Verf. phot.

Padrebucht zusammen, so gelangt man zu der Auffassung, dass dieses Gebiet frische Spuren vulkanischer Tätigkeit aufweist. Vergleicht man die obengenannten Tuffe mit den von QUENSEL[1] beschriebenen roten Tuffen von der Cumberland Bay, so scheinen die letztgenannten nicht so empfindlich gegen Verwitterung zu sein, wie besonders die Palagonittuffe.

Hydrothermale Bildungen.

Ein aragonithaltiges Gestein vom Ufer gleich südlich vom Yunquegipfel dürfte als hydrothermal umgewandelter Basalt angesehen werden. (Fig. 6.) Das Handstück ist ein von weissen Streifen durchzogenes scharfgrünes Gestein, das u. d. M.

---

[1] L. c. p. 266.

grosse Augitkristalle in einer völlig zerflossenen Serpentinmasse zeigt. Das Präparat ist von Aragonitbändern durchzogen. Dieses Gestein muss als ein stark umgebildeter Olivinfels bezeichnet werden. QUENSEL[1] hat ganz frische Gesteine von letztgenanntem Typus angetroffen und beschrieben. Vielleicht kann die Aragonitbildung hier eine Andeutung geben, auf welche Weise der Olivin chemisch umgewandelt worden ist.

Auf derselben Stelle wurde auch eine reine Kalksinterbildung gefunden, was darauf hinweist, dass diese Gegend in späterer Zeit postvulkanischen Prozessen hydrothermaler Natur ausgesetzt gewesen ist.

In Fig. 7 ist eine eigentümliche Bildung dargestellt, wie sie auf dem offenen

Fig. 4. Das Vaqueriatal. Wasserfall über den säulenförmig abgesonderten doleritischen Basalt.

Plateau bei Puente vorkommt. Es sind lange, in einem »Sandfeld» aufrechtstehende rohrähnliche Bildungen, Aragonit, Pyroxen, Magnetit sowie etwas Olivin in einem Zement von Karbonat enthalten. Die wahrscheinlichste Deutung dieser Phänomene ist wohl, dass mit Calciumkarbonat gesättigte thermale Gewässer über eine Vegetationsdecke geflossen sind, wobei Wurzeln etc. mit einer Kruste von oben angegebener Zusammensetzung überzogen wurden.

Santa Clara.

An dem Südende von Masatierra liegt die kleine Insel Santa Clara. Von Santa Clara selbst ist keine Probe mitgebracht, dagegen von der kleinen Insel Morro de los alelies, die bei tiefstem Wasserstand mit der Hauptinsel zusammen-

---

[1] L. c. p. 265.

Fig. 5. Handstück vom Vaqueria-gang. Verf. phot.

hängt. Sowohl in Dünnschliff wie in Handstück zeigt dieses Gestein, das als fast vertikale Gänge auftritt, eine völlige Übereinstimmung mit einem der dichten Basalte von Masatierra vom Gipfel des Cerro Negro SO von Yunque, 190 m ü. d. M. Ursprüngliche Plagioklaseinsprenglinge von bis zu 2 mm Länge sind oft so stark kaolinisiert, dass beim Schleifen nur die Hohlräume übrig geblieben sind und dem Gestein ein falsches, schlackiges Aussehen verleihen. Hierbei ist interessant, dass der Feldspat der Grundmasse sich frisch beibehalten hat. Die Olivine sind natürlich völlig in Serpentin umgewandelt. Das ganze Präparat ist von Ilmenitskeletten durchwachsen.

Masafuera.

Etwa 180 km westlich von Masatierra erhebt sich die Insel Masafuera. Abweichend von Masatierra in Bezug auf die einheitliche Mineralzusammensetzung der Gesteine liefert Masafuera Beispiele petrographisch weit verschiedener Typen. Basalte mit den dazugehörenden Gangformen von ungefähr gleichem Mineralbestand wie die auf Masatierra vorkommenden gibt es zwar auch hier, ausserdem finden sich aber auch an Erzmineralien stark übersättigte Basalte, sowie den Trachytandesiten sich nähernde Gesteine. Am interessantesten ist jedoch das Vorkommen von reinen Alkaligesteinen, wie z. B. die von QUENSEL angeführten Natrontrachyte.

Natrontrachyt.

Leider ist das einzige mitgebrachte Handstück dieses Gesteins von einem losen Block am Fuss der Steilwand von Tierras Blancas abgeschlagen. SKOTTSBERG hat indessen mündlich berichtet, dass zahlreiche Blöcke desselben Gesteines in den Talusbildungen von Tierras Blancas vorkommen, und dass, soweit er verstehen konnte, dasselbe hellgraue Gestein den ganzen oberen Teil der Steilwand bildet; seiner Kartenskizze nach zu urteilen tritt dasselbe bereits 400 m ü. d. M. auf. Dies ist von Bedeutung für das Feststellen der Eruptionsfolge, die später kurz erwähnt werden soll.

Das Gestein besteht aus gleichmassigen Körnern und ist sehr reich an Feldspat. Die Feldspatleisten erreichen eine Länge von 0,3—0,4 mm. Sie sind gut parallelorientiert und verleihen dem Gestein eine trachytoidale Struktur. Da Albitzwillinge nicht vorhanden sind und der Feldspat durch die Anlagerung der dünnen Individuen unscharfe Begrenzungen zeigt, konnte eine genaue Bestimmung desselben nicht ausgeführt werden. Die Lichtbrechung hält sich im allgemeinen etwas über Kollolith ($n = 1,535$), stellenweise ist das Relief jedoch ganz verschwunden. Um eine nähere Kenntnis von den Feldspaten zu bekommen, ist eine Alkalibestimmung des Gesteins ausgeführt worden. Diese ergab 3,45 % K_2O und 7,34 % Na_2O. Dies würde einem Gehalt von 20,44 % Ortoklas und 62,27 % Albit im Gestein entsprechen. Auf Grund der Lichtbrechungsverhältnisse dürfte jedenfalls neben einem Kali-Natronfeldspat auch ein saurer Plagioklas der Oligoklasreihe vorhanden sein.

Eine geringere Menge Pyroxen tritt ebenfalls auf. Die durchschnittliche Ausdehnung desselben ist 0,1 mm, die Farbe ist gelbbraun, die kristallographische Ausbildung schlecht entwickelt. Eine Auslöschung von $c:x = 40°$ (ungef.) deutet auf Augit. Schliesslich war auch Magnetit vorhanden, der öfters fliessende Begrenzung der graubraunen Glasbasis gegenüber zeigt.

← Aragonitband, von einem Augitindividuum überquert

Fig. 6. Hydrothermal umgewandelter Olivinfels von dem Yunque. — Vergr. 12,5 ×. Verf. phot.

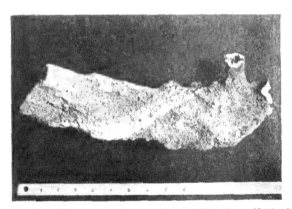

Fig. 7. Sinterbildung von Puente. Massstab in Cm. Verf. phot.

Der von QUENSEL[1] beschriebene Natrontrachyt ist ungefähr 1200 m ü. d. M. gefunden worden und zeigt bei einem Vergleich einige Abweichungen. Das Handstück scheint im Gegensatz zu dem obenbeschriebenen etwas verkieselt zu sein. U. d. M. bemerkt man sofort, dass der Pyroxen hier abweichend von dem vorerwähnten farblos ist. QUENSEL bezeichnet denselben als Diopsid. Ferner ist die farbige Glasbasis nicht vorhanden.

[1] L. c. p. 283.

Andesit

Von dem Berggipfel »Las Torres», 1370 m u d M, und in losen Blocken von dem Bergrucken NO von der genannten Stelle 1200 m u d M sind Handstucke von einem feldspatreichen aschgrauen Gestein mitgebracht worden. Obwohl etwas olivinreicher, stehen dieselben den von QUENSEL[1] beschriebenen, einem 1100 m u d M liegenden Niveau entnommenen Trachytandesiten sehr nahe. Als Einsprenglinge kommen Feldspat und Olivin vor, u d M zeigt der erstgenannte eine Zusammensetzung von $Ab_{38}An_{62}$ und erreicht eine Korngrosse von 3—4 mm. Die Olivine sind etwas kleiner. Sie werden im allgemeinen nur ca 1 mm in Diameter und sind wenig verandert, nur an den Randern zeigt sich eine schwach gelbe Farbe, wo die Umwandlung begonnen hat. In der Grundmasse dominiert der Plagioklas mit einer Ausdehnung von ca 0,1 mm. Die Pyroxene und Magnetite sind noch kleiner, im allgemeinen nur 0,05 mm. Die Magnetite sind vollig idiomorph. Die Klassifizierung hiehergehorender Gesteine ist etwas unsicher. Die trachytoidale Struktur konnte auf einen gewissen, nicht wahrnehmbaren Alkali gehalt in der Grundmasse deuten. Genugende Grunde, sie als Trachytandesite zu bezeichnen liegen jedoch nicht vor.

Sehr interessant ist ein bei Correspondencia (1420 m u d M) genommenes Gestein. Mikroskopisch zeigt dieses Handstuck ein aschgraues, porphyrisches Aussehen, doch sind einige Partien bedeutend dunkler. Als Einsprenglinge kommen Feldspat und Olivin vor. U d M zeigt der erstgenannte eine Zusammensetzung $Ab_{42}An_{58}$ und erreicht eine Korngrosse von durchschnittlich 2 mm bei einer max.-Lange von 5 mm.

Der Olivin ist vollig frisch, die Einsprenglinge treten aber in zwei verschiedenen Entwicklungen auf. Dies steht im Zusammenhang damit, dass das Gestein, wie bereits erwahnt, nicht vollig homogen ist. Die dunkleren Partien erweisen sich bei mikroskopischer Untersuchung als bedeutend magnetit- und ilmenitreicher als der ubrige Teil des Gesteins.

In den dunkleren Schlieren finden sich nun Olivine mit Magnetiteinschlussen vollgesteckt. Besonders an den Randern ist der Magnetit so reichlich vorhanden, dass die Olivinkorner vollig opak sind. Sowohl aus diesem Grunde als auch infolge der abgerundeten Form der Mineralkorner scheint es, als ob diese Olivin korner einer kraftigen Resorption ausgesetzt gewesen waren. Nahelegend ist nun, dass diese dunkleren Schlieren mit ihrem grosseren Eisengehalt Ruckstande aufgeloster Bruchstucke sind, welche ursprunglich zu dem Typus gehorten, die einem schlackigen Basalt vom Gipfel des Inocentas entsprechen, der spater beschrieben werden soll.

In einer Entfernung von kaum 1½ mm von einem der erwahnten Olivinkorner treten Individuen des anderen Typus auf. Diese sind ganz einschlussfrei, vollig idiomorph mit scharfen Begrenzungsflachen, erreichen einen Durchschnitt bis zu 4 mm und entsprechen vermutlich der intratellurischen Olivingeneration des Hauptgesteins.

Der Feldspat in der Grundmasse der helleren Schlieren tritt in Stengeln von ca 0,14 mm Lange auf und verleiht durch seine Parallelorientierung dem Gestein eine Fluidalstruktur. Die Zusammensetzung desselben ist $Ab_{46}An_{54}$. Im ubrigen enthalt die Grundmasse Magnetit und Pyroxen.

Die Grundmasse der dunkleren Partien unterscheidet sich von der obenge-

---
[1] L c p 282

nannten durch ihren Gehalt an Ilmenit, leicht erkennbar an seinem tafelförmigen Habitus. Ausserdem kommen hier feine Nadeln vor, welche aus einem ziemlich stark lichtbrechenden Mineral bestehen. Dasselbe ist pleochroitisch von braungelber bis gelbgrüner Farbe und weist parallele Auslöschung auf. Wegen der kleinen Dimensionen der Körner konnte eine sichere Bestimmung derselben nicht ausgeführt werden. Mit grösster Wahrscheinlichkeit liegt hier nur eine feinblättrige Ausbildung von Ilmenit vor.

Basaltische Laven

Auf dem Uferplateau an der Ostseite der Insel bei dem Casastal steht ein feinkörniger Basalt mit porphyrischen Feldspat und Olivineinsprenglingen an. Die Feldspäte erreichen eine Länge von 0,9 mm und erweisen sich als Plagioklase mit einer Zusammensetzung von $Ab_{40}An_{60}$ und stimmen also mit dem Feldspat der Masatierra Basalten überein. Die von QUENSEL[1] erwähnten, stark basischen Feldspatkerne habe ich nicht angetroffen. Die Olivinkörner erreichen in diesem Präparat eine Grösse von 0,3—0,4 mm und sind etwas iddingsitumgewandelt. Von den Mineralien in der Grundmasse werden die Plagioklase am grössten, 0,08 mm. Der Pyroxen ist dagegen so klein, dass eine nähere Bestimmung sich nicht ausführen liess. Er erscheint in kleinen, viereckigen, farblosen Körnern, meistens zusammen mit dem Magnetit.

Diesem Gestein sehr nahe verwandt ist dasjenige, welches am Ufer des MonoTales ansteht. Makroskopisch sind die beiden Gesteine einander sehr ähnlich. U. d. M. tritt jedoch ein Unterschied auf, und zwar indem die Grundmasse des Monobasaltes hier bedeutend mehr Olivin enthält, weshalb man dieses Gestein auch wegen der zahlreicheren Olivineinsprenglinge als einen Olivinbasalt bezeichnen muss, während sich das erstgenannte den Feldspatbasalten nähert.

In Quebrada del Óvalo, ungefähr 150 m ü. d. M., steht eine säulenförmige Basaltkuppe an, die dem Tal seinen Namen gegeben hat. Sie ist oben horizontalzerklüftet, während weiter unten eine prismatische Vertikalzerklüftung ansetzt. Vorausgesetzt, dass die Kuppe aus ein und demselben Gesteine besteht, kann dies als ein gutes Beispiel der von IDDINGS[2] dargetanen Veränderung in der Richtung für den kleinsten Schrumpfwiderstand innerhalb des erstarrten Gesteins angesehen werden.

Die Handstücke sind den unteren Teilen der 20—30 m hohen Säule entnommen und bestehen aus einem porphyrischen Olivinbasalt. Die Einsprenglinge sind Olivine von ca. 0,6 mm Durchmesser. Dieselben sind an den Rändern dunkelrot, kaum durchleuchtend, was wahrscheinlich durch einen Gehalt an freiem Fe_2O_3 verursacht wird. Untenstehende Photographie (Fig. 9) stellt einen dieser übrigens sehr sparlich vorkommenden Einsprenglinge dar.

Die Grundmasse ist der des vorstehend erwähnten Olivinbasalts völlig gleich, nur etwas gröber. Der Plagioklas, ein Labrador, erreicht eine Länge von ca. 0,12 mm, das ganze Präparat ist parallelorientiert. Besonders hervorgehoben sei, dass das Olivin in der Grundmasse nicht rotpigmentiert ist. Im übrigen findet sich Magnetit und der farblose Pyroxen.

---

[1] S. p. 276.
[2] J. P. IDDINGS, The columnar structure in the igneous rocks of Orange Mountain, N. J. Amer. Journ. 31 (1886), p. 321.

Der höchste Berg auf Masafuera ist der Inocentes. Von dem Gipfel, ca. 1500 m ü. d. M., wurde ein rötlicher, sehr schlackiger porphyrischer Basalt mitgebracht, der sich besonders durch seinen hohen Gehalt an Erzmineralien auszeichnet.

Unter dem Mikroskop erwies sich die Grundmasse als hyalopilitisch. Die Einsprenglinge bestehen hauptsächlich aus grossen, im ersten Augenblick vollständig opaken Körnern von ca. 3 mm Durchmesser. Bei genauerer Untersuchung erweisen sich jedoch mehrere als stellenweise durchsichtig. Diese Teile besitzen

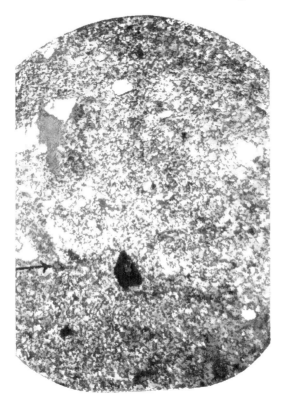

Fig. 8 a. Das heterogene Gestein von Correspondencia. Dunklere Partien oben und unten sichtbar. — Vergr. 10×. Photo. E. DAHLSTRÖM.

die hohen Interferenzfarben des Olivins, dazu weisen die Körner auch im übrigen den Habitus des Olivins auf. Bei Beobachtung in konvergentem polarisiertem Licht bei einem Achsenaustritt wurde keine Krümmung des Achsenbalkens beobachtet, weshalb der Achsenwinkel nahezu 90° sein dürfte. Dies deutet auf eine für Basalte normale Zusammensetzung von Olivin mit verhältnismässig niedrigem Eisengehalt.

Kand. S. LANDERGREN führte eine Eisen- und Titanbestimmung der Gesteinsarten aus, wobei folgende Werte erhalten wurden: 18,82 % Fe_2O_3 und 3,59 % TiO_2. Dies entspricht einem Gehalt von 6,81 % Ilmenit und 15,44 % Magnetit. Diese Zahlen sind natürlich zu hoch, da Fe auch in den geringen Mengen Olivin, Pyroxen und Glasbasis enthalten ist, die sich in dem Gestein befinden. Es ist jedoch besonders interessant, dass, obgleich das Magma eisenübersättigt war, das Eisen die Konstitution des Olivins nicht nennenswert beeinflusste.

Von solchen magnetitübersättigten Olivinen spricht Doss[1] in einer Beschreibung von Basalten aus Syrien: »In diesen Gesteinen beherbergt der porphyrische Olivin eine derartige Menge von Magnetitkörnern, dass dieselben meist die Hälfte, zuweilen ungefähr $^4/_5$ des ganzen Kristalldurchschnittes einzunehmen scheinen». An einer späteren Stelle schreibt er: »Das Extrem hiervon tritt dann ein, wenn der

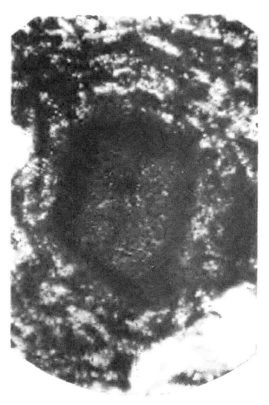

Fig. 8 b. Detail von Fig. 8 a bei →. — Vergr. 210×. Zu beachten ist die parallele Anordnung des Magnetits. Photo. E. DAHLSTRÖM.

Olivinkrystall einen breiten, völlig opaken, schwarzen Saum von Magneteisen besitzt». Das Phänomen stimmt mit dem vorliegenden vollkommen überein, nur dass hier der entgegengesetzte Fall vorliegt, indem das ganze Korn vollständig opak sein kann, auch in sehr dünnen Präparaten.

REITER[2] hat sich mit der Zusammenschmelzung von Olivin und Magnetit beschäftigt und sagt: »Bei Abkühlung tritt eine gewisse Übersättigung ein. Vom Magnetit scheidet sich ein Teil ab, dann wird der übersättigte Olivin ausgeschieden ...

---

[1] B. Doss, Die basaltischen Laven und Tuffe der Provins Haurân und vom Diret et-Tulûl in Syrien. T. M. P. M. Bd. 7 (1886), p. 483—484.

[2] L. c. p. 232.

Wir erhalten hiemit also Magnetite in zonarer Anordnung in den nachher entstehenden Olivinen eingeschlossen;...»

Die umstehende Photographie (Fig. 10) zeigt, wie der Magnetit parallel angeordnet ist, sodass die durchsichtigen Partien in Streifen auftreten.

Unter den Einsprenglingen kommt, wenn auch selten, hier und da ein Feldspatindividuum vor, dessen Zusammensetzung ungefähr $Ab_{40}An_{60}$ ist; es handelt sich also um einen Labrador, unbedeutend abweichend von dem Feldspate der übrigen Gesteinsarten.

Die basischen Plagioklase der Grundmasse zeigten zum Teil unscharfe Begrenzungen, durch die Anlagerung der dünneren Individuen verursacht.

Die Pyroxene sind bedeutend kleiner und erreichen einen Durchschnitt von ca. 0,02—0,03 mm, wenn auch einzelne stengelige Individuen etwas grösser werden

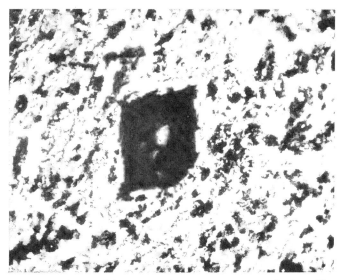

Fig. 9. Rotpigmentierte Olivineinsprenglinge. Basalt von El Óvalo. — Vergr. 56×. Photo. Hj. Olsson.

können. Von diesen kommen zwei verschiedene Ausbildungen vor. Der eine (normale) ist mit den in den beschriebenen basaltischen Gesteinen auftretenden Pyroxen indentisch und vermutlich als Diopsid zu betrachten, da er beinahe farblos und kaum pleochroitisch bei einer Auslöschung von ca. 45° ist. Der andere Typus ist braungelb und tritt besonders um die Löcher herum, niemals zusammen mit dem erstgenannten Typus auf, stellt aber wahrscheinlich nur eine Pigmentierung desselben dar. Auch hierin zeigt das Gestein eine grosse Analogie mit den vorerwähnten, von Doss beschriebenen Basalten. Er sagt auf Seite 481: »Hier besitzen die in der Nähe der von Kalkspat ausgefüllten Hohlräume gelegenen Augite eine goldgelbe Farbe;...».

Im übrigen besteht die Grundmasse aus kleinen, idiomorphen Magnetitkörnern, Ilmenit und Glasbasis. Der ganze Gebirgskamm soll aus diesem ausgesprochen basischen Gestein bestehen.

Bereits mikroskopisch zeigt ein anderes Handstück, das vom Strandabhange nahe des Casatales abgeschlagen ist, eine auffallende Ähnlichkeit mit dem Inocentesgestein. (Laut Angabe von SKOTTSBERG soll das ganze östliche Ufer aus diesem Gesteinstypus bestehen, abwechselnd mit den obenerwähnten Feldspatbasalten.)

Auch hier treten magnetitführende Olivine auf, wenn auch spärlicher. Die Feldspate sind dieselben und besteht der einzige Unterschied darin, dass das Gestein glasreicher ist, weshalb der in dem letztgenannten Gestein vorkommende Pyroxen nicht mit Bestimmtheit hat wahrgenommen werden können. Nimmt man an, dass dieses Gestein einer rascheren Abkühlung ausgesetzt gewesen ist als das vorgenannte, kann man dasselbe diesem gleichstellen und möglicherweise eine Andeutung über eine nicht unbedeutende Ausbreitung der fraglichen stark basischen Gesteinsart finden.

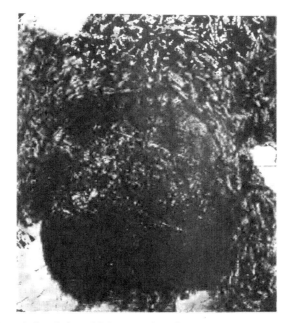

Fig. 10. Magnetitübersättigte Olivinsprenglinge im Basalt von Inocentes. Verf. phot.

Umstehende Tabelle ist eine Zusammenstellung über die Veränderlichkeit der effusiven Masafuera-Gesteine im Verhältnis zum Niveau der Fundstätten. Die Gesteine sind nach abnehmender Basisität geordnet und dabei das Material SKOTTSBERG's wie auch dasjenige QUENSEL's berücksichtigt.

Zwar fallen die Lavabetten etwas nach NNO ab, doch dürfte mit Rücksicht auf den geringen Umfang der Insel die umstehende Tabelle ein gutes Bild der Eruptionsfolge gewähren, wobei die ältesten Gesteine beim Meeresniveau, also links beginnen.

Vor allem verstösst der stark basische Basalt aus der Höhe von 1500 m ü. d. M. gegen die unter Zugrundlegung der Eruptionsfolge vorgebrachte Theorie, dass die Gesteine hier gravitativ differenziert sein sollen. Die Gesetzmässigkeit, die QUENSEL bei diesen Gesteinen gefunden zu haben glaubte — mit den sauren und alkalireichen als den jüngsten — scheint mir schwerlich mit diesen Beobachtungen in Übereinstimmung gebracht werden zu können.

	0	1	2	3	4	500	6	7	8	9	1000	11	12	13	14 1500
Natrontrachyte						o							x		
Andesite												x	o		o o
Basanit									x						
Basalte Feldspat-	xo														
Olivin-	oo	o													
Erzubersattigte Basalte	o														o

m ü d M

Die Verteilung der Effusivgesteine der Insel Masafuera
o bezeichnet Das Material SKOTTSBERG's
x » » » QUENSEL's

Es ist selbstverständlich denkbar, dass die in den tieferen Teilen des Zuflusskanales versunkenen schweren Magmas zuletzt herausgestossen wurden, doch spricht gegen diese Annahme das bereits in einer Höhe von 400 m u d M auftretende alkalische Gestein

Schliesslich ist aus der Tabelle zu ersehen, dass aus einer Höhe von 500—1000 m überhaupt kein Material untersucht ist. Die Masafuera Gesteine sind jedenfalls in Hinblick auf den Mineralbestand so verschiedenartig, dass eine nähere Untersuchung der noch unbekannten Höhenlagen wichtige Aufschlüsse ergeben dürfte

First printed February 25th, 1924
Reprinted without change April 13th, 1954

3 Additional Comments on the Geology of the Juan Fernandez Islands

By

PERCY QUENSEL

Contents

	Page
Introduction	37
Main Geological Features	40
Petrology of the Volcanic Formations	44
Masatierra	45
Masafuera	56
Regional Relations	
Tectonic Connections	74
Petrographic Connections	77
General Conclusions	79
Acknowledgements	82
Tables of Analyses	83
Bibliography	86

Introduction

The Juan Fernandez Islands consist of Masatierra, Masafuera and Santa Clara. In many publications the name Juan Fernandez has been used to denote Masatierra only, the other islands then being indicated by the names as above.

The largest island, Masatierra, situated 660 km from and nearly due west of Valparaiso, measures 95 square km. Masafuera, 170 km further westward is 64 square km. The small island Santa Clara, close to Masatierra is only 5 square km in area.

During more or less casual visits to Juan Fernandez stray observations have been recorded on geological features of the islands. In all cases they refer to Masatierra. It may be of interest in this connection to give a summary recount thereof.

The first samples of volcanic rocks of Masatierra were, as far as known collected by Lord COCHRANE in January 1823. He was returning to Europe after 5 years service as admiral in Chilean service during the war of independence. The ship at his disposal, Colonel Allen touched at Masatierra for two days. Mrs MARIA GRAHAM, a passenger on board, has in her diary given the following details, recorded by THOMAS SUTCLIFFE in his book Crusoniana 'Lord

Cochrane brought from the summit (1 500 feet) a piece of black porous lava, and under it he found some dark hardened clay full of cells the inside of which appear slightly vitrified. The island seems chiefly composed of this porous lava, the strata of which, being crossed at right angles by a very compact black lava, dip on the eastern side of the island about 22° and on the west side 16°, pointing to the centre of the island as an apex." (1, p 198)

In 1830 C. BERTERO published some observations under the title 'Notice sur l'Histoire naturelle de l'ile Juan Fernandez'. With regard to geological questions he says "Je pense qu'un géologue n'y trouverait que du basalte dans les états, même dans celui de la plus parfaite décomposition, plusieurs blocs sont parsemés d'une cristallisation particulière a laquelle on donne, je crois, le nom d'olivine. Il n'y a pas de trace de volcan, les pierres qu'on prend pour de la lave, et dont quelques unes ressemblent assez aux scories ou de la pierre ponce, ne sont, a mon avis que du basalte decomposé, on trouve aussi cette roche sous forme sphérique, et composée de couches concentriques " (2, p 345 compare in the latter respect Fig 10 on page 52 of this paper)

A. CALDCLEUGH, who accompanied Captain P. PARKER KING on the surveying voyages of H M S Adventure and Beagle on their first expedition 1826-1830, read before the Geological Society of London on Jan 5th, 1831, a statement on 'The geology of the island of Juan Fernandez'. In the Proceedings of that year the following account of Caldcleugh's discourse is given "The author could discover no trace of a volcano, said to exist here by former visitors, all the rocks, according to him, consist of basaltic greenstone and trap of various mineralogical structure both amorphous and vesicular, together with trappean concretions no other contained minerals being observable except olivine and chaux carbonatée métastatique. It is further mentioned that the basalt in parts is almost columnar and in others has a peaked and serrated outline the mass being, here and there, traversed by dykes. Owing to the peculiar character of this basalt and especially from the great quantity of olivine the author compares its age with that of the basalt of Bohemia the Rhine, the Vivarais and Beaulieu in Provence" (3, p 256 also published in the Phil Mag and Annals of Philosophy, Vol IX 1831, p 220)

Captain King recapitulates Caldcleugh's narrative, as given above, with the addition "In captain HALL's interesting journal there is a list of geological and mineralogical specimens, of which one from Masafuera is named vesicular lava" (4, p 304) The ultimate destiny of these specimens is unknown

Members of the Dumont d'Urville expedition, when visiting Masatierra in 1838, collected and specified several different samples of the lavas from the island (5, p 114) The material for the new analyses of basalts from Masatierra which LACROIX recently caused to be made and which will be referred to later on, are evidently from this collection, as Lacroix says they were made from specimens collected by the Dumont d'Urville expedition G GRANGE records some observations as follows "Toutes les roches appartiennent a diverses variétés de trapp et de diorite basaltique amorphes et vésiculaires, on ne trouve dans ces roches volcaniques aucun autres minéraux que de l'olivine et de la chaux metastatique

La roche basaltique s'y présente le plus souvent en couches superposées, quelquefois en escarpements interrompus et fractionnés et sont traversés par des dikes d'éjections plus modernes. Le basalt forme des pics élevés dans l'Ile et sur quelques points prend une disposition prismatique fort remarquable' (6, p 39)

In 1896 L H PLATE published a paper 'Zur Kenntnis der Insel Juan Fernandez' Plate was a zoologist and the paper deals with the zoology of Masatierra, but some introductory remarks refer to geological observations from which the following instances may be quoted "Das Gestein der Insel ist ausschliesslich vulkanischer Natur und besteht aus schwarzer, basaltischer Lava, der an einzelnen Stellen weissliche oder röthliche Tuffe eingelagert sind   Die Insel fällt fast überall mit senkrechten Wänden, deren Höhe zwischen 100 und 300 m schwankt, gegen das Meer zu ab und nur in den Hafen der Ansiedelung (Bahia Cumberland), dem Puerto Ingles, dem Puerto Frances und der Bahia de la Vaqueria erstrecken sich die Thäler bis an die Kuste, so dass man in diesen Stellen ohne Mühe vom Meer in das Innere der Insel vordringen kann   Die Lavawände sind deutlich geschichtet   Betrachtet man nun vom Meer aus eine (solche) Lavawand, so erkennt man sofort dass sie geschichtet ist, denn sie wird in ganzer Ausdehnung von zahlreichen horizontalen Linien durchsetzt   Diese horizontalen Linien sind wohl der Ausdruck des successiven Aufbaues der Insel   Aus einem submarinen Krater ergossen sich Lavaströme und breiteten sich auf dem Grund des Oceans aus   Die Eruptionen wiederholten sich häufig, und so floss eine Lavaschicht über die andere, um später zum Teil über die Oberfläche des Meeres gehoben zu werden   Ohne Zweifel war die Insel in früheren Erdperioden sehr viel grosser   Eine Untersuchung des Meeresbodens zwischen Masatierra und Masafuera wird vielleicht später den Beweis bringen dass die beiden Inseln, welche jetzt 92 Seemeilen von einander liegen, ursprunglich nur eine einzige bildeten oder doch wenigstens die höchsten Punkte desselben submarinen Plateaus darstellen und daher gleichzeitig entstanden sein mussen" (7, p 221)

The observations, hitherto recorded, have hardly more than historical interest As little attention had been paid to the geology of the Juan Fernandez Islands before the last decade of the past century, these casual comments have, however, here been included to evade oblivion

The first observations of any importance regarding the rocks of Masatierra are based on specimens collected by members of the Challenger Expedition in 1876 A RENARD has given a description thereof in a paper titled 'Rocks of the Island of Juan Fernandez (This name here signifies Masatierra) He says that "the rocks which have been submitted to examination all belong to the basalt type, and it seems probable that the whole island is made up of those rocks that we are about to describe The rocks, which form the central mass of the island, appear in the specimens as dolerites or as common basalts Among the specimens collected on the coast of Juan Fernandez it is necessary to mention a greyish very scoriaceous rock from which stand out large crystals of plagioclase of a waxy and milky appearance This rock is a dolerite with large vesicules Under the microscope the fundamental mass, in which the plagioclase crystals are embedded, has a dolerite structure. The felspar crystals show large extinction angles (38°—41°) which may be compared with those of bytownite. The sections of the mineral are cracked and pervaded with zeolite matter which forms an irregular network. This matter which looks slightly grey when seen by ordinary light, remains obscured between crossed nicols. The olivine, of which large sections are seen, is uniformly changed into a red hematite these sections, however, still show extinctions like those of the unaltered olivine" (8 p 176) The characteristic change of olivine to iddingsite in the basalts, which will be treated below in some detail is here evidently noted by Renard, though by him named hematite For the rest his description mostly refers to the colour and texture of different samples of dolerite and basalt

In 1886 L. DARAPSKY published a short report on detached rounded lumps of magnesite from Bahia del Padre in Masatierra, locally known as "piedras de campana" but named "Glockenstein" by the author (9). R. POHLMANN later (1893) described this singular formation in rather more detail and discussed its origin (10)

An account of some geological and petrographical observations by J. SCHULZ and R. POHLMANN, participants in FEDERICO JOHOW's expedition to the islands in 1891 has been published by the latter as an introduction to Johow's monograph 'Estudios sobre la Flora de las Islas de Juan Fernandez' (11, p 1)

As a member of the Swedish Magellanian Expedition of 1907—1909 I had the opportunity, together with Professor SKOTTSBERG of visiting the islands in 1908 and later described the rock specimens then collected in a paper 'Die Geologie der Juan Fernandezinseln' (12) In 1916—17 Skottsberg again visited the islands and collected specimens from some new localities These were subsequently described by I HAGERMAN under the title 'Beitrage zur Geologie der Juan Fernandez-Inseln' (13)

Since Skottsberg's visit in 1917, no further exploration in the field has been published concerning the geology of the islands in question And, with the exception of four recent analyses of lavas from Masatierra from collections made by members of Dumont d'Urville's 'Voyage au Pole Sud et dans l'Océanie' in 1838, commented on by LACROIX (14, p 64) no further observations have, as far as known, been published on the geology or petrography of the Juan Fernandez Islands On the other hand questions relating to their lithological connection with other intra-pacific islands and their geophysical position in relation to eastern-pacific volcanic centres has been the subject of repeated discussions during later years

Main Geological Features

The two islands Masatierra and Masauera present very different aspects with regard to their bulk configuration Masatierra exhibits a rugged appearance of isolated jagged cliffs (Fig 2) The highest peak, El Yunque, is 927 m On the clear cut shore bounded escarpments one can distinguish many hundred lava beds overlying one another In thickness they can vary from some few metres up to 20 m or more

Fig. 1. Perspective view of Masafuera from the East. Reproduced from F. Johow, Estudios sobre la flora de las Islas de Juan Fernandez, Santiago de Chile 1896.

Masafuera presents notable dissimilarities to Masatierra. Its dome shaped, sharply bounded outline with an approximately oval circumference and its imposing height give an impression of a volcanic configuration deviating from that of Masatierra. On the west side of the island the cliffs fall all but perpendicularly for over 1 000 m. The shore line below is a stony and sandy reach, in part named Loberia vieja on account of the number of fur seals found there at certain seasons. The eastern coastline has a very different appearance. As the highest ridge lies towards the west, the fall on this side is not so precipitous. Instead it is traversed by numerous narrow and steep sub-parallel erosion valleys (quebradas). Attempts to ascend the higher parts of the island can only be made from the eastern side by means of these quebradas, a climb which is anything but easy going (Fig. 3). The highest peak is 1 500 m.

The sketch in Fig. 1 gives an excellent conception of the singular configuration of Masafuera's eastern escarpments.

The Juan Fernandez Islands are exclusively formed of volcanic material, in many respects of much the same nature as in other volcanic islands of the eastern Pacific. All indications tend to show that they are of late origin. Both VON WOLF (15, 1929, p. 771) and J. BRÜGGEN (16, p. 59) consider them to be late tertiary or pleistocene in age. Lacroix says regarding all the non-coralline islands of the southern central Pacific: "leur âge précis est indeterminé, mais il est certainement tertiaire, pleistocène ou même, dans certains cas, recent" (14, p. 55).

No signs of recent activity have been found on the Juan Fernandez Islands. That the immediate environs have recently been subjected to sub-marine volcanic activity is, however, evident from a narrative, published in the Report of the Challenger Expedition as follows: "In 1835 Masatierra appears to have been governed by a Mr SUTCLIFFE, an Englishman in Chilean service. He was present when the earth-quake took place on the 20th of February of that year, of which he gives the following account: At 11.30 a.m. the sea rose over the mole and afterwards retired, leaving the greater part of Cumberland Bay dry, so much so that old anchors on the bottom became clearly visible. The earth then began to shake violently, and a tremendous explosion was heard, the sea still receding in immense rollers, which afterwards returned, violently rising to such a height that the settlement was literally covered and washed away, when the sea again receded. The phenomenon occurred four times, causing much destruction, uprooting trees and drowning cattle. Shortly after the explosion, a large column, some-

Fig. 2. The south slope of the high ridge along the western half of Masatierra as seen from Portozuelo. Photo C. Skottsberg.

what resembling a water-spout, was seen ascending from the sea off point Bacalao, which proved to be smoke, but at 7 p.m. volcanic flames were visible through the smoke, which lasted till 2 a.m. on the 21st. The depth of the water on the spot, where the eruption took place, was from 50 to 80 fathoms; no alteration in the depth was detected after the eruption had subsided" (17, p. 818). Sutcliffe has published an account of the 'earthquake' in a separate publication (18) and reproduced a sketch of the sub-marine eruption (19, p. 387).

It is obvious that these narratives must refer to a sub-marine volcanic explosion. CHARLES DARWIN also mentions the phenomenon in his 'Geological Observations on the Volcanic Islands' (20, p. 149). Renard gives the position of the explosion as 1 English mile from the island and remarks "that the close proximity of a volcanic centre seems therefore to be implied" (8, p. 176).

The sub-marine eruption must be taken as conclusive evidence that the immediate neighbourhood of the Juan Fernandez Islands has been the seat of volcanic action within the last 115 years. A point of further interest is that the explosion was simultaneous with violent earthquakes on the Chilean coast, as Darwin already observed (see p. 75).

Brüggen refers to some further observations of sub-marine eruptions in the vicinity of the Juan Fernandez Islands, recorded by FR. GOLL in his paper 'Die Erdbeben Chiles' (Münchener Geogr. Studien 1904, Nr. 14). The following denotements by GOLL are taken from Brüggen (16, p. 332):

Fig. 3. Quebrada del Varadero on the east coast of Masafuera. Photo C. Skottsberg.

"Según Goll se produjo, el 12 de febrero de 1839 una erupción submarina y maremoto a unas 120 km al este de la Isla de Mas a Tierra. El mismo autor cita la observación siguiente hecha en un punto un poco más austral: 'En octubre de 1867, se sintió un temblor submarino en 34° 55′ S y 77° 38′ W (unas 100 millas SE de Juan Fernández) después el buque navegó durante dos horas por agua de color blanco lechoso, habiendo mucho pescado muerto en la superficie.' Se trata probablemente del mismo fenómeno que describe JOSÉ M. POMAR en la forma siguiente, aunque dice que el punto se halla a 100 millas al SW en vez de SE de Juan Fernández: 'En 1867, el capitán SIMPSON de la barca británica Coronella navegaba en el Pacífico con mucha calma y vientos contrarios, con excepción de un fuerte viento acompañado de siete temblores que se produjeron como a 100 millas al SW de la Isla de Juan Fernández; durante dos horas navegó por agua tan blanca como leche, sondeó, pero no tocó fondo en 100 pies de profundad; vió muchos pescados muertos y una gran cantidad de pajaros por todas partes. Agregaba el capitán Simpson que si hubiera estado 10 millas más adelante, el choque hubiera sido peor y hubiera causado averías al buque.'"

Concerning the earthquake of Vallenar in the province of Atacama on the 10th of Nov. 1922 Bruggen cites BAILEY WILLIS' observations on the contemporaneous volcanic activity on San Felix.

Bruggen concludes his opinion on the submarine explosions, given above, as follows: "A la teoría del origen de los tsunamis por erupciones submarinas podría objetarse que serían erupciones muy excepcionales ya que consistirían en una sola o muy pocas explosiones que causan las pocas olas sísmicas, apagándose luego la actividad. En realidad se tratará solamente de las primeras explosiones que abren la chimenea para la salida de la lava o de los gases y que tienen la fuerza suficiente para causar el tsunami. También en otro sentido las erupciones submarinas se distinguen de las de los volcanes de los Andes, que sólo excepcionalmente entran en actividad durante los terremotos. Los volcanos submarinos parecen estar en relación más estrecha con los focos sísmicos de los grandes terremotos chilenos." (16, p. 332)

Petrology of the Volcanic Formations.

The following description of the rocks of Masatierra and Masafuera is based on specimens collected by myself in 1908 and by SKOTTSBERG in 1917. In many cases the two collections supplement one another and help to elucidate to a certain degree the distribution of the somewhat varying types of the lava flows.

The specimens from Masatierra in both collections give conclusive evidence that this island in the main is formed of a rather uniform series of basaltic lava beds, only diverging in respect of coarser or finer grain or of a higher or lower content of olivine. The specimens from Masafuera on the other hand indicate more obvious dissimilarities in the composition of the rocks at different levels.

In the following the principal petrological features of the two islands will first be treated. Under a later heading references will be made to resemblances in various respects to other volcanic islands of the eastern Pacific.

Masatierra

Lat. 33° 37½' S., Long. 78° 50' W.

The two collections of specimens from Masatierra by Skottsberg and myself have partly been taken from different localities. The central parts of the island are however sparsely represented. Somewhat more complete series of rock samples originate from the heights around Bahia Cumberland (Ensenada de San Juan Bautista), Puerto Frances and Portezuelo as well as from Bahia del Padre. From the adjacent small island Santa Clara there is only one specimen. It is not easy to single out the local distribution of the different lava beds on account of the unconnected localities from which specimens have been collected. Some characteristic features may however be found which indicate that certain types of lavas are restricted to localised areas. To some extent one may then draw conclusions regarding the sequence of the volcanic eruptions.

The predominating rocks of Masatierra are olivine basalts, differing only in their content of olivine. Lava beds from around Puerto Frances are exceptionally rich in this mineral, the content of which can reach 40 vol % of the rock (Fig 6). Such rocks, with an extreme content of olivine, I named picrite basalts in my earlier paper (12, p 265). Lacroix originally named such basalts 'picrite feldspatique' but later discarded this name, substituting for it the name oceanite[1], under which name he includes the basalts of the Juan Fernandez Islands with an exceptionally high content of olivine (14 p 65). Since the name picrite basalt, as originally defined in my former paper, has later been adopted[2], I will retain this name for the rocks in question, with the name oceanite as synonym.

From the extremely olivine-rich basalts around Puerto Frances there is every transition over intermediate types to feldspar basalts without any olivine at all or with only a very insignificant amount thereof. Such rocks, however, have a relatively limited distribution on Masatierra. In general one may say that types with a very high content of olivine are restricted to lower elevations whereas higher up more normal olivine basalts predominate.

A second feature of dissimilarity in the basalts is found in their texture. Many of the lava beds show a coarse grained ophitic texture and may be classed as dolerites, and have been so named by Hageman and myself in our previous papers. Such rocks are usual around Puerto Frances and Bahia Cumberland as well as at Vaqueria and Tres Puntas. Specimens from all these localities are in outward appearance very much alike. In general these rocks, in contrast to other lavas, are singularly fresh. Only the olivine often shows a dark brown rim, indicating an incipient alteration to iddingsite (cf 12, p 260).

The doleritic basalts seem only to occur at lower horizons, where the lava beds generally attain their greatest thickness. All the specimens thereof at hand are from between sea level and 200 m. A sample in Skottsberg's collection from Bahia Cumberland (Fig 7) and another from Vaqueria are both from 150 m above sea

---

[1] The name oceanite was first proposed by Lacroix in 1923 in Mineralogie de Madagascar Vol III, p 49. The name is given 'a cause de leur abondance dans les iles du Pacifique".
[2] Holmes, Q J Geol Soc 172, 1916, p 231, Washington Am J of Sc V 1923 p 471

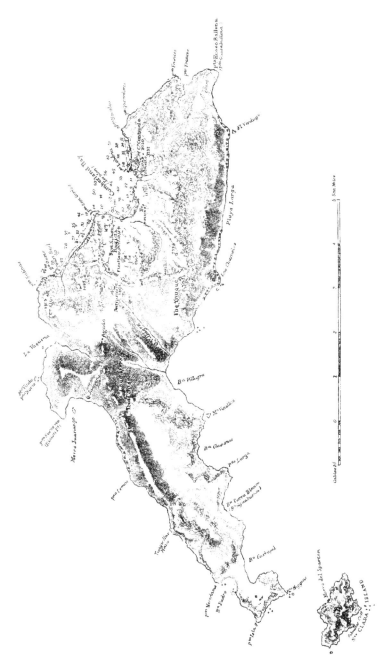

Fig. 4. Masatierra. Map by Fernando Amador de Amaya of 1795 with corrections from the Chilean Gov. chart of 1921. Scale 1 : 103 970.

Fig. 5. Basaltic lava beds. Western head of Bahia Cumberland, Masatierra. Photo C. Skottsberg.

level. The two specimens are in texture and mineral composition identical. A third sample from Tres Puntas is from 200 m. Specimens in my earlier collection were taken from the lower lava beds in the quebradas around Puerto Frances.

As no scoriaceous or slaggy development is to be seen in the upper or lower parts of the doleritic beds, which have a very coarse-grained texture, they may well represent intrusions between previously consolidated lava flows, in accordance with what DALY has assumed to be the case with similar doleritic rocks in Hawaii (R. Daly, Differentiation in Hawaii, Journ. of Geology, Vol. 9, 1911, p. 291).

The doleritic basalts and the picrite basalts have much the same mineralogical composition. The only essential difference is the higher content of olivine in the picrite basalts. The other rock-forming constituents in both rocks are labradorite, a pleochroic Ti-augite and magnetite.

In the picrite basalts (oceanites) from around Puerto Frances as well as in the olivine basalts in general the phenocrysts of olivine are often more or less altered to iddingsite. In some cases only insignificant rests of olivine are left; the iddingsite pseudomorphs, however, still retain the crystal habit of the olivine. To the petrogenetic problem of iddingsite as representing a deuteric mineral I will return later in connection with equivalent alterations in certain lava beds of Masafuera, where the 'iddingsitisation' has gone further and there gives the rocks a very characteristic aspect (see p. 60).

In the picrite basalts from Puerto Frances inclusions of dunite occur. The large olivine crystals of this rock are singularly fresh, without any signs of even

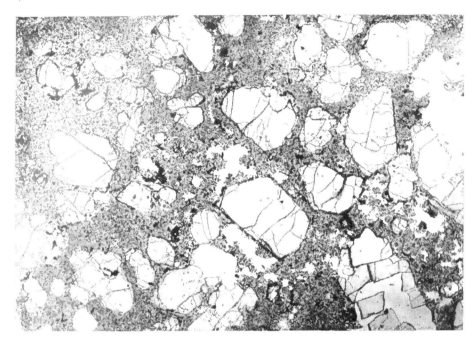

Fig. 6. Picrite basalt (oceanite). × 9. Puerto Frances, Masatierra.

Fig. 7. Doleritic basalt. × 37. Bahia Cumberland, Masatierra.

a periferic alteration to iddingsite which is otherwise usual in the olivine of the surrounding basaltic lavas.

At higher levels the basalts have a more normal character. Large phenocrysts of olivine, or olivine and feldspar, lie in a more or less glassy groundmass of augite, olivine and labradorite with abundant small grains of magnetite. Ilmenite in tabular form or in skeleton crystals is now often present. Most of these lavas are vesicular, scoriaceous or slaggy. The cavities are in many cases rimmed or filled with opal.

The occurrence of basalts of this type is widespread up to the highest parts of the island, and they are without doubt the dominant lavas of Masatierra.

Somewhat divergent lava beds seem, however, to predominate at intermediate horizons. All the specimens at hand of this type are holocrystalline rocks of an ash grey colour, aphanitic and aphyric in texture (Fig. 8). They generally show a characteristic light zone of weathering and a tendency to develope a columnar structure (Fig. 9). The fine-grained mineral assemblage consists of augite, labradorite and very abundant magnetite in small euhedral crystals, evenly dispersed throughout the rock. Ilmenite is also generally present in skeleton crystals. Stray small grains of olivine may in some cases be observed; in other specimens olivine is completely absent. In vesicular lavas of this type the cavities are again more or less filled with opal (Fig. 8 b).

These lava beds, which represent the only specific feldspar basalts of Masatierra, are found at heights between 400 and 500 m (Cordon Chifladores 400 m, Portezuelo 500 m). At an elevation below 100 m at Punta Larga in the more western part of the island the same type has been found, but then in the form of a dike, which may signify a channel for the analogous lavas at higher levels.

The very characteristic aspect of these rocks seems to indicate that they represent a definite epoch of intrusion intermediate between the doleritic basalts and picrite basalts of the lower parts and the scoriaceous olivine basalts of the higher horizons. An analysis has been made of a very similar rock from Masafuera, which confirms its classification there as a feldspar basalt (see p. 66).

Lacroix's four new analyses of basaltic lavas from Masatierra indicate that the analysed rocks are similar in composition. It is regrettable that the specimens all originate from Bahia Cumberland. Probably the members of the d'Urville expedition only brought back samples from that locality and these were therefore the only specimens available in Paris for Lacroix's analyses. On the other hand the insignificant dip of the lava flows on Masatierra ($15—20°$) may infer that the analysed rocks can be taken as representative in chemical composition for the basal basalts of the island. Microscopic determinations of corresponding specimens from the other localities point in the same direction.

With the exception of the ultra femic picrite basalts from Puerto Frances and the inclusions therein of dunitic rocks, and the light grey feldspar basalts of intermediate horizons, we may conclude that the dominant rocks of Masatierra consist of rather normal olivine basalts deviating principally in texture and in a varying content of olivine.

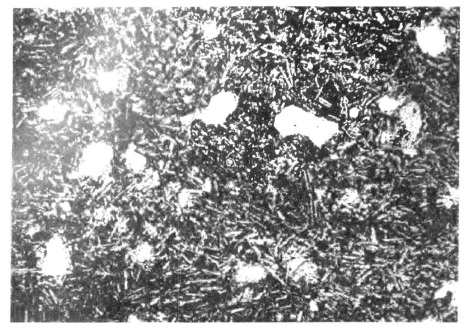

Fig. 8 a. Vesicular aphyric feldspar basalt columnar structure. × 30. Portezuelo, Masatierra (see Fig. 9).

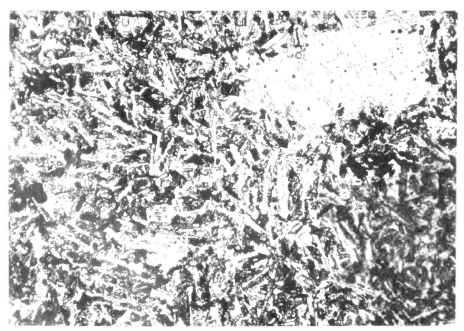

Fig. 8 b. Same specimen as Fig. 8 a, magnified × 65. Vesicle in upper right corner filled with opal. Portezuelo, Masatierra.

Fig. 9. Northern wall of the Portezuelo Pass, showing columnar structure of feldspar basalt Fig. 8 a'. Photo C. Skottsberg.

Fig. 10. Spheroidal weathering of basalt. Bahia Cumberland, Masatierra. Photo C. Skottsberg.

Quantities of pyroclastic material are found interbedded between the lava flows all over the island. Pöhlmann has described such products from Bahia del Padre as follows: "Überall sieht man Decken von basaltischem, meist säulenförmig abgesondertem Eruptivgestein mit Schichten von vulkanischem Auswurfsmaterial wie Asche, Lapilli, Bomben u. s. w. wechsellagernd.

Eine solche aus Lapilli und Bomben zusammengesetzte Schicht von mehreren Metern Mächtigkeit an der rechten Seite der Bucht in der Nähe der sog. Kapelle gelegen, liefert das Material der sog. 'Glockensteine'. Der Vorgang ihrer Bildung ist, kurz gesagt, folgender: zunächst entstehen traubige und nierförmige Concretionen zwischen den losen zusammengefügten vulkanischen Massen; diese weissen Knollen (Fig. 12) gelangen beim Absturzen der Schichten an den Strand und erhalten als Rollsteine durch die Thätigkeit des Wassers ihre gerundete Form" (10, p. 321).

I have previously noted that the lava beds of the eastern parts of the island are also often interbedded with agglomeratic layers (12, p. 257).

Some stray occurrences of superficial tuffs seem still to have evaded destruction by erosion. When Renard says that "amongst the specimens collected at Juan Fernandez (Masatierra) by the Challenger Expedition in 1875, we have not found any specimen which might belong to any recent eruption, no tuffs, no volcanic ash are to be found and everything seems to prove that they have been washed away by the waves and the atmospheric agencies" (8, p. 176), this last conclusion seems questionable. Hagerman refers to two specimens in Skottsberg's collections as representing recent tuffaceous material. The one he describes as "ein poröses, dichtes Gestein von El Puente, dem Istmus zwischen der Padrebucht und Carbajal und ist ein Palagonittuff mit einigen sporadischen Augit und Magnetitkörnern. Der andere Tuff stammt von dem nördlichen Ufer der Padrebucht, von wo einige umgewandelte Olivinbasalte herrühren" (13, p. 26). As these specimens have been collected without any observations regarding their petrological position one cannot draw any conclusive evidence as to their age, but the specimens from both the localities have every appearance of being recent pyroclastic sediments.

I have previously described rocks from Bahia Cumberland, filling out the greater part of the bay, which I assumed to be of recent tuffaceous origin. The description was given as follows: "In den zentralen Teilen von Cumberland Bay liegen noch ziemlich mächtige, meist lebhaft rot gefärbte Tufflager, die sehr stark umgewandelt sind. Bruchstücke von Olivinkristallen, lapilliartige Lavabruchstücke, Erzkörner und Glas liegen in einer Grundmasse, die aus einer weichen mit Messer schneidbaren, roten lateritähnlichen Lehmsubstanz besteht, die durch Verwitterung aus dem ursprünglichen Tuffmaterial hervorgegangen sein dürfte. Überall in den Tuffsedimenten ist eine deutliche Lagerung sichtbar" (12, p. 266). It is over 40 years since I visited the locality and naturally I cannot now rely on any personal recollection. The inundation in connection with the volcanic disturbance of 1835 referred to above (p. 41), may have wrought such havoc, that superficial deposits could have been re-formed. But the composition of the formation, as well as my notes from the field, offer indications that the tuffaceous material of Bahia Cumberland also represents pyroclastic sediments of recent volcanic origin.

Even if only trivial remains of tuffaceous formations indicative of late volcanic activity on the island, are left, the submarine explosion of 1835 confirms without doubt that the area in the immediate vicinity has at that time been subjected to disturbances of volcanic nature.

Some rocks from around Bahia del Padre deserve special notice. Schulze and Pohlmann have observed the deviating nature of the rock assemblage and the latter has commented thereon as follows: 'De suma importancia para esplicar la formacion jeolojica de Masatierra es la entrada á Bahia del Padre situada en la parte suroeste de la isla. Aqui se observa debajo de las capas basálticas ya descritas un grand macizo de roca compacta verdosa, que es andesitica. Segun la opinion de Schulze[1] que, a me parecer, es correcta, esta roca verdosa es la mas antigua de la isla. En ningun otro punto, ni en Masatierra, ni en Masafuera se ha observado una configuracion jeolojica analoga a la mencionada (11 p. 4).

The rocks referred to by Pohlmann certainly show a divergent aspect. But I do not think they can be taken as representing rocks belonging to a more ancient formation than the lavas around, nor that they should be classified as andesites as Pohlmann has assumed. I have as the result of microscopical examination of the rocks come to the conclusion that the deviating character is the result of post volcanic alterations through thermal processes. In my earlier paper I have given in some detail the reasons for this conclusion (12, p. 266), and

---

[1] Dr. Schulze died before publishing his observations.

Fig. 11. Volcanic [...] nerate, Bahia Cumberland, Masatierra. Photo C. Skottsberg.

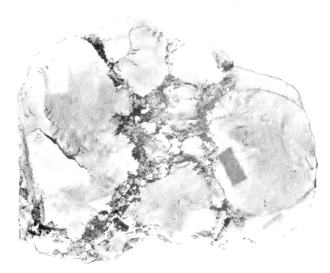

Fig. 12. Lumps of magnesite the so-called Glockenstein. Nat. size, Bahia del Padre, Masatierra. Reproduced from P. Quensel, 12, p. 269.

Fig. 13. Scoriaceous lava with newtonite and bole. Nat. size, Bahia del Padre, Masatierra. Reproduced from P. Quensel, 12, p. 269.

will in this connection only summarize the facts. The   s in question are very fine-grained and of a greenish colour. The abundant cl   age plains are coated with epidote and calcite. Pyrite is finely dispersed thr   out the rock. Under the microscope one can see that original phenocrysts of   th olivine and augite are more or less completely changed to serpentine and c   orite. The matrix consists of olivine, augite, plagioclase, magnetite and ilmenite — i.e., the usual mineral assemblage of the basaltic lavas. The greater part of the silicates are, however, very much altered to serpentine, chlorite and prehnite. Secondary albite and some scapolite is also present together with abundant pyrite. Small cavities are filled with epidote and calcite. In the slaggy lavas in the immediate vicinity larger cavities are filled with a purely white clay like substance which was found to be newtonite. In intimate association with this mineral is nearly always found a yellowish waxy substance which shows every resemblance to what mineralogically may be signified as bole (Fig. 13). It is very brittle with a conchoidal fracture. In water it readily disintegrates into small angular fragments. This bole mineral is also found filling cracks, or occurs in smaller masses in the cavities of the basalts around the bay.

In the agglomeritic lavas of the vicinity large cavities are filled with hard compact magnesite. As early as 1886 Darapsky described this mineral by the name "Glockenstein" and gave an analysis thereof which shows it to be an exceptionally pure magnesite (9, p. 113). Without doubt the magnesite is primarily derived from olivine, the decomposition being caused by the same processes as have changed the basaltic lavas nearby.

The whole aspect of the rocks from Bahia del Padre, with magnesite, calcite, serpentine chlorite, scapolite and pyrite as secondary minerals, seems without doubt to indicate that the lava beds in question have been subjected to alterations in connection with thermal processes during some intermediate phase of volcanic activity on the island. There seems no reason to classify them as andesites of an older formation, as is done by Schulze and Pohlmann.

In a specimen collected by Skottsberg from the shore south of El Yunque, Hagerman also found evidence of a far reaching decomposition. Under the heading 'Hydrothermale Bildungen' he gives the following description: "Das Handstuck ist ein von weissen Streifen durchzogenes schartgrunes Gestein das u d M grosse Augitkristalle in einer vollig zerflossenen Serpentinmasse zeigt. Das Praparat ist von Aragonitbandern durchzogen. Dieses Gestein muss als ein stark umgebildetes Olivinfels bezeichnet werden" (13, p. 27). The large olivine crystals of the dunite found as inclusions in the picrite basalt at Puerto Frances, show on the contrary, no signs of secondary alteration (see p. 47). There is therefore no doubt that the highly decomposed 'Olivinfels' described by Hagerman has succumbed to a later decomposition of much the same nature as has been active around Bahia del Padre.

Masafuera

Lat. 33° 52′ S., Long. 80° 54′ W.

The lavas of Masafuera present a more varying aspect than those of Masatierra and contain several types of petrographic interest. They have however, hitherto only been summarily described in the papers by myself (12, p. 274) and by Hagerman (13, p. 28).

The rocks which predominate at lower levels are mostly vesicular to slaggy basalts. They are well represented around the Quebrada de las Casas. At higher levels the basalts consist of more compact lava beds. In contrast to the basalts

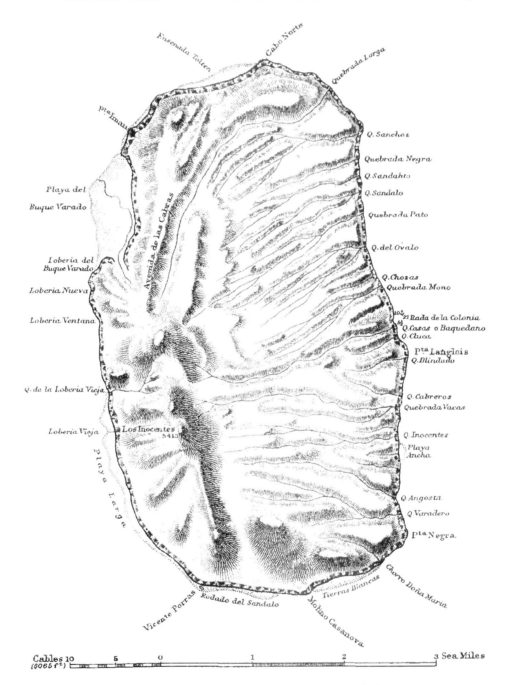

Fig. 14. Masafuera. From the Chilean Gov. chart of 1921. Scale 1 : 70 000.

Fig. 15. View of the interior of Quebrada de la Loberia vieja towards the shore. Photo C. Skottsberg.

of Masatierra, olivine is more scarce in the dominant basalts of Masafuera, but is singularly rich in the basaltic dikes which in hundredfold vertically traverse the island.

The rocks prevailing at heights up to c. 1 000 m may for the greater part be classified as dark vesicular feldspar basalts, with large phenocrysts of labradorite (Ab 45, An 55). Olivine is scarce as phenocrysts but occurs in varying amount in the groundmass together with augite, labradorite and magnetite in a dark, glassy matrix (Fig. 16).

In many specimens of the vesicular lavas the vesicles are filled or lined with zeolite minerals. In some samples the vesicles present, from the outward rim, first a coating of glass, followed by chalcedon and chabasite and a central replenishment of well developed natrolite spherolites.

At an elevation of about 1 000 m a lava bed of a very different aspect is met with. In contrast to the dark basalts of lower horizons, the rock now in question is light grey in colour. Large phenocrysts of olivine (up to 5 mm in diameter) and labradorite are uniformly distributed in a very fine-grained groundmass, consisting of augite, slender laths of labradorite, abundant small grains of magnetite and a small amount of a nearly colourless glass (Fig. 17).

In outward appearance this lava has a very singular aspect. The surface feels rough and grainy which, together with the light grey colour, at first gives the impression that the rock would have a trachytic or trachy-andesitic compo-

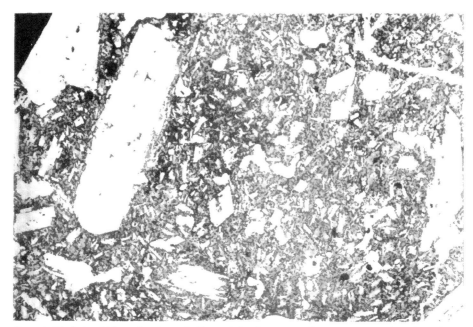

Fig. 16. Vesicular feldspar basalt. × 8. Normal development under 1000 m elevation, Masafuera.

sition. The analysis (Table I, No. 7), however, shows that the lava must be assigned to the basaltic group, though in many respects it obviously differs from all the dark basaltic rocks of lower elevations on the island. With some hesitation, in my former publication I referred the rock to the basanite group, assuming that a content of virtual nepheline might be concealed in the groundmass, which was readily affected when treated with HCl. This circumstance Lacroix assumes to be characteristic for the basanitoid lavas of the Pacific, where he says the nepheline often "n'est pas exprimée; elle est restée a l'etat potential dans la verre. La poudre des ces roches, traitée par HCl s'attaque plus au moins facilement" (C. R. 169, 1919, p. 402). BARTH has, in his paper 'Pacificite, an anemousite basalt', suggested that the virtual nepheline may be concealed in the plagioclase in the form of carnegieite. For such basalts he proposes the name pacificite, or if olivine is present, olivine pacificite and on account of my former description, refers the lava in question from Masafuera to the pacificite group (21, p. 60; 22, p. 380, 510).

In publishing the description of the rocks from the Juan Fernandez Islands in my earlier publication the analyses were not recalculated according to modern methods. This has been done now and the results recorded in the appendixed table of analyses. With regard to the rock, then tentatively named basanite, the calculated norm shows no nepheline and an excess of 1.99 % of aluminium. This, together with a content of 3.36 % H_2O, gives the impression that the rock is decomposed. On this account Lacroix, in reproducing my analyses of the Juan Fernandez rocks, omitted this analysis, "car les résultats ne correspondent pas

Fig. 17. Olivine basalt. Nat. size. Elevation c. 1 000 m. Masafuera. The olivine phenocrysts more or less completely altered to deuteric iddingsite.

à la composition minéralogique décrite; le calcul fait voir qu'il s'agit d'une roche altérée" (14, p. 65).

A renewed scrutiny of the rock has offered new aspects regarding its petrologic and petrographic position. The essential point has been that the large olivine phenocrysts are altered to such a great extent to iddingsite. We have every intermediate phase from a more or less broad rim of iddingsite around a kernel of perfectly fresh olivine to complete pseudomorphs of iddingsite, retaining the crystal habit of the olivine. The circumstance that the kernels of olivine are absolutely unaltered, leads to the conclusion that the iddingsite is not a product of normal weathering but a deuteric mineral, derived during a final stage of cooling of the lava in which it occurs.

During later years several papers have been published, in which the origin of iddingsite has been discussed in detail. The conceptions, there put forth, to all intent conform with the characteristic features of the lava from Masafuera. As the petrogenesis of the rock in question is of a certain interest, some significant quotations may be given, relating to the formation of iddingsite from different localities.

Ross and SHANNON summarize their conclusions as follows: "Iddingsite is not confined to weathered surfaces; its development shows no proximity to joint cracks and evidences of weathering in associated minerals is entirely absent. Thus it is concluded that iddingsite is not a product of ordinary weathering but a deuteric mineral, that is to say the result of metasomatic processes associated with the later stages of a cooling magma." They also emphasize that the magma must have come to rest before iddingsite formed, for though it is a very brittle mineral, it is never fractured or distorted by flow (U. S. National Museum, Proc. 67, 1925, Art. 7, p. 18).

AUROUSSEAU comes to the conclusion that "iddingsite is the result of oxidation processes that acted rapidly on the olivine during the liberation of copious active volatile phases at the time of eruption (Linnean Soc of N S W , Proc 51, 1926 p 617)

Finally EDWARDS in his paper 'The formation of iddingsite says "It is concluded, therefore, that iddingsite forms during or after extrusion, according to the temperature of the magma at the time of extrusion, and that, if the magma has cooled sufficiently before extrusion, not enough iron oxides are left in the residual volatiles for iddingsite to be formed" (Am Min 23, 1938 p 281)

The formula for iddingsite is given by Ross and Shannon as $MgO \cdot Fe_2O_3 \cdot 3 SiO_2 \cdot 4 H_2O$ with magnesia replaced in part by CaO, approximately in the ratio 1 4 The calculated composition according to this formula includes 7 90 % H_2O^- and 7 90 % H_2O^- (ibid p 17)

All the authors, now quoted, come to the same conclusion that the formation of iddingsite cannot be regarded as the result of normal weathering processes but that the mineral must be of deuteric origin, formed during the later stages of a cooling magma. The development of abundant iddingsite in the lava flow from Masatuera leads to the same conclusion. I may also remark that most of the photomicrographs, representing different stages of alteration from olivine to iddingsite published in Pl I—II in Ross and Shannon's paper, correspond in nearly every detail with equivalent alterations in the lava from Masafuera (Fig 18) As iddingsite according to the formula of Ross and Shannon contains 15 80 % H_2O, we may conclude that an appreciable amount of the 3 46 % H_2O, according to the analysis of the lava in question (Table I No 7), enters the iddingsite molecule

Another singular alteration in the iddingsite basalt in question is also worthy of notice. The slender labradorite laths in the groundmass as well as some phenocrysts of the same mineral are found to be more or less completely altered to an isotropic substance, though retaining their crystal habit perfectly intact. I had observed this circumstance in my former publication on the Geology of the Juan Fernandez Islands (12, p 278) and then came to the conclusion that the invading material was glass formed through fusion of the feldspars in the volcanic vent (Fig 19)

Dr OTTO MELLIS has kindly undertaken a renewed investigation of this isotropic alteration product. At first he also came to the conclusion that it consisted of glass, formed by fusion of the feldspars during a period of high-temperature autometamorphism. A more detailed study, however, led to different conclusions. Dr Mellis gives the result as follows "Repeated determinations showed that the refractive index of the isotropic material lies between 1 49 and 1 50 These values must exclude the presence of glass, formed by fusion of a labradoritic feldspar The index of refraction should according to Franco and Schairer in such a case lie between 1 53 and 1 54 (Journ of Geology, Vol 59 1951, p 266) A further evidence in this respect is that, when treated with HCl, the isotropic matter readily gelatinized, which is not in accordance with what one can assume to be the case with glass, formed by fusion of a basic plagioclase Opal must for the same reason be excluded as a possible component Continued investigations resulted in the conclusion that the alteration of the feldspars in the iddingsite

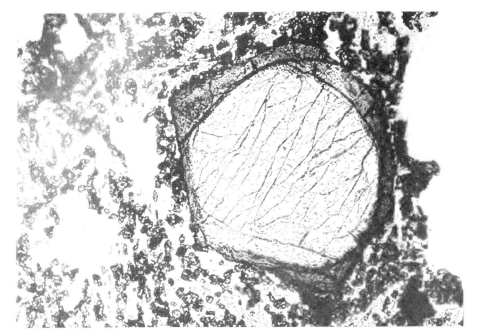

Fig. 18. Iddingsite forming sharp outer borders around unaltered olivine. × 100. From specimen Fig. 17. Elevation 1 000 m. Masafuera.

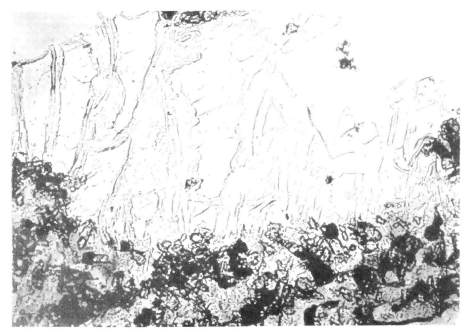

Fig. 19. Phenocryst of labradorite, traversed by a zeolitic matter. × 170. From specimen Fig. 17. Masafuera.

basalt must be attributed to an invasion of zeolitic matter. As there seems to be a slight difference in refractive indices in the alteration product, this is probably a mixture of different zeolites or related material. It has, however, not been possible to determine the definite nature of the zeolites. The fact that they show no sign of birefringence indicates that they must belong to the isotropic group or to those of very near zero birefringence."

It is of interest to note that Renard evidently has observed a very similar circumstance in a lava flow from Masatierra when he says that sections of a basic feldspar from a greyish very scoriaceous lava under the microscope are seen to be cracked and pervaded with zeolitic matter, which forms an irregular network. This matter, which looks slightly grey when seen in ordinary light, remains obscured between crossed nicols." This description might as well refer to the zeolitisation of the lava bed from Masatuera, especially as Renard in the same lava mentions olivine uniformly changed to iddingsite (Renard says hematite, S p 176)

It therefore seems probable that lava beds, in which the content of olivine has been more or less changed to deuteric iddingsite, also have succumbed to a high degree of zeolitisation. The fact that the large phenocrysts of olivine, only rimmed with iddingsite, show no signs of alteration, whereas the feldspars in the same section may be completely altered to an isotropic substance of zeolitic composition, must indicate that also the zeolitisation of the rock has taken place at an early stage and cannot be attributed to periods of normal weathering or later thermal activity.

In consequence of the changes in chemical composition which must have taken place in connection with the formation of iddingsite and the zeolitisation of the lava, it is no longer possible to establish the primary composition of the rock in question. Though the whole aspect of the lava bed so obviously differs from the normal olivine basalts on Masafuera there is evidently not reason enough with any degree of certitude to classify the rock as an olivine basanitoid. The presence of alkaline rocks on Masafuera must for the present therefore, be restricted to the occurrence of the soda-trachytic lava flows now to be described.

At an elevation between 1 000 and 1 100 m there occur rocks of quite another type. In outward appearance they are dense aphanitic and aphyric in texture and of a light yellowish green colour. The dominant minerals are an acid plagioclase and, subordinate orthoclase. Olivine, a light green diopsidic pyroxene and ore minerals are sparingly found in small individuals between the feldspar laths which have a well-defined trachytoid orientation (Fig 20). An analysis of this rock was made for my former description and is reproduced in the annexed table of the analyses of the Juan Fernandez rocks (Table I, No 8). I named the rock soda-trachyte.

On my survey I had assumed that rocks of this composition only existed on and formed the highest parts of the island, as at that time no higher elevations were reached. New specimens in Skottsberg's later collection disprove my earlier supposition in two essential respects. In the first place rocks of much the same

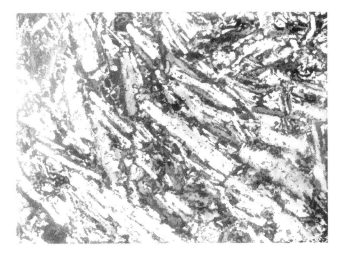

Fig. 20. Soda trachyte. × 50. Elevation c. 1050 m. Masafuera.

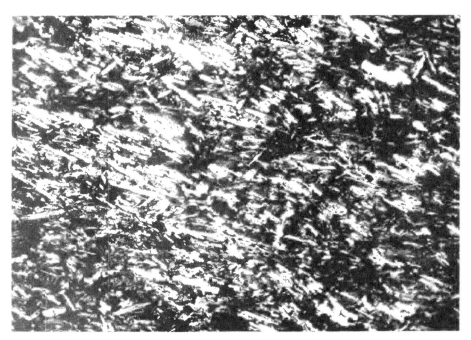

Fig. 21. Soda trachyte (boulder). × 30. Nic. +. Elevation about 400 m.
Tierras Blancas, Masafuera.

character as the soda-trachyte have now been found at lower levels. Secondly, Skottsberg reached the summit of the island and was there able to establish that basaltic lavas occupy the whole highest part of the island.

The new find of a rock, closely related to the soda-trachyte from higher levels, was a loose boulder at the foot of Tierras Blancas. According to Skotts-

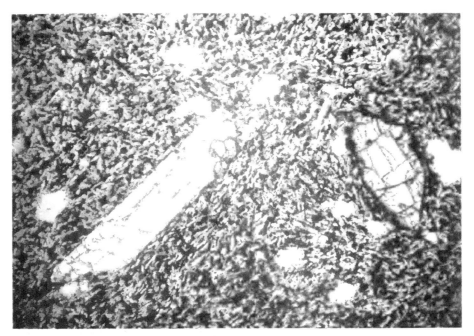

Fig. 22. Vesicular phyric feldspar basalt with stray phenocrysts of olivine. 30. Analysed specimen from 1 420 m elevation. Masafuera.

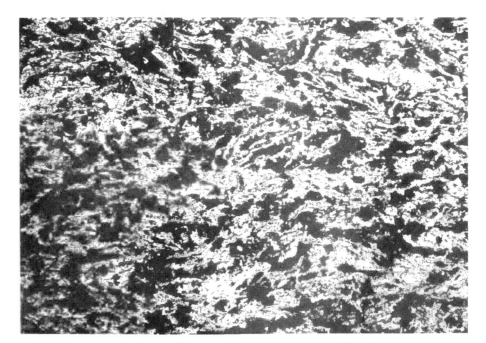

Fig. 23. Aphyric feldspar basalt. Columnar structure. × 50. Elevation c. 150 m. El Ovalo, Masatuera.

berg's information, boulders of this character were very numerous in the talus under a steep escarpment and can here hardly have originated from higher elevations than about 400 m.

In outward appearance this rock shows an aspect different to the compact soda trachyte between 1 000 and 1 100 m which on account of its dense texture at first sight gives the impression of a quartzitic rock. The new specimen has on the other hand a rough, loose grained structure. Minute intergranular cavities in the rock are seen under the microscope to be filled with limonitic matter. But allowing for this structural dissimilarity the rocks from the talus below Tierras Blancas seem to be closely related to the soda-trachyte as described above (Fig. 21). Taking into consideration the seemingly horizontal position of the lava beds of Masafuera the conclusion must be that lavas of soda trachytic composition have been emitted at different times and that they have alternated with lavas of more normal basaltic composition (see p. 71).

Specimens of the rocks from between 1 100 and 1 400 m present again a different aspect. Five samples from 1 100, 1 200, 1 300 and 1 420 m all have very much the same appearance. They are all phyric lavas of an ash grey colour. Feldspar and more rarely, olivine occur as phenocrysts in a groundmass of basic plagioclase, augite and abundant magnetite. In a somewhat vesicular specimen from 1 100 m olivine is also present as sporadic grains in the groundmass.

The groundmass has in most of the specimens a trachytic texture the narrow laths of feldspar circuiting the phenocrysts in a more or less well defined manner (Fig. 22).

In my previous paper I named the rocks of this nature trachyandesite. Hagerman says, referring to much the same specimens in Skottsberg's collection "Die Klassifizierung hiehergehöriger Gesteine ist etwas unsicher. Genügende Gründe sie als Trachyandesite zu bezeichnen liegen jedoch nicht vor" (13 p. 30). Hagerman names the rock andesite in his paper.

These rocks evidently have a rather wide distribution on Masafuera, probably forming the whole complex of lava beds between 1 100 and 1 420 m. To certify their petrographic position an analysis has now been made of a typical specimen (Table I, No. 5). The calculated norm and Niggli values definitely classify the rock as a feldspar basalt, in many respects of similar composition as some of the analysed basalts from Masatierra (Table I No. 1—4). A difference of interest is the still lower content of K_2O, the Niggli value k is now 0.08 against 0.15—0.20 in the basalts from Masatierra.

These phyric feldspar basalts from Masafuera in general aspect also very much resemble the aphyric feldspar basalts from between 400—600 m elevation on Masatierra. Occasionally at lower levels they also on Masafuera may be aphyric in texture (Fig. 23). They seem also in several respects to correspond to certain phyric and aphyric basalts from the Hawaiian Islands, as described by WASHINGTON (Petrology of the Hawaiian Islands I Kohala and Mauna Kea Am J of Sc V, 1923, p. 487). To this question I will return under a concluding heading dealing with the chemical and petrological connections between the rock of the Juan Fernandez Islands and other volcanic islands of the eastern Pacific.

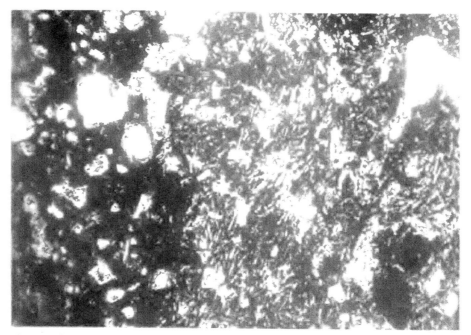

Fig. 24. Olivine basalt, supersaturated with iron oxide. × 35. Vesicular flow-breccia. Los Inocentes, elevation c. 1 500 m , Masafuera.

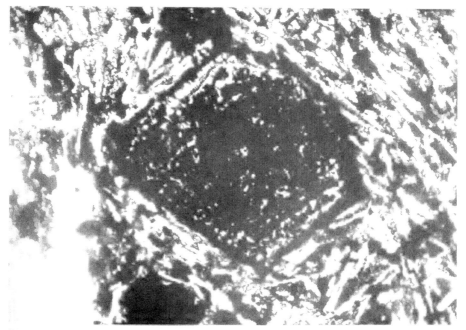

Fig. 25. Olivine phenocryst from specimen Fig. 24. × 110. Specks and streaks of unaltered olivine as rests in a pseudomorph after olivine. Los Inocentes, Masafuera.

Fig. 26. Disintegrated phenocryst of olivine, caused by high temperature oxidation. The rim around the olivine crystal is hematite. Within the olivine the light grains are mineral components, formed by exsolution. × 150. Los Inocentes, Masafuera. Photo P. Ramdohr.

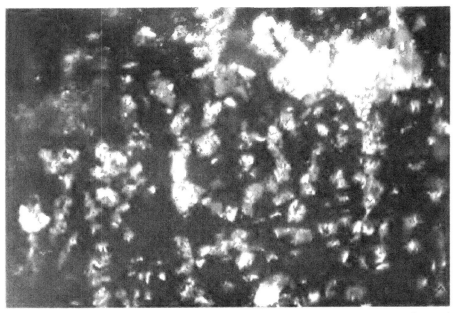

Fig. 27. Part of disintegrated olivine phenocryst, enlarged × 600. Against the dark background of olivine the exsolution product is seen in the form of small composite grains consisting of hematite light and a darker undefined component. Larger light grains see Pl. II, Fig. 1. Photo P. Ramdohr.

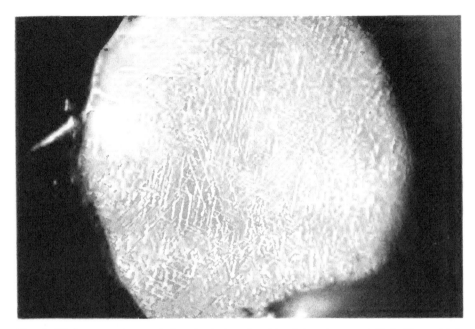

Fig. 28. High-temperature exsolution of spinel, enclosed in olivine phenocryst Pl. I, Fig. 2. Light lamellae, according to Ramdohr probably magnetite in groundmass of excess spinel. × 600. Photo P. Ramdohr.

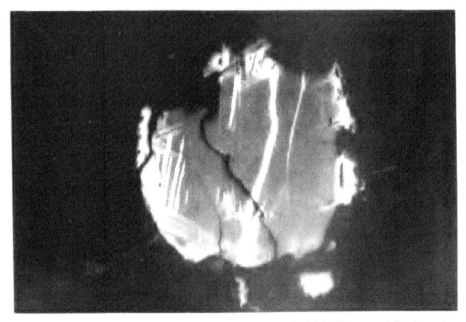

Fig. 29. Magnetite in groundmass of the lava bed as seen in Pl. I, Fig. 1 partially changed to hematite (martite). × 500. Photo P. Ramdohr.

An observation of importance with regard to the distribution of different lava beds on Masafuera is the find of a deviating type of olivine basalt from Los Inocentes. According to Skottsberg's observations such lavas probably occupy the highest part of the island, representing elevations above 1 420 m. The few samples brought back are highly scoriaceous flow breccias containing a high content of iron oxides (Fig. 24). Hagerman has in the preceding publication of this series given a description of these lavas which he characterizes as slaggy olivine basalts with large olivine phenocrysts, supersaturated with magnetite (13, p. 35).

The phenocrysts of olivine are under the microscope found to be almost opaque, due to the precipitation of new-formed ore minerals. A varying amount of residual olivine is, however, nearly always to be observed in the form of specks or streaks (Fig. 25). No signs of alteration are to be observed in this olivine. Optical determinations indicate that only a low content of about 8 % FeO is present in the molecule.

The groundmass consists of slender laths of labradorite, small grains of augite, magnetite, ilmenite and pseudobrookite in a dark brown glass matrix.

To determine the mineral composition of the pseudomorphs after olivine Professor S. GAVELIN and Dr UYTENBOGAARDT kindly undertook to examine some polished sections of the rock. Professor P. RAMDOHR (Heidelberg) contemporaneously supervised a section for the same reason. It thereby became apparent that the seemingly opaque constituent was not magnetite and that the mineral assemblage of the pseudomorphs was of a complicated nature. Professor Ramdohr has taken four photomicrographs thereof and kindly put them at my disposal. They are reproduced in Fig. 26—29 with Ramdohr's explanatory notes. In Fig. 26 the essential components can be observed. A rim of hematite is seen to encircle an idiomorphic crystal of olivine with specks of disintegrated minerals. In the enlarged microphotograph Fig. 27 these minerals are seen in the form of small lighter grains uniformly distributed against the dark background of olivine. One can now observe that the grains consist of two constituents. The one component is hematite. Repeated attempts have been made to determine the second component both in polished sections and with X-ray powder photographs. No conclusive evidence regarding the true nature of this mineral has, however, been attained.

The singular alteration of the olivine phenocrysts must in all probability be connected with the same processes as have controlled the formation of the deuteric iddingsite, though in the samples at hand this mineral is not extant. Edwards seems to have described a very similar formation in the iddingsite-bearing basalts from two Victorian localities in Australia. After concluding that the iddingsite must have been formed before the ultimate consolidation of the lava flow, Edwards says "In some instances, however, the action has gone further, and a rim of iron oxid is formed on the outer margin of the iddingsite. Eventually all the original olivine vanishes and the iddingsite, which had formed a rim about it, is completely replaced by magnetite. It is essential for the formation of iddingsite that the magma should not only be rich in water vapour, but that it should have differentiated in such a manner as to give rise to an iron-rich final fluid" (Am. Min. 23, 1938, p. 280). A photomicrograph in the text shows, according to Edwards, "a pseudomorph of iron ore after iddingsite, itself a pseudomorph after olivine".

These suppositions seem also referable to the very similar formation on Masafuera. The lava bed in question contains 33.86 % FeO according to determination by LANDERGREN (13, p. 33). This is more than double the content of FeO in any other basalts of the Juan Fernandez Islands. There seems little doubt that the pseudomorphs in question have formed under much the same conditions as advanced by Edwards. This is furthermore supported by the nearly identical appearance of the photomicrographs of the pseudomorphs from the Australian localities and from Masafuera, in both cases in connection with lavas containing iddingsite. Edwards assumes that, via an intermediate stage of iddingsite, the ultimately formed component is magnetite. As narrated above, this is not the case in the lava from Masafuera, where the pseudomorphs are found to be of a more complicated composition, formed without iddingsite as an intermediate phase.

All the observations given above seem to indicate that the iddingsite bearing basalt from elevations about 1 000 m as well as the flow breccias from the highest elevations on Masafuera have been subjected to an automorphic re mineralisation, prior to the final consolidation of the magma. This would suggest that the volcanic eruptions have been interposed by periods, during which the lava in a molten state has temporally stagnated in the volcanic vent under conditions which in connection with active volatile phases have led to the formation of such deuteric minerals as iddingsite and to the partial high temperature exsolution of the olivine phenocrysts.

The conclusions which may be drawn regarding the distribution of the different lavas of Masafuera would be now that rocks of more normal basaltic composition, principally feldspar basalts, occupy the lower and intermediate elevations of the island, whereas the highest parts consist of an olivine basalt, supersaturated with iron oxides. At some intermediate elevations lavas of a more alkaline character are found in the form of at least two beds of soda-trachyte, interposed between dominant flows of basaltic lavas.

Horizontal distribution of different types of lava on Masafuera

in m × 100	0	1	2	3	4	5	6	7	8	9	10	11	12	13	14	1500
Olivine basalt supersaturated with magnetite																×
Light grey phyric feldspar basalt												×	×			
Soda trachyte			×							×						
Iddingsite bearing phyric olivine basalt									×							
Dark phyric and aphyric feldspar- and olivine basalt	×	×	×	×												

Fig. 30. Picrite basalt (masafuerite). Dike rock. Nat. size. Lobería vieja, Masafuera.

Hagerman has recorded in his paper in tabular form his conception of the horizontal distribution of the different lavas of Masafuera. This is reproduced on p. 71 with some slight corrections on the base of renewed examination.

My former supposition that the basaltic lavas only occur up to an elevation of about 1 000 m, from there on being succeeded by more alkaline rocks of soda-trachytic composition, is no longer in agreement with more recent observations, based on Skottsberg's new collections. Any thought of gravitative differentiation to explain the sequence of the volcanic rocks, which I tentatively proposed in my former publication, must in the light of later observations be discarded now.

The numerous basaltic dikes, traversing the whole island in a West-East direction, are worth special notice as representing rocks exceptionally rich in olivine. In this respect they exceed the most olivine-rich picrite basalts from Puerto Frances on Masatierra. BOWEN has commented on these rocks as follows: "One other rock may be mentioned in this connection. It is a picrite basalt from Juan Fernandez, a dike, not a lava, but quenched so as to reveal the fact of its origin. In it is shown the highest amount of normative olivine (53 %) of any rock termed basalt by the author describing it. Great crystals of olivine lie in an aphanitic ground composed mainly of plagioclase and augite (Fig. 30—32). Some of the olivine basalts of this island group are, locally at least, about as rich in olivine as this dike, but they have not been analyzed. Their high olivine content is invariably due to an increased amount of phenocrysts of olivine about 1 cm in diameter. Plainly these crystals were not in solution in the dike or flow material at the time of its intrusion or extrusion. This

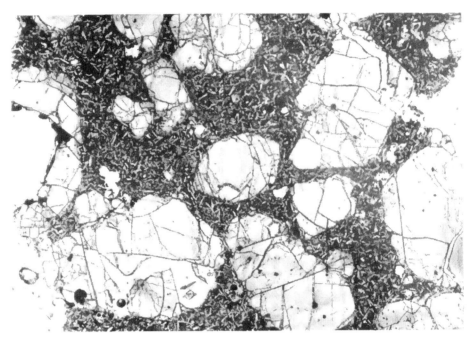

Fig. 31. Masafuerite dike. × 9. Loberia vieja, Masafuera.

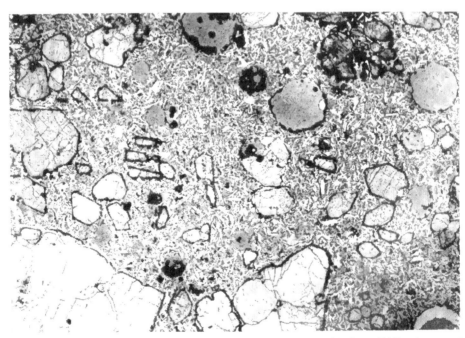

Fig. 32. Masafuerite dike. × 9. Analogous to sample Fig. 31 but with rims of iddingsite around all phenocrysts of olivine. Loberia vieja, Masafuera.

fact does not prove that they were not in solution in that material at an earlier time. But if one finds the condition shown by these basalts to be invariably true of all rocks rich in olivine, which have suffered quenching, one must conclude that large amounts of olivine occur in solution in magmatic liquids. A survey of igneous provinces leaves no question that such rocks do have this character, that is, they always contain either all of their olivine or all in excess of a quite small amount (apparently some 12—15 %) as relatively large phenocrysts. They, therefore, force acceptance of the stated conclusion" (23, p. 163). The quotation above refers to purely theoretical questions but indicates the extreme position these rocks hold in petrographic classification with regard to the abnormally high content of olivine in basaltic lavas. JOHANNSEN has named these rocks masafuerite, with the following argument: "The picrite basalt from Masafuera of the islands of the Juan Fernandez group is a most extraordinary rock. While this particular rock occurs as a dike, on the adjacent island of Masatierra, for example at Puerto Frances, there is a similar rock in the form of a lava flow with large olivine crystals in a groundmass containing more or less the same mineral. I am placing the rock among the hypabyssals on the basis of the occurrence on Masafuera. To all olivine-melabasalt dikes which contain more olivine than any other mineral and in addition carry basic plagioclase and augite, I should like to apply the name masafuerite" (24, p. 334).

We already have the name picrite basalt for the lava flows of much the same composition on Masatierra, with Lacroix's name oceanite as synonym, given with the following definition: "les roches basaltiques porphyriques à olivine sont parfois extraordinairement riches en péridot, dans l'échantillon analysé, tous les grains de ce minéral se touchent, ils sont réunis par une petite quantité de plages de labrador, englobant des microlites d'augite et des lames d'ilmenite" (14, p. 44). Johannsen has restricted the name masafuerite to aschistic dike rocks of a picrite basaltic magma.

These dikes may represent, at least in part, transmission channels for the upper basalt beds, supersaturated with iron oxides. A significant feature in this respect is that they contain numerous 'schlieren' of darker colour, due to abundant minute grains of magnetite. These streaks may indicate relics from a magmatic flow, subsequently consolidated in the shape of the olivine basalt supersaturated in iron oxides, which now forms the highest parts of the island. At a later period the channels may then have been filled with the melanocratic magma, which now characterizes them as such singular rocks. Sequent intrusions of this nature might lead to phases of crystallisation in accordance with Bowen's conception of these dikes as quenched rocks, referred to above.

Regional Relations.

Tectonic Connections.

In the introductory lines I already noted that during recent years as well as in older reports speculations have been offered regarding connections in one or other respect between the Juan Fernandez Islands and the volcanic islands of the eastern Pacific. Some quotations may be given.

CHARLES DARWIN already expressed views regarding geotectonic connections between the Juan Fernandez Islands and, on the one side, the South American continent, on the other, the Galapagos Islands. In his 'Observations on the volcanic islands and parts of South America' he says: "Some authors have remarked that volcanic islands occur scattered, though at very unequal distances, along the shores of the great continents, as if in some measure connected with them. In the case of Juan Fernandez, situated 330 miles from the coast of Chile, there was undoubtedly a connection between the volcanic forces acting under this island and under the continent as was shown during the earthquake of 1835. The islands, moreover, of some of the small volcanic groups, which border the continents, are placed in lines, related to those along which the adjoining shores of the continent trend, I may instance the lines of intersection at the Galapagos' (20, p. 144).

In his paper 'Constitution lithologique des îles volcaniques de la Polynésie Australe' LACROIX gives expression to much the same trend of thought when he writes: ' Particulièrement interessantes sont les îles volcaniques qui se trouvent à une plus ou moins distance de l'Amérique du Sud, les îles Juan Fernandez, San Felix et San Ambrosio, et enfin Galapagos, puis au large de l'Amérique centrale, l'île Clipperton. Bien que la connaissance de la lithologie de ces îles soit loin d'être complètement éclaircie, on peut à present assurer que leurs laves diffèrent de celles des Cordillères des Andes, c'est-à-dire de la série circumpacifique et montrer qu'elles se rattachent à la serie intrapacifique ' (14, p. 64).

In 'La Face de la Terre' EMMANUEL DE MARGERIE refers to the same subject as follows: "Le Relay de la marine des Etats Unis a signalé, au large de Valparaiso 5 651 mètres. A l'ouest de ces fosses sont situées les deux îles volcaniques anciennes de San Felix et San Ambrosio au Sud de ces îles le croiseur Chilien Présidente Pinto a trouvé, sur une etendue de 760 km, des profondeurs si faibles qu'il est probable qu'une crete sous marine, orientée à peu pres N—S, s'allonge dans la direction de l'île Juan Fernandez' (25, III, p. 1359).

In his 'Description and Geology' of San Felix and San Ambrosio, BAILEY WILLIS writes: 'San Felix and San Ambrosio are volcanic islands in the South Pacific Ocean, San Felix being situated in latitude 26°15′ south and longitude 80°7′ west of Greenwich and San Ambrosio lying about 16 km to the east-south-east. They are about 500 miles west of Chañaral on the east coast of Chile, and the same distance due north of the group of Juan Fernandez and Mas a fuera. The South Pacific charts show several rocks or islets and some whose existence is recorded as doubtful, which, with the above named islands, form an archipelago strewn on a narrow submarine ridge that extends along the meridian of 80 degrees west from about 36 degrees south to 26 degrees south, the ridge being defined by the 2 000 meter contour line. Knowing that all these islands and islets are peaks of volcanoes, we may suspect that there are more of them than we can see, but this must remain an unverified guess until detailed soundings can be made. The depth of the ocean in this region, which lies west of the Richards Deep, varies from 4 000 to 5 000 meters. The islands, therefore represent the summits of volcanoes probably sixteen to eighteen thousand feet or more in height — that is to say, they compare with the volcanoes of the Andes, which are situated on the other side of the deep" (26, p. 365).

In an interesting paper on the geology of Galapagos, Cocos and Easter Island, L. J. CHUBB has published some noteworthy remarks on the regional relations of the volcanic islands of the eastern central Pacific. He writes as follows: "Under the east central Pacific there lies a vast area, the Albatross Plateau, under depths of less than 2 000 fathoms, though on all sides the depths exceed this figure. No islands rise from the central part of this plateau, but at each end is an archipelago that appears to have been built up on a set of intersecting fissures, the Marquesas at the western end, and the Galapagos at the eastern. On or near its southern margin too there are several volcanic islands, including the Mangareva (Gambier) Archipelago, Pitcairn, Easter, Sala y Gomez and the Juan Fernandez Islands.

"It is suggested that the plateau constitutes a resistant block which has withstood lateral pressure that has been brought to bear on it from all sides, that around its margin it has become cracked and fissured, and that on the fissures volcanic islands have been erected. That these islands owe their origin to a common cause is suggested by the similarity of their structure and geological history, so far it is known. Petrographically, too, these islands resemble each other and differ from most of the other Pacific islands. The most striking characteristics of their rocks are the almost complete absence of nepheline bearing types and the presence of virtual free silica in many.

"Cocos, St. Felix and St. Ambrose islands are constituted in part of nepheline rocks, and for this reason they are regarded as lying, not on the resistant block, but beyond its eastern margin. Petrographically they resemble the Society Islands and Austral Islands which lie to the west of the plateau.

"It is thought that beyond the margins of the block the crust is more pliable and has yielded to pressure with the formation of anticlines and synclines. Volcanoes that have produced nepheline bearing rocks have been erected on the anticlines. The folds have tended in the western area to migrate from southwest to northeast with a wavelike motion proved by the history of their coral reefs. There is not sufficient evidence, however, to determine whether the folds which probably underlie Cocos, St. Felix and St. Ambrose islands have suffered a similar movement" (27, p. 43).

JUAN BRÜGGEN has recently in his book 'Fundamentos de la Geologia de Chile' discussed the geotectonic position of the Juan Fernandez Islands. He writes: "Esta zona (la region situada al este de Lhco en Arauco) de dislocaciones tan extrañas a la structura de la Cordillera de los Andes, coincide con la region donde una ancha loma submarina se desprende del continente. Encima de la loma se levantan las islas Juan Fernandez y mas al norte las de San Ambrosio y San Félix.

Parece que se trata de una antigua cordillera que se separo del actual conti nente entre Magellanes y Arauco y que se hundió posteriormente A esta cordillera o simplemente zona continental, que llamaremos 'Tierra de Juan Fernández, se deberá el término de las capas de la Quiriquina en el sur de Arauco y también el hecho que sedimentos marinos de Eoceno no se conozcan más a sur

Pero en el Oligoceno, cuando la costa del piso de Navidad se extendió hasta la región de Ypun (45° L S), se había hundido una gran parte de la Tierra de Juan Fernández, conservándose probablemente cierta extención en la vecindad de las islas volcánicas, cuyas rocas se formaron solo más tarde en erupciones posteriores A juzgar por el grado de denudación y en vista de las actividades volcánicas recientes en Más a Tierra y San Felix, la parte volcánica de estas islas se había formado en el Terciario superior, probablemente en el Plioceno cuando existía todavía un resto de la antigua Tierra de Juan Fernández, de la cual inmigró la flora del Eoceno Cuando más tarde se hundió también este resto, sobresalían solamente las partes volcánicas, constituyendo las islas de Juan Fernández que servían de refugio para la flora" (16, p 59)

The references now given suffice to show how the position of the Juan Fernandez Islands has from different points of view been geotectonically connected with other volcanic islands or groups of islands of the eastern Pacific

Petrographic Connections

In many papers of recent years, petrological and petrographical connections between the rocks of the Juan Fernandez Islands and those of other volcanic islands of the Pacific Ocean have also been the subject of discussion The types of lava which in this respect have been of special interest are the extremely melanocratic picrite basalts (oceanites of Lacroix) and their occasional combinations with more alkaline rocks A short summary of the literature on this subject may be given first

We may conveniently begin with the islands of San Felix and San Ambrosio, which geographically lie nearest The distance is 760 km due north of Juan Fernandez H S WASHINGTON has given a petrographical description of the rocks I may quote some lines from his general conclusions "It would appear from the specimens brought back by Willis that the lavas of San Felix volcano are, so far as known, only of two kinds — a decidedly sodic trachyte and a somewhat variable nepheline basanite, which seems to be highly vitreous There is little doubt that the yellow tuff is derived from a nephelite basanite magma closely similar to that of the flows The prominent characteristic of these two types of lava is their high content in alkalies, especially in soda, while high titanium and phosphorus appear to be other constant characters of minor but still considerable interest This conclusion as to the generally highly sodic character of the San Felix lavas is subject to the limitations imposed by the absence of specimens from the lower flows and from various parts of the island Such basaltic lavas, especially if highly vitreous, may appear megascopically to be very uniform and yet modally and chemically very diverse It is, therefore, possible that earlier lowermost flows are less sodic and more typically basaltic than the upper, which were the ones examined." Washington continues 'In this predominantly highly sodic character of the lavas San Felix appears to differ widely from other Pacific islands. At Masafuera, it is true, both soda trachyte (and nepheline basanite)[1], closely like those of San Felix, occur but these are accompanied by basalt and picrite basalt, whereas at the neighbouring Juan Fernandez (Masatierra) the lavas appear to be, to judge from Quensel's description, only olivine basalt with neither trachyte nor basanite. Trachyte, also highly sodic, occurs at several other Pacific volcanic islands as do also nephelite basanite and similar rocks high in soda but at all of them the predominant lavas are more or less normal basalts or andesites, so that the general magmatic character is basaltic — that is to say, sodi-calcic, somewhat modified by distinctly sodic facies. (26, p 382)

Referring to the trachyte of San Felix Washington says that 'in thin section the rock shows a somewhat peculiar texture, which resembles that of the trachyte of Masatuera described by Quensel, that of Puu Anahulu on the island of Hawaii and of the trachyte of Lahaina on Maui. The texture seems to be rather usual in the trachytes of the Intra Pacific volcanic islands. Ill defined laths of alkali feldspar make up most of the rock. Most of these are arranged irregularly, but here and there flow texture is evident.' (26, p 375)

In several places in his paper 'La constitution lithologique des iles volcaniques de la Polynésie Australe' Lacroix compares the petrographic character of the lavas of the Juan Fernandez Islands with those of other volcanic islands of the Pacific. Concerning the basalts of the Galapagos Islands he observes that they "offrent l'analogie la plus grande avec les basaltes de Masatierra et avec ceux des iles Gambier, c'est-à-dire avec les plus calciques des basaltes du Pacifique et les plus pauvres en potasse" (14, p 68). And further on in the same paper "Les iles Juan Fernandez se groupent au voisinage des iles Marquises et l'on a vu qu'il faut comparer ce que l'on sait des roches des îles Galapagos aux donnees concernant ceux des îles Gambier" (14, p 77).

These conclusions of Lacroix refer to the normal basalts of Masatierra and are founded on the four new analyses of such basalts. The similarity in respect of the Gambier Islands, however, goes a step further, as Lacroix describes from there associated with more normal basalts, typical oceanites (picrite basalts), which, as we have seen, also occur on Masatierra.

A third author who has brought the Juan Fernandez rocks under discussion with reference to chemical similarities with other volcanic islands of the Pacific is CONRAD BURRI. Under the title 'Chemismus und provinziale Verhältnisse der jungeruptiven Gesteine des pazifischen Oceans und seine Umrandung' he coordinates under the heading "Typus Hawaii" (in contrast to "Typus Tahiti"), the rocks of Hawaii, the Leeward group, Juan Fernandez and Samoa, remarking that the Juan Fernandez, San Felix and San Ambrosio lavas are good representatives of the group, the basanite from Masafuera, however, showing a small deficiency

[1] This name now discarded see p 63)

in $al - alk$ (28, p 177) — This deficiency is now explained by the fact that the analysed specimen has attained an abnormal chemical composition through the formation of deuteric minerals (see p 60)

A second part of Chubb's paper on the geology of Galapagos Cocos and Easter islands contains the "Petrology of the Galapagos Islands by C RICHARDSON Under a concluding heading he says "The Juan Fernandez Islands are the only islands on which both types of basalt (porphyric with dominant phenocrysts of olivine or with basic plagioclase) are found in addition to soda trachyte similar to that occurring in the Galapagos Archipelago Although oceanites (and basanitic lavas) are also present the Juan Fernandez Islands are petrologically closer to the Galapagos than any other islands' (27, p 64)

General Conclusions

A characteristic feature of the volcanic rocks of the Pacific is the universal predominance of sodium over potassium LACROIX says that in this respect "toutes les roches étudiées presentent la commune caracteristique d etre plus riche en soude qu'en potasse' (14, p 55) BURRI comes to the same conclusion based on recalculations of all available analyses He states that the Niggli value k is always under 0 4 and for the most typical regions of volcanic rocks of the intra-Pacific Ocean under 0 25 (28, p 173)

The value k in the four new analyses from Masatierra in no case exceeds 0 20 (average 0 17) And the light grey basalt from Masafuera has a still lower content of K_2O (Niggli value k 0 08) Therefore, with regard to low percentage of potassium the basaltic lavas of both Masatierra and Masafuera must be considered in this respect as representative for the basalts of the volcanic islands of the Pacific

In other respects the petrographic relationship between Juan Fernandez and other intra-pacific islands has been interpreted somewhat differently The reason is, however, easy to explain In some cases only the basaltic rocks of Masatierra have been taken into consideration, in other cases special notice has been given to the soda-trachytic lavas of Masafuera as indicating a casual presence of more alkaline rocks Since no rocks of alkaline character occur on Masatierra, this island has petrographically been connected most closely with the Gambier and Marquesas Islands as, according to Lacroix, representing les plus calciques des basaltes du Pacifique et les plus pauvres en potasse ' (14, p 68 and 77)

In chemical composition the basaltic lavas of the Juan Fernandez Islands also show similarities with some of the basalts from the Hawaiian Islands Several analyses of phyric and aphyric feldspar basalts from Kohala and Maunakea as well as from Kilauea, published by Washington are very similar to those of the basalts from Juan Fernandez (Am J of Sc 5, 1923, p 482—87 and 6, p 341) It can be suggestive that together with both ancient and recent lavas of Kilauea, Washington also describes chrysophyric picrite basalts of much the same character as those from Masatierra and Masafuera Another similarity can be given WHITMAN CROSS has described, together with the normal basalts soda-trachyte from Maui and Anahulu on the first island in connection with a 'picritic basalt (U S Geol Survey, Prof Paper 88, 1915, p 26—28) This corresponds exactly to the rock assemblage of Masafuera

Petrographic description of the Hawaiian basalts from the mentioned localities is, also in other respects found to agree with both megascopic and microscopic features of the basalts of Juan Fernandez Washington describes an aphyric basalt from Kohala as follows "The type is a light grey, almost aphanitic lava, except that some rare, very small feldspar phenocrysts may be present, and a few phenocrysts of olivine are seen in most specimens The texture is rough and trachytic, so that the rock would probably be considered an andesite or trachyte in the field Most specimens are dense and very fine grained or aphanitic, but vesicular forms may occur' (l c, p 485) This description might as well refer to the light grey basalts of Masafuera at elevations between 1 100 and 1 400 m, which I also, before an analysis was made tentatively denoted as a trachyandesite (12, p 282)

Although certain lavas of Hawaii evidently present similarities with the basalts from Juan Fernandez, the general assemblage has, however, a different character According to Washington 'olivine-free labradorite basalts constitutes the most abundant type followed in abundance by andesine basalt and then by oligoclase andesite" (Am J of Sc 6 1923, p 355) The high percentage of andesine basalt and andesite denote a magmatic sequence differing from that of the non-alkaline lavas of more southern latitudes of the Pacific It may, therefore, be advisable for the present to comply with Lacroix when he says "Les roches de cette ile (Hawaii) constitueraient une division speciale, ayant une originalite propre' (14 p 76)

If we take into consideration the assemblage of olivine and feldspar basalts and soda trachytic lavas on Masafuera as a characteristic feature for this island it seems evident that, as Richardson already has assumed, the rocks of the Galapagos Archipelago display the closest similarities According to the analyses, published by Richardson, both the basalts and the soda trachyte are in chemical composition very similar to equivalent rocks of Masafuera Also soda trachyte is of the same scarce occurrence in the Galapagos Islands as on Masafuera the only sample being collected by Darwin on the Beagle voyage of 1835 Richardson says "Juan Fernandez are the only islands on which both types of basalt are found in addition to soda trachyte similar to that occurring in the Galapagos archipelago' (27, p 64) The low content of potassium is in common for the basalts from both island groups

On the other hand we must evidently exclude any petrographical relationship between Juan Fernandez and San Felix—San Ambrosio where the lavas have, as far as is known, a more pronounced alkaline composition, classified by Washington as soda trachytes and nepheline basanites (l c, p 382) Richardson says "The Juan Fernandez are petrologically closer to the Galapagos than are any other islands Both are situated comparatively near the American coast of the Pacific but their similarity is not shared by San Felix and San Ambrosio islands, or any other islands on that side of the Pacific" (27, p 64) Lacroix comes to the same conclusion He finds the closest connection with San Felix—San Ambrosio to be the highly alkaline rocks of Tahiti in the mid Pacific (14, p 77) Though lying geographically nearest Juan Fernandez the rocks of San Felix—San Ambrosio evidently represent lavas of a more alkaline composition, with the exception of Cocos Island, not otherwise met with among the volcanic islands of the eastern Pacific

We may conclude, therefore, that the lavas of the Juan Fernandez Islands in chemical composition, and to a certain degree also with regard to their general aspect and fluctuations in petrographic character must be regarded as most closely associated with the rocks of Galapagos and in some respects also with some rock assemblages of the Hawaiian Islands, and in the more central parts of the Pacific Ocean, with the Gambier and Marquesas island groups

These connections are purely based on petrographical and chemical similarities It is of interest to find how these connections coincide with Chubb's more theoretical ideas regarding the regional distribution of the volcanic islands of the Pacific I refer to the quotation above (p 76) and will here only recapitulate the following 'No islands rise from the central part of this plateau (the Albatross plateau), but at each end is an archipelago that appears to have been built up on a set of intersecting fissures the Marquesas at the western end, and the Galapagos at the eastern On or near its southern margin too there are several volcanic islands, including the Mangareva (Gambier) archipelago, Pitcairn, Easter Sala y Gomez and the Juan Fernandez islands '

An approximately symmetrical distribution of alkaline and non alkaline rocks of the volcanic islands in the Pacific, which are situated between Lat $0°$ and $35°$ S may, therefore, be assumed to encircle the Albatross plateau, itself so obviously unendowed with any islands The outward lying connections would then include San Felix-Ambrosio and Cocos on an eastern marginal zone and the Austral and Society Islands on the western margin The rocks of these islands all have a pronounced alkaline character and have been referred by Lacroix to 'la serie nephelinique' of the Pacific islands Inward zones of connection would include Juan Fernandez—Galapagos and the Gambier (Mangareva) and Marquesas island groups, characterized by absence of nepheline-bearing types and the presence of virtual free silica in many Lacroix unites them as belonging to 'la serie sans nephéline' (14, p 59)

A plausible explanation of these circumstances might be that tectonic disturbances at different intervals have located cracks and fissures around a resistant block, represented by the Albatross plateau Volcanic eruptions of different magmatic composition have then been localised to different areas the alkaline lavas being restricted to peripherical dislocations in contrast to the non-alkaline lavas, located along inner lines of connection Easter Island and Sala y Gomez, composed of lavas of a deviating type and composition may have been orientated by intersecting fissures along other trends

The climax of volcanic activity on all these islands belongs to past periods of probably late tertiary or pleistocene age However, several of the islands bordering the American continent still manifest obvious indications of volcanic nature On San Felix volcanic gases were issuing from a crevice on the southern rim in May 1923 Bailey Willis says "In this sense and to this extent we may consider San Felix an active volcano" (26, p 370) The Galapagos Islands are still the seat of volcanic eruptions As late as 1925 lava flows reached the sea, pouring over the 100 foot cliffs (27, p 9) The Juan Fernandez Islands on the other hand show no signs of recent volcanic activity but, as recorded above, one, and possibly, several sub-marine explosions have taken place in their immediate vicinity during the past century

The formation of fissures in locating the position of the volcanic islands bordering the South American continent may be conceived to be connected with dislocations of the oceanic sub-stratum as an after sway of displacements during the formation of the continental mountain ranges Time connections between violent earthquakes on the continent and volcanic activity on some of the adjacent islands are significant in this respect

However, much of what has been said regarding connections of the volcanic islands of the Pacific, whether founded on petrological or petrographical similarities or on geotectonic orientation, must still be considered as conjectural For the present, we must agree with Daly that "a glance at the larger aspects of Pacific petrology shows how pitifully slight is our knowledge of the island petrography Now is not the time for settled convictions Now is the time for concerted, persistant effort, leading to a thorough exploration of the Pacific archipelagos, under the auspices of a single institution with a staff of cooperating observers" (R Daly, Petrography of the Pacific Islands Bull Geol Soc of America, 27, 1916, p 331)

Acknowledgements.

The writer is indebted to Professor P RAMDOHR, Heidelberg, and to Professor S GAVELIN and Dr W UYTENBOGAARDT for friendly cooperation in determining the ore minerals Professor Ramdohr has taken some photomicrographs of the same and kindly put them at my disposal for reproduction

Dr O MELLIS has helpfully co-operated in taking most of the other photomicrographs The landscape photographs have kindly been put at my disposal by Professor C SKOTTSBERG They are taken by him on his visits to the Juan Fernandez Islands in 1908 and 1917

A grant from the foundation LARS HIERTAS MINNE is gratefully acknowledged

Mineralogical Department, University of Stockholm,
March 1952

Table I

Analyses of the rocks from the Juan Fernandez Islands

	Masatierra I—IV				Masafuera V—VIII			
	I	II	III	IV	V	VI	VII	VIII
SiO_2	46.08	46.10	46.50	47.62	46.51	43.37	43.47	63.43
TiO_2	3.48	3.80	3.04	3.42	3.25	1.03	2.68	0.28
Al_2O_3	15.98	16.54	13.34	16.24	16.68	8.48	17.30	18.64
Fe_2O_3	2.75	5.48	5.34	4.74	4.30	2.91	6.87	2.78
FeO	8.83	7.25	6.71	7.14	8.17	11.00	7.09	1.02
MnO	0.23	0.24	0.11	0.18	0.18	0.13	0.07	0.09
CaO	10.54	10.64	10.04	10.60	8.85	5.03	6.09	1.68
BaO	—	—	—	—	0.01	—	—	—
MgO	6.53	4.58	8.89	4.41	6.40	25.93	8.60	1.38
Na_2O	3.61	2.94	2.32	2.60	2.80	1.33	2.53	6.77
K_2O	1.36	0.88	0.63	0.68	0.36	0.58	0.74	3.82
P_2O_5	0.32	0.30	0.29	0.36	0.46	0.19	0.27	0.18
Cr_2O_3	—	—	—	—	—	—	0.13	—
F	—	—	—	—	0.15	—	—	—
Cl	—	—	—	—	0.08	0.08	0.18	0.04
S	—	—	—	—	—	trace	0.12	0.01
$H_2O^{-105°}$	0.34	0.96	1.63	1.24	1.09	—	—	—
$H_2O^{+105°}$	0.05	0.37	1.39	1.61	1.06	0.19	3.36	0.24
	100.10	100.08	100.23	99.84	100.35	100.25	99.48	100.35

I Olivine basalt (dolerite) Masatierra, Bahia Cumberland Raoult anal
II Olivine basalt Masatierra, Bahia Cumberland Raoult anal
III Olivine basalt Masatierra, Bahia Cumberland Raoult anal
IV Aphyric basalt Masatierra, Bahia Cumberland Raoult anal
V Feldspar phyric basalt Elevation 1420 m Masafuera A M Bystrom anal
VI Picrite basalt (Masafuerite, Oceanite) dike rock Masafuera N Sahlbom anal
VII Iddingsite basalt Elevation 1000 m Masafuera N Sahlbom anal
VIII Soda trachyte Elevation 1200 m Masafuera N Sahlbom anal

Analyses I—IV have been made for A Lacroix from specimens collected at Bahia Cumberland by members of Dumont d'Urville's expedition in 1854 These analyses were first published in Lacroix' paper Constitution lithologique des iles volcaniques de la Polynesie Australe in 1927

Analysis No V is new, representing a sample of the abundant light grey feldspar basalts at higher elevations on Masafuera

Analyses VI—VIII are produced from my earlier paper on the geology of the Juan Fernandez Islands (No 12)

Analyses calculated as water free.

	I	II	III	IV	V	VI	VII	VIII
SiO_2	46.21	46.68	47.83	48.60	47.36	43.34	45.27	63.36
TiO_2	3.49	3.85	3.12	3.49	3.31	1.03	2.79	0.28
Al_2O_3	16.03	16.75	13.72	16.57	16.99	8.48	18.02	18.62
Fe_2O_3	2.76	5.55	5.49	4.84	4.38	2.91	7.15	2.78
FeO	8.86	7.34	6.90	7.29	8.32	10.99	7.38	1.02
MnO	0.23	0.24	0.11	0.18	0.18	0.13	0.07	0.09
CaO	10.55	10.78	10.35	10.82	9.01	5.03	6.34	1.68
BaO	—	—	—	—	0.01	—	—	—
MgO	6.55	4.64	9.15	4.50	6.62	25.91	8.96	1.38
Na_2O	3.62	2.98	2.39	2.65	2.85	1.33	2.64	6.76
K_2O	1.36	0.89	0.65	0.69	0.37	0.58	0.77	3.81
P_2O_5	0.32	0.30	0.30	0.37	0.47	0.19	0.28	0.18
Cr_2O_3	—	—	—	—	—	—	0.14	—
F	—	—	—	—	0.15	—	—	—
Cl	—	—	—	—	0.08	0.08	0.19	0.04
	100.00	100.00	100.00	100.00	100.00	100.00	100.00	100.00

Molecular proportions ($\times$ 100).

	I	II	III	IV	V	VI	VII	VIII
SiO_2	76.94	77.72	79.64	80.92	78.85	72.16	75.37	105.49
TiO_2	4.36	4.81	3.91	4.36	4.13	1.29	3.48	0.35
Al_2O_3	15.72	16.43	13.72	16.25	16.67	8.32	17.68	18.27
Fe_2O_3	1.73	3.47	3.44	3.03	2.74	1.82	4.48	1.74
FeO	12.33	10.22	9.60	10.15	11.58	15.30	10.27	1.42
MnO	0.32	0.34	0.15	0.25	0.25	0.18	0.10	0.13
CaO	18.84	19.22	18.42	19.29	16.06	8.97	11.30	2.99
BaO	—	—	—	—	0.01	—	—	—
MgO	16.24	11.51	22.69	11.16	16.17	64.26	22.22	3.42
Na_2O	5.84	4.81	3.85	4.27	4.60	2.14	4.26	10.90
K_2O	1.44	0.94	0.69	0.73	0.39	0.62	0.82	4.04
P_2O_5	0.22	0.21	0.21	0.26	0.33	0.13	0.28	0.13
Cr_2O_3	—	—	—	—	—	—	0.09	—
F	—	—	—	—	0.79	—	—	—
Cl	—	—	—	—	0.23	0.23	0.54	0.11

Norms.

	I	II	III	IV	V	VI	VII	VIII
Q	—	0.14	0.40	4.25	0.66	—	—	4.49
C	—	—	—	—	—	—	1.99	0.79
or	8.08	5.23	3.84	4.06	2.17	3.45	4.56	22.48
ab	18.14	25.22	20.19	22.39	24.12	11.22	22.33	57.45
an	23.48	29.71	24.81	31.29	32.49	15.47	29.62	7.12
ne	6.76	—	—	—	—	—	—	—
di	21.78	17.39	19.32	16.00	7.43	6.65	—	—
hy	—	6.28	16.84	7.59	19.20	3.51	23.40	3.43
ol	10.46	—	—	—	—	53.07	1.58	—
ap	0.74	0.71	0.71	0.87	1.11	0.44	0.67	0.45
il	6.62	7.30	5.93	6.62	6.27	1.96	5.28	0.53
mt	4.01	8.03	7.97	7.02	6.34	4.21	10.37	2.78
hm	—	—	—	—	—	—	—	0.86
cm	—	—	—	—	—	—	0.20	—
sal.	56.39	60.30	49.24	61.99	59.44	30.14	58.50	91.93
fem.	43.61	39.71	50.77	38.01	40.35	69.84	41.50	8.05

Quantitative system.

			or:ab:an
I.	III:5:3:4	Camptonose	16.14:36.55:47.31
II.	III:5:4:4	dosodic	8.69:41.92:49.39
III.	III:5:4:4	dosodic	7.86:41.34:50.80
IV.	III:5:4:4	dosodic	7.03:38.78:54.19
V.	III:5:4:5	persodic	3.69:41.03:55.28
VI.	IV:1:1:4	doferrous	11.44:37.23:51.33
VII.	III:5:4:4	dosodic	8.07:39.51:52.42
VIII.	I:5:2:4	Laurvikose	25.91:65.88:8.21

Niggli values.

	I	II	III	IV	V	VI	VII	VIII
si	103.7	110.4	105.1	118.7	110.7	69.8	99.7	236.3
qz	−35.5	−22.4	−18.9	−10.5	−17.3	−41.0	−27.1	+2.3
al	21.2	23.3	17.8	23.9	23.4	8.0	23.4	40.9
fm	43.6	41.2	51.9	40.5	47.0	80.6	55.0	18.9
c	25.4	27.3	24.3	28.3	22.6	8.7	14.9	6.7
alk	9.8	8.2	6.0	7.3	7.0	2.7	6.7	33.5
c.fm	0.58	0.66	0.47	0.70	0.48	0.11	0.27	0.35
ti	5.88	6.83	5.16	6.40	5.80	1.25	4.60	0.78
p	0.30	0.30	0.28	0.38	0.66	0.13	0.26	0.29
k	0.20	0.16	0.15	0.15	0.08	0.22	0.16	0.27
mg	0.50	0.40	0.58	0.40	0.48	0.77	0.53	0.40
o	0.11	0.24	0.17	0.22	0.16	0.04	0.22	0.41
w	0.21	0.40	0.41	0.37	0.32	0.19	0.46	0.69

Bibliography

1. TH SUTCLIFFE Crusoniana Manchester 1843
2. C BERTERO Notice sur l'Histoire naturelle de l'île Juan Fernandez Annales des Sciences Naturelles, Paris 1830, Tome XXI, p 345
3. A CALDCLEUGH On the Geology of the Island of Juan Fernandez Geol Soc of London, Proceedings, Vol 1, 1826—1833 p 256 (Also published in Phil Mag and Annals of Philosophy, Vol IX, 1831, p 220)
4. P PARKER KING Narrative of the surveying voyages of H M S Adventure and Beagle Vol 1 Proceedings of the first expedition 1826—1830, p 304
5. J DUMONT D'URVILLE Voyage au Pôle Sud et dans l'Oceanie Histoire du Voyage, III, 1842, p 114
6. J GRANGE Geologie, Mineralogie et Geographie physique du Voyage Dumont d'Urville, Voyage au Pôle Sud et dans l'Oceanie, 2^e Partie, 1854, p 39
7. L PLATE Zur Kenntnis der Insel Juan Fernandez Verh der Gesellschaft für Erdkunde zu Berlin Band XXIII, 1896, p 221
8. A RENARD Report on the rock specimens collected on the Oceanic Islands during the voyage of H M S Challenger Rocks of Juan Fernandez Report of the Challenger Expedition, Vol II, 1889, No 15 (Also published in French under the title Notice sur les roches de l'île de Juan Fernandez' Bull Acad Belgique, tome 10, 1885, p 569)
9. L DARAPSKY Über den Glockenstein von Juan Fernandez Verh des deutschen wissenschaftlichen Vereins zu Santiago, 1886, Heft 3, p 113
10. R POHLMANN Das Vorkommen und Bildung des sog Glockensteins (Magnesit) Ibid Band II 1893, Heft 5—6
11. —— Noticias preliminares sobre las condiciones jeograficas i jeolojicas del Archipielago Publ in I Johow Estudios sobre la Flora de las islas de Juan Fernandez Santiago de Chile 1896, p 1
12. P QUENSEL Die Geologie der Juan Fernandezinseln Bull Geol Inst of Upsala, Vol XI, 1912, p 252
13. I HAGERMAN Beiträge zur Geologie der Juan Fernandezinseln The Natural History of Juan Fernandez and Easter Island Vol I, 1924
14. A LACROIX La constitution lithologique des îles volcaniques de la Polynesie Australe Mem Acad des Sciences Paris Tome 59, 1927
15. F VON WOLF Vulkanismus Stuttgart Teil I, 1913, p 290 Teil II, 1929, p 771, 805
16. J BRÜGGEN Fundamentos de la Geologia de Chile Santiago de Chile 1950, p 59, 326, 332
17. I H TIZARD, H N MOSELEY, J G BUCHANAN and J MURRAY Narrative of the cruise of H M S Challenger Vol I, 1885, p 818
18. T SUTCLIFFE The earthquake of Juan Fernandez as it occurred in the year 1835 London 1839
19. —— Sixteen years in Chile and Peru from 1822 to 1839 London 1841, p 387 (with a sketch of the sub marine explosion)
20. CH DARWIN Geological observations on the volcanic islands of South America, visited during the voyage of H M S Beagle London 1876 p 144
21. I BARTH Pacificite, an anemousite basalt Journ Washington Acad of Sc Vol XX, 1930, p 60
22. —— Mineralogical Petrography of the Pacific lavas Am J of Sc Vol XXI, 1931, p 380, 510
23. L BOWEN The evolution of igneous rocks Princeton 1928, p 163

24 A. JOHANNSEN: Petrography, III, p. 334
25 F. DE MARGERIE: La face de la Terre III, p. 1359
26 BAILEY WILLIS and H. S. WASHINGTON: San Felix and San Ambrosio, their geology and petrography. Bull Geol Soc of America Vol 35, 1924, p. 365
27 L. CHUBB and C. RICHARDSON: Geology of Galapagos, Cocos and Easter Islands. Bernice P. Bishop Museum, Honolulu Bull. 100, 1933, p. 13, 17, 64
28 C. BURRI: Chemismus und provinciale Verhaltnisse der jungeruptiven Gesteine des pacifischen Oceans und seiner Umrandung. Schw. Min.-petrogr. Mitt. Band 6, 1926, p. 177

Unfortunately an interesting paper by GORDON A. MACDONALD on the 'Hawaiian Petrographic Province', published in the Bull Geol Soc of America (60 2, 1949, p. 1588), in which comparisons with Juan Fernandez and other Central Pacific Islands are discussed, has evaded my attention until this paper was already in print.

4. A Geographical Sketch of the Juan Fernandez Islands.

By

C SKOTTSBERG

The Juan Fernandez Islands were discovered on the 22nd November, 1574, by the Spanish navigator JUAN FERNANDEZ who called them Las Islas de Santa Cecilia They consist of two islands, distant from each other, Masatierra with its satellite Santa Clara, and Masafuera Masatierra lies 360 miles W of Valparaiso, Masafuera 92 miles W of Masatierra According to the charts the position of the light in Cumberland Bay on Masatierra is 33°37′15″ S and 78°49′50″ W, and of the summit of Masafuera, 33°46′ S and 80°46′ W

The islands are of volcanic origin and considered to be late Tertiary They show no signs of recent activity, but a submarine eruption near Pta Bacalao in Masatierra is reported by Sutcliffe to have occurred in 1835, and another E of this island by Goll in 1839 (BRUGGEN pp 326, 332) Sutcliffe (1, Plate p 387) published a drawing of the eruption, the landscape is a pure flight of fancy Some visitors have wanted to recognize a number of extinct craters To this question I shall return later When Ulloa thought that he saw flames bursting from the summit of Mt Yunque, he certainly made a mistake

No geographer has, as far as I know, visited the islands, but many notes on their configuration and topography are found in the narratives of early navigators as well as in the official reports to the Oficina Hidrográfica in Valparaiso by the Commanders of surveying ships Certain observations on the former distribution of the forests were referred to in an earlier paper (Skottsberg 3) Many popular descriptions of the nature and life on Masatierra have appeared (see Bibliography), some also paying attention to Masafuera The latest, by JORGE GUZMAN PARADA, contains much useful material and will often be referred to here

Comments on some earlier descriptions and maps of Masatierra

The most interesting account of this island from the 18th century is found in WALTER's narrative of Captain (later Lord) ANSON's voyage The illustrations are, even if not quite so accurate as the author thinks, vastly superior to the contemporaneous ones in Ulloa's work Plate XIV is a prospect from E, including Santa Clara (called Goat I), the rock El Verdugo (Monkey Key) and part of the north coast of Masatierra, seen under almost right angle and with the conspicuous mountains in correct position Plate XV is a map, not bad in its main features, of the mountains only Mt Yunque appears. The names on the map are Monkey Key, East Bay (Pto' Frances), the Spout (a cascade not far from Pta Bacalao) West Bay (Pto Ingles) and Sugarloaf Bay (Vaqueria). Woods cover the east half, the treeless west half erroneously includes the still well wooded Villagra valleys. Plate XVI is a Special of Cumberland Bay, of which Pl XVII gives a good view, and Pl XVIII shows the Commodore's camp in the valley later named in commemoration of his visit. Masatierra was the rendezvous of Anson's squadron and brought salvation to the remnants of the crews, of which the greater part had fallen a victim to scorbut. The winter months of 1741 were spent here and the ships refitted.

ANTONIO DE ULLOA's narrative is accompanied by a panorama of the south side of Masatierra showing Mt Yunque, Mt Pirámide, Co Negro and Damajuana, but other details cannot be identified. The map (Plate IV) is a rough sketch. Three bays have names, Puerto del Ingles, Englishman's harbour, very likely named to commemorate Selkirk as the cave called "Robinson's grotto" is found here, Puerto Grande de Juan Fernandez (Cumberland Bay) and Pucito de Juan Fernandez (Pto Frances). Some other (nameless) coves are indicated, e.g. Pangal. Three rivers empty in the harbours.

I do not know the circumstances under which the survey by FRANCISCO AMADOR DE AMAYA was made. It resulted in a map published in 1795 which has formed the basis of the charts still in use, but it may not have been known to THOMAS SUTCLIFFE, whose book "Crusoniana" (1843) is accompanied by a map with more details than the older ones, with regard to the coast line it is inferior to Anson's. Sutcliffe was Governor of the islands in the 1830's. There are many names, but as I have not seen Amaya's original map I do not know which are new. Cumberland Bay is called Port of Juan Fernandez, West Bay, Ulloa's Puerto del Ingles, Selkirk Bay, and East Bay French Bay. Sugar loaf Bay (Vaquería) is called Sandal Bay, an interesting name, perhaps most of the sandal wood was obtained here in Sutcliffe's time. West of this place we find Desolation Bay, a well chosen name, now called Bahia Juanango. Herradura, undoubtedly an old Spanish name, is known now as Bahia del Padre, La Punta is Pta de la Isla. The east cape, now Pta or Cabo Hueso de Ballena, is called Pta de Juanango. On the south coast we find Caravajal (Carvajal), Loberia, Villagra, Chamelo and Monkey I. These names are, however, misplaced. Sutcliffe's Carvajal is Bahia Tierra Blanca, a name placed by him inland at the foot of the hills (where it belongs), the two bights on both sides of "Loberia", B Chupones and B Villagra, are nameless, the former is also called Tierras Amarillas on some charts, a name used by Sutcliffe for a tract of land back of his Tierras Blancas. Villagra is located east instead of west of Mt Yunque, and Chamelo used for the coast now called Playa Larga. The interior shows some topographical features, a mountain range can be followed from east cape to beyond the misplaced Yunque, and north of this is a short row of hills, corresponding to Cordon Central, which

---
[1] *Abbreviations* B = Bahía (bay), C = Cordon (range, ridge), Co = Cerro (mountain), L = Loberia (sealing grounds), M = Morro (small islet, rock), Pta = Punta (point, cape) Pto = Puerto (port, harbour), Q = Quebrada (narrow valley, gorge), V = Valle (valley).

separates "Anson's vale" from "Lonsdale" (now Valle Colonial). A name not found on any other map is "Kay's town", the settlement in Cumberland Bay. This name was given by Sutcliffe in commemoration of one JOHN KAY who, through his technical skill, greatly furthered the textile industry in England and whose biography appears in "Crusoniana". The Salsipuedes ridge and the ridge between Pto Ingles and Vaqueria are marked, while the conspicuous crest uniting Yunque and Salsipuedes has disappeared altogether. The topography of the western section is poor, only Tres Puntas placed in correct position. The name "Puente" is misplaced, but certainly refers to the elevated isthmus between Carvajal and Herradura.

Some later surveys and maps.

From time to time the Chilean Hydrographic Office despatched a vessel to the islands as part of the work on a "derrotero" for the entire coast of the Republic. The reports were published in the Anuario Hidrográfico de la Marina de Chile. LOPEZ (1876) mainly repeats older statements with regard to distances, size of the islands, altitudes etc., VILL (1878) concentrated his attention on the possibilities of making Masatierra productive. VIDAL GORMAZ (1881) little more than copied Lopez. The chart was not much improved. More information on the nature of the coast, the serviceableness of the harbours and anchorages, landmarks etc. are found in the compiled "Instrucciones nauticas" of 1896. For Cumberland Bay the original Spanish name Bahía San Juan Bautista is used and some other early names are preferred, Bahía del Este, B del Oeste, Pan de Azucar (Sugar-loaf, also Cerro Alto) and B Pan de Azucar (Vaqueria), etc. GUNTHER's report of 1920 has little to add to the Instrucciones. A new chart had now been published and is reproduced in a very small scale. The distances between certain points indicated by Gunther agree rather well, with regard to the east section of Masatierra, with those on my map, while considerable difference is noted in the length of the long, narrow western section, 12.96 km according to Gunther, 10.25 on my map, so that the total length between Pta de la Isla and Pta Hueso Ballena becomes 22.2 and 18.5 km, respectively.

From American, French and English sources the well-known editor of geographical and nautical works L. FRIEDERICHSEN of Hamburg compiled a new map to accompany Ermel's popular account of his visit to Masatierra (1889). The central portion is much disfigured, but the general trend of the mountain ranges more or less correct, the details, however, erroneous in many cases. Most of the names used are Spanish. Some are still in use on the British and Chilean charts, where, however, Punta is used for Cabo. C del Padre, C Iunquillar (Tinquillar), C Lemos, Morro Juanango, C de los Negros (now also called Pta Suroeste), B de la Vaqueria, C Salinas, Sal si puedes, C San Carlos, C Lobería C Bacalao, C Pescadores, C Frances, Corrales de Molina (a series of hanging gorges E of Mt Yunque), Morro Viñillo, Bahía Chupones, C O'Higgins. Some of the names on Friederichsen's map are now forgotten. Bahía de la Fé (= B Juanango), El Palillo (west head of Pangal), C Madurgo (W of the east cape, here called

C Guasabullena a corruption of Hueso de Ballena), Morro Caletas (= El Verdugo), C Chupones (now Pta Larga), Bahia Aguabuena [now Tierra Blanca, but modern charts have Pta Aguabuena between T Blanca and Carvajal (Coqbajal of Friederichsen)] The topography is much clearer and more correct than in any of the earlier maps With the exception of Cerro Alto and Yunque no names of mountains have been put in

R POEHLMANN s short description of the islands, with special reference to the geology, serves as an introduction to Johow's well known work on the natural history Johow's map of Masatierra, based on 'recientes trabajos recopilados por la Oficina Hidrográfica en 1895", gives a very unsatisfactory idea of the topography

Amador de Amaya s map of 1795, with additions and corrections by the British (no 1383) and Chilean navies, remained the basis of all charts until 1917, when I handed over my notes and sketches to the Oficina Hidrográfica From 1918 on several editions have appeared Pta Suroeste replaces Friederichsen s Pta de los Negros, but the latter should be preferred because not this point but Pta de la Isla is the south-west point of Masatierra For Monkey Key El Verdugo is sanctioned, Cabo Chamelo is replaced by Los Chamelos, referring to the rocks outside, Cabo Viudo by C Norte, with the rock in front called Morro Viudo E of Co Tres Puntas Co Chumacera appears More important is that, for the first time, the valleys between Pto Frances and Pta Pescadores have been indicated and named On the Special of Cumberland Bay is the new name Cordón de las Cabras for the ridge generally called C Central The British chart 'with corrections from the Chilean Gov chart of 1921' reproduced by Quensel (2 p 46) shows the topography more distinctly than the former except of the east section, where all the improvements have been omitted A new name is Pta Meredavia for Pta del Padre The latest edition, revised up to March 1953, is identical, but for the topography a different technique has been used

The names used by Guzmán in his text do not always agree with those on the map He has taken up Herradura for Bahia del Padre, which is all right, but when he called Bahia Juanango 'Ensenada Pan de Azucar, cuyo nombre lo debe a su islote Juanango" — the conical Morro — he made a mistake, because the name Pan de Azucar belongs to Vaqueria and refers to Co Alto

During our expedition I tried to sketch the distribution of the forest, using the chart as a basis The position of the boundaries was determined with help of simultaneous aneroid and temperature readings, the same observations were made at sea level before and after every excursion and the elevations calculated from tables I had received from the late Professor AXEL HAMBERG This method does not, of course, give exact results, but it gives more reliable figures than the altimeter Our large series of photographs has been a great help Nevertheless the need of a map, based on a real survey, was deeply felt, and when, in 1951, I was going to put my notes in shape for publication, I approached the Chilean government through the Swedish Legation in Santiago and asked for assistance from the Chilean Air Force This was most generously granted During a flight on April 8, 1952, Masatierra was photographed, unfortunately it was rather late in the season and much of the island was hidden by clouds.[1] Though some corrections could be made along the south coast and around Cumberland Bay, the result was not what I had hoped for. A second attempt was planned, but had to be given up, and the work was discontinued. Fortunately the Swedish engineer Mr. BIRTH FRODIN, then a resident of Santiago and a most helpful channel during my negotiations with the authorities, had been invited to join the first flight, and his series of Kodachrome pictures, most of them taken from the plane, was graciously put at my disposal. They have proved to be of very great help, the reproductions here will, I dare say, testify to their high value. A comparison with our photographs allowed me to identify practically every single forest patch shown, and their size and shape was almost the same in 1952 as in 1917. With the aid of all this material a new sketch map, reproduced here in reduced size, was drawn (fig. 1). I want to emphasize that this map is a s k e t c h only.

Main geographical features.

Masatierra can be inscribed in an obtuse angled, isosceles triangle with the hypotenuse (the distance from Pta Isla to Pta Hueso Ballena) 12.5 nautical miles (23 km) long on the sea chart and the greatest width (from Pta Salinas to Los Chamelos) 4.2 miles (7.8 km), circumference 34 miles (= 53 km), area 93 sq. km. These are the figures generally quoted, but others are also found: length 15.5, width 3.75 miles (Lopez), 22 and 8 km (Frmel), 25 and 9 km (Branchi), etc. The figures obtained from my map are: length (= hypotenuse) 18.5 km width 7 km, area 75.2 sq. km.

Masatierra is a deeply eroded and very rugged mountain range (fig. 2) rising abruptly from a submarine ridge running S—N and bordered by deep water, the bathymetrical conditions will not be discussed here. There is hardly any level land on the island worth speaking of. Where the soil is not covered by forest, as on the barren seaward slopes of the valleys, on the coast escarpments and on the precipitous ridges rising high above the continuous forest cover, hundreds of lava beds overlying one another can be distinguished, varying in thickness from a few m (in cases less than one) up to 20 or more (Quensel 2 p. 40). The location of the main summit ridge and, as a consequence, the trend of the valleys, depends on the dip of the lava beds. From the east highland to Mt Yunque and from Pta San Carlos to Co Alto, the tilt is N to NE, above Pto Frances 14—18° (fig. 13), at Centinela and Pangal about 20°, between San Carlos and Pto Ingles 12—13° (fig. 3), at Co Alto 20° or a little more. From the east end to in-

[1] One of Mr. Frodin's photographs of Masatierra seen from the air in 2 000 m altitude was reproduced in the daily paper "Dagens Nyheter". The explanation says: " ... covered with white clouds that later lifted, enabling us to map the islands accurately". And in the text we read: "We flew to and fro over Masatierra and took series of photographs which will be put together to form maps in scale 1:15 000. We had the good luck to get the summits quite free from clouds". This story is confirmed by Mr. Frodin's kodachromes which show the central and northern parts of Masatierra very clear. On the aerial map in 1:28 500, submitted to me by the Chilean Air Force, the island is, however, more or less covered with clouds, and not one of the conspicuous mountains could be identified with certainty.

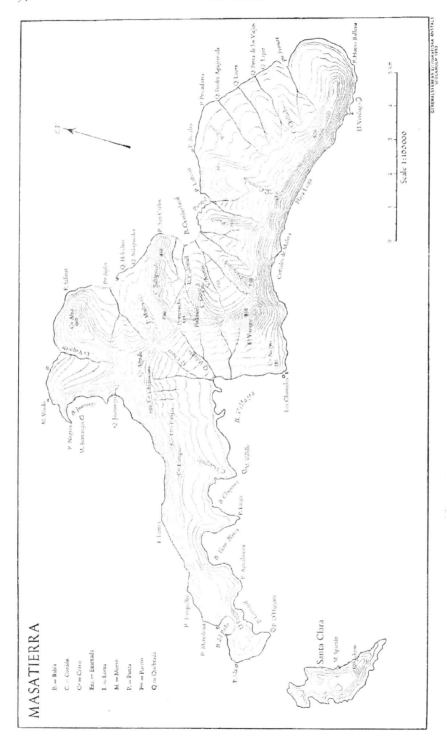

Fig. 1. Map of Masatierra and Santa Clara. After Skottsberg.

Fig. 2. Eastern half of Masatierra, seen from the air. — Photo B. Frödin 3/1 1952.

Fig. 3. End of Cordón Salsipuedes close to Pta San Carlos, showing the dip of the lava beds. At the foot of the ridge the Cemetery. — Photo C. Skottsberg 3/1 1917.

cluding the Yunque massif, the crest follows the south coast, an imposing barranca several hundred m high, with almost vertical gorges. As a rule the saddles are impassable (figs 11, 14, 31). From the saddle between Yunque and Pirámide (figs 21, 22) the ridge turns NNW and in a shallow curve runs right across the widest part of the island. The reason is that the beds, at least the middle and upper ones, are horizontal, at the foot of Mt Yunque a very insignificant tilt of 5—9° was observed in one place (fig 7). The central part of the island receives the greatest precipitation and erosion has worked inland from two opposite directions, but the Cumberland valley system has been considerably more deepened than the Villagra system. The ridge is 600 to 700 m high in this section. A narrow pass, Portezuelo de Villagra, often spoken of as "Selkirk's lookout", forms the only practicable passage between the two sides of the island. West of Vaqueria the ridge reaches the north side of the island, turns SW and follows the coast, rising to at least 500 m in the highest peaks, then getting lower and lower and disappearing as we approach El Puente, flat and sandy and only 50 m above sea level. The small peninsula forming the extreme west of Masatierra is crowned by a hill at least twice as high. At Carvajal the beds appear to be horizontal (fig 47), but E of the isthmus they are tilted SE, and consequently all the valleys trend toward the south coast. The dip is slight.

The change in position of the backbone, combined with its decreasing elevation, has a profound influence not only on the morphology, but, as a consequence of the direction of the prevailing winds, also on the local climate and thereby on the vegetation. Climatic dates will be found in my paper on the vegetation (3 pp 812—818), the common wind direction is SE to SW (together 78 %). Along the east and central section the air currents are suddenly forced up over crests 500—900 m high, cooled and condensed, and rain drenches the ridges (fig 4). This is the forest country, where the deep valleys are covered with verdure. The region around Mt Yunque may be shrouded in mist while all the country west enjoys sunshine. Very often the lower cloud limit is knife sharp (Skottsb 3 fig 2 on p 808). Fig 4 shows clouds also over the West and on Santa Clara. But W of Cerro Chumacera, where the main ridge forms the upper edge of the long northern escarpment, the air does not hit a high, precipitous wall but rises gradually, and the elevation is too modest to allow the rain-bringing clouds to gather except now and then during the winter months. This is the barren, treeless, grass-covered land.

Geology and morphology

No extensive geological survey has been made in these islands. Our knowledge is mainly based on QUENSEL's short visit in 1908, when he studied the stratigraphy at a limited number of places and later gave an account of the geology, petrography and mineralogical composition of the rocks, but his material was too small to allow us to trace the different kinds of strata from one end of the island to the other. For my own part I had no geological training, but during our 1916—17 campaign I collected rock specimens in many places. They

Fig. 4. Masatierra and Santa Clara (right, behind the promontory) seen in SW from 3000 m alt. — Photo B. Frödin ⁵¹/₁ 1952.

were described by HAGERMAN. The joint material served Quensel for a renewed study, enlarged to a discussion of the geotectonic connection between Juan Fernandez and other volcanic islands of the East Pacific.

Even a casual visitor cannot fail to observe the difference in appearance and colour between the lower brownish, yellowish and reddish slopes and profiles and the higher, light to dark gray ridges; see the water colour sketch in Skottsb. 2, opposite p. 52. These two horizons can be followed from the east end to Tres Puntas, possibly to Cerro Enrique, but no samples were brought from the extreme western section with the exception of a few from Bahía del Padre. The island is "in the main formed by a rather uniform series of basaltic lava beds, only diverging in respect of coarser and finer grain or of a higher or lower content of olivine" (Quensel 2 p. 44). Rocks with a very high content of olivine (picrite basalts) seem to be restricted to lower elevations; higher up more normal basalts, less rich in olivine, predominate, but between the two extremes there is every transition. Of the lower lava beds, up to 200 m above sea level, "many show a coarse-grained ophitic texture and may be classed as dolerites" (l.c. p. 45); these lavas have been traced from Pto Frances to Tres Puntas. The dolerites are very resistant and show, at least where observed by me, a columnar structure. They form thresholds in some of the valleys. The most conspicuous ones were met with in Vaquería (fig. 5) — a piece of a column was figured by Hagerman p. 28 — and on the south side of the island below Chumacera and Tres Puntas. At Chumacera the bed is about 3 m thick. The pillars appear as long and narrow,

Fig. 5. Vaquería valley, Masatierra, showing bed of doleritic basalt. — After a photograph bought in Valparaiso.

Fig. 6. Spheroidal weathering of basalt, Valle Colonial, Cumberland Bay. — Photo C. Skottsberg ²/₄ 1917.

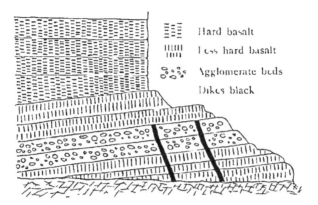

Fig 7 Diagrammatic sketch of a profile of the seaward base of Mt Yunque Height c 350—400 m

3 sided prisms The dolerites have a very fresh appearance and are supposed to represent intrusions between previously consolidated flows (Quensel 2 pp 45, 47)

The lava beds at lower elevations in east and central Masatierra are interbedded with agglomerate layers, formed by tuffaceous material as explained by Quensel and illustrated by his fig 11 (2 p 54) The photograph was taken near the entrance to Anson's valley at approximately 50 m above sea level In a clayey ground mass of a deep brick-red colour hard blocks of various shapes and sizes are embedded, showing spheroidal weathering, l c fig 10 is a fine example from the same bed Another, from the floor of Valle Colonial near the trail to Portezuelo, is seen in my fig 6 The entire exposed surface weathers in this fashion, the soft ground mass is washed out and carried into the sea and the hard blocks left lying The same kind of agglomerate is found also in other valleys Stratification is quite distinct in the profile illustrated by Quensel His opinion is that these beds are pyroclastic sediments of recent volcanic origin According to my notes the volcanic agglomerate was observed overlayered by hard, gray basalt in Pto Frances and at the seaward base of Mt Yunque (fig 7) In the profoundly eroded Cumberland valleys all the upper strata have been removed

All through the island the lower horizons are traversed by vertical dikes of hard lava striking approximately N—S Nowhere are they better observed than on the imposing perpendicular escarpment between Vaqueria and Juanango bay, where the wall is ribbed with innumerable dikes which, thanks to their greater hardness, project above the rim to form a serrated edge (figs 8, 9)

The geology of Bahia del Padre was considered by POEHLMANN to be of particular interest and importance The lowermost bed at the entrance to the bay was identified by him as an andesite representing a much older formation than the overlaying basalts and tuffs and exposed only in this place, but Quensel came to the conclusion that we have no reason to classify these beds as andesites of an older formation (1 p 266, 2 p 56), they "have been subjected to alterations in connection with thermal processes during some intermediate phase of volcanic activity'

Fig. 8. The escarpment between Vaquería and Juanango, Masatierra, showing the numerous vertical dikes. — Photo C. Skottsberg 26/8 1908.

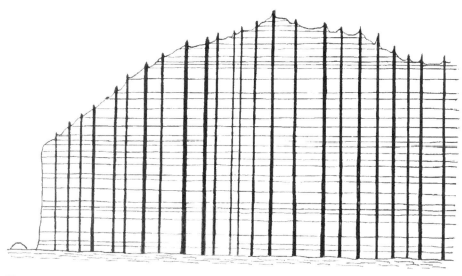

Fig. 9. Diagrammatic sketch of part of the escarpment between Vaquería and Juanango; comp. fig. 8. Dikes black; in nature they do not run quite so regularly.

Fig. 10. El Puente seen from the shore in Bahía del Padre, Masatierra. — Photo C. Skottsberg 15/1 1917.

Fig. 10 shows the profile of the Puente. The foot of the cliff is more or less hidden under talus material. A tuff bed overlayers a sequence of basalt and agglomerate beds; one of these, rather distorted, can be followed righ across the slope on Pl. 102: 1, Skottsb. 3. The tuff was described by Hagerman p. 26. It resembles a coarse-grained sandstone and disintegrates easily. The Puente (figs. 45, 46) and the adjacent slopes on both sides are covered with white, mobile sand where small dunes and ripplemarks announce wind action, and the wind carries the sand out into the bay. On the sand, standing more or less upright, are numerous peculiar more or less tube-shaped concretions (see fig. 7 in Hagerman's paper). Hagerman p. 29 calls them sinter concretions formed by a number of minerals in a cement of $CaCO_3$: "Die wahrscheinliche Deutung dieser Phänomene ist wohl, dass mit Calciumkarbonat gesättigte thermale Gewässer über eine Vegetationsdecke geflossen sind, wobei Wurzeln etc. mit einer Kruste von oben angegebener Zusammensetzung überzogen wurden." This should bear witness of late volcanic activity contemporaneous with the existence of a more humid climate than the present one, permitting a vegetation cover to thrive. Now there are neither any hot springs saturated with lime nor is this region covered with native plants; the Puente is a field of pure sand with large patches of weeds along the edge (fig. 46). There are indications that the west part subsided in geologically recent time, when Masatierra and Santa Clara hung together. With greater elevation rains were more frequent and where the land is now barren, it bore shrubs and trees.

More normal olivine basalts, less rich in olivine than the rocks characteristic of the lower horizons, are "widespread up to the highest part of the island" (Quensel 2 p 49) They are dark gray and as a rule vesicular, scoriaceous or slaggy, but they are hard, more resistant to denudation, and form the elevated crests and crags all along the ridges At intermediate horizons, approximately between 400 and 500 m (Cordon Chifladores 400 m, Portezuelo 500 m), feldspar basalts seem to predominate (Quensel l c) These lavas are ash gray, aphanitic and aphyric in texture and have a tendency to develop a columnar structure Rocks of the same type were found near Pta Larga at less than 100 m in the form of a dike, "which may signify a channel for the analogous lavas at higher levels" These beds are supposed to "represent a definite epoch of intrusion, intermediate between the doleritic basalts and picrite basalts of the lower parts and the scoriaceous olivine basalts of the higher horizons ' Very likely the thick bed seen on Pl 97 2 in Skottsb 3, about 450 m above sea level, belongs to this type I admit that the photograph selected by Quensel to illustrate this formation (fig 9, p 51) has the same outward appearance, but the altitude is approximately 625 m, and as this place is out of reach — the climber cannot depend on the shallow-rooted shrubs and ferns — no specimens were taken there, the samples I brought came from 500 to 575 m and whether or not the beds are intermediate is impossible to tell, as no rocks from a higher elevation than 575 m have been examined The samples from this level are vesicular aphyric feldspar basalts We know nothing about the mineralogical composition of the rocks forming the highest summit Mt Yunque rises about 350 m above Portezuelo de Villagra

A geographical reconnaissance of Masatierra.

Pta Hueso de Ballena, where we shall start our circuit of the island, plunges abruptly into the sea, forming an escarpment of perhaps 300 m A dominant feature of the coast is that talus deposits are insignificant or lacking, so that the surf is able to undermine the wall and to excavate caves Only in the coves where a valley has been eroded down to sea level a beach is found which leaves a passage along the foot of the escarpment

Between the east cape and the Frances valley the land rises to 500 m or more Some shallow quebradas, filled with forest, descend north toward the sea but do not reach very far down (fig 11)

Pto Frances does not deserve to be called a harbour, it offers no protection even as an occasional anchorage (Instrucc náut p 226) It is a small, open cove facing N and E, but with winds from other quarters landing is easy The beach consists of rounded stones and coarse shingles, here as elsewhere the surf removes all minor particles The lower slopes of the valley are very barren, the soil is exposed or covered with patches of weeds, and the marks of running water and the tracks of cattle are everywhere to be seen (fig 12) Some little distance from the shore and about 50 m above sea level is a small shack The streambed occupies the entire narrow bottom of the broadly V-shaped valley to which sev-

Fig. 11. Most easterly part of Masatierra, seen from the air, looking east. The detached, conical rock is El Verdugo. Ridges *a* (centre) and *b*. — Photo B. Frödin ⁵/₁ 1952.

Fig. 12. Pto Frances seen from a spur about 350 m above the sea. — Photo C. Skottsberg ¹³/₁₂ 1916.

Fig. 13. Ridge *a* overlooking the E branch of Frances valley. — Photo C. Skottsberg 17/4 1917.

Fig. 14. Pto Frances, W valley-branch. Left, *c*; right, *d*. — Photo C. Skottsberg 17/4 1917.

Fig. 15. Prospect of the E part of Masatierra, seen toward SE from an airplane at low elevation, showing the land from Pto Frances to Quebr. Pesca de los Viejos; between them, the small and steep Q. Lapiz. The dotted line follows the crest of Cordón Chifladores. From left to right ridges a, b and c. — Photo B. Frödin $^8/_4$ 1952.

Fig. 16. Continues fig. 15, to Pta Pescadores. From left to right Quebr. Lapiz, Pesca de los Viejos, Laura and Piedra Agujereada; ridges a, b, c, d. — Photo B. Frödin $^8/_4$ 1952.

eral quebradas belong, filled with maqui-infested grazed luma forest[1] lower down but higher up with fine primeval stands. Some gullies cut deep into the ridge and end in an impassable saddle, on the south side is a precipice. Figs 13 and 14 show two of these gorges. Fig 15 is a general view of the Frances system, the letters *a*, *b* and *c* denote three conspicuous crests, easy to identify also on figs 11, 13, 14 and 16. The stream has some water also during the drier summer half year.

From Pto Frances the coast runs in an almost straight line to *Pta Pescadores* (Fishermen's point). The trail crosses three valleys Pesca de los Viejos, Laura and Piedra Agujereada, none of which has been eroded down to the sea (fig 16), but all have been cut back deep and widened to form a basin furrowed by numerous small tributaries. To call these valleys "apenas unas grietas", as Guzmán does (p 26), is not to do them justice.

Cordon de los Chifladores (Whistlers' ridge, fig 16) is, as most of the ridges extending N—S, wide near the sea and narrows inland, in the steeper rise up toward the crest approaching the knife edge type. As everywhere along the north side of the island the country near the coast is treeless. Possibly the forest never went clear down to the cliff. This question was raised by Johow and commented on by me (3 p 800). I forgot then to mention Fimel's theory that, as the islands are so much younger than the mainland, a vegetation cover has not yet had time to spread to the coast! There is no need for a discussion. On C Chifladores the first forest is met with about 300 m above the sea, covering the ridge another 50 m and then passing into the usual low scrub.

Near the seaward slope of the ridge is a dry crevice where a few stunted lumas linger. We named it *Q del Lapiz* (because I lost a pencil there).

Q de la Pesca de los Viejos (Old folks' fishing place, fig 17) had very little water in the stream in December and not much more in April. Along the outer slopes the inclination is gentle, the middle section is steeper, up to 35°. Scattered trees are remnants of the once closed forest. The interior is well wooded up to the main ridge. Not much maqui was seen in this valley.

Q de Laura (fig 18). Near the sea the valley sides slope 23—24°, a little farther inland about 30°. None of these valleys is deeply eroded. There was some water in the stream in December, but nothing in April when the picture published in Skottsb 3 fig 32 on p 889 was taken.[2] Fig 18 shows the valley in August. The outer section is desert like, the soil naked or covered with weeds, but a few solitary trees may be seen. The slope facing E is more barren than the opposite slope. The interior is filled with good, thick stemmed forest.

A high, well wooded crest, rising to at least 650 m, forms the background of *Q de la Piedra Agujereada* (fig 19) which got its name from a rock pierced

---

[1] For some of the leading species the local names are used. Canelo, *Drimys confertifolia*, Chonta, *Juania australis*, Luma, *Nothomyrcia fernandeziana* (Masatierra) and *Myrceugenia Schulzei* (Masafuera), Maqui, *Aristotelia maqui* chilensis, a maical is a maqui grove. Naranjillo, *Fagara mayu* Masatierra and *F. externa* (Masafuera), Pangue, *Gunnera peltata* Masatierra) and *G. Masafuerae* (Masafuera)

[2] The text is incorrect. The photograph was taken by the author 17.4 1917

Fig. 17. Quebr. Pesca de los Viejos, looking S; ridge *d*. — Photo C. Skottsberg $^{17}/_1$ 1917.

Fig. 18. Quebr. Laura, looking N. — Photo K. Bäckström Aug. 1917.

Fig. 19. The interior of Quebr. Piedra Agujereada. — Photo K. Bäckström Aug. 1917.

by a hole (aguja, needle). The exterior section (see Skottsb. 3 fig. 33 on p. 890) has the same character as in the valleys mentioned, while the interior is filled with fine forest covering the ridges on both sides and above 400 m very damp and rich in tree-ferns. The vegetation cover acts as a sponge and only a minor part of the precipitation will feed the stream, its lower course being dry during the summer; in winter the water rushes down to the sea as a cascade, mentioned by Anson ("The Spout") and referred to in Instrucc. náut. p. 227, where it is said to run quite dry at the end of the winter.

El Rabanal (rábano = *Raphanus sativus*, formerly abundant here) is very unlike the other valleys with its wide, almost level floor; in Johow's time it was densely wooded, but in 1905 it was ravaged by fire, and the forest never came back. In March 1917 the dry soil was covered with the dead stalks and innumerable young rosettes of *Silybum marianum* (see Skottsb. 3 fig. 34 on p. 891). Pl. 86 (l.c.) shows the same spot in August, when a vigorous new growth had sprung up. The shadow across the *Silybetum* indicates the streambed. There are a few dying lumas, maqui is plentiful in the quebradas, succeeded toward the interior by degraded luma-canelo forest. Higher up are better stands (l.c. Pl. 94: 1).

Rising at an angle of about 85° *Pta Bacalao* forms the end of the Centinela ridge. It got its name because the bacalao ("stock-fish"), the commonest and most valuable fish in these waters (fig. 100), is very abundant here.

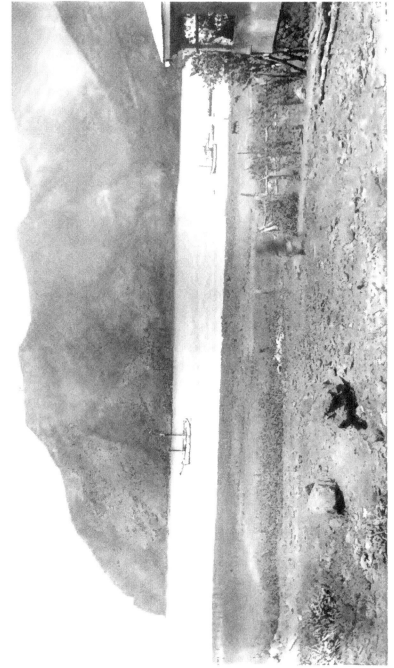

Fig. 20. Pta Bacalao and Cordón Centinela, seen from the Colony. The wireless station on top of the ridge. Right, entrance to Pangal. — Photo C. Skottsberg 17/4 1917.

Fig. 21. View W from the summit of Centinela ridge, c. 780 m, toward Mt. Yunque and Mt. Pirámide (right), in front of Yunque Mt. Damajuana; below Pirámide the crest between Quebr. Minero and Pangal. — Photo C. Skottsberg [11]/4 1917.

Cordón Centinela (Sentinel ridge). The broad northernmost part of this ridge forms a small meseta, upon which, 320 m above the sea, stands the wireless station[1] (fig. 20). The ridge, which is steep on both sides (45—55°), is very barren and shows the stratification on the yellowish-gray lava beds very plainly. A zigzag trail, cut in the rock, leads from Pangal to the station, where one has a splendid view of Cumberland bay and the mountains behind (fig. 27). Following the ridge, which gradually gets very narrow, we have the rare opportunity to walk right across the island to the top of the main ridge and to look down on the south coast, almost 800 m below our feet (fig. 21). The gradient is gentle all the way up, from 5° a little south of the station to about 20° farther up. From about 300 m there is forest on both sides, closing over the ridge a little higher up. A very dense scrub covers the crest (l.c. Pl. 90: 2).

Pta Lobería (lobo, seal; place where sealing was practised in old times) and *Pta San Carlos* (fig. 27) are the headlands of Cumberland bay. The distance between them is about 2 km.

Bahía Cumberland or *San Juan Bautista* is the only harbour in the islands where large ships find good anchorage; see the charts and descriptions by Walter, Sutcliffe, Lopez, Vidal Gormaz, Günther etc. The bay is open toward N and NE,

---

[1] Acc. to Guzmán p. 16 not used now.

Fig. 22. Cumberland Bay from Pta Lobería to Cordón Central, seen from the air in 1000 m elevation. From left to right, Pangal, Cordón Escarpado, Quebr. Minero-Damajuana, La Damajuana, Valle Anson with El Yunque. — Photo B. Frödin 8/4 1952.

but winds from these quarters are uncommon also during the winter. The sudden squalls coming down through the valleys with great force should be looked out for. Four valleys end in the bay, from E to W Pangal, Minero-Damajuana, Anson and Colonial. The scenery round the bay is very impressive, a semicircle of bold mountains, green gorges and gray precipices (figs. 22, 27). Many of the names quoted by Guzmán are unknown to me, for inst. Cordón de la Falda Larga ("falda" in the sense of "long skirt"), perhaps = the back wall of Q. del Minero, Picacho con la Piedra con Letras (?Cerro Pirámide), Cerro de los Muñoces, Picacho de la Mona (= she-monkey) and Cerro el Tope ("top"). Pico Central, a long established name, is not mentioned by Guzmán.

El Pangal. The entrance to this picturesque gorge is crossed by the trail to Centinela, but it is also easy to land on the stony beach. The main branch is a blind alley and the only true canyon on Masatierra, recalling on a small scale the magnificent gorges of Masafuera. The U-shaped gorge ends in a high wall, luxuriant with verdure, through which a small waterfall leaps down. The altitude of the valley bottom at the foot of the fall is only about 200 m. Pls. 78, 87 and 98 (Skottsb. 3) give a good idea of the vegetation with its stately tree-ferns and giant pangues (*Gunnera peltata*) which gave its name to this valley. No wonder that WALPOLE found that the "rhubarb" grew so luxuriantly on Masatierra, that it was too coarse to be good! Above the waterfall the valley widens and is filled with primeval forest (l.c. Pl. 89: 1). A branch with a patch of forest comes down from the Centinela ridge (fig. 23).

Fig. 23 Centinela ridge and Pangal, seen from the slope of Salsipuedes above the Cemetery. — Photo B. Frödin ²⁹/₁ 1952.

Cordón Escarpado (= steep ridge) with its Picacho, 365 m high (fig. 22), separates Pangal from the next valley.

Q. del Minero (Miner's v.) comes down to the water rather steeply (figs. 22, 24). We did not survey this valley, but to judge from the colours on the Kodachrome film only the higher slopes have native luma forest, the lower being covered by maqui. There were no plantations here in 1916—17. A steep spur separates Q. Minero from

Q. de la Damajuana (figs. 25, 26). The lower slopes have been cleared, but between 150 and 200 m elevation a dense macal fills the bottom, followed by a mixed luma-maqui forest and finally a belt of native wood.

La Damajuana (The Demijohn, figs. 25, 26) is a very characteristic landmark. The cone crowns a short, high and narrow spur, continued toward the sea by a long ridge, which is barren on the west side. This ridge can be followed up to the base of the cone, alt. c. 430 m, and from there round the bend into the valley and up to c. 530 m. The gradient is steep, nowhere under 35°. There are ledges of harder rock, on both sides with a small waterfall, the first at 230 m when going up the valley. The sides of the cone are precipitous, the height 2338 ft (739 m) according to the English chart, 712 m on the latest Chilean map, but only 570 m according to Branchi; this figure is too small. As far as I know this mountain has not been ascended. An attempt should be made from the south.

Valle de Anson drains the loftiest part of Masatierra and is watered by two

Fig. 24. Quebr. del Minero. — Photo C. Skottsberg 25/12 1916.

permanent streams. Bounded by Damajuana on the east and by Cordón Central on the west it is dominated by the square Yunque massif (figs. 22, 31). Due to the scant water supply in the side gullies near the sea, the distal part of the valley floor inclines steeply, whereas the middle section has been levelled, being almost horizontal at the small clearing known as *Plazoleta* (or Plazuela) *del Yunque* ("small square"), situated about 220 m above the sea (Skottsb. 3 Pl. 89: 2), but from here the gradient gets very steep. It is evident from the pictures in Walter's narrative that quite some clearing was done by Anson's party, very likely as far up as to Plazoleta, and there is little native forest below this point. In 1916—17 the trail went through an extensive macal, and the lower slopes near the sea were barren. Very few people lived in this valley (fig. 27).[1] The forests of the interior were in good condition and the upper montane type luxuriated below the saddle between Damajuana and Yunque from 400 to 600 m.

El Yunque (The Anvil) presents, from all directions, the same venerable appearance (figs. 21, 22, 25, 31, 51). The walls are everywhere steep with gradients

---

[1] Plazoleta is where, in 1930, HUGO WEBER went to live all alone as a modern Robinson, as told in his interesting book. He built a hut, cleared the ground, made a garden and raised chickens. He married in 1932, built a more substantial home and extended his cultivations. In 1942 he left the island and settled on the mainland. The little farm is still his property but without a tenant, and I am told by Dr. GUILLERMO KUSCHEL that the place was overgrown with *Rubus ulmifolius* when he visited the island a few years ago.

Fig. 25. Damajuana and Yunque from the trail to Pangal, looking SW. — Photo C. Skottsberg 11/4 1917.

from 55° to 70°, in places almost perpendicular. The exact height is not known; the figures vary from 1700 ft (537 m, Walpole) to 983 m (Viel); Branchi has 805 m, the English chart 3005 ft (913 m), the new Chilean 915 m, Instrucc. náut. 927 m. The first ascent was made in 1795, a second shortly after, the third in 1923, after which the attempt has been repeated with success a few times (Guzmán p. 30). Only the route from the Damajuana-Yunque saddle seems to lead to the summit. The figure 838 m (doubtless too high) on Friederichsen's map corresponds to a small pinnacle set on the saddle, the "Camote" (= sweet potato, bulb). The ascent, which is difficult and dangerous, was described by TENZ, who was the first to give us any information on the topography and plant life of the summit; see Skottsb. 3 pp. 897—898.

Cordón Central (figs. 22, 27, 31, 99). From the broad gable of Mt. Pirámide, E of its centre, this sharp-edged ridge runs down to the coast, separating the Anson and Colonial valleys and widening to a fan-shaped, barren and sandy front, sloping down to the stony beach. *Pico Central*, c. 570 m, marks the end of the harder basalts belonging to the upper horizons; l.c. Pl. 89: 2, Johow Pl. IV.

Valle Colonial (V. del Polvorín of Guzmán; p. = powder-house), the seat of the village, is the only valley on Masatierra that approaches maturity. The floor rises gently to the foot of Mt. Pirámide, a distance of about 2 km, and is watered

Fig. 26. Mt. Damajuana seen from Anson's valley. In the foreground a section through an agglomerate bed. — Photo C. Skottsberg $^{25}/_{12}$ 1916.

Fig. 27. Valle Colonial seen from the Centinela ridge, c. 350 m above sea level. Left, Cordón Central; above, Portezuelo de Villagra and Cordón Salsipuedes, ending in the vertical escarpment of Pta San Carlos, behind which, on the west side of Pto Ingles, towers Cerro Alto. — Photo C. Skottsberg 17/1 1917.

by two permanent streams, which receive several small tributaries from the surrounding gullies. The valley bottom was cleared of its native forest centuries ago; already 80 years ago practically nothing was left below 250 m. Macales and maqui-luma stands fill the interior, and only farther up the gullies we find better forest. Material washed down from the sides have contributed to build the wide, stony and sandy beach, the largest piece of level ground on this island (figs. 3, 20, 27). I cannot remember having heard of any names for the streams. Guzmán mentions 3 streams emptying in Cumberland Bay, Arroyo del Hospital, A. de la Turbia (turbio = turbid) and A. de la Reina; the first is, I suppose, where Anson had his hospital.

El Pirámide (figs. 21, 29, 31), separated from Mt. Yunque by a narrow saddle (W Portezuelo del Yunque), towers above the colony. Johow's Pl. V dates from von Rodt's reign and shows the scenery when no village existed. The figure 809 m on Friederichsen's map stands for the summit of Mt. Pirámide. From both N and S the ascent is rather steep, 40—50° the first stretch, but gets more gentle higher up, 25—20°; toward the valleys on both sides the slopes are precipitous (Skottsb. 3 Pl. 91).

Portezuelo de Villagra (fig. 28). No visitor, even if he only has a single day at his disposal, fails to visit this famous spot with the Selkirk memorial tablet. The

Fig. 28. Portezuelo de Villagra, seen from above the settlement in Valle Colonial. — Photo C. Skottsberg ³⁰/₁₂ 1916.

altitude of the pass is generally stated to be 550 m; an average of 20 aneroid readings gave 593 m. which I believe is too much; about 575 ought to be approximately correct. The north "door-post" rises with an angle of 80° (Quensel 2 fig. 9 on p. 51), the south is formed by the slope of Mt. Pirámide; see fig. 29, a transverse profile with a gradient on either side of about 70°. The trail across has, in some places, been worn down in the red forest soil and has been deeply eroded by running water. From the saddle one has a grand view of the south side of Masatierra from Mt. Yunque to Pta O'Higgins and Santa Clara (figs. 49, 50).

* * *

A volcanic island, especially if considered to be of late Tertiary origin, often has craters or shows other signs of recent activity, and it is not surprising that visitors to Masatierra have tried to locate old centres of eruption. Walpole writes p. 93: "We skirted up the western side, which shows three semicircular craters, whose sides toward the sea are broken down, thus forming bays within their basins. Of these, Cumberland Bay is the central . . ." The other two were, I presume, Pto Frances and Pto Ingles (if not Bahía del Padre). And Quensel (1 p. 256), referring to Cumberland Bay, speaks of "die lockeren Tuffmassen, die noch einen alten Kraterboden bedecken . . ." and p. 257: "Mächtige, oft rot gefärbte Tuffablagerungen füllen den Talboden, was darauf hindeutet, dass es sich nicht um ein Erosionstal,

Fig. 29. South side of Portezuelo with the Selkirk memorial tablet, seen from the pass. — Photo C. Skottsberg $^{25}/_{12}$ 1916.

sondern um eine teilweise erhaltene Kraterbildung handelt." Finally, 'Ob das westlich von dem Portezuelo sich öffnende cirkusförmige Tal auch eine Kraterbildung darstellt, lässt sich nicht entscheiden. In einer vorläufigen Mitteilung habe ich diese Möglichkeit angedeutet, und vieles scheint mir darauf hinzudeuten, dass ursprünglich ein Doppelkrater hier gestanden hat, wobei gerade der enge Rücken des Portezuelo die Scheidemauer bildet.' This was written after our visit in August 1908, and at that time I shared my companion's opinion (1 p 136) During my later expedition, when I came to know most of the island better, I arrived at a different conclusion (see e g 2 p 57) The geological structure is the same all the way from Pto Frances to Bahia Juanango, we find the same agglomerate beds more or less well exposed in the valley bottoms, but nobody would be inclined to deny that they are typical erosion valleys where denudation thanks to the scant supply of running water, is very slow, in many cases abrasion has worked faster than erosion In Pto Frances the stream has barely managed to lower its bed down to sea level near the coast In Pto Ingles, where the surrounding ridges are very high, the distal part of the valley has been widened and levelled, and quite some alluvial soil has been formed The same procedure is, I think, responsible for the formation of the Cumberland valley system, there is nothing that speaks in favour of a crater theory or against its origin as the result of erosion The streams drain the wettest part of the island, where erosion is greater and faster and accumulation a factor of some consequence As I said, my first impression was that the Colonial valley was the old crater and its wall formed by Cordón Central, Mt Piramide and the Salsipuedes ridge, and I think this also was what glimmered in Quensel's mind However, the thick, stratified deposits of brick-red, deeply weathered tuff with "Bruchstücke von Olivinkrystallen, Lapilli artige Lavabruchstücke, Erzkörner und Glas" also occur in Anson's valley, separated from Valle Colonial, the supposed crater, by the over 500 m high Cordon Central which runs down to the shore of the bay I mentioned above that my photograph of the section through an agglomerate bed published by Quensel was taken in Anson's valley Either this is another broken down crater, or the deposits are ejections from the 'Colonial" volcano This would make us postulate that the Anson valley had been excavated even to a lower level than the present one when the volcano was active, and this seems questionable In his second paper Quensel quotes his earlier discussion (p 53) and adds "It is over 40 years since I visited the locality and naturally I cannot now rely on any personal recollection", and 'But the composition of the formation, as well as my notes from the field, offer indications that the tuffaceous material of Bahia Cumberland also represents pyroclastic sediments of recent volcanic origin" He refers to the submarine eruption 1835 off Pta Bacalao I willingly admit that I lack the necessary training to get to the bottom with a geological problem, but my observation near the foot of Mt Yunque (see above p 99) suggests that the agglomerate bed underlying the basalt is of the same nature as the formation in Cumberland Bay With regard to Villagra, there is no semicircular valley corresponding to the opposite one, for only on the north and east sides are ridges resembling a crater wall Until a geologist-vulcanologist has had an occasion to study the island it is better to leave the question of the nature of Cumberland Bay open

Fig. 30. Cordón Salsipuedes from Cumberland Bay, with the still wooded quebradas nos. 3 to 5 (counted from Pta San Carlos; beyond, the deep Quebr. Gutierrez. — Photo B. Frödin $^{29}/_1$ 1952.

Fig. 31. Cumberland Bay in SSE, seen from the air. From left to right Quebr. Minero-Damajuana, Damajuana, Portezuelo del Yunque, Valle Anson, El Yunque, El Pirámide with Cordón and Pico Central, Salsipuedes with Pta San Carlos. — Photo B. Frödin $^3/_4$ 1952.

Fig. 32. From the trail across the Salsipuedes highland, looking SE. Photo C. Skottsberg 21/1 1917.

Cordón Salsipuedes forms the western boundary of Cumberland Bay and runs from the main range to *Pta San Carlos* (figs. 3, 27, 31), along the east side of the Salsipuedes highland between the bay and Pto Ingles. Whether the name, which means "get out, if you can", was originally applied to the coastal escarpment, 380 m high on Friederichsen's map, I cannot tell. A well-worn zigzag trail, also used as a bridle-path, unites the colony with Pto Ingles and crosses the ridge at about 410 m. From here it is not difficult to follow the ridge up to over 700 m; who attempts to continue until the rib abuts on the backbone takes his life in his hands, for the ridge is a knife-edge, studded with crags. Already at about 600 m it is only 1—2 m wide, and the rise, quite gentle farther down, increases to 25—30°. As we climb, scrub, brushwood and forest succeed each other on the slopes.

The declivity facing the Colony is sculptured by a series of shallow gullies, of which the two nearest to the coast are treeless, whereas the others are wooded. A comparison between fig. 30 from 1952 and Skottsb. 3 Pl. 90: 1 from 1916 makes it clear that the forest patches have undergone no perceptible change in size. The floor of the fourth quebrada (counted from Pta San Carlos) slopes 30°; the forest is of an open, degraded luma-canelo type with much maqui. There is no water in these gullies. The gullies of the main ridge, Q. Gutierrez and Q. del Monte Maderugo, were thickly wooded in 1917 (monte maderugo = forest full of timber).

The trail to Pto Ingles ascends the buttress between the gullies no. 2 and 3, descends on an undulating slope (fig. 32), crosses *Loma de los Muñoces* and descends rather abruptly into V. Ingles. The quebradas coming down from the main ridge are filled with a remarkable *Dicksonia* forest near the range — note Q. Helechos ("Fern gully") — followed by luma groves and macal, I refer to my description, 3 p. 909. Fog is a very important climatic factor here.

Pto. Ingles offers no protection and is not used as a harbour (fig. 33). As a rule there is a heavy swell and the boulders on the beach are shifted to and fro making landing uncomfortable, perhaps dangerous. Close to the east headland a rock projects, separating a miniature cove from the main bay. The beach is a steep wall of boulders, but with a tolerably calm sea landing is easy at the foot of the rock, which is pierced by a tunnel, "una roca agujereada sobre una playa de piedras grandes", as this place is described in Instrucc. naut. p. 229, referring to Selkirk, Guzmán calls the tunnel "la portada del Solitario" (p. 23). Through the tunnel or, at high tide, across the rock, we gain the bay, and immediately to the left, about 5 m above sea level (Branchi) is the famous "Robinson's cave", a favourite goal for visiting tourists (fig. 34). It is hardly probable that the cave, described in some detail by Guzman l. c., served the recluse as his permanent abode.

Fig. 35 is a general view of the valley seen from an airplane, but this picture does not show the extent of the beach flat and of the wide, gently sloping valley floor. The stream has water at all seasons. A ridge extending halfway down the valley divides it in two, the east branch comes from a crescent shaped saddle, equally conspicuous from both sides of the island (figs. 35, 36) and reported to be impassable. The dividing cordón can be followed along the crest up to about 550 m, where it gets so narrow that further advance becomes too hazardous (see Skottsb. 3 Pl. 90 2). All the low land in the valley (fig. 36) has been cleared by fire and the forest replaced by extensive weed fields, but in the branch valleys and side gullies is some good forest, where a few chonta palms have been spared (Skottsb. 3 Pl. 88). There is much naranjillo, but little maqui. The continuous cover of herbs and grasses testifies that erosion is slight, and so is the inclination of the cleared valley floor. It would perhaps be possible to reforest this valley with luma and other native trees. At present (or at least in 1917) it is grazed, a tropilla is seen in fig. 36.

Cerro Alto boldly terminates the dividing ridge between Pto. Ingles and Vaqueria (figs. 37, 38). Possibly this ridge gives access to the summit which is about 600 m high, an older figure says 627 (Friederichsen, Johow). All other sides are almost or quite perpendicular. Patches of forest are seen on the flanks of the cone.

Bahia de la Vaqueria serves, as the name suggests, as a cattle ranch. The cove is useless as an anchorage, but landing is easy enough with a calm sea. There is no level beach, the stream, which is permanent, gropes its way between a wall of boulders of all sizes. Fig. 39 is a general view of the valley seen from the air. The outer part is grass land with scattered trees on the slopes, closing to form groves higher up, the interior is densely wooded (Skottsb. 3 fig. 35 on p. 894). The animals in Vaqueria have been left to run wild, and the visitor should look out for the bulls.

As far as I could see, the geological structure is the same as in Cumberland Bay, with the same red volcanic agglomerate, and it was during our visit to Vaqueria that I began to doubt the crater character of the former. Halfway up the valley

Fig. 33. Pto Ingles with the foot of Cerro Alto (note tilt of the strata). Mrs. S. seated on an old Spanish gun. — Photo C. Skottsberg $^{20}/_1$ 1917.

Fig. 34. The cave ("Robinson's grotto") in Pto Ingles. — Photo P. Quensel $^{25}/_8$ 1908.

Fig. 35. The surroundings of Pto Ingles, seen from the air; note the crescent-shaped saddle overlooking the south coast of the island. — Photo B. Frödin 8/4 1952.

Fig. 36. The gently sloping floor of Valle Ingles with the main range in the background; right, the dividing ridge where, in 1908, the last living *Santalum* grew. — Photo K. Bäckström 1917.

Fig. 37. Cerro Alto, seen from Cordón Salsipuedes. The small eminence above the escarpment is the same shown at the extreme right in fig. 38. — Photo C. Skottsberg 8/12 1916.

Fig. 38. Cerro Alto seen from a point on the crest of the central ridge in Valle Ingles, c. 400 m above sea level, looking N. — Photo C. Skottsberg 19/1 1917.

Fig. 39. The Vaquería cove and valley, seen from the air. Left, Cerro Alto, right, ridge between Vaquería and Juanango; the top of Cerro Chumacera visible behind. — Photo B. Frödin 8/4 1952.

1 Co Agudo; 2 El Pirámide; 3 El Yunque; 4 Co Chumacera; 5 Co Tres Puntas; 6 V. Villagra; 7 Villa Alemana; 8 M. Juanango; 9 V. Juanango.

Fig. 40. Bahía Juanango with Pta Negros and Morro Juanango, seen from the air looking SE. — Photo B. Frödin 8/4 1952.

we meet the conspicuous dolerite bed mentioned above (p. 97 and fig. 5). A passage across the steep rocky and scrub covered ridge leads us down into the Juanango valley.

The spectacular escarpment between Vaqueria and Pta Negros was described and illustrated above (p. 99 and fig. 8). Near the entrance to Vaqueria is a low rock and a little farther west, off *Pta Norte*, another called *Morro del Viudo* (Widower's rock). These rocks rest on a submarine abrasion terrace, clearly distinguishable at low tide. The coast wall projects west in a long, narrow and curved spur, not unlike a saw-blade, *Pta de los Negros*, and SE of this lies *Morro Juanango* (fig. 40).

Bahia del Juanango is a wide bight, protected against winds from N and E, but otherwise open. Seen from some distance out to sea it looks forbidding, and the name "Desolation Bay" seems well chosen, but on a closer view two green quebradas come in sight, *Villa Alemana* (Germantown), accessible with difficulty, and Q. Juanango.

Q. del Juanango. The beach in the little cove is of the same kind as in Vaqueria, a low escarpment and large, angular stone blocks, but with a suitable wind landing is easy. My diary calls these blocks "conglomerate", without much doubt identical with the agglomerate found in Vaqueria. The valley is full of weeds near the sea, but as it isn't grazed native grasses are abundant farther in. At about 200 m above the sea are the first forest patches, and a little higher up, at the small waterfall, is good forest. The threshold is, I suppose, formed by the same dolerite bed as in Vaquería, but I did not bring any specimens.

From *Juanango* to *Bahía del Padre* the coast escarpment trends SW in wide, slightly concave curves to *Pta Lemos* and *Pta Tunquillar* and thence to *Pta Meredazia*, the east head of B. del Padre. Figs. 41 and 42 make further descriptions superfluous. Two conspicuous mountains tower high above the coast line, Chumacera and Tres Puntas, overlooking both sides of the island, the latter with its three peaks ought to be a fitting goal for expert climbers (fig. 43). On the slope of Chumacera are found the most westerly forest patches on Masatierra, from here the country is treeless.

Bahia del Padre (Parson's Bay) got its name from the configuration of the rock W of the entrance. The old Spanish name *B. Herradura* (Horseshoe B.) is still used by some authors. The diameter is about 250 m. It is a convenient harbour for small boats, but the entrance, guarded by rocks, is narrow (fig. 44). Landing on the beach of sand and shingles (Skottsb. 3 Pl. 102 1) is comfortable with a moderate swell, but may be difficult. The cove is a natural amphitheatre, but we do not find very much of the "risueñas representantes del mundo vegetal" praised by Guzmán (p. 24), except a patch of salt meadow (*Salicornia*) along the beach, because the flora is poor and mainly consists of weeds, among which the gilly flowers are conspicuous. Nowhere is the climate drier. *El Puente* was described and illustrated above (p. 101, fig. 10), the flat, sandy surface is seen on figs. 45 and 46, the former showing the wind-polished tuff beds.

Looking at the maps and photographs one is struck by the peculiar appearance of B. Padre. It is evident that it is no valley, no result of erosion. Branchi wrote (p. 168) "Un cráter muy pronunciado puede suponerse en la Bahia del Padre", and

Fig. 41.

Fig. 42.

Figs. 41—42. North coast of western Masatierra from B. Juanango to Pta Lemos, seen from Quebr. Juanango. Cerros Chumacera (note patches of luma), Tres Puntas and Enrique. — Photo C. Skottsberg 9/1 1917.

Fig. 43. Cerro Tres Puntas. — Photo Hans Frey.

Fig. 44. The entrance to Bahía del Padre. — Photo C. Skottsberg ¹³/₁ 1917.

I am tempted to endorse his opinion. Both Quensel and Hagerman came to the conclusion that the rocks have been subject to post-volcanic thermal processes, and Hagerman, after a description of the palagonite tuff from Puente, writes: "Stellt man diese verschiedenen Bildungen aus der Nähe der Padrebucht zusammen, so gelangt man zu der Auffassung, dass dieses Gebiet frische Spuren vulkanischer Tätigkeit aufweist" (p. 26).

On the naked sand we found many living beetles (no reference is made to them in vol. III) and empty shells of four species of landshells, *Fernandezia tryoni* Pilsbry, *Succinea fernandi* Reeve (also in sand at Tierra Blanca), *S. texta* Odhner and *S. semiglobosa* Pfeiff. (also in sand on Santa Clara). These delicate creatures of the humid forests are entirely unfamiliar to these dry and barren surroundings, and it is difficult to account for the presence of these shells here as well as at Tierra Blanca and on Santa Clara. Are they a testimony of a more humid climate permitting some kind of brushwood to exist, a period during which the concretions mentioned above (p. 101) were formed? Or did dwarf trees such as *Dendroseris litoralis*, *Rea pruinata* and *Chenopodium Sanctae Clarae*, on which landshells lived, grow here in historical time but before goats were introduced? Certain facts do speak in favour of this theory. A few specimens of *Rea* and *Dendroseris* still occur on the south coast of Masatierra, particularly on M. Viñillo and on M. Juanango, where the goats cannot get them. What did this now barren country look like when the islands

Fig. 45. View from Puente, looking S. Wind-eroded tuff beds and sand. Behind, Pta O'Higgins with its morro, in the background Santa Clara. — Photo K. Bäckström 13/1 1917.

Fig. 46. Mobile sand on Puente, in the foreground a dense growth of weeds, mainly *Chenopodium multifidum*. C. S. as measure. — Photo K. Bäckström 15/1 1917.

were discovered. Not as to-day I am sure, but more or less like Morro del Spartan at Santa Clara, as already suggested by Johow p. 261. I would think that 80, in some valleys 90 per cent of the soil is now occupied by introduced weeds. We have no reason to believe that there was a desert when the immigration of aliens began.

It is to be regretted that we did not study how the shells found did occur, if only on the surface or also deeper down embedded in the sand. And we have to find out if landshells live on the plants mentioned above.

*   :   .

With *Pta de la Isla* we reach the end of the north coast. Time did not permit us to visit the small peninsula W of El Puente, and we shall now proceed along the south side of Masatierra.

Pta O'Higgins, watched by a nameless morro (small skerry), and the inhospitable coast cliffs of *Bahia Carvajal* are seen in fig. 47. With a NW wind boats engaged in langost fishing at Santa Clara find shelter here. From *Pta Aguabuena* to Co Negro the coast shows several well-marked bights.

Bahía Tierra Blanca or *Tierras Blancas* has its name from the white sand above the bay. Just as the other bays on this coast it is bordered by cliffs and beaten by a never resting surf. To land anywhere on this side of the island is possible only under very exceptional conditions (fig. 48).

Pta Larga (Long Pt) separates Tierra Blanca from the next bay, in the background rises a rounded hill which I take to be identical with Guzmán's *Co Enrique*. From a distance it seems to be formed by basalts of the higher horizons, but no specimens were brought.

Bahia Chupones derives its name from "chupon", in Chile a vernacular name for *Greigia sphacelata* Reg. (Bromeliaceae), which has edible fruits (chupar = suck), and applied by the fishermen of Masatierra to the extremely rare *Hesperogreigia* as well as to *Ochagavia*, in this case the former, an inhabitant of the wettest and loftiest ridges, is not to be thought of, whereas the latter, a typical xerophyte, very likely occurs here, even if we did not observe it W of Tres Puntas where it covers rock faces (see Skottsb 3 Pl. 97). The slopes round the bay are grassland, in the western half almost pure *Avena barbata*, otherwise with extensive patches of the native *Stipetum*. All streambeds in this western section are dry most of the year.

Loma Escarpada[1], 385 m high where we crossed it near the main range, separates B. Chupones from Villagra Bay, this taken in a wide sense. Off the point lies *Morro Viñillo* (viñilla means 'small hill planted with vines", but the name must refer to something quite different in this case), the gradient of the surface shows the tilt of the lava beds (fig. 49).

Bahia de Villagra and its valleys, the bay taken in a wide sense and

---

[1] In my field notes I called this ridge "Cordon Escarpado", and this name also appears on the Chilean chart, and on my map I had used the same name for the ridge between Pangal and Q. Minero, and as it was published in this sense (Skottsb 3 pp. 890, 915), I have renamed the other ridge Loma Escarpada.

Fig. 47. View from Puente toward Bahía Carvajal and Pta O'Higgins. Behind, Santa Clara. — Photo K. Bäckström 15/1 1917.

Fig. 48. Bahía Tierra Blanca seen from Pta Larga. — Photo C. Skottsberg 5/1 1917.

Fig. 49. View from Portezuelo de Villagra looking SW, with Santa Clara in the background, Morro Viñillo in the middle, right the south coast of Masatierra from Bahía Villagra to Pta O'Higgins. — Photo C. Skottsberg $^{18}/_{12}$ 1916.

extending from M. Viñillo to Los Chamelos. The broad slopes E of Loma Escarpada, locally known as Los bajos de Villagra, are strewn with lava boulders and furrowed by dry, stony streambeds. In the background two very conspicuous mountains, already seen on the north coast, *Co Tres Puntas* and *Co Chumacera* (Rowlock Mt., with a deep vertical slit), rise to a height of perhaps 500 m (Branchi's figure 650 is certainly too high). In the dry streambed below Tres Puntas we found a patch of pangue, which reaches its farthest west here. Chumacera looks like an enormous rock slab standing on end. At the foot water was found also during the dry season, and here is the westernmost luma forest on this side, and below a threshold (see above p. 97 and Skottsb. 3 fig. 36 on p. 896) with a small waterfall a grove of *Boehmeria*. The next gully has forest down to about 300 m above the sea. Fig. 50 gives a good idea of the nature of this country.

On all the earlier charts and maps the bay is presented as forming a regular curve, but the aerial survey proved that this is not the case; see fig. 2. The coast cliffs are lower here than farther west, but there are very few places where it is possible to get down to the water. It can be done not far from Cerro Negro, where we found access to the beach.

Villagra is watered by three permanent streams and densely wooded. The scenery is even more grand than on the Cumberland side, with the sequence of

Fig. 50. View from Portezuelo de Villagra looking W. From W to E Cerros Enrique, Tres Puntas and Chumacera. — Photo C. Skottsberg 10/1 1917.

summits from *Co Agudo* (sharp) to Mt. Yunque, more imposing perhaps from this side than from any other (fig. 51). A peak between Agudo and Chumacera is called Oreja del Conejo (Rabbit's ear) by Guzmán. The higher slopes are precipitous, with gradients of 60—70° and sculptured with numerous hanging gullies, carrying water after every rain, when many little cascades tumble down from the summit of Mt. Yunque (fig. 2) between the carpets of ferns and pangue. The Villagra valleys have not been levelled by erosion as much as Valle Colonial, V. Ingles or V. Anson; the inclination in the middle and lower sections is 20—30°. The forest in *Q. de la Choza* (responsible for this name is a small shack below the lower timber-line, l.c. Pl. 85: 1) and on the slope of Mt. Pirámide (l.c. Pl. 91) is primeval; it extends up to the level of the Villagra pass and is very wet and rich in species. Some maqui is seen here and there at lower elevations. The forest comes to a sudden stop 200—250, in cases 300 m above the sea. On a former occasion (3 p. 895, Pl. 85: 1) I have discussed the nature of this timber-line. Below the forest degraded grass-land with foreign grasses and herbs dominates over the natural *Stipetum*. Along the streams a fringe of pangue runs down toward the sea (l.c. Pl. 85: 2). Nobody lives in Villagra, but it is grazed over by cattle on the lower slopes.

Mt. Yunque has already been described; I shall add here what Tenz l.c. has to say about the summit. "Se ve arriba una altiplanicie muy extensa y suavemente inclinada hacia oeste a poca profundidad, de forma rectangular, rodeada

Fig. 51. El Yunque seen from the Villagra slope c. 175 m above sea level. — Photo C. Skottsberg 9/1 1917.

Fig. 52. South coast of Masatierra from Cerro Negro to beyond Corrales de Molina. After a water-colour sketch by the author.

de cordones en los cuales sobresalen varias cimas. Desde ellas nacen, en distintas direcciones, quebradas en que corren cristalinas vertientes." The buttress projecting S is prolonged to a ridge ending in a low cone, *Co Negro*, 190 m high (one reading only; l.c. Pl. 92: 1).

From *El Yunque* to *El Verdugo* the main ridge of the island presents the picture of a sky-high rock wall (figs. 2, 11, 52). E of Mt Yunque several nearly vertical, trough-shaped gorges have been dug out, each with a cascade and a patch of forest and known as *Corrales de Molina* (corral = enclosure; probably named for Padre IGNACIO MOLINA, an Italian-Chilean naturalist of the 18th century and author of a Compendio in which 3 plant species from Masatierra were mentioned). Goat-hunters cross the ridge here and descend into the gullies, which have been described with much detail by Weber who went there several times. Fig. 52 shows that it is no easy going. Hence follows a naked vertical wall, exposing the regularly stratified lava (fig. 52, right). Along the shore *Playa Larga* extends, marked "Low beach" on the English chart, presumably a low abrasion ledge. The country farther E is a succession of cliff walls and gorges; see figs. 2 and 11. The sinister name *El Verdugo* (executioner, hangman, fig. 11) reminds of the dangers on this coast, where no light warns the sailor.

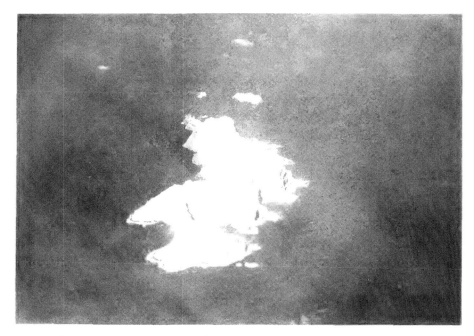

Fig. 53. Santa Clara from the air, looking SE. — Photo B. Frödin ⁸/₄ 1952.

Santa Clara.

Santa Clara or Goat Island is a barren, desolate islet separated from Masatierra by a shallow, about 1500 m wide strait, dreaded for its strong currents and turbulent waters. The depth is 19—20 fathoms according to Anson's map; I sounded 20—45 m.

The older literature gives little information about this island, but it was described in some detail by Guzmán pp. 48—53, to whom the reader is referred. Various bays and morros are mentioned, with names probably given by the fishermen. The circumference of the island is said to be 9 km, the area 500 hectares. Measurements on the new map gave a length of 3.5 km, a maximum width of 1.25 km and an area of 2.5 sq. km. This map is based on the aerial survey of 1952 and on Mr. Frödin's photographs (fig. 53) The length profile is seen in its full extension on fig. 48. A comparison shows that all the older maps are very defective.

The island is everywhere bordered by steep cliff walls (fig. 53). Above is a sandy table-land, studded with hills, of which the easternmost, incorrectly placed on other maps, is about 375 m high (366, Lopez). Guzmán calls it Co Negros, but as we have one Co Negro on the south coast of Masatierra, I named it *Cerro Johow* in commemoration of the author of the well-known work on the flora of Juan Fernandez. Close to the coast are several morros. The west side of the island is beaten by a heavy surf and inaccessible, but on the inner side, behind M. del Spartán, landing is — but not always — possible.

On Anson's map of 1741 Santa Clara is shown as covered with some kind of arboreous vegetation. Walter does not tell if a landing was made, but the name Goat I shows that there were goats on the island, and Ulloa's map of 1742 leaves it treeless. Just as Johow we found the place very barren and the vegetation mostly formed by weeds with *Avena* in dominance, all very dry during the summer. When Gunther says that there were "algunos árboles en la pendiente del este" he either did see some specimens of *Dendroseris* on the cliffs above the water or refers to *Morro Spartan* (also called M de los Aleltes, fishermen are said to have collected seeds of *Matthiola* in B del Padre and to have scattered them on Santa Clara). Relics of the original flora found a refuge on the morro, which is separated from the island by a channel less than 10 m wide and blocked by huge boulders which are exposed at low tide. The current rushes through the narrow channel, and to judge from the vegetation the goats are unable to cross. I believe that Johow (p 261) was right in assuming that, before the introduction of this pest, Santa Clara must have looked much like M Spartán. The altitude of the island is sufficient to catch the trade clouds, as shown on fig 4, and we are told that rains are not unfrequent during the winter months (Johow p 261), giving origin to an abundant vernal flora of annuals. During our brief visit in January we did not see any trace of water, but we read in Instrucc náut p 230 that a stream leaps over the cliff at the NW point, a statement repeated by Guzman who calls it *Chorro de Doña Maria* (p 50).

To judge from our passing observations, the geology is the same as of western Masatierra, uncounted, light yellowish or brownish volcanic beds traversed by numerous vertical dikes of a hard gray basalt. I regret having neglected to bring samples of the lava beds for comparison with the rocks from Puente. The dike rock was described by Hagerman p 28 and found to be identical with the basalt from the top of Co Negro. The sample came from a dike on M Spartán. We landed at the foot of this dike which forms a flight of steps leading to the table-land of the morro, see Skottsb 3 p 924 and Pl 103. The dikes project as flat slabs above the softer beds.

Masafuera, former surveys and maps.

Until our visit in 1917 Masafuera was much less known than her sister island. It had been inhabited more permanently only during the period of the penal settlement 1909—1913, a misfortune that befell this ocean castle a second time in 1927—1930. Only few scientists have visited Masafuera.

Of the early navigators few paid a visit to this island. One of Commodore Anson's captains, on his way to Cumberland Bay, happened to come up under Masafuera and reported that the island was not, as former navigators had imagined, a barren rock, but "almost every where covered with trees and verdure, and was near four miles in length". He had not been able to land, but added that "it appeared to him far from impossible, but some small bay might be found on it, which might offer sufficient shelter for any ship desirous of refreshing ashore" (Walter p 134). As four ships of the squadron were missing the Com-

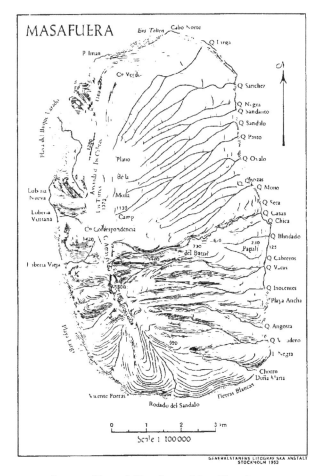

Fig. 54. Map of Masafuera. After Skottsberg.

modore sent a sloop to Masafuera to look for them there, and when she returned after a fruitless search, during which the island was circumnavigated, a report was drawn up with the first real description of the island. Anchorage had been found on the north side close to the shore but protected from S only (l. c. p. 156). Pl. XXI is a view of the NE side of "Masa-Fuero", as the name is spelled. It shows the table-land up to the highest hills well forested, and we have little reason to doubt that such was the situation 200 years ago. Four places along the coast are marked with the letters *a*, *b*, *b* and *c*, *a* seems to indicate a reef, *b* and *b* are the entrances to two of the canyons. I believe that *a* also indicates Q. Casas and that *b* are Q. Ovalo and Q. Sanchez. *c* is the waterfall coming down from Q. Larga. Pl. XXII, pretending to show the west side, is less easy to read. I think that it represents the north-west section of the coast from Cabo Norte south toward Loberia Vieja, but nothing like the perfectly cylindric tower on the extreme right in the picture exists — the only thing I can think of is a very irregular rock close to the beach in Lobería. The promontory in the middle is Buque Varado. Groups of trees are seen only above this place and above Lobería Nueva.

Ulloa found the island very inhospitable: "La Isla de *afuera de Juan Fernandez* es toda muy alta, y tan escarpada, y escabrosa que no tiene parage conmodo para desembarcar" (p. 287). On a former occasion (3 p. 796) I quoted the narratives of Byron and Carteret. The island was well wooded in 1765.

The hydrographic expeditions despatched by the Oficina in Valparaiso paid little attention to Masafuera. When Lopez reports that the island was "cubierta de arbolado" in 1875 (p. 67) he must have included the *Dicksonia* jungle on the slopes of Mt Inocentes. Johow (p. 96) asserts that the luma was common all over the island except near the coast and in the highland, but this does not necessarily mean that it formed extensive woods. We find the same statement in Instrucc. naut. of 1896. It is not known when the destruction of the forest started in earnest, but it is probable that the exploitation of the sandal-wood, which led to its complete extermination, had serious consequences for the forest as such. The names of two valleys and a place on the south coast testify that a species of *Santalum* grew on the island. The possibility that forest fires have ravaged the woods must not be forgotten. Foreign grasses spread into the cleared spaces and prevented the germination of the seeds of the native trees. The direct influence of the goats, introduced, I believe, during the 17th century, remains to be found out. They greedily devour the arboreous Compositae and the endemic herbs, but I cannot tell if they eat the leaves of the luma, naranjillo and canelo. I can testify from my own experience that there was better forest in 1908 than in 1917, an undisputable consequence of the activity of the convicts during the intermediate period. Nevertheless Gunther (1920) repeats the old statement that Masafuera was covered with trees.

In 1895 the Oficina Hidrografica published the first map showing the principal topographical features. New dates had been provided by Johow. During our visit in 1917 we soon discovered that this map was too defective to be used as a basis for a map of the vegetation, and we did what we could to correct it. The result was a sketch put at the disposal of the Oficina, which used it for a new chart. When the flight over the islands was undertaken in 1952 Masafuera was covered by clouds. A new map is urgently needed.

Main geographical features

In shape and general appearance Masafuera differs profoundly from her sister island. The island (fig. 54) is a solid rectangular block with slightly rounded corners, tilted NE so that the escarpment along the west side is very much higher than on the east side, where it is quite respectable (figs. 55—57). The table land is traversed by numerous parallel deep valleys running NE—E (figs. 57, 58), the high west wall by a number of precipitous gorges, this side has much the same appearance as the south side of Masatierra E of Mt Yunque (fig. 52).

Fig. 55. North half of Masafuera looking W. Quebr. de las Casas at the extreme left. — Photo K. Bäckström Feb. 1917.

The question may be raised if not the eroding forces have been more active in bygone times than they appear to be at present when so many of the streams are dry or carry very little water during the summer half year. If it is true, and this is believed by many, that the Ice Age was characterized by high precipitation values, the climate of Juan Fernandez, otherwise not much influenced by the glaciation in the southern Andes, must have been more rainy than now and, as a consequence, the eroding forces stronger. The end of the Pleistocene left the islands much as we see them now.

The coast lacks bays, there is no harbour, not even a sheltered cove to accomodate small craft. The landing places from where the interior can be reached are the entrances to Q. Sanchez and Q. Casas, but only under favorable conditions with regard to wind and sea. It happens that an expedition has to return with its errand unaccomplished. Abrasion has created a terrace along the west side, continued by a reef studded with rocks (fig. 59). At the foot of the coast cliffs a talus has accumulated, sloping down to a beach where the surf washes out the finer material leaving the boulders. It is possible to scramble along the shore from Q. Sanchez south round the island and from there north along the west side to the north extremity of the Lobería Vieja plain, separated from the Lobería Ventana beach by an impassable obstacle. Figs. 60 and 61 show that it is no easy going, and with a heavy swell it may not be possible to pass the southeast corner of the island. The opportunity to make this circuit round $^3/_4$ of the shore and to proceed from one canyon entrance to the next greatly simplifies matters for the surveyor where, in contradistinction to Masatierra, boats cannot be used to move from one place to another.

The longitudinal axis is directed N by W—S by E. The statements regarding the size of the island vary a great deal. 9 miles (14.4 km) by 4 miles (6.4 km) with a circumference of about 46 km and an area of 85 sq. km, all according to Lopez, 11.7 by 7.4 km (Johow's map), Bianchi, 10 by 6 km, area 84 sq. km, Gunther, 9.25 by 6 km, and Guzmán, 17(!) by 7 km, a circumference of 55 km and an area of 85 sq. km. The figures taken from my map are 10.3 by 6.2 km and the area 57.6 sq. km.

Geology and morphology

In 1908 Quensel, the only geologist who ever visited Masafuera made a hasty survey of the rocks along the coast from Q. Casas to Lobería Vieja and north of Casas from the shore to perhaps 1300 m altitude. His field notes and specimens served him for a description of the principal geological features. In structure the two islands differ considerably. Both are built up of innumerable volcanic beds of varying thickness and tilted about 20°, both exhibit two more or less distinct horizons, both are traversed by vertical dikes, but here the resemblance ends. On Masatierra the lower strata consist of lavas very rich in olivine, interbedded with tuffaceous deposits, deeply weathered and denuded, resulting in the formation of V shaped valleys. The lower horizon of Masafuera consists of hard, dark gray to black vesicular feldspar basalts (Quensel 2 p. 58), less rich in olivine and very resistant to the denuding forces. These rocks prevail up to approximately 1000 m. My notes from 1917 contain a statement that W of Vicente Porras, where Playa Larga begins, a bed of "conglomerate" was observed traversed by harder dikes, but unfortunately no specimen was preserved. In a paper not quoted by Quensel, who did not mention the occurrence of agglomerate beds on Masafuera, R. A. PHILIPPI described 14 rock samples collected by Germain, most of them "losen, von der Höhe heruntergerollten Blocken entnommen". I doubt that anybody will be able to identify these rocks from Philippi's unscientific description, but two of the samples suggest the occurrence of tuffaceous deposits, they consist of "Rapilli" cemented together.

At about 1000 m a lava bed of a different aspect was met with, a light gray, "iddingsite bearing phyric olivine basalt" (Quensel 2 pp. 58—63). Between 1000 and 1100 m a rock of quite another type occurred, described as a light yellowish green soda trachyte. Apparently a closely related type is found also at lower levels, boulders of this rock are so common in the talus along the south shore that the place was called Tierras Blancas. Quensel arrived at the conclusion that "lavas of soda trachytic composition have been emitted at different times and that they have alternated with lavas of more normal basaltic composition" (2 p. 66).

The upper horizon, from about 1100 to 1400 m, is formed by dense, ash gray feldspar basalts, which probably form the whole upper complex of lava beds with exception of the summit of Mt Inocentes, these rocks very much

Fig. 56. East coast of Masafuera between Pta Negra and Playa Ancha, with entrance to Q. del Varadero. — Photo C. Skottsberg 21/2 1917.

Fig. 57. Part of the east side of Masafuera seen from the air. The highland is covered with thick fog. — Photo B. Frödin 8/4 1952.

Fig. 58. View from the high land above Las Chozas looking toward the Ovalo, Pasto and Sándalo valleys. — Photo C. Skottsberg 3/2 1917.

Fig. 59. The shore at Lobería Vieja with a crag on the reef. — Photo K. Bäckström 17/2 1917.

Fig. 60. At the landing-place in Las Casas. Our party is about to embark, assisted by the crew of the schooner. — Photo K. Bäckström 15/3 1917.

Fig. 61. As fig. 60, showing beach of large boulders. — Photo K. Bäckström 15/3 1917.

Fig. 62. Slope of Mt. Inocentes seen from Cordón Atravesado, c. 1350 m above sea level. — Photo C. Skottsberg $^{15}/_2$ 1917.

resemble the hard basalts between 400 and 600 m on Masatierra (l.c.). The summit of Mt. Inocentes consists of a still different rock, a slaggy olivine basalt supersaturated with iron oxides (l.c. p. 70). The extension and thickness of this bed is unknown.

As on Masatierra numerous vertical dikes traverse Masafuera, in this case in W—E direction. The rock is extraordinarily rich in olivine and the dikes may represent, at least in part, channels for the beds forming the summit of the island (l.c. p. 74).

The difference in geological structure between the two islands helps, I think, to explain the profound difference in morphology. The streams, eroding deeper and deeper into the land, have excavated valleys which, in their distal parts, are V-shaped, with steep sides, which rapidly become steeper inland, where the perfect U-shape is retained in the canyon, with the entire narrow width of the gently sloping bottom occupied by the streambed. In the innermost part, where the land reaches its greatest elevation and the precipitation its highest figures, lateral erosion has widened the valley and a fan-shaped series of hanging gorges has been formed. The canyon ends in a high, almost vertical wall with a waterfall. Figs. 63—65, 68—71, 73, 75 and 77 serve to illustrate the valley formation. In the northern, drier and less high half of the island no deep canyons were formed. The ridges left standing between the valleys are very unlike the ridges

Fig. 63. Entrance to Quebr. de las Casas. — Photo K. Bäckström Feb. 1917.

Fig. 64. In the Casas canyon after a few days of dry weather. The rhubarb-like plant is *Gunnera Masafuerae*. — Photo K. Bäckström Feb. 1917.

Fig. 65. Looking down into the interior of Casas canyon from the crest of Cordón del Barril. — Photo K. Bäckström 1/2 1917.

Fig. 66. The grass-covered table-land between the Casas and Vacas valleys, looking N. The stone-building, an observation post overlooking the ocean, dates from the first convict settlement. — Photo C. Skottsberg $^{19}/_2$ 1917.

in Masatierra, because the hard basalt layers have not been removed by denudation, but are left as a cover right down to the sea, forming gently sloping, wide plains. Farther inland the ridge gradually narrows. See figs. 57 and 58. Beds of greater resistance form ledges along the valley slopes and thresholds across the streambed.

The south half of Masafuera.

Shrouded in clouds most of the time, *Los Inocentes* rises above the west wall, an imposing dome forming the south half of the island. Opinions have differed very much regarding the altitude: 2000 m on the older charts as well as on Johow's map, 1836 (Lopez), 1850 (Viel; 850 is a misprint), 2300 (v. Rodt), 1624 (Branchi) and 1840 (Guzmán). My single reading, carefully worked out, gave only 1500 m, a figure possibly too low. Toward W, N (fig. 62) and NE the summit falls precipitously; it is connected with the north table-land by a ridge, C. Atravesado, bordered on both sides by a precipice and so narrow that the stretch above the Vacas valley, where a pinnacle rises from the knife-edge, is not passed by the goats. Above Casas the highest point is c. 1370 m. Where Ermel got the idea from that the summit is covered with eternal snow (p. 113) is hard to understand.

Fig. 67. Cordón del Barril, looking W toward C. Atravesado. Note goat track along the ridge. — Photo C. Skottsberg ¹/₂ 1917.

Q. de las Casas, once the headquarters of the convict settlement and the ordinary landing-place, is called Q. Baquedano by Guzmán, commemorating the corvette frequently sent to the outlying islands of the Republic. From the beach, bordered by lofty headlands down to the water, we enter the valley, which is about 200 m wide here, with slopes receding under an angle of 40—45° (fig. 63). It gradually narrows so that the streambed offers the only access into the canyon. After a downpour the stream overflows and the valley is closed; a couple of days with dry, sunny weather and the bed, filled with boulders of all sizes, resting on the bedrock, lies dry, with pools of crystal clear water in the depressions and back of the thresholds (fig. 64). The most spectacular part of the gorge begins about 1 km from the entrance, where the width at the bottom may fall below 10 m, while the walls are many hundred m high (fig. 65). From a botanist's viewpoint Casas is one of Nature's conservatories; see Skottsb. 3 pp. 639—640 and Pl. 110. Johow called this place "El Pangal", and nowhere is the pangue (*Gunnera Masafuerae*) more luxuriant (l.c. Pl. 111). About 2 km from the

Fig. 68. Entrance to Quebr. de las Vacas. — Photo C. Skottsberg 13/2 1917.

entrance and 210 m above the sea the passage is obstructed by a threshold damming up a deep pool which cannot be passed round, and into this pool the water comes down in a cascade. Q. Casas drains C. Atravesado. The eroding power of the current is great, and I suppose that the stream is more or less permanent during the winter half year, but it must have taken a very long time to dig a gorge 1000 m deep through the hard basalt.

C. del Barril. Between Casas and Vacas lies a sloping, triangular tableland, about 1.5 km wide along the top of the coastal escarpment, which is 125 m high in this place, and extending west c. 2 km, where the cordón proper begins. The ruin seen on fig. 66 lies 190 m above the sea; the tilt, corresponding to the dip of the lava beds, is 20° F. Three small gullies break the monotony of the grass-land, Q. Chica, Q. Blindado and Q. Cabreros. *Q. Chica* (=small) is very shallow and dry, but some luma trees are seen. *Q. del Blindado* (B. means ironclad cruiser, but may have a very different significance here) is much larger and the water comes down over a threshold about 500 m upstream and has dug out a miniature canyon. There is good forest between 400 and 500 m and some groups of trees a little farther down. There is some forest also in *Q. de los Cabreros* (Goat-hunters' valley). Where the narrowing rocky Barril ridge, which has its name from a barrel-shaped monolith, begins, the elevation is 730 m. By and by the crest gets very narrow, but the rise is gentle, and there is a goat track all the way up to C. Atravesado (fig. 67). The ridge slopes 50—60° on both sides and we look down into the Casas and Vacas canyons (figs 65, 69) From C Atravesado the road N to Plano de la Mona lies open

Q de las Vacas (= cow, this place name is old, but no cattle existed on the island in 1908 Reintroduced in 1909, they had been killed off before 1917 and were introduced again in 1927) Following the beach south from Casas past *Pta Langlois* we reach the entrance to this second large canyon, which drains the highest part of Mt Inocentes It happened that when Casas was dry, the Vacas stream was still alive The entrance is quite picturesque thanks to the deep side valley separated from the main quebrada by a high spur ending in a sharp peak (fig 68) The interior has the same morphology as Casas, fig 70 shows the drainage basin viewed from the Barril ridge, fig 71 a typical, low threshold of harder basalt Some witches' cauldrons were observed (fig 72)

Little Vacas is accessible to a point about 1 km from the sea, where a very high cliff barrier impedes further progress

The easiest way to reach the table land S of Vacas is to climb a low barranca at *Playa Ancha*, a level stretch of stony beach, from where Q *de los Inocentes* with its untouched forest and fern groves is gained without difficulty Crossing this valley high up we climbed the Inocentes-Vacas ridge which leads to the top To our surprise we were not stopped by the fern forest we had reason to expect judging from our experience farther south, the stony and rocky ridge was covered with Alpine heath which continued right to the Inocentes summit The ridge can also be gained from Little Vacas The slope is, as seen on fig 68, steep, but it is terraced, and on our return we made a quick descent here

From the ridge south of Q Inocentes a good view is obtained across the interior of the narrow Q *Angosta* (fig 73) The morphology is the same as in Casas and Vacas, but the valley got its name because it is narrower than any other, only about 5 m wide at the bottom, a magnificent blind alley where, c 1 km from the entrance, we are confronted with a precipice and waterfall once more The photograph shows the columnar structure of the threshold At the foot of the waterfall the vegetation is, as in all these gorges, luxuriant

Quebr del Varadero (varadero = ship-yard, which does not fit here, varar also = to be stopped, and a strong surf may prevent passing the escarpment south of the canyon entrance) Our first attempt to ascend Mt Inocentes was made from this valley at the place seen in fig 74, where we gained the ridge at 400 m above sea level On account of the slippery grass the climb was a little hazardous To begin with, the ridge itself was easy until, at c 740 m, the treeferns, which had begun to appear on the sides, gathered on the very crest, forming an impenetrable thicket Having crawled through the soaking wet barricades of decaying trunks under the closed roof of the fronds and made perhaps 500 m in an hour, we had to give up The altitude was c 950 m and *Dicksonia* continued in every direction as far as we could see from a solitary canelo rising above the fern roof

A short walk into the Varadero gorge offers a strikingly wild scenery (fig 75) A picture of the short and narrow side valley was published by Quensel (2 fig 3 on p 43) Gradients of 60—80° are the rule in these gorges

Fig. 69. Looking down into the Vacas Canyon from the Barril ridge. — Photo K. Bäckström 1/3 1917.

Fig. 70. Innermost part of the Vacas canyon, seen from the top of Cordón Barril. — Photo K. Bäckström 1/3 1917.

Fig. 71. A low threshold in the Vacas canyon. — Photo C. Skottsberg 13/2 1917.

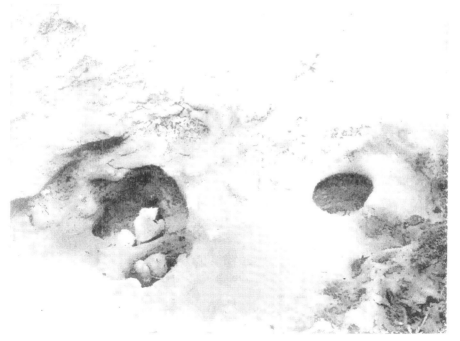

Fig. 72. Two witches' cauldrons in the Vacas canyon. — Photo C. Skottsberg 13/2 1917.

Fig. 73. A view of the interior of Quebr. Angosta, seen from the ridge N of this valley, 550 m above sea-level. — Photo C. Skottsberg 9/3 1917.

The south coast. The strip of beach is narrow S of Varadero, and the escarpment reaches an imposing height at *Pta Negra* (fig. 56). A short km beyond this point a gorge with a cascade is passed, *Chorro de Doña María*, whether the same lady to whom the chorro on Santa Clara was dedicated I cannot tell. The talus W of this place derives its name, *Tierras Blancas*, from the light colour of the deposits. Along *Rodado del Sándalo* (rodar, to make a turn) the land rises gently; the shore is fringed by a reef, on which the sea breaks with a thundering roar (fig. 76). At *Vicente Porras* we arrive on the west coast. The long and broad abrasion terrace, *Playa Larga*, was referred to above (p. 142); a level plain like this is a rare phenomenon on Juan Fernandez. At Lobería Vieja, "the old sealing grounds", where some fur-seals were still to be seen, the width is $1\frac{1}{2}$ cable (277.5 m) according to Günther, a figure in good accordance with our estimation. Several hanging gorges face the playa, coming down from Inocentes and C. Atravesado, and two streams find their way across the plain to the sea. One of the gorges, described as *Q. de la Lobería Vieja* (Skottsb. 3 p. 941) was surveyed by us. The entrance is barred by very large boulders, and one has to climb along the wall to get into the valley. Quensel published a photograph of the entrance (2 fig. 15 on p. 58). The short canyon ends in the ever-present cliff wall with its waterfall (fig. 78). The altitude of the valley floor is only c. 190 m.

A short but impassable stretch prevents us from reaching the remaining

Fig. 74. Entrance to Quebr. del Varadero, from where, up the south wall left an ascent was made. The knob on the extreme right is shown in fig. 75. — Photo C. Skottsberg $^{21}/_2$ 1917.

Fig. 75. Looking into the Varadero canyon. — Photo C. Skottsberg $^{21}/_2$ 1917.

Fig. 76. Coast of Masafuera between Tierras Blancas and Vicente Porras. — Photo K. Bäckström 16/2 1917.

"loberías", *L. Ventana* (= window, a hole in the rock), *L. Nueva* and *L. del Buque Varado*.

Playa del Buque Varado ("the beach of the stranded ship") is a wide tongue formed by the talus deposits; probably one or several landslides have occurred here, where the barranca is of formidable height and steepness (fig. 78). A stream coming from the gullies above has cut a winding bed (fig. 82).

Ensenada Toltén is a shallow open cove W of *Cabo Norte*. When it is impossible to approach the east coast boats anchor here, where landing, as a rule, meets with little difficulty. Consequently, numerous weeds mix with the native herbs and grasses covering the slopes at the foot of the barranca. Unfortunately Toltén is quite unfit as a base camp, as the highland cannot be reached, nor is there a passage along the shore to Q. Sanchez.

The table-land N of Q. de las Casas.

The *Plano de la Mona* ("she-monkey's plain"), a name of unknown origin (there are no monkeys on Juan Fernandez), and the rim of the coast escarpment can be reached from several valleys. The usual route takes us up a zigzag trail from Casas, across a dry gully and through the large, branched and well forested *Q. del Mono* (another queer name) to the abandoned convict settlement *Las Chozas*, situated among the remnants of luma forest 550—650 m above sea

Fig. 77. Interior of the Lobería Vieja canyon. — Photo C. Skottsberg 17/2 1917.

Fig. 78. Pta del Imán and Playa del Buque Varado, seen from the sea looking S. — Photo C. Skottsberg 16/3 1917.

level; another 50—100 m and the undulating grass-, fern- and pangue-covered Mona plain, crossed by many little gullies, dry during the summer, lies open in every direction (fig. 79). At one of the tributaries to Q. Pasto, 1130 m above the sea, a pool of water in the rocky stream-bed made the place a convenient camp site ("Campo Correspondencia"). A short walk brings us to the edge of the plain and to Las Torres (Towers), c. 1370 m, and Co Correspondencia, c. 1420 m. Fig. 80 is a view of one of the Lobería gorges seen from Correspondencia. The Alpine flora is well represented on these hills. Near the top of the high western barranca some shallow depressions almost lack vegetation (fig. 81). The soil is clayey and the surface, which shows distinct signs of water erosion, strewn with stones and cracked in places. Some small boulders rested on short pillars of clay. The ground is perhaps flooded during the winter. I was told that patches of snow have been observed here, but this needs corroboration. Wind erosion might be responsible for the formation of the small "tables".

Avenida de las Cabras, "Goat Avenue", is a well-beaten track running along the very edge of the abyss from C. Atravesado to Co Verde. From about 1100—1250 m alt. one looks down on Buque Varado (fig. 82) and *Q. del Imán* (Magnet gorge, fig. 83). One of the former inmates of the convict settlement told me that he had been employed cutting a trail down the precipice to Buque Varado, where also huts were built, but we saw no signs of either. There are

Fig. 79. View across Plano de la Mona toward the Larga and Sanchez valleys, elev. 940 m. — Photo C. Skottsberg 25/2 1917.

Fig. 80. Looking down into one of the upper gorges of Quebr. Lobería from an altitude of c. 1400 m. — Photo C. Skottsberg 14/2 1917.

Fig. 81. Small depression at the west edge of the Masatierra table-land, c. 1400 m; naked soil, on the stones mosses and lichens. Left, a patch of *Lophosoria*. — Photo C. Skottsberg 15/2 1917.

Fig. 82. Looking down on Playa del Buque Varado from c. 1200 m. — Photo C. Skottsberg 7/3 1917.

Fig. 83. Quebr. del Imán seen from c. 1100 m. Left, Buque Varado. — Photo C. Skottsberg 7/2 1917.

Fig. 84. Plano de la Mona, looking N, with Cerro Verde in the background. — Photo C. Skottsberg 7/3 1917.

Fig. 85. Looking S toward Lobería Nueva from Avenida de las Cabras N of Buque Varado. — Photo C. Skottsberg 7/3 1917.

Fig. 86. Quebr. del Mono seen from the beach. — Photo C. Skottsberg 8/3 1917.

only scattered patches of trees on this side, while ferns especially *Lophosoria*, pangue, grass etc form a more or less continuous cover. A picture taken from a point between Buque Varado and Imán gives some idea of the scenery (fig. 85).

At the north extremity of the plain stands a green, rounded hill, *Cerro Verde* (fig. 84), mentioned as Pico Norte in Instrucc. náut. p. 230 and said to be 1340 m high. This figure is too high, I believe.

From Cabo Norte to Q. de las Casas

The coast cliffs from *Cabo Norte* to the Sanchez shore are almost perpendicular and about 300 m high. Half way a cascade tumbles down to the beach in two leaps, coming from the gap of *Q. Larga*. Just as the other valleys on the east side this has a forest belt above c. 300 m and grass-land below. Here the trees cover also part of the ridge between Larga and Sanchez, apparently the largest continuous patch of luma forest on Masafuera.

Q. de Sanchez is very long, narrow and twice furcate, and there is forest in all the branches. None of the other valleys is quite destitute of trees. The small *Q. Negra* (also called Q. del Plan Negro) does not reach the shore. *Q. del Sandalito* and *Q. del Sándalo* do not seem to offer anything of particular interest. The talus slope permits a fairly comfortable passage as far south as to the large *Q. del Pasto*. "Pasto" means pasture, and there is better grass-land with abundant native grasses along this part of the coast than anywhere else. Pasto is a large valley with its sources near the edge of table land. The main stream runs over a high threshold. S of Pasto a land-slide is crossed before reaching *Q. del Ovalo*, which derives its name from a conspicuous hill inside the entrance, a good example of columnar structure. The passage is a little fatiguing until we are opposite *Q. del Mono*, another big valley emptying its waters through a narrow crevice (fig. 86). From here going is easy to Casas, where we have completed our circuit of the island.

Human influence on Juan Fernandez

The discovery of the two virgin and uninhabited islands in 1574 was soon followed by the first inroad into its living world. If we are to believe the historians cited e.g. by Guzmán, Fernandez returned and settled on Masatierra where he introduced 60 Indians (Weber), a few goats and pigs and devoted himself to agriculture, fishing and sealing. His stay is said to have been short, but his goats remained and multiplied. After Fernandez' death the island was turned over to the Order of Jesuits, and, in the beginning of the 17th century, the first fruit-trees were planted and vegetables introduced (Weber p. 162). During the "era of the buccaneers" the islands served as a place of refreshment, but the damage was, I daresay, confined to the surroundings of the harbours. Their first visit is said to have taken place in 1680. A change for the worse came when L'Hermite reported that the precious sandal wood was abundant. I refer to Johow's instructive account of the history of this ill-fated tree, pp. 127—131. L'Hermite's visit took place in 1624, and already at the middle of the century a lucrative traffic was

Fig. 87. Ruins of the old Spanish fort in Cumberland Bay. — Photo C. Skottsberg ²⁹/₁ 1917.

in full swing between the islands and Perú. Toward the middle of the 18th century there cannot have been very much left on either island, or the sandal-wood should not have escaped Anson and his men who spent months there and must have known of the former trade.

The hunt for sandal-wood ended in the extermination of this species and had, I presume, serious effects on the forest in general, with the final result that all the lower slopes became cleared of trees, leaving the field open for an invasion of weeds; Ulloa for instance was struck by the abundance of *Avena*.

Having suffered serious losses from the raids of the martial English navigators the Spaniards took possession in 1750 and made up their mind to transform Masatierra into a stronghold. I shall not dwell upon the history, enough said that in 1779 7 places were fortified. Part of the walls in Cumberland Bay are still standing (fig. 87), and old guns lie about in other places (fig. 33). Nor have I any good reason to retale the melancholy history of the time when Masatierra served as a prison for banished patriots during the years of resurrection and later. Its rôle as a depository for undesirable citizens came to a definite close in 1855. Then came the tenants.

A source of destruction of the forest, not at all negligible, were the frequent visits of American whalers during the 19th century who called to supply themselves with water, wood and goats' meat. The large herds of goats had been a great asset during the era of the corsairs, and in order to stop this traffic mastiffs were landed as early as in 1686 or 87 (Burney IV p 210) The result was that the goats had become very shy at the time of Anson's visit, he estimated them to be about 200 only, but the dogs were plentiful, savage and dangerous His men saw no dogs on Masafuera, whereas goats abounded, but later dogs were introduced also to this island which was spoken of as "Isla de Perros" There were some dogs left when Johow went to Masafuera in 1892, but none in 1908 In 1830 they were exterminated on Masatierra Freed from their worst enemies, the goats increased in number, in 1877 Viel estimated them at 3000 The new lessee von Rodt persecuted them for the sake of their hide, and in 1892 the number had sunk to about 1000, while there were 200 on Santa Clara and 4000 on Masafuera if these figures are reliable is hard to tell We came across a small herd on the south side of Masatierra in 1917, and once in a while a daring hunter brought down a buck from the inaccessible crags where they liked to hide themselves At that time they enjoyed the protection of the Government — the descendants from Robinson Crusoe's goats were regarded as sacred They were abundant on Masafuera, and even if their number was reduced during the time of the convict station, they soon recovered To judge from what Weber tells us the island swarmed with goats after the departure of the convicts in 1930, and they went right down to the beach Their damage to the indigenous vegetation (and thereby to the fauna) cannot be estimated nor disputed Their ravages had left their marks everywhere, and several peculiar endemic plant species were on the verge of extinction in 1917

Beside goats Juan Fernandez brought pigs which ran wild, but they were killed off long ago, nor are there any wild asses left, while cattle and horses came to stay I suppose that ever since the first Spanish colony 200 years ago domestic animals have existed on Masatierra In 1813 there were 1000 sheep, 100 goats, 500 cows, 200 horses, 10 mules and 40 pigs (Guzman p 178), but a decade later very few seem to have been left Again the Government stocked the island (Sutcliffe 2 p 206), and in 1833 there were 350 sheep, 120 tame goats, 70 cows, 15 horses, 8 mules and 30 pigs (Guzmán l c), but the tenants took no interest in farming, and in 1860 Mackenna registered 15 sheep, 98 cows, 15 horses and 15 mules only In 1878 and 1892, only horses remained

It is easy to understand that the early visitors got a very favourable impression of Masatierra, its agreeable climate, volcanic soil, evergreen forests, luxuriant verdure and good water, and concluded that the island was fertile if only its natural resources were utilized Certainly they did not fail to observe that there was very little level and moderately sloping land, but the valleys of Cumberland Bay and Pto Ingles must have looked inviting We can also understand that in those times it did not occur to anybody that the living world was unique, but it is strange that educated people like Governor Sutcliffe or Mrs GRAHAM could dream of Masatierra as fit not only to feed a considerable population but to be able to export its products Mrs Graham, cited by Sutcliffe (2), wrote in 1824 "The island might maintain easily 2000 persons, exchanging the surplus of beef, wines, brandy, for bread and clothing, and its wood and water would render it invaluable as a port." And Sutcliffe (1 pp. 442—443) cites a letter written to him by one MANUEL DE SALAS Sept. 1, 1835, when Sutcliffe had been appointed governor.

"The clays and soils of various colours brought to my memory the minerals of Golconda and Brazil — their (the islands') geographical position places them in a like situation and renders probable the same effects and equal productions. One occurs to me which might be of great importance, such is the making of bricks, of which immense quantities are brought from England and the United States, and for which you have all the elements in abundance, there are, the firewood, the clays, and, above all, the idle hands."

Still the tenants, who succeeded each other, did not coin money. Guzmán made an estimation of the arable land, 110 hectares on level ground, 70 on the lower slopes, in addition there were 20 on Santa Clara and 100 on Masafuera, and, if the forest was cleared, grazing land of much greater size would be obtained. The colonists took no interest in cattle. Lopez argued (1878) that if the tenant were more enterprising, he would go in for cattle and sheep, of which the island could maintain 10000 — the expectations had grown! Viel's report (pp. 19—22), founded on his observations in 1877 — a few days I presume — reflects the ideas of his time regarding the future of Masatierra. He admits that its fertility was more apparent than real although chonta and sandalwood grew in the forests, both highly appreciated for their valuable wood and a possible source of a small trade — it was 50 years since anybody saw a sandal tree! A road around the island would become a great asset, because various industries could be started in different places. Timber was plentiful, but the contract forbade the lessee to use it, because the disappearance of the forest would endanger the water supply. Viel's personal opinion was that this danger did not exist, "the island, situated in mid-ocean, accumulates the clouds and condensation produces the rains which feed the streams and irrigate the land, thus there is no reason why the lack of trees would have a contrary effect".[1] He forgot all about erosion. He recommended to His Excellency to authorize the lessee to utilize the forest, besides, he wrote, "if dead trees are left lying, the fresh growth will be poor and raquitic(!)", one cannot help wondering why, after thousands of years, when the fallen logs were left to decay, there was still dense, healthy forest. Unfortunately, "the quality of the native timber was not good, for which reason it should be better gradually to replace the indigenous trees by better ones, which later would become a source of income to the Republic. Pines should be planted at once on a large scale, it would be wise to take advantage of the present tenant who would be glad to look after the plantations, provided that some minor behalves which wouldn't in any way harm the State or render his contract more favourable were conceded him".[1] It was necessary to supply good timber, if not, the whalers would cease to come. Fruit-growing ought to be improved, wheat grew well, potatoes could be exported to northern Chile with great gain. In this connection Viel says that zarzaparilla — here = *Acaena argentea*, a noxious weed — was common and

---

[1] Translated from Spanish.

maqui not less abundant, it is not clear whether or not he regarded them as a source of wealth

As a more promising industry than forestry Viel recommends raising cattle. The island could easily maintain 1000, during the Spanish time there had been 800, and now the number of domesticated animals was 98 cows and 50 horses, but many had run wild. The 3000 wild goats ought to be protected by a closed season, 800 skins had been exported recently. Apparently the fur seals did not, in his opinion, need protection 'the output was mediocre, a consequence of the settlers not being sufficiently intelligent and industrious'[1] — he forgot that the poor result of sealing was a consequence of ruthless persecution during a century. The average number of seals killed per annum was 700 — one would call this a fair number considering the small size of the islands. Fishing was neglected, only very little salted or dried fish had been exported. There was plenty "langosta", and it ought to be made into preserves. Viel concludes his report with the following words "El estado actual es bien lamentable." Had the Government listened to his recommendations the situation would have become much more lamentable.

Of this official report to the Minister of Finance and to the Governor of Valparaiso FELLENBERG published a translation, but he protests against Viel's belief that the disappearance of the forest would not harm the water supply. As an appendix he published 3 letters from the new tenant, addressed to his relatives in Bern.

ALFRED VON RODT, of Swiss descent, an ex officer in the Austrian army and a well-educated gentleman, settled on contract on Masatierra as tenant of the islands. Encouraged by the many favorable reports on their resources, he expected to make his fortune, and he had some money to invest in the enterprise. His first letter, written shortly after his arrival and dated June 5 1877, contains dates on the size and position of the place, he tells that there were 7000 wild goats and pasture for 1000 head of cattle and that he intended to start "verschiedene Industrien". Evidently he went to work without delay, on March 13, 1878, he writes that he had timber worth 3000 Dollars ready to be shipped to the coast. He reported from Masafuera 17 6 1878 that this island was considerably larger than Masatierra (!) and that there were large forests and the most beautiful grasslands where it would be easy to feed 20000 sheep. He had killed more than 700 fur seals.

The castle in the air vanished, von Rodt never founded any new industries on Masatierra, there never was a sheep farm on Masafuera. He lost his money, but he remained true to his beloved Masatierra, where it is easy enough to make a living, but perhaps not a fortune. The von Rodt dynasty was still going strong when we visited the islands, the sons of Alfred made their living as lobster[2] fish-

---

[1] Translated from Spanish

[2] Professor KARL LANG, head of the Dept of Evertebrates in the Nat Hist Museum, Stockholm, on my request kindly made a diligent search for an English equivalent to the Spanish word langosta as name of the large Decapod *Jasus Lalandei* formerly known as *Palinurus frontalis*, which from a scientific viewpoint is no real lobster. He reports that *Palinurus vulgaris* and related forms are called "rock lobster", "spiny lobster" is another name. For the sake of brevity "lobster" or "langosta" will be used here.

ers, cultivated their corn fields and gardens and reared a new crop of sturdy fishermen.

The damaging influence of von Rodt's reign on the native flora and fauna must not be overrated. It is true that the maqui spread, but also that the goats decreased in number. The population remained very small, and the cultivated soil did not extend much. In comparison with recent disasters the encroach during the last decades of the 19th century was of little significance, except, perhaps, with regard to the chonta palm, one of Nature's great treasures. And BURGER tells us (p. 111) that when von Rodt failed to "develop" the islands, he became a protector of their nature.

In 1877 the population of Masatierra counted 64 persons, 29 of whom were male, children not included (demographic figures taken from Guzmán p. 37), in 1878 74 (22), in 1879 141 (51), and in 1880 147 (55) — the rise probably due to the arrival of labourers contracted by the tenant. Then it began to sink, 82 (24) in 1885, 61 (23) in 1886. In 1885 the German merchant ALEXANDER ERMEL visited Masatierra as partaker in a tourist excursion. As many before and after him he fell for the beauty of the scenery and he returned with fantastic ideas of the value of the natural resources, which nobody had understood to utilize properly.[1] Consequently he did not hold a very high opinion of von Rodt. Even barren Santa Clara became fertile in Ermel's eyes. For Masafuera only no great future was in store, it was too inaccessible. "Daher wird Masafuera für die Zukunft allein die traurige Bestimmung haben, als ein in Wolken eingehüllter, schauriger Felsen dazustehen, dessen Nähe die Seefahrer soviel als möglich vermeiden werden" (p. 115).

In spite of the very short duration of his visit (3 days), Ermel judged himself competent to discuss the economic importance of the islands for Chile. Masatierra might well serve as a health resort. Its principal industry would be fishing. Here he was, as the future showed, right, and the same is true when he argues that the seals needed protection. In former days the seals had been extremely abundant, not only the fur seal, but also the sea elephant. L. Heremite saw thousands of sea lions and seals (Burney III p. 18). Walter reports on the "sea lions", which occurred in large herds, but Pl. XIX shows that his "sea lions" were sea elephants. Ulloa tells us (p. 287) that "the beaches and rocks were everywhere crowded with seals in such abundance that no free space was left where one could walk, they did not leave a passage between them".[2] Captain ROGERS (1709) says that a compact string of seals lined the beach of Cumberland Bay (Guzmán p. 215). The main slaughter of the fur seal commenced in 1797, it is reported that in 1801 a single ship carried one million skins to the London market. If this be

---

[1] These illusions have been very tough. In an American newspaper (Meridian Star, Miss.) the following paragraph appeared on March 1, 1928: "Crusoe island fruitful — Juan Fernandez Island, on which Alexander Selkirk the reputed original of Robinson Crusoe, lived for four years, is one of the most fruitful spots in South America, according to a recent survey. Every known plant seems to grow there. One Frenchman who was shipwrecked there 40 years ago refuses to leave." No comments needed, but the climax is priceless.

[2] Translated from Spanish.

true it is a wonder that sealing could be practised with a profit over a period of 40 years. The seals have disappeared from Masatierra, the sea elephant is extinct in the waters of Juan Fernandez. As I told above, we found a small herd of fur seals at Loberia Vieja. Since 1891 it is protected by law, to what effect I shall not say.

But let us return to Ermel. Even if fishing ranked first, the wealth of the land was by no means contemptible: timber and fuel, chonta, sándalo, charcoal, "womit Herr von Rodt in den ersten Jahren seiner Pachtzeit einen lohnenden Anfang gemacht hatte", all kinds of fruit, probably also grain and wine, and breeding cattle, llamas and vicuñas should be tried. He also underlined Masatierra's strategic position.

However, nothing happened except that the population continued to dwindle, reaching its lowest figure, 35 (12), in 1893. When Johow revisited the islands in 1895 it had grown to 54. In 1891—92 Johow headed an official commission and he outlined a program for the future management of the islands. This document was published in his book, pp. 267—274. It is not without interest, and a summary will be given here. It begins by stating that the utilization must be based on the principal marine products, the langosta (*Jasus Lalandei*), confined to Juan Fernandez and the Desventuradas Islands (San Ambrosio and San Felix), and the bacalao (*Polyprion prognatus*), also absent from the coast of the mainland. Even the latter would become a valuable article of export, the more so because it is one of the worst enemies of *Jasus*. The waters abound in many other kinds of savoury fishes. When, however, the commission recommends to repeal the law of 1891, prohibiting the destruction of the fur seals, with the motive that seals are the most dreaded enemies of the fishes, no responsible authority in our days would agree. Poachers can be relied upon to keep the number of seals down.

Johow states that agriculture will never become profitable, for the simple reason that there is very little arable land and that the soil, once deprived of its natural vegetation cover, will be subject to erosion. Wheat should be imported from the mainland and land utilization limited to cultivation of potatoes and vegetables for local consumption. Nothing is said of the aspects as grazing land. There were very few animals in Johow's time. After these introductory remarks the commission proceeds to answer a number of questions.

With regard to the administration, some kind of authority should be established on Masafuera. A small steamer would become necessary to serve the communications between Masatierra and Valparaiso. An "inspector de colonización" should be appointed. The question whether it would be necessary to prohibit the cutting of chonta and sándalo is answered in the affirmative. Johow estimated the number of full grown chontas at 100 to 150, and he had occasion to visit the last living sándalo. They were already under provisional protection and it was recommended "no solo por motivos meramente ideales o sea cientificos, sino tambien por consideraciones de carácter comercial i economico" that the law should remain in force and violation be subject to severe penalty. "No seria, a nuestro juicio, exajerado castigar la destruccion de un solo ejemplar de chonta o de sándalo como delito de robo comun, i prohibir tambien su corta bajo pretesto cientifico." And the commission made public that, at repeated occasions, the crew — they forgot to add "and officers" — of vessels belonging to the Armada Nacional had possessed themselves of large quantities of chonta trunks — with the assistance of the colonists. (Such is the attitude of the majority of people all over the world that if an individual stands before the last living specimen of a plant or animal, he will grab it, because if he doesn't, someone else will have it.)

In the 1890's there were no plantations needing protection, but in Johow's opinion the existence of the native forest was jeopardized by the ravages of a parasitic fungus, *Antennaria scoriadea* Berk (Limacinia fernandeziana Neger et Johow), and he feared that it would "concluir poco a poco con la vejetacion de muchas quebradas." The fungus is still plentiful, but its killing capacity was, as far as I could see, greatly overrated. The commission recommended to make punishable to set the woods on fire, and to enjoin the inhabitants and visitors in need of wood to use only the fallen trunks. If I remember right there later was a regulation that only the maqui could be used for fuel. In the report nothing is said about the damnable habit of visitors to rob the forest of the stately endemic tree-ferns which, always without success, they tried to plant in their gardens on the mainland. Ermel saw the lifeboats of his ship return laden with young chontas and tree ferns and looking like gardens afloat. I have witnessed the same traffic myself, but I do not know if it still flourishes — there is a long way now to the young chontas and to the tree ferns.

A question if fishing with dynamite ought to be forbidden was answered in the affirmative, but not because it would reduce the fish supply very much — though it is admitted that the demand for fish might be greater in the future — but rather because "la dinamita manejada por personas de poca o ninguna ilustracion, facilmente orijina funestos incidentes." With regard to the langosta no scarcity had made itself felt, but it was recommended to leave it in peace during the breeding season.

Among the remaining questions, of which many were referred to specialists and not answered by the commission, one is of interest. It was recommended to exterminate the wild dogs and the native buzzards on Masafuera. The motive was to take better care of the goats, still considered to be an important source of meat, the meat is, I admit, very palatable. A bounty was therefore suggested. Nobody will grieve the loss of the wild dogs, they are not good company, but in the case of the buzzard, *Buteo erythronotus exsul*, the care for the goats gets in conflict with the interests of science. In his catalogue of the insular Ornis Johow remarks that the "aguiluchos quizas representan una variedad endémica si no una especie distinta de la del continente" — nevertheless he would not hesitate to exterminate it. Had he known the flora of Masafuera better, he would have been less kindly disposed toward the goats.

Finally the commission underlines the urgent need of regular communications with the mainland with rapid steamers permitting the products of the fishing industry to arrive fresh at their destination.

Thus the wants and needs were stated, but little was accomplished. The wild dogs on Masafuera were exterminated, but fortunately the buzzard escaped

Fig. 88. The boat harbour in Cumberland Bay. — Photo C. Skottsberg 4/12 1916.

Fig. 89. Lobster fishers working for Recart y Doniez by their boats during the closed season. Cumberland Bay. — Photo K. Bäckström Dec. 1916.

Fig. 90. The take is brought into the Recart y Doniez factory; left, live lobsters; right, the metal cooking baskets. — Photo C. Skottsberg 9/1 1917.

Fig. 91. The harbour in Cumberland Bay, showing three schooners at anchor, a motor launch and a number of fish-chests used for storing the take until shipped alive to Valparaiso. — Photo C. Skottsberg 2/1 1917.

Fig. 92. The village in Cumberland Bay, seen from the slope of Salsipuedes. — Photo C. Skottsberg 21/3 1917.

Masafuera got no supervisor, the management of the forests continued as before, the chonta continued to be cut unlawfully — a common occupation during the winter months, Weber says p. 116 — nothing was done for the fishing industry, no steamer came and went to the benefit of the inhabitants. Life went on as before.

Let us return to the langosta. Ever since the days of the discovery of the islands this magnificent crayfish had been appreciated as very good eating, and at Anson's time the beaches literally swarmed with large-sized specimens. No instrument was needed to catch any amount in one or two feet of water. How long this happy state of affairs lasted I do not know, nowadays the best catch is made in depths from 40 to 80 meters. In spite of the value of this marine product, which from time to time was shipped to the mainland, none of the tenants had the means to organize the industry on a larger scale. A company was formed in 1893, but even with a catch of 35 to 40 thousand annually and exporting some 40 000 tins of preserved tails, the business did not pay, and a new company formed in 1900 also failed (see Guzmán p. 209). In 1914 Messrs. Recart y Doniez started their establishment. We had the very best opportunity to watch the fishing from the catch of the sharks used as bait to handling the langosts in the factory (figs. 88—91) and to the export of the living animals, in the company of which we made our return voyage to Valparaiso onboard one of the schooners. The stern is built as a well with free circulation of the water, and

Fig. 93. *Carica papaya* in the garden of Mr. Charpentier, Valle Anson. — Photo C. Skottsberg 11/4 1917.

if the passage could be completed in 2 1/2 to 3 days all went well, but in too calm or too bad weather the motor alone did not help very much, the crossing was slow and it happened that very few of the lobsters arrived alive. Two minor companies were also in operation. The closed season was strictly observed. On the 2d of January at 6 a.m. a rifle shot signalled the open season, and the launches towed a string of boats, each party rushing to gain the best grounds which it monopolized during the season. Recart y Doniez also held the licence to fish at Masafuera and sent a schooner thither several times. I don't remember having heard that any kind of fish was exported at that time, but fish was the staple food on the island. About 200 people lived there, most of the men being employed by the companies. The village in Cumberland Bay (fig. 92) looked quite inviting with its neat, if not always too well kept houses, vegetable gardens, fruit trees and flower-beds, set among exotic trees like araucarias, eucalypts, poplars, pines, *Albizzia*, *Eriobotrya* and so forth. Johow has published a paper on the plants cultivated in the islands, and also a list in his book pp. 263—266. With the exception of the fig and the quince most of the fruit trees yielded indifferent fruits. The climate is of the Mediterranean type, but at the same time pronouncedly oceanic, and the lack of a period of real warm weather seemed to be responsible for the failure of *Citrus* fruits. The more surprising was it to find the papaya in cultivation in a garden belonging to a colonist of French descent.

Fig. 94. Threshing the wheat with a tropilla of horses, Cumberland Bay. — Photo K. Bäckström 1917.

Fig. 95. Chaff before the wind. Same place as fig. 94. — Photo K. Bäckström 1917.

Fig. 96. A rodeo in Cumberland Bay. — Photo K. Bäckström 1917.

The specimens were small, and so were the fruits, which we had no opportunity to taste (fig. 93). This seems to be the only tropical tree thriving in this warm-temperate climate. Several ornamental plants have become naturalized in the neighbourhood of the village, e.g. *Zantedeschia aethiopica*, *Pelargonium* spp., *Tropaeolum majus*, *Matthiola incana* and *Lochnera rosea*.

Wheat-fields were few and small and harvesting methods quite primitive; see figs. 94 and 95. Most of the flour was imported, and there was also a shortage of potatoes. Unfortunately the number of animals had increased very much, much more than would be deemed necessary, but milk-cows were few. Imported wine was the daily beverage, here as in other parts of Chile. Herds of cattle roamed through all the valleys from Pto Frances to Vaquería on the north and from the foot of Mt. Yunque to Puente on the south side of the island. I regret having neglected to ask their number; every animal had its owner. Fig. 96 shows a rodeo in Cumberland Bay. Only the herd in Vaquería was left to run wild. Horses were seen in some valleys, but I cannot remember having seen any sheep, and we were never offered mutton.

After 1917 the population remained about the same for years, but in 1930 it had increased to 298, of which 155 were male, including the boys. Ten years later it had grown to 434 (225).

I shall leave Masatierra for the present and try to follow the fate of Masafuera.

Fig. 97. View from the south slope of Casas valley, Masafuera, showing the headquarters of the first convict settlement. — Photo K. Bäckström Feb. 1917.

The first house was built in 1867 (Weber). Goat-hunters or fishermen used to visit the island. In 1908 we found some people staying there, but there was no permanent settlement. The next year saw a radical change. The full history is told by Guzmán pp. 87—101. A short summary is given here. Guzmán begins with the following words: "Tal vez la descripción de la flora natural de la isla de Más Afuera que hiciera el sabio sueco Skottsberg, hizo creer a un Ministro de Justicia del Presidente Pedro Montt, que dicha isla era el sitio ideal para la fundación de un presidio agrícola." Certainly Guzmán is joking, the more so as I tried on my return to start a campaign in favour of preserving the native flora and fauna — not the goats however! — and never said a word about Masafuera as a suitable place for agricultural or any kind of commercial experiments. Two months later a decree was signed, transforming the island into a settlement of criminals, and in April 1909 "Carcel Pedro Montt" received its first inmates and soon after a second lot, together 170. For the State it was no cheap affair to erect substantial headquarters at the entrance to Casas valley, to build a jetty in the turbulent water of the so-called landing-place and a schooner to serve the colony, but the parents of the scheme were optimistic and thought that once in operation, the establishment would soon become self-supporting, a miracle to be performed by cutting trees and cultivating the soil. Goats were plentiful and easy to get hold of, at least to begin with. "Tal era la convicción que tenían los creadores del presidio en la feracidad de la estéril Más Afuera, que al alcalde se le designó con el singular título

Fig. 98. The ruined forest and village of Las Chozas, Masafuera. — Photo K. Bäckström Feb. 1917.

de Director y Jefe de Cultivos", Guzmán writes. This official was a thrifty fellow, but he could not call up arable land where there was none. Houses were built in many places, vegetables sown and potatoes planted, cattle introduced and killed surreptitiously by the convicts, but much food had to be imported, and when the boarders obtained permission to send for their wives or relatives to keep them company the population rose to 350 persons. Good luck did not favour this humanitarian enterprise, the situation on the island became, to say the least, unpleasant, the schooner was shipwrecked and lost, and in 1913 Masafuera was abandoned. The buildings in Casas were in tolerably good condition in 1917 (fig. 97), but the wooden huts more or less fallen to pieces. Ruined forests, abandoned potato fields and a host of new weeds told the story (fig. 98). Of domestic animals only two horses could be discovered. We caught them because we could use them.

But, as Guzmán says, "los juristas no podían aceptar que una Naturaleza tan pródiga en helechos y en plantas sub-alpinas, no fuera generosa también para con las legumbres, hortalizas y frutales . . . ", and in 1927 "Prisión Carlos Ibañez" was established, this time not reserved for ordinary criminals — in addition 150 political offenders were exiled to Masafuera. More trees were cut, new houses built, new seeds sown, but the harvest was no richer than before, and in 1930 the colony was discontinued. Guzmán seems to fear a repetition of this sad story, to judge from his concluding remark " . . . el hombre con sus disposiciones legales

Table 1

Lobster catch 1940—46 After Guzmán

	Number	Gross weight in kg		
		Total	Living	Tinned
1940	109 250	112 531	15 533	96 998
1941	103 695	100 590	14 415	86 175
1942	134 589	112 531[1]	20 903	91 628
1943	62 287	64 160	14 929	49 231
1944	27 959	28 600[2]	11 947	16 633
1945	23 516	24 220	13 643	10 557
1946	56 431	58 120	—	—

y con su persistencia, indiferente del pasado, espera el momento propicio para construir un nuevo penal, sobre las ruinas del séptimo presidio" (there had been 5 on Masatierra).

On January the 16th, 1935, President ARTURO ALESSANDRI signed a decree making the Juan Fernandez Islands (together with Easter I.) a National Park, and two German residents, Weber and CARLOS BOCK, both addicted to the study of the fauna and flora, were appointed honorary forest inspectors. Bock soon died, and Weber left the islands after some years. The regulations were strict, had they been followed the goal for which I had fighted so many years, supported by Chilean colleagues, would have been attained. The rules did not infringe upon the reasonable rights of the colonists, nor was the fishing industry affected. In order to collect specimens of the indigenous plants and animals, also for scientific purposes, a license was required. No permanent habitations could be erected on Masafuera and Santa Clara. It is evident that Weber, in spite of his earnest intentions, did not quite understand what effective conservation involves or he would not have written the following words (p. 138) "Die Tierwelt von Juan Fernandez war leider sehr spärlich, es sollte mehr Leben in die schweigsamen Wälder kommen" — it did not occur to him that the introduction of foreign animals, even a few birds, would disturb Nature's balance in a way never properly to be foreseen.

Unfortunately a law has little effect without adequate means to enforce it. Without money and men with authority a conservation program cannot be realized, and in the case before us there was neither. Serious inroad upon the forests might, however, be prevented, and with the declining lobster industry and the non existent possibilities to expand agriculture there seemed to be no danger that more people would settle on Masatierra. But what happened? Guzman's interesting account gives the answer, l.c. p. 37.

---

[1] This figure, which is identical with the figure for 1940, must be incorrect. In all other cases save one (1941) the average weight of the langosts slightly exceeded 1 kg, and it was very little below that weight in 1941.

[2] On p. 202 Guzman quotes a very different figure: 47 238 kg obtained during the period Jan.—Aug. The balance cannot, I am sure, have been consumed locally, because the people fish for the companies, so that some other explanation has to be found.

Fig. 99. The central part of Masatierra, seen from the air and showing the cultivations and plantations around Cumberland Bay; from left to right V. Colonial, V. Anson and Quebr. del Minero. — Photo B. Frödin ³/₄ 1952.

In 1940 the population amounted to 434 persons (225 men and boys), in 1943 771 (198 men; the number of women was 123, of children no less than 450); 1944 shows a drop to 653, a result, one would think, of the heavy drop in the number of lobsters caught. In 1948 the population was about 600. The total export of lobster, living and tinned, is shown in Table I (after Guzmán).

As we see, the proportion of preserved lobsters underwent a rapid decrease during these years; the export of live animals was undoubtedly more profitable. The reasons for the sudden rise in total output in 1946 are not known to me, nor if it indicated a reliable increase or just a transient improvement; after 1946 no figures have been available to me.

The growth of the population between 1940 and 1943 cannot have had anything to do with the fishing industry, and the drop from 1943 to 1944 does not run parallel with the quantity of lobsters; besides, the effect would not show before 1945, when no census was taken.

More people meant more houses, more gardens, more timber and fuel used, etc. The effect is shown by comparing figs. 24, 27 and 92 with 22, 30 and 99. In 1917 the lower slopes of Q. del Minero were barren, in 1952 there were plantations; Anson's valley, where few people lived in 1917, bears sign of much activity, and the aspect of the settlement in the Colonial valley has changed a great deal from 1917 to 1952. Everybody welcomes that the devastated slopes near the sea, where erosion is a serious problem, have been planted, nobody objects to the growth of the population as long as fishing provides a decent livelihood for the majority. This, however, is not the case. The time has come when the old dreams to utilize the land, fostered by well meaning patriots, are coming true. The statistics tell us that Masatierra is being transformed into a cattle and sheep farm, a new and strange type of National Park. In 1945 the island had 5000 sheep, 600 head of cattle, 500 tame (?) goats and 300 horses, and even if the horses and cows mostly graze the open country with grasses and herbs, mainly introduced weeds, they do not despise the light forest which, and this was easy to observe already in 1917, suffers. The habits of the sheep and goats are different, wild sheep were observed by Weber in the thirties (p. 116). There are no fences and nothing to prevent these animals to run wild among the crests, where it is difficult to follow them. No palatable plant species is likely to escape these gluttons and in contradistinction to the naturalist, they need no license. It goes without saying that they will take to the mountains when, at the end of the drier season, food becomes scarce. Guzmán recommends introducing new kinds of grasses, better adapted to the climate, a measure probably unheard of in combination with the management of a national park. It should not be forgotten that one Mr. OTTO RIEGGEL, "el gran amigo de las ciencias naturales" as Guzmán calls him, celebrated the creation of the national park by introducing 6 pairs of rabbits (!) which, as everywhere else, will take what the sheep leave, nor that a particularly dangerous weed, the zarzamora (*Rubus ulmifolius*), a wellknown pest on the mainland, was introduced on purpose to be used as living fences. The success was complete. The thrushes took care of the dispersal of the fruits, invasion is going on everywhere, and I have just been told that the entire Plazoleta del Yunque presents the picture of an impenetrable "living fence". From the same source I have the information that the unlawful cutting of the Chonta has not been stopped — I doubt that anybody tried to stop it — but is going on just as before and with the same method: before a tree is felled a cut with an ax is made near the base in order to know the thickness of the wood cylinder, if it is too thin to be of value the tree is left standing, a potential victim of fungus attacks.

It remains to be mentioned that 17 colonists settled on Masafuera some years ago (72 persons in all). Their principal occupation is said to be lobster fishing.

Basing his opinion on his personal knowledge of the islands and on a wealth of material from various sources, Guzmán discusses the present situation and the possibilities to improve it. There can be no doubt that he is interested in the preservation of the nature, but it is also evident that he greatly underrates the dangers jeopardizing the survival of the indigenous flora and fauna. The pros and cons in agriculture and silviculture are set forth in detail. In his appreciation of the fruit produced he differs considerably from Johow who did not hold a very high opinion of the quality, and our impression was not too favourable. Oranges and lemons, not grown in our time, are said to prosper in the valleys — this may be true, but what are the fruits like? The wheat of poor quality according to Johow, is excellent, which must mean that new strains have been introduced. A circumstance in favour of agriculture, Guzmán says, is that as a national park all the land belongs to the State, and the concessioned farmer needs not worry about rents or amortizations. On the other hand, Guzmán continues, the factors rendering agriculture difficult are also conspicuous. The men working for the companies — there are three of them, but the Recart y Domez Co. was taken over "en estado ruinoso" by Cia Santa Sofia — earn much more money than the farm hands, with the result that everybody prefers to be a fisherman. The schooners cannot accommodate the export of fruit or vegetables. Good soil is rare and shallow, because the islands are too young (!). The zarzamora is taking possession of the best agricultural soil and is becoming a serious problem. The strong winds are another inconvenience to be overcome by planting hedges.

The most serious obstacle is the very limited extension of arable land, referred to above p. 171, 300 hectares, in 9 different localities, including Masafuera and Santa Clara, might be utilized, with an annual output of cereals amounting to 2300 quintales. If 800 are reserved for local consumption and 300 for seed corn, 1200 remain for export (l.c. p. 160) to compete on the market with millions of quintales produced on the mainland, and having to carry the cost of freight! It it disgusting to find that such imaginary hopes have been carried from generation to generation. How much of the land is level? Almost nothing. And what would happen if the slopes, where the inclination rarely falls below 15 to 20°, and the soil is very thin, are plowed? The badly eroded areas seen everywhere give the answer. When Guzmán recommends the declivities for tree planting he gets on safer ground. And he believes that reforestation, large olive plantations and the creation of orchards and artificial meadows would transform Masatierra into an "alegre huerto isleño, deleite de los turistas" (l.c. p. 164).

Masatierra is already blessed with sheep, cattle, goats and rabbits, all in excess — will it also be necessary to add a host of tourists? Guzman holds a very high opinion of the attractions of Juan Fernandez. He quotes "el célebre viajero Carlos Rowsel" (I regret never having heard his name before) who once said that if Masatierra were situated 60 instead of 360 miles from Valparaiso it would be "la Reina de los Balnearios" in the Pacific — and this in spite of the fact that there is not the slightest trace of a bathing beach on the island. And when Guzmán compares Juan Fernandez to Hawaii and finds that the one is just as marvellous as the other, he has lost all contact with reality. I should add that I happen to be very well acquainted with both, and that nobody could appreciate the beauties of Juan Fernandez more than I do. Call it a miniature Hawaii if you like, but deprived of the tropical luxuriance, the colourful Royal history of the natives, the white, palm-shadowed beaches of coral sand, the gigantic mountains and active volcanoes, not to mention the comfort and luxury offered by the busy cities, the large hotels, beautiful camp sites, excellent motor roads and easy and rapid communications by sea and air with the outside world! The nature of the indigenous living world is, in principle, of the same type in the two cases, but incomparably richer and more varied in Hawaii — there is room for half Masatierra in the caldera of Haleakala. To the average tourist Masatierra remains Robinson Crusoe's island — this is its main attraction. I have no doubt that the traffic will grow and the tourists become a moderate source of income which nobody will envy the kind and hospitable colonists, but I am afraid that Guzman is too optimistic when he thinks that the day is near when Juan Fernandez will become "el balneario habitual de los soñadores del mundo" (p. 229) and when large passenger planes will land on the big aerodrome on Masatierra. At present not even a tiny plane is able to land without crashing, but there are some places where an autogiro could come down safely. The roadstead in Cumberland Bay is so far the only place where a plane (a Catalina) has alighted, but with a high wind and a heavy swell the situation gets unpleasant. The level land by the sea in front of the colony is the only place where a small airport could be constructed. Its length will be 500 m or, if the front slope of Cordon Central with the old prison caves be blasted, perhaps 800 m, but the buildings belonging to the fishing companies and a good many other houses would have to disappear. On the table land of Masafuera, about 1200 m above sea level, another airport could be built at enormous cost, another one, probably a little cheaper, on the Loberia plain. Neither would serve any sensible purpose if not a strategic one. Let us limit our plans of making Juan Fernandez a popular goal of the tourist to an improvement of the communications and to a couple of modest guest-houses — and to impress on the visitor that he finds himself in a sanctuary where he has to keep his hands off. An unknown number of plants and animals barely manage to hold their own, and obviously many are on the verge of extinction, pronouncedly stenotopic as they are. The trail to Portezuelo ought to be improved and kept in repair, for everybody will want to see Selkirk's Lookout, to read the memorial tablet and behold the grand views. And there is no point within easy reach where the endemic flora is — or was, at least, in 1917 — better displayed.

* * *

If we want to preserve a unique living world of very great scientific interest and as such belonging not to a single country but to the whole world, these are the rules:

to limit plantations and fields to the waste land on the north side of Masatierra,

to encourage gardening for local consumption,

to declare war on the introduced noxious weeds, goats and rabbits,

greatly to reduce the number of domestic animals and to keep them out of the native forest,

to reduce the number of wild goats on Masafuera and keep it on a minimum or, which would be the best, to exterminate them,

to teach the inhabitants not to disturb Nature's equilibrium,

to enforce the Law of Jan. 31, 1935, by appointing a sufficient number of salaried supervisors and guardians.

Human influence has cut its mark deep and it has changed the natural scenery greatly without adding to its beauty. In part this has been inevitable, if man was to live on the islands, but there has been and is too much senseless destruction. This is the more to be regretted as the welfare of the population need not at all depend on either breeding cattle or sheep farming. Once the lobster meant

Fig. 100. Large specimen of bacalao, Cumberland Bay. The gentleman is Don NATALIO SANCHEZ, subdelegado civil and the highest authority in the islands at the time of our visit. — Photo K. Bäckström 1917.

everything. Today we can speak with Guzmán of the "Crepusculo de la langosta". The situation is alarming, he calls for measures to put an end to the decline, and he proposes certain ways and regulations. I would like to add that in a case as serious as this the best thing to do is to proclaim the whole year a closed season during a sufficiently long period. An industry based on the enormous supply of fish, with the bacalao (fig. 100) heading the list, would, if carefully handled become a profitable enterprise. A ship with modern equipment would bring the frozen fish to the mainland where it would find a ready market. The new methods of cold storage permit deep frozen food, fish not excepted, to keep absolutely fresh during any length of time. Beside the bacalao, the most abundant of all and considered to be the most delicious, there are several other kinds of commercial value unknown on the coast of Chile. I shall add one more remark. Cumberland Bay ought to be an ideal place for a biological station. The fauna and flora, terrestrial as well as marine, offers a wide field for scientific research, no less important from a practical viewpoint.

The present management of these precious islands is not in good accordance with the intrinsic meaning of the Law and, in some cases, directly violates it. If the responsible authorities do not change their attitude, Juan Fernandez will become a second Saint Helena and a disgrace to an enlightened world.

Speaking as on behalf of the Chilean nation, I would like to say, with a slight alteration what Guzmán said about the threatened langosta (p. 223)

No permitamos que nuestras islas se transformen en el recuerdo de una riqueza extinguida en forma irreparable. Así lo exige nuestro prestigio de nación civilizada, así lo esperan de nosotros las generaciones futuras.

December 1953

Bibliography

ANDERSON, G. W. A new, authentic and complete collection of voyages round the world. London. No date. (BYRON's and CARTERET's visits to Juan Fernandez.)
ANSON, G. A voyage round the world in the years 1740—44. Compiled by RICHARD WALTER. London 1749.
BRANCHI, F. C. La Isla de Robinson. Valparaiso 1922.
BRUGGEN, M. J. Fundamentos de la geologia de Chile. Santiago 1950.
BURNEY, JAMES. A chronological history of the discoveries in the South Sea or Pacific Ocean. London. Vol. III (1813, L'Heremite), IV (1816).
BÜRGER, O. Die Robinson-Insel. Leipzig 1909.
ERMEL, A. Eine Reise nach der Robinson-Crusoe-Insel. Hamburg 1889.
FRODIN, B. Expedition på svenskt uppdrag kartlade sagoön i Stilla havet. (Expedition on Swedish initiative mapped the fairy isle in the Pacific Ocean.) Dagens Nyheter $^{29}/_4$ 1952.
GRAF MARIN, A. Problemas económicos de Juan Fernandez. Departamento General de la Producción. Oficina de Enlace Agricola. Memorandum 158. Santiago, 29 de Abril de 1944. (Typewritten.)
GRAHAM, MARIA. Journal of a residence in Chile during the year 1822. London 1824.
GUNTHER, F. Derrotero de la costa de Chile. V. Anuario Hidrográfico de la Marina de Chile 32. 1920.
GUZMAN PARADA, J. Cumbres oceánicas. Santiago. No date.

HAGERMAN, E. H. Beiträge zur Geologie der Juan Fernandez-Inseln. Nat. Hist. of Juan Fernandez and Easter Island I: 1. 1920.

HAWKESWORTH, J. An account of the voyages undertaken... for making discoveries in the Southern Hemisphere. I. London 1783. (Byron's and Carteret's journeys.)

Instrucciones nauticas de la costa de Chile. Anuario Hidrográfico de la Marina de Chile XX. 1896.

JOHOW, F. Estudios sobre la Flora des Islas de Juan Fernandez. Santiago 1896.

JUAN, G. Y ULLOA, A. DE Relación historica del viage a la America meridional. Pt. 2, vol. III. Madrid 1748.

LOPEZ, JUAN F. Esploracion de las islas esporádicas de la costa de Chile. Anuario Hidrográfico de la Marina de Chile II. Santiago 1876.

PHILIPPI, R. A. Geognostische Beschaffenheit der Insel Masafuera. Neues Jahrb. für Mineralogie etc. Stuttgart 1857.

PHILIPPSON, A. Die Erosion des fliessenden Wassers und ihr Einfluss auf die Landschaftstypen. Geogr. Bausteine herausgeg. von Dr. HERMANN HAACK. Gotha 1914.

POEHLMANN, R. Noticias preliminares sobre las condiciones jeográficas i jeolójicas del Archipiélago (de Juan Fernandez). In Johow, Estudios.

QUENSEL, P. (1) Die Geologie der Juan Fernandez Inseln. Bull. Geol. Inst. of Upsala XI. 1912.

—— (2) Additional Comments on the Geology of the Juan Fernandez Islands. Nat. Hist. of Juan Fernandez and Easter Island I: 3. 1952.

SKOTTSBERG, C. (1) The Wilds of Patagonia. London 1911.

—— (2) Till Robinson ön och världens ände. Stockholm 1918.

—— (3) The vegetation of the Juan Fernandez Islands. Nat. Hist. of Juan Fernandez and Easter Island II: 20. 1953.

SUTCLIFFE, TH. (1) Sixteen years in Chile and Peru from 1822 to 1839. London 1841.

—— (2) Crusoniana or Truth versus Fiction, elucidated in the history of the Island of Juan Fernandez. Manchester 1843.

TENZ, O. Una ascensión emocionante a la cumbre del Monte Yunque. El Mercurio 8/3 1921. Valparaiso.

VIDAL GORMAZ, F. Jeografia nautica de la Republica de Chile. Anuario Hidrografico de la Marina de Chile VII. 1881.

VIEL, O. Islas de Juan Fernandez. Anuario Hidrográfico de la Marina de Chile IV. 1878.

WALTER, R. See ANSON.

WALPOLE, F. Four years in the Pacific in Her Majesty's ship "Collingwood", from 1844 to 1848. London 1850.

WEBER, HUGO Signalmaat Weber. Zehn Jahre auf der Robinson-Insel. Reutlingen 1940.

Addition

This paper was in page proof when my friend Mr. G. LOOSER sent me a report written by Dr. ALBERTO GRAF MARIN, Head of the Oficina de Enlace Agrícola in Santiago, and kindly put at my disposal (see Bibliography). Dr. Graf Marin visited Masatierra in January 1944 in order to inform himself of the economic situation of the population, 452 persons in 1943, a figure very different from the one quoted by Guzmán for the same year, 771, both cannot be correct. Graf Marin judged the living conditions to be comparatively good, even if much remained to be improved in the way of housing, teaching, medical care, entertainment, travel facilities, etc. It goes without saying that lobster fishing gave the main income, again, there is a discrepancy between his figures and those of Guzmán. 84 100 lobsters shipped to the mainland in 1943, whereas the total catch was 62 287 according to Guzmán. The average annual profit derived from the export of wool was about $1/6$ of the income from fishing, the number of sheep 3000. Finally, some mutton was sold to Cia Oto Hnos, apparently the only fishing enterprise in operation (comp., however, p. 187). With regard to the lobster Graf Marin was told that it breeds the year round whence follows that the fears later expressed by Guzmán would seem groundless and a closed season — after 1931 1/6—30/9 — unnecessary.

Although Graf Marin recognizes the fishing industry as the main source of wealth he revives the old dream of Masatierra as a future rich farming country, and his plans were drawn up without regard to the fact that Masatierra forms part of a National Park, protected by a law which, nevertheless, he does mention in passing. He recommends to import farmers from the region of Concepcion, where the climate is similar. As the soil, save for the houses and gardens, is fiscal property, anybody is entitled to supply himself with wood in the forest — only maqui is used for fuel, however. The forest should be subject to economic management by multiplying the few good timber trees and by introducing new ones, the Mediterranean cork-oak is particularly recommended beside *Acacia melanoxylon* and *Pinus radiata*. Of the endemic trees two are (or rather were) of commercial value, the chonta palm and the sandalo; the former — and also the latter, if it could be rediscovered — ought to be propagated in nurseries and planted on a grand scale. He tells us that the last living sandal tree seen by Johow in 1892 and by me in 1908 was ordered by the Subdelegado VERA in 1918 or 19 to be cut down — but in 1916 I was assured by the same man who brought me to the tree in 1908 that it had died and the wood been taken care of. I have no reason whatsoever to doubt the correctness of his statement.

With regard to the black pest *Antennaria* (Limacinia) Graf Marin shares my opinion that Johow exaggerated its dangerousness. A more serious enemy of the luma is an insect, *Saissetia oleae*, and he recommends the introduction, successfully arranged for on the mainland by himself, of its parasites.

Even if various fruits can be produced in sufficient quantity to be exported — the water-supply is good and the streams might be canalized and used for irrigation — raising live stock should constitute the main occupation of the farmers, but it is jeopardized by the spread of the zarzaparilla (*Acaena argentea*) and of the zarzamora (*Rubus ulmifolius*). They ought to be exterminated, which is just as desirable from the naturalist's viewpoint, but much easier said than done. In order to improve the pasture alfalfa and new and more nutritious foreign grasses should be introduced. Above all, to stimulate general utilization of the land and to prevent that a single thrifty person take possession of most of it, the island ought to be parcelled and the size of the lots fixed with regard to their rentability. The total value of Masatierra, settlements not included, is said to be 220 000 pesos, of Masafuera 120 000 (considerably more to day that 10 years ago). From a scientific and scenic viewpoint the value of these islands cannot be expressed in figures — it is inestimable. If the plan set forth in Graf Marin's interesting report materializes, Juan Fernandez will stand as a unique example of a National Park, the home of a unique fauna and flora, offered for sale

THE NATURAL HISTORY OF JUAN FERNANDEZ AND EASTER ISLAND

EDITED BY DR. CARL SKOTTSBERG

VOL. I

GEOGRAPHY, GEOLOGY, ORIGIN OF ISLAND LIFE

PART III

5. C. SKOTTSBERG: Derivation of the Flora and Fauna of Juan Fernandez and Easter Island.

Part III completes vol. I.

UPPSALA 1956
ALMQVIST & WIKSELLS BOKTRYCKERI AB

5 Derivation of the Flora and Fauna of Juan Fernandez and Easter Island

By

C SKOTTSBERG

With 1 Map

Part I

THE JUAN FERNANDEZ ISLANDS

Chapter I

Composition, distribution and relationships of the Flora

The statements made below are based on the results laid down in vol II of this work and in a number of papers published from time to time prior to the survey in the field undertaken by myself and collaborators during a three months' stay in the islands, Dec, 1954–March, 1955 Later on some minor changes will have to be made in the lists of the Vascular Plants, but as they will not alter the conclusions drawn I have preferred not to include them here, more so as the species in question, some of them at least, have to be subjected to a close taxonomical study With regard to the Cryptogams, to be referred to a number of specialists, the revision of the collections will take some time but even if a few new species will be described, and other additions made to the lists, the proportions between the various geographical elements will, I think, remain much the same

1 Angiospermae.

In the islands 42 families are represented of which one, *Lactoridaceae*, is endemic and monotypic Until recently Juan Fernandez (Masatierra) was the only oceanic island possessing an endemic family but after the discovery of the genus *Degeneria*, which forms the monotypical family *Degeneriaceae*, it shares this honour with Fiji the Fiji group is, however, not as "oceanic", in the current sense of this word, as Juan Fernandez

The largest families are Compositae with 28 (13 gen), Cyperaceae with 14 (7 gen), and Gramineae with 13 species (10 gen), but these are very large families almost everywhere, Campanulaceae (2 gen) and Juncaceae have 6 (2 gen, but some species of *Juncus* may not be truly indigenous), Rubiaceae 5 (4 gen),

Umbelliferae 5 (3 gen.), Chenopodiaceae 4 (2), Myrtaceae 4 (4), Piperaceae 4 (1), Rosaceae 4 (3), Solanaceae 4 (2), and Urticaceae 4 (3), Caryophyllaceae 3 (2), Cruciferae 3 (1), Gunneraceae 3 (1), Halorrhagidaceae 3 (1), Berberidaceae 2 (1), Bromeliaceae 2 (2), Convolvulaceae 2 (2), Labiatae 2 (1), Leguminosae 2 (1), Plantaginaceae 2 (1), Rutaceae 2 (1), Scrophulariaceae 2 (2), represented by 1 species only Aizoaceae, Boraginaceae, Callitrichaceae, Empetraceae Ericaceae, Euphorbiaceae, Flacourtiaceae, Iridaceae, Lactoridaceae, Loranthaceae, Palmae, Ranunculaceae, Rhamnaceae, Santalaceae, Saxifragaceae, Verbenaceae, Winteraceae, 17 families or 40 % of the entire number. Some of the families are altogether small, but others are large and widespread also in Andean America— as, for instance, Umbelliferae Hydrocotyloideae (*Azorella*), Caryophyllaceae, Cruciferae, Labiatae, Leguminosae (*Adesmia Cassia*), Plantaginaceae, Scrophulariaceae (*Calceolaria*), Boraginaceae (*Plagiobotrys* and related genera), Euphorbiaceae Iridaceae (*Sisyrinchium*), Ranunculaceae, Rhamnaceae, Verbenaceae The absence of such families as Amaryllidaceae, Asclepiadaceae Fagaceae, Geraniaceae, Lauraceae, Liliaceae, Nolanaceae, Onagraceae, Orchidaceae, Oxalidaceae, Polygonaceae, Portulacaceae, Valerianaceae and Violaceae is noteworthy, being more or less well, some of them very well, represented on the Chilean mainland

Of the 42 families Masatierra possesses 39, seven of these also found on its satellite Santa Clara, and Masafuera 30, 12 are confined to Masatierra (Plantaginaceae also on Santa Clara) and 3 to Masafuera 27 are common to Masatierra and Masafuera The families are, in contradistinction to the genera and species, evenly distributed over the group, as shown by the list of Genera and Species, Table I

The number of genera is 89, of these 71 are found on Masatierra, 9 on Santa Clara and 54 on Masafuera, 35 are known from Masatierra only, including those known from Santa Clara, all also found on Masatierra, 18 are confined to Masafuera, 36 shared by both islands Expressed in percentage Masatierra 39 3 %, Masafuera 20 2 %, Masatierra + Masafuera 40 5 % Thus less than one half of the genera are common to both islands The floristic difference between them is partly explained by the difference in altitude and thereby in climate— Masafuera has an alpine and subalpine flora for which there is no room on Masatierra, partly by the more varied topography of this island, which has a richer flora The difference becomes particularly obvious when endemism is considered

Of the 89 genera, 17 (19 %) are endemic, of these 12 (70 6 %) are confined to Masatierra, 1 (5 9 %) to Masafuera and 4 (23 5 %) found on both islands, see Table II

Of 71 genera known from Masatierra 16 (22 5 %) are endemic to the islands, of 54 found on Masafuera, 5 (9 3 %), of 35 genera only found on Masatierra, 12 are endemic (34 3 %), the corresponding figures for Masafuera are 18, 1 and 5 5 % and, for the genera occurring on both islands, 36, 4 and 11 1 % These figures serve to illustrate the great difference in the distribution of the endemic genera commonly looked upon as representing the most ancient element among the Angiosperms in Juan Fernandez

Of the total number of species, 147, 99 are found on Masatierra, 9 on Santa

Table I

Endemics bold faced, endemic genera in capital letters

	Masatierra	Santa Clara	Masafuera
Abrotanella **crassipes** Skottsb	−	−	+
Acaena ovalifolia Ruiz et Pav	+	−	+
— **masafuerana** Bitter	−	−	+
Agrostis **masafuerana** Pilger	−	−	+
Apium **fernandezianum** Johow	+	−	−
Azara **fernandeziana** Gay	+	−	−
Berberis **corymbosa** Hook et Arn	+	−	−
— **masafuerana** Skottsb	−	−	+
Boehmeria **excelsa** Wedd	+	−	−
Callitriche Lechleri (Hegelm) Fassett	+	−	−
Calystegia tuguriorum R Br	−	−	+
Cardamine chenopodiifolia Pers	+	−	−
— flaccida Cham et Schlechtd	−	−	−
— **Kruesseli** Johow	−	−	+
Carex **berteroniana** Steud	+	−	+
— Banksii Boott	−	−	+
CENTAURODENDRON dracaenoides Johow	+	−	−
Centella triflora (Ruiz et Pav) Nannf	+	−	−
Chaetotropis chilensis Kunth	+	−	−
— imberbis (Phil)	+	−	+
Chenopodium **crusoeanum** Skottsb	+	−	−
— **nesodendron** Skottsb	−	−	+
— **Sanctae Clarae** Johow	−	+	−
Chusquea **fernandeziana** Phil	+	−	−
Cladium scirpoideum (Steud) Benth et Hook f	+	−	−
Colletia **spartioides** Bert	+	−	−
Coprosma Hookeri (G Don) W R B Oliver	+	−	−
— **pyrifolia** (Hook et Arn) Skottsb	+	−	+
CUMINIA eriantha Benth	+	−	−
— **fernandezia** Colla	−	−	−
Cyperus eragrostis Lam	−	−	+
— reflexus Vahl	−	−	−
Danthonia collina Phil	+	−	−
DENDROSERIS litoralis Skottsb	+	+	−
— **macrantha** (Bert) Skottsb	+	−	−
— **macrophylla** D Don	−	−	+
— **marginata** (Bert) Hook et Arn	+	−	−

	Masatierra	Santa Clara	Masafuera
Dichondra repens Forst	+	—	—
Drimys **confertifolia** Phil	+	—	+
Dysopsis **hirsuta** (Muell Arg) Skottsb	+	—	—
Eleocharis fuscopurpurea (Steud) H Pfeiff	+	—	—
Empetrum rubrum Vahl	—	—	+
Erigeron **fruticosus** DC	+	—	+
— **Ingae** Skottsb	—	—	+
— **Innocentium** Skottsb	—	—	+
— **luteoviridis** Skottsb	—	—	+
— **rupicola** Phil	—	—	+
— **turricola** Skottsb	—	—	+
Eryngium **bupleuroides** Hook et Arn	+	—	—
— **inaccessum** Skottsb	+	—	—
— **sarcophyllum** Hook et Arn	—	—	+
Escallonia **Callcottiae** Hook et Arn	+	—	—
Euphrasia **formosissima** Skottsb	—	—	+
Fagara **externa** Skottsb	—	—	+
— **mayu** (Bert) Engl	+	—	—
Galium **masafueranum** Skottsb	—	—	+
Gnaphalium spiciforme Sch Bip	—	—	+
Gunnera bracteata Steud	+	—	—
— **Masafuerae** Skottsb	—	—	+
— **peltata** Phil	+	—	—
Halorrhagis **asperrima** Skottsb	—	—	+
— **masafuerana** Skottsb	—	—	+
— **masatierrana** Skottsb	+	—	—
Hedyotis thesiifolia St Hil	+	—	—
Hesperogreigia Berteroi Skottsb	+	—	—
HESPEROSERIS gigantea (Johow) Skottsb	+	—	—
JUANIA australis (Mart) Drude	+	—	—
Juncus capillaceus Lam	+	—	—
— dombeyanus Gay	+	—	—
— imbricatus Laharpe	+	—	—
— planifolius R Br	+	—	—
— procerus E Mey	+	—	—
Koeleria micrathera (Desv) Griseb	+	—	—
LACTORIS fernandeziana Phil	+	—	—
Lagenophora Hariotti Franch	—	—	+
Libertia formosa Grah	+	—	+

	Masatierra	Santa Clara	Masafuera
Lobelia alata Labill	−	−	+
Luzula masafuerana Skottsb	−	−	−
Margyricarpus digynus (Bitter) Skottsb	+	−	−
MEGALACHNE berteroniana Steud	+	−	−
— masafuerana (Skottsb et Pilger) Hubbard ms	−	−	+
Mimulus glabratus H B K forma	−	−	−
Myrceugenia Schulzei Johow	−	−	−
Myrteola nummularia (Poir) Berg	−	−	+
Nertera granadensis (L fil) Druce var	−	−	+
Nicotiana cordifolia Phil	−	−	+
NOTHOMYRCIA fernandeziana (Hook et Arn) Kausel	+	−	−
OCHAGAVIA elegans Phil	+	−	−
Oreobolus obtusangulus Gaud	−	−	+
Parietaria humifusa Rich	+	−	+
Paronychia chilensis DC	+	−	−
Peperomia berteroana Miq	+	−	+
— fernandeziana Miq	+	−	+
— margaritifera Bert	+	−	−
— Skottsbergii C DC	−	−	+
Pernettya rigida DC	−	−	+
PHOENICOSERIS berteriana (Dene) Skottsb	+	−	−
— pinnata (Bert ex Dene) Skottsb	+	−	−
— regia Skottsb	−	−	+
Phrygilanthus Berteroi (Hook et Arn) Reiche	+	−	−
Piptochaetium bicolor (Vahl) Presl	+	−	−
Plantago fernandezia Bert	+	−	−
— truncata Cham var	−	+	−
PODOPHORUS bromoides Phil	+	−	−
Ranunculus caprarum Skottsb	−	−	+
REA micrantha Bert ex Dene	+	−	−
— neriifolia Bert ex Dene	+	−	−
— pruinata (Johow) Skottsb	+	+	−
Rhaphithamnus venustus (Phil) B L Robins	+	−	+
RHETINODENDRON Berterii (Dene) Hemsl	+	−	−
ROBINSONIA evenia Phil	+	−	−
— gayana Dene	+	−	−
— gracilis Dene	+	−	−
— Masafuerae Skottsb	−	−	−
— thurifera Dene	+	−	−

	Masatierra	Santa Clara	Masafuera
Rubus geoides Sm.	−	−	+
Salicornia fruticosa Kunth	+	+	+
Santalum **fernandezianum** F. Phil.	+	−	+
Scirpus cernuus Vahl	+	−	+
— nodosus Rottb.	−	−	+
SELKIRKIA Berteroi (Colla) Hemsl.	−	−	−
Solanum **fernandezianum** Phil.	+	−	−
— masafueranum Bitter et Skottsb.	−	−	+
— robinsonianum Bitter	+	+	+
Sophora **fernandeziana** (Phil.) Skottsb.	+	−	−
— masafuerana (Phil.) Skottsb.	−	−	+
Spergularia confertiflora Steud.	−	−	+
— masafuerana Skottsb.	−	−	+
Stipa (Nassella) laevissima (Phil.) Speg.	+	−	+
— neesiana Trin. et Rupr.	+	−	−
SYMPHYOCHAETA macrocephala (Dene) Skottsb.	+	−	−
Tetragonia expansa Murr.	−	+	+
Trisetum chromostachyum Desv.	+	−	−
Ugni **Selkirkii** (Hook. et Arn.) Berg	+	−	−
Uncinia brevicaulis Thouars	−	−	+
— costata Kuekenth.	−	−	+
— Douglasii Boott	+	−	+
— phleoides Pers.	−	−	+
— tenuis Poepp.	−	−	−
Urtica **fernandeziana** (Rich.) Ross	−	−	−
— Masafuerae Phil.	−	−	+
Wahlenbergia **Berteroi** Hook. et Arn.	+	+	−
— fernandeziana (A. DC. p.p.) Skottsb.	−	−	−
— Grahamae Hemsl.	+	−	−
— Larrainii (Colla) Skottsb.	−	−	−
— Masafuerae (Phil.) Skottsb.	−	−	+
YUNQUEA Tenzii Skottsb.	+	−	−

Clara, and 74 on Masafuera, 68 = 46.3 % (68.7 % of 99) are restricted to Masatierra, 1 = 0.7 % to Santa Clara, and 47 = 32 % (63.5 % of 74) to Masafuera, 4 = 2.7 % are common to Masatierra and Santa Clara with the exclusion of Masafuera, 4 = 2.7 % found in all three islands and 23 = 15.6 % on Masatierra and Masafuera excluding those also occurring on Santa Clara. Thus only 27 species = 18.4 % are reported from both Masatierra and Masafuera, a surprisingly small

Table II

Distribution of the endemic genera

	Masatierra	Santa Clara	Masafuera
Centaurodendron	+	−	−
Cuminia	+	−	−
Dendroseris	−	−	+
Hesperoseris	−	−	+
Juania	+	−	−
Lactoris	+	−	−
Megalachne	+	−	+
Nothomyrcia	+	−	−
Ochagavia	+	−	−
Phoenicoseris	+	−	+
Podophorus	+	−	−
Rea	+	+	−
Rhetinodendron	+	−	−
Robinsonia	+	−	+
Selkirkia	+	−	−
Symphyochaeta	+	−	−
Yunquea	+	−	−

number, for even if we pay due attention to the physiographic difference between them, it tells a story of effective isolation with little possibility for an exchange across the 92 miles of water separating them.

Of the total number of species (147), 101 are endemic = 68.7 %, of the 99 species found on Masatierra, 66 (66.7 %) are endemic in Juan Fernandez, the corresponding figures for Masafuera are 74 and 47 (63.5 %), and for Santa Clara 9 and 5 (55.5 %). Thus endemism plays about the same rôle in all cases, and this is apparent also when local endemism is considered. Of the 68 species restricted to Masatierra 50 (73.5 %) are local endemics, of the 47 species restricted to Masafuera, 34 (72.3 %), the single species restricted to Santa Clara is endemic. Of the 27 species common to Masafuera and Masatierra 13 (48 %) are endemic in Juan Fernandez. If, to the 68 species restricted to Masatierra, 4 also found on Santa Clara are added, the figures are 72 and 73.6 %. Of the total number of endemic species (101), 50 are, as we have seen, confined to Masatierra (49.5 %), 3 (3 %) to Masatierra + Santa Clara, 1 (1 %) to Santa Clara, 34 (33.7 %) to Masafuera, 12 (11.9 %) common to Masatierra and Masafuera, and 1 (1 %) found on all three islands. The difference between Masatierra and Masafuera stands out even more clearly. It is less pronounced when we come to the 46 non endemic species, only on Masatierra 18 (39.1 %), on Masatierra and Santa Clara 1 (2.2 %), only on

Masafuera 13 (28 3 %), on Masatierra and Masafuera 11 (23 9 %), and on all three islands 3 (6 5 %) However, several of the species restricted to Masatierra are, perhaps, not truly indigenous whereas the indigenous character of the species only recorded from Masafuera cannot be doubted, 11 of them are mountain plants With regard to the former, some were commented upon by JOHOW In his table "Contingente B Especies autoctonas, pero no endémicas", pp 221–222, he mentions several species regarded as doubtful natives 3 species of *Gnaphalium*, *Mimulus*, *Solanum furcatum* (= *robinsonianum*) *Tetragonia expansa*, *Spergularia rubra* (= *confertiflora*), *Parietaria humifusa*, *Trisetum chromostachyum* and *Danthonia collina* With the exception of *Gnaphalium* spp I have listed them as native There seems to be little reason to regard *Tetragonia*, a wide-spread thalassochorous plant, as anthropochorous, and the *Spergularia* is known only from Juan Fernandez and Desventuradas Is *Danthonia* gave me the impression of being just as autochthonous as *Piptochaetium* and the two species of *Stipa*, and I find no good reason to exclude either *Mimulus*, *Parietaria* or *Trisetum* (this never seen by us) With regard to *Solanum 'furcatum'* (not *furcatum* of DUNAL) I share JOHOW's doubts It was described by BITTER as *S robinsonianum*, a Morella microspecies of *S nigrum* L coll and found on all three islands This assemblage as represented on the mainland has never been seriously studied Possibly *S robinsonianum* is a case of the same kind as the dandelion discovered on the islands in 1917 and described as *Taraxacum fernandezianum* Dahlst, a microspecies of the Eurasiatic *Vulgaria* There cannot be the slightest doubt that it is an alien introduced from Chile, where these weeds have not been studied From JOHOW's list I have excluded *Bahia*, *Amblyopappus*, *Erythraea*, *Monocosmia* and *Phalaris* Further some species not recorded from Juan Fernandez by JOHOW or earlier authors, but for the time being listed as native by me are under strong suspicion *Juncus capillaceus* and *planifolius* *Centella* and *Hedyotis*, perhaps also *Paronychia* If, in the future, we shall be able to purify the list the percentage of endemic species will rise to 72 % or even more

The genera richest in species are *Erigeron* with 6, *Juncus*, *Robinsonia*, *Uncinia* and *Wahlenbergia* with 5, and *Dendroseris* and *Peperomia* with 4 species each eight genera have 3, 15 two and 59 only one species The average number of species to a genus is 1 65

The systematical position of the endemites and the distribution of the genera and species also found elsewhere

Gramineae

Stipa L About 250 sp (BEWS) widespread both hemisph, subtrop–temp

neesiana Trin et Rupr Mex to Boliv and Chile, Braz, Argent, Urug Polymorphous (*249 771*)

laevissima (Phil) Speg Peru, Chile, Argent With a number of S Amer sp referred to a separate genus (*Nassella*)

Piptochaetium Presl 20, N Amer to extratrop S Amer
    bicolor (Vahl) Desv Chile, Valdivia, Braz, Argent

Podophorus bromoides Phil In 227 referred to *Brachyelythrum* Beauv and *Aphanelythrum* Hack as the nearest relatives Mr C E HUBBARD kindly informed me that it resembles the former in a number of important features and that he regards both genera as belonging to a relatively ancient group of grasses The distribution of *Brachyelythrum* is disjunct after a well known pattern *B erectum* (Schreb) Beauv, N E Amer, and *B japonicum* Hack ex Honda, China, Korea, Japan PILGER (*198*) brings this genus to Festuceae-Festucinae next to *Aphanelythrum*, placing *Podophorus* with the Brominae

Chaetotropis Kunth 2 (?3)
    imberbis (Phil) Near the following
    chilensis Kunth Peru, Chile, Braz, Argent, Urug

Agrostis L About 125, very wide spread in temp and cold climates
    masafuerana Pilger "Gehort in die Verwandtschaft von *A canina* L In der Tracht *A magellanica* Lam sehr ahnlich" (PILGER *197*) This is recorded from Magell, Falkl, N Zeal (*55*) E B H BROWN (*35* I 84) says that his *A rapensis* from Rapa Id is "very closely allied" to *magellanica*, but to judge from his illustrations they seem to have little in common

Trisetum Pers About 65, N and S temp (also S Braz)
    chromostachyum Desv Centr–S Chile

Danthonia DC About 100, essentially southern (S Amer, S and E Afr, Austral, N Zeal), but extending north to N Amer, S Eur, and India
    collina Phil S Chile

Koeleria Pers 60 (DOMIN), N temp, S E Austral, Tasm, N Zeal, S Amer And to Patag, Falkl
    micrathera (Desv) Griseb S Chile

Megalachne Steud 2 very distinct sp, *berteroniana* Steud and **masafuerana** (Skottsb et Pilg) Hubbard ms Reduced to *Bromus* by PILGER (*197*), but restored to generic rank in his posthumous paper on the system of the Gramineae (*198*)

Chusquea Kunth About 100 (?) sp Mex to Argent and S Chile
    fernandeziana Phil Related to Chilean species

Cyperaceae

Cyperus L A world wide, essentially tropical genus of about 600 sp (KUKENTHAL)
    eragrostis Lam (vegetus Willd) N and Centr Amer to Braz, Urug, Argent and S Chile, Easter I Often introduced and perhaps not indigenous in Juan Fernandez
    reflexus Vahl Mex and Tex to Braz, Argent and S Chile Indigenous

Scirpus L About 400 cosmopolitan
    nodosus Rottb Circumpolar, S temp zone Recently the Chilean plant was segregated as *S molinianus* Beetle, but I am unable to recognize this as specifically distinct (*326*)

cernuus Vahl Subcosmopolitan and of variable habit, south to Fueg and Falkl

Eleocharis R Br A worldwide genus of about 150 sp (SVENSON)

fuscopurpurea (Steud.) H Pfeiff S Chile Listed before as a subspecies or variety of *H maculosa* (Vahl) R Br (W Ind–Braz)

Oreobolus R Br An austral-circump genus of 6 sp, extending north to Malaysia and Hawaii

obtusangulus Gaud Andes of Colomb and Ecuad to Fueg Falkl

Cladium R Br 48 (KÜKENTHAL), widespread, trop-subtrop with preponderance S E Asia–N Guin–Austral–N Zeal, north to Hawaii, W Ind, Braz 2 boreal sp

scirpoideum (Steud.) Benth et Hook f Nearly related to *C angustifolium* (Gaud) Benth et Hook f (N Guin Tahiti, Hawaii)

Uncinia Pers 32, circump–austr-subantarct with outposts north of the Equator in Centr Amer and Philipp Is, greatest concentration of species in N Zeal

brevicaulis Thouars S Chile to Fueg, Falkl, Trist da C, St Paul and Amsterd Is

Douglasii Boott

costata Kuekenth Related to the former

phleoides Pers Andes from Colomb to S Chile and Patag

tenuis Poepp Centr Amer?, Andes of Chile to Fueg

Carex L About 1500, worldwide, but comparatively few trop sp

Banksii Boott Andes of Centr Chile to Fueg Belongs to the boreal section Frigidae-Fuliginosae of KÜKENTHAL

berteroniana Steud Sect Echinochlaenae of KÜKENTHAL, with few exceptions (Austral, Tasm, Norfolk I and one Chilean sp) confined to N Zeal

Palmae

Juania australis (Mart.) Drude Affinities undoubtedly trop Andean Included in the Iriarteae by DRUDE, but perhaps nearer to the Morenieae, or possibly regarded as type of a separate subtribe HUTCHINSON brought *Juania* next to *Ceroxylon*, following BENTHAM and HOOKER, CROIZAT (71) remodelled Morenieae, including *Juania* and the Mascarene *Hyophorbe* otherwise linked with Chamaedoreae

Bromeliaceae

Hesperogreigia **Berteroi** Skottsb 2 or perhaps more sp Subtrop Andean, related to *Greigia* (8 sp, Costa Rica, Venez–S Chile) LOOSER called *Hesperogreigia* monotypical, because my paper (240) had escaped him, if not, he would not have written "¿Quiza de la afinidad de Greigia?" (170 291) Inspired by L B SMITH he suppressed *Hesperogreigia* in an appendix to his paper (p 299), an attitude I cannot take The two genera differ very much [1]

---

[1] Sepals free Pericarp thin Seed testa thin with a thick coat of mucilage forming a massive pulp Raphe inconspicuous Scales with irregular more or less isodiametric cells   *Hesperogreigia*

Sepals connate into a tube Pericarp fleshy Testa very hard, without mucilage Raphe very conspicuous Scales with long and narrow cells radiating from centre   *Greigia*

Ochagavia elegans Phil. Very near the Chilean genus *Rhodostachys*, see 229:110 and 249:774.

Juncaceae

Luzula DC. A worldwide essentially temp. and mainly boreal genus of about 80 sp., also represented on trop. mountains and in the S Braz. highland, south to Fueg., Falkl. and N Zeal.

    masafueriana Skottsb. Nearly related to some Andean sp. (Mex., Boliv.–Fueg.) needing taxonomic revision.

Juncus L. Mainly temp.–subtrop., about 225. Well represented S hemisph. (about 50), especially Austral. and N Zeal., less so temp. S Amer.

    imbricatus Laharpe Ecuador–S Chile, Braz., Argent., Urug.

    capillaceus Lam. Ecuador, Centr. Chile, Braz., Argent., Urug. Introduced

    procerus E. Mey. S Chile

    dombeyanus Gay Peru, Chile, Braz., Argent., Urug.

    planifolius R. Br. S Chile, Austral., Tasm., N Zeal. Introduced

Iridaceae

Libertia Spreng. 5 sp., 3 Chile, 2 N Zeal.

    formosa Grah. S Chile

Piperaceae

Peperomia Ruiz et Pav. Possibly over 1500, pantropical.

    berteroana Miq. Extremely like *P. tristanensis* Christoph. from Gough I., see 245.

    margaritifera Bert. ex Hook. Possibly related to *P. Reineckei* C. DC. (Samoa)

    Skottsbergii C. DC. Allied to the former.

These species form a separate subgenus *Tildenidium* Skottsb. (247), which seems to stand closer to palaeotropical than to neotropical groups. *P. berteroana* and *tristanensis* show affinity to *P. urvilleana* A. Rich. (Austral., N Zeal., Lord Howe I., Norfolk I.) and *P. Ventenatii* Miq. (Java).

    fernandeziana Miq. Central (Fiar Jorge, Talinay) and S Chile (Valdivia). Belongs to subgen. *Sphaerocarpidium*.

Urticaceae

Urtica L. About 40 sp. widely scattered in temp. zones on both hemisph., well represented in Amer. (13, Mex.–Fueg.)

    Masafuerae Phil. Related to *U. echinata* Benth. (Ecuador)

    fernandeziana (Rich.) Ross A very distinct species without near relatives (WLDDLLL)

Boehmeria Jacq. About 100, trop.–subtrop.

    excelsa (Bert. ex Steud.) Wedd. Seems to be more nearly related to Pacific than to American species. Very similar to *B. dealbata* Cheesem. (Kermadec Is.)

Parietaria L. Some 30 sp., in all parts of the globe. Several medit.-orient., others N. and S. Amer., one (*P. debilis* Forst.) supposed to be widely distributed.

humifusa Rich. Chile. Until now listed as *debilis* which, in WEDDELL's monograph, is a collective species. I have shown (*241*) that FORSTER's species from Australia, New Zealand and Polynesia has little to do with the forms referred to this but occurring elsewhere and that none of the specimens from S. Amer. seen by me belong to true *debilis*. Pending a revision of the genus, *humifusa* is a correct name for the Chilean plant.

Loranthaceae

Phrygilanthus Eichl. About 30, bicentric. Mex.-Braz. and Chile, Argent., Urug., Austral., N. Zeal., N. Guin., Philipp. Is.

Berteroi (Hook. et Arn.) Reiche. Related to Andean sp.

Santalaceae

Santalum L. 18, Austral.-N. Guin. 5, Melan. 2, Polyn. 2, Hawaii 7, Bonin 1, and the following. See *236* and *270*.

fernandezianum F. Phil. Extinct. Belongs to sect. *Polynesica* Skottsb., not, as has been said (*111*), related to *S. freycinetianum* of Hawaii which belongs to a different section (*270*).

Chenopodiaceae

Chenopodium L. Over 250, world-wide, but essentially temp.

Sanctae Clarae Johow, **crusoeanum** Skottsb. and **nesodendron** Skottsb. On my request Dr. P. AELLEN, who created sect. *Skottsbergia* to receive the three island endemics, sent me the following remarks: "Ich würde sagen, dass die drei Arten zu keiner der uns heute bekanntgewordenen Arten irgendwelche verwandtschaftliche Züge und Beziehungen aufweisen. Es sind völlig isolierte Typen, Relikte eines im Meere versunkenen Florenreiches." Evidently Dr. AELLEN does not support the idea that they are related to *paniculatum* Hook (N. Amer., Peru–Chile) or *oahuense* Meyen (Hawaii), which latter has the same arboreous habit.

Salicornia L. Widely distributed, about 30 sp.

fruticosa L. (*peruviana* Kunth) Taken in a wide sense Mediterr., S. Afr., W. Ind., Polyn. *peruviana*, W. coast of S. Amer. to S. Chile.

Aizoaceae

Tetragonia L. About 25 sp. Strongly represented in S. Afr., several sp. in Chile.

expansa Murr. Coasts and islands of the Pacific, Braz.

Caryophyllaceae

Spergularia Presl. A widely scattered genus of about 40 sp., numerous in Chile.

confertiflora Steud. San Ambrosio. Related to species from Centr. Chile.

masafueiana Skottsb. Related to the former and to *S. media* (L.) Presl.

Paronychia L. About 40, scattered in temp. and subtrop. regions
    chilensis DC. Centr.–S. Chile, S. Braz., Argent.

Ranunculaceae

Ranunculus L. Probably over 300, world wide, particularly boreal, numerous sp. N. Zeal.
    caprarum Skottsb. Apparently with distinct relations in New Zealand, not near boreal or S. American species (*229* 125, *173*)

Berberidaceae

Berberis L. About 540 sp. distributed over the N. hemisph. and extending south along the Andes to Fueg., also S. Braz.
    corymbosa Hook. et Arn. Referred to sect. *Corymbosae* Schneid. (3, trop. And.) Not close to Chilean species
    masafuerana Skottsb. Near the former

Winteraceae

Drimys Forst. 40, 29 N. Guin., 6 Austral., 1 Borneo–Philipp. Is., 3 Mex.–Fueg., and the following
    confertifolia Phil. Near *D. Winteri* Forst. (Centr. and S. Chile to Fueg.)

Lactoridaceae

Lactoris fernandeziana Phil. With regard to the position of the family systematists disagree, some bringing it to *Polycarpicae*, others to *Piperales*. GUNDERSEN (*120*) asserts that it belongs to the latter, but it differs from this in very important characters

Cruciferae

Cardamine L. About 130, world wide, essentially temperate, many Chilean sp.
    chenopodiifolia Pers. Boliv., Braz., Argent. Urug.
    flaccida Cham. et Schlechtd. Centr. and S. Amer. to S. Chile
    Kruesselii Johow. Related to *C. vulgaris* Phil. (S. Chile)

Saxifragaceae

Escallonia Mutis. About 50, Colomb.–Fueg., Braz., Argent., Urug.
    Callcottiae Hook. et Arn. Occupies a rather independent position among the Chilean sp. (*158*)

Rosaceae

Rubus L. A very large, temp. and trop. montane genus, richly developed in the N. hemisph.
    geoides Sm. S. Chile to Fueg., Falkl.
Margyricarpus Ruiz et Pav. 4 or 5, trop. Andes to Patag.

digynus (Bitter) Skottsb. Near *M. pinnatus* (Lam.) O. K. (Peru, Chile, S. Braz., Argent.)

Acaena L. An austral genus of over 100 sp., the majority in S. Amer., 12 Austral.-N. Zeal., single sp. Calif., Hawaii, the Cape, etc.
    masafuerana Bitter. Near *A. antarctica* Hook. f. (Magell., Fueg.)
    ovalifolia Ruiz et Pav. subsp. *australis* Bitter. S. Chile to Fueg., Falkl. Perhaps accidentally introduced to Juan Fernandez.

Leguminosae

Sophora L. 70–80, Old and New World, sect. *Tetrapterae* ("Edwardsia") austral-circump., 17 closely related species
    fernandeziana (Phil.) Skottsb. and *masafuerana* (Phil.) Skottsb. Very near the Chilean "*tetraptera*" (*S. macnabiana* Phil.) not identical with *S. tetraptera* Ait. from N. Zeal.

Rutaceae

Fagara L. Over 200, pantrop., a large palaeotrop. group well represented in the S. Pacific (Austral., N. Caled., Polyn.), extending north to Hawaii. The two Juan Fernandez species *F. mayu* (Bert., Hook. et Arn.) Engl. and *externa* Skottsb., which are very closely allied, form the sect. *Mayu* Engl. Related to W. Pacific sp.

Euphorbiaceae

Dysopsis Baill. 3, 1 in Ecuador [*D. paucidentata* (M. Arg.) Skottsb.], 1 in S. Chile [*D. glechomoides* (Rich.) M. Arg. p. p.], and the following
    hirsuta (M. Arg.) Skottsb.

Callitrichaceae

Callitriche L. Widely distributed in the N. hemisph., austral circump., south to Austral. and S. Chile but absent from the southern half of Afr.
    Lechleri (Hegelm.) Fassett. S. Chile to Magell. (249, 781)

Rhamnaceae

Colletia Comm. 17, Andean and extratrop. S. Amer.
    spartioides Bert. ex Colla. A well marked species, related to Chilean and other S. Amer. forms.

Flacourtiaceae

Azara Ruiz et Pav. 20–21 sp., 18–19 Chile, 1 Braz., 1 Argent.
    fernandeziana Gay. Closely related to *A. serrata* Ruiz et Pav. (S. Chile)

Myrtaceae

Ugni Turcz. 15, Mex., Centr. Amer., Andes, south to Chiloé, Venez., Braz.
    Selkirkii (Hook. et Arn.) Berg. Probably related to species in Centr. Amer. and Venez., perhaps also to *U. Candollei* (Barn.) Berg from Chile, not very close to *U. Molinae* Turcz (S. Chile, KAUSEL in litt.)

Myrteola Berg 12, Colomb.–Chile
    nummularia (Poir.) Berg Chile, Cord. Linares to Fueg., Falkl.

Nothomyrcia Kausel A monotypical genus, related to Chilean genera
    fernandeziana (Hook. et Arn.) Kausel

Myrceugenia Berg About 40, trop. Andes, S. Braz. (many sp.) and about 20 in Chile, south to Chiloe
    Schulzei Johow Related to *M. plampes* (Hook. et Arn.) Berg (S. Chile)

Gunneraceae

Gunnera L. About 30 sp. Subgen. Pangue, 16 sp. Costa Rica, Colomb.–S. Chile, Magell., Braz., Hawaii 2 sp., but some more, of doubtful taxonomic status, have been described. Other subgenera in the Andes of Colomb to Chile, south to Fueg and Falkl., Urug., S. and Centr. Afr., Malays.–Philipp. Is., N. Zeal., Tasm.
    peltata Phil. and **Masafuerae** Skottsb. related to Andean sp.
    bracteata Steud. Seems to come closer to the Hawaiian *G. kauaiensis* Rock than to S. Amer. species

Halorrhagidaceae

Halorrhagis Forst. About 80, the great majority Austral–N. Zeal., single sp. scattered north to Indonesia, Philipp. Is., China and Japan, and east to Rapa and J. Fern.
    asperrima Skottsb., *masatierrana* Skottsb. and *masafuerana* Skottsb. belong to Subsect. *Cercodia* and are closely related to *H. erecta* (Murr.) Schindl. (N. Zeal.) and other Austral and N. Zeal sp. All J. Fern. forms were formerly incorrectly identified with *erecta*

Umbelliferae

Centella L. 29, 19 Afr., Madag., 1 China, 2 Austral., 5 trop. Amer. and the widely dispersed *C. asiatica* (L.) Urb.
    triflora (Ruiz et Pav.) Nannfeldt Centr and S. Chile, formerly included under *asiatica* Introduced?

Eryngium L. About 230, in all parts of the world, but with two centres W. Eur.–Medit. and trop.–subtrop. Amer. Poorly represented in N. Amer. and Australas.
    bupleuroides Hook. et Arn., *inaccessum* Skottsb. and *sarcophyllum* Hook. et Arn. form a special sect. *Fruticosa*, but differ mainly in being arborescent from the species occurring on the mainland

Apium L. About 30, in all parts of the world
    fernandezianum Johow A well-marked species, probably not nearly related to the Chilean species, but showing some affinity to *A. prostratum* Labill. (Austral.) or *australe* Thouars (Tristan da C.)

Ericaceae

Pernettya Gaud. About 12, 6 or 7 Mex. and Centr. Amer. and along the Andes to Fueg. and Falkl., 1 Galapag. Is., 2 N. Zeal., 2 Tasm.
    rigida (Bert.) DC. A well-marked sp. (252)

Empetraceae

Empetrum L. A bipolar genus, *E. nigrum* L. north, *E. rubrum* Vahl south, but according to GOOD the latter is represented in the Subarctic by special forms. See 249, 781.
  rubrum Vahl. Andes of S. Chile and Argent. to Fueg. and Falkl., Tristan da C.

Convolvulaceae

Dichondra Forst. 5, trop.-subtrop. Amer., 1 N. Zeal., and the following
  repens Forst. Widely spread over both hemispheres, north to N. Amer. and China, south to S. Chile and N. Zeal.
Calystegia R. Br. 10–20, temp.-subtrop. in all parts of the world
  tuguriorum R. Br. S. Chile (Hantelmanni Phil.) and N. Zeal.

Boraginaceae

Selkirkia Berteroi (Colla) Hemsl. According to JOHNSTON (148) very near *Hackelia* Opiz, a genus centering in western N. Amer., with outposts in S. Amer. and Euras., *H. revoluta* (Ruiz et Pav.) Johnst. Peru to Boliv. and Argent.

Verbenaceae

Rhaphithamnus Miers 2, one in Centr. and S. Chile. Near *Citharexylon* L., a neotrop. genus of about 20 sp., Mex. and W. Ind. to Boliv. and Braz.
  venustus (Phil.) B. L. Robins. A very distinct species

Labiatae

Cuminia Colla 2. An isolated genus, referred to *Prasioideae* by EPLING (90), a palaeotropical group best developed in Hawaii, but whereas *Cuminia* has the drupe of this tribe, it has the corolla of *Stachyoideae-Menthinae*, where BRIQUET placed it, BURGER'S statement that the flowers are "Lippenbluten" (41, 23) is erroneous
  fernandezia Colla and **eriantha** Benth. Perhaps united by intermediate forms

Solanaceae

Solanum 1 Probably over 1000, in all parts of the world, richly represented in trop. Amer., many in Chile
  fernandezianum Phil. Related to S. *tuberosum* L. coll.
  masafueranum Bitter et Skottsb. A very well marked Morella
  robinsonianum Bitter. See above p. 200

Nicotiana L. 60, 45 Amer., Calif.-Mex., And. S. Amer. (Ecuad.-Perú-Chile, Braz.-Argent.-Patag.), 15 Austral. (1 N. Caled. etc.)
  cordifolia Phil. Belongs to the *Rustica* group, confined to trop. Amer. and Australas., and related to *N. Raimondii* Macbr. (Andes of S. Perú), *solanifolia* Walp. (N. and Centr. Chile) and *paniculata* L. (Peru, N. Chile) Dr GOODSPEED expressed his opinion (in litt.) that the *Rustica* complex originated in the region now occupied by western Bolivia and Perú and extended to the 'Juan Fernandez land', becoming isolated during the final uplift of the Andes or possibly even earlier

See also *112*. F. B. BROWN (*35* III 262) suggested an affinity between *cordifolia* and *fatuhivensis* F. B. Brown (Marquesas), but they belong to different subgenera and the latter is referred to *N. fragrans* Hook. from N. Caled. as a variety (*112*).

Scrophulariaceae

Mimulus L. About 130, widely dispersed, predominantly western N. Amer. (80 Calif.), south to S. Chile, 2 Afr., Madag. 4 E. Asia 5 Austral., Tasm., N. Zeal.

  glabratus H. B. K. N. Amer. to Boliv., Argent and Chile, polymorphous, the island form very close to var. *parviflorus* (Lindl.) Grant (*114*).

Euphrasia L. About 100, bor. circump. with isolated populations in the S. Andes, south to Fueg. and Falkl., and in Austral.-N. Zeal., the gap between E. Asia and Australia bridged over by trop. mountain stations, see map *78* 224.

  formosissima Skottsb. The fact that this species is very unlike the *Trifidae* of Chile makes it particularly interesting. In *229* 169 I emphasized the difference between *formosissima* and the *Australes* of N. Zealand and placed it nearer to the boreal *Semicalcaratae*. WETTSTEIN, in his contribution to my paper (l. c. 209), expressed the opinion that it could be attached to a Japanese group of species, intermediate between Australes and Semicalcaratae. The question was taken up by DU RIETZ who thinks, with good reason I believe, that I overrated its relations to boreal species (*77* 533) and that, in most respects, it is more nearly related to N. Zealand forms.

Plantaginaceae

Plantago L. About 270, world-wide, essentially temp.

  fernandezia Bert. The nearest relative appears to be *P. princeps* Cham. et Schld. of Hawaii. Both belong to sect. *Palaeopsyllium* scattered over the S. hemisph. and extending north to N. Amer., Hawaii and S. Eur. N. Amer. 5, S. Amer. 1, S. Eur. 2, Afr. 5, St. Helena 1, Madag. 1, Lord Howe I. 1, Auckl. Is. 1, Rapa 2, and Hawaii 9.

  truncata Cham. Centr. and S. Chile. PILGER distinguished the island form as a separate subspecies close to ssp. *firma* Pilger, but I doubt that it deserves the rank assigned to it, and it is even possible that it is a very late arrival in the islands.

Rubiaceae

Hedyotis L. A large pantrop. genus.

  thesiifolia St. Hil. Trop.-subtrop. S. Amer., in Chile south to Chiloe. Very likely not truly indigenous in J. Fern.

Nertera Banks et Sol. 10–12, centering in N. Zeal. (4 endem. sp.), north to Malaya and Hawaii, Tristan da C., S. Amer. from Falkl. and Fueg. to Colomb. and Mex.

  granadensis (L. fil.) Druce. A polymorphous species, reported from S. Amer., Tristan da C., Austral., Tasm., N. Zeal., Java and Hawaii—see *244*, where I pointed out that it is heterogeneous but that the plant from Masafuera seems to be identical with the form common in Magell. and Falkl.

Coprosma Forst. 90, a western Pacific genus centering in N. Zeal. (39) and distributed from Australia to Malays., Melan and Polyn with a secondary centre in Hawaii (18), entirely absent from Amer

Hookeri (G Don) W R B Oliver (*192*) Forms a separate monotypical section

pyrifolia (Hook et Arn) Skottsb Belongs to a section of 8 Polyn sp (4 Tahiti, 1 Cook Is, 1 Rapa, 1 Pitcairn, 1 J Fern)

Galium L World wide, essentially boreal Over 500 have been described, almost $1/4$ of these Medit-Orient, about 50 in S Amer, mostly along the Andes and extending south to Fueg, Falkl and S Georgia

masafueranum Skottsb Related to *G criocarpum* Bartl DC and *trichocarpum* DC (both Coquimbo–Cord Linares), the fruit as in *masafueranum* covered with straight hookless hairs

Campanulaceae

Wahlenbergia Schrad Essentially S African, about 230 sp (9 S Amer, 10 S Eur-Orient 2 or 3 St Helena, 20 trop Afr, 6 Madag-Mascar, 150 S Afr, 9 As, 1 N Guin, 8 Austral, 8 N Zeal, 5 J Fern)

Larrainii (Bert ex Colla) Skottsb, *fernandeziana* A DC p p and *Grahamae* Hemsl are closely related to each other

Masafuerae (Phil) Skottsb approaches the former, but has the large tuber of the following

Berteroi Hook et Arn occupies a rather independent position

Most African species are annuals and quite unlike the island species and these have little in common with the single Chilean or the other American forms, nor with those from Australia or N Zealand, even if there is a superficial likeness between *W Masafuerae* and a couple of perennial S African species such as *W Ecklonii* Buek and *oxyphylla* A DC On the other hand the resemblance between the J Fernandez and St Helena species is quite striking, and in spite of the difference in the number of carpels the ovary being trimerous in the former and dimerous in the latter, the possibility of a common origin cannot be dismissed The number of carpels in the genus varies between 2 and 5, in most species they are 3 HEMSLEY (*127* 61) regarded the St Helena species as allied to African and Juan Fernandez species

Lobelia L 350–370, particularly numerous in Amer and Afr, less so in As, Austral and Oceania, 2 in Eur

alata Labill S Chile, S Afr, Austral A sea side sp

Compositae

Lagenophora Forst A bicentric austr-subantarct genus of 16 sp, most numerous in Austral-N Zeal Fiji, Rapa, extending north to Philipp Is and Hawaii

Hariotii Franch Andes of S Chile to Fueg

Erigeron L A large bor-temp genus Ind Kew lists about 700 sp as valid, half of them in N Amer and about 100 in S Amer, where the genus is richly developed along the Andes, south to Patag, Fueg and Falkl Not few are known from trop mountains in the W and E hemispheres, very few reported from

Australia. One species is found on Rapa, related to the Juan Fernandez species according to BROWN (35 III 338).

fruticosus DC. and *luteoviridis* Skottsb. are related to each other.

Ingae Skottsb., *Innocentium* Skottsb.[1] and *turricola* Skottsb. form another group.

rupicola Phil. stands apart from all other species.

VIERHAPPER (see 229 182) suggested that the island species are allied to Andine species, but also that *E. fruticosus* comes very close to *F. lepidotus* Less. of Hawaii; this is, however, now referred to *Tetramolopium* by SHERFF. There is no *Erigeron* in Hawaii.

Gnaphalium L. A large subcosmopol., essentially temp. genus needing revision.

spiciforme Sch. Bip., comp. 229 187-188. Patag.-Fueg. The assemblage to which the alpine species of Masafuera belongs is in a state of taxonomic confusion. The identity with the Magellanian plant may be doubted, but I am convinced that the island form cannot be referred to either *americanum* Mill., *purpureum* L., *spicatum* Lam. or *mucronatum* Phil. which, together with *consanguineum* Gaud., are regarded as forms of a single polymorphous taxon.

Abrotanella Cass. An austr. subantarct. genus of 20 sp., the majority in N. Zeal. with the subantarct. islands (9) and W. Patag.-Fueg.-Falkl. (5), of the remainder 1 in Austral., 2 Tasm., 1 N. Guin., 1 Rodriguez I., and the following

crassipes Skottsb. Very near *A. Moseleyi* Skottsb. nom. (W. Patag.), see 229 189-190.

Robinsonia DC. BENTHAM (20 460) remarks on *Robinsonia* and *Rhetinodendron*: "Although their connexion with Eusenecioneae seems greater than with any other subtribe or tribe, yet in their dioecious capitula, in the presence of small free anthers without pollen in the female floret and some other points they approach the subtribe Petrobieae of Helianthoideae." The idea was rather attractive, because the Petrobieae inhabit St. Helena and S. America. Another suggestion mentioned the Hawaiian *Dubautia* and *Raillardia*, but they are not dioecious. Recently an undisputable relative was discovered in New Guinea: *Brachionostylum* Mattfeld (178 27-28).

Von *Senecio*, dessen pacifische Arten unserer Pflanze recht nahe kommen, unterscheidet sich diese Gattung wesentlich durch die Zweihausigkeit und weiter in Zusammenhang damit durch die Form der Griffelschenkel der Scheibenbluten, die dei Fegehaare ganz entbehren und vorn nicht gestutzt sondern abgerundet sind. Diese Merkmale hat sie aber mit den auf Juan Fernandez endemischen Gattungen *Robinsonia* und *Rhetinodendron* gemeinsam, von denen sie sich uberhaupt durch kein generisches Merkmal unterscheidet. Aber die Ubereinstimmung erstreckt sich sogar auf kleinere Merkmale, wie den leicht hinfalligen Pappus, die kurzen, aber verhaltnismassig sehr breiten, etwas vorspringend gestreiften Zungen, die Form der durch ein kleines Becherchen gekronten Achaenen, und schliesslich die Wuchsform und Verzweigungsart bei beiden schliesst der schopfig beblatterte Stengel mit dem Blutenstande ab, wahrend der Fortsetzungsspross aus der Achsel eines der oberen Laubblatter unter dem Blutenstande entspringt und diesen bald zur Seite drangt. So bleibt als einziger Unterschied der durch die sehr verschiedene Blattform bedingte habituelle Eindruck.

---

[1] Described as a variety of the former and now raised to specific rank.

Die Blutenkopfe sind bei *Robinsonia* erheblich zahlreicher und kleiner, kurz und breit glockenformig, bei unserer Pflanze aber schmalglockig

Wurden diese Sippen demselben pflanzengeographischen Gebiete angehoren, so wurde man sie sicher nicht generisch trennen konnen Was hier aber wesentlich dazu zwingt, ist, dass die Zweihausigkeit, die ja hier die wesentliche Ubereinstimmung bedingt, bei den Kompositen zu den verschiedensten Malen in den verschiedenster und auch in denselben Gruppen entwickelt wurde und daher keineswegs als Kriterium fur eine generische Verwandtschaft angesehen werden kann

To this I shall remark that nobody would think of uniting *Robinsonia* and *Rhetinodendron*, because they differ in essential floral characters *Brachionostylum* is to judge from the description and plate XC B (only ♀ known), closely related to *Robinsonia* but not to *Rhetinodendron* The mode of growth is not quite the same, for in *Robinsonia* (as well as in *Rhetinodendron*) 2 or 3 innovations are developed, and none of them continues the mother axis Besides *Brachionostylum* has petiolate, penninerved leaves of a type current in dicotyledons and widely different from the sessile, linear-lanceolate, broadly clasping and parallel veined leaves of *Robinsonia*

    gayana Dcne and ***thurifera*** Dcne are a pair of related species
    evenia Phil and ***Masafuerae*** Skottsb form another pair
    gracilis Dcne stands more isolated

Symphyochaeta (DC) Skottsb See *249* 785
    macrocephala (Dcne) Skottsb

Rhetinodendron Meisn *Berteri* (Dcne) Hemsl See above

Centaurodendron diacaenoides Johow Not, as has been supposed, just an arboreous *Centaurea*, but differing materially in flower structure (*243*)

Yunquea Tenzii Skottsb See *237* 163

Dendroseris C Don An isolated genus, perhaps distantly related to *Thamnoseris* Phil from Desventuradas Is, but probably not to *Fitchia* Hook fil BENTHAM stated (20 480) that the achenes of *Dendroseris* differ from those of the Cichorioideae in general, and that also the involucre and the habit are different With regard to the achenes this is certainly true of *Dendroseris* s str, and also of *Phoenicoseris*, whereas they are of a rather normal type in *Rea* and *Hesperoseris* All are devoid of paleae, which are present in *Thamnoseris* and *Fitchia*, a distinctive feature pointed out by BENTHAM, but the awned achenes of *Fitchia* differ from those of all the other genera mentioned In spite of the profound discrepances in such important characteristics as inflorescence, involucre, receptacle and stigma *Thamnoseris* has more in common with the *Dendroseris* assemblage than with other genera

    macrophylla D Don, ***macrantha*** (Bert ex Dcne) Skottsb, ***marginata*** (Bert ex Dcne) Hook et Arn and ***litoralis*** Skottsb, all lumped together by JOHOW, are well marked species comp *229* 201-204

Phoenicoseris Skottsb, *249* 787
    pinnata (Bert ex Dcne) Skottsb and ***berteriana*** (Dcne) Skottsb (Masatierra) are closely related but quite distinct, ***regia*** Skottsb (Masafuera) differs from both in leaf shape, but fertile specimens have not been found

Rea Bert ex Dene, p. p. See 219, 788.

nernfolia Dene. Little is known of this, but it is undoubtedly a very good species, *micrantha* Bert. ex Dene and *pinnata* (Johow) Skottsb. are near relatives but good species (comp. 229, 207).

Hesperoseris Skottsb. *gigantea* (Johow) Skottsb. See 219, 788.

Vicarious species

VIERHAPPER (276) distinguished between true and false vicarism. True vicarists have arisen from a common initial species and become differentiated either within the limits of the area this once occupied or after penetration into a different habitat, followed by isolation, whereas in the case of pseudo-vicarism they have a different origin, a second species may invade the area of the first and colonize such parts of the area as are unsuitable to the latter. Very often the term "vicarious" has been taken in a much wider sense: any two related species replacing each other in separate areas were called vicarious, and phytogeographers used the term to designate two plant species, related or not, that played corresponding rôles in two closely allied plant communities, in this case *Nothomyrcia fernandeziana* and *Myrceugenia Schulzei*, which form the bulk of the forest in Masatierra and Masafuera, respectively, are vicarists, although they belong to different genera. Species not fulfilling the conditions claimed by VIERHAPPER were called "substitute species".

WULFF (291, 66-67) devotes considerable space to a discussion of vicarism. He agrees with VIERHAPPER: true vicarism is a result of one taxon breaking up into two, adapted to different habitat conditions. CAIN (42, 265) expresses himself in slightly different words, but their meaning is the same: "closely related allopatric species which have descended from a common ancestral population and attained at least spatial isolation." He summarizes statements made by DRUDE, DILLS, WULFF and SETCHELL, who called species vicarious if they were only slightly discontinuous morphologically but widely so geographically; certainly anybody would call them vicarists but use the same term for a pair of intimately related forms of which one inhabits granite and the other limestone within the same geographical area.

I am afraid that, in most cases, we know very little or nothing at all of the ancestry of species we are used to call vicarious, let it be that we have reason to assume that they have differentiated out of a common population some time in the past. This is, at least, the situation in Juan Fernandez. Here I should perhaps refer to what CAIN (l. c. 276) calls polytopic species, i.e. when the same taxon occurs in two or more discrete areas, disjunction being the result either of dispersal from one original centre or of the breaking up of an area through subsidence or formation of some other kind of barrier, upon a close investigation it has been shown in many instances that slightly different forms within the original population happened to become isolated and appear as examples of true vicarism.

JOHOW (150, 233) held forth that 6 species endemic in Masatierra correspond to 6 other species endemic in Masafuera, but he did not use the term vicarious

These were (the species from Masatierra mentioned first) *Dendroseris macrantha-gigantea* (belong to different genera), *Wahlenbergia Berteroi-tuberosa* (= *Masafuerae*, not very closely related), *Myrceugenia fernandeziana-Schulzei* (different genera), *Eryngium bupleuroides-sarcophyllum* (only distantly related), *Cardamine alsophila* (= *flaccida*)-*Kruesselu* (not nearly related), and *Urtica glomeruliflora* (= *fernandeziana*)-*Masafuerae* (belong to different sections). There is not among them a single example of either vicarism or pseudo-vicarism in the sense of VIERHAPPER.

In 1914 (227) I distinguished 4 pairs of vicarists in Juan Fernandez *Dendroseris macrantha-gigantea*, *Myrceugenia fernandeziana-Schulzei*, *Gunnera peltata-Masafuerae*, and *Peperomia margaritifera-Skottsbergii*, the flora of Masafuera was at that time little known. Of these pairs the last two still hold good, the species replace each other from a taxonomical as well as from a sociological viewpoint, nevertheless I am not prepared to argue that they arose out of *one* initial species, several species may have been involved, for they differ in a number of minor characters and all we can say is that they make the impression of coming from the same stock. On the basis of our present knowledge of their taxonomy the following nine pairs are distinguished, the species replace each other, call them vicarious or substitute: *Berberis corymbosa-masafuerana*, *Chenopodium crusoeanum-nesodendron*, *Dendroseris macrantha-macrophylla*, *Fagara mayu-externa*, *Gunnera peltata-Masafuerae*, *Halorrhagis masatierrana-masafuerana*, *Peperomia margaritifera-Skottsbergii*, *Robinsonia evenia-Masafuerae*, and *Sophora fernandeziana-masafuerana*. As regards *Berberis*, *Fagara*, *Halorrhagis* and *Sophora*, perhaps also *Gunnera*, *Peperomia* and *Robinsonia*, the two members of a pair are closely related, but in the case of *Halorrhagis* the situation is complicated because there is a third species, endemic in Masafuera, *H. asperrima*, *masafuerana* seems, however, to be a better match for *masatierrana* than *asperrima*. As we have seen, there is also a third species of *Chenopodium*, endemic to Santa Clara, very likely formerly occurring also on Masatierra but extinct there. Of the 3 species of *Dendroseris* inhabiting Masatierra, *marginata* and *litoralis* form a pair of one inland and one coast species.

An unbalanced flora

It has always been argued that an island flora, where the number of species is small compared with the number of genera and many large and widely distributed families, well developed under different conditions, poorly represented or altogether absent furnishes one of the best proofs of the absolute oceanity of its abode, and Juan Fernandez is no exception from this rule. I have mentioned this above (p. 194) pointing out that most of these families have numerous genera and species on the opposite mainland, thus Caryophyllaceae 20 genera, Compositae some 130, Cruciferae 28, Leguminosae 22, Scrophulariaceae 18, Umbelliferae about 30, and so forth, and examples of important families in Chile not found in the islands were also given. This state of things calls for an explanation. JOHOW paid much attention to it, as he believed that the islands had been isolated from the very beginning he blamed chance in all cases where, according to the current opinion, the diaspores were adapted for dispersal across a wide expanse of water. He mentions Compositae Labiatiflorae, Calyceraceae, Valerianaceae, Cactaceae, Orchidaceae and Dioscoreaceae as good examples. In other cases he blames the diaspores as in Nolanaceae, Leguminosae, Violaceae, Fagaceae, Amaryllidaceae and Liliaceae.

Also with reference to life forms the island flora makes an impression of being unbalanced, a fact already discussed at some length in 251 825–830, I shall only repeat that woody species are in overwhelming majority and annuals almost absent, whereas they are very numerous, also proportionately, on the mainland. Already in 1914 (227) I argued that climatic differences alone do not offer an explanation and that historical causes must be taken into account.

Geographical elements

In his survey of the flora p. 229–232 JOHOW discussed its composition and distinguished various elements. The endemic genera and a few peculiar endemic species of non endemic genera form his first (and most ancient) group, the second group contains the remainder of endemic species (a) markedly distinct, (b) nearly related to continental species. Both groups make up 'Contimjente A'. The third group, "Contimjente B", contains the species found elsewhere, all occurring in South America except *Halorrhagis "alata"*. America is claimed as the source of the endemic element as well. "tanto las especies del primero como las del segundo grupo pertenecen, con la única excepcion del *Santalum*, a jéneros representados, si no en Chile, a lo menos en alguna parte de la costa occidental de Sud América"— this did not, however, apply to the isolated Compositae, to *Lactoris* etc., which JOHOW regarded as originated from ancestors to be looked for in the Tertiary flora of Chile. *Halorrhagis*, *Santalum* and *Coprosma*, mentioned later, were supposed to have immigrated from western Pacific.

It serves no purpose to go into detail, when JOHOW wrote his book our knowledge of the flora was too defective to allow him to arrive at anything like safe conclusions. The same may be said of my 1914 paper (227) even if my short visit to the islands revealed the existence of an up till then unknown element. Four main groups were distinguished. I. Old Pacific (ENGLER's Altoceanisches Element), comprising genera or species supposed to have a long history behind them within the precincts of the Pacific and lacking near relatives, subdivision A, Endemic genera, with 11 sp., and Non endemic genera with 10 sp., subdivision B with allied species in Hawaii, Polynesia, Australia and New Zealand, 16 endemic species—the genus *Dendroseris* was also placed here—and 1 non endemic (*Halorrhagis*). Group II, called Neotropical, contained 6 endemic species, *Cuminia* and *Juania* were included here. Group III, called Chilean, was the largest and was divided into 3 lots A, very distinct species, 18 (*Ochagavia* placed here), B, less well marked species, 11, C, also found in Chile, 28, but among them were 6 not now regarded as native. So far the main difference between this arrangement and JOHOW's lies in the greater number of species with supposed west Pacific connections. Finally Group IV, Subantarctic Magellanian, 4 species, was added.

The study of our 1916–1917 collection added many species not known before and gave rise to a fresh analysis of the vascular plants (239), of which a short summary is given here (translated from French) The ferns are not included below

1. Neotropical and Andean element Species either found in Chile (with one exception, c) or endemic but allied to Chilean species, 47
   a) in Central or S Chile, 20
   b) in the Magellan region, but not of subantarctic character, 3
   c) in South America, but not in Chile, 1
   d) endemic species of non-endemic genera, 21
   e) „   ,   „ endemic   „ , 2
2. Element consisting of wide-spread species, also inhabiting Chile, 5
3. Neotropical element, not represented in Chile, 7
   a) endemic species of non-endemic genera, 3
   b) species belonging to endemic genera, 4
4. Magellanian - Old Antarctic element, 27
   a) subantarctic species, 10
   b) austral species, 5
   c) endemic species allied to subantarctic species, 7
   d) endemic species not allied to subantarctic species, 5
5. Pacific element, 59
   a) isolated endemic species of wide genera, 21
   b) endemic species belonging to genera or sections of west to central Pacific distribution or, if belonging to wide genera, then more closely related to Pacific species, 17
   c) species of isolated endemic genera with supposed transpacific relations, 18
   d) species of endemic genera with unknown relations, 3

This analysis was based on my memoir on the Phanerogams published in 1922 (*229*) Since that time several pending questions have been restudied, additional plant material has come to hand, and recent monographs have been consulted The results were communicated above, and we shall now proceed to the following arrangement of the angiosperms

I Andine-Chilean element — 69 (46 9 %)

a Endemic species (34) In two cases, *Ochagavia* and *Nothomyrcia*, also the genus endemic, but nearly related to Chilean genera Chaetotropis imberbis, Chusquea fernandeziana, Uncinia Douglasii and costata, Hesperogreigia Berteroi, Ochagavia elegans, Luzula masafuerana, Phrygilanthus Berteroi Spergularia masafuerana, Cardamine Kruesselii, Escallonia Callcottiae, Margyricarpus digynus, Sophora fernandeziana and masafuerana, Dysopsis hirsuta Colletia spartioides, Azara fernandeziana, Nothomyrcia fernandeziana, Myrceugenia Schulzei, Gunnera peltata and Masafuerae, Apium fernandezianum Pernettya rigida, Rhaphithamnus venustus Solanum fernandezianum, masafueranum and robinsonianum, Galium masafueranum, Erigeron fruticosus, luteoviridis, Ingae, Innocentium, turricola and rupicola

b Known from continental Chile, many also in other parts of S America or of still wider distribution (33) Stipa neesiana and laevissima, Piptochaetium bicolor Chaetotropis chilensis, Trisetum chromostachyum Danthonia collina, Koeleria micrathera Cyperus eragrostis and reflexus Scirpus cernuus and nodosus, Eleocharis fuscopurpurea Uncinia phleoides, Juncus imbricatus, capillaceus, procerus, dombeyanus and planifolius, Libertia formosa, Salicornia fruticosa, Tetragonia expansa,

Peperomia fernandeziana, Parietaria humifusa, Paronychia chilensis, Cardamine flaccida, Callitriche Lechleri, Centella triflora, Dichondra repens, Calystegia tuguiorum, Mimulus glabratus, Plantago truncata, Hedyotis thesiifolia, Lobelia alata

c Also known from San Ambrosio Spergularia confertiflora

d S American, but not reported from Chile Cardamine chenopodiifolia

II Subantarctic-Magellanian element —15 (10 2 %)

a Endemic (4) Agrostis masafuerana, Drimys confertifolia, Acaena masafuerana, Abrotanella crassipes

b Not endemic, in several cases extending north along the Andes (11) Oreobolus obtusangulus, Uncinia brevicaulis and tenuis, Carex Banksii, Rubus geoides, Acaena ovalifolia, Myrteola nummularia Empetrum rubrum, Nertera granadensis, Lagenophora Hariotii, Gnaphalium spiciforme

III Neotropical element —19 (12 9 %)

a Belonging to endemic genera without or with only distant relations to the present Andean flora but presumably of neotropical ancestry (5) Megalachne berteroniana and masafuerana, Podophorus bromoides (only tentatively referred here), Centaurodendron dracaenoides, Yunquea Tenzii

b Belonging to endemic genera of undoubted neotropical affinity (2) Juania australis, Selkirkia Berteroi

c Endemic species belonging to widespread genera and presumably of neotropical ancestry (7) Urtica fernandeziana, Chenopodium Sanctae Clarae, crusoeanum and nesodendron, Eryngium bupleuroides, inaccessum and sarcophyllum

d Endemic species of unquestionably neotropical parentage (5) Urtica Masafuerae, Berberis corymbosa and masafuerana, Ugni Selkirkii, Nicotiana cordifolia

IV Pacific element —26 (17 7 %)

Affinities along the route New Zealand–Australia–Melanesia–Polynesia–Hawaii all endemic

a The genus endemic (9) Cuminia fernandezia and eriantha, Robinsonia gayana, thurifera, evenia, Masafuerae and gracilis, Symphyochaeta macrocephala, Rhetinodendron Berterii

b Only the species endemic (17) Cladium scirpoideum, Carex berteroniana Peperomia margaritifera and Skottsbergii, Boehmeria excelsa, Santalum fernandezianum, Ranunculus caprarum, Fagara mayu and externa, Gunnera bracteata, Halorrhagis asperrima, masatierrana and masafuerana, Euphrasia formosissima, Plantago fernandezia, Coprosma Hookeri and pyrifolia

V Atlantic - S African element —6 (4 1 %) Endemic

Peperomia berteroana Wahlenbergia Larrainii, fernandeziana, Grahamae, Masafuerae and Berteroi

VI Eu-Fernandezian element —12 (8 2 %)

Isolated endemics of unknown parentage, the Cicoriaceous genera forming a natural group

Lactoris fernandeziana, Dendroseris macrophylla, macrantha, marginata and litoralis, Phoenicoseris pinnata, berteriana and regia, Rea nerifolia, miciantha and pruinata, Hesperoseris gigantea.

The differences between this arrangement and the one of 1934 are considerable, but partly at least more apparent than real. Group 1 of 1934 corresponds (if we exclude (b), which from a purely geographical point of view has to go to the present group II) to I, but *Selkirkia* has now been placed in III, a group corresponding to the 3d element of 1934. Group 4 was rather heterogeneous and included, beside Magellanian species, several bicentric ones and some endemics of austral circumpolar affinity now referred to I a. Group 5, Pacific element, included the new groups IV–VI and part of III.

II. Pteridophyta

Six families (taken in the old sense) are represented, Ophioglossaceae only on Masatierra, Lycopodiaceae only on Masafuera. The number of genera is 23, 21 (91.3 %) are found on Masatierra and the same number on Masafuera, 3 on Santa Clara. Two genera are confined to Masatierra (8.7 %) and 2 to Masafuera, 19 (82.6 %) shared by both islands, 3 of them also known from Santa Clara. A single genus (*Thyrsopteris*) is endemic in Juan Fernandez and found on Masatierra and Masafuera.

Of the 53 species listed 43 occur on Masatierra, 3 on Santa Clara and 45 on Masafuera. Only 8 species are restricted to Masatierra, 15.1 % (18.6 % of the total found there) and 10 to Masafuera, 18.9 % (22.2 % of the total), 35 (66 %) are found on both.

There are 18 endemic species (34 %), of which 16 inhabit Masatierra and 14 Masafuera, no endemic is found on Santa Clara. Of the endemics 4 are confined to Masatierra and 2 to Masafuera, 12 having been recorded from the two islands, in percentage 22.2, 11.1 and 66.7 %, respectively.

A high percentage of ferns is to be expected in "oceanic" islands, whether or not isolated from the beginning, and Juan Fernandez is no exception from this rule, for of the 200 vascular plants 26.5 % are Pteridophytes.

Of the 35 species also found elsewhere 4 are confined to Masatierra, 8 to Masafuera and 23 found on both islands, 3 of these also on Santa Clara, in percentage 11.4, 22.9 and 65.7, respectively. The differences in percentage between endemic and non endemic species is due to the occurrence, in the highland of Masafuera, of a few mountain ferns not found on the other island. But whether our analysis bears upon families, genera or species the distribution over the archipelago is very much more even than the dispersion of the angiosperms, and this is of course what we have every reason to expect. Also, the number of species to a genus is greater, 2.3.

The systematical position of the endemites and the geographical distribution of the genera and species also found elsewhere.

Hymenophyllaceae

Trichomanes L. coll. The island species belong to *Vandenboschia* Copel., a pantrop. and circum-austr. genus of about 25 sp., extending north to N. Amer., Engl. and Japan.

philippianum Sturm. "One of the most distinct species of *Trichomanes* its cellular structure quite unique" (CHRISTENSEN 62 3) — Also in S. Chile (see l.c. 2).

Ingae C. Chr. Belongs to the neotrop. *pyxidiferum* group.

exsectum Kze. S. Chile, south to Chiloe. Near the neotrop. *T. tenerum* Kze.

Serpyllopsis v. d. Bosch. A monotypical genus without near relatives (COPELAND 69 37).

caespitosa (Gaud.) C. Chr. (var. *fernandeziana* C. Chr. et Skottsb., slightly different from the forms described from the mainland). Falkl. and Fueg. to S. Chile.

Hymenoglossum Presl. Monotypical and without near affinity to any known genus (COPELAND l.c.)

cruentum (Cav.) Presl. S. Chile, Valdivia to 49° s. lat.

Hymenophyllum Sm. coll.

a. *Mecodium* Presl. About 100, pantrop. and austral, with several sp. in N. Zeal., north to Sakhalin.

cuneatum Kze. S. Chile, Valdiv.-W. Patag., Marquesas Is., Rapa. Near *H. polyanthus* Sw., a variable pantrop. sp.

caudiculatum Mart. Peru, S. Braz., S. Chile, Valdiv.-49° s. lat.

fuciforme Sw. S. Chile to W. Patag. A very distinct sp., referred to *Mecodium* with considerable doubt (COPELAND 66 95).

b. *Hymenophyllum* s. str. About 25, austr. circump. with outlying stations in W. Eur. and Japan, *H. peltatum* (Poir.) Desv. widely scattered in slightly different forms.

pectinatum Cav. S. Chile, Valdiv.-Fueg. An aberrant species, COPELAND 69 34.

falklandicum Bak. W. Patag., Fueg., Falkl., S. Georgia. Related to *peltatum* which if *falklandicum* really belongs to *Mecodium*, where COPELAND placed it 66 94 also must be brought here; *peltatum* is known from extratropical regions of both hemispheres and also reported from Chile (perhaps = var. *Menzusii* (Presl) C. Chr. 61 4), by CHRISTENSEN also quoted for Juan Fernandez—he must have forgotten that in 62 11 all material from there was referred to *falklandicum*.

rugosum C. Chr. et Skottsb. Related to *H. tunbridgense* (L.) Sm., W. Ind., Venez., Chile, Atl. islands, Mediterr., S. Afr., Austral., Tasm., N. Zeal.

c. *Sphaerocionium* Copel. A pantrop. and austral genus of about 50 sp. richest developed in trop. Amer.

ferrugineum Colla. S. Chile, Valdiv.-Fueg. Related to the pantropical *H. ciliatum* Sw. and belonging to a small austral tricentric group of closely allied species, *H. Franklinae* Col. (N. Zeal., probably = *ferrugineum*, CHRISTENSEN 61 5),

Table III

List of species

Endemics bold faced, endemic genera in capital letters

	Mt	SC	Mf
Adiantum chilense Kaulf	+	+	+
Arthropteris **altescandens** (Colla) J. Sm.	—	—	+
Asplenium dareoides Desv.	+	—	+
— obliquum Forst. var.	+	+	+
— **macrosorum** Bert. ex Colla	+	—	+
— **stellatum** Colla	+	—	+
Blechnum auriculatum Cav.	+	+	+
— chilense (Kaulf.) Mett	+	—	+
— **cycadifolium** (Colla) Sturm	—	—	+
— longicauda C. Chr.	—	—	+
— **Schottii** (Colla) C. Chr.	+	—	+
— valdiviense C. Chr.	+	—	.
Cystopteris fragilis (L.) Bernh.	—	—	+
Dicksonia **berteriana** (Colla) Hook.	+	—	—
— **externa** Skottsb.	—	—	+
Dryopteris **inaequalifolia** (Colla) C. Chr.	—	—	+
Elaphoglossum Lindenii (Bory) Moore	+	—	—
Gleichenia cf. litoralis (Phil.) C. Chr.	—	—	+
— pedalis (Kaulf.) Spr.	+	—	—
— quadripartita (Poir.) Moore	—	—	+
Histiopteris incisa (Thunb.) J. Sm.	+	—	+
Hymenoglossum cruentum (Cav.) Presl	+	—	+
Hymenophyllum caudiculatum Mart.	+	.	+
— cuneatum Kze.	+	—	+
— falklandicum Bak.	—	—	+
— ferrugineum Colla	+	—	+
— fuciforme Sw.	+	—	—
— pectinatum Cav.	+	—	+
— plicatum Kaulf.	+	—	+
— **rugosum** C. Chr. et Skottsb.	+	—	+
— secundum Hook. et Grev.	—	—	+
— tortuosum Hook. et Grev.	+	—	+
Hypolepis rugosula (Labill.) J. Sm.	+	—	+
Lophosoria quadripinnata (Gmel.) C. Chr.	+	—	+
Lycopodium magellanicum Sw.	—	—	+
— scariosum Forst.	—	—	+
Ophioglossum **fernandezianum** C. Chr.	—	—	—
Pellaea chilensis Fee	+	—	+
Polypodium magellanicum (Desv.)	+	—	—

	Mt	Sc	Mf
— intermedium Colla	+	—	+
— lanceolatum L.	+	—	+
— Masafuerae Phil.	—	—	+
— trichomanoides Sw.	+	—	—
Polystichum **berterianum** (Colla) C. Chr.	+	—	+
— vestitum (Forst.) Presl	.	—	+
Pteris berteroana Ag.	—	—	+
— chilensis Desv.	+	—	+
— semiadnata Phil.	+	—	+
Serpyllopsis caespitosa (Gaud.) C. Chr.	+	—	+
THYRSOPTERIS elegans Kze.	+	—	+
Trichomanes exsectum Kze.	+	—	+
— Ingae C. Chr.	+	—	—
— philippianum Sturm	+	—	—

acruginosum (Thouars) Carm. (Tristan da C. and N. Amsterd. I.) and *Marlothii* Brause (Cape).

d. *Meringium* Copel. About 60, S. Chile, Afr., Ceylon, Formosa, N. Guin., N. Zeal., Fiji.

secundum Hook. et Grev. S. Chile, Valdiv.–Fueg.

plicatum Kaulf. See 249 763. S. Chile, Valdiv.–W. Patag.

tortuosum Hook. et Grev. S. Chile, Valdiv.–Fueg., Falkl.

Cyatheaceae

Thyrsopteris elegans Kze. Unanimously regarded as a very ancient type (BOWER, SEWARD, BERRY, WINKLER, COPELAND, etc.) BERRY (27 88) pointed out that *Cyatheoides thyrsopteroides* Berry is remarkably similar to *Thyrsopteris*, it was, however, found sterile, and he adds that most of the fossils formerly referred to *Thyrsopteris* are based on too slender evidence. SEWARD (220 221) says "Thyrsopteris is very closely allied to certain Jurassic Ferns from the Yorkshire coast and many other places geological evidence points to a remote antiquity, and its present isolation is in all probability the last phase in its history of a direct derivative of a widely scattered Jurassic type." COPELAND called it "a relic from the time when *Dicksonia* and *Cyathea* had a common ancestor" (69 48) and he thinks that it is allied to *Culcita* Presl. He brought *Thyrsopteris* to his large and possibly very heterogeneous family Pteridaceae, where also *Dicksonia* is placed.

WINKLER's statement that *Thyrsopteris* is found on Masafuera only (287 472) is erroneous.

Lophosoria Presl. One polymorphous species.

quadripinnata (J. F. Gmel.) C. Chr. Trop. and subtrop. Amer., Mex.–Chile and south to W. Patag., 49° s. lat. The taxonomical status of the various forms remains to be settled. The island form (or forms, for there seems to be some dif-terence between the plants of Masatierra and Masafuera) is certainly unlike the form inhabiting Chile, see *62* 16

Dicksonia L'Herit 24, 1 Mex, 3 Centr Amer to Colomb, 1 Ecuad -Braz, 2 Perú, 1 St Helena, 1 Malays, 4 N Guin, 2 Austral -Tasm, 3 N Zeal 3 N Caled, 1 Fiji-Samoa

berteroana Colla and **externa** Skottsb are very near each other and closely related not to the Andean group but to *D lanata* Col from N Zeal CHRIST (*59* 154) further quotes as relatives *D antarctica* Labill (Austral), *Blumei* (Kze) Moore (Indones, Philipp), *grandis* Ros (N Guin) and species from N Caledonia and the South Sea islands

Polypodiaceae

Cystopteris Bernh 15, 1 boreal, 10 Ind -China, Japan, N Zeal, 2 Eur, 1 S Braz

fragilis (L) Bernh coll A wide spread, polymorphous sp, found in all parts of the world (83° n lat to S Georgia) except Australia The form occurring on Masafuera presumably related to a form from the mainland (*62* 18)

Dryopteris Adans Sens u C Chr about 1200 sp, s str COPELAND about 150, "an assemblage of genera that must be segregated in their entirety before of use for a study of distribution (COPELAND *69*)

inaequalifolia (Colla) C Chr Belongs to a neotrop group and comes nearer to tropical forms than to the south Andean *D spectabilis* (Kaulf) C Chr, which extends south to Chile

Polystichum Roth About 225 widely spread, numerous in E As

berterianum (Colla) C Chr Near *P adiantiforme* Forst, spread through the S temp zone, north to W Ind

vestitum (Forst) Presl coll S Amer (also Chile), Austral N Zeal

Arthropteris J Sm About 20, palaeotrop, recorded from trop Afr, north to Arab, Madag, Australas, north to Philipp Is, New Caled Fiji, Samoa best developed N Guin, N Caled and Madag

altescandens (Colla) J Sm Closely related to Pacific forms (*62* 21)

Asplenium L 650–700, cosmopolitan

obliquum Forst var *chondrophyllum* (Bert) Mett Typical *obliquum* reported from S Chile, Austral and N Zeal

macrosorum Bert ex Colla Distantly related to neotrop sp, see *62* 23

stellatum Colla Belongs to the pantrop *lunulatum* group, see *62* 24

dareoides Desv (magellanicum Kaulf) S Chile, Fueg, Falkl Closely related to *A alvarezense* Rudm Brown of Diego Alvarez (Tristan da C), see *61* 13

Blechnum L 180–200, essentially southern

auriculatum Cav Temp S Amer, common in Centr and S Chile and related to *B australe* L (S Afr)

valdiviense C Chr Chile, south to Chiloé Related to *B lanceolatum* (R Br) Sturm from Austral and N Zeal As regards the nomenclature, see *169* 54, and *249* 764

Schottii (Colla) C Chr Stands near *B attenuatum* (Willd) C Chr (S Afr, E Austral, Polyn) and *meridense* (Kaulf) C Chr (trop Amer) see *62* 27 *chilense* (Kaulf.) Mett. Centr. Chile to W. Patag., Falkl. Belongs to the *capense* group (S. Afr., Indomal.), see *62* 27 and *169* 47.

cycadifolium (Colla) Sturm. Almost too near *B. magellanicum* (Desv.) Mett. (S. Chile to Fueg. and Falkl.), both related to *B. tabulare* (Thunb.) Kuhn (S. and E. Afr., Madag., Mascaren.)

longicauda C. Chr. Very near *B. Sprucei* C. Chr. from trop. S. Amer. (Ecuad. Boliv., Braz.), see *250*. HICKEN records it from Tucumán in Argent. (*133* 246), a statement overlooked also by CHRISTENSEN.

Pellaea Link. About 80, the majority in S. Amer. (south to Chile), S. Afr. and islands N. Amer. north to Canada, N. Zeal.

chilensis Fée Very close to *P. nivea* (Poir.) Prantl (Ariz.–Chile), see *62* 30.

Hypolepis Bernh. A pantrop. genus of 45–50 sp., half of them trop. Amer. several Afr. and surrounding islands, others N. Guin.–E. As. and Austral.–Polyn.

rugosula (Labill.) J. Sm. Centr. and S. Chile, the typ. sp. Austral, N. Zeal, var. *villososcida* (Thouars) C. Chr. (*61* 6) on Tristan da C., *Polypodium viscidum* Roxb. from St. Helena very likely is another variety.

Adiantum L. 200–225, widely distributed but most numerous in S. Amer.

chilense Kaulf. Peru-Chile, Patag., Falkl.

Pteris L. 270–280, mainly trop. but extending north to S. Eur. and south to S. Afr., Tasm. and N. Zeal.

chilensis Desv. Near *P. leptophylla* Sw. (S. Braz.)

semiadnata Phil. S. Chile, Valdiv.–Huafo I. A distinct sp., possibly related to *P. pulchra* Schlechtd. from Mexico.

berteroana Ag. Related to *P. comans* Forst. (Austral., Tasm., N. Zeal) and particularly to *P. endlicheriana* Ag. (Norfolk I.)

Histiopteris (Ag.) J. Sm. An assemblage of trop. and austr. circump. forms which according to CHRISTENSEN cannot claim to be regarded as different species (*62* 36), whereas COPELAND (*69* 60) speaks of local, derived species (a concentration in Indomal.–Polyn.) differing sufficiently from the following polymorphous taxon

incisa (Thunb.) J. Sm. Chile, S. Afr., Tristan da C., Austral., Tasm., N. Zeal, Polynes.

Polypodium L. coll. World-wide, Ind. Fil. registers more than 1100 sp. The genus is now generally broken up, most radically by COPELAND, who segregates numerous genera partly restored from synonymy.

a *Grammitis* Sw. About 150, an essentially southern genus, reaching north to West Indies and Bonin Is. and richest developed in New Guinea.

magellanica Desv. S. Chile, Valdiv.–Fueg. and Patag. (Rio Negro), Tristan da C., Marion I. In *62* 36 as *P. Billardieri* (Willd.) C. Chr. var. *magellanicum* (Desv.) C. Chr., but later restored to specific rank by CHRISTENSEN *61* 18. Distribution of *Billardieri* Austral., Tasm., N. Zeal., Auckl. and Campb. Is., Lord Howe and Norfolk Is., St. Paul and N. Amsterd. Is., Kerguel.

b *Synammia* Presl. According to COPELAND *69* 184 only one species, *S. Feuillei* (Bert.) Copel. (*Polypodium trilobum* Cav.), but I fail to see how we could exclude the island species *intermedium* Colla [*translucens* (Kze) Fée] JOHOW united *P trilobum* Cav and *californicum* Kaulf with *translucens*, and they seem to belong to the same small group, to which also *P Espinosae* Weatherby (Chile, Atacama) must be referred

c *Polypodium* s str, about 75 sp, mainly N hemisph and neotrop

Masafuerae Phil S Peru to N Chile (Antofagasta), Argent, comp *149* 14 and *168* 33 Very close to *P pycnocarpum* C Chr (Mex–N Chile)

d *Xiphopteris* Kaulf About 50, pantrop

trichomanoides Sw Trop Amer A puzzling record (see *249* 766)

e *Pleopeltis* Humb et Bonpl About 40, pantrop, the following sp widespread

lanceolatum L Mex and W Ind to subtrop S Amer (also in Chile), St Helena, Tristan da C, Afr, Madag, Indomal, Hawaii

Elaphoglossum Schott A pantrop genus of more than 400 sp, very numerous in And S Amer, 4 sp on Tristan da C, and many sp in Polyn and Hawaii

Lindeni (Bory) Moore Mex to Ecuad and Braz

Gleicheniaceae

Gleichenia Sm About 130 sp, the majority of them referred to *Sticherus* (Kaulf) Ching, to which also the species in J Fern belong about a dozen sp spread over the austral zone, 5 Chile, one extending to Falkl, 1 S Afr, 1 Madag, Mascaren and Seych Is, 1 Tasm, 1 Tasm and N Zeal, 2 N Zeal

quadripartita (Poir) Moore S Chile to Fueg

pedalis (Kaulf) Spreng S Chile south to Chonos Is

cf *litoralis* (Phil) C Chr Hardly identical with this little known species and perhaps only a form of *G pedalis*

Ophioglossaceae

Ophioglossum L 28 sp recognized by CLAUSEN (*64*), the genus "scattered with remarkable uniformity over the habitable globe" (COPELAND *69* 12)

fernandezianum C Chr Not very near *O japanense* Mart (Colomb, Braz) as CHRISTENSEN thought but close to *O scariosum* Clausen from Peru, Dept Junin

Lycopodiaceae

Lycopodium L A large world wide genus, badly ill-treated by NESSEL, who listed several undistinguishable species in J Fern, see *249* 766

magellanicum Sw S Chile to Fueg, Falkl, S Georgia, Marion I, Kerguel

scariosum Forst Chile, Valdiv–Guaytecas Is (*L gayanum* Remy), N Zeal, Trop Andes, Braz (*L Jussieui* Desv) See l c 767

In his treatment of the geographical groups distinguished by him, JOHOW included the ferns—no Fern Allies were at that time known from Juan Fernandez All were classified as American except 3, *Dicksonia berteroana*, said to be similar to a species from Fiji, *Pteris berteroana* (identified with *comans*), and "*Asplenium longissimum* Blume", the species now known as *Blechnum longicauda* In 1914 (*227*) I went a step further, to my "Altpazifisches Element" 5 species were referred, to the Trop American 5, and all the rest to the Chilean In 1934 I attempted a more detailed subdivision (*239*, here translated from French)

1. Neotropical and Andean element. Species either found in Centr. and S. Chile or endemic but allied to Chilean species, 28
    a) in Chile, 22
    b) in the Magellan region, but not of subantarctic character, 3
    d) endemic species of non endemic genera, 3
2. Element consisting of wide-spread species, also inhabiting Chile, 2
3. Neotropical element, not represented in Chile, 7
    a) non-endemic species, 1
    b) endemic species of non endemic genera, 6
4. Magellanian Old Antarctic element, 9
    a) non-endemic Magellanian species, 2
    b) ,,   ,, Old Antarctic but not Magellanian species, 4
    c) endemic species allied to subantarctic species, 2
    d) ,,   ,, not allied to subantarctic species, 1
5. Pacific element, 5
    a) isolated endemic species of wide genera, 1
    b) endemic species belonging to genera or sections of west to central Pacific distribution, 3
    d) species of endemic genus with unknown relations, 1

A modified arrangement is attempted below, corresponding to the analysis of the angiosperms.

I Andine-Chilean element —34 (64.1 %)

a Endemic species (5, 9.4 %): Hymenophyllum rugosum, Polystichum berterianum, Blechnum cycadifolium, Pellaea chilensis, Polypodium intermedium.

b Known from continental Chile, many also in other parts of S. America or of still wider distribution (29, 54.7 %): Trichomanes exsectum, Hymenoglossum cruentum, Hymenophyllum cuneatum, caudiculatum, fuciforme, pectinatum, ferrugineum, secundum, plicatum and tortuosum, Lophosoria quadripinnata, Cystopteris fragilis, Polystichum vestitum, Asplenium obliquum, Blechnum auriculatum, valdiviense and chilense, Hypolepis rugosula, Adiantum chilense, Pteris chilensis and semiadnata, Histiopteris incisa, Polypodium magellanicum, Masafuerae and lanceolatum, Gleichenia quadripartita, pedalis and cf. litoralis, Lycopodium scariosum.

II Subantarctic-Magellanian element —4 (7.5 %)

Not endemic, extending north but not beyond Centr. Chile: Serpyllopsis caespitosa, Hymenophyllum falklandicum, Asplenium dareoides, Lycopodium magellanicum.

III Neotropical element —9 (17 %)

a Endemic species (7, 13.1 %): Trichomanes philippianum and Ingae, Dryopteris inaequalifolia, Asplenium macrosorum and stellatum, Blechnum longicauda, Ophioglossum fernandezianum.

b Not endemic (2, 3.8 %): Polypodium trichomanoides, Elaphoglossum Lindenii.

IV West Pacific element —5 (9.4 %)

Affinities in Australia, New Zealand and Oceania, not in America. All endemic: Dicksonia berteroana and externa, Arthropteris altescandens, Blechnum Schottii, Pteris berteroana.

V. Eu-Fernandezian element —1 (1.9 %)

Endemic genus without affinities among the living ferns: *Thyrsopteris elegans*.

As could be expected, the Chilean element is stronger among the ferns than among the angiosperms, followed in great distance by the neotropical, which also is comparatively stronger, whereas the Magellanian and the Pacific are less important, especially the latter; long distance advocates would expect the opposite, because ferns ought to travel across the ocean much more readily than flowering plants.

III. Musci

The following list is based on BROTHERUS' paper in vol II (*34*) and on his treatment of the group in the 2nd edition of Natürl. Pflanzenfam. In many cases the figure for the number of species (in brackets) is too low, as numerous mosses have been described in later years, but I have refrained from searching the literature. Much information was obtained from HERZOG's work (*129*) and in pt 2 of IRMSCHER's book (*143*). I am indebted to Dr HERMAN PERSSON for kind assistance.

Mt = Masatierra, Mf = Masafuera

Ditrichaceae

Pleuridium Brid. (about 30) Widespread, mainly temperate
  Robinsonii (Mont.) Mitt. Chile, Urug. Belongs to a S. Amer. group —Mt

Ditrichum Timm (about 50) In all parts of the world
  affine (C.M.) Hampe S. Chile and Patag., E. Austral., N. Zeal., Auckl. Is. Not listed in *210*, where *D. elongatum* (H.f. et W.) Mitt. is quoted for Chile, Austral., Tasm. and N. Zeal. —Mt, Mf
  longisetum (Hampe) Jaeg. S. Chile to Fueg. —Mf

Ceratodon Brid. (2, one trop.)
  purpureus (L.) Brid. Cosmopol. —Mt, Mf

Pottiaceae

Hymenostomum R. Br. (50–60) All over the world
  kunzeanum (C.M.) Broth. S. Chile —Mt

Gymnostomum Hedw. (10) All over the world
  calcareum Bryol. germ. Eur., Afr., As., N. Amer., S. Amer. Ecuad.-Chile, Austral., Tasm., N. Zeal. —Mt, Mf

Trichostomum Hedw. (81) Cosmopolitan
  brachydontium Bruch Eur., Caucas., N. Afr., Macaron., Mascar., Japan, N. Zeal., but not mentioned in *210* —Mf

Dicranaceae

Amphidium Nees (10) Very widely distributed
  cyathicarpum (Mont.) Broth. Ecuad.-Chile, S. Georgia, Afr., E. Austral., Tasm., N. Zeal. —Mt, Mf

Dicranella Schimp (60) All continents, numerous S Amer and As
    costata Broth —Mt, Mf

Oncophorus Brid (8) Southern S Amer, Eur, E As, Ceylon
    fuegianus Card Patag -Fueg —Mf

Dicranoloma Ren (76) Almost exclusively S hemisph, austr subantarct, 1 S Afr
    fernandezianum Broth Near *D Dusenii* Broth (S Chile) —Mt
    capillifolium Broth S Chile-Fueg —Mt
    capillifolioides Broth Near the former —Mf
    Menziesii (Tayl) Par S Chile, F Austral, Tasm, Norfolk I, N Zeal, Chatham Is, Auckl Is —Mt
    Billardieri (Schwaegr) Par Peru-Fueg, Falkl, S Afr, Austral, Tasm, N Zeal, Auckl and Campb Is—Mt, Mf
    nigricaule Angstr S Chile, south to Fueg —Mf

Campylopus Brid (about 500) All over the world, mainly trop -subtrop
    introflexus (Hedw) Mitt N Amer, S Amer, Ecuad to Urug and Fueg, islands of W and E Afr, Ascens, St Helena, Tristan da C, Marion I, Austral, Tasm, N Zeal, Auckl, Campb and Antipodes Is, Pacific islands —Mt
    truncatus C M Chile —Mt
    polytrichoides De Not W and S Eur, N Afr, Mascar —Mt
    aberrans Broth A very peculiar sp —Mt, Mf
    areodictyon (C M) Mitt Centr and S Amer, Venez -Boliv —Mf
    subareodictyon Broth Related to the former —Mf
    blindioides Broth —Mf

Thysanomitrium Schwaegr (31) Trop -subtrop, especially Old World, extending south to the austr subantarct zone
    Richardi Schwaegr Centr and S Amer to Chile —Mt, Mf
    leptodus (Mitt) Broth [*Campylopus clavatus* (R Br) H f et W] Ecuad, Chile, Austral, Tasm, N Zeal, Auckl and Campb Is —Mt, Mf

Dicnemonaceae

Eucamptodon Mont (7) Chile (1), Austral (1), N Caled (4), N Zeal +N Caled (1)
    perichaetialis Mont S Chile to Magell —Mf

Fissidentaceae

Fissidens Hedw (over 700) All continents, very numerous in trop zones
    fernandezianus Broth —Mt, Mf
    crassicuspes Broth Related to *F crassipes* Wils (Eur Mediterr, Madeira) —Mt
    rigidulus Hook f et Wils Ecuad -W Patag, Austral, Tasm N Zeal —Mt, Mf
    leptochaete Dus Chile —Mt
    maschalanthus Mont Chile, south to W Patag —Mt, Mf
    pycnotylus Broth Very near the former —Mt
    asplenioides (Sw) Hedw Centr Amer to Peru, S Chile and Braz, W Afr, Macaron, Tristan da C, Indomal, Queensl, N Zeal —Mt

Leptodontium Hampe (80) Most numerous in Amer, 40% And
    fernandezianum Broth Related to *L. luteum* (Tayl) Mitt (trop And)—Mf
Didymodon Hedw (91) Subcosmopol, mainly temp, essentially Amer Mex-Centr Amer-Peru and Chile, 1 Antarct
    calymperidictyon Broth —Mt
    linearis Broth —Mf
Tortula Hedw (220) Subcosmopol, mainly temp
    scabrinervis (C M) Mitt Chile —Mt
    flagellaris (Schimp) Mont Chile —Mt
Grimmia Ehrh (230) Subcosmopol but rare in the trop zones
    phyllorhizans Broth —Mt
Rhacomitrium Brid (80) As *Grimmia*
    subnigritum (C M) Par W Patag-Fueg —Mf
    symphyodontum (C M) Jaeg S Chile to Fueg and Falkl, S Afr, Kerguel, Tasm, N Zeal Not listed for N Zeal in *210* —Mt, Mf
    striatipilum Card S Chile to Fueg, S Georgia, N Zeal (*210*) —Mf
    lanuginosum (Hedw) Brid Cosmopol —Mf
    loriforme Dus W Patag —Mf
    convolutum Mont S Chile to W Patag —Mf

Ptychomitriaceae

Ptychomitrium (Bruch) Furnr (62) Of wide distribution in temp zones
    fernandezianum (Mitt) Jaeg —Mt, Mf

Orthotrichaceae

Zygodon Hook f et Tayl (about 100) N and Centr Amer (6), trop S Amer (40), S Chile and Argent (20), Eur (4), trop Afr (2), trop As (6), E Austral-N Zeal (10)
    intermedius B et S S Amer, Afr, Monsoon reg, Austral, Tasm, N Zeal —Mt (*264*) *Z obovalis* Mitt, a doubtful species (*313*, 139) is supposed to be identical with *intermedius*
    Menziesii (Schwaegr) W Am S Chile, Austral, Tasm, N Zeal —Mt
Stenomitrium (Mitt) Broth (2) Peru, Chile
    pentastichum (Mont) Broth Peru-W Patag —Mf
Ulota Mohr (43) N and S temp zones, 1/3 Chile, some N Zeal
    fernandeziana Malta (*313*) Near *U rufula* (Mitt) Jaeg (Chile-W Patag, Argent, N Zeal) —Mf
Macromitrium Brid (415) Trop-subtrop, special groups Chile-Patag and E Austral-Tasm-N Zeal
    hymenostomum Mont S Chile-Fueg —Mt
    saxatile Mitt —Mt, Mf
    fernandezianum Broth Related to *M asperulum* Mitt (Tasm, N Zeal, not in *210*) —Mt
    Masafuerae Broth Near the former —Mf

Funariaceae

Funaria Schieb (200) A world wide genus
    hygrometrica (L.) Sibth Cosmopol —Mt, Mf

Bryaceae

Mielichhoferia Hornsch (100) Widely distributed, centering in the Andes
    longiseta C M Ecuador —Mt
Bryum Dill (about 800) All over the world
    Lechleri C M Chile —Mf
    fernandezianum Broth Related to *B Crucgeri* Hampe (neotrop) —Mt, Mf

Leptostomaceae

Leptostomum R Br (11) S Chile (2), Indomal, Austral, N Zeal Norfolk I Campb I
    Menziesii (Hook) R Br S Chile to W Patag and Fueg —Mf

Eustichiaceae

Eustichia (Brid) Mitt (8) 6 Mex.–S Chile, 1 S Afr, 1 islands of E Afr
    Poeppigii (C M) Par S Chile-Magell —Mt, Mf

Rhizogoniaceae

Rhizogonium Brid (27) Austr -circump (S Amer, S Afr, Austral, N Zeal, Polyn), extending into the N hemisph, 1 pantrop
    Novae Hollandiae Brid var *patagonicum* Card et Broth W Patag the typical sp Austral, Tasm, N Zeal —Mt
    mnioides (Hook) Schimp Colomb -Fueg, E Austral Tasm, N Zeal —Mf

Bartramiaceae

Anacolia Schimp (7) W N Amer -trop Andes (5), 1 Medit, 1 Ethiop
    subsessilis (Tayl) Broth Mex -Ecuad —Mt, Mf
Bartramia Hedw (110) Subcosmopol, a few sp subantarct circump
    aristata Schimp Chile —Mt, Mf
    patens Brid W Patag -Fueg, Falkl, S Georgia, Kerguel E Austral Tasm, N Zeal —Mf Not mentioned in *210*, where *B halleriana* Hedw, widely distributed in the N hemisphere, is credited to Patag, Fueg, Austral, Tasm and N Zeal —Mf
    fernandeziana Card —Mt
Philonotis Brid (174) Subcosmopol, two monotyp sections in S Amer
    krauseana (C M) Jaeg Centr Chile to W Patag —Mt, Mf
    glabrata Broth Related to the former —Mt
    scabrifolia (Hook f et Wils) Broth Circump -subantarct, forming a separate section Ecuad -Fueg, Falkl, S Georgia, S Afr, Marion I, Kerguel, Austral Tasm, N Zeal, Auckl and Campb Is —Mt, Mf
    vagans (Hook f et Wils) Mitt Forms a separate section Chile-Fueg, S Georgia —Mf (an aberrant form)
Breutelia Schimp (104) Best developed trop mountains, rare N Amer numerous austr -subantarct
    Masafuerae Broth —Mf

Hedwigiaceae

Rhacocarpus Lindb. (24). Centr. Andes and Braz. mountains etc., almost confined to the S. hemisph.
  Humboldtii (Hook.) Lindb. Mex., W. Ind., Colomb.-And. Patag., Fueg., Falkl., Centr. Afr., Madag., Réunion, Austral., Tasm., N. Zeal. A polymorphous sp.- - Mf

Cryphaeaceae

Dendrocryphaea Par. et Schimp. (4). Austr. subantarct., 2 Chile, 1 Argent.-Patag., 1 Tasm.-N. Zeal.
  cuspidata (Sull.) Broth. S. Chile.—Mf
Cyptodon Par. et Schimp. (6). 2 Austral.-N. Zeal., 1 N. Caled., 2 Fiji-Samoa-Tonga, 1 J. Fern.
  crassinervis Broth. Close to *C.* (*210* under *Cryphaea*) *dilatatus* (Hook f. et Wils.) Par. (E. Austral., N. Zeal.)—Mf

Lepyrodontaceae

Lepyrodon Hampe (6–8). 1 bicentric (Chile-Fueg., E. Austral. Tasm., N. Zeal., Campb. I.), 2 or 3 trop. Andes to Braz. and Argent., 2 or 3 Chile, 1 N. Zeal.
  parvulus Mitt. Centr. and S. Chile.—Mt, Mf
  tomentosus (Hook.) Mitt. Colomb.-Peru, Braz., Argent., W. Patag.—Mt
  implexus (Kze) Par. Chile, south to Fueg.—Mt

Ptychomniaceae

Ptychomnium Hook. f. et Wils. (9 or 8 if *cygnisetum = aciculare*). Austral subantarct., extending north to Braz. and Hawaii, Argent and Chile to Fueg., E. Austral., Tasm., N. Zeal. and subant. islands, Lord Howe I., N. Caled., Polyn.
  subaciculare Besch. Chile, south to Fueg.—Mt
  falcatulum Broth. Related to the former.—Mt
  ptychocarpum (Schwaegr.) Mitt. Chile, south to W. Patag.—Mf

Neckeraceae

Weymouthia Broth. (3–4). Austr.-circump., Hawaii.
  mollis (Hedw.) Broth. Centr. and S. Chile to Magell., E. Austral. Tasm., N. Zeal.—Mt, Mf
Leptodon Mohr (4). Afr. and islands (3), and the following.
  Smithii (Dicks.) Mohr. Argent., Chile, S. Eur., Caucas., Afr., Macaron., E. Austral. N. Zeal.—Mt Mf
Neckera Hedw. (127). Widely distributed trop.-subtrop., extending south to Chile and N. Zeal.-Auckl I.
  rotundata Broth. A very distinct sp.—Mf
Porothamnium Fleisch. (51). 1 W. N. Amer., 41 Centr. and S. Amer., extending south to Patag., 7 trop. Afr., 1 Ceylon, 1 N. Zeal.
  fasciculatum (Sw.) Fleisch. W. Ind. Colomb.-Peru, Braz.—Mf
  arbusculans (C. M.) Broth. Chile, Patag.—Mf

Thamnium Bryol eur (33) N Amer, W and S Eur, Macaron, S Afr, N and E As, Indomal, Austral, N Zeal, Melan The Juan Fernandez species belong to a southern section

    rigidum (Mitt) Broth —Mt
    latinerve (Mitt) Broth —Mt
    Caroli Broth Related to *rigidum* —Mt
    Ingae Broth Very near the former —Mt
    crassinervium (Mitt) Broth —Mt
    proboscideum Broth Near the former —Mt
    assimile Broth Very near the former —Mt
    confertum (Mitt) Broth —Mt

Pilotrichella (C M) Fleisch (37) Pantrop
    macrosticta Broth A very distinct sp —Mf

Hookeriaceae

Distichophyllum Dozy et Molk (93) Essentially austral, extending south to Austral, Tasm, N Zeal well represented Indomal region

    subelimbatum Broth —Mt
    assimile Broth Near the former —Mt
    fernandezianum Broth Related to *D rotundifolium* (Hook f et Wils) Broth (Chile, Patag, F Austral, Tasm, N Zeal) —Mf

Pterygophyllum Brid (32) Mainly S hemisph, 6 S Chile-Fueg, 25 Austral-Tasm-N Zeal, 2 of these also S Amer

    anomalum (Schwaegr) Mitt Fueg —Mt Perhaps only an extreme water form of the following (137 85)
    obscurum (Mont) Mitt S Chile to W Patag, Falkl, Tasm —Mf
    tenuinerve Broth Very near the former —Mt
    denticulatum (Hook f et Wils) Mitt W Patag-Fueg, Falkl, E Austral, Tasm, N Zeal, Auckl and Campbell Is —Mt Not included in 210, where *P dentatum* (Hook f et Wils) Mitt is supposed to occur in Chile and Fuegia

Eriopus (Brid) C M (25) Some trop Andes, 1 S Afr, numerous N Zeal

    leptoloma Broth Related to *E apiculatus* (Hook f et Wils) Mitt (S Chile-Fueg, Austral, Tasm N Zeal) —Mt, Mf
    grandirets Broth Near the former —Mf

Lamprophyllum Schimp Monotypical, more or less distantly related to neotrop genera

    splendidissimum (Mont) Schimp S Chile and W Patag —Mf

Hypopterygiaceae

Lopidium Hook f et Wils (16) 14 paleotrop, 2 S Amer (Braz, Chile)
    concinnum (Hook) Fleisch Chile, south to W Patag, Austral, Tasm N Zeal, Auckl Is —Mt

Hypopterygium Brid (61) Widely distributed N and S Amer, Afr, As, Indomal, one small group austr-bicentr

Thouinii (Schwaegr.) Mont. S. Chile–Fueg. Belongs to a group of 4 sp. (3 Chile, 1 N. Zeal.) —Mf

Rhacopilaceae

Rhacopilum Palis. (51) Pantrop., mainly southern, south to N. Zeal.
  fernandezianum Card. S. Chile. Related to *R. tomentosum* (Sw.) Brid (trop.-subtrop. Amer.) —Mt, Mf

Thuidiaceae

Thuidium Bryol. eur. (161) All over the world, especially in humid mountain climates
  Masafuerae Broth. Related to *T. fulvastrum* (Mitt.) Jaeg. (Tristan da C., N. Zeal. but not included in *210*) and to the following sp. —Mf
  Valdiviae Broth. S. Chile —Mt, Mf

Amblystegiaceae

Sciaromium Mitt. (22) Mainly austral, the majority southern S. Amer., 1 Cape, 2 China, 2 E. Austral, 1 N. Zeal., the single N. Amer. sp. forms a separate section Sect. Aloma 6 (1 Boliv. 2 Fueg., 2 E. Austral, 1 N. Zeal.)
  pachyloma (Mont.) Par. S. Chile-W. Patag. —Mt, Mf

Hypnaceae

Stereodon Mitt. (7) 2 Mex., 1 Chile, 4 mountains of Asia
  Lechleri (C. M.) Mitt. Centr. Chile to W. Patag. —Mt
Isopterygium Mitt. (170) Widely distributed, preponderately trop.-subtrop.
  fernandezianum Broth. Related to *I. tenerum* (Sw.) Mitt. (neotrop.) —Mt

Sematophyllaceae

Rhaphidostegium (Bryol. eur.) De Not. (106) Subcosmopol., trop. and temp. The Chilean species sometimes regarded as belonging to a separate genus *Rhaphido-rhynchium*
  Masafuerae Broth. Similar to *R. cyparissioides* (Hornsch.) Besch. (Braz.) —Mf
  aberrans Broth. Similar to *R. callidum* (Mont.) Jaeg. (S. Chile to W. Patag.) —Mt, Mf
  caespitosum (Sw.) Jaeg. W. Ind., trop.-subtrop. S. Amer. —Mt, Mf
  caespitosoides Broth. Related to the former —Mt
  brachycladulum Broth. —Mt
Rigodium Kze. (19) Trop.-subtrop. Amer., 2 Afr.
  toxarium (Schwaegr.) Schimp. Trop. S. Amer. to W. Patag. —Mt, Mf
  arborescens (C. M.) Broth. S. Chile-W. Patag. —Mt, Mf
  hylocomioides Card. et Broth. Patag. —Mf
  robustum Broth. —Mt
  Looseri Ther. Related to *R. gracile* Rén. et Card. (Costa Rica) —Mt
  tamarix C. M. (elegantulum Card.) S. Chile-W. Patag. —Mt
Rhynchostegium Bryol. eur. (130) Temp.-subtrop., almost cosmopol.
  complanum (Mitt.) Jaeg. Centr. Chile —Mt, Mf
  tenuifolium (Hedw.) Jaeg. Urug., S. Chile, E. Austral, Tasm., N. Zeal —Mt

Catagoniopsis Broth. Monotypical, related to *Catagonium* (S. hemisph.)
 bertcroana (Mont.) Broth. Centr. Chile —Mt

Hypnodendraceae

Hypnodendron Lindb. (28) Chile (2), Indomal., Austral., Polyn., Hawaii
 microstictum Mitt. Chile —Mf

Polytrichaceae

Oligotrichum Lam. et DC. (13) Widely scattered: 2 W. N. Amer., 4 Chile, single sp. Braz., trop. Andes, Arct. alp., Eur., bor.-circump.
 canaliculatum (Hook.) Mitt. var. The typical sp. in S. Chile —Mt
Psilopilum Brid. (17) A bipolar genus, tricentric in the S. hemisph.
 antarcticum C. M. Boliv., Fueg., Falkl., S. Georgia, Kerguel. —Mf
Polytrichadelphus (C. M.) Mitt. (22) Centering in the Andes (17), 1 W. N. Amer., 1 Braz. 2 Magell., 1 subant.-bicentric
 magellanicus (L.) Mitt. Patag., Fueg., Falkl., E. Austral., Tasm., N. Zeal., Auckl. and Campb. Is. —Mf
Dendroligotrichum (C. M.) Broth. Monotypical
 dendroides (Brid.) Broth. Peru, S. Chile south to Fueg., N. Zeal. —Mf

The geographical distribution of the mosses is less well known than of the vascular plants, and some of the species now considered to be endemic in Juan Fernandez will perhaps be discovered on the mainland. No specialist ever visited the islands, where most likely further species, endemic or known from elsewhere, will be found. Species now only recorded from Masatierra may be found on Masafuera, and vice versa.

The 131 species of mosses hitherto recorded from Juan Fernandez belong to 65 genera (2:1), all known from elsewhere, 48 species (36.6 %) are endemic, a high figure in a spore bearing group, higher than for the Pteridophytes (34 %). On Masatierra 84[1] were collected, 50 of these (38.1 %) not found on Masafuera, where 81 were recorded, of which 47 (35.9 %) are restricted to this island, 34 (26 %) are known from both islands. No mosses have been reported from Santa Clara.

The mosses are less evenly distributed than the ferns, presenting a higher degree of local endemism, but this may be due to insufficient knowledge of their distribution. Endemics are more local than non-endemics, of the former (48), 24 (50 %) are only known from Masatierra, and 16 (33.3 %) only from Masafuera, 8 (16.7 %) being found on both islands, of the non endemics (83), 26 inhabit Masatierra (31.3 %), 31 Masafuera (37.4 %) and 26 (31.3 %) both islands. Endemics are proportionately more numerous on Masatierra, where 32 species or 38 % are endemic, the figures for Masafuera are 24 and 29.6. It is remarkable that all the 8 species of *Thamnium* are endemic on Masatierra.

For two reasons it is a difficult task to segregate with sufficient accuracy the

---
[1] BROTHERUS p. 420 records *Rhacomitrium subnigritum* from both islands, but the locality quoted for Masatierra is situated on Masafuera.

various geographical elements of which the flora is made up many of the non-endemic species have a more or less wide distribution, and the accurate systematic position of the endemic ones is, in many cases, uncertain or quite unknown, where no information was given by their author and nobody has studied them after him, I have not ventured to find a place for them. Thus 11 species had to be left out, bringing the number down to 120, on which the percentages have been calculated. Even so it stands to reason that the arrangement below cannot be definite because many doubtful points remain to be cleared by the bryologist.

As to the 83 non-endemic species the main thing is whether, regardless of their total distribution, they have been found in S. America or not, in consequence of the geographical position of Juan Fernandez they must be referred to one of the American groups I–III. No less than 25 % are austral or subantarctic and bicentric, their origin if antarctic or not, will not concern us here.

The geographical elements
I Andine-Chilean element —77 (64.2 %)

a Endemic species (15) Dicranoloma fernandezianum and capillifolioides, Fissidens pycnotylus, Didymodon calymperidictyon and linearis, Ulota fernandeziana, Philonotis glabrata, Ptychomnium falcatulum, Distichophyllum fernandezianum, Pterygophyllum tenuinerve, Eriopus leptoloma and grandiretis, Thuidium Masafucrac, Rhaphidostegium aberrans, Rigodium robustum.

b Also known from Chile, rarely extending to the extreme south (57) Pleuridium Robinsonii, Ditrichum affine and longisetum, Hymenostomum kunzeanum, Amphidium cyathicarpum, Dicranoloma capillifolium, Menziesii and nigricaule, Campylopus truncatus, Thysanomitrium Richardi and leptodus, Eucamptodon perichaetialis, Fissidens rigidulus, leptochaete, maschalanthus and asplenioides, Tortula scabrinervis and flagellaris, Rhacomitrium loriforme and convolutum, Zygodon intermedius and Menziesii, Stenomitrium pentastichum Macromitrium hymenostomum, Bryum Lechleri, Leptostomum Menziesii, Eustichia Poeppigii, Rhizogonium mnioides, Bartramia aristata, Philonotis krauseana and vagans, Rhacocarpus Humboldtii, Dendrocryphaea cuspidata, Lepyrodon parvulus and implexus, Ptychomnium subaciculare and ptychocarpum, Weymouthia mollis, Leptodon Smithii, Porothamnium arbusculans, Lamprophyllum splendidissimum, Lopidium concinnum, Hypopterygium Thouini, Rhacopilum fernandezianum, Thuidium Valdiviae, Sciaromium pachyloma, Stereodon Lechleri, Rigodium toxarium, arborescens, hylocomioides and tamarix, Rhynchostegium complanum and tenuifolium, Catagoniopsis beteroana, Hypnodendron microstictum, Oligotrichum canaliculatum, Dendroligotrichum dendroides.

c Cosmopolitan (5) Ceratodon purpureus Gymnostomum calcareum, Campylopus introflexus, Rhacomitrium lanuginosum, Funaria hygrometrica.

II Subantarctic-Magellanian element —13 (10.8 %)

All non endemic, found in the far south, many going north to the latitude of Valdivia or even farther, several occur on the Falkland Is., South Georgia or other subantarctic islands and not few reappear in New Zealand, etc.

Oncophorus fuegianus, Dicranoloma Billardieri, Rhacomitrium subnigritum, symphyodontum and striatipilum, Rhizogonium Novae Hollandiae, Bartramia patens, Philonotis scabrifolia, Pterygophyllum anomalum, obscurum and denticulatum, Psilopilum antarcticum, Polytrichadelphus magellanicus.

III Neotropical element — 14 (11.7 %)

Recorded from tropical America but not from Chile, or related to tropical species.

a Endemic (8) Campylopus subareodictyon, Leptodontium fernandezianum, Bryum fernandezianum, Pinnatella macrosticta, Isopterygium fernandezianum, Rhaphidostegium Masafuerae and caespitosoides, Rigodium Looseri.

b Non-endemic (6) Campylopus areodictyon, Mielichhoferia longiseta, Anacolia subsessilis, Lepyrodon tomentosus, Porothamnium fasciculatum, Rhaphidostegium caespitosum.

IV West Pacific element — 13 (10.8 %)

Endemic species, allied to S.W. Pacific species (Australia, Tasmania, New Zealand etc.) but, as far as known, not to S. American species. Macromitrium fernandezianum and Masafuerae, Cyptodon crassinervis, Distichophyllum subelimbatum and assimile, Thamnium rigidum, latinerve Caroli, Ingae, crassinervium, proboscideum, assimile and confertum.

V Atlantic element — 3 (2.5 %)

a Endemic Fissidens crassicuspes
b Not endemic Trichostomum brachydontium, Campylopus polytrichoides.

Endemic species of unknown position Dicranella costata, Campylopus aberrans and blindioides, Fissidens fernandezianus, Grimmia phyllorhizans, Ptychomitrium fernandezianum Macromitrium saxatile, Bartramia fernandeziana, Breutelia Masafuerae Neckera rotundata, Rhaphidostegium brachycladulum.

The dominance of a South American element is self evident, groups I to III make up 86.7 %. It is hard to draw a line between I and II the Magellanian species are supposed to have come from the far south, and theirs is a more southern area, but many of the species referred to I *b* may have had the same history though, at present, they do not reach so far south.

The Atlantic element is artificial. *Fissidens crassicuspes* is, if BROTHERUS is right, related to a species that has its nearest station on Madeira, but the genus is a very large one, and another connection may be found. *Campylopus polytrichoides* is an Atlantic species with its nearest locality on Madeira, its presence on Masatierra is indeed surprising. *Trichostomum brachydontium* is scattered over half the globe, with its nearest stations in Macaronesia, but it extends not only to and beyond the Mediterranean region, but turns up on the island of Reunion, in Japan and on New Zealand. Have we to do with isolated remnants of a once more continuous area, or is it still to be discovered in other places? Is it a bipolar species?

Of the species left aside for the present, *Dicranella costata* (many in S Amer), *Ptychomitrium fernandezianum* (other sp in the Andes), *Macromitrium saxatile* (many in S Amer), *Bartramia fernandeziana* and *Breutelia Masafuerae* (many austral sp) may turn out to belong to an American element The occurrence in Masatierra of 8 endemic species of *Thamnium* is astonishing, for not one is quoted for South America, whereas related species are found in Australia–New Zealand, Oceania and Malaysia, for this reason I have referred the species in Masatierra to the Pacific element

IV Hepaticae

No handbook equal to BROTHERUS comparatively modern account of the mosses exists of the Hepaticae SCHIFFNER's treatment of this group in the 1st edition of Naturl Pflanzenfamilien is too antiquated to be of much use Much important information is, however, found in HERZOG's work (*129*) as well as in DOMIN's paper (*76*), and also in this case Dr PERSSON kindly helped me, but to search the voluminous special literature of the last thirty years was not to be thought of The number of species given is, in many cases at least, too low, but I don't think this matters very much

The following list is based on EVANS' and HERZOG's papers (*93*, *130*) with a few alterations (*131*) Several species credited to Juan Fernandez by STEPHANI (*333*) but not mentioned by HERZOG are included here, some of them are, perhaps, identical with other species

Marchantiales

Plagiochasma Lehm et Lindenb (about 20) Mostly trop –subtrop
 rupestre (Forst) St Cosmopol , also Chile —Mt, Mf
Reboulia Raddi (1)
 hemisphaerica (L) Raddi Cosmopol, also Chile —Mt, Mf
Lunularia (Mich) Adans (1)
 cruciata (L) Dumort S Amer , also Chile, Medit Eur, Atl islands, Afr, Austral —Mt, Mf
Marchantia L (about 50) Subcosmopol , numerous trop
 polymorpha L Cosmopol , also Chile —Mt, Mf
 berteroana Lehm et Lindenb Chile south to Fueg , Falkl , St Helena S Afr , Marion I Kerguel , Austral, Tasm , N Zeal —Mt, Mf
 foliacea Mitt S Chile, Tasm , N Zeal —Mt, Mf

Metzgeriales

Riccardia S F Gray (140–150, but much higher figures are given) N temp 6, trop Amer 43, Afr 14, trop As –Oceania 53, austr -subantarct 35
 fuegiensis Massal S Chile to Fueg —Mf
 breviramosa (St) Evans Falkl —Mt, Mf
 adglutinata Evans —Mt, Mf
 insularis Schiffn St Paul and New Amsterd Is —Mt
 variabilis Evans S Chile —Mt

leptostachya Evans Related to the former. —Mt
nudinutia (St) Evans S Chile to W Patag. —Mf

Metzgeria Raddi (about 50) Well developed trop, some widely spread N hemisph in oceanic climates

decrescens St S Chile to W Patag. —Mf

decipiens (Massal.) Schiffn et Gottsche Centr Chile to W Patag, Austral, N Zeal, Antipodes Is —Mt, Mf

multiformis Evans Closely related to the former. — Mt, Mf

violacea (Ach.) Dumort Centr and S Chile, Fueg, Argent, W and S Afr, N Zeal, Antip Is Brought to *M decipiens* as a variety by HODGSON (*136* 278).—Mf

Hymenophytum Dumort (5) S Amer, Ind, Austral, Tasm, N Zeal, Melanes

flabellatum (Labill.) Dumort Colomb, Chile, Austral, Tasm, N Zeal, N Caled, Fiji —Mf

Symphyogyna Nees et Mont (39) Trop and austral

circinata Nees et Mont Centr and S Chile —Mt, Mf

Hochstetteri Nees et Mont Falkl —Mt, Mf

hymenophyllum (Hook) Nees et Mont Trop Amer, Chile, Austral, Tasm, N Zeal —Mt, Mf Probably identical with *S podophylla* (Thunb) Mont et Nees from Centr and S Africa (S ARNELL, ms)

Pallavicinia S F Gray (about 25) Trop.–subtrop Colomb, Indomal, Kerguel, N Zeal

xiphoides (Tayl) St N Zeal —Mf

Monoclea Hook (2, 1 trop Amer)

Forsteri Hook S Chile-W Patag, N Zeal —Mt, Mf

Androcryphaea Nees (1, Noteroclada Tayl)

confluens (Tayl) Nees Mex, Colomb-Chile, south to Fueg, Braz, Argent, Falkl, Kerguel —Mf

Fossombronia Raddi (26) Trop.–subtrop, extending into cooler regions

fernandeziensis St —Mt

Anthocerotales

Anthoceros L (about 140) Mainly trop

Skottsbergii (St ex p.) Evans —Mt, Mf

Megaceros Campb (about 40) Mex, W Ind, S Amer south to Chile, Réunion, Indomal-N Zeal, Oceania

fuegiensis St W Patag–Fueg Related to neotrop sp —Mt, Mf

Jungermanniales

Solenostoma Mitt (30) Subcosmop, but now partly referred to *Aplozia* Dum, partly to *Plectocolea*

crassulum (Mont) St S Chile —Mf

obtusiflorum St —Mt

rostratum St —Mf

Jamesoniella Spruce (20) Mainly trop.–subtrop (1 Engl) but also important in the austral zone

colorata (Lehm.) Spruce Centr. Amer., S. Amer. south to Fueg., Falkl., Tristan da C., S. Afr., Marion I. Kerguel. L. Austral., Tasm., N. Zeal., Auckl., Campb. and Antipodes Is. —Mt, Mf
maluina St. Falkl. —Mt
ocnops St. S. Chile, south to Fueg., S. Georgia —Mt
grandiflora (Lehm. et Gottsche) Spruce Colomb.–Chile, south to Fueg., Tristan da C., Marion I., Tasm. —Mt

Anastrophyllum Nees (31) Very widely distributed
leucocephalum (Tayl.) Spruce Venez., Peru, Fueg. —Mf

Acrobolbus Nees (11) Essentially austral. 2 S. Amer., 1 subantarct., 1 Himal., 7 Austral., N. Zeal., N. Caled.
exasus (Mitt.) Schiffn. W. Patag., Fueg. Kerguel. —Mf

Anastrepta (Lindb.) Schiffn. (4) 2 southern S. Amer., 1 Alaska–Eur.–E. As.–Hawaii, 1 Himal.
bifida St. S. Chile Valdivia, Magell. —Mt, Mf

Plagiochila Dumort. (about 1000) Very few bor. zone, trop., particularly neotrop. but well represented southern S. Amer.
gayana Gottsche S. Chile —Mt
fasciata St. Chiloé —Mt, Mf
hyadesiana Besch. et Massal. S. Chile, Fueg. —Mt, Mf
deformifolia St. W. Patag. —Mf
chiloensis St. S. Chile to W. Patag. —Mf
rectangulata St. W. Patag. —Mf
remotidens St. S. Chile, Magell. —Mf
fuscobrunnea St. Almost too closely related to *P. rubescens* Lehm. et Lindenb. (Syn. *P. chilensis* St. according to HERZOG *130*) —Mt, Mf
pudetensis St. Chiloe —Mt
homomalla St. W. Patag. —Mf
ncesiana Lindenb. S. Chile south to Magell. —Mt
riparia St. W. Patag. —Mt, Mf
squarrosa St. W. Patag. —Mt, Mf
robusta St. W. and L. Patag. Fueg. —Mf
elata Hook. f. et Tayl. Fueg. —Mf
Notarisii Lehm. Falkl. —Mt, Mf

Tylimanthus Mitt. (25) S. hemisph., best represented Australia. 1 W. Ind.
limbatus St. W. Patag. —Mt
silvaticus St. —Mf
densiretis Herz. —Mf
bilobatus St. —Mt

Mylia S. F. Gray (40–50) The majority neotrop. mountains (Mex., W. Ind., Centr. and S. Amer. south to Magell.), 4 Afr., 1 S. Georgia
repens (Mitt.) Herz. Magell., N. Zeal. —Mf
fuscovirens (Tayl.) St. See *130* 714. Centr. and S. Chile to Fueg. —Mf
ligulata (St.) Herz. W. Patag. —Mt

Lophocolea Dumort (250-300) Worldwide, main concentrations subantarct S Amer (60), S As-Oceania (35), and Austral-N Zeal (70)
    rotundifolia St W Patag, Fueg, Falkl —Mf
    fernandeziana St Centr Chile (Coquimbo) —Mt, Mf
    pallidevirens (Tayl) St Centr (Coquimbo) and S Chile to W Patag, Fueg, Falkl, Marion I —Mt, Mf
    papulosa St —Mt
    attenuata St S Chile to W Patag —Mt, Mf
    textilis Tayl W Patag -Fueg, Falkl —Mf
    divergenticiliata St S Chile W Patag, Fueg —Mt, Mf
    muricata Nees W Ind, S Braz, Centr and S Chile to W Patag, S Afr, Réunion, Java, N Guin E Austral, N Zeal —Mf
    angulata St —Mt
    chilensis St Chile —Mf
    submuricata Herz Near *muricata*, but also very close to *L fragrans* Tayl (atl-mediterr, 130 720) —Mt, Mf

Chiloscyphus Corda (150-200) Trop-subtrop, best developed S hemisph (about 50 Austral-Tasm-N Zeal, 8 subantarct Amer)
    integrifolius Lehm et Lindenb Centr Chile to Fueg —Mt Mf
    lobatus St W Patag, Fueg —Mf

Saccogyna Dumort (9-10) Braz 2, Chile 1, Eur -Macaron 1, Indomal-Polyn 2, Tasm-N Zeal 3 Hawaii
    squarristipula Herz S Chile to W Patag —Mt

Marsupidium Mitt (about 40) Austr circump, subantarct Amer, Austral-N Zeal
    piliferum St S Chile, E Austral, N Caled —Mt, Mf

Adelanthus Mitt (7) Widely scattered W Ind, Ecuad, Chile, Eur, St Helena
    sphalerus Hook f et Tayl W Patag-Fueg —Mt

Bazzania S F Gray (230) Worldwide
    cerina (St) Fulford S Chile, W Patag Falkl, Tristan d C —Mt, Mf
    peruviana (Lehm et Lindenb) Trev Peru, Chile to W Patag —Mt

Lepidozia Dumort (about 200) World-wide, but few north temp, most numerous trop-subtrop, many austr subantarct (70-80)
    sejuncta (Ångstr) St Mex, W Ind, S Braz, Azor, W and S Afr, Tasm —Mf
    bicuspidata Massal Centr Chile, W Patag, Fueg —Mt
    pseudozoopsis Herz S Chile to W Patag (*131* 51) —Mt
    fernandeziensis St S Chile (*130* 725) Near *L plumulosa* and *Lindenbergii* St (N Zeal) —Mt
    plumulosa Lehm et Lindenb S Chile to W Patag and Fueg, Falkl, N Zeal, Auckl Is, Antipodes Is —Mt
    fragillima Herz Related to Chilean species —Mt
    disticha St —Mt
    Jacquemontii St Centr Chile-Magell, Fueg —Mt, Mf

Herberta S F Gray (15) Widely scattered
    runcinata (Tayl) Herz S Chile to W Patag —Mt
Lepicolea Dumort (5) Scattered S hemisph
    ochroleuca (Spreng) Spruce S Braz, S Chile to Fueg, Cape —Mt, Mf
Lepidolaena Dumort (12) S temp and cold zones
    magellanica (Lam) Schiffn S Chile to Fueg, E Austral, Tasm, N Zeal —Mf
Trichocolea Dumort (32) 1 Bor zone, 19 trop Amer, 7 trop As-Oceania, 5 Austral-N Zeal
    opposita St Near *T australis* St (N Zeal) —Mt
    verticillata St S Chile to W and F Patag —Mt, Mf
Schistochila Dumort (83) Essentially southern austral-subantarct (20), Afr (7), Indomal-Oceania (35), Austral-N Zeal (21)
    berteroana (Hook) St S Chile —Mt, Mf
    Skottsbergii St Related to *S stratosa* (Mont) St (S Chile to Fueg) —Mt, Mf
    pachyla (Tayl) St W Patag-Magell —Mt
    splachnophylla (Tayl) St W Patag-Fueg, N Zeal —Mf
Balantiopsis (Nees) St (17) 1 Braz, 1 Queensl, the remainder austr subantarct
    cancellata (Nees) St S Chile to W Patag —Mf
    chilensis St S Chile to W Patag —Mf
    purpurata Mitt S Chile Determination uncertain —Mf
    hians Herz —Mt
    lancifolia St —Mt
Radula Dumort (220) Mainly trop-subtrop Bor zone (Eur, N Amer, 7), trop-subtrop Amer (66), Afr (37), Indomal-Oceania (69), Austral-N Zeal (29), subantarct (15)
    hastata St S Chile to Fueg —Mf
    microloba St S Chile —Mt, Mf
    Duseni St S Chile to W Patag —Mf
    Mitteni St Falkl —Mt, Mf
Madotheca Dumort (153) Trop-subtrop Amer (45), trop As-Oceania (67), Austral-N Zeal etc (12)
    chilensis Lehm et Lindenb var *fernandeziensis* Herz Centr Chile (Coquimbo, main sp S Chile to W Patag) —Mt, Mf
    subsquarrosa Nees et Mont S Chile to Fueg —Mt
Frullania Raddi (500–600) World-wide, but mainly trop and southern N Amer (35)
    Ecklom Spr (crassa Herz) Centr Chile to W Patag, W and S Afr —Mt
    chilensis St S Chile to W Patag —Mt
    lobulata Hook f et Wils W Patag, Fueg —Mf
    magellanica (Spreng) Web et Nees Centr and S Chile to Fueg, Tristan da C Tasm, Campb I —Mt, Mf
    stipatiloba St Centr Chile to W Patag —Mt

Lopholejeunea Spruce (74) Trop and austral, trop Amer (13), trop Afr (17), trop As.-Oceania (38), Austral-N Zeal (6)
    spinosa St.—Mt, Mf

Brachiolejeunea Spruce (65) Trop Amer (26), Chile (1) Afr (10), trop As.-Oceania (22), Austral-N Zeal (6)
    spruceana (Massal.) St. S Chile-Magell.—Mf

Harpalejeunea Spruce (57) Trop Amer (36), Chile (2), Afr (2), As.-Oceania (8), Austral-N Zeal (9)
    oxyota (Mont.) St. Centr (Coquimbo) and S Chile to W Patag Tristan da C —Mf
    setifera (St.) Herz Magell —Mf

Strepsilejeunea Spruce (47) Trop Amer, south to Chile (19), Afr (6), As (7), Austral-N Zeal (7), subantarct (8)
    acuminata (Lehm et Lindenb) St. S Chile —Mt
    squarrosula Herz —Mf
    macroloba Herz —Mf

Siphonolejeunea Herz (1)
    nudicalycina Herz Centr Chile (Coquimbo, *131* 65)—Mt, Mf

Lejeunea Lib (190) Pantrop, scarce toward the south
    reticulata Herz Related to Chilean sp —Mt, Mf

Aphanolejeunea Evans (13) Trop –subtrop
    asperrima St. S Chile —Mt
    diaphana Herz Centr Chile (Coquimbo, S ARNELL ms)—Mt

Cololejeunea Spruce (about 80) Mainly trop
    Skottsbergii Herz Nearly related to a species from N Zealand —Mt, Mf

Colura Dumort (30) Trop to subantarct, Amer (8), Magell (2), Eur (1), Afr (2), Indomal (16)
    bulbosa Herz W Patag (*131* 66) —Mf

The 124 Hepaticae, of which 25 (20.2 %) are endemic, belong to 47 genera (2.6:1), 27 are thallose, 97 foliose None have been reported from Santa Clara

Of the 27 *thallose* species 21 have been recorded from Masatierra and 23 from Masafuera, 4 (15 %) are known from Masatierra only, 7 (25 %) restricted to Masafuera 16 common to the two islands Of the 5 endemics 2 have been found on Masatierra only, 3 on both islands Endemism is stronger on Masatierra (25 %) than on Masafuera (13 %)

Of the 97 *foliose* species 59 occur on Masatierra and 67 on Masafuera, 30 (30.9 %) are restricted to Masatierra, 38 (39.2 %) to Masafuera, 29 (29.9 %) are found on both islands Endemic species 20 (21.6 %), of these 9 only on Masatierra, 5 only on Masafuera and 6 found on both islands

Of the 59 species recorded for Masatierra 15 are endemic in the islands (25.4 %), the corresponding figures for Masafuera are 67, 11 and 16.4 % After the discovery of *Siphonolejeunea* on the mainland of Chile there is no endemic genus in Juan Fernandez

Of the *total* number of species, 124, 80 occur on Masatierra and 90 on Masafuera, of these 20 (25 %) and 14 (16 5 %), respectively, belong to the endemic element, 34 species are restricted to Masatierra (27 4 %), 44 to Masafuera (35 5 %) and 46 (37 1 %) shared by the two islands The corresponding figures for the endemic species are Masatierra 11 (44 %) Masafuera 5 (20 %), both islands 9 (36 %), and for the non endemics 23 (23 2 %) 39 (39 4 %) and 37 (37 4 %) Of the 99 species also found elsewhere Masatierra has 60 and Masafuera 76 This island is richer in non endemic species many of which belong to higher altitudes

Geographical elements

I Andine-Chilean element — 97 (78 3 %)

a Endemic (20) Riccardia adglutinata and leptostachya, Metzgeria multiformis, Solenostoma obtusiflorum and rostratum, Plagiochila fuscobrunnea, Tylimanthus silvaticus, bilobatus and densiretis, Lophocolea papulosa, angulata and submuricata, Lepidozia fragillima and disticha, Schistochila Skottsbergii, Balantiopsis hians and lancifolia, Strepsilejeunea squarrosula and macroloba, Lejeunea reticulata

b Also known from Chile and not restricted to the extreme south (73) Marchantia berteroana and foliacea Riccardia fuegiensis, variabilis and nudimitra, Metzgeria decrescens, decipiens and violacea, Hymenophytum flabellatum, Symphyogyna circinata and hymenophyllum, Monoclea Forsteri, Androcryphaea confluens, Solenostoma crassulum, Jamesoniella colorata and grandiflora, Anastrophyllum leucocephalum, Anastrepta bifida, Plagiochila gayana, fasciata hyadesiana, deformifolia, chiloensis rectangulata remotidens pudetensis homomalla, neesiana, riparia, squarrosa and robusta, Tylimanthus limbatus, Mylia repens, fuscovirens and ligulata, Lophocolea fernandeziana, attenuata, divergenticiliata, chilensis and muricata, Chiloscyphus integrifolius, Saccogyna squarristipula, Marsupidium piliferum, Bazzania cerina and peruviana, Lepidozia bicuspidata, pseudozoopsis, fernandeziensis, plumulosa and Jacquemontii, Herberta runcinata Lepicolea ochroleuca, Lepidolaena magellanica, Trichocolea verticillata, Schistochila berteroana, Balantiopsis cancellata chilensis and purpurata, Radula hastata microloba and Duseni, Madotheca chilensis and subsquarrosa, Frullania Lekloni, chilensis, magellanica and stipatiloba, Brachiolejeunea spruceana, Harpalejeunea oxyota, Strepsilejeunea acuminata, Siphonolejeunea nudicalycina, Aphanolejeunea asperrima, Colura bulbosa

c Cosmopolitan (4) Plagiochasma rupestre, Reboulia hemisphaerica, Lunularia cruciata, Marchantia polymorpha

II Subantarctic-Magellanian element — 18 (14 5 %)

All non-endemic Riccardia brevinamosa, Symphyogyna Hochstetteri, Megaceros fuegiensis, Jamesoniella maluina and oenops, Acrobolbus excisus, Plagiochila elata and Notarisii, Lophocolea rotundifolia, pallidevirens and textilis, Chiloscyphus lobatus, Adelanthus sphalerus, Schistochila pachyla and splachnophylla, Radula Mittenii, Frullania lobulata, Harpalejeunea setifera

III Neotropical element — 5 (4 0 %)

a Endemic (4) Fossombronia fernandeziensis, Anthoceros Skottsbergii, Lopholejeunea spinosa, Aphanolejeunea diaphana

b Not endemic Lepidozia sejuncta

IV West Pacific element — 3 (2.4 %)

a Endemic (2) Trichocolea opposita, Cololejeunea Skottsbergii
b Not endemic Pallavicinia xiphoides

V Known from St Paul and New Amsterdam Is — 1 (0.8 %)

Riccardia insularis

The American element is in absolute dominance, 120 species, 96.8 %, belong to elements I–III. The Pacific group is very small, but as we shall find later, many species are austral and bicentric.

Table IV

Comparison between the Angiosperms, Pteridophytes and Bryophytes. Figures in %

A, Andine Chilean, M, Magellanian, N, Neotropical, P, West Pacific

	A	M	N	P
Angiosperms	46.9	10.2	12.9	17.7
Pteridophytes	64.1	7.5	17.0	9.4
Mosses	64.2	10.8	11.7	10.8
Hepatics	78.3	14.5	4.0	2.4

The lower percentage of Mosses in A, as compared with the Hepatics, may be due to imperfect knowledge of the distribution and to the fact that 11 moss species had to be left out of consideration.

V Lichenes.

What I have said above when dealing with the Bryophytes holds good of the Lichens in a still higher degree no lichenologist ever visited Juan Fernandez, and a non specialist is bound to pass over many species, collecting crustaceous lichens growing on hard basalt is not easy and generally time absorbing. Our collection is listed after ZAHLBRUCKNER (*296, 297*) where also the species found by other collectors, but not found by us, are included. Some changes had to be made, for instance, ZAHLBRUCKNER did not distinguish between *Sticta* and *Pseudocyphellaria* on my request, Dr R SANTESSON kindly revised the nomenclature. Some determinations in these and other genera were corrected by him (see vol II 886) Later he went over the proof sheets of this paper and added further corrections. I thank him for generous assistance.

It is to be regretted that ZAHLBRUCKNER did not indicate the distribution of the non-endemic species, and the statements in his Catalogus are too general. I have tried to collect further data from a number of papers on the flora of Chile and the Subantarctic and Antarctic regions (*1, 32, 73, 139, 176, 177, 182, 184, 295, 327-329*) but it was beyond my possibilities to search the entire literature. Dr A H MAGNUSSON, who kindly took the trouble to go over my list, supplied much useful information

SC = Santa Clara

Verrucariaceae

Verrucaria Schrad. (about 270). All parts of the world.
  microspora Nyl. N. Amer., Chile, Eur., Jap.—Mt.

Microglaena Koerb. (37). Eur., except 1 Braz., 1 Socotra, and the following.
  fernandeziana Zbr.—Mt, SC.

Dermatocarpaceae

Normandina Nyl. (1).
  pulchella Nyl. N. and S. Amer., south to Fueg., Eur., Afr., St. Paul s I., As., Hawaii, N. Zeal.—Mt.

Pyrenulaceae

Arthopyrenia Mass. (150). Trop.-subtrop.
  Cinchonae M. Arg. Widely distributed in the trop. zone, also Hawaii—Mt.
  aduexa M. Arg. var. **leptosperma** Zbr. The typ. sp. Braz.—Mf.
  planorbis M. Arg. Trop.-subtrop., also Hawaii—Mt.

Porina M. Arg. (235). All over the globe, south to N. Caled. and N. Zeal.
  fernandeziana Zbr. Belongs in the vicinity of *P. chlorotica* (Ach.) M. Arg., a cosmop. sp.—Mt.
  rufocarpella Zbr.—Mt.
  depressula Zbr. Possibly related to *P. exserta* M. Arg. (Braz.)—Mt, Mf.

Pyrenula Ach. (170). Widely distributed in the trop. zone.
  aspistea Ach. Trop., also Hawaii—Mt.
  mammillana Trev. Trop., Hawaii, S. Chile—Mt.
  Kunthii Fée. Trop.—Mt, Mf.

Astrotheliaceae

Pyrenastrum Eschw. (18). Trop.
  chilense Mont. Chile.—Mt.

Sphaerophoraceae

Sphaerophorus Pers. (8). Of wide distribution, centering S. hemisph.
  melanocarpus (Sw.) DC. Almost cosmop., Chile, south to Fueg., Falkl., N. Zeal., Auckl. and Campb. Is.—Mt, Mf.

Arthoniaceae

Arthonia Ach. (about 370). The majority trop.-subtrop.
  Cytisi Massal. var. **meridionalis** Zbr. The typ. sp. Eur.—Mt.
  subnebulosa Zbr. Related to *A. ephelodes* Nyl. (N. Caled.) and *scutula* Krmph. (Braz.)—Mt.
  berberina Zbr. Related to *A. varia* (Ach.) Nyl. (trop. Amer.)—Mt.
  complanata Fée. Pantrop., also Hawaii, Chile—Mt.

Graphidaceae

Graphis Adans. (about 280). The majority trop.-subtrop.
  intricata Fée. Widely distributed trop. zone—Mt.
  Dumastii Spreng. Trop.—Mt.

Phaeographina M Arg (80) Trop-subtrop
    sculpturata M Arg Trop-subtrop, S Amer, N Zeal —Mt

Chiodectonaceae

Enterostigma M Arg (2) 1 trop Amer and the following
    Skottsbergii Zbr —Mf

Dirinaceae

Dirina Fr (12) Of wide distribution
    limitata Nyl Chile —Mt

Lecanactidaceae

Schismatomma Fw et Koerb (80) Mainly warmer countries
    accedens (Nyl) Zbr Chile —Mt

Chrysotrichaceae

Byssocaulon Mont (5) Austral-Oceania
    niveum Mont Subtrop, north to Japan, south to Chile and N Zeal —Mt

Thelotremaceae

Ocellularia Spreng (over 100) Mainly warmer regions
    subdenticulata Zbr —Mf
Thelotrema (Ach) M Arg (over 100) Mainly warmer regions
    lepadinum Ach Widely distributed, also Hawaii, Chile, south to Fueg, N Zeal, Auckl Is —Mt, Mf

Diploschistaceae

Diploschistes Norm (30) Cold-temp, trop-alp
    actinostomus (Pers) Zbr N and S temp, Hawaii —Mt
    scruposus (Schreb) Norm N and S temp, S Chile, south to Fuegia —Mt

Gyalectaceae

Dimerella Trev (39) Mostly trop
    lutea (Dicks) Trev Widely distributed, also S Chile, Patag, Haw —Mt, Mf
Gyalecta Ach (60-70) Mainly colder climates
    jenensis (Batsch) Zbr N Amer, Eur, N Zeal —Mt
Pachyphiale Loennr (4) 2 S W Eur, 1 bor-temp, and the following
    cornea (With) Poetsch et Schiedem Eur, Chile —Mt

Coenogoniaceae

Coenogonium Ehrenb (30) Centr and trop S Amer, Afr, trop As, Austral
    velutinum Zbr S Chile (comm by R SANTESSON) —Mt
Racodium Fr (1)
    rupestre Pers N and S Amer (Staten I, comm by R SANTESSON), Eur —Mt

Collemaceae

Lemmopsis (Vain.) Zbr. (4) 1 temp. N. Amer. + Eur., 2 S.W. Eur., and the following
   polychidioides Zbr. —Mt

Physma Massal. (10) W. Ind., trop. As., Japan, Austral., N. Caled.
   chilense Hue Chile —Mt

Leptogium (Ach.) S. F. Gray (over 100) All over the world
   moluccanum (Pers.) Vain. Widely scattered, Hawaii also Chile —Mt, Mf
   tremelloides (L. fil.) S. F. Gray Trop.-temp. in Chile south to W. Patag., S. Georgia —Mt
   cyanescens (Ach.) Koerb. Temp.-subtrop., e.g. Hawaii, S. Amer. —Mt, Mf
   phyllocarpum (Pers.) Mont. Trop.-subtrop., S. Amer. Chile S. Afr., Philipp., Australia —Mt
   Menziesii (Sm.) Mont. Mount. of trop. Amer., Hawaii, Chile south to Fueg., Falkl., S. Georgia —Mf
   callithamnion (Tayl.) Nyl. Trop. Amer. —Mt

Pannariaceae

Parmeliella M. Arg. (40) Widely scattered, warm and cold climates
   nigrocincta (Mont.) M. Arg. Chile, south to Fueg., W. Afr. islands, Hawaii, Austral., N. Zeal. —Mt, Mf
   symptychia (Tuck.) Zbr —Mt
   pycnophora (Nyl.) R. Sant. var. *subdivisa* (Zbr.) R. Sant. W. Patag. (329). The typ. sp. N. Zeal. —Mt

Pannaria Del. (about 60) Widely spread over the world
   fuegiensis Zbr. Fueg. —Mt
   hilaris Zbr. —Mt
   rubiginosa Del. Scattered, e.g. Hawaii, Chile, Falkl., St. Helena Campb. I. —Mt
   rubiginosa var. **vulcanica** Zbr. Perhaps specifically distinct —Mt

Massalongia Koerb. (2, 1 E. As.)
   carnosa (Dicks.) Koerb. Mount. of N. Amer. and Eur., Falkl., N. Zeal. —Mf

Psoroma Nyl. (about 60) Mainly cold and temp., centering in N. Zeal. etc.
   vulcanicum Zbr. —Mf
   cephalodinum Zbr. —Mt
   pholidotum (Mont.) M. Arg. Chile, south to Fueg. —Mt
   sphinctrinum (Mont.) Nyl. S. Amer., also Chile south to Fueg., N. Zeal. —Mt, Mf
   dasycladum Zbr. —Mt
   angustisectum Zbr. —Mt

Stictaceae

Lobaria Schreb. (70) Mainly warmer countries
   crenulata (Del.) Trev. Trop. Amer., south to Chile, Hawaii Austral.-Oceania —Mt

Pseudocyphellaria Vain (with Sticta about 200) Humid trop to temp climates
    argyracea (Del) Vain Chile, S Afr, Madag, Mascar, Malays, Hawaii, N Zeal, Polyn —Mt, Mf
    intricata (Del) Vain S Amer Chile south to Fueg, Falkl, Ireland Macaron, Mascar, Cape, Tristan da C, Hawaii —Mt
    fragillima (Bab) S Amer Austral, N Zeal, Auckl and Campb Is —Mt
    subvariabilis (Nyl) Vain Philipp, Austral, N Zeal —Mt
    chloroleuca (Hook f et Tayl) Du Rietz S Chile to Fueg, N Zeal —Mf
    cinnamomea (Rich) Vain S Chile to Fueg Austral, Tasm, Philipp —Mt, Mf
    berteroana (Mont) —Mt
    hirsuta (Mont) Malme S Amer, Chile south to Fueg —Mt
    Guilleminii (Mont) S Chile-Fueg —Mt
    gilva (Ach) Malme S Chile to Fueg, Falkl, S Afr, Australia —Mt
    mougeotiana (Del) Vain Warmer countries, Hawaii, also Chile —Mt, Mf
    aurata (Ach) Vain Trop-subtrop, N Amer, Chile, W Eur, St Helena, Hawaii, Austral —Mt, Mf
    nitida (Tayl) Malme S Chile to W Patag, Fueg —Mf
    endochrysea (Del) Vain S Chile to Fueg, Falkl, S Georgia Austral N Zeal, Auckl and Campb Is —Mt, Mf
    Durvillei (Del) Vain S Chile to Fueg, Falkl, N Zeal —Mt
    flavicans (Hook f et Tayl) Vain W Patag-Fueg, Philipp, Hawaii Australia —Mt
    Freycineti (Del) Malme S Chile to Fueg, Falkl, S Georgia, Austral, Tasm, N Zeal Campb and Antipodes Is —Mt, Mf
    Richardi (Mont) Raes W Patag-Fueg, N Zeal, Auckl Is —Mt

Sticta Schreb
    Weigelii (Ach) Vain Widespread, also Hawaii, S Chile to Fueg, Austral, N Zeal —Mt
    lineariloba (Mont) Nyl S Amer, south to Magell —Mt
    latifrons A Rich Chile, N Zeal —Mt
    laciniata (Huds) Zbr S Amer —Mt

Nephroma Ach (27) N and S temp
    plumbeum Mont Chile —Mt
    cellulosum (Sm) Ach S Chile to Fueg, Tasm N Zeal —Mt
    antarcticum (Wulf) Nyl S Chile to Fueg, Tasm —Mt, Mf
    australe A Rich S Chile, N Zeal —Mt

Peltigera Pers (20) World-wide
    rufescens (Neck) Humb Cosmop, Patag, Fuegia, Falkl, S Georgia —Mt
    polydactyla (Neck) Hoffm Cosmop, Chile, south to Fueg, Falkl, Tristan da C, Marion I, Kerguel, Auckl and Campb Is —Mt, Mf

Lecideaceae

Lecidea (Ach) Th Fr (1000 or more) Preferably cold or temp climates
    avium Zbr Related to *L aeruginosa* Nyl (Chile) —Mt

inactiva Zbr —Mt
cyanosarca Zbr —Mt Mf
leucoplaca M Arg Chile —Mt
leucozonata Zbr —Mt
enteroleuca Nyl Temp Eur, etc St Helena, etc —Mt, Mf
latypea Ach Temp widely distributed —Mt
viridans Lamy Eur —Mt
mutabilis Fée N and S Amer, also Chile, W Eur —Mt
uterica Tayl S Amer, also Chile —Mf

Catillaria (Ach) Th Fr (about 150) Widespread N and S hemisph
intermixta Arn Widespread, south to N Zeal —Mt
melastegia (Nyl) Zbr S Amer, Chile south to Fueg N Zeal —Mt, Mf
endochroma (Fee) Zbr N and S Amer —Mt
leucochlora (Mont) Zbr Chile —Mt, Mf
theobromina Zbr —Mt

Megalospora Mey et Flot (about 50) Warmer regions
versicolor (Fee) Zbr var **microcarpa** Zbr The typ sp S Amer, N Zeal —Mt

Bacidia (De Not) Zbr (at least 200) World-wide
endoleuca Kickx Almost cosmop, also S Amer, N Zeal —Mt, Mf
arceutina (Ach) Arn var **hyposcotina** Zbr The typ sp Eur —Mt
delapsans Zbr Hawaii —Mt
subluteola (Nyl) A Zbr Braz —Mf

Lopima Th Fr (about 80) Mainly temp
bullata (Mey et Flot) Zbr Ecuador Chimborazo —Mf

Lopadium Koerb (about 50) Almost cosmop
leucoxanthum (Spreng) Zbr var **albidius** Zbr The typ sp subtrop, south to Austral and N Zeal Hawaii —Mt
sp, different from the former, described as *Myxodictyon lopadioides* by ZAHLBRUCKNER p 383 Chile —Mt

Rhizocarpon DC (about 90) Cosmopol, cold to temp climates
geographicum (L) DC Cold and temp, both hemisph, Patag, Fueg, Falkl, Kerguel, W Antarct —Mf
microspermum Zbr Similar to the following sp —Mf
obscuratum (Ach) Massal var **deminutum** Zbr The typ sp cold and temp climates —Mf

Phyllopsoraceae

Phyllopsora M Arg (25) Trop –subtrop
parvifolia (Pers) M Arg Widespread, also Chile, Hawaii and N Zeal —Mt

Cladoniaceae

Baeomyces Pers (34) Majority trop, 7 N Zeal
chilensis (Mont) Cromb Chile —Mt, Mf

Cladonia (Hill) Vain (about 280) All over the world
pycnoclada (Pers) Nyl Boliv, S Chile to Fueg, Falkl, Tristan da C —Mt,

Mf To this belongs *C alpestris* of ZAHLBRUCKNER 296 370, a species not occurring in the south hemisphere (SANTESSON 327 and in letter)

    bacillaris (S F Gray) Nyl Very widespread, Chile, Fueg Falkl, Campb I —Mt

    didyma Vain Mex -Fueg, Austral, N Caled Hawaii —Mt

    coccifera (L) Willd Very widespread, Chile, Patag, Fueg, Falkl, Tristan da C, W Antarct —Mt, Mf

    aggregata (Sw) Ach N and S Amer, Chile to Fueg, Falkl St Helena, S Afr Madag, Auckl and Campb Is, Macquarie I, Asia Hawaii —Mt, Mf

    furcata (Huds) Schrad Cosmopol, Chile to Fueg, Falkl, S Georgia, W Antarct, Antipodes Is, Hawaii —Mt

    gracilis (L) Willd Cosmopol, Chile to Fueg, Falkl, S Georgia, Tristan da C, Hawaii Kerguel, W Antarct —Mt, Mf

    pyxidata (L) Fr Cosmopol, Chile to Fueg, Falkl, Tristan da C, Kerguel, St Paul's I, Hawaii —Mf

    fimbriata (L) Fr Cosmopol, Chile to Fueg, Falkl, Marion I, Kerguel, W Antarct, Auckl and Campb Is, Hawaii —Mt, Mf

    pityrea (Flk) Fr Cosmopol, Falkl Tristan da C, Hawaii —Mt, Mf

Stereocaulon Schreb (about 90) N and S temp, trop -subtrop mountains

    patagonicum M Lamb S Chile and Patag to Fueg, Falkl —Mt, Mf

    ramulosum (Sw) Raensch N and S Amer, Chile south to Magell, N Zeal —Mt, Mf

    implexum Th Fr S Amer, south to Fueg, N Zeal —Mt, Mf (f *compactus* (Zbr) M Lamb)

Acarosporaceae

Acarospora Massal (over 200) World-wide

    smaragdula (Wahlenb) Massal var N temp —Mf

    xanthophana (Nyl) Jatta S Amer mountains —SC

Pertusariaceae

Coccotrema M Arg (1)

    granulatum (Hook f et Tayl) R Sant n comb (C curbitula M Arg, Porina granulata Hook f et Tayl) Chile Valdiv -Fueg, Ceyl, Jap, Philipp, N Zeal —Mt

Pertusaria DC (about 200) World-wide

    leioplaca (Ach) Schaer Cosmop —Mf

    polycarpa Krph var **monospora** Zbr The typ sp Braz —Mf

    hadrocarpa Zbr Similar to *A cerebrinula* Zbr (Falkl) —Mt, Mf

    Skottsbergii Zbr Related sp in Chile —Mt, SC

Melanaria Erichs (15) N and S Amer, Eur, S Afr As, N Zeal

    melanospora (Nyl) Erichs S Amer, also Chile —Mt, SC Mf

Lecanoraceae

Lecanora Ach (over 200) World-wide

    masafuerensis Zbr Close to *L submersa* (Fee) Vain (Braz) —Mf

coarctata (Sm.) Ach. Widespread temp., Chile —Mf
atra (Huds.) Ach. Cosmop., Chile, Falkl., Hawaii —Mt, Mf
Ingae Zbr. —Mt, Mf
albellina M. Arg. var. **validior** Zbr. The typ. sp. Fueg. —Mf
dispersa (Pers.) Flk. Widespread N. hemisph. —Mt, Mf
polytropa (Ehrh.) Ach. Cosmop., Chile, Falkl., W. Antarct., Hawaii —Mf
chrysoleuca (Sm.) Ach. W. Arct., Eur. mountains, Antarct., etc. —Mt
saxicola (Poll.) Ach. N. Amer., Eur., ?Chile —Mt

Placopsis Nyl. (31) Widely distrib., but mainly austral, 18 southern S. Amer.
chilena M. Lamb. Chile —Mf
fuscidula M. Lamb. S. Chile to Fueg., Tristan da C. —Mt, Mf
parellina (Nyl.) M. Lamb. Boliv. And., Chile to Fueg., Java, S. Austral., N. Zeal., Hawaii —Mt
gelida (L.) Ach. Circumpol. Arct. and temp. oceanic, Chile, Tristan da C., Kerguel., Java, N. Zeal., Hawaii —Mf (var. *subreagens* M. Lamb, but identity doubtful)

Candelariella M. Arg. (27) N. and S. Amer., Eur.
vitellina M. Arg. Widespread, Chile, Falkl., Hawaii —Mt, Mf

Myxodictyon Massal. (3, 1 Australia)
chrysostictum (Tayl.) Mass. Chile, N. Zeal. —Mt *M. lopadioides* Zbr. 296:383 is a species of *Lopadium* (SANTESSON in letter)

Parmeliaceae

Parmelia (Ach.) De Not. (about 400) World-wide
laevigata (Sm.) Ach. Widespread temp. and trop., also Hawaii and Chile —Mt
laevigatula Nyl. Braz. —Mt
revoluta Flk. Widespread temp.-trop. Also Hawaii —Mf
cetrata Ach. Very widespread temp. and trop., also Hawaii —Mt, SC, Mf
saxatilis (L.) Ach. Widespread, in Chile south to Fueg., Falkl., W. Antarct. —Mt
conspersa (Ehrh.) Ach. Cosmop., also Hawaii, Falkl. —Mt, SC, Mf
abstrusa Vain. Braz. —Mf
perlata Ach. Widespread, also Hawaii and S. Chile —Mt
nilgherrensis Nyl. Trop.-subtrop. —Mf
pilosella Hue N. Amer. to Mex., Eur. —Mt, Mf
piloselloides Zbr. —Mt
cetrarioides Del. Very widespread —Mf
microsticta M. Arg. Trop. Amer. —Mt
caperata (L.) Ach. Temp. zones, Chile, Hawaii —Mt, Mf
soredica Nyl. Calif., Mex. —Mf

Menegazzia Mass. (30) Few north hemisph., majority S. Amer. (11) and Austral.-Tasm.-N. Zeal. (14)
sanguinascens (Raes) R. Sant. (328:11, Parmelia pertusa (Schrad) Schaer in 296:389) Valdiv. to Fueg. —Mt, Mf

Ramalina Ach. (about 100) World wide
    linearis (Sw.) Ach. Warmer regions, Chile, Fueg., Falkl., N. Zeal.—Mt
    usnea (L.) Howe Jr. Trop.-temp., N. Amer., Chile —Mf
Usnea Wigg. (about 100) Cosmop.
    dasypogoides Nyl. Rodriguez I.—Mt, Mf
    florida (L.) Hoffm. Very widespread, also Chile —Mf
    subtorulosa (Zbr.) Motyka Easter I.—Mf
    angulata Ach. N. Amer., south to Mex., S. Amer. to Chile —Mf

Caloplacaceae

Blastenia (Massal.) Th. Fr. (about 60) World wide
    fernandeziana Zbr.—Mt, SC
    ferruginea (Huds.) Massal. —Mt. Determination probably incorrect acc. to Dr. MAGNUSSON
Bombyliospora De Not. (25) Mostly trop.-subtrop.
    dolichospora (Nyl.) Zbr. Chile —Mt
Caloplaca Th. Fr. (over 100) World wide
    clandestina Zbr.—Mf
    Selkirkii Zbr.—Mt, Mf
    rubina Zbr. Easter I.—Mt, SC, Mf
    isidioclada Zbr.—Mf
    subcerina (Nyl.) Zbr. var. **aurantiaca** Zbr. Trop.—Mf
    elegans (Link) Th. Fr. var. *australis* Zbr. Chile, W. Patag. The typ. sp. cold to temp. N. and S. hemisph.—Mt, SC, Mf
    orthoclada Zbr. In the vicinity of *C. Felipponei* Zbr. (Urug.)—Mf

Teloschistaceae

Teloschistes Norm. (12) World wide
    flavicans (Sw.) M. Arg. Widespread trop.-subtrop., in S. Amer. south to Fueg., Falkl.—Mt

Buelliaceae

Buellia De Not. (about 200) World wide
    concinna (Stzbgr.) Th. Fr. var. *oceanica* Zbr. The typ. sp. Eur.—SC
    siphoniatula Zbr. Similar to *B. posthabita* (Nyl.) Zbr. (Colomb.) and *falklandica* Darb. (Falkl.)—Mt
    stellulata (Tayl.) Mudd Cosmop. Chile, Kerguel.—Mt, SC, Mf
    halophila M. Arg. Australia—Mt
    halophiloides Zbr. Easter I.—Mt
    fernandeziana Zbr. Easter I.—Mt
    masafuerana Zbr.—Mf
    barrilensis Zbr.—Mf

Physciaceae

Pyxine (Fr.) Nyl. (16) Warmer regions
    curvatula Zbr.—Mt

Physcia (Schreb.) Vain. (100-150) Cosmop., most numerous temp. regions
   picta (Sw.) Nyl. Widespread trop.-subtrop. Also Hawaii —Mt

Anaptychia Koerb. (30) Widespread mainly warmer regions
   hypoleuca (Muhlb.) Massal. Widespread, also Hawaii —Mt
   pectinata (Zbr.) R. Sant. Patag. (Nahuelhuapi), Fueg.—Mt

Hymenolichenes

Cora Fr. (8) Trop.-subtrop.
   pavonia (Sw.) Ir. Mex.-Chile, south to Fueg., St. Helena —Mt Mf

The list includes 194 species, 103 (53 %) of these are restricted to Masatierra, including 3 also found on Santa Clara, 2 (1 %) have only been encountered on this islet, 39 (20 %) only on Masafuera, 50 (25.7 %) are listed for both islands, 6 of them also found on Santa Clara. The number of endemic species is 36 (18.5 %), a number likely to be reduced when the lichen flora of South America becomes better known: some species described by ZAHLBRUCKNER as endemic in Juan Fernandez have later been found on the mainland or on Hawaii. New discoveries will, on the other hand, be made in the islands.

Masatierra has 153 species, of which 26 (17 %) are endemic in Juan Fernandez, the corresponding figures for Santa Clara are 11 and 3 (27.3 %) and for Masafuera 89 and 15 (16.8 %). Masatierra is richer in lichen species than Masafuera: this may have something to do with the greater variety of substratum offered by the numerous species of trees and shrubs inhabiting only Masatierra. Of 100 corticolous species 62 are restricted to Masatierra, 16 to Masafuera and 22 occur on both islands, thus 84 species have been collected on the former and only 38 on the latter.

The greater wealth of Masatierra is also shown in the number of endemic species found only on Masatierra, 21 (of 36) or 58.3 %, 3 were found also on Santa Clara. The figure for Masafuera is 10 = 27.7 %, of these 5 belong to the highland above 1000 m. Only 5 species (14 %) have been found on both islands. I suppose that the superiority of Masatierra depends on the greater variation of habitat. Future research will, I suppose, yield numerous additional species, but I do not expect that the relation between the islands will be much altered.

It is difficult to arrive at a geographical classification of the lichens because in too many cases only very general information is given: "in the tropics", "in warmer regions", "in temperate regions" and so forth, and "cosmopolitan" is used too generously. Statements suggesting the most surprising disjunctions are not uncommon, some are probably due to wrongly named specimens. Unfortunately the lichen flora of Chile is not very well known. I have tried to find out if a species called cosmopolitan has been recorded for Chile. Many world-wide lichens have been found in Juan Fernandez, if also found in Chile they were referred to the Chilean element.

I Andine-Chilean element — 106 (62.4 %)

a Endemic species supposed to be most nearly related to Chilean species (7) Psoroma vulcanicum, cephalodinum, dasycladum and angustisectum, Pseudocyphellaria berteroana, Lecidea avium, Pertusaria Skottsbergii

b Also known from Chile (88) Verrucaria microspora, Normandina pulchella, Pyrenula mammillana, Pyrenastrum chilense, Sphaerophorus melanocarpus, Arthonia complanata, Dirina limitata, Schismatomma accedens, Byssocaulon niveum, Thelotrema lepadinum, Diploschistes scruposus, Dimerella lutea, Pachyphiale cornea, Coenogonium velutinum, Racodium rupestre, Physma chilense, Leptogium moluccanum, tremelloides, cyanescens, phyllocarpum and Menziesii, Parmeliella nigrocincta and pycnophora var., Pannaria rubiginosa, Psoroma pholidotum and sphinctrinum, Lobaria crenulata, Pseudocyphellaria argyracea, intricata, cinnamomea, hirsuta, Guilleminii, gilva, mougeotiana and aurata, Sticta Weigelii, lineariloba and latifrons, Nephroma plumbeum and australe, Peltigera rufescens and polydactyla, Lecidea leucoplaca, mutabilis and icterica, Catillaria melastegia and leucochlora, Rhizocarpon geographicum, Phyllopsora parvifolia, Baeomyces chilensis, Cladonia pycnoclada, bacillaris, didyma, coccifera, aggregata, furcata, gracilis, pyxidata, fimbriata and pityrea, Stereocaulon ramulosum and implexum, Coccotrema granulatum, Melanaria melanospora, Lecanora coarctata, atra and polytropa, Placopsis chilena, fuscidula, parellina and gelida, Candelariella vitellina, Myxodictyon chrysostictum, Parmelia saxatilis, laevigata, conspersa, perlata and caperata, Menegazzia sanguinascens, Ramalina linearis and usnea, Usnea florida and angulata, Bombyliospora dolichospora, Caloplaca elegans, Buellia stellulata, Theloschistes flavicans, Coia pavonia

c Widespread to cosmopolitan species expected to occur on the mainland of Chile (11) Diploschistes actinostomus, Pseudocyphellaria fragillima, Sticta laciniata, Catillaria intermixta and endochroma, Bacidia endoleuca, Pertusaria leioplaca, Parmelia revoluta, cetrata and cetrarioides, Physcia picta

II Subantarctic-Magellanian element — 14 (8.2 %)

a Endemic Pertusaria hadrocarpa

b Also in W Patagonia, Fuegia etc (13) Pannaria fuegiensis, Pseudocyphellaria chloroleuca, nitida, endochrysea, Durvillei, flavicans Freycinetii and Richardi, Nephroma cellulosum and antarcticum, Stereocaulon patagonicum, Lecanora albellina (endem var), Anaptychia pectinata

III Neotropical element — 26 (15.3 %)

Endemic, or found or expected in South America, but not recorded for Chile

a Endemic (5) Arthonia subnebulosa and berberina, Enterostigma Skottsbergii, Lecanora masafuerensis, Caloplaca orthoclada

b Not endemic, some perhaps to be expected in Chile (14) Arthopyrenia Cinchonae, adnexa and planorbis, Phaeographina sculpturata, Leptogium callithamnion, Megalospora versicolor (endem var), Bacidia subluteola, Toninia bullata, Acarospora xanthophana, Pertusaria polycarpa (endem var), Parmelia laevigatula, abstrusa and microsticta, Anaptychia hypoleuca

c Widespread tropical-subtropical species, probably also occurring in South America (7) Pyrenula aspistea and Kunthii, Graphis intricata and Dumastii, Lopadium leucoxanthum (endem var), Parmelia nilgherrensis, Caloplaca subcerina (endem var)

IV Pacific element — 7 (4 1 %)

Pseudocyphellaria subvariabilis, Bacidia delapsans Usnea subtorulosa, Caloplaca rubina, Buellia halophila, fernandeziana and halophiloides

V Boreal element — 16 (9 4 %)

a Endemic Lemmopsis polychidioides

b Not endemic (15) Arthonia cytisi (endem var), Gyalecta jenensis, Massalongia carnosa, Lecidea enteroleuca latypea and viridans, Bacidia arceutina (endem var), Rhizocarpon obscuratum (endem var) Acarospora smaragdula, Lecanora dispersa, chrysoleuca and saxicola Parmelia pilosella and soredica, Buellia concinna (endem var)

VI Only reported from Juan Fernandez and Rodriguez I

Usnea dasypogoides

The following 22 endemic species had to be left out, their taxonomic relations being unknown Microglaena fernandeziana, Porina depressula fernandeziana and rufocarpella, Ocellularia subdenticulata, Parmeliella symptychia, Pannaria hilaris Lecidea inactiva, cyanosarca and leucozonata, Catillaria theobromina, Rhizocarpon microspermum, Lecanora Ingae, Parmelia piloselloides, Blastenia fernandeziana, Caloplaca clandestina, Selkirkii and isidioclada Buellia siphomatula masafuerana and bairilensis, Pyxine curvatula — further, Lopadium sp, and the dubious Blastenia sp have been excluded The percentages were calculated with 170 as a total

VI. Fungi.

Our knowledge of the fungus flora is very limited and time did not permit us to pay due attention to this group Of *Basidiomycetes* about 40 species were identified by ROMELL (*207*) including those enumerated by JOHOW (several species doubtful) Endemic species few KEISSLER's list of *Ascomycetes* (*159, 160*), with additions by ARWIDSSON (*311*), short as it is — only 31 species — gives some idea of the relation between the geographical elements Of the 29 named species, 9 were known before from S America (mostly Chile) and 1 from N America 5 are widespread and 5 endemic, one of these belonging to an endemic genus *Limacinia scoriadea* (Berk) Keissl is also known from Chile, Java and New Zealand Three of the endemic genera of Compositae have their special rusts the endemic *Euphrasia* is attacked by the same *Uredo* that is found on two species of sect *Trifidae* in Chile, *Azara fernandeziana* by the rust known from *A integrifolia* in Chile, and *Rubus geoides* is accompanied by the same parasite as in Fuegia (*159*)

Of *Gasteromycetes* only 2 named species were reported, of these *Ileodictyon gracile* Berk is of geographical interest S America, S Africa, Australia and New Zealand, the second species was known before from N America and Samoa (*102*)

The *Myriophyta*, 18 species, are more or less cosmopolitan (*101*)

I have tried above to indicate where the native plants have their nearest stations outside the islands or, if endemic, where their closest relatives occur. Statistics like this serve to assign to a local flora its position within a certain floristic region and, when dealing with an oceanic island, to trace the sources from where its living world is likely to have been derived. The position generally assigned to Juan Fernandez is that of an outpost from South America. In ENGLER'S Syllabus the islands form the "Gebiet von Juan Fernandez und Masafuera" under "Zentral- und sudamerikanisches Florenreich", it is characterized thus: "Gattungen vorzugsweise verwandt mit denen der chilenischen Ubergangsprovinz", i.e. Central Chile and the Valdivian forest region, ENGLER's transitional belt between the Andean and Magellanian provinces. GOOD (*109*) distinguished a "Region of Juan Fernandez" under his "Neotropical Kingdom", giving it the same rank as the "Amazone Region", the "Andean Region", etc. We have seen that there is an unmistakable floristic agreement between Juan Fernandez and South Chile, but also that it is far from complete, and both ENGLER and GOOD were well aware of the presence of elements that had little to do with the flora of the mainland. They were barely recognized by JOHOW (see above p. 215) who, with his faith in unlimited transoceanic dispersal, paid little attention to them, they were too few to disturb the Chilean picture. Not until the flora had become better known did its strange features stand out in a clearer light. It is surprising that GUILLAUMIN who knew and quoted the synopsis published in vol. II of this work (*229*) failed to recognize them. In his paper on the floristic divisions of the Pacific he states that Juan Fernandez lies outside Oceania and he includes it in his discussion only for the sake of comparison. The flora is characterized as follows (*118*: 931): "Sur 142 Phanérogames indigenes, la moitié sont endemiques mais apparentees aux espèces chiliennes, les autres sont cosmopolites ou Sudamericaines, surtout chiliennes." It is not easy to understand how he arrived at this conclusion. On the other hand, some authors were led astray by the *difference* between the islands and the continent. ERMEL, who got his impression from a short visit to Masatierra, wrote (*91*: 48)

> muss die Zusammengehorigkeit dieser Insel zum amerikanischen Festlande, zu welcher Ansicht deren geringe geographische Entfernung von selbst hinleiten konnte, aufs nachdrucklichste in Abrede gestellt werden, weil die beiderseitige Flora and Fauna zu grosse Verschiedenheiten aufweist, wo wir an geeigneter Stelle die notigen Beweise beibringen werden. Die Gestaltung der Flora ordnet die Inselgruppe vielmehr dem australischen Weltteile zu, von dem der grosste Teil heruntergegangen ist.

It is hardly necessary to mention that his proofs were based on his ignorance of the composition of the island flora and very likely also of the floras of Australia and Chile.

Chapter II

Sources of the island flora as judged by the total distribution of the geographical elements distinguished, with special reference to the composition of the Chilean flora.

I have attempted above to describe the distribution of the non endemic species, to state where the endemics have their relatives, if any and to distinguish a number of geographical elements. Now I shall proceed a little further and look at the matter from a wider horizon. A species was called Chilean because it is found also in Chile or has its relatives in the south Andean flora, or it was referred to a Magellanian group because it occurs only in the farthest south of the continent and so forth, but in order to know something of the genesis and history of each group we cannot stop here. We shall find that our "Chilean element", Chilean from our insular viewpoint, consists of several types, each with its own distribution pattern. To speak with WULFF (291 203), until now we occupied ourselves with the *geographic* elements, now we shall try to trace the *genetic* ones "species grouped according to their region of origin thus reflecting the genesis of a given flora". He very properly adds "To determine the region of origin of a species"—and indeed also of a genus or family—"is often a very difficult matter, requiring a monographic study." With regard to Juan Fernandez, the genetic elements are congruent to WULFF's 'migration elements'.

I. Angiospermae.

Of the two species of *Stipa*, *neesiana* is distributed from Mexico through the tropical Andes to Central Chile and east to Brazil, Argentina and Uruguay, *laevissima* (Nassella) a typical Andean species, the former is neotropic, the latter Chilean, extending north into Peru and east into Argentina. Almost the same area is occupied by *Piptochaetium bicolor*, a genus limited to extratropical South America.

Podophorus is a unique anomaly without known neotropical affinities, as it were, a far travelled member of an Arcto tertiary flora, if its affinity with *Brachyelytrum* hits the mark, in PILGER's opinion it sides with *Megalachne*.

The species of *Chaetotropis* were referred to the neotropical group—"tropical" not to be taken in a purely climatic sense, because a species included under this heading may just as well be subtropical and even extend into a temperate zone.

Agrostis masafuerana and the bicentric *A magellanica* were linked together, but only provisionally, because in a large and world-wide genus like *Agrostis* the relationships cannot be safely judged without a thorough taxonomic genetic study of the whole genus. Assuming that PILGER was right, Antarctica becomes involved, and the two species—and probably others as well—should be classified as "Old Antarctic", or, as I now prefer to term them, Antarcto-tertiary (corresponding to Arcto-tertiary). An Antarcto-tertiary taxon is not necessarily of Antarctic ancestry, strictly spoken it certainly should be, but there are numerous cases where the point of origin was either the South American or the Australasian-New Zealand centre, and Antarctica only served as a transcontinental route of migration.

Trisetum chromostachyum is Chilean, but the genus is both N and S temperate, perhaps originally Arcto-tertiary? *Danthonia collina* and *Koeleria mucrathera* also are Chilean, but the distribution pattern of the genera indicates that Antarctica eventually was involved in their history.

Megalachne, temporarily referred to *Bromus* but once more stated to be an independent genus, is a relict type with unknown history, eventually a remnant of a pre-Andean flora (comp. above p. 217).

The genus *Chusquea* belongs to the neotropical element in the flora of Chile, and the same is true of the species of *Cyperus*. *Scirpus nodosus* and *cernuus* are circumpolar seaside plants and most likely thalassochorous, if Antarctica had a share in their earlier history is impossible to say, but it is not improbable. *Eleocharis* is another large world-wide genus, perhaps too wide-spread to allow us to locate its place of origin.

Oreobolus. The Antarcto-tertiary character of *Oreobolus* can hardly be disputed, it is often referred to as a classical example of an Antarctic genus. Of the 6 species recognized by KÜKENTHAL, 1 (with 2 varieties) is found in S and E Australia, Tasmania and New Zealand, 2 in N E New Guinea, one of them extending to Borneo, 1 in N Sumatra and Malacca, 1 in Hawaii, and *O. obtusangulus* in Chile from the cordilleras of Valdivia to Fuegia, the Falkland Is. and Juan Fernandez. [A seventh species, *O. pfeifferianus* Barros, was identified by KÜKENTHAL (164 VIII) with *pumilio* var. *pectinatus*].

Cladium (164 XII) is wide ranging but it is not cosmopolitan in spite of the large areas occupied by *C. mariscus* L. and its varieties, among which *jamaicense* is circumpolar and distributed also south of the equator. The main distribution of subg. *Machaerina* (incl. Vincentia), where *C. scirpoideum* of Juan Fernandez belongs, is palaeotropical with 11 species (Madagascar, Mascarene Is., Australia, Lord Howe I., New Guinea, Indonesia, Oceania), 5 are neotropical (W. Indies, Brazil). Its austral character is clear enough. The closest relative of *scirpoideum* is not an American species but *C. angustifolium* (Gaud.) Benth. et Hook. fil. (New Guinea, Tahiti, Hawaii). Subg. *Baumea*, with 29 scattered from Australia, where there are 18 species, over the Indomalayan region west to Ceylon, north to Hongkong and Japan, east to Melanesia and Hawaii, has 15 in Australia–Tasmania–New Zealand and 1 in the region of Madagascar and Mascarene Is. Together the two subgenera cover the 3 sectors, the African, the Australian-Malaysian and the American. In the centre of this vast area lies Antarctica or, as it were, Gondwana Land. The history of *Cladium* may well lead back to the Mesozoic, and it seems natural to refer the genus to the Antarcto-tertiary element. The same applies to *Uncinia*, one of the generally recognized Antarctic genera, represented in Juan Fernandez by 5 species, 2 of them endemic. Within the South American sector are 13 species distributed along the Andes with a concentration toward the south, one species going north as far as Mexico and the West Indies, 1 extending east from Fuegia to the Falkland Is and Tristan da Cunha. On the opposite side of Antarctica are 18 species, 14 of these indigenous in New Zealand, where 8 are endemic, the remainder scattered along the route Macquarie I–Auckland and Campbell Is–Tasmania–Australia–New Zealand–Lord Howe and Norfolk Is, one New Zealand species reappears in Hawaii, another on Kerguelen and New Amsterdam I, and Marion I has an endemic species. Finally, 2 species are found in New Guinea, one of them also reported from Borneo, and the Philippines have 1 endemic species. Both sections of subg. *Eu-Uncinia* are represented in America, only Stenandriae in the opposite sector. The monotypical subg. *Pseudocarex* is Magellanian.

It is not easy to find one's way through the labyrinth of the enormous and still growing genus *Carex*, world wide but unbalanced as the tropics are poor in species in comparison with the temperate and cold zones. Our two island species, the endemic *C. berteroniana* and the south Andean *Banksii*, belong to different sections and different geographic groups, the former to sect Echinochlaenae of 20 species 16 are endemic in New Zealand (one with a variety on Norfolk I), 1 in Australia, 1 in Tasmania, the little known Chilean *C. lamprocarpa* Phil and *C. berteroniana* are far flung outposts, but it lies near at hand to assume that they or their ancestors migrated across Antarctica. *C. Banksii* belongs to Frigidae-Fuliginosae, a boreal group centering in Eurasia with one species in Pacific North America, but I cannot tell if *Banksii* comes near this species.

The systematic position of *Juania australis* was briefly discussed in 229 109 and above p. 202, but whether we bring it to Morenieae or Iriarteae or let it form a separate subtribe it remains a member of the neotropical element. HUTCHINSON followed BENTHAM and HOOKER in placing it next to *Ceroxylon*, but this genus is polygamo-monoecious and the stigma becomes basal in fruit. To me CROIZAT's opinion lacks foundation, he solves what he calls "a hopeless conflict among taxonomists" (71 85) by deriving *Juania* from "a massive center of origin of angiospermy at the Mascarenes" (p 103)

Ochagavia and *Hesperogreigia* belong to an Andean neotropical assemblage of genera, with close relatives in Chile

To judge from BUCHENAU's monograph of the Juncaceae in Pflanzenreich *Luzula masafuerana* must be referred to a group of Andean species, *L. racemosa* Desv (Mex–S Chile), *excelsa* Buch (Boliv), *Hieronymi* Buch (Argent), *Leyboldtii* Buch (Chile), and *chilensis* Nees et Mey (Chile, south to Fuegia), but in the same group we find *L. spicata* (L.) DC (Arct circump and Alpine) and *abyssinica* Parl (Ethiop, Brit E Afr), and the possibility that the Andine species are of boreal origin should be considered. On the other hand much speaks in favour of a southern origin of Juncaceae: the subantarctic genera *Marsippospermum* and *Rostkovia*, the isolated *Prionium* in South Africa, endemic Andine genera like *Oxychloe* and *Patosia*, well marked endemic species of *Luzula* in New Zealand and the Magellanian region, and the subantarctic-bicentric *Juncus scheuchzerioides* group. It is true that 4 of the 5 *Juncus* species reported from Juan Fernandez—some of them perhaps not native—inhabit the Andes, 3 going east to Brazil, Argentina and Uruguay, the fifth, *J. planifolius*, shared by Chile and Australia-Tasmania-New Zealand, but it is also true that even if we look for the origin of the family in Antarctica, a possibility pointed out by WEIMARCK (*281*), we must count with secondary centres of evolution in the boreal zone where the overwhelming majority of sections and species are found. Some 50 species are in the South hemisphere with main centres in South Africa (20) and Australia (17).

Libertia with 3 species in Chile and 2 in New Guinea-Australia-New Zealand tells a story of an Antarctic past, and the group Sisyrinchineae has a stronghold in the South, where the genera concentrate, *Sisyrinchium* itself centres in South America, where 4 small genera are endemic (*Symphyostemon, Chamaelum, Solenomelus* and *Tapeinia*), South Africa is another stronghold (*Aristea, Witsenia, Bobartia, Klattia* and *Cleanthe*), and 3 (*Orthosanthus, Diplarrhena* and *Patersonia*) are found in the East Australian - Indomalayan region, but this does not entitle us to derive Iridaceae from the far south.

Of the 4 island species of *Peperomia* only *P. fernandeziana* (Chile) is neotropical, while the other species appear to be more nearly allied to palaeotropical ones (Java, Australia, Oceania), *P. berteroana* occupies a unique geographical position (p. 203). The genus is of tropical origin and centres in America, but if we try to understand the history of the endemic species of Juan Fernandez, the possibility of Antarctica as a migration route should be considered.

Whereas *Urtica masafuerana*, one of the few indigenous annuals, is related to a species from Ecuador, *U. fernandeziana* with the habit of a miniature tree (*229: 862*) appears to lack near relatives. The family is, I suppose, of tropical origin, but the actual centre of *Urtica* is in the north temperate and subtropical zones, there are 14 species in Eurasia, including the Mediterranean region, and 7 in North and Central America with a secondary centre in the Andes (Colomb.-Fueg. 6), 3 species are tropical (Braz.-Urug., Ethiopia, Java). There are a few species in the south hemisphere, 2 S. Afr., 1 Australia, 2 N. Zeal. and 1 Auckl. Is. *U. fernandeziana* seems to represent an ancient type.

Boehmeria excelsa was described by BURGER (*41*) as an elegant shrub which came from S. America, it is a clumsy tree and not related to neotropical species. It comes nearest to *B. dealbata* (Kermadec Is.) and points west, not east.

Parietaria humifusa (Chile), see above p. 204. Belongs to a neotropical group which has not been cleared up (*241*) but is also closely related to the Australian-Polynesian *debilis* of FORSTER WIDDIII's *debilis* is a mixture of varieties scattered over the globe and most likely consists of several good species.

Phrygilanthus Berteroi. The family Loranthaceae is tropical, but *Phrygilanthus* is of Antarctic origin. Of the 7 sections, 4 (about 20 species) are American and range from Lower California to S. Chile, 1 with 2 species belongs to Australia and New Zealand, 1 (1 species) to New Zealand, and 1 has one species in Australia, another in New Guinea and a third in the Philippines—a typically austral-bicentric genus.

The genus *Santalum* ranges from Australia and Melanesia to Micronesia and Malaysia and east to Polynesia and Hawaii with a distant outlying station in Juan Fernandez, see TUYAMA's map (*270*). Of the 4 sections distinguished by

TUYAMA (who divided my section *Eusantalum* in 2 and referred the Hawaiian Eusantala to a separate section *Solenanthus*), *Eusantalum* s. str. is the largest with 9 species, *Solenanthus* and sect. *Hawaiensia* (together 8) confined to Hawaii (incl. Laysan), and sect. *Polynesica* (2, with varieties) to Polynesia. In this section the extinct *S. fernandezianum* occupies a rather independent position. "Aber woher kam der fremdartige Eremit Santalum?" BURGER (41 221) exclaims "zweifelsohne fern aus ostindischen Meeren, wo die Wiege seines altberühmten Geschlechtes steht"—nothing could give a wronger idea of the history of the sandalwoods, because everything points toward Antarctica as their cradle. There are related endemic genera in Australia, *Mida* in New Zealand, *Exocarpus* ranges from Australia across Polynesia to Hawaii, and several endemic genera are at home in temperate S America (*Arjona*, *Iodina*, *Ovidia*, *Quinchamalium*, and *Nanodea* in the extreme south and in the Falkland Is.) one is tempted to regard the family as of Antarctic ancestry, but with *Thesium* in mind it might be safer to speak of a special Antarcto-tertiary centre.

The 3 endemic species of *Chenopodium* were commented upon above (p. 204). In general appearance they are very like the Hawaiian *oahuense* but the specialist opines that they are not nearly related to this nor to other species. I can find no better place for them than in a neotropical group.

Salicornia fruticosa, taken in a wide sense, is a thalassochorous plant scattered along tropical and subtropical coasts, the same is the case with *Tetragonia expansa* in the S. hemisphere, but while *Salicornia* is a worldwide genus, *Tetragonia* has a stronghold in South Africa and several endemic species in Chile.

Spergularia is a wide-ranging, but mainly boreal genus with a vigorous branch in Andean America but absent from Australia, New Zealand and Oceania. The 2 island species, of which *S. confertiflora* is also found on San Ambrosio, are closely related to Chilean species. *Paronychia* has about the same distribution pattern as *Spergularia*, but is poorly represented in S. America.

Ranunculus caprarum. A very large essentially boreal-temperate genus with well-stocked branches in S. America and on New Zealand. The Masafueran endemic stands apart from its American congeners and approaches certain New Zealand species, perhaps also the Hawaiian ones. An Antarctic migration route seems probable.

Berberis corymbosa and *masafuerana* belong to a small section confined to the tropical Andes and not extending to Chile, where we have many other species. The present area of the Berberidaceae testifies to its Arcto-tertiary character, it centres in E and S Asia and ranges far south only in America, where 3 species reach Fuegia.

Of the six genera of Winteraceae (253), *Bubbia* has 2 species in Australia, 1 on Lord Howe I., 8 in New Caledonia and 19 in New Guinea, *Belliolum* 4 in New Caledonia and 4 in the Solomon Is., *Pseudowintera* 2 in New Zealand, *Exospermum* 2 and *Zygogynum* 6 in New Caledonia, and *Drimys* 6 in Australia (1 also in Tasmania), 29 in New Guinea and 1 on Borneo, Celebes and in the Philippines, all these belonging to sect. *Tasmania*, the other section, *Ludwigia*, is American with 4 species, *D. confertifolia* endemic in Juan Fernandez. This section is a distant branch of an Australasian family and ranges from the uttermost south along the mountains to Mexico and to Roraima in Brazil. That Antarctica once played a role in the history of *Drimys* is proved by the Tertiary fossils discovered in West Antarctica.

Lactoris is generally looked upon as a primitive member of the Ranales and claimed to belong to the most primitive element in the island flora. It has no relatives in America. It is no typical member of the Magnoliales, an Arcto-tertiary order, which it needs a CROIZAT to derive from the Antarctic. Geographically, *Lactoris* is a parallel to *Degeneria* of Fiji, but the affinities of the latter are not questionable and they have little in common. It lies near at hand to think of the small family Lardizabalaceae endemic in Chile. HUTCHINSON regards Lactoridaceae as "closely related to the Winteraceae, of which it is probably a reduced derivative" (*140* II 85)—but is the perfect trimery a result of reduction? And are not the never quite closed carpels an indication of primitiveness? I daresay most systematists agree that the Polycarpicae, whether regarded as *one* order or split up, are among the oldest living angiosperms. The distribution of Winteraceae and the occurrence in the South Hemisphere of small isolated families as Degeneriaceae Lactoridaceae and Lardizabalaceae suggests that the Antarctic continent was one of the centres of evolution.

Cardamine is a world-wide, mainly temperate and essentially boreal genus, extending into the tropics and south to Fuegia and New Zealand. The 3 island species, one of them endemic, were commented on above (p. 205).

Among the numerous Chilean species of *Escallonia*, *E. Calleottiae* stands a little apart from the rest (*158*), the genus is spread along the Andes and extends to Brazil and Uruguay. The subfamily Escallonioideae is austral circumpolar. *Tribeles* (1 S Chile-Fueg.), *Valdivia* (1 S Chile) *Forgesia* (1) and *Berenice* (1), Reunion *Anopterus* (2, Tasm. E Austral), *Cuttsia* (1 E Austral), *Argophyllum* (10 E Austral, N Caled), *Colmeioa* (1 Lord Howe I), *Carpodetus* (1 N Zeal., N Guin), *Quintinia* (15 Austral-N Guin-N Caled, Philipp), *Pottingeria* (1 N E Ind)—a distribution suggesting an Antarctic origin.

Rubus geoides has a single near relative *R. radicans*, in S Chile. They differ very much from the numerous north temperate and tropical montane species and form their own section or subgenus, and their resemblance to the Tasmanian *R gunnianus* Hook. Icon Plant III is no proof of affinity. They seem to represent an isolated offshoot from the north which has become cut off from its source of origin and found its way into the subantarctic zone.

Acaena Nobody if not CROIZAT would argue that *Rosaceae* are a southern family, but this cannot prevent us from assuming that the *Sanguisorba* assemblage of genera has gone through part of its evolution at least in the far south. BITTER (*31*) distinguished 10 sections I, 13 species, S Amer, II, 1, The Cape, III, 2, 1 S Amer, 1 Hawaii IV, 1, S Amer, V, 8, 6 S Amer, 1 J Fern, 1 Tasm, VI 1, S Amer, VII, 28, 26 S Amer, 1 Calif, 1 Tasm VIII, 64 58 S Amer, 1 Tristan da C, 1 N Amsterd I, 3 N Zeal, 1 N Zeal-Tasm-Austral-N Guin, IX, 1, N Zeal, and X, 2, N Zeal Two Magellanian species occur on S Georgia and 1 on Kerguelen The circumpolar distribution shows no gaps About 70 %

of the species inhabit extratropical S America, but many of them are so closely related that they are little more than microspecies and in not few cases based on one or two specimens from a single locality, and the number of separable taxa will perhaps be reduced when more material becomes available. Be this as it may, 7 sections are represented in America, 5 in the Australian–N Zealand area, 3 are common to both, one of them ranging to the African sector, where another section is endemic. As regards *A masafuerana* see p 206 above I suppose we can draw no other conclusion from this distribution than that *Acaena* is an Antarcto-tertiary genus, 2 sections having developed numerous species in the Andes and Patagonia

Margyricarpus a small Andean genus is so closely allied to *Acaena* that they have produced a bigeneric hybrid in Juan Fernandez. Two more genera are found in the Andes, *Tetraglochin* and *Polylepis*. In S Africa we have the large genus *Cliffortia*. The remaining genera *Sanguisorba*, *Poterium* and *Bencomia* (Macaronesia) belong to the N hemisphere

Sophora sect Tetrapterae is austral circumpolar. New Zealand (3 species), Chatham I (1), Lord Howe I (1), Austral Is (1), Rapa (1) Marquesas (1), Hawaii (1), Easter I (1), Juan Fernandez (2), Chile (2, *S macrocarpa*, however, rather unlike all the others), Diego Alvarez (1), and Réunion (1). With the exception of *macrocarpa* and the Hawaiian *chrysophylla* the remaining species used to be united under *tetraptera* Ait, otherwise endemic in New Zealand They are very closely related, but distinct, it is of minor importance if we call them species or geographical subspecies. Unless we believe that *S tetraptera* was carried by water from island to island and was transformed into a new species wherever it landed, we must look upon Antarctica as a one time centre of a polymorphous population, which radiated in various directions, we shall not discuss here how this may have happened. We have not to do with litoral but with inland plants, the pods are adapted to float, assisted by the four narrow wings, JOHOW says, but some of the forms have no wings at all, and even if they have, the pods open on the tree and discharge their seeds

Fagara mayu and *externa* form their own section. When BURGER said (41 19) that *Fagara* had migrated to Juan Fernandez from the primeval forests of Peru and Colombia he overlooked that the affinity is with palaeotropical rather than with neotropical species, there are numerous species scattered from Australia and New Caledonia to Polynesia and Hawaii, where many are endemic. Rutaceae were perhaps represented in the Antarctic in Tertiary times, and we have too look for a route across to the American sector

The family *Euphorbiaceae* is pantropical, let alone that *Euphorbia* has attained a world wide distribution and flourishes also in temperate climates. *Dysopsis* is Andean, *Seidelia* (2) and *Leidesia* (1) South African the fourth genus of the *Mercurialis* group *Mercurialis* (8), ranges from North Europe to the Mediterranean and is found in E Asia. The southern genera seem to be more closely connected mutually than with *Mercurialis*. The disjunctions are interesting and difficult to explain, unless we can find good reason to look for a common source in the Antarctic

The systematical position of *Callitriche* has been discussed many times, but we know nothing of its history or where it started. The genus is world wide, but many species are not wide spread and some are quite local, among them *C. Lechleri*, which may have been carried to Juan Fernandez from the mainland by accident.

The tribe Colletieae of the otherwise wide ranging *Rhamnaceae* is called austral antarctic by SUSSENGUT (Naturl Pflanzenfam. 2nd ed.), except *Adolphia* (Mexico–U S A) the genera are distributed over Andean and extratropical S America, centering in Chile, and *Colletia spartioides* finds its place with the Andean element. It should be mentioned that *Discaria* (11) extends south to Fuegia and reappears in Australia (1) and New Zealand (1), suggesting transantarctic migration from America.

The family *Flacourtiaceae* is tropical, *Azara* is neotropical with about 19 species in Chile, 1 in Brazil and 1 in Argentina. The tribe to which it belongs is well developed in the south hemisphere tropical America and Africa, Madagascar and neighbouring islands, Asia, New Guinea and (*Xylosma*) Oceania to Hawaii, but Antarctica may not at all be involved in its history.

Myrtaceae. A very large world wide and tropical-subtropical family. Of the subfamily Myrtoideae, some 2400 species, 75 % are American, the remainder scattered over Asia, Africa, Australia and Oceania. The Leptospermoideae, some 850, are restricted to Australasia with the single exception of *Tepualia*, monotypical and endemic in the Chilean rain forests, south to West Patagonia, a most interesting case of disjunction. BERRY (26) regards the family to be of American origin and to have attained its present distribution before the close of the Cretaceous. Basing his conclusions on fossil evidence he thinks that during the cooling down of the climate during late Tertiary the ancestral stock of Myrtoideae withdrew from North America to the neotropical zone, the Australian Leptospermoideae represent the remnants of the Cretaceous radiation during which numerous new types became evolved. Some of these eventually invaded Antarctica and *Tepualia* survives on Chilean soil.

The Juan Fernandez Myrtoideae are closely linked to Andean types. For *Ugni Selkirkii* and *Myrteola nummularia* see p. 206. *Nothomyrcia*, now restricted to Masatierra, may or may not have inhabited a larger area. *Myrceugenia* has about 20 species in Chile.

Gunneraceae (often placed as a subfamily under Halorrhagidaceae) is a classical example of a tricentric Antarcto-tertiary type. Its long and complicated history is reflected in its taxonomic differentiation. *Gunnera* is composed of 6 subgenera. *Pangue* is the largest with 10 species ranging from Costa Rica to S Chile, 1 in Brazil, 3 in Juan Fernandez and 2 in Hawaii. *Perpensum* is monotypical with separate varieties in S Africa, British E Africa and Madagascar, *Ostenia* an aberrant monotype endemic in Uruguay. *Misandra* includes 3 species, one extending from Colombia to Fuegia and Falkland, one restricted to the S Chilean Andes and one to subantarctic America. *Milligania* has 8 species in New Zealand and 1 in Tasmania. The monotypical *Pseudogunnera* inhabits New Guinea, Java, Sumatra and the Philippines. No subgenus is found in more than one sector. It is surprising that the geographically isolated Hawaiian species are closely related to the species of Juan Fernandez. We know other examples of this connection, but to construct a route between Hawaii and Juan Fernandez meets with serious obstacles, and *Pangue* may have reached Hawaii along a quite different route. The evolution and differentiation of the subgenera very likely took place in Antarctica.

SCHINDLER (Pflanzenreich) expressed his opinion of the history of *Halorrhagidaceae* thus: "Aus der geographischen Verbreitung der ursprünglichsten Halorrhagaceen, nämlich der Gattung Halorrhagis, ist mit Sicherheit zu folgern, dass die Familie antarktischen Ursprungs ist." It is not easy to see how he arrived at this conclusion, though I think it is correct, because at that time the endemic species of Juan Fernandez were unknown, they passed as *H. erecta*, a New Zealand endemic, and this, incorrectly attributed also to Juan Fernandez and Chile, had been carried there on purpose. "Der Standort auf Juan Fernandez und in Chile ist kein ursprünglicher, sondern durch die auch in Neuseeland erfolgende Verwendung der Pflanze als Futterpflanze erklärt." But there was no *Halorrhagis* on the mainland, and the species indigenous in Juan Fernandez were not used as forage, let it be that the introduced animals eat them. *Halorrhagis*, eminently Australian (59 out of 80 species) and with 7 species in New Zealand extends north to Indomalaya, Micronesia S.E. China and Japan and east to Rapa (not known to SCHINDLER) and Juan Fernandez—see ILYAM's map of distribution (*271*). The genus "well illustrates the not infrequent extension of an Australasian group far north of the equator, and the much rarer condition of occurrence in Juan Fernandez but not in continental America (*109* 108). *Halorrhagis* shows the same distribution pattern as *Santalum*.

Centella is essentially African, see above p. 207, the distribution is tricentric with some remote stations. The widespread *C. asiatica* is scattered over a broad belt but not reported from America. Very likely the Hydrocotyloideae, a separate family according to some authors, are of Antarctic origin, but *C. triflora* may well have reached Juan Fernandez with the traffic from Chile.

The peculiar endemic species of *Eryngium* differ so much in habit from all other species of this large and widespread genus that they have been referred to a separate genus, a rank to which they are not entitled. *Eryngium* concentrates in the Mediterranean region and in tropical South America, where also the island species belong, in spite of their arborescent habit, to quote TURMLI (*269* 130) "Se rattachant à la Region chilienne, on cite les especes de Juan Fernandez *E. bupleuroides, sarcophyllum* et *inaccessum*, plantes, du moins pour les deux premieres, arbustives s'opposant radicalement aux autres especes des territoires voisins"—but *inaccessum* also is a dwarf tree, more so I would say than *sarcophyllum*. I doubt that they descend from herbaceous continental forms, they belong to an ancient type and find their proper place with the neotropical element.

The tribe Apioideae-Ammineae is very widely spread, with a concentration in the North hemisphere, *Apium* distributed also in the south temperate zone, and *A. graveolens* L. is frequently regarded as bipolar species. I don't believe that any of the southern forms should be included, they are, however, in need of revision. *A. fernandezianum* is a well-marked species, related, but not very closely, to a series of forms, probably good species reported from subantarctic America, Falkland, Tristan da Cunha, Australia, etc. and possibly descending from an old Antarctic stock.

Pernettya 13 species 8 Mexico and Centr America to Chile, south to Fuegia and Falkland 1 Galapagos Is, 2 in Tasmania and 2 in New Zealand, *P. rigida* is linked to Andean species, but very distinct (252). The genus is more diversified in the American sector, and this seems to be where it originated, having reached New Zealand across the Antarctic, if not with *Gaultheria*, well developed in New Zealand, descending from a common Antarcto tertiary stock.

Empetrum is a bipolar genus the family most likely of boreal origin Concerning *E. rubrum* see 249 781.

Of the 7 *Dichondra* species 5 are neotropical, 1 endemic in New Zealand and *D. repens* (incl *sericea*) spread round the world. It is common on the coast of Chile and possibly adventitious in Juan Fernandez. The occurrence of an endemic species in New Zealand suggests that Antarctica witnessed part of its history.

Calystegia About 25 species have been described, scattered over the globe, *C. sepium* sensu lat reported from America, Eurasia, N Africa, Australia, New Zealand, Easter I, etc. and evidently very easily naturalized. The plant found on Masafuera and also on the mainland was described as *C. Hantelmannii* Phil and later identified with *tuguriorum* from New Zealand, see 249 783. If this is correct, *C. tuguriorum* offers one of the very few cases of a species restricted to Chile and New Zealand, but even if they are kept apart, they present a remarkable case of disjunction.

Selkirkia Berteroi, the only representative of Boraginaceae, so richly developed on the mainland, was regarded as an isolated, Old Pacific type (227 31, 224 593) until JOHNSTON (148) showed that it comes close to *Hackelia* and differs from this principally by its arboreous habit. With *Urtica fernandeziana*, the species of *Eryngium* etc. I refer it to the neotropical element.

Rhaphithamnus venustus is of neotropical ancestry (see above p 208), the second species is common in Centr and S Chile.

BRIQUET placed *Cuminia* in the Stachyoideae-Menthinae next to *Orcosphacus* Phil, a shrub of the high Cordillera in the boundary region between Chile and Argentina, but this genus has a schizocarp of four nuts. It has also been compared with *Bystropogon* L'Hérit (Canary Is, Colomb–Peru, different sections). EPLING (using the fancy name *Johowia*) referred *Cuminia* to Prasioideae, an ancient group showing great disjunctions *Prasium* Mediterranean, *Stenogyne*, *Phyllostegia* and *Haplostachys* in Hawaii, *Bostrychanthus* and *Gomphostemma* in Asia, *Cuminia* differs in the shape of the corolla (see above p 208) but even so it seems to represent a palaeotropic element in the island flora.

Solanum fernandezianum is a distinct species of indubitable neotropical and Andean ancestry. With regard to *S robinsonianum*, see above p 200.

Nicotiana cordifolia has, according to GOODSPEED (112 347), its closest resemblance, in flower structure as well as in general habit, to *N Raimondii* Crosses with this species and with *solanifolia* gave evidence of fundamental affinities between the island endemic and species of the mainland to the north (l c)

Mimulus is essentially a western N American genus with few species elsewhere, the somewhat polymorphous *M glabratus* ranges from N America to Bolivia, Chile and Argentina

The different opinions on the systematic position of *Euphrasia formosissima* have already been referred to above Within the area of the geographically isolated Chilean-Magellanian *Irifidae* occurs the semicalcarate *E perpusilla* Phil (S Chile) Both would indicate a road from the Australian-New Zealand area across the Antarctic to America, just as the tropical mountains of Malaysia served as a road between Asia and Australia as DE RIETZ thinks (77 536) "The *Euphrasia* population of Juan Fernandez may therefor very well have formed the northern end of a population so far south that the lack of close relationships between *E formosissima* and the species of Middle Chile is fully explained and the semicalcarate anthers of the more southern *E perpusilla* may be the last South American remnant of this old connection " Another question, not yet answered, is this are the very well marked *Trifidae*, reaching from subantarctic America to the Andes of S Chile, likewise descendants from a remote southern population or did they originate in Chile?

Plantago fernandezia is another arborescent member of a herbaceous worldwide genus and often cited as an example of a mysterious connection between Hawaii and Juan Fernandez but if we look at the total distribution of sect *Palaeopsyllium* (see above p 209) its character of an austral group is revealed, even if it extends north to N America and S Europe In the south it is circumpolar, and the route from New Zealand (Auckland Is) via Rapa to Hawaii can be traced —a radiation from Antarctica seems not unthinkable

Plantago truncata, represented in Juan Fernandez by an endemic (?) variety, belongs to the large section *Novorbis* and needs no further comments

The neotropical *Hedyotis thesiifolia* is a recent addition to the flora and may have been accidentally introduced

Vertera is an austral-circumpolar genus allied to *Coprosma* and best developed in New Zealand where 5 species occur, 4 of them endemic, the fifth is *N granadensis* (depressa), claimed to be very widely spread One species is endemic in Tristan da Cunha Recent observations tend to show that *granadensis* includes taxonomically distinct forms, the Malaysian plant is not identical with the Andean, and other forms will perhaps become distinguished after a critical revision Be this as it may, the genus is Antarcto tertiary and, if we link Tristan da Cunha with Africa, tricentric

Coprosma is a parallel to *Halorrhagis* but differs in being present in Hawaii, another difference is that the species of Juan Fernandez do not have their closest relatives in New Zealand or Australia—*Hookeri* forms its own section, *pyrifolia* is of Polynesian affinity As the genus is absent from America as well as from Africa it should lie near at hand to refer it to a West Pacific element, a position favoured by the relationships of *pyrifolia*, and to the believers in transoceanic migration combined with evolution of local endemics wherever *Coprosma* happened to land this is the only course to take, even if the sudden appearance of an isolated type like *Hookeri* becomes somewhat embarrassing. With an extension north and east of an Antarctic borderland *Coprosma* could pass as of Antarcto-tertiary origin.

C. pyrifolia offers a good example of an incorrect taxonomic position leading to false conclusions. It was described as *Psychotria* and referred to a neotropical group; it came, as BURGER writes (*41* 20), "von den Urwäldern Perus und Colombias".

Of the more than 500 species described under *Galium* about 400 are distributed over the boreal zone and some 50 or 60 are known from South America extending from the tropical Andes to Fuegia, the Falkland Is and South Georgia, about 30 are African, the remaining species being divided between India, Malaysia, Australia, New Zealand etc. *Galium* is a boreal genus with a strong representation along the Andes, a not uncommon case. *G. masafueranum* is allied to species from the mountains of Central Chile, probably also to species found farther north. Nothing indicates that Antarctica ever had a share in the history of this genus.

Whether Campanulaceae Lobelioideae evolved in the tropics or in the far South will not be discussed here. The remarkable concentration of arboreous genera two of them large, in Hawaii, has given rise to much speculation, and the occurrence of other endemic genera in Polynesia as well as the Australian affinity of *Brighamia* of Hawaii have led some authors to look for the origin of the subfamily (or family) in the Antarctic. In our special case we can leave this question aside because *Lobelia alata* is a widely distributed seaside species, tricentric in the South Hemisphere.

The distribution of *Wahlenbergia*, a large and widespread genus, is interesting. It is essentially southern; of the about 230 species described 150 are South African and 20 tropical African, 6 are reported from Madagascar and the Mascarene islands. North it extends to the Mediterranean, the Orient and Asia, together some 25 species. Scattered species are known from New Guinea (1), Australia (7), New Zealand (7), Lord Howe I (2) and St Helena (3). Species are few in America (North Amer 1, South Amer 8), a single species, *W. gracilis*, ranges over the south hemisphere.

If we look at the related genera, some 13 in number, the dominant position of South Africa becomes still more conspicuous 7 are exclusively or preponderantly South African, 1 is from tropical Africa, F Indies and Brazil, 4 Asiatic and 1 from S E Europe, all according to the old synopsis in Naturl Pflanzenfam. Our island species are, as we have seen, not matched in Africa, nor in America or other parts of the world except on St Helena, see above p 210. All known facts suggest that the genus had a long and complicated history in the far south and that S Africa is a secondary centre where evolution has been progressive and prolific in species formation. It is important to remember that our island forms are not a group of closely related taxa but that *W. Masafuerae* and particularly *Berteroi* stand apart from the rest. The distribution of the genus can hardly be explained without admitting Antarctica into the picture.

The distribution of *Lagenophora* clearly testifies to its Antarctic origin 3 Magellanian species, one of them also on Tristan da Cunha and one on Masafuera, 7 in New Zealand, 2 in Australia, one of these north to the Philippines, 1 in Fiji and 3 in Hawaii, the four Pacific ones connected with *L. Billardieri* Cass (Austral), whereas the Magellanian species point toward *L. pumila* Cheesem and *petiolata* Hook. fil. (New Zealand).

In *Erigeron* we meet again with a large boreal genus strongly represented along the Andes and ranging south to Patagonia, Fuegia and Falkland, 135 species are reported from Eurasia, incl. India, 345 from North America, 35 from Centr America and the W. Indies, 95 from S. America, 10 from Africa, 8 from Australia and a single species from Oceania (Rapa), *E. rapensis* F. B. H. Brown, and this is compared with our island species. To judge from the description it has the same habit as these, a shrub about 3 dm tall with the leaves in terminal rosettes. In Hawaii the genus is represented by *Tetramolopium*, which is very close to *Erigeron*, VIERHAPPER (229 182) suggested that the Juan Fernandez species came near the Hawaiian *E. lepidotus* Less., which is now referred to *Tetramolopium*, and that we ought to look for relatives among the Andine and Mexican forms. Among our island species *E. rupicola* differs much in habit from the rest, but all belong together and most likely represent a special branch of the Andine *Erigeron* flora which, in its turn, comes from a boreal stock.

To what I said above about *Gnaphalium spiciforme* nothing can be added at present. Chile is well provided with poorly limited species related to *G. purpureum* L., most of them are badly known. Their boreal parentage can hardly be doubted.

Abrotanella resembles *Lagenophora* in its distribution, but is absent from Oceania, the majority inhabits New Zealand with its subantarctic islands (9 sp.), 1 is found in Victoria, 2 in Tasmania, 1 in New Guinea and 5 in S. America (W Patagonia to Fuegia and Falkland), in addition, one is found on Rodriguez I. The genus is, as it were, tricentric and its Antarcto tertiary character indisputable.

The concentration of isolated arborescent Compositae in the Pacific was emphasized by BENTHAM, the main groups of the family are represented among them, and the accumulation of endemic genera in Hawaii and Juan Fernandez has led to much discussion. The enormous development and differentiation in the family on American soil is an undeniable fact, but simply to derive the endemic Pacific genera from America as did GUPPY (*121*) does not seem possible. Speculations (comp f inst SETCHELL *219*) led back to Antarctica but not until *Brachionostylum* was discovered in New Guinea and found to be nearly related to *Robinsonia* of Juan Fernandez were we able to stand on tolerably firm ground.

With regard to *Centaurodendron* to which *Yunquea* seems to be related, the situation is different. *Centaurea* and all the genera of Centaureinae belong to the Old World with the exception of a single species in N. America and a few in the Andes, south to Centr Chile. The group ranges over Europe with a stronghold in the Mediterranean, the Orient, Ethiopia and through Centr Asia to Japan. The Chilean species of *Centaurea* belong to the *Plectocephali*, but *Centaurodendron* differs not only from this section but from all in sex distribution (*243*). It serves no purpose to say that *Centaurodendron* descends from some continental *Centaurea* which became arboreous under insular conditions, because the character of the ray floret is entirely opposed to such a theory and *Centaurodendron* seems to be a more ancient type than *Centaurea*, a relic from an epoch previous to the final uplift of the Andes.

The four Cichoriaceous genera, to which *Thamnoseris* of the Desventuradas Is shows some slight affinity are even more isolated. The only other genus to which they bear some resemblance is the Polynesian *Fitchia*, but the differences are too profound to allow us to visualize an Antarctic Pacific ancestry of the *Dendroseris* group and it remains us to link it with the neotropical element.

Referring to the synopsis given above the Phanerogams are rearranged in the following way according to their supposed source of origin.

I Antarcto-tertiary element —62 sp (42.2 %)

1 Distribution pattern austral circumpolar, bicentric or tricentric —33 sp

a Endemic species (17) Cladium scirpoideum, Uncinia Douglasii and costata, Carex berteroniana, Luzula masafuerana, Drimys confertifolia, Phrygilanthus Berteroi, Acaena masafuerana, Sophora fernandeziana and masafuerana, Gunnera peltata, Masafuerae and bracteata, Apium fernandezianum (?) Pernettya rigida, Plantago fernandezia, Abrotanella crassipes

b Species also found on the continent (16) Danthonia collina, Koeleria micrathera (?) Oreobolus obtusangulus, Uncinia brevicaulis, phleoides and tenuis, Juncus imbricatus, capillaceus, acutus, dombeyanus and planifolius, Libertia formosa, Acaena ovalifolia, Centella triflora, Nertera granadensis, Lagenophora Harioti

2 Genera only found in S America but supposed to be of Antarctic origin. The species are endemic Escallonia Callcottiae, Margyricarpus digynus —2 sp

3 Endemic genera or species as far as known without continental American affinities, either suggesting an ancient Antarcto Pacific track east from Australasia without reaching America, or having arrived along the road over the Scotia Arc without leaving any traces in the present S American flora —21 sp

a Belonging to endemic genera (7) Robinsonia gayana, thurifera, evenia, Masafuerae and gracilis, Symphyochaeta macrocephala, Rhetinodendron Berterii

b Endemic species of genera of wider distribution (14) Peperomia berteroana, margaritifera and Skottsbergii, Santalum fernandezianum, Bochmeria excelsa, Ranunculus caprarum, Fagara mayu and externa, Halorrhagis asperrima, masatierrana and masafuerana, Euphrasia formosissima, Coprosma Hookeri and pyrifolia

4 Endemic species with relatives in the African sector only Wahlenbergia Larrainii, fernandeziana, Grahamae, Masafuerae and Berteroi —5 sp

5 Endemic family, possibly of old Antarctic, perhaps pre Tertiary ancestry Lactoris fernandeziana —1 sp

II Neotropical-Andean element —54 sp (36.7 %)

1 Endemic genera or species of neotropical parentage, non endemic species South American —31 sp

a Belonging to endemic genera (4) Juania australis, Ochagavia elegans, Nothomyrcia fernandeziana, Selkirkia Berteroi *b* Endemic species of non-endemic genera, some of wider distribution (14) Chaetotropis imberbis, Chusquea fernandeziana, Hesperogreigia Bertcroi, Urtica Masafuerae, Dysopsis hirsuta, Colletia spartioides, Azara fernandeziana, Ugni Selkirkii, Myrceugenia Schulzei, Rhaphithamnus venustus, Solanum fernandezianum, robinsonianum and masafueranum, Nicotiana cordifolia.

c Species also found on the continent (13) Stipa neesiana and laevissima, Piptochaetium bicolor, Chaetotropis chilensis, Cyperus eragrostis and reflexus, Eleocharis fuscopurpurea, Peperomia fernandeziana, Parietaria humifusa, Myrteola nummularia, Mimulus glabratus, Plantago truncata, Hedyotis thesiifolia.

2 Endemic genera or endemic sections of wide ranging genera without relatives in the present continental flora but supposed to descend from extinct neotropical ancestors —23 sp.

a Belonging to endemic genera (16) Podophorus bromoides, Megalachne berteroniana and masafuerana, Centaurodendron dracaenoides, Yunquea Tenzii, Dendroseris macrophylla, macrantha, marginata and litoralis, Rea nerifolia, micrantha and pruinata, Phoenicoseris pinnata, berteriana and regia, Hesperoseris gigantea.

b Belonging to endemic sections (7) Urtica fernandeziana, Chenopodium Sanctae Clarae, crusoeanum and nesodendron, Eryngium bupleuroides, inaccessum and sarcophyllum.

III Arcto-tertiary element —23 sp (15 6 %)

Genera essentially boreal but extending south along the Andes or reappearing in S America.

a Endemic species of wide ranging genera (13) Agrostis masafuerana, Spergularia confertiflora (also Desventuradas) and masafuerana, Berberis corymbosa and masafuerana, Cardamine Kruesselii, Galium masafueranum, Erigeron fruticosus, luteoviridis, Ingae, Innocentium, turricola and rupicola.

b Species also found on the continent (10) Trisetum chromostachyum, Carex Banksii, Paronychia chilensis, Cardamine chenopodifolia and flaccida, Rubus geoides, Callitriche Lechleri, Empetrum rubrum, Calystegia tuguriorum (?), Gnaphalium spiciforme.

IV Palaeotropic element —2 sp (1 4 %)

Endemic genus Cuminia fernandezia and eriantha.

V Austral element of wide-ranging seaside species —6 sp (4 1 %)

Scirpus nodosus and cernuus, Salicornia fruticosa (peruviana), Tetragonia expansa, Dichondra repens, Lobelia alata.

Even if Antarctica is recognized as an important source of evolution of both plants and animals and as a centre from where large-scale migration took place, a percentage of 42 may seem surprisingly high, and I admit that some genera or species have been referred to group I with considerable hesitation This does not, with very few exceptions, apply to I 1, 22 4 % of the total or 53 2 % of I *Luzula* and *Juncus* were placed here because the family was regarded as Antarctic, but even if this be true it is possible that the sections including our species are of boreal origin and has spread south. *Pernettya* is a bicentric genus, but it is much better developed in America and may have originated with *Gaultheria* in the Antarctic. The same should apply to *Nicotiana* according to MERRILL (*306*, *310*) who thinks that its actual distribution was attained in the Tertiary period by way of Antarctica; however, *N. cordifolia* cannot be removed from II 1 b and find a better place with I 1 a. On the other hand, a truly Antarctic genus may have produced numerous species in one sector and few in another, or the few may be a remnant of a larger population. In group I 3 *Peperomia berteroana* calls for attention. As I have shown (*245*) it is so close to *P. tristanensis* that their common origin cannot be doubted and that little prevents us from regarding them as forms of *one* species, very distinct but clearly related to the other two species endemic in Juan Fernandez, and they point west. This is the reason why all three were referred to I. *Wahlenbergia* (I 4) is another mysterious case, but as it is neither boreal nor palaeotropical or neotropical but South African (and on St Helena), only a far southern ancestry remains to explain the disjunction.

Of the endemic genera belonging to group II 1 only *Juania* is taxonomically isolated. *Rhodostachys* of Chile is brought to *Ochagavia* by some authors, and *Selkirkia* comes very near *Hackelia*. With regard to the endemic Cichoriaceous genera authors' opinions differ. BENTHAM looked upon the arborescent Pacific Compositae as relics of an old Polynesian flora but did not refer directly to Antarctica as source; GUPPY (*121*) quoting BENTHAM believed that, with the Hawaiian Lobelioideae, they belonged to an ancient flora of the Pacific which had originated in America and gained dominance during what he termed "Age of Lobeliaceae" and "Age of Compositae", respectively. Antarctica seems not to have meant anything at all to him but as I have discussed his ideas in some detail in an earlier paper (*248*), I shall not enter upon this subject here.

Calystegia tuguriorum is doubtful case, but few people will be inclined to think that it originated independently in Chile and New Zealand.

In a paper of 1928 (*218*) SETCHELL discussed what he called the two principal elements in the Pacific flora, the Indomalayan and the "Subantarctic". With this he did not understand what, from a geographical viewpoint, I call subantarctic, nor the species of old Antarctic genera found in the bogs of Hawaii, the Pacific flora with which he was particularly concerned, but the group he later (*219*) called "the Old pacific and antarctic element", for it included also the arboreous Lobeliaceae and Compositae, which he believed had a common origin in high southern latitudes. They had migrated north along different lines, the Compositae taking an easterly course along the route Juan Fernandez–Hawaii, the Lobeliaceae, which are absent from Juan Fernandez but have left traces in Polynesia, a more westerly; a third line is called the Dammara (Agathis)–Podocarpus line, an Australasian line running over Fiji. What interests us here is that the isolated genera of Compositae were regarded as Antarctic. As we have seen, I did not venture to include the Cichoriaceous genera, but I cannot assure that SETCHELL was wrong.

Before quoting some other authors who have paid special attention to the Antarctic problems I want to add a few remarks on the relations between the far South and South America–Juan Fernandez. The Antarctic flora invaded the American continent, advancing especially along the rising Andes and in some cases extending north of the Equator. It must have been a climatically diversified flora, for the great southern continent must have had coast and inland, lowland and mountain climates and consequently the Antarctic plants in S. America have varying claims on moisture and heat. The less exacting plants are concentrated in West Patagonia, Fuegia and the Falkland Is., rising higher and higher as they advance north along the Cordillera, whereas such as require more favourable temperature conditions are found farther north in S. Chile and in the montane region of the tropical Andes. Father RAMBO, a wellknown expert on the flora of S. Brazil, called my attention (letter of Nov. 30, 1953) to an Antarctic element in the highlands of Rio Grande do Sul, where such genera as *Acaena*, *Margyricarpus*, *Escallonia*, *Gunnera*, *Drimys* and *Phrygilanthus* are represented; in 202, 30 he mentions *Araucaria angustifolia*, *Podocarpus Lamberti*, *Drimys Winteri*, *Acaena fuscescens*, *Fuchsia regia*, *Gunnera manicata*, and *Griselinia ruscifolia*, elements which, in his opinion, constitute the last remnants of the old flora that inhabited the southern lands united until early Tertiary times.

HILL (134) was cautious in his judgment of the importance of Antarctica in the history of the plant world. He quotes SEWARD who had pointed out that a number of families now largely in the South Hemisphere were present in the North Hemisphere already in Mesozoic times and that this would lead us to derive them from there, which most likely is true in certain cases. He also refers to SMUTS, who looked at the "ancient lands of the Southern Hemisphere" as the cradle of the peculiar S. African flora, and HILL formulates the following question (p. 1497):

Did the angiosperms originate in the north and migrate southwards and then, having reached the south, evolve along special lines in lands comparatively isolated from the land masses in the north, or did certain groups first appear in the South Hemisphere in an ancient Antarctic Continent and become dispersed northward into our present-day New Zealand, Australia, South America and South Africa?

With regard to Juan Fernandez he finds that

the present flora suggests that at one time these islands formed part of the Antarctic continent or were united to the extreme south of Chile, a view which is shared by Jhering and Joly, who believe that such a connection may have existed in early Tertiary times and that Kerguelen Island was probably part of a large land mass at the same period

and he continues

It seems also likely, on geological evidence, that Antarctica extended in the Tertiary epoch towards Tasmania and Australia, and so to Asia, and towards New Zealand, and the distribution of certain present-day plants in the Australasian region lends considerable support to such an extension (p. 1479)

Nevertheless, the problem is not as simple as it might seem to be.

We must be prepared to modify our views extensively in those cases which appear to afford fairly certain evidence of distribution from a Southern centre, but from the evidence available it seems probable that such genera as *Calceolaria, Jovellana, Fuchsia, Ourisia, Pelargonium Caltha, Lilaeopsis, Gunnera, Hebe, Pernettya, Azorella, Drapetes* and other Thymelaeaceae, *Nothofagus Eucryphia, Laurelia,* probably the Proteaceae, some of the Ericaceae   may have originated in some continental area in the South Hemisphere, whence their descendants spread northwards

It is of course possible that in early times many of the plants from which these Southern Genera evolved belonged to the Northern region and gradually migrated to the south and having reached the Southern regions they there, in a state of some isolation, evolved peculiar types which in their turn spread again northwards   without however crossing the Equator and reaching the North Hemisphere On this view we may perhaps best regard many of the present day genera which are now only found in the South Hemisphere (p 1480)

He adds,

It may be almost impossible in these latter days to make any certain pronouncement as to which natural families or genera, if any, actually originated in the Southern Hemisphere, when it is remembered that there have been a succession of alternations of warm temperate and cold glacial periods at various geological epochs not only in the Arctic but also in the Antarctic regions

He thinks that the cold spells gave rise to an extensive migration south and north, respectively, but he did not recognize the glaciations as contemporary in the two hemispheres

Of other modern authors, W H CAMP (43) interests us here My Antarcto-tertiary element lists *Drimys* as a classical example of an Antarctic genus, in fact, the entire family Winteraceae is supposed to be of Antarctic origin On CAMP's map, however, the original seat of the family is placed in the region of the old Bering Land bridge, from where tracks lead south through Asia to Australia-Tasmania and through western N America to S America The related Magnoliaceae are circumboreal and have left numerous fossil remains in the north Another map shows *Laurelia, Eucryphia, Luzuriaga* and *Jovellana*, all as a rule considered to be Antarctic here CAMP has two alternatives one track leading from the north as in *Drimys*, another from the south Other southern families shown on his maps are Tetrachondraceae, Eucryphiaceae, Centrolepidaceae, Epacridaceae (Hawaii inadvertently left out), Stylidiaceae, Restionaceae, Liliaceae Milliganieae, Philesiaceae, Halorrhagidaceae and Gunneraceae He emphasizes the fact that of the natural families, some 300 in number, 103 have a fairly restricted range, and that 80 of these are on the South Hemisphere I shall quote him in full

In the majority of instances an analysis of a group indicates that the primitive members are on the southern part of the group's range If we were to follow the well-known dicta of Matthews we could conclude that these primitive forms were "driven" unto the southern land mass extremities by the more highly specialized, better adapted, and more recently derived groups of the north The natural corollary to this, therefore, is that we should find the majority of the peculiar specialized and more recently derived families farthest away from the primitive forms However, as can quite easily be seen in the angiosperms, in most instances this is not the case I therefore incline to the conclusion that these southern land masses are not only the original homes of the great majority of our basic angiosperm groups, but that also it has been on these same southern land masses where the greater part of their primary evolutionary divergences took place (pp. 180–181),

and he continues,

It seems likely that the angiosperms, as a group, arose on this southern land mass contemporaneously with the Paleozoic of the northern (Holarctic) land mass and that the divergences of the basic, generalized familial groups had been accomplished in this southern land mass certainly by the mid-Mesozoic.

This would make the Jurassic the great period of ascendency of the angiosperms.

CAMP's theory does not, at least at first sight, agree too well with his opinion on the origin of the Magnoliales, always regarded as a primitive group though not of restricted range: the Winteraceae have a stronghold in New Guinea–Australia–New Zealand, and the actual distribution of this family testifies to a southern origin.

Recently STEBBINS (257) took up the question of the history of the Ranales. He points out (p. 8) that this order

includes a high proportion of species which on the basis of all characteristics must be placed not only in monotypic genera but even in monogeneric or digeneric families. They are obviously relict types of which the close relatives have long been extinct. Finally, distributional studies show that the genera and species are at present strongly concentrated in eastern Asia and Australasia, and at least one family, the Winteraceae, may have radiated from the latter center (A. C. Smith 1945). This family was dispersed through the Antarctic regions.

We cannot deny the possibility that New Guinea was the birthplace of types that now generally pass as Antarctic, a theory first advanced by Miss GIBBS (106) and perhaps strengthened by the sensational discovery there of a great number of *Nothofagus* species, but it is quite clear that, if they are bicentric, they must have migrated across what is now the Antarctic continent in order to arrive in S. America, which again compels us to assume that connections were established on both sides, and the existence of fossil plants belonging to taxa now living in the two sectors furnishes additional evidence that Antarctica took an important part in their history. Anyhow, *Nothofagus* survives in greater variation in New Guinea than either in New Zealand or in Chile, though these are situated nearer to the Antarctic continent.

Before Antarctica was recognized as a possible centre of evolution, the Holarctic region was claimed as the great and only cradle of temperate plant families which spread south during the Tertiary just as in pre-Tertiary times, tropical families had extended to the present Arctic. GORDON (113), although he finds undeniable proofs of an old Antarctic radiating centre, carefully scrutinizes the possibility of a northern origin of temperate types now found in the south, referring to OLIVER's theory that a genus like *Nothofagus* originated in N. America and that two tracks lead south, one to subantarctic America, one across the Bering land to Australia and New Zealand, but he doesn't think it probable that we can explain the disjunctions of numerous taxa in the south in this way and that the chances for cool climate types to cross the broad and well stocked tropical belt must have been small.

To me it would seem more acceptable to fall back on an ancient pantropical flora, spread from pole to pole before any temperate zones had become sharply delimited and when the distribution of land and sea was quite different from what it is now. With the appearance of distinct climatic belts a sorting out of meso- and microthermic groups followed, and these belts, both north and south, started to produce their own particular new groups which dispersed toward the equatorial zone and eventually met and passed it where mountain ranges offered a passage. This is in agreement with FLORIN's opinion (95) that the temperate floras, angiosperms as well as gymnosperms, developed independently throughout the Tertiary period in the north and south hemispheres. The march of Antarcto-tertiary types north corresponds to the march of Arcto-tertiary types south.

Recently Antarctica and the far south in general as the birthplace of the world's floras has found an eloquent advocate in LEON CROIZAT (71), who throws all other speculative authors in the shade. His ideas were criticised by SPARRE (256), but, as Juan Fernandez is regarded by CROIZAT as "one of the most interesting domains of general phytogeography", I cannot pass him in silence.

The original southern plant world, CROIZAT says, spread over the globe in a way not to be deducted from the present map we have to go back to the map as it looked during the Cretaceous but he does not tell which of the constructions he prefers only that he dismisses WEGENER's theories, that everybody who devotes himself to the study of plant migrations should pay attention not only to the present configuration of the continents goes without saying. His own ideas of Cretaceous geography in the south are expressed on p. 252.

> It is most probable, sure we would venture to say, that an ancient shore connected every land in the deep south of our maps, not only, but that the lands, now vanished, but once extant between the approach of Kerguelen Islands and Magellania are the ultimate hub of angiospermous dispersal

Here extends the Patagonian-Mascarene baseline with its two triangles, Natal-Kerguelen-Tristan da Cunha (the Afro-antarctic triangle) and Ceylon-Madagascar-Mascarenes, the "hub" spoken of above. CROIZAT points at South Georgia as a proof of the existence of an old Antarctic flora.

> The theory that a nebulous 'Glacial Epoch' killed off very nearly all the ancient vegetation of the antarctic islands is shown to be false by the comparatively large plant-world still endemic in South Georgia, indeed a sizeable flora if we consider that it thrives in what is now hardly better than a glaciated mountain straight out of the ocean (p. 255)

Now, CROIZAT otherwise deals with the phanerogams only, there is not a single endemic species in South Georgia, but there are many endemic bryophytes and lichens. And he forgets to mention that the "nebulous" glacial epoch has left its very distinct marks there, because we know that the lowland was ice-covered where the phanerogams now form closed communities and that it is very improbable that the higher flora survived. It is surprising that, in this connection, he does not mention Kerguelen where endemic genera such as *Pringlea* and *Lyallia* surely survived.

A second baseline indicates the extension of an Antarcto-Gondwana in the S. Indian Ocean, a third lies along 60° S and runs from south and east of Chatham Is. to contact S. America. From these centres the angiosperms started to disperse during late Jurassic and very early Cretaceous times through three "gates" in three main streams, the West Polynesian, the Magellanian and the African gate. Many of the genera occurring in Juan Fernandez, endemic or not, are mentioned by CROIZAT, several of them are, also in my opinion, of Antarctic origin.

Oreobolus Instead of allowing it to enter S. America through the "Magellanian gate" CROIZAT makes a circuit along his Pacific baseline from New Zealand to Fuegia.

Juania I have already discussed the taxonomic position of this genus which CROIZAT derives from a Mascarene centre in company with related Andine genera. HUTCHINSON linked it with *Ceroxylon* to form a tribe Ceroxyleae, CROIZAT remarks that

this may be better taxonomy, we do not know, but does not change substances in the least. The ingredients that make up the Morenieae, Iriarteae and Ceroxyleae are all from the same kitchen. In one case *Hyophorbe* speaks, in another so does the face of dispersal. Everything in the end rhymes to the very same. With or without *Hyophorbe*, seasoned with this or that sauce, the stew does not change. classification of such a genus as this is bound forever to remain the plaything of opinion (pp. 456–457),

a statement quite characteristic of this author's method of approaching a phyto-geographical problem.

Peperomia has its stronghold in tropical America where a number of subgenera are found. To CROIZAT the genus is Pacific and Juan Fernandez one of the starting-points of its dispersal toward the heart of S. America, the four island species leading straight to north Chile. He based this opinion on YUNCKER who wants to bring them to subgen. *Sphaerocarpidium*, where, however, only one of them belongs, while the other three, as was brought forth above (p. 259), point west, one of them intimately related to *P. tristanensis*, which, unexpectedly it is true, brings the Antarctic within sight. In a footnote CROIZAT admits that I may be right in my opinion of the taxonomic position of *P. berteroana*, none the less he finds the contact Juan Fernandez–Tristan not at all peculiar. *Empetrum* is another example, both "a mere aspect of the standard dispersal between Africa and South America" (p. 102). But this 'standard dispersal', as discussed by ENGLER, refers to a number of tropical genera and families bearing witness of a transatlantic bridge. In CROIZAT's opinion the track Mascarenes–Africa–America was a very important route.

Palms and Peperomias are pantropical and range south to New Zealand and central Chile, and there are many endemic palm genera on the Indian and Pacific islands south of the Equator whence follows that the field is open for speculation and that the possibility of a primary centre in the south may be discussed without breaking the rules of the game, but to derive exclusively neotropical families from a Mascarene centre cannot fail to cause astonishment. CROIZAT, dealing with Cactaceae, Bromeliaceae, Rapateaceae etc.—and in an earlier chapter he asserts that Malesherbiaceae also had their starting point in Africa—says that

to credit groups of the kind with "American" origin steps must be taken as a preliminary which no one trained in precise thinking will encourage. *Rhipsalis* is doubtless a Gondwanic genus because it is rooted within the triangle Ceylon–Madagascar–Mascarenes. It well may have reached Brazil and the West Indies from West Africa. the baseline of the Cactaceae squarely rests between Patagonia and the Mascarenes, and if

Rhipsalis is Gondwanic it is likely, to say the least, that the archetypes of the family itself stem from the *Afroantarctic* triangle (pp. 364, 365).

Much could be said to this, but I shall confine myself to remarking that the claims of *Rhipsalis* outside America to true citizenship are still under suspicion and that the existence of this specialized type of angiosperms in the Gondwana flora needs proofs of some sort. But CROIZAT does not stop here. On p. 523 we read

Considering that the New World is *uniformly* at the receiving end of angiospermous tracks throughout the first epoch of migration we are drawn to conclude that none of the primary angiosperms ever originated in the Americas.

But who will tell us where the first angiosperms were evolved? We have to go back to times when "the Americas", as we know them, did not exist and where, just as everywhere else, all centres of origin are secondary. I cannot see that his opinion that the primary centre must be looked for in an "Afroantarctic triangle" rests on a stable foundation, but everybody will agree when he formulates the following recommendation to the "phytogeographers of the Academic school" "Look, and keep silent awhile ere you speak."

Phrygilanthus and *Santalum*, compare what will be said below about *Coprosma* *Dysopsis* Antarctic according to CROIZAT p. 51, I regarded it as neotropical

'A large part of the Ericaceae originated with the Empetraceae in the Afroantarctic Triangle', CROIZAT writes p. 381 That the Antarctic has been used as a migration route of the Gaultherioideae seems certain, let alone where the family or complex of families had its beginning CROIZAT finds that the occurrence of a species of *Pernettya* in Juan Fernandez and of another in Galápagos is

one of the most interesting aspects of the Gaultherioideae a track of this nature is nothing unusual, of course, because dispersals of this extent and nature are commonplace between the vicinity of Juan Fernandez and Hawaii, not to speak of the Galapagos and the Revilla Gigedos (pp. 167, 168).

We have examples of a floristic "contact" between Juan Fernandez and Hawaii, but they are very few and to call this type of dispersal commonplace is an inadmissible exaggeration of facts. The American area of *Pernettya* extends from Fuegia Falkland to Mexico, and its presence on Juan Fernandez and Galápagos, outlying stations west of the continent, is not surprising, we need not construct a special east Pacific track to explain them, nor assume that "the South Pacific is a fundamental center of the Ericaceae"

I have mentioned *Empetrum* and the boreal centre of Empetraceae, also that CROIZAT wants them to have followed the same stream as Ericaceae "they begin their visible dispersal only westward from the Cape region" (p. 349), "with the present Atlantic as the axis of their distribution" (p. 353) *Empetrum* used to pass as a classical example of bipolarism, but to those who still believe that bipolarity exists CROIZOT says 'bipolarism, as we know, is a bugaboo of academic phytogeography"—I am afraid that some of us didn't know that.

The case of *Cuminia* (for which CROIZAT uses the fancy name *Johowia*), whether or not to be linked with the Old World and Hawaiian Prasioideae, is embarrassing

my discussion with F. B. H. BROWN (237) made CROIZAT remark that "the debate proved futile, as could be anticipated. To attempt a solution and to discuss possible routes of migration is called 'obvious nonsense'".

Of the presumable history of *Euphrasia* enough has been said above. In CROIZAT's opinion there cannot be the question of a north-south track from Asia across Malaysia to Australia and New Zealand; his map fig. 6 shows the centre far south in the Pacific from where tracks lead east to S. America and west to New Zealand and Australia and thence from there to Eurasia and along the Aleutian arc to N. America.

From the hypothetical "main angiospermous center" south of Madagascar, where *Plantago Palaeopsyllium* was born, one branch leads west around S. America to Juan Fernandez, another east to Polynesia and from there to Hawaii, alternatively reached directly from Juan Fernandez. I preferred the first alternative, but even if the circumpolar distribution suggests an Antarctic origin I can see no good reason to place the starting point south of Madagascar.

Coprosma is one of the standard Antarctic dispersal types but lacking in Africa and in continental America. From its distribution CROIZAT draws the following conclusions

This dispersal shows a) An Antarctic range in the southern Pacific which fed *Coprosma* to all lands between Juan Fernandez and E. Java, b) This range could possibly reach Hawaii from West along the line East Malaysia–Hawaii, c) The trend of this type of dispersal is all westward from the Americas (Juan Fernandez to New Zealand, Australia, New Guinea, Malaysia) ultimately veering again eastward to reach Hawaii (p. 101)

To make Juan Fernandez the source of *Coprosma* in New Zealand is utterly impossible and the statement is not in agreement with CROIZAT's map, fig. 29 which shows a baseline along lat. 60° between the longitudes of New Zealand and Fuegia and arrows pointing west to New Zealand and northeast to Juan Fernandez.

I am not going to enter upon a discussion of the origin of a world wide family like Compositae, I shall only quote the following sentence "The perfect circumpolar distribution of *Taraxacum magellanicum* in itself tells us where is to be sought the ultimate origin of the Compositae" (p. 63). Even if it is true that this interesting dandelion also inhabits New Zealand, the conclusions would seem too far-reaching.

I shall conclude this discussion with a summary of a recent paper by AXELROD (15) who gives us a palaeontologist's view on angiosperm evolution.

The cradle of angiosperms stood in the tropical belt, the width of which has undergone considerable change during the geological ages. The angiosperms originated and evolved in uplands during Permian to Triassic times and gradually descended to the lowlands to replace the vanishing floras now extinct or represented by such remnants as the Cycadophyta. Fossil records, especially of pollen, make it probable that many families existed in early Jurassic, and from middle Cretaceous, when angiosperms had gained dominance over gymnosperms and ferns, the presence of numerous families belonging to very different orders bear witness of a long history. By that time three different lowland floras had developed, the

Tropic, Arcto-, and Antarcto Cretaceous, and it is the latter that interests us here. AXELROD emphasizes that numerous data allow us to conclude that many families and genera generally regarded as having evolved in the temperate zones originated in the tropics.

The data seem to support the view that angiosperms have not had an exclusively holarctic source, or a wholly austral center of origin. They were being assembled in both regions by the gradual adaptation of basic tropical groups to extratropical conditions during the long period of Permo-Triassic down to the Cretaceous. On this basis the Arcto-Cretaceous and Antarcto-Cretaceous floras of higher temperate latitude represent vegetation types whose genera were derived largely by the long and continued differentiation of successively derivative members of original tropical and border-tropical angiosperms. From this standpoint, the temperate regions to the north (holarctic) and south (antarctic) are subordinate or secondary centers in early angiosperm evolution.

The conclusions we can draw from this are (1) that the origin and primary seat of the angiosperms was in the tropics before anything like the present map existed, (2) that this tropical flora gradually gave birth to a temperate flora also in the south, (3) that Antarctica became the centre of a varied Antarcto-tertiary flora which spread north and over S. America reached the region where now stands Juan Fernandez.

II Pteridophyta

Owing to their great age and perhaps also to their greater faculty of dispersal many of the genera and some species have attained a very extensive range making it difficult or impossible to assign them to one of the elements proposed in the subdivision of the angiosperms. Of 23 genera found in Juan Fernandez, 16 are very wide spread, some of them belong to the largest fern genera, and even if we avail ourselves of the generic concept used by COPELAND (69), the situation remains practically the same. To COPELAND 50-75 % of the living ferns are of austral or Antarctic ancestry; we shall see to what extent this is true of the Juan Fernandez flora.

With regard to the Hymenophyllaceae COPELAND remarks (67 174) that "no other plant family of its size and diversity is quite so conspicuously Antarctic in origin as this one".

Trichomanes-Vandenboschia is pantropical, as 2 of the 3 insular species are decidedly neotropical in their affinities, also *T. philippianum* is referred to the same element.

Serpyllopsis is subantarctic American and best attached to an Antarcto-tertiary element.

Hymenoglossum should perhaps be referred to the same element, but its relations are just as unknown as those of *Serpyllopsis*.

Hymenophyllum Mecodium is a pantropical group, also represented in New Zealand, *cuneatum* and *caudiculatum* are most likely of neotropical origin and this may be true also of *fuciforme*. *H. pectinatum* stands, COPELAND says, apart from the other species, but I can find no good reason to call in Antarctic, while the distribution of *Sphaerocionium ferrugineum* and its near relatives testifies to their Antarctic origin in spite of their affinity to *ciliatum* (comp. above p. 219). *Hymenophyllum* s. str.

as limited by COPELAND 1938 (66) does not include *falklandicum* (*Mecodium* according to COPELAND p 94), though it is closely akin to *peltatum*, and *H rugosum* "is to *H tunbridgense* what *H falklandicum* is to *H peltatum*" (62 13) According to CHRIST (59 146), *peltatum* and *tunbridgense* are essentially Antarctic-andine but found north as far as Mexico, also reported from S Africa and New Zealand, extending in insular climates to western Europe The conclusion would be that also *falklandicum* and *rugosum* should be brought to the Antarctic group

Hymenophyllum Merungium secundum, *plicatum* and *tortuosum* are subantarctic-American in their present distribution, *Merungium* is austral and extends north to tropical Asia, and its origin most likely Antarctic

Thyrsopteris Mesozoic fossils supposed to come near this genus have been reported from the boreal zone, besides, from the Tertiary in Chile (see below p 399) HILL (134 1477) calls it "a remnant of a once widespread group which migrated southwards, possibly in Cretaceous times, from the Northern Hemisphere" With regard to its present unique station COPELAND (67 175) writes

> As Juan Fernandez can hardly have evolved so peculiar a fern, its most reasonable origin, as a Juan Fernandez fern, is Antarctica, whether directly or through southern Chile European fossils have been referred to this genus, but Juan Fernandez was not colonized from Europe

Lophosoria is exclusively neotropical at present, but if we are to believe, as COPELAND thinks, that the Cyatheaceae derive from Antarctica, it is unlikely that *Lophosoria* would be an exception

The Antarctic origin of *Dicksonia* seems very clear to judge from its actual distribution pattern To what was said above p 222 I shall add that along the track New Zealand–Australia–New Caledonia–Fiji(–Samoa)–Malaysia 14 species are found, along the Andean path 9, and that the species of Juan Fernandez are not linked with the neotropical but with southwest Pacific species

The present distribution of the genus *Cystopteris* suggests a boreal origin

In its wide as well as in its more restricted sense *Dryopteris* is world-wide and COPELAND's remark (67 181) that he has little doubt that the group as a whole is of southern origin (see also 69 122) is perhaps little more than a guess I think we can take it for granted that hundreds of species have evolved in the neotropical region, where the single Juan Fernandez species *D inaequalifolia* has its relatives

Polystichum Eastern Asia is the centre of greatest concentration, the section occurring there is, in COPELAND's opinion, the least primitive, and we have a number of southern bi or tricentric forms, among them *P vestitum* coll The endemic *P berteroanum* is very close to the circumpolar *adiantiforme* To quote COPELAND "The case for an Antarctic origin of *Polystichum* is so clear that the evidence has long been familiar even to those hesitant to draw the obvious conclusion" (67 181), and, "The distribution testifies clearly to its Antarctic origin" (69 109)

Arthropteris is the only fern genus found in Juan Fernandez which is absent from continental America, but otherwise typically austral Its Antarctic origin is beyond doubt, and *A. altescandens* has its nearest allies in Oceania, comp. above p. 222.

Asplenium. COPELAND points out that some groups at least are southern and that perhaps the same applies to the whole genus: "it migrated in its present form from Antarctica" (69 167). Of the species found in Juan Fernandez, *obliquum* is austral-bicentric, *stellatum* close to neotropical species, *macrosorum* most likely of neotropical affinity, *dareoides* comes very near *alvarezense* from Tristan da Cunha and is not, as has been suggested, related to the boreal *ruta muraria*.

Blechnum. According to COPELAND (69 157) no fern genus is more conspicuously austral in its present distribution and thus more evidently Antarctic in origin. Of the 6 species found in Juan Fernandez *auriculatum*, *chilense* and *cycadifolium* belong to an Afro-american group, *Schottii* and perhaps also *valdiviense* of austral circumpolar type, and *longicauda* intimately related to the neotropical *Sprucei*, even so it cannot blur the picture of an old Antarctic genus.

Pellaea is an austral tricentric genus extending north to Canada, but *P. chilensis*, endemic in Juan Fernandez, but dangerously close to a widespread American species, belongs to a group that, according to COPELAND (69 70), is best allowed to form a separate genus; I have brought it to the neotropical element.

Hypolepis is pantropical, especially neotropical, but numerous species are scattered in the equatorial and austral zones: Africa with neighbouring islands, Malaysia and north to Japan, Australia–New Zealand–Lord Howe–Melanesia–Hawaii —when COPELAND said "without surviving Chilean representatives" he forgot *rugosula*. This species is bicentric or, including *Polypodium villososcudum* of Tristan, tricentric; there is another variety on St. Helena. Thus when COPELAND 67 177 calls *Hypolepis* "an old antarctic genus now at home chiefly in the Tropics but with two of its paths still occupied", we can add that also the third path is indicated.

Adiantum is most numerous in S. America, and *A. chilense* and related species tell us nothing of the earlier history of the genus, COPELAND 69 78 "I suppose that at least the most of the extant species are of Antarctic ancestry, but the genus is old and may have lived elsewhere without interruption", in 67 178 he says that "Antarctica has played a major part in its history", but that the genus "may include elements surviving from other floras and from an age prior to the great dispersal from the south". I refer *A. chilense* to the neotropical group.

Pteris. The great wealth of species is in the tropics and only few extend as far south as to south Chile, S. Africa and New Zealand. *P. chilensis* is of neotropical character, perhaps also *P. semiadnata*, while *berteroana* belongs to a group regarded by COPELAND as Antarctic to judge from its distribution pattern (see above p. 223).

Histiopteris incisa is a pantropical and circum-austral, polymorphous fern with a number of "local derived species" (COPELAND) in Indonesia and Polynesia. The genus is, COPELAND says (69 60) "evidently old enough to be a migrant from Antarctica".

Polypodium is an aggregation of unities of different origin and history. *Grammitis* is, in COPELAND'S opinion (67 184), "a plain Antarctic case", and *G. Billardieri* "surrounds Antarctica more closely and completely than does any other fern' (69 211 see above p 223), it was at that time supposed to be circumpolar, but is replaced in S America by *P magellanicum* As mentioned above, I believe that if a genus *Synammia* with *Polypodium Feuillei* as the typical species is accepted, the endemic *P intermedium* finds its place with this, but I fail to see why COPELAND (68) regards *S Feuillei* as "clearly Antarctic", whereas the nearly related *Goniophlebium* is called "a northern genus Of the remaining species *P Masafuerae* and *P* (Xiphopteris) *trichomanoides* are neotropical and *P* (Pleopeltis) *lanceolatum* pantropical but not reported from Australia and not indicating an Antarctic origin

We have no good reason to look for an Antarctic ancestry of *Elaphoglossum*, though COPELAND thinks that it "may have come from the south" (67 185), and *E Lindenii* is a neotropical species

The species of *Gleichenia* occurring in Juan Fernandez belong to *Sticherus*, a genus segregated by some modern authors, 11 species are scattered over the austral zone, and in COPELAND's opinion Gleicheniaceae are 'obviously and entirely of Antarctic ancestry' (69 26), or "entirely Antarctic at some stage of its history" (67 173), how this should be explained I cannot tell unless he means that the family characters first evolved in the Antarctic, secondary centres of evolution having become established in the tropics The genetic relations between the species inhabiting the three sectors (see above p 224) should be studied Meanwhile I shall refer the 5 species occurring in southern S America to the Antarcto tertiary element

The *Ophioglossaceae* are an ancient family, "scattered with remarkable uniformity over the habitable globe' (COPELAND 69 12) In 67 167 he paid special attention to *Botrychium australe* R Br which has the peculiar distribution Argentina, Australia Tasmania and New Zealand and 'may be regarded as an obvious immigrant from the south" It is surprising that the species found in Patagonia and Fuegia is not this, but the northern *B lunaria* L We have no reason to regard *Ophioglossum fernandezianum* as coming from the south

Lycopodium was not discussed by COPELAND *L magellanicum* is subantarctic-circumpolar, and part of the history of the genus may have been enacted in Antarctica, the more so as *L scariosum*, which belongs to another section, is bicentric

With reference to the discussion above the Pteridophytes are arranged as follows

I Antarcto-tertiary element — 32 sp (66 4 %)

1 Distribution pattern austral circumpolar, bicentric or tricentric — 20 sp

a Endemic species (2) Hymenophyllum rugosum Polystichum berterianum

b Species also found in S America (Chile), many of them with a wider distribution (w) in the S hemisphere (18) Hymenophyllum secundum, plicatum, tortuosum, ferrugineum and falklandicum (w), Polystichum vestitum (w), Asplenium obliquum (w) and dareoides, Blechnum valdiviense and chilense Hypolepis rugosula (w), Histiopteris incisa (w), Polypodium magellanicum (w) Gleichenia pedalis, quadripartita and cf litoralis, Lycopodium magellanicum (w) and scariosum (w)

2 Species belonging to genera endemic in S America but supposed to be

of Antarctic origin: Serpyllopsis caespitosa, Hymenoglossum cruentum(?), Lophosoria quadripinnata. —3 sp.

3. Endemic species without near relatives in America, suggesting either an ancient southern Pacific west-east path or an Antarctic-Magellanian track now not occupied: Dicksonia berteroana and externa, Arthropteris altescandens, Blechnum Schottii, Pteris berteroana. —5 sp.

4. Species closely related to S. African ones. —2 sp.
  a Endemic: Blechnum cycadifolium
  b Also on the mainland: Blechnum auriculatum

5. Endemic species very nearly related to a neotropical species: Blechnum longicauda. —1 sp.

6. Endemic genus without affinities to living genera: Thyrsopteris elegans. —1 sp.

II. Neotropical-Andean element —20 sp. (37.7 %)

a Endemic species (8): Trichomanes Ingae and philippianum, Dryopteris inaequalifolia, Asplenium stellatum and macrosorum, Pellaea chilensis, Polypodium intermedium, Ophioglossum fernandezianum.

b Also on the mainland, restricted to Chile or more wide ranging (10): Trichomanes exsectum, Hymenophyllum cuneatum, cauduculatum, fuciforme and pectinatum, Adiantum chilense, Pteris chilensis and semiadnata, Polypodium Masafuerae and lanceolatum.

c Non-endemic neotropical species not found in Chile (2): Polypodium trichomanoides, Elaphoglossum Lindenii.

III. Arcto-tertiary element —1 sp. (1.9 %)

Also in Chile: Cystopteris fragilis var.

The Antarctic element is considerably larger than in the angiosperms, 60.4 % against 42.2, the neotropical being of the same size, 37.7 and 36.7 %. On the other hand, the boreal element is very insignificant (even open to doubt). No living pteridologist has a wider general knowledge of the ferns than F. B. COPELAND, and even if his new system does not appeal to everybody, we are bound to pay attention to his theories. In several of his writing he points, as we have seen, to Antarctica as the main source. On the other hand he admits that

ferns existed well over the world longer ago than I have would try to explain their presence as immigrants from Antarctica, and must be supposed to have maintained continuous existence elsewhere. This being so, the preponderance of ferns of apparent Antarctic origin in the world to-day is surprising indeed (67. 188).

This origin is not readily revealed in the large and world-wide families and genera, the best proofs are furnished by small families restricted to high southern latitudes and bi- or tricentric in distribution—most of these families have been created as a result of the modern splitting process. With a single southern genus in a large tropical family we cannot feel on safe ground, and if in a large tropical genus only a solitary species is southern, we are not inclined to classify the genus as Antarctic in origin. But, COPELAND remarks, if the ferns as a group were of tropical origin they would be expected to be far more abundant northward where the land areas increase than southward where the land decreases — and very much so — in size, and this would be still more so if they were of northern origin. The conclusion is that if a family or genus is mainly southern to-day, this fact is a strong indication of its Antarctic origin and that, if the present range is wholly southern, the evidence becomes almost conclusive. If the more primitive families or genera are found to be characteristically southern, a southern seat of old fern evolution is almost demonstrated (*68* 626). But when it comes to the large families, their history may be much more difficult to read

A large family, even if of southern origin, cannot possibly be predominantly southern in present distribution, because tropical and northern species must outnumber the whole flora of Antarctic America, or even of New Zealand (*67* 158)

With this he wants to say, I suppose, that a vigorous family has invaded the tropics and also extended north under rapid evolution of genera and species concealing the primary origin, he believes this evolution to have been so rapid that the period since the Miocene has been sufficient to create most of the existing species and a large part of the genera and for their spread over any expanse of suitable land area (l c)

We have no evidence that the Tropics as a whole were at any past time unfit for ferns; and the assumption that this has been the chief place of evolution obviates the necessity of assuming and explaining migration in latitude. It is only when we open our eyes to anomalies in present distribution that appeal to other places of evolution becomes necessary (*67* 163)

Great geographical disjunctions, of which the Juan Fernandez fern flora offers many examples, are such anomalies, and they seem to show that Antarctica has taken a very important part in fern history

III. Musci.

In his analysis of the Magellanian moss flora CARDOT (*48*) distinguished an Antarctic element and he believed in a common origin of the floras of Magellania and New Zealand (p 44) HERZOG (*129*) found that Juan Fernandez has "eine fast vollständig austral antarktische Moosvegetation", but also possesses "ein paar tropisch anmutende Arten *Thysanomitrium Richardi Porothamnium fasciculatum, Pinnatella macrosticta* und ein *Rhacopilum*". The monotypical Chilean genus *Lamprophyllum* was also mentioned as a genus of tropical ancestry. A circumpolar austral antarctic element is said to dominate in the moss flora of Patagonia and Fuegia, characteristic genera, also represented in Juan Fernandez, are *Dicranoloma, Ulota, Dendrocryphaea, Leptodon, Ptychomnium, Weymouthia, Distichophyllum, Pterygophyllum, Eriopus, Hypopterygium, Sciaromium*, perhaps also *Catagoniopsis* and *Psilopilum*. IRMSCHER (*143*) gives many examples of austral-bicentric taxa *Lepyrodontaceae, Polytrichadelphus, Weymouthia, Pterygophyllum, Sciaromium* sect. *Aloma, Hypopterygium* sect *Stenobasis, Hypnodendron*, and species of *Distichophyllum, Tortula, Macromitrium* and *Mielichhoferia*

The synopsis pp. 226—233 led to a classification according to the actual geographic distribution. We have to look for austral antarctic species and genera in the Andine-Chilean, Subantarctic Magellanian and Pacific groups, thereby I have tried to follow the same principles as applied before. Many of the endemic species are difficult to place because their author did not compare them with other species or discuss their position, i. i. belonging to large and widespread genera were left out (see list p. 235). The 8 species of *Thamnium*, all endemic, were tentatively included in group IV. In Natürl. Pflanzenfam. 2d ed. BROTHERUS enumerates 34 species, but none at all are quoted for S. America. Sect. I is entirely austral, with a single species in tropical Asia (Sumatra, Java, Borneo, Philippines), 2 are found in Australia and New Zealand, 1 in New Caledonia and 8 in Juan Fernandez. Of sect. II, 3 species are southern (New Hebrides, E. Australia–New Zealand, New Zealand–Java–Sumatra), the remainder scattered over the boreal zone, 3 N. America, 3 mediterr.–macaronesian, 1 England, 1 W. Europe to Japan, 2 Caucasus, 9 E. Asia.

The total number of species included in the following synopsis is 120.

I. Antarcto-tertiary element — 67 sp. (55.8 %)

1. Bicentric or tricentric (t) distribution: Ditrichum affine, Amphidium cyathicarpum, Dicranoloma Billardieri (t) and Menziesii, Campylopus introflexus (t), Thysanomitrium leptodus, Fissidens rigidulus and asplenioides (t), Rhacomitrium symphyodontum (t), Zygodon intermedius and Menziesii, Rhizogonium Novae Hollandiae and mnioides, Bartramia patens (t), Philonotis scabrifolia (t), Rhacocarpus Humboldtii (t), Weymouthia mollis, Leptodon Smithii (t), Pterygophyllum obscurum and denticulatum, Lopidium concinnum, Rhynchostegium tenuifolium, Polytrichadelphus magellanicus, Dendroligotrichum dendroides —24 sp.

2. Endemic or also found in Chile and restricted to the S. American sector, in either case with Australian-Neozelandic relations, with the exception of Eustichia —30 sp.

   a. Endemic species (9): Dicranoloma fernandezianum, capillifolioides and nigricaule, Ptychomnium falcatulum, Distichophyllum fernandezianum, Pterygophyllum tenuinerve, Eriopus leptoloma and grandiretis, Thuidium Masafuerae.

   b. Also in Chile (21): Ditrichum longisetum, Dicranoloma capillifolium, Eucamptodon perichaetialis, Rhacomitrium subnigritum and striatipilum, Macromitrium hymenostomum, Leptostomum Menziesii, Eustichia Poeppigii (other species in America and Africa), Dendrocryphaea cuspidata, Lepyrodon parvulus, tomentosus and implexus, Ptychomnium subaciculare and ptychocarpum, Pterygophyllum anomalum, Hypopterygium Thouinii, Thuidium Valdiviae, Sciaromium pachyloma, Catagoniopsis berteroana, Hypnodendron microstictum, Psilopilum antarcticum.

3. Endemic species of presumably Australasian and Polynesian affinity not or more distantly related to American species: Macromitrium fernandezianum and Masafuerae, Cryptodon crassinervis, Thamnium rigidum, latinerve, Caroli, Ingae, crassinervium, proboscideum, assimile and confertum, Distichophyllum subclimbatum and assimile —13 sp.

II. Neotropical element — 26 sp (21.7 %)

a Endemic species (11) Campylopus subareodictyon, Leptodontium fernandezianum, Didymodon calymperidictyon and linearis, Bryum fernandezianum, Pinnatella macrosticta, Isopterygium fernandezianum, Rhaphidostegium Masafuerae and caespitosoides, Rigodium robustum and Looseri.

b Also in S. America (15) Gymnostomum calcareum (widely dispersed), Campylopus areodictyon, Thysanomitrium Richardi, Mielichhoferia longiseta, Anacolia subsessilis, Porothamnium fasciculatum and arbusculans, Lamprophyllum splendidissimum Rhacopilum fernandezianum, Stereodon Lechleri, Rhaphidostegium caespitosum, Rigodium toxarium, arborescens, hylocomioides and tamarix.

III. Chilean element — 24 sp (20.0 %)

a Endemic species (4) Fissidens pycnotylus, Ulota fernandeziana, Philonotis glabrata, Rhaphidostegium aberrans.

b Also in Chile, mostly southern (17) Pleuridium Robinsonii, Hymenostomum kunzeanum Oncophorus fuegianus, Campylopus truncatus, Fissidens leptochaete and maschalanthus, Tortula scabrinervis and flagellaris, Rhacomitrium loriforme and convolutum, Stenomitrium pentastichum Bryum Lechleri, Bartramia aristata Philonotis krauseana and vagans, Rhynchostegium complanum, Oligotrichum canaliculatum.

c Cosmopolitan (3) Ceratodon purpureus, Rhacomitrium lanuginosum, Funaria hygrometrica.

Note — On p. 234 *Campylopus introflexus* was placed here, it was transferred to I 1 on account of its circumpolar distribution in the far south, from where it may have invaded the tropics and migrated north, but it is perhaps just as probable that it is an old pantropical species which has spread both north and south.

IV. Atlantic-Mediterranean element — 3 sp (2.5 %)

Comp above, p 235

a Endemic Fissidens crassicuspes
b Not endemic Campylopus polytrichoides, Trichostomum brachydontium

We have seen above that HERZOG regarded the moss flora of Juan Fernandez as almost entirely austral antarctic and that the tropical element was small. Most likely he added the species forming my Chilean element, because they are concentrated in the moist southern part of the country and in several cases range south into the subantarctic zone which is, however, no proof of their Antarctic ancestry. A species like *Porothamnium arbusculans* is as far as I know, restricted to Chile and Patagonia, but the genus is essentially tropical, *Stereodon Lechleri* extends from S. Chile to W. Patagonia, but is the only species reported south of the Equator. *Rigodium* is American except 2 species found in Africa and essentially tropical. On the other hand it is difficult to draw a limit between groups II and III, but the species with a southern area are so numerous that I felt obliged to make this distinction. The Atlantic element will perhaps disappear when the distribution becomes better known.

The bi- or tricentric species found in Juan Fernandez represent a minor fraction only of the mosses common to S America and New Zealand SAINSBURY's new Flora (270) contains nearly 60 species with this type of distribution, and to these some occurring in Australia and Tasmania, but not in New Zealand, may be added *Ditrichum affine, Trichostomum brachydontum, Rhacomitrium symphyodontum, Bartramia patens*, and *Pterygophyllum denticulatum*, listed for New Zealand by BROTHERUS (37) are not recorded by SAINSBURY

Consequently, what Miss FULFORD (see below p 289) says about the Hepaticae is true also of the mosses

IV Hepaticae

In an interesting paper on the distribution of the Hepaticae DOMIN (76) lays stress upon that they are just as specialized geographically as the flowering plants, and

einen uralten, heutzutage in den gemassigten und kälteren Gebieten sozusagen erstarrten, sich von ihren ganz speziellen Standorten nicht weiter ausbreitenden, wenig anpassungsfähigen Typus darstellen, welcher auf der nordlichen Hemisphare seinen Entwickelungsgang in weit zurückliegenden Epochen durchgemacht und bereits zur Tertiarzeit in den Hauptzugen beendet hat (p 3)

He thinks that the evolution still continues in the tropics Numerous genera are widespread, but the majority of genera and species inhabit the tropical and south temperate rain forests in America, Africa (perhaps not so rich?), Malaysia, Australasia and Oceania Austral antarctic genera mentioned by DOMIN are *Schistochila, Balantiopsis, Adelanthus* (hardly austral), *Lophocolea, Chiloscyphus, Trichocolea* and many genera with their greatest wealth of species in the tropics are well represented in the temperate and cool south such as *Riccardia Symphyogyna, Plagiochila, Madotheca, Lepidozia, Radula, Frullania*, while few, in cases very few, species are found in the boreal zone From HERZOG s handbook the following genera may also be quoted as tropical-austral, or essentially or exclusively southern *Hymenophytum, Acrobolbus Tylimanthus, Jamesoniella, Saccogyna, Lepicolea* and *Marsupidium*, to mention only genera also found in Juan Fernandez *Lepidolaena* is restricted to the south temperate and cold zones In the following arrangement I have been guided by these authors

I Antarcto-tertiary element —84 sp (67 7 %)

1 Bicentric or tricentric (t) species Marchantia berteroana (t) and foliosa, Riccardia insularis, Metzgeria decipiens and violacea (t), Hymenophytum flabellatum, Symphyogyna hymenophyllum, Monoclea Forsteri, Pallavicinia xiphoides, Jamesoniella colorata (t) and grandiflora (t), Acrobolbus excisus Mylia repens, Lophocolea pallidevirens and muricata (t), Marsupidium piliferum, Bazzania cerina, Lepidozia sejuncta (t) and plumulosa, Lepicolea ochroleuca (t), Lepidolaena magellanica, Schistochila splachnophylla, Frullania magellanica (t) —23 sp

2 Restricted to the American sector, endemic in Juan Fernandez or also found on the mainland, connected with species in the Australia-New Zealand sector —61 sp

a Endemic (17) Riccardia adglutinata and leptostachya, Metzgeria multiformis, Tylimanthus silvaticus, bilobatus and densiretis, Lophocolea papulosa, angulata and submuricata, Trichocolea opposita, Schistochila Skottsbergii, Balantiopsis hians and lancifolia Lopholejeunea spinosa, Strepsilejeunea squarrosula and macroloba, Cololejeunea Skottsbergii

b Also found in Chile (44) Riccardia fuegiensis, breviramosa, variabilis and nudimitra, Metzgeria decrescens, Symphyogyna circinata and Hochstetteri, Jamesoniella maluina and oenops, Tylimanthus limbatus, Mylia fuscovirens and ligulata, Lophocolea rotundifolia, fernandeziensis, chilensis, attenuata, textilis and divergenticiliata, Chiloscyphus integrifolius and lobatus, Saccogyna squarristipula, Adelanthus sphalerus Lepidozia bicuspidata, pseudozoopsis, fernandeziensis and Jacquemontii, Trichocolea verticillata, Schistochila berteroana and pachyla, Balantiopsis cancellata, chilensis and purpurata, Radula hastata, microloba, Mittenii and Dusenii, Madotheca chilensis and subsquarrosa, Frullania Eckloni, chilensis, lobulata and stipatiloba, Brachiolejeunea spruceana, Strepsilejeunea acuminata

II Neotropical element — 13 sp (10 5 %)

a Endemic (3) Fossombronia fernandeziensis Anthoceros Skottsbergii, Lejeunea reticulata

b Also in tropical South America, extending to Chile, or southern but presumably of tropical origin (10) Megaceros fuegiensis, Androcryphaea confluens, Anastrophyllum leucocephalum, Bazzania peruviana Harpalejeunea oxyota and setifera, Siphonolejeunea nudicalycina, Aphanolejeunea asperrima and diaphana, Colura bulbosa

III Chilean element — 27 sp (21 8 %)

Chilean species without tropical connection, nor suggesting Antarctic relations

a Endemic (5) Solenostoma obtusiflorum and rostratum, Plagiochila fuscobrunnea Lepidozia fragillima and disticha

b Also in Chile especially in the south (18) Solenostoma crassulum, Anastrepta bifida, Plagiochila gayana, fasciata, hyadesiana, deformifolia chiloensis, rectangulata, remotidens, pudetensis, homomalla, neesiana, riparia, squarrosa, robusta clata and Notarisii, Herberta runcinata

c Cosmopolitan (4) Plagiochasma rupestre, Reboulia hemisphaerica, Lunularia cruciata, Marchantia polymorpha

Even if not the Juan Fernandez Hepatics are almost entirely Antarctic as HERZOG thinks, the Antarcto tertiary element is proportionally larger than in any other group, and it is not impossible that genera like *Megaceros* or *Harpalejeunea*, the island species of which were referred to the neotropical element, are Antarctic, and that this is true also of *Bazzania*, represented in I and II, but on the other hand we must admit that pantropical genera like *Riccardia, Anthoceros, Megaceros, Bazzania, Lepidozia, Radula, Madotheca Frullania* etc may have extended far south during a warmer period and given rise to important groups all around the circumpolar belt, and that we have to show that such disjunct southern groups are interrelated in such a manner that we can derive the genera from a common Antarctic centre. This is a problem that only an expert and all round hepatologist can solve. In our island case the result may be that the Antarctic element will shrink and the Neotropical swell, we may have to merge the Chilean element in the Neotropical. Disregarding the cosmopolitan species, anthropophilous and anthropochorous and very likely of recent introduction, we find that the bulk of the Chilean species is formed by the 14 species of *Plagiochila*, we need a critical revision of this gigantic assemblage before we shall know anything of its origin and history. Also small but widely scattered genera offer difficulties. *Anastrepta*, *Adelanthus* and *Herberta*, for instance.

The discontinuous distribution of many southern genera and several species was commented upon by Miss FULFORD (10; 846).

The distribution patterns indicate that they were contemporaries at a time when free migration was possible between South America, Africa, Australia, New Zealand and the Sikkim area in N.E. India. They also indicate that the Antarctic Continent has been of great importance in the distribution of genera and identical species in South America, the Antarctic Islands (*read* Subantarctic), Australia—New Zealand and probably Africa.

Finally, let us repeat our comparison of the four phyla analyzed. No obviously Arcto tertiary (Boreal) species were distinguished among the Hepaticae. The Chilean element accepted in the mosses and hepatics has been combined with the Neotropical to form a Neotropical-Chilean group (NC), A, Antarctic, B, Boreal.

Table V

	A	NC	B
Angiosperms	42.2	36.7	15.6
Pteridophytes	60.4	37.7	1.9
Mosses	55.8	11.7	2.5
Hepatics	67.7	32.3	—

V Lichenes.

Unlike the Archegoniates the Lichens offer insuperable difficulties when we try to trace eventual centres of origin and evolution. Of 67 genera represented in Juan Fernandez no less than some 55 have a wide, in cases world-wide distribution, they are called cosmopolitan, subcosmopolitan, tropical, temperate and so forth, and with regard to about 70 species the situation is the same. Only in a very limited number of instances a genus, or a group of related species is, to judge from its present distribution, concentrated to a limited area, tempting us to consider it a centre of evolution. On the other hand we must not forget that lichens are lichenized fungi, modern lichenologists do not regard them as a special phylum but range them with the different fungus orders and families according to the taxonomic position of the fungus component. Nothing prevents us from assuming that the same lichen species originated in different places widely apart where both fungus and microscopic alga happened to be present at the time when lichen-forming fungi existed as independent organisms. Nor should it be forgotten that numerous green and bluegreen algae are cosmopolitan and that the fungus spores as well as the thallogenous diaspore (in fact more important for dispersal) of lichens are quite resistant and adapted to long-distance transportation, also that they have a greater facility to get established where they happen to land than the spores of ferns and bryophytes.

During early Tertiary times—and certainly much earlier—South America had a rich and varied lichen flora of tropical and subtropical character. With the gradual climatic differentiation and the evolution of cold-resistant forms the rising Andes provided stations for both northern and southern lichens, migrations in both directions helped to equalize the Boreal-arctic and Austral-antarctic floras and furthered the origin of a bipolar element.

With our present insufficient knowledge of the distribution of the lichens all we can say with regard to a majority of species or genera is that they are tropical–subtropical or temperate and either northern or southern, it is rarely possible to decide in favour of the north or the south as a primary source of the Andean temperate flora. The exceptions from this rule are few for instance, genera like *Pachyphiale*, *Lemmopsis* and *Massalongia* may be classified as northern, while *Byssocaulon*, *Pseudocyphellaria*, *Nephroma* and *Stereocaulon* are southern or, if bipolar, have a southern centre making it permissible to conclude that the Antarctic continent has played an important part in their history and that the bicentric distribution of so many species, also in the larger genera, testifies to an Antarctic origin or at least indicates that a transantarctic migration route once existed. Thus I have ventured to distinguish an Antarcto-tertiary element also in the Chilean–Juan Fernandez lichen flora. Here as in other groups the possibility that a bicentric species may have reached its stations from the north must be taken into account, that a circumglobal species has reached southern Chile and New Zealand is no proof of a transantarctic connection.

Below an attempt is made to distribute the Juan Fernandez lichens among geographical-genetic groups. Only 164 species could be included. No place at all could be assigned to many of the endemic species—see above p. 254—and the following non-endemic ones with their disjunct areas were also excluded: *Baeidia delapsans*, *Usnea dasypogoides* and *subtorulosa*, *Caloplaca rubina*, *Buellia halophiloides* and *fernandeziana*.

The arrangement proposed is far from satisfactory and will, I am sure, be subjected to criticism. With our very imperfect knowledge of the real distribution of lichens called "wide-spread" or even "cosmopolitan", mistakes in assigning a species to a certain element are unavoidable. Thus, many were referred to group I with great hesitation because it is impossible to decide if they have reached their austral bicentric stations (south Chile, New Zealand) independently from the north, or if Antarctic routes are involved. The species lumped under IV surely represent several different distribution patterns.

I Antarcto-tertiary element —58 sp (35.4 %)
b, Austral bicentric t, Austral tricentric species

a Endemic species (5) Psoroma vulcanicum, cephalodium, dasycladum and angustisectum, Pseudocyphellaria berteroana

b Non endemic (53) Sphaerophorus melanocarpus, Phaeographina sculpturata (b), Byssocaulon niveum (b), Leptogium phyllocarpum (b), Parmeliella nigrocincta (t) and pycnophora Pannaria fuegiensis and rubiginosa (b), Massalongia carnosa, Psoroma pholidotum and sphinctrinum (b), Lobaria crenulata (b), Pseudocyphellaria argyracea (t), intricata (b) fragillima (b), subvariabilis (b), chloroleuca (b), cinnamomea (b), hirsuta, Guillemini, gilva (t), mougeotiana, aurata (t), nitida, endochrysea (b), Durvillei (b), flavicans (b), Freycinetii (b) and Richardi (b), Sticta Weigelii (b), linearilobа, latifrons (b) and laciniata, Nephroma plumbeum, cellulosum (b), antarcticum (b) and australe (b), Catillaria melastegia (b), Megalospora versicolor (b), Phyllopsora parvifolia (b), Cladonia pycnoclada, didyma (b) and aggregata (t) Stereocaulon patagonicum, ramulosum (b) and implexum (b), Coccotrema granulatum (b), Lecanora albellina, Placopsis chilena, fuscidula (b) and patellina (b), Myxodictyon chrysostictum (b), Buellia halophila (b)

II Andean tropical to temperate element —54 sp (32.9 %)

a Endemic species (9) Arthonia subnebulosa and berberina, Enterostigma Skottsbergii, Coenogonium velutinum, Lecidea avium, Pertusaria hadrocarpa and Skottsbergii, Lecanora masafuerensis Caloplaca orthoclada

b Non endemic (45) Arthopyrenia cinchonae, adnexa and planorbis, Pyrenula aspistea, mammillana and Kunthii Pyrenastrum chilense, Arthonia complanata, Graphis intricata and Dumastii, Dirina limitata, Schismatomma accedens, Thelotrema lepadinum, Dimerella lutea, Physma chilense, Leptogium moluccanum, tremelloides, cyanescens, Menziesii and callithamnion, Lecidea leucoplaca and icterica, Catillaria endochroma and leucochlora, Bacidia endoleuca and subluteola, Toninia bullata, Lopadium leucoxanthum, Baeomyces chilensis, Acarospora xanthophana, Pertusaria polycarpa, Melanaria melanospora, Parmelia laevigatula, abstrusa, nilgherrensis, soredica and microsticta, Menegazzia sanguinascens, Usnea angulata, Bombyliospora dolichospora, Caloplaca subcerina, Theloschistes flavicans, Physcia picta, Anaptychia pectinata, Cora pavonia

III Boreal element —14 sp (8.5 %)

a Endemic Lemmopsis polychidioides

b Non endemic (13) Verrucaria microspora, Arthonia cytisi, Gyalecta jenensis, Pachyphiale cornea, Racodium rupestre, Lecidea enteroleuca and viridans, Bacidia arceutina, Acarospora smaragdula, Lecanora dispersa and saxicola, Parmelia pilosella, Buellia concinna

IV Pantemperate-Bipolar to Cosmopolitan element —38 sp (23.2 %)

Normandina pulchella, Diploschistes actinostomus and scruposus, Peltigera rufescens and polydactyla, Lecidea latypea and mutabilis, Catillaria intermixta,

Rhizocarpon geographicum and obscuratum, Cladonia bacillaris, coccifera, furcata, gracilis, pyxidata, fimbriata and pityrea, Pertusaria leioplaca, Lecanora coarctata, atra, polytropa and chrysoleuca, Placopsis gelida, Candelariella vitellina, Parmelia laevigata, revoluta, cetrata, saxatilis, conspersa, perlata, cetrarioides and caperata, Ramalina linearis and usnea, Usnea florida, Caloplaca elegans, Buellia stellulata, Anaptychia hypoleuca.

Chapter III

Composition, distribution and relationships of the Fauna.

There are no indigenous reptiles, amphibians, freshwater fishes or mammals on the islands, of the introduced mammals, goats, rats and mice were naturalized centuries ago and during the last 20 years also rabbits and *Nasua rufa*.

Aves.

LÖNNBERG (174) names in brackets used by GOODALL-JOHNSON PHILIPPI (110).

Indigenous land-birds

Turdus magellanicus King (*T. falklandii magellanicus*). Both islands. North Chile to Patagonia and Fuegia, according to *51* V 224 not known to be migratory. "More richly coloured with buff below than specimens from the mainland available to me", LÖNNBERG wrote l.c. 3, a colouring characteristic of *T. falklandicus* (Quoy et Gaim), comp. *51* V pl XIII. In *110* this is called *T. f. falklandii* and the island form is referred to *magellanicus*.

Anaeretes fernandezianus (Phil.) (Spizitornis f.) Endemic on Masatierra. *Anaeretes* is a neotropical genus of 7 species (Ecuador to N. Argentina and Chile). *A. fernandezianus* is related to a Chilean species.

Aphrastura masafuerae Phil et Landb. Endemic on Masafuera. A second species ranges from Centr. Chile to Patagonia and Fuegia.

Cinclodes oustaleti Scott ssp *baeckstroemi* Lönnb. Both islands, endemic but very near the typical species (Antofagasta—Chiloé). A genus of 13 species (Ecuad. to Argent., Patag., Falkl. Is.).

Eustephanus fernandensis (King as *Trochilus*) Gould (Thaumaste f.) Endemic, forming an endemic genus according to *110* 300. "Coloración totalmente diferente de la de cualquier Picaflor que habita el continente." These authors leave open the question whether or not *E. leyboldi* Gould of Masafuera is distinct but list it as *Th. f. leyboldi* and the form from Masatierra as *Th. f. fernandensis*. LÖNNBERG p. 7 gave good reasons for considering them as identical. The humming-bird seems to be extinct on Masafuera.

Eustephanus galeritus Mol (as Trochilus, Orthorhyncha sephanoides Lesson et Gainot 1827—but MOLINA's name must be about 50 years older, Sephanoides s, *110*) Masatierra and on the mainland from Centr. Chile to Fuegia. Said to migrate to the coast and spend the winter there (*174*), a statement not quoted by GOODALL.

Asio flammeus Pontoppidan (*A. f. suinda* Vieillot) Masatierra. The typical species almost cosmopolitan, *suinda* ranges over South America from Venezuela to Fuegia.

Cerchneis sparverius (L.) ssp. *fernandensis* Chapm (*Falco s. f.*) Masatierra, endemic, the species distributed from North America and the West Indies to northern South America, another ssp. in Chile. A genus of 28 species and very wide distribution but not recorded for Oceania.

Buteo erythronotus King ssp. *exsul* Salvin (*B. polyosoma e.*) Endemic on Masafuera, an accidental visitor to Masatierra, typical *erythronotus* ranges from Peru to the Magellan Straits and Falkland. On Masafuera the principal food of the buzzard are rats, mice and young goats (kids), all introduced by man, but it has been observed attacking petrels and thrushes. A widespread genus of 33 species (Amer., Furas., Austral., Ocean.)

Breeding sea-birds

Fregetta grallaria Vieillot. Masatierra and Santa Clara and also Desventuradas (San Ambrosio), coasts and islands of the Indian and Pacific Oceans. 4 species, subtropical-tropical seas.

Puffinus creatopus Coues. Masatierra and Santa Clara, California–S. Chile where it breeds on Mocha I. and islands in the vicinity of Chiloé. Migrates during the winter to Peru and along the coast north to Alaska, returning south in November. The genus (28 sp.) is world wide.

Pterodroma neglecta Schleg. Masatierra and Santa Clara, also on San Ambrosio and further reported from Lord Howe and Kermadec Is. Strolls north during the winter. A genus of about 30 species spread over the south hemisphere and extending north to the north Atlantic and to Japan.

Pterodroma externa Salvin (*P. e. externa*) Endemic on Masafuera, migrates north as far as Costa Rica. Another race breeds on Tristan da Cunha, a third on Kermadec Is.

Pterodroma cooki Gray ssp. *defilippiana* Gigl. et Salvin. Endemic to Santa Clara, Masatierra and Desventuradas. Typical *cooki* on New Zealand, *P. cooki orientalis* Murphy on the coast of Peru and Chile, but breeding places unknown, *defilippiana* is said to extend its flights to Peru.

Pterodroma cooki ssp. *masafuerae* Lonnb. (*P. leucoptera Masafuerae*) Masafuera, endemic. At first LONNBERG felt inclined to identify the bird with *P. c. leucoptera* "in spite of the zoogeographical difficulties for such a theory" (p. 15), LONNBERG's opinion is strengthened by the fact that, whereas *defilippiana* and *leucoptera* are surface-breeding like *neglecta externa* and *masafuerae* are burrowing.

Two aliens are naturalized in the islands, a melanistic form of *Columba livia* Briss. in the 18th century and now common, and *Lophortyx californicus* Shaw et Nodd. introduced 1912 or 1913. Several landbirds have been observed as accidental visitors, *Crymophilus fulicarius* and *Buteo obsoletus* migrants from the north and *Belonopterus chilensis*, *Cathartes* sp., *Cygnus melanocoryphus*, *Haematopus ater* and *Circus maculosus* from the opposite coast. Petrels, albatrosses, Cape pigeons and penguins are occasionally seen around the islands but do not breed there

Of the 15 species breeding on the islands 3 are endemic, of the remaining 12, 6 are represented by endemic subspecies of which, however, 2 also breed on the Desventuradas Islands Including these, 60 % of the birds are endemic, a high figure in animals as mobile as birds are Otherwise, the poverty of the island ornis is noteworthy, as also the fact that the affinities of the landbirds are all with S America

With regard to the actual distribution we can distinguish the following two groups

I South American (especially Chilean) group -- 10 sp

a Endemic (6) Anaeretes fernandezianus, Aphrastura masafuerae, Eustephanus fernandensis, Cinclodes oustaleti baeckstroemii, Cerchneis sparverius fernandensis, Buteo erythronotus exsul

b Not endemic (4) Turdus magellanicus, Eustephanus galeritus, Asio flammeus, Puffinus creatopus

II South Pacific group — 5 sp

a Endemic (3) Pterodroma externa externa, cooki defilippiana and cooki masafuerae

b Not endemic (2) Fregetta grallaria, Pterodroma neglecta

The first group includes of more tropical birds *Anaeretes*, *Cinclodes* and *Eustephanus*, and of more temperate *Turdus*, *Asio*, *Cerchneis*, *Buteo* and *Puffinus* Of the endemic species *Eustephanus fernandensis* is the most notable, in certain characters a unique type in the family Trochilidae The second group is of particular interest as including, beside the widespread frigate-bird, four species of *Pterodroma* not breeding on the mainland, where, perhaps, a special race of *P cooki* breeds The genus is essentially austral-circumpolar, as it were tricentric, with Tristan da Cunha representing the African sector Cases like those of *P neglecta* and *externa* call for a common source and suggest that *Pterodroma* belongs to an Antarcto tertiary element which inhabited the coasts and islands of Antarctica in preglacial times

Oligochaeta

MICHAELSEN (*181*) regards all the earth worms of Juan Fernandez as adventitious The single strictly South American *Kerria saltensis* was, he believes, introduced from Chile with the human traffic, and this is also true of the three species of *Allolobophora*, introduced to Chile from Europe, and by *Frederica galba* The occurrence of *Pachydrilus verrucosus* offers more interest It was known from Great Britain, the Hebrides, SW Africa and Fuegia, everywhere living on the seashore, on Masatierra it was not found on the beach but inland in a freshwater stream

Hirudinea

The leech discovered in 1917 in the highland of Masafuera was described as a new species of the Australian genus *Philaemon*, *Ph skottsbergi* L Joh (*147*)

Whether or not the two species described from Samoa and Madagascar, respectively, belong to *Philaemon* remains to be settled. JOHANSSON expressed some doubts with regard to the position of the Juan Fernandez leech and after his death the question was taken up by NYBELIN who showed that it should form a separate genus *Nesophilaemon* (*188*). With its allies it forms a small austral group, possibly of old Antarctic ancestry. It must, of course, have a host, it was found in the extremely wet *Dicksonia* forest, where *Pterodroma cooki masafuerae* makes its burrows, the only possible host existing here (see also *147* 442). Truly no leech has been collected on the bird, but extremely few specimens of this have been taken care of and examined.

Crustacea

Amphipoda (*56*)

Orchestia chilensis (chilicnsis) Milne-Edw. Both islands, terrestrial and found from near the shore to almost 600 m altitude. It is a bicentric species, known also from Chile and New Zealand.

Isopoda (*277*)

Beside 3 cosmopolitan species 2 endemic ones have been found, both belonging to widespread genera, *Ligia litiginosa* and *Philoscia mirifica*, the latter referred to a new subgenus.

Arachnoidea

Araneae (*22*)

I am indebted to Professor A. B. TULLGREN, who supplied much information on the distribution of the genera. BERLAND lists 24 species, of which 4 are cosmopolitan and also occur in Chile, of the remaining 20 one, belonging to the very large and widely spread genus *Araneus* and perhaps new, was left unnamed. The other 19 are enumerated below. Here as in the following + signifies an endemic species, + + an endemic genus. Mt = Masatierra, SC = Santa Clara, Mf = Masafuera.

Ariadna maxima Nicolet Chile — Mt, Mf. The genus widely distributed (N and S Amer, Afr, E Ind, Australia)

– *Theridion Baeckstroemi* Berl —Mt. The genus is cosmopolitan

Th. gracile Keyserl Chile —Mf

+ *Lephthyphantes Fernandezi* Berl —Mf. A cosmopolitan genus, but only a single species recorded for S America (Patagonia)

+ *Macrargus pacificus* Berl —Mt. The genus is known from northern N America and Europe, but TULLGREN (in litt.) doubts that it has a wide distribution in America, thus, its appearance in Juan Fernandez is rather unexpected

+ *M. australis* Berl —Mt

+ *Leptorhoptrum* (?) *Plateri* F. Cambr —Mt. Doubtfully referred to this European genus, from which it differs in certain characters. "l'épigyne est d'un type tout à fait différent" (22 430)

+ *Tmeticus Defoei* F. Cambr —Mt. The genus used to be quoted from N America and Europe, but TULLGREN informed me that a great many species are now referred to other genera

Meta nigrohumeralis F Cambr —Mt, endemic (see l c 430) The genus is known from all continents

+ *Selkirkiella alboguttata* Berl —Mt The genus is related to the neotropical *Gnolus*, known from Peru, Brazil and Chile and appears not to be restricted to Juan Fernandez, BERLAND has seen a very closely related species from Valdivia (22 432)

Mecysmauchenius segmentatus Simon Patagonia and Fuegia —Mt A genus of 2 species, the second one from the Magellanian region

+ *Misumenops Sjoestedti* Berl —Mt An American, especially N American genus

+ *Gayenna Skottsbergi* Berl —Mt A S American, especially Chilean genus of numerous species

G maculatipes Keyserl Chile —Mt

+ *Oxysoma Delfini* Simon —Mt A S American genus

+ *Philisca ornata* Berl —Mt A subantarctic magellanian genus extending north into Chile

+ *Ph ingens* Berl —Mt

+ *Lycosa Fernandezi* F Cambr —Mt The genus is cosmopolitan

Erophrys quilpuensis Simon Centr Chile —Mt The genus is known from Centr and S America, Europe, S Africa and Japan

Of the 19 species enumerated 13 or perhaps 14 are endemic in the islands, 15 (11 or 12 endemic) are restricted to Masatierra, 3 (2 endemic) to Masafuera and a single Chilean species found on both islands The only conclusion we can draw from these figures is that most likely only a minor part of the spiders occurring on the islands is known It is quite possible that there is a marked difference between the two islands, but it is not probable that Masafuera is so poor and that Santa Clara is devoid of spiders Only a short visit was paid to this islet

The fauna makes the impression of being almost entirely neotropical or, at least, S American with the exception of the two species of *Macrargus*, which are of boreal parentage, of the doubtful *Leptorhoptrum* nothing can be said The presence of a southern, eventually Antarctic element is indicated by *Mecysmauchenius*, possibly also by *Philisca*, but so far there is no sign of a bicentric group Whether it can be distinguished in subantarctic America I cannot tell

Acarina

TRÄGÅRDH (268) enumerates 28 species, of which 2 are cosmopolitan, the remainder endemic He points out that the collection, the first ever made in Juan Fernandez, undoubtedly represents only a small part of the acarofauna this is evident already from the fact that not a single species came from Masafuera or Santa Clara Whether the cosmopolitan species are late arrivals or not is impossible to tell, but very likely they are This would mean that the entire acarofauna is endemic, and new investigations will not change its independent character unless some species are discovered on the mainland Of the 23 indigenous genera only one—probably a second will have to be described—is endemic and several have a wide distribution.

The scant knowledge of this neglected group in these regions, particularly in Oceania, is to be regretted, it certainly does not yet lend itself to zoogeographical speculations. Nevertheless it deserves to be mentioned that *Eutergus similis* Trag belongs to a genus hitherto recorded only from New Zealand and that *Phyllhermannia dentata* Trag is related to a neozelandic species, the genus is also found elsewhere.

Pseudoscorpionidea (19)

++*Asterochernes vittatus* Beier —Mt The genus has its greatest resemblance to *Thalassochernes* Beier from New Zealand
+*Chelanops insularis* Beier —Mt
+*Ch. kuscheli* Beier —Mt Related to a Chilean species
+*Geogarypus bucculentus* Beier —Mt
+*Parachernes kuscheli* Beier —Mt, Mf
++*Protowithius fernandezianus* Beier —Mf
+*P. robustus* Beier —Mt

Neotropical elements are present, but species with their relatives in the Australian-Polynesian region are in dominance and part of the fauna shows notable archaic characters (l c 205).

Myriapoda

The very small and incomplete collection—no specimens were brought from Masafuera or Santa Clara—was studied by VERHOEFF (274). In order to get some information on the distribution of the genera I asked Dr OTTO SCHUBART of Piiassununga, Brazil, for assistance, and he most liberally put his wide knowledge of this group at my disposal (letter, Aug 27, 1954). Several changes had to be made in the nomenclature the names used by VERHOEFF, if different, have been put in brackets.

Diplopoda

Brachyiulus pusillus Leach (*Microbrachyiulus litoralis* Verh) Indigenous in western Europe, adventitious in N America and Argentina.

Brachydesmus superus Latzel A European species, adventitious in N America and Argentina.

+*Aulacodesmus insulanus* (Verh) Schubart (*Semnosoma*, Verh) Endemic A genus of 16 species, distributed over Chile and Argentina and belonging to the austral family Sphaerotrichopidae (S Amer, S Afr, Madag, Nossi Bé, Austral, Tasm, N Zeal, N Caled, Hawaii).

Nopoiulus venustus Meinert (*pulchellus* Leach) Widely distributed in Europe, introduced to N America and Chile.

Cylindroiulus frisius oceanicus Verh Typical *frisius* (*C. Oweni* Bollman) introduced to N America, Argentina (also in forma *oceanicus*), S Africa and St Paul's I.

Chilopoda

+ *Nesogeophilus laticollis* (Attems) Schubart (Geophilus, Verh.) Endemic. The genus, which has not been reported from S. America, includes after the latest revision by ATTEMS (as subgenus of *Geophilus*) 11 species (1 S W Austral., 1 N Zeal., 1 N Caled., 1 Annam, 3 Jap. and 2 Eur.)

— *Nesogeophilus baeckstroemi* (Verh.) Schubart (Geophilus, Verh.) Endemic.

Schizotaenia alacer (Pocock) Silvestri Chile, south to Fuegia, Argentina. A genus of 6 species (3 Chile and Argent to Patag., Fueg., 1 E. Austral. 1 N Zeal., 1 Chatham Is.)

Lithobiomorpha africana Porat (Lamyctes insignis Pocock, insignis baeckstroemi Verh.) Widely distributed over Africa, also Tristan da Cunha, St. Paul s I., S W Australia and Hawaii. The genus very wide-ranging [N Amer., W Ind., S Amer. (also Chile), Afr., E Ind., Austral., Tasm., N Zeal., Chatham Is., N Caled., Kermadec Is., Guam, Hawaii]

If we exclude the 4 species regarded, rightly I presume, as introduced with the human traffic, 5 species remain. 3 of these endemic in Juan Fernandez. This is indeed a very small number, but in spite of being so few, they tell a story of an austral circumpolar, presumably Antarcto-tertiary element.

Collembola

Of the 8 species distinguished by SCHOTT (*216*), the first ever collected in Juan Fernandez, 2 inhabit Chile, 3 are known from various parts of the world and 3 endemic. As long as so little is known about the distribution of this group it does not lend itself to zoogeographical speculations. The occurrence of widely dispersed boreal species in S. America and other parts of the south hemisphere (Australia, New Zealand etc.) is noteworthy, but whether their wide range is due to the great age of Collembola or a result of later dispersal is unknown.

Thysanura (*222 293*)

+ *Isolepisma annectens* Silvestri —Mt, Mf. The specific epithet refers to the intermediate position between *Isolepisma* and *Heterolepisma*, the species is compared with forms known from Africa and Australia.

+ + *Kuschelochilis Ochagaviae* Wygodz —Mt. A monotypical endemic genus related to *Allomachilis* and *Nesomachilis* from Australia, but not, as far as known, to an American genus.

Among the Invertebrates treated above the endemic leech offers great interest. Of Arachnoidea the Pseudoscorpionidea include a remarkable Antarcto-tertiary element, whereas the true spiders, strangely enough, are quite disappointing in this respect, even more so than the centipedes.

Insecta.

In order to get an idea of the zoogeography of the island insects I asked a number of specialists for information on the general distribution of genera and species. For their readiness to supply me with the necessary data I am much obliged to Dr OLOF AHLBERG, Stockholm (Thysanoptera), Dr KJELL ANDER, Linköping (Orthoptera), Dr PER BRINCK, Lund (Coleoptera), Mr NILS BRUCE, Gårdby (Coleoptera), Dr LARS BRUNDIN, Stockholm (Coleoptera), Mr FELIX BRYK, Stockholm (Lepidoptera), Dr W. E. CHINA, London (Hemiptera), Dr K.-H. FORSS-LUND, Stockholm (Trichoptera), Dr G. J. KERRICH, London (Hymenoptera), Dr K. PRINCIS, Lund (Orthoptera), Mr BO TJEDER, Falun (Neuroptera) and Dr B. P. UVAROV, London (Orthoptera).

JOHOW (150) enumerates 26 species of insects from Juan Fernandez, some finds may, I presume, have escaped his notice, but probably not many, and it is evident that the entomofauna was very little known at that time. During our survey 1916-17 a fair number of insects were collected and many novelties were described in vol. 3 of this work, but the collection gave the impression of being very fragmentary. The intense collecting undertaken in 1951 and 1952 by the Rev. Dr GUILLERMO KUSCHEL revealed, however, the existence in the islands of a surprisingly rich and varied insect world. As Dr ALEXANDER, the wellknown specialist on Tipulidae, expresses himself (4 35) "Father Kuschel's collecting has completely revolutionized our knowledge of the insect fauna of the islands in many groups, including the crane flies"—only 3 species were known, the number now amounts to 37.

Until now only a part of Dr KUSCHEL's large material has been worked up by specialists, and I can only refer to what has been published (142, 208, 292, 293, 309, 314), but for some groups we now have sufficient data to form an opinion of the zoogeographical position of the islands as far as the insects go. At the end of 1954 Dr KUSCHEL joined my new expedition to the islands and brought back a third very large collection. When all his material has been studied, the insect fauna of Juan Fernandez will be better known than that of most isolated islands. At present about 340 indigenous species have been recorded, of which about 230 (70 %) are regarded as endemic. Dr KUSCHEL (letter Oct. 16. 1955) calculates that of a total of about 600 species collected by him, about 360 still await publication. Among them are 25-30 flies, probably over 50 butterflies, many endemic, at least 180 beetles (more than 120 weevils, of which 4 have been introduced accidentally, the remainder being endemic), and some 40 hymenopters.

Orthoptera

Dermaptera (225)

+*Euborellia annulipes* (Lucas).—Mt, SC, Mf. The genus S. Amer., T. Afr., Orient, Ind., Ceylon, Tasm.

Anisolabis Bormansi Scudd. Galápagos Is., Easter I.—Mt. A large genus of world wide distribution.

Saltatoria (58, 225)

+*Hoplospyrnum Skottsbergi* Chopard.—Mt. An American genus, the species related to species from N. America and Chile.

Trimerotropis ochraceipennis Blanch. Chile.—Mt. The genus is American

Corrodentia

Isoptera

+ *Kalotermes gracilignatus* Emerson — Mt. The only Termite known from Juan Fernandez. "The wing venation is close to that of *Kalotermes brouni* Froggatt from New Zealand" (8; 393).

Mallophaga (266)

Puffinus creatopus and *Pterodroma neglecta* and *externa* are infested with the same mallophagous parasites found on these and related birds in other regions. A new *Halipeurus* is mentioned but not described.

Thysanoptera (3)

Aeolothrips fasciatus L. Boreal — Mt.
– *Physothrips Skottsbergi* Ahlb. — Mt. The genus is distributed over N. America, Europe, W. Asia and Australia.
+ *Sericothrips ineptus* Ahlb. — Mt. Perhaps nearest to a Californian species. The genus is otherwise confined to Europe, where it is widely spread.
Thrips tabaci Lindem. N. America — Mt. The genus known from N. America, Eurasia, N. Africa and Australia.

The two non endemic species may have been introduced accidentally. Both were found in the spathe of *Zantedeschia aethiopica*, cultivated and naturalized.

Neuroptera (185, 92, 125)

– – *Conchopterella kuscheli* Handsch. — Mt.
+ *C. maculata* Handsch. — Mt.
Gayomyia falcata (Blanch.) Chile, Argentina — Mt. Mf. A small S. American genus.
+ *Hemerobius Stoestedti* Navás (H. fumosus Esb.-Peters., H. nigrinus Esb.-Peters.) — Mt. An almost world wide genus, absent from the S. hemisphere except for the Andean region (Colomb., Peru, Boliv. Braz., Argent., Chile).
– *H. Skottsbergi* Navás — Mt, Mf.

Trichoptera (214)

+ *Australomyia masatierra* Schmid — Mt. The genus is known from Chile, Patagonia and Falkland Is.
+ *A. masafuera* Schmid — Mf.
Verger Porteri Nav. Centr. Chile — Mt. A Chilean genus.

Lepidoptera (13)

A great number of genera and species will have to be added when Dr. KUSCHEL's material has been determined.

Tineomorpha

Gelechidae
++ *Apothetoeca synaphrista* Meyr —Mt. The genus is closely allied to the large and widespread *Gelechia* (N. and S. Amer., Galap., Palearct., Macaron., S. Afr., Australia)

Oecophoridae
+ *Depressaria relegata* Meyr. —Mt. Near a species from the Andes of Ecuador. The genus is Holarctic and also found in S. Africa.
Endrosis lactella Schiff.— Mf. Widely spread, domestic

Tineidae
Monopis crocicapitella Clem.—Mt, Mf. In most parts of the globe, domestic

Pyralimorpha

Pyralidae
+ *Crambus fernandesellus* Hamps.—Mt. A world wide genus
Elasmopalpus lignosellus Zell. Centr. and S. Amer.—Mt.
Ephestia kuehniella Zell. Widespread, domestic
++ *Fernandocrambus Baeckstroemi* Auriv.—Mt, Mf. The genus nearly related to *Crambus*
+ *F. brunneus* Auriv.—Mt
+ *F. fuscus* Auriv.—Mt
++ *Juania annulata* Auriv.—Mt. Similar in some ways to *Ptochostola* Meyr. (S. Afr., Australia)
Nomophila noctuella Schiff. Cosmopol.—Mt. Mf, adventitious
+ *Pionea fumipennis* (Warren) Hamps.—Mt. A world wide genus
Scoparia Ragonoti Butl.—Mt, Mf. Chile. A very widespread genus

Geometrina

Geometridae
+ *Eupithecia halosydne* Prout —Mt. A widespread genus, but not found in Australasia
+ *E.* (?) *inepta* Prout —Mt
+ *E. physocleora* Prout —Mt
+ *Lobophora insularis* Auriv.—Mt. An essentially Palaearctic genus

Tortricidae
+ *Crocidosema insulana* Auriv. – Mt. A S. American genus
+ *Eulia griseiceps* Auriv.—Mt. The genus Holarctic, also in Hawaii, few elsewhere
+ *E. Robinsoni* Auriv.—Mt
+ *E. striolana* Auriv.—Mt

Noctuina

Noctuidae
Copitarsia turbata Herr.-Sch. Venezuela, Colombia —Mt. The genus in Mex., Centr. and S. Amer. (Argent., Chile)
Feltia malefida Guen. Amer. (south to Chile), Macaronesia —Mt

+ *Hoplotarsia magna* Auriv. —Mt. Related to *Copitarsia*
Leucania impuncta Guén. Chile —Mt. A bipolar genus (Palaearct., N. Zeal.)
+ *Lycophotia Baeckstroemi* Auriv. —Mt. The genus widespread (Arct., Amer., Eur., S. Afr., Madag., N. Zeal.)
L. messium Guen. Chile, Patag. —Mt.
Rachiplusia nu Guén. Patag., Urug., Argent., Chile —Mt.
Syngrapha gammoides Blanch. Chile —Mt, Mf. A Palaearctic genus, Mex., S. Amer.

Rhopalocera

Pyrameis carye Huebn. Widespread in S. America and probably introduced in Juan Fernandez —Mt.

Diptera (84, 142)

Acroceridae (208)
+ *Ogcodes kuscheli* Sabr. —Mt. A temperate genus, recorded from all continents, but only 2 species known from the mainland of S. America

Anthomyzidae (128)
Anthomyza cursor (Kieffer) Cosmopol., also S. Chile —Mt.

Calliphoridae (255)
Callynthopyga humeralis (Walker) Souza L. et Alb. (C. Selkirki I ndeil.) Chile (Concepcion) —Mt, Mf
Paralucilia fulvicrura (Desvoidy) Aub. et Baxt. —Mt, SC, Mf
Sarconesia chlorogaster (Wiedem.) Arrib. Chile, Easter I. —SC, Mf
Sarconesiomima bicolor Souza L. et Alb. Chile (Santiago) —Mt, SC A monotypical genus

Cecidomyidae (84, 100)
+ + *Psadaria pallida* Enderl. —Mt, Mf Related to *Campylomyza* Meigen

Chloropidae (209)
Hippelates australis Sabrosky [*H. (Cadrema) metallicus* Enderl. non Beck. (= *H. flavipes* (Loew) Sabr.)] Ecuad., Peru, Argent., Chile —Mt, probably adventitious

Culicidae
Culex interfor Dyar —Mt, Mf

Dolichopodidae (126)
+ *Hydrophorus kuscheli* Harmston —Mt
H. poliogaster (Phil.) Harmston Chile —Mt, SC
+ *Sympycnus fernandezensis* Harmston Near a Chilean sp. —Mt, Mf

Ephydridae (289)
Dimecoenia caesia (v. d. Wulp) Wirth Argent., Uruguay —Mt, SC
— *Discocerina fumipennis* Wirth —Mt Near a Chilean sp.
Hyadina certa Cresson Chile —Mt, Mf
Hydrellia vulgaris Cresson Guatem., Boliv., Chile —Mt

—Scatella angustipennis Wirth —Mf An almost Cosmopolitan genus
—S. argentifacies Wirth —Mt
+S. brachyptera Wirth —Mt
+S. decemguttata Wirth —Mt, SC, Mf
+S. discalis Wirth —Mt
+S. fernandezensis Wirth —Mt
+S. kuscheli Wirth —Mt, Mf
—S. lutea Wirth —Mt
+S. marginalis Wirth —Mt
+S. masatierrensis Wirth —Mt
+S. minima Wirth —Mt
+S. nanoptera Wirth —Mt
+S. pallida Wirth —Mt
+S. pilimana Wirth —Mf
+S. stenoptera Wirth —Mt
—S. vittata Wirth —Mt
+Scatophila fernandeziana Wirth —SC
S. medifemur Wirth Chile (Coquimbo) —Mt, SC

Heleidae (288)

+Dasyhelea australis Wirth —Mt, Mf Near a Chilean sp., genus cosmop.
+Forcipomyia tenuisquamipes Wirth —Mt A widespread genus (N. and S. Amer., Eur., Afr., Austral.), one species common to Paraguay and Australia
+F. sanctaeclarae Wirth —Mt, SC

Helomyzidae (128)

Blaesochaetophora pictuornis (Bigot) Henn. S. Chile —Mt
Prosopantrum flavifrons Tonn. et Mall. (Cnemospathis Baeckstroemi et Schoenemanni Enderl.) Chile, S. Africa, New Zealand —Mt, Mf

Lonchaeidae (128)

Lonchaea patagonica Malloch Chile —Mt

Muscidae (128)

Austrocoenosia ignobilis (Stein) Hennig Chile —Mt
Craspedochaeta limbinervis (Macq.) Hennig S. Chile —Mt, Mf
Delia platura v. sanctijacobi (Bigot) Hennig Chile —Mt, Mf
Euryomma peregrinum (Meigen) Hennig Peru, Chile —Mf
Fannia anthracina (Walker) Hennig Chile —Mt
F. canalicularis (L.) Cosmopol., also in Chile —Mt, Mf
F. punctiventris Malloch S. Chile —Mt
Fucellia intermedia Lundbeck (Egeria masatierrana et masafuerana Enderl.) Eur., Oceania —Mt, Mf
Hydrotaea cyaneiventris Macq. Chile —Mt, Mf
Limnophora patagonica Malloch S. Chile, Patag. —Mt
+Notoschoenomyza kuscheli Hennig —Mt, Mf
Ophyra caerulea Macq. Centr. Chile to Fueg. —Mt

+ *Schoenomyzina endent* Hennig —Mf
+ *Syllimnophora lispomima* Hennig —Mt, Mf

Mycetophilidae (100)

+ *Exechia furcilla* Freem —Mt Near a Chilean species, world-wide genus
+ *Leia malleolus* Freem —Mt Allied to a species reported from Bolivia, Peru and Brazil the genus world wide
Macrocera funerea Freem Chile —Mt A world wide genus
+ *Mycetophila angustifurca* Enderl —Mt, Mf The genus world wide
M conifera Freem Chile —Mf
M cornuta Freem Chile —Mt
M flavolunata Freem Chile —Mt, Mf
M (?) insecta Freem Chile —Mt
M spinosa Freem Chile —Mf
+ *M subfumosa* Freem —Mt
− *Paraleia nephrodops* (Enderl s n Selkirkius) Freem —Mt
P nubilipennis Walker Chile —Mf The genus neotrop, Austral, Tasm
Sciophila ochreata Phil Chile —Mt A world-wide genus

Piophilidae (128)

Piophila casei (L) Cosmopol, domestic —Mt, Mf
P foveolata Meigen Cosmopol —Mt

Phoridae (84)

+ *Lioyella juanfernandezica* Enderl —Mt, Mf A European genus

Phrynidae (128)

Phryne fuscipennis Macq S Chile —Mt, Mf

Platypezidae

Microsania pallipes Meigen Cosmopol —Mf

Psychodidae (84, 212)

Psychoda cinerea Banks Cosmopol, also Chile —Mt A widespread genus
+ *P masatierrensis* Satchell —Mt, Mf Possibly = the following
+ *P minutissima* Enderl —Mt
P severini Tonnoir Widespread in temperate regions —Mt, Mf

Sarcophagidae (255)

Hypopygia varia (Walker) Townsend Chile —Mt, SC, Mf

Scatopsidae (84, 100)

+ + *Masatierra ferruginea* Enderl —Mt Related to the European *Rhaeboza* Enderl FREEMAN does not mention *Masatierra*
Scatopse fuscipes Meigen —Mt, Mf A world-wide genus
S notata (L) Cosmopol, introduced with the traffic —Mt

Sciaridae (100)

+ *Bradysia fusca* Freem —Mt, Mf A world wide genus

+ *B. media* Freem — Mt, Mf
+ *Merianna kuscheli* Freem — Mt, Mf. Another species in Brazil
− *Psiloscaia nitens* Freem — Mt

Simuliidae (294)

+ *Gigantodax kuscheli* Wygodz — Mt, Mf. An essentially Chilean Patagonian genus with single species as far north as Mexico

Sphaeroceridae (84, 204)

Archiborborus submaculatus Duda. S Chile, Patag — Mt
++ *Gyretria binodatipes* Enderl — Mt. The genus is perhaps identical with *Skottsbergia* Enderl, and this is merged into *Leptocera* by RICHARDS who, however, does not list the two *Gyretria* species described by ENDERLIN but not found in Dr KUSCHEL's material
+ *G. crassicosta* Enderl — Mf
Leptocera brachystoma (Stenhammar) Richards Cosmopol, also in Chile — Mt, Mf The genus is widespread and well represented in S America
+ *L. cultellipennis* (Enderl ut Skottsbergia) Richards — Mt
L. darwini Richards Chile, Argent — Mt, Mf
L. divergens Duda Peru, Boliv, Chile, Argent — Mt, SC
+ *L. duplicata* Richards — Mt
+ *L. ellipsipennis* Richards — Mt
L. flavipes (Meigen) Richards Eur, N Afr — Mt
L. mediospinosa Duda Cosmopol — Mt
L. pectinifera (Villen) Richards Eur, Falkl Is — Mt
L. pulchripes Duda Argent, Parag, Urug — Mt
++ *Phthitia alexandri* Richards — Mt The genus must be very near *Leptocera*
+ *Ph. selkirki* (Enderl ut Pterodrepana) Richards — Mt
− *Ph. venosa* Enderl — Mt

Syrphidae (96)

Allograpta exotica (Wiedem) (A. Skottsbergi Enderl) Neotropical. An American genus of at least 16 species, the majority in S America — Mt, SC, Mf
− *A. robinsoniana* Enderl — Mt, Mf
Melanostoma fenestratum (Macq) Fluke Chile — Mt An American genus
+ *M. Lundbladi* (Enderl ut Carposcalis) Fluke — Mt
Eristalis tenax (L) Cosmopol, also in Chile — Mt, Mf
Sterphus aurifrons Shannon Chile — Mt

Tachinidae (70)

Incamyia chilensis Aldrich Chile — Mt, SC, Mf A S American genus
− *Phantasiosiphona kuscheli* Cortés — Mt A Centr American genus

Tendipedidae (288)

Anatopynia vittigera Edw S Chile, Patag — Mf A world wide genus
+ *Clunio fuscipennis* Wirth — Mf A large wide ranging genus
+ *Hydrobaenus fernandezensis* Wirth — Mt, Mf The genus world wide

H. pratorum (Goetgeb.) Coe. England, Chile, Patag.—Mt

H. pusillus (Eaton) Coe. England, Kerguelen—Mt

+ *Podonomus acutus* Wirth—Mf. A genus of numerous species in southern S. America, few elsewhere (Eur., N. Amer.)

+ *P. discistylus* Wirth—Mt. Mf.

P. kiefferi (Garrett) Edwards. Brit. Columb. Chile, Fui.—Mf

+ *P. kuscheli* Wirth—Mf

P. nigrinus Edwards—S. Chile—Mf

+ *P. selkirki* Wirth—Mt. Mf

Tanytarsus flavipes (Meigen) Townes. N. Amer., S. Amer., also Chile, Eur.—Mt

Tipulidae (4)

Ctenoptera pilipes (Fabricius) Cosmopol.—Mt, SC, Mf

+ *Limonia* (Dicranomyia) *affabilis* Alex.—Mt. Mf. A very large and wide-ranging genus

+ *L. amphionis* Alex.—Mt

+ *L. aviciasta* Alex.—Mt

+ *L. harpax* Alex.—Mt

+ *L. kuscheliana* Alex.—Mt

+ *L. masafuerae* Alex.—Mf

+ *L. pedestris* Alex.—Mf

+ *L. selkirki* Alex.—Mt. Mf

+ *L. stuardoi* Alex.—Mt

L. trituberculata Alex. S. Chile, Patag.—Mt. SC (an endemic variety)

+ *L. venatrix* Alex.—Mt

+ *L. veneris* Alex.—Mf

+ *L. yunqueana* Alex.—Mt

+ *Molophilus amphacanthus* Alex.—Mt. A world-wide genus well developed on the mainland

+ *M. antimonus* Alex.—Mt. Mf

+ *M. appressospinus* Alex.—Mt

+ *M. araferus* Alex.—Mt

+ *M. canopus* Alex.—Mt

+ *M. defoeanus* Alex.—Mf

+ *M. distifurcus* Alex.—Mt

+ *M. filiolus* Alex.—Mt

+ *M. filius* Alex.—Mt

+ *M. masafuerae* Alex.—Mf

+ *M. multifidus* Alex.—Mt

+ *M. neptunus* Alex.—Mt

+ *M. pectinifer us* Alex.—Mt

+ *M. rectispinus* Alex.—Mt

+ *M. selkirkianus* (Enderl. ut *Archimolophilus*) Alex.—Mt

+ *M. styx* Alex.—Mf

+ *M. tridens* Alex.—Mt
+ *M. variatus* Alex.—Mf
+ *M. junquensis* Alex.—Mt
+ *Shannonomyia kuscheli* Alex.—Mf. An American genus, well represented also in Chile and extending north to Canada.
+ *Sh. masatierrae* Alex.—Mt
+ *Sh. selkirkiana* Alex.—Mt
+ *Tipula baeckstroemi* Alex.—Mt. The genus world wide.

Coleoptera

As yet little has been published about the beetles collected by Dr. KUSCHEL, to judge from what is known the number of island species no doubt will be multiplied.

Anobiidae (195)

Anobium punctatum De Geer. Cosmopol., introduced.—Mt. Beside the typical species an endemic ssp. described by Pic (Mt)
A. striatum Ol. Cosmopol., introduced.—Mt
+ *Calymmaderus atronotatus* Pic.—Mt, Mf. Near a Chilean species. Numerous species in N. and S. America.
++ *Masatierrum impressipenne* Pic.—Mt, Mf. A genus near *Megorama* Fall, a small N. American genus.
Stegobium (Sitodrepa) *paniceum* (L.) Cosmopol., domestic.—Mf
Xyletomerus pubescens ssp. *kuscheli* Pic.—Mt. the ssp. endemic. A north American genus.
X. pubescens var. *picitarsis* Pic (fumosus var., Pic).—Mt. The variety endemic.

Anthribidae (153)

++ *Opisolia lenis* Jordan.—Mt. Related to *Eucyclotropis* Jordan (Centr. and S. Amer.)

Bostrychidae (166)

Neoterius pulvinatus Blanch. Chile.—Mt. A small genus reported from Peru and Chile.
Prostephanus sulcicollis Fairm. et Germ. Chile.—Mt

Carabidae (5, 260)

Bembidium inconstans Solier. Chile.—Mt. A world wide genus.
B. punctigerum Solier. Chile.—Mt
Laemosthenes complanatus Dejean (Pristonychus, Gory, Andrewes). Cosmopol., also Chile, introduced.—Mt, Mf
+ *Metius eurypterus* Putzeys.—Mf. A S. American genus, mostly in the far south.
M. flavipes Dejean. Chile.—Mt, SC
+ *M. kuscheli* Straneo.—Mt
+ *M. ovalipennis* Straneo.—Mf

+ *Pterostichus kuscheli* Straneo —Mt A world-wide genus
+ *Pt. selkirki* Andrewes —Mt, SC
+ *Pt. skottsbergi* Andrewes —Mt
+ *Pt. walkeri* Andrewes —Mt
+ + *Trachysarus basalis* Straneo —Mt The genus presumably endemic (260 138)
+ *T. bicolor* Straneo —Mt
+ *T. emdeni* Straneo —Mt
+ *T. kuscheli* Straneo —Mt
+ *T. ovalipennis* Straneo —Mt
+ *T. pallipes* Germ —Mt, Mf
+ *T. punctiger* Andrewes —Mf
+ *T. serveus* Andrewes —Mf
+ *Trechisibus backstroemi* (Andr.) Straneo —Mf An American genus
T. femoralis Germ. Chile —Mt (end. ssp.), SC
+ *T. kuscheli* Jeannel —Mt
+ *Variopalpus ausoei* Reed —Mt, SC

Chrysomelidae (282, 18)

+ + *Minotula fernandeziana* Bechyné —Mt The genus is related to *Hypnophila* (W. Eur.–Japan)
+ *M. kuscheli* Bechyné —Mt
+ *M. nitens* Weise —Mt

Cioidae (166)

+ *Cis bimaculatus* Germ —Mt A world-wide genus
+ *C. fernandezianus* Lesne —Mt
+ *C. rufus* Germ —Mt

Cleridae (213)

Necrobia rufipes De Geer Cosmopol —Mt, introduced

Coccinellidae (282)

Eriopis opposita Guér. Chile —Mt The genus ranges from Vancouver I. to Patag. and Fuegia

Colydiidae (200)

+ *Pycnomerodes masafuerensis* Pope —Mf Beside the two Juan Fernandez species there is a third in New Zealand
+ *P. masatierrensis* Pope —Mt
+ *Pycnomerus insularis* Grouvelle —Mt The genus N. and S. Amer., E. Ind., Japan, Australia, N. Zeal. (numerous), Samoa
+ *P. germaini* Pope —Mf

Cryptophagidae (36)

Cryptophagus atomarioides Grouv. (Selkirki Bruce[1]) Chile —Mt A world-

---
[1] Letter 19.9.1954

wide genus, the subg. *Mnionomus*, where the island species belong, in Eur., N and Centr. Afr., Macaron., Centr. Asia probably also N Amer.

+ *C. Skottsbergi* Bruce —Mt
+ *C. splendens* Bruce —Mt
+ + *Cryptosomatula longicornis* Bruce —Mf
+ *Loberostheina convexum* Bruce —Mt Beside the island species 3 in Bolivia and 2 in Chile
+ *L. discoideum* Bruce —Mt

Curculionidae (*12*) Dr KUSCHEL, who specializes in this family, estimates the number of species collected by him to exceed one hundred.

+ - *Anolethrus gracilis* Auriv —Mt
+ - *Apteronanus dendroscaridis* Auriv —Mt
- *A.* (?) *gunnerae* Auriv —Mt
Aramigus Fulleri Horn A widespread noxious beetle —Mt
+ *Caulophilus* (?) *nigrirostris* Auriv —Mt The genus in southern U S A, Centr and S America. It does not exist on Juan Fernandez (KUSCHEL in litt.)
+ *Cyphometopus masafuerae* Auriv —Mt 3 species in Chile, where the island species most likely also occurs (KUSCHEL in litt.)
+ + *Juanobia ruficeps* Auriv —Mt
+ - *Juanorhinus Robinsoni* Auriv —SC
Otiorrhynchus rugosostriatus Goeze W and S Europe —Mt, accidentally introduced via Chile
+ - *Pachystylus dimidiatus* Wollaston —Mt
+ *P. nitidus* Auriv —Mt
+ *Pachytrogus crassirostris* Wollaston —Mt
+ *Pentarthrum affine* Wollaston —Mt A widespread genus, found on many oceanic islands
+ *P. nigropiceum* (Phil.) Auriv —Mt
+ *P. nitidum* Wollaston —Mt
- *P. rufoclavatum* Auriv —Mt Close to *P. apicale* Broun from New Zealand.
+ - *Platynanus arenarius* Auriv —Mt
- *P. Backstroemi* Auriv —Mt
+ *P. hirsutissimus* Auriv —Mt
+ *P. quadratifer* Auriv —Mt
+ *P. sericatus* Auriv —Mt
+ *P. Skottsbergi* Auriv —Mt
+ *Strongylopterus nitidirostris* Auriv —Mt The genus is also found in Chile and New Caledonia
S. ovatus Boh Chile —Mt, Mf

Dermestidae (*104*)

Dermestes vulpinus L Cosmopol., introduced —Mt

Dytiscidae (*299, 117*)

Anisomeria bistriata Brullé Chile —Mt The genus known from Tristan da Cunha

+*Lancetes Baeckströmi* Zimmerm.—Mf. The genus austral bicentric
Rhantus signatus ssp. *kuscheli* Guignot.—Mt, Mf. An endemic variety of a Chilean species

Lathridiidae (196)

i *Corticarius curtipennis* Pic—Mt. Near *C. dimidiatus* Belon (Boliv., Chile) An essentially European genus

C. subfasciatus Reitt. Chile—Mt

Melasidae (308)

+*Pseudodiacritus Selkirki* Flet.—Mt. An Argentine genus

Mycetophagidae (196)

Mycetophagus chilensis Phil. Chile—Mt. The genus in Eur., Asia, Afr. and Amer.

Nitidulidae (196, 107)

+*Cnips acuta* Gillogly—Mt. A Chilean genus
i *C. atrata* Gillogly—Mt
+*C. diversa* Pic—Mt
+*C. fernandezia* Gillogly—Mt
+*C. mucronis* Gillogly—Mt

Scarabaeidae (215)

Aphodius granarius L. Cosmopol., domestic—Mt
Pleurophorus caesus Creutz. Reported from N. Amer., Chile, Eur., Orient, Madagascar—Mt, introduced

Scolytidae (309)

Gnathotrichus corthyloides Schedl. Chile—Mt. The genus in N. and S. America
Phloeotribus milleri Schedl. Peru and Chile—Mt

Staphylinidae (25)

+*Atheta Robinsoni* Bernhauer—Mt. Near a Brazilian species. A cosmopolitan genus of about 2000 species

i *Eleusis semirufa* Fairm. et Germ.—Mt. A genus of about 150 species, S. Amer. (also Chile), Austral., N. Zealand

+*Medon crusocanus* Bernhauer—Mt. A cosmopolitan genus of about 500 species

+*Ocyusa Baeckströmi* Bernhauer—Mt. About 40, mainly Palaearctic

Philonthus nitidipennis Solier. Chile—Mt. A cosmopolitan genus of about 800 species

+*Trogophloeus Skottsbergi* Bernhauer—Mt. A cosmopolitan genus of about 350 sp.

Temnochilidae (196)

+*Phanodesta orbrata* (Blanch.) Includes *Ph. angulata* Reitt.—Mt, SC. A Chilean genus

+*Ph. robusta* Pic—Mt
+*Ph. variegata* Germ.—Mt

Tenebrionidae (104, 196)

Blapstinus punctulatus Solier S. Amer., also Chile.—Mt, SC. Numerous species in N. and Centr. Amer., some in S. Amer.

+*Ennebocus Baeckstroemi* Pic.—Mt. Near a species from Panama. The genus Mex.—Colomb., Tasmania

Nycterinus gracilipes Phil. Chile.—Mt. Numerous species in Chile.

Hymenoptera

Aphelinidae (211)

Aphelinus jucundus Gahan N. America.—Mt, Mf

Bethylidae (191)

+*Cephalonomia skottsbergi* Brues.—Mt
±—*Lepidosternopsis kuscheliana* Oglobin.—Mt
—*Perisierola maculicornis* Oglobin.—SC. A widely distributed genus of about 25 species
+*P. sanctae clarae* Oglobin.—SC

Braconidae (187)

+*Apanteles evadne* Nixon.—Mt, Mf. A wide spread genus
+*A. morroensis* Nixon.—SC
Aphaereta minuta (Ns.).—Mt
—*Opius kuscheli* Nixon.—Mt, Mf
—*O. scabriventris* Nixon.—Mt

Dryinidae (191)

±*Haplogonatopus insularis* Oglobin.—Mt. A genus of 6 species (N. Amer., J. Fern., Australia, Pacif. Is.)
—+*Idologonatopus nigrithorax* Oglobin.—Mt. A genus related to the former

Elachertidae (211)

——*Kuschelachertus acrasia* De Santis.—Mt, Mf
+*Pseudelachertus semiflavus* De Santis.—Mt. The genus otherwise Australian

Encyrtidae (211)

±*Hemencyrtus kuscheli* De Santis.—Mt, Mf. A neotropical genus

Entedontidae (211)

+*Achrysochris bicarinata* De Santis.—Mt, Mf
Euparacrias phytomyzae (Brethes) De Santis Chile, Argentina.—Mt introduced
+*Omphalomorphella elachertiformis* De Santis. Said to come near an Australian sp.—Mt, Mf

Eulophidae (211)

—*Diaulomyia calvaria* De Santis.—Mt, Mf. Allied sp. in Australia

Formicidae (283)

Ponera trigona Mayr var *opacior* Forel N Amer, W Ind, Chile, Argent —Mt The typical species in Brazil Probably spread with the traffic

Prenolepis obscura Mayr ssp *vaga* Forel Melanesia —Mt The typical species Java, Australia, Hawaii, another variety N Guinea and Melanesia

Tetramorium guineense (Fabricius) An African ant, now widely spread with the human traffic —Mt

Ichneumonidae (206)

Enicospilus purgatus Say Temperate N and S America —Mt, Mf An almost world-wide genus (Amer, Eur, Afr, Austral, N Zeal, Hawaii)

+*Hemiteles Baeckstroemi* Roman —Mt An almost world-wide genus, less rich in the tropics

+*H masafuerae* Roman —Mf

+*Holocremna* (?) *juaniana* Roman —Mt The genus is known from Europe

Metelia (Paniscus) *gerlingi* Schiottky Chile —Mt Range of genus very wide, including S Amer, Falkl Is, Rodriguez, Austral N Zeal

Stilpnus gagates Grav var *Robinsoni* Roman —Mf The typical species in Europe, the genus also in N America and Greenland

Triptognathus aequicinctus Spin Chile —Mt

Mymaridae (190)

Anagrus incarnatus Hal Palaearctic —Mf, undoubtedly introduced

++*Cremnomymar fernandezi* Oglobin —Mt

+*C imperfectus* Oglobin —Mt

++*Nesopolynema caudatum* Oglobin —Mt

Polynema fuscipes Hal Palaearctic —Mf, supposed to have been accidentally introduced

++*Scolopsopteron kuscheli* Oglobin —Mt

Rhynchota

Heteroptera

Anthocoridae (21)

+*Buchananiella decura* Bergroth —Mt Related to *B continua* B White from Madeira, other species reported from Tasmania and Hawaii

Lyctocoris campestris Fabr Cosmopolitan, probably adventitious —Mt

Lygaeidae (21, 161)

++*Murymenus kuscheli* Kormilev —Mt Most nearly related to *Metagerra* B White from New Zealand (KORMILEV)

+*M seclusus* Bergroth —Mt

+*Nysius Baeckstroemi* Bergroth —Mt, Mf An almost cosmopolitan genus with numerous species in New Zealand and Melanesia, east to Samoa, greatest concentration in Hawaii *N Baeckstroemi* is closer to *N Huttoni* B White from New Zealand than to any American species (KORMILEV)

++*Robinsonochoris tingitoides* Kormilev —Mt Forms a separate tribe

Miridae (50)

++*Derophthalma fernandeziana* Carv.—Mt. A neotropical genus (Braz., Argent., Urug.)

+++*Kuscheliana masatierrensis* Carv.—Mt.

Nabidae (21)

Nabis (Reduviolus) *punctipennis* Blanch. Chile—Mt, Mf. A world-wide genus

Reduviidae (292, 310)

Empicoris (Ploeariodes) *rubromaculatus* (Blackb.) Almost cosmopolitan—Mt, probably adventitious

+*Metapterus additus* Wygodz.—Mt. A wide ranging genus (Amer., also Chile, S. Eur., N. Afr., W. Asia)

+*M. kuscheli* Wygodz.—Mt

+*M. masatierrensis* Wygodz.—Mt

Ploiaria chilensis (Phil.) Kuschel—Mt, Mf. Almost cosmopolitan, also in Chile and probably adventitious in Juan Fernandez

Homoptera

Aphididae (communicated by Dr. KUSCHEL). 4 introduced species on garden plants

Cicadellidae (57)

++*Evansiella kuscheli* China.—Mt

Delphacidae (314)

+*Nesosydne sappho* Fennah.—Mt. A genus known before from south and central Pacific islands including Hawaii, but never reported from America

+*N. minos* Fennah.—Mt, Mf

+*N. orcas* Fennah.—Mt

+*N. calypso* Fennah.—Mt, Mf

+*N. philoctetes* Fennah.—Mt, Mf

+*N. vulcan* Fennah.—Mt

+*Delphacodes kuscheli* Fennah.—Mt. A widely distributed genus

+*D.* (Sogata) *selkirki* (Muir) Fennah.—Mt

Jassidae (21)

++*Alloproctus amandatus* Bergroth.—Mf

Some zoogeographical statistics

Orthoptera.—Of the four species known 2 are endemic but of American affinity, one a Chilean species and one reported from Galápagos Is. and Easter I.

Neuroptera.—Endemism strong, 4 species of 5, 2 forming an endemic genus, the fifth an American species. Relations presumably Andean

Lepidoptera.—Of the 26 indigenous species 18 (69 %) are endemic, and there are four endemic genera. Of these, *Apothetoeca* and *Fernandocrambus* are related to world wide genera also represented in S. America, *Hoplotarsia* to an American genus, the systematic position of *Juania* has not been stated. Together they include 6 species. Of the remaining 12, 7 belong to genera with a large to world-wide area including at least some part of America, and one belongs to an American genus. *Luzla* (3 sp.) and *Lobophora* are essentially boreal. The 8 non-endemics are found in Chile or in some other part of S. America.

The total absence of all indigenous Rhopalocera is remarkable.

Diptera.—At present 157 named species belonging to 27 families have been reported. Nine or ten species at least have been introduced with the human traffic, 147 are thought to be indigenous and of these 94, 64 %, are endemic. Considering our insufficient knowledge of the dipterofauna of Chile too much weight should not be laid on these figures, but even if quite a few of the insular endemics will, in the future, be discovered on the mainland, I trust that a fair number will remain, sufficient to show the peculiar character of the fauna. Besides it can be foreseen that Dr KUSCHEL's new material will bring to light some remarkable additions.

The fauna is not a haphazard crowd of wind-drifted flies. It gets its stamp less from the few endemic genera—of 10 new genera proposed by Enderlein only 4 remain—than from the presence of six non-endemic, S. American or more wide-ranging genera with six or more species each, *Molophilus* with 19 (all end.), *Scatella* with 16 (all end.), *Limonia* with 13 (12 end.), *Leptocera* with 10 (3 end.), *Mycetophila* with 7 (2 end.) and *Podonomus* with 6 (4 end.) together 71 species of which 56 (79 %) are endemic.

The Neotropical Chilean character of the fauna is obvious. This is what we expect quite apart from what we may think about the history of the fauna, but the almost total absence of even a small austral-circumpolar or Pacific element is noteworthy, the only examples would be *Prosopantrum flavipes* (austral tricentric) and *Fucellia intermedia* said to be distributed over "Oceania". There are some striking cases of disjunction, suggesting bipolarity (*Liojella Hydrobaenus, Podonomus Kiefferi*), but the distances will perhaps be lessened when the distribution becomes better known.

Coleoptera.—I want to emphasize that of Dr KUSCHEL's collections only 5 families have been worked out, it is to be regretted that no list of the Curculionids is available. On the other hand I believe that the beetles inhabiting the Chilean mainland are better known than the flies and some other insect groups so that the proportion between endemics and non-endemics will not undergo very great change in the future.

The number of named species hitherto reported from Juan Fernandez is 103, belonging to 19 families, perhaps little more than $1/3$ of the species found there. Eleven species are anthropochorous. Of the remaining 92 no less than 74 are endemic—80 %, only 20 % having been found elsewhere. Future research will alter these figures, I suppose, a number of island endemics will be stated to extend to Chile and vice versa, but on the other hand we have good reason to expect that practically all Curculionids collected but not yet described will prove to be endemic, of 22 indigenous species enumerated by AURIVILLIUS 21 were described as new.

So far 49 indigenous genera are cited, of which 10 are endemic, five of these are Curculionids.

The non-endemic species are, with one exception—*Syletomerus pubescens*, a N. American species represented by 2 endemic varieties—also found in Chile. As yet no austral bicentric or tricentric species have been found. However *Pycnomerodes* with 2 species in Juan Fernandez, 1 in New Zealand and none elsewhere, as well as *Pycnomerus*, *Strongylopterus*, *Lhasis* and *Enneboeus* suggest the existence of a small austral, possibly Antarctic element, even if the area in cases extends north of the Equator.

Hymenoptera.—The 35 registered species, 5 of them adventitious, cannot represent but a minor portion of the fauna. Just as in all other insect groups endemism is strong, 23 species are endemic (76.6%) and of the 26 genera 6. The affinities were, as a rule, not indicated by the authors, very likely they are with some exceptions with S. American forms. *Haplogonatus* is essentially southern, *Prenolepis obscura* is a southern, mainly Pacific ant. *Aphelius jucundus* and *Stilpnus gagates* are said to be boreal but in these as in other similar cases the possibility of accidental introduction must be considered.

Hemiptera.—The 21 indigenous species—there are 7 adventitious ones—are by no means a fair representation of the Rhynchota inhabiting the islands. Dr KUSCHEL's collection contains twice as many species, more than half of them endemic, of the 21 named species 20 are restricted to Juan Fernandez. Where 3 of the 4 endemic genera have their relatives I cannot tell, but the fourth, *Micrymenus*, is most nearly allied to a genus in New Zealand. *Buchananiella* is quoted for Madeira, Tasmania and Hawaii but not from America, *Nysius*, a world wide genus, has a stronghold in New Zealand and in the Pacific, and the single island species stands nearer to a species endemic in New Zealand than to its American congeners. It seems likely that we have to do with an austral-antarctic element.

Mollusca

The following synopsis is based on information supplied by Professor NILS ODHNER who put his unique knowledge of this group at my disposal. The additions and changes in his earlier list (*189*) are entirely due to him, and I thank him for invaluable assistance. Possibly the new material brought back by our 1954–55 survey will give additional taxonomic results, but they will not alter the zoogeographical position of the fauna.

Endodontidae

+ +*Amphidora helicophantoides* Pfeiff.—Mf. The genus (only 2 species known) is related to *Stephanoda*.

+*A. marmorella* Pfeiff.—Mf.

−*Charopa* (Endodonta s. lat.) *involuta* Odhner.—Mf. Numerous species, Polyn., N. Guin., Austral., N. Zeal.

+*C. occulta* Odhner.—Mf.

+*C. skottsbergi* Odhner.—Mf.

+ *Punctum conicum* Odhner —Mt. A genus of a rather small number of species, in various parts of the world.

+ *P. depressum* Odhner —Mt

+ *Radiodiscus masafuerae* (Odhner) Pilsbry —Mf. An American genus of few species, found in N. America (Arizona) and in S. America, south to Patagonia.

+ *Stephanoda antispira* Pfeiff —Mt. About 30 species in western S. America (Chile, south to Fuegia).

+ *S. ceratoides* Pfeiff —Mt

+ *S. quadrata* Férussac —Mt

+ *S. selkirki* F. A. Smith —Mt

+ *S. tessellata* Muchli —Mt, Mf

Helicidae

Helix aspersa Muell. Cosmopol. introduced to Chile —Mt

Limacidae

Agriolimax agrestis L. Very widespread, introduced to Chile —Mt, Mf

Limax arborum Buch.-Chant. As the former —Mt, Mf

Milax gagates Diaparn. As the former —Mt, Mf

Succineidae (subfam. Succineinae)

+ *Succinea cumingi* Reeve —Mt. *Succinea* is taken in its old sense, it has been split up, and the Juan Fernandez species belong to a group which must bear a different name. It is reported from N. America, Panamá, Galap. Is., St. Helena, S. Africa, Hawaii and Tahiti.

+ *S. fernandi* Reeve —Mt

S. fragilis King (syn. *S. texta* Odhner) Hawaii —Mt

S. gayana (D'Orbigny) Odhner —Mt

+ *S. masafuerae* Odhner —Mf

+ *S. pinguis* (Pfeiff) Reeve —Mf

+ *S. semiglobosa* Pfeiff —Mt, SC

Tornatellinidae

+ *Fernandezia bulimoides* Pfeiff (incl. *consimilis* Reeve) —Mt

+ *F. conifera* Reeve —Mt

F. cylindrella Odhner —Mt. Possibly identical with *Tornatellina* (*Elasmatina*) *tussita* Anton, credited to Opara I.[1]

F. diaphana King —Mt

+ *F. expansa* Pilsbry —Mt

+ *F. inornata* Pilsbry —Mt

F. longa Pilsbry —Mt

− *F. philippiana* Pilsbry —Mt

+ *F. splendida* Anton —Mt

F. tryoni Pilsbry —Mt

+ *F. wilsoni* Pilsbry —Mt

---

[1] Rapa seems to be the name commonly used.

+ *Tornatellina aperta* Odhner —Mt A Pacific genus of over 50 species, ranging from E. Ind. and Japan over Micron., Polyn. (incl. Hawaii), Melan. (Kermadec Is., N. Caled.) to Austral. and N. Zeal.

T. bilamellata Anton Recorded from Oparu I.

+ *T. callosa* Odhner —Mt

+ *T. conica* Anton —Mt

+ *T. plicosa* Odhner —Mt

T. reclusiata Petit —Mf According to ODHNER probably identical with *T. tri-rita* Anton

+ *T. trochiformis* (Beck) Pfeiff —Mt

T. trochlearis (Beck) Pfeiff Oparu I.—Mt

+ *Tornatellinops minuta* (Anton) Pilsbry et Cooke —Mt A Pacific genus of 22 species, reported from Japan, Philipp. Is., Polyn. and N. Zeal.

Zonitidae

Hyalinia alliaria Miller A widely distributed anthropochorous species.—Mt

H. cellaria Miller As the former —Mt Mf

Forty-six species are enumerated, of these 6 have been introduced through the human traffic. Of the remaining 40, 35 (87.5%) are supposed to be endemic, 13 belong to the two endemic genera. The occurrence of *Succinea fragilis* in Hawaii and Juan Fernandez and nowhere else in surprising, and 4 species are credited to Oparu (Rapa) Island, but the distribution is perhaps not too well known. The poverty of Masafuera, where only 5 species have been collected, 3 of them restricted to this island, is, I daresay, only apparent. Additional forms have been found later and still await study. On Santa Clara only empty shells of a Masatierran species were found. This islet seems entirely unfit for land shells.

Only two well-defined geographical groups are distinguished to which a third of wider extension is added.

I American element —8 sp

Amphidoxa (2), Radiodiscus (1), Stephanoda (5).

II Pacific element —23 sp

Charopa (3), Fernandezia (11), Tornatellina (8), Tornatellinops (1).

III Austral (or more widespread) element —9 sp

Punctum (2), Succinea (7, see above).

Chapter IV

Continental and Oceanic islands.

For a clear distinction between the two main kinds of islands WALLACE (*278*) is as a rule referred to as the leading authority. From a geographic-geological viewpoint an island, usually neovolcanic or coralline, which does not stand upon a continental shelf, is called oceanic. If situated on the shelf there is a strong possibility that, at some period of its existence, it has formed part of the continent. This is e. g. the case with the Falkland Islands. A truly oceanic island lacks a continental basement of old, granitic or sedimentary rocks, at least, their presence has not been demonstrated. It is, on all sides, surrounded by deep water and a rise of perhaps thousands of metres is required to bring it into contact with a continent. MAYR (*179*), however, argues that from a biological viewpoint, every island, whether situated on a continental shelf or not, is oceanic which has received its entire living world across the open ocean—consequently it must be shown that every kind of organism present on the island has or once had the faculty of migrating across the sea and establishing itself, either the species actually found or their ancestors.

It goes without saying that the answer to the question "continental or oceanic" should in the first place be looked for in the history of the oceans. With regard to the Pacific our knowledge of its origin and history is incomplete, and even if modern oceanographical research has supplied a wealth of information on the hydrography, the nature of the sediments and so on, large parts of the southern Pacific are little known and soundings so few that we cannot form but a very general idea of the bathymetrical conditions and the configuration of the bottom. The northern half is of course far better known. As it is, we must admit that little or nothing has come to light that is opposed to the theory of the permanence of the Pacific Ocean. It is, with few exceptions, from the biologists' camp that the theory has been attacked, particularly by phytogeographers; the majority of zoologists seem to accept the conclusions arrived at by physiographers and geologists. It is easy to understand, however, that many biogeographers, struck by the perplexing disjunctions in the distribution of plants and animals, started to build bridges across wide expanses of sea, in cases with a generosity that led to absurdities. I have no reason to enter into details, our problem concerns Antarctica, southern South America and Juan Fernandez, but even so it seems worth while to quote a number of modern scientists, mainly geographers and geologists who have expressed their opinion on the nature and history of the Pacific Ocean.

Geotectonics of the Pacific Basin.

BAILEY WILLIS (*284*) thinks that a suboceanic pressure works against the continents surrounding the Pacific, resulting in an expansion of the suboceanic mass and a deepening of the basin which, in its turn, has a displacing effect on the continental margin. He summarizes p. 367–368:

The consideration of the general facts of the geotectonics of the Pacific basin thus leads us to regard the great ocean as a dynamic realm, within which the peculiar characteristics of its rocks have facilitated the internal forces of the earth. The effects have been as a whole to deepen the basin in consequence of the expansion of the underlying rocks. The expansion has in turn crushed the continental margins and raised the great cordilleras. Geologic studies of the mountain ranges have demonstrated that the actual orogenic period began in the Jurassic or possibly somewhat earlier in the Mesozoic. Of the earlier periods we know but little, but the fragmentary records indicate that periods of orogenic activity alternated with those of quiescence.

WILLIS did not question the permanence of the basin, what interests us here more particularly is his belief in the instability of the marginal regions.

In H. E. GREGORY's view the Pacific basin inside the deep troughs is an old sink and it follows that all the islands within this sink are truly oceanic. Considering geological evidence alone there has been no significant change in the position of Polynesian land masses since Pleistocene, most likely since early Tertiary time. "There is no geologic evidence that any Polynesian island stood in Jurassic or Cretaceous seas" (*115* 1673). Still he thought that due regard should be taken to objections raised by other branches of science, and he did not extend the unaltered permanent basin outside the deep troughs. When, a little later, another prominent geologist, J. W. GREGORY (*116*), expressed a different opinion, this attracted a good deal of attention. The Pacific had, he says, been claimed to have existed in its present shape and size throughout geological time, a hypothesis almost universally adopted by geophysicists and geologists, but from a biological viewpoint this theory did not satisfy. GREGORY was no believer in large-scale transmarine migration of either plants or animals and consequently inclined to consider the arguments put forth by the opponents to the permanence theory. He counted with a number of Pacific seas separated by stretches of land, and he looked upon the region where atolls serve as proofs of subsidence, a subsidence which gradually enlarged the basin until it reached its present size, as originally continental.

ANDREWS (*6*) who was a firm believer in successful transoceanic migrations of all kinds of organisms and knew more about geology than most biogeographers, shared H. E. GREGORY's opinion: islands situated within the area bounded by the ocean deeps such as Hawaii, Marquesas, Society and Juan Fernandez, all differing in their geological structure from the continents, are oceanic. Parts of ANDREWS' interesting paper deserve to be quoted here:

> An examination of the continental blocks proper and the great western island arcs suggests that they have had similar histories, whatever great differences may otherwise exist between them. Japan, Eastern Australia, New Zealand, New Guinea, Fiji may be taken as examples. Each has a foundation of ancient folded and metamorphosed sediments, such as conglomerates, grits, quartzites, sandstones, slates, shales, and limestones, and each of these foundations has been subjected to marked plutonic intrusions of granitoid nature. Upon this foundation have been accumulated sediments similar to those mentioned above, together with lavas not only of basic but also of acid types. These, in turn, have been folded, overthrust, and invaded by plutonic rocks. This generalization is true even though as yet no consensus exists concerning the age, or ages, of the folded sediments and plutonic intrusives of the foundation rocks. It would appear, however, that the foundation rocks of the island arcs which occur marginally to the continents of Asia and Australia are not as old as the earliest members of the continental nuclei. This leads to the consideration of island arcs situated more centrally within the Pacific Ocean. For this purpose, these may be considered as including all the Pacific islands lying oceanward of the great island arcs mentioned above. The principal examples include the Hawaiian Islands, the Marquesas, Juan Fernandez, Easter Island, the Society Islands, the Cook Group, the Line Group, Micronesia, Samoa, and the Ladrone, Caroline, and Pellew groups, Tonga and the Hebrides occupy a peculiar position, mentioned below (p. 202—3).

Field observations show that these islands have had histories which present marked differences from those of the continents and their marginal island arcs. Thus, they appear to be composed almost entirely of volcanic material, mainly basic, together with "coral reef" formations, whereas granitoid intrusives and acid lavas are lacking, together with the sediments invariably associated with "continental" areas. And not only is this so, but the volcanic ejectamenta of these inner groups do not appear to contain fragments of granitoids and sediments such as might be expected from volcanos discharging through a foundation of rock formations such as compose the continents (p. 203).

Another interesting feature is the peculiar topography of that portion of the Pacific floor which separates the great island arcs and lands of "continental" character from the more central groups. Thus, on the American side of the Pacific, the "continental" lands are separated from the groups—such as Hawaii, the Marquesas, the Society Islands, and Juan Fernandez—by a series of deep discontinuous ocean trenches, practically collinear (p. 203).

The question is whether these trenches are of quite the same nature and date from the same period as the deeper trenches arranged oceanward from the great western island arcs. It is unfortunate for the advocates of a "continental" origin of the Juan Fernandez flora that these islands are situated on the wrong side of the trench. However, the Galápagos Islands occupy a similar position and still they have been claimed, on good grounds, once to have been united with Central America. In this connection another quotation from ANDREWS with regard to the New Hebrides and Tonga is of interest.

Island groups which are difficult to place exactly in this scheme are the New Hebrides, Tonga, and possibly the Pellews and the Ladrones. A profound deep lies between New Caledonia and the New Hebrides, and this is suggestive of a noncontinental origin of the group. On the other hand, the occurrence of mineral deposits such as copper, iron, and nickel, of large kauri, fig, myrtaceous, and other trees, and of animals such as lizards, turtles, ducks, pigeons, and parrots, suggests that they may well have formed, at some earlier time, portions of a continental margin which later became involved in a powerful movement within the marginal Pacific, resulting in the gradual submergence of these outer portions, the present Hebrides, Tonga, and so on, being built upon such sinking area. This certainly is suggested for the New Hebrides and for Tonga, while the Pellew and Ladrone islands also have had complex histories, which would well repay close attention, in their structural, petrological and biological aspects (p. 203).

An additional point of interest is the association of great ocean deeps with youthful volcanic zones, and inasmuch as the trough and crest of an earth undulation are parts of the same structure, it is a legitimate inference that the great Pacific deeps or trenches are relatively youthful structures (p. 203).

ANDREWS summarized his idea of the Pacific basin in a number of points which, with very slight verbal alterations, form the introduction to his paper on the origin of the Pacific insular floras (7 613–14).

1. The continents bordering the Pacific have been larger, at various times, than they are at present.

2. The great bordering island arcs of the Pacific—such as the Aleutians, Japan, the Philippines, the Netherlands East Indies, New Guinea, Fiji, New Caledonia and New Zealand—have been connected directly with the continental lands. Certain of these

island groups—such as Fiji, New Caledonia, and New Zealand—appear to have been isolated at much earlier periods than others, such as New Guinea, the East Indies, and Japan.

3. The ancient borderlands of the continents have, in part at least, suffered undulatory submergence. Compensatory forms are the deep ocean trenches, on the one hand and the mountain ranges of the continents, on the other.

4. The Pacific is a relatively deep and unstable area whereas the Atlantic—with the exception of the broad intersected belt of activity directed toward the equator—has on the whole, been relatively stable since the Palaeozoic.

5. The western area of the Pacific appears to possess a more complex structure than the eastern, owing to the earth's rotation, the width and weakness of the Pacific base and the resistance opposed to this activity by the stable continental masses of Eurasia and the Australian-Sahul area.

6. The islands of the Pacific lying within the area bounded by the ocean trenches have not had continental histories, nor do they appear ever to have had actual and direct land connections with the continents.

7. The New Hebrides and Tongan Islands, and possibly also the Pellew and Marianne groups, appear to partake in some measure of the nature both of "continental" and "oceanic" islands.

We shall have occasion to return to ANDREWS' opinion on the origin and history of Pacific floras. Here it seems convenient to draw attention to the numerous submarine cones called "guyots" recently discovered in the sea between Hawaii and the Marianas and discussed by HESS (*132*). About 160 flat-topped peaks, presumably truncated volcanic islands rise from 9000 to 15000 feet above the deep sea bottom. In most cases their flattened summit was sounded in about 800 fathoms. HESS' working theory is that they were formed on land, sunk to their present level and levelled by sea action—this would mean that they stood with their summit at sea level long enough to be exposed to wave action. Thus, drowned reefs could be expected, but no such are reported: the guyots are, HESS thinks, very ancient structures dating from a "proterozoic episode of vulcanism", they are of pre Cambrian age and consequently do not lend themselves to biological speculations. There may, however, have existed later islands, both Palaeozoic and Mesozoic but all have disappeared beneath the surface of the ocean, either built up again by reef building organisms or sunk to a depth where these cannot live. The high volcanic islands are very young, perhaps not even Tertiary but Pleistocene or recent, because the rocks could rarely be proved to be of Tertiary age. We shall see by and by that the endemic insular floras and faunas cannot be anything like recent. "Oceanic islands", HESS continues, "are and have always been slowly sinking relative to sea level" as a consequence of the accumulation of bottom sediments causing the water level to rise. The red clay increases 1 cm in 10000 years, the globigerina ooze the same amount in 5000 years. Thus millions of years are needed to account for even a very moderate submergence. Besides, raised shore lines are, in many cases, unmistakable proofs of local emergence. The melting of the great inland ices ought to have had a greater influence.

Finally, let us listen to one of the foremost authorities on geophysics, GUTENBERG (*123*). He finds (p. 7) that there is growing accumulation of evidence that the Pacific basin shows unique features which are not duplicated in any other oceanic or continental area of the earth. There is no feature on the surface of the earth which compares in dimensions and importance with the Marshall line within which the younger eruptive rocks are basaltic rather than andesitic. This discontinuity in the material of the crustal layers is called here the boundary of the Pacific Basin.

This is in conformity with what I have quoted above from other sources. However,

certain areas of the Pacific Ocean (near its borders, for example) at least part of the region between South America and the Easter Island rise, or between the Marianas and the Asiatic continent, show indications of continental layers. For the latter petrographical and geophysical evidence agree.

As seen on the map, GUTENBERG goes a good way beyond the Juan Fernandez-San Ambrosio rise, but the Easter Island shield which, excepting the vicinity of this island, is covered by very deep water, belongs to the wide basaltic centre where continental layers are lacking—in contrast to the Atlantic where "granitic layers of the continents continue far out under the bottom ... probably at least some continental rocks underlie its bottom throughout its area".

Turning to the speculations of biologists I shall quote some representatives from the two opposite camps. ARLDT (*8*) did not draw his conclusions merely from facts of distribution but compiled a wealth of geological, palaeontological, bathymetrical dates and so on, and constructed a series of maps illustrating the distribution of land and sea through earth's history. A Cretaceous Oceania united South America with Australia + New Zealand; it disappeared during Eogene and left the west coast of South America in the same position as to-day. From what he says about Juan Fernandez it appears that he regarded these islands as continental (see below p. 376), while still admitting the possibility of oversea migration from the coast. CAMPBELL was for a long time a supporter of the land-bridge theory. He regarded the Hawaiian Islands as formerly much larger and more closely connected with land masses to the southwest, having become isolated during early Tertiary time coincident with the uplift of the great cordilleras (*44*). Later when discussing the Australasian element in the Hawaiian flora he expresses himself very positively: "We are justified in assuming the former existence of landmasses of considerable size, connecting more or less directly both Australia and New Zealand with Hawaii" (*45* 221), and when, for the third time, he took up the history of the Hawaiian flora, he expressed himself as follows (*46* 181):

We may assume that the Hawaiian Archipelago, as it now exists, is but a remnant of a much larger land-mass which has been in subsidence for a long period, and that extensive subsidence has also occurred throughout Polynesia, and to a lesser degree in Australasia. One argument for this assumption is the great development of coral reefs in the Pacific, especially in Polynesia and northeastern Australia. The existence of active coral reefs involves continuous subsidence and the absence of large land-masses in mid Pacific, with the innumerable small coral islands and reefs, can be explained most satisfactorily on the theory that the latter are remnant of submerged land masses of large size—possibly even of continental dimensions.

It is surprising that, fourteen years later, he was converted to wegenerianism in the form modified by Du Toit, thinking that "this theory would best explain most of the problems in the geographical distribution of the floras of the Southern Hemisphere" (*47* 70)—he seems to have forgotten how badly Hawaii fits into the picture.

GUILLAUMIN, in his paper on the floristic regions of the Pacific (*118*), devotes a chapter to its geotectonic history.

> Un vaste continent parallele a l'equateur a du relier les regions australiens, canaque et neozelandaise a l'Amerique du Sud tandis que la region malayo polynésienne et le domain hawaiien, formant peut-être un continent en etaient separes.

The dissolution and disappearance of this hypothetical continent took place before the end of the Jurassic, so that its direct influence on the distribution of angiosperms must have been slight, ARLDT's "Oceanis" was more useful. The Melanesian extension of Australia-New Zealand, including Fiji, Kermadec Tonga etc., persisted longer and is perhaps better founded, but when GUILLAUMIN thinks that his hypotheses "ne sont pas en contradiction avec les donnees geologiques ni avec ce qu'on sait du relief sousmarin du Pacific", he moves on unsafe ground. Most authors who deny any considerable reduction of the surface of the Pacific admit that Melanesia forms an exception. Thus GUPPY (*121*) who otherwise is a firm believer in oversea migration thinks that "we should rope in Fiji with all the large islands westward and southward as originally continental" because they lie inside the gymnosperm line. All non coniferous ones are excluded. GERMAIN (*105* 973) goes much farther. Discussing the Hawaiian region he thinks that it may have extended far eastward. The distribution of some animals, for instance the eel, proves that Hawaii was "part of an oriental Pacific continent perhaps also united with the Juan Fernandez and Easter islands", and he suggests that many of the Polynesian elements in Hawaii travelled by way of South America and Juan Fernandez (p 1009).

Among botanists SETCHELL, pointing to the evidence furnished by geology, expresses his opinion on Pacific paleogeography in the followings words:

> I see no necessity of postulating any fundamental changes from the point of view of the permanence of the Pacific Ocean as such, and the purely volcanic origin probably in Tertiary times, of the islands existing in it, in much the same position as we now find them (*219* 301).

Another prominent botanist who has strong claims to the title "Defender of the Oceanic Faith", is FOSBERG. He refuses to recognize any Pacific islands at all as continental, even Fiji (*98* 164 etc), though the flora is "plutot de nature continentale" it is not necessary to count with terrestrial connections to explain its characteristics. Among zoologists, MAYR (*179*) and ZIMMERMAN (*298*) belong to the same camp, and so do most of them, but it happens that certain animal groups, particularly the land molluscs, offer serious difficulties and have led otherwise conservative zoogeographers to take refuge in "a mid Pacific land". So for instance MUMFORD (*183* 247)

Evidence with regard to the nature and distribution of land snails is of the utmost importance, for it is from the nature of the land-snail fauna in Polynesia that Mr PILSBRY has reached the conclusion that the whole of Polynesia with Hawaii, was once a great continental land mass *Partula*—an ancient generalized type of land snail—is widespread in Polynesia and Melanesia and not elsewhere, whereas many groups (e g Helicidae and Arionidae) found widely spread in the world are absent in Polynesia etc Professor Buxton is of the opinion that Pilsbry has been more successful than any other writer in establishing a case for the early existence of a mid-Pacific continent

But how early or how late? To explain the absence of modern land molluscs we may have to go back to late Tertiary times only, and we should need other proofs of a distribution of land and sea sufficiently different from the present one, perhaps they will be found But we cannot simply fill out the Pacific basin with land and leave the surrounding continents unaltered Often enough due regard was not taken to such circumstances SWEZEY (*262*), who for his own part believed that the entire insect fauna of Hawaii owed its presence to accidental migration quotes two of the authors of "Fauna Hawaiiensis" who did in his opinion without any reason, build bridges where they found that they needed them MEYRICK and Lord WALSINGHAM MEYRICK, an authority on Microlepidoptera when stating that among the endemic Hawaiian genera three were of south Pacific affinity postulated "the former existence of a considerable land area (now submerged) between New Zealand and South America", a land mass which compares to ARLDT s South Pacific bridge—such a land still exists and is not submerged Antarctica! —and he also believed in a "Palaeonesia" extending from Rapa to Hawaii and from Pitcairn Island to the Society and Cook groups Little room is left for the water of the ocean, but he does not argue that these land masses were contemporaneous Lord WALSINGHAM who based his opinion on the distribution and relationships of the Microlepidoptera regarded the Hawaiian Islands as representing the summits of mountain ranges formerly belonging to a continent, "a lost Pacifica", if not accepted, 'some other theory possibly even less acceptable must be devised'—equally beyond the possibility of exact proof

It is easy to understand that, in all these discussions and speculations, Hawaii in its isolated position and with its rich flora and fauna should be the object of the main interest, and I shall end this chapter with a review of E H BRYAN's recent contribution, "The Hawaiian Chain" (*40*), equally instructive as popularly written BRYAN believes in a continental Melanesia but regards Hawaii as oceanic, but this does not prevent him from accepting the Leeward islands as remnant of a long deeply submerged ridge nor from admitting that the Hawaiian Islands proper may have been greater and, in part at least, united The chain is supposed to have emerged first at its extreme western end where we now only find the remnants of once larger islands It appeared some time during Tertiary, the formation proceeding toward the east, with the island of Hawaii, where ejection of lava still occurs as the youngest link the chain having been completed by the end of the Pliocene BRYAN, who has a wide knowledge of the Hawaiian fauna, is no friend of land bridges and less so of submerged continental masses, but unlike many other zoologists he admits that it is very difficult to explain the fauna without the help of some kind of closer contact with other lands. He looks around for bridges in the shape of "stepping stones", just as MAYR does, "temporarily connected or sufficiently close together". "It is," he continues "a long distance between Guam and Fiji and Tahiti and Hawaii, but if there were numerous other islands spread conveniently between ", speaking of the weevils of Necker Island and of Nihoa, Wake and Laysan where, with the exception of Nihoa with its endemic palm and Laysan, once the home of an endemic form of *Santalum*, no suitable host plants exist, he finds strong evidence for their representing 'the last remnants of former forest insects, surviving along a route of migration, a land bridge of the past"—this applies, I daresay, to an earlier connection between the links of the broken Hawaiian chain. However, it seems to me that rows of "conveniently spaced stepping stones", sufficient to offer routes of migration from several directions, involve tectonic movements of considerable magnitude. Few conscientious bridge-builders would argue that, for instance a solid land mass extended from Melanesia and Indonesia to Hawaii as a continuous open road, it might have risen gradually from west to east—when the land upon which the present Hawaiian Islands were built, was above the sea, the western part of the bridge had disappeared, all that was left was a detached, "advanced" portion of a borderland, the home of a facies of the Australian-Malaysian fauna and flora, which gradually took possession of the rising volcanic soil of Hawaii.

Chapter V

The Pacific Ocean and Continental Drift.

It serves no purpose to dwell here at any length on WEGENER's original hypothesis, with which every biogeographer is familiar, but it may be useful to scrutinize its bearing on Pacific problems in general and Juan Fernandez in particular. Before the breaking up of Pangaea, the Pacific Ocean was twice as wide as now, an enormous water desert where no islands enlivened the seascape. The entire sial crust revolved west, where festoons were successively split off from the Asiatic-Australian land mass, got stuck in the sima forming one island arc after the other, bordered on their outside by deep trenches. The Americas travelled at a greater speed away from Europe-Africa, and the Pacific became less wide. It is true that most of the island chains in the Pacific trend NW–SE, but there are many islands that do not follow this pattern, among them Juan Fernandez, nevertheless, even if he did not expressly state this, it seems clear that WEGENER regarded all of them to be of the same origin. In an earlier paper (*231*) I referred briefly to what he said about Juan Fernandez, here I shall quote him in full (*280*: 116):

Die pazifischen Inseln (mitsamt ihrem submarinen Unterbau) werden in der Verschiebungstheorie als von den Kontinentalschollen abgelöste Randketten betrachtet, die bei der allgemeinen, vorwiegend westlich gerichteten Bewegung der Erdkruste über den Kern allmählich nach Osten zurückgeblieben sind. Ihre Heimat wäre hiernach, ohne auf

Einzelheiten einzugehen, auf der asiatischen Seite des Ozeans zu suchen, der sie jedenfalls in den betrachteten geologischen Zeiten erheblich näher als heute gelegen haben müssen. Die biologischen Verhältnisse scheinen dies zu bestätigen. So haben nach Grisebach und Drude die Hawaiinseln eine Flora, die am nächsten verwandt nicht mit Nordamerika ist, das ihnen doch am nächsten liegt, und von dem heute Luft- und Meeresströmung herkommen, sondern mit der alten Welt. Die Insel Juan Fernandez zeigt nach Skottsberg gar keine Verwandtschaft mit der doch so nahen Küste von Chile, sondern mit Feuerland, Antarktika, Neuseeland und den anderen pazifischen Inseln. Doch sei hervorgehoben, dass die biologischen Verhältnisse auf Inseln allgemein schwerer zu deuten sind als diejenigen auf grösseren Landräumen.

In the 3rd edition p. 59 we read after "Inseln": "Dies passt vorzüglich zu unserer Vorstellung, dass Südamerika, nach Westen wandernd, sich ihr erst in letzter Zeit so weit genähert hat, dass der Florenunterschied auffallend wird." In the following editions this sentence was excluded.

Certainly I never said anything like that and I fail to see where WEGENER got his strange ideas, just as many other writers I have pointed out that the Andean-Chilean element is stronger than any other. Even to a firm believer in the festoon theory the Juan Fernandez and Desventuradas Islands ought to offer insuperable difficulties. WEGENER built his theory on the island arcs accompanying the Asiatic-Australian continental border, geologically these arcs are continental, but when he came to island chains like Hawaii, the Marshall Islands and the Society Islands —and we can add Marquesas, Tuamotu etc.—all of which are situated outside the deep trenches, neovolcanic and regarded as built up from the depths of the ocean—he was driven to assume that they have a sialic basement hidden under the basaltic layers. He thinks that this assumption is supported by pendulum observations, the force of gravitation being greater over the islands than over the open ocean where, of course, a sial cover is incompatible with his displacement theory.

WEGENER's theories were taken up by DU TOIT and presented in a modified form (81), I shall quote his attitude toward the festoons.

As WEGENER has observed, they are all comparable in size, regular, linked together en echelon and convex to the Pacific, each shuts off a large portion of sea and fronts an oceanic deep, while the concave side bears a row of volcanoes. To Suess we owe the conception of the development of successive arcuate asymmetrical fold-waves migrating outwards from the more stable "Amphitheatre of Irkutsk", which led to progressive expansion of Asia towards the Pacific. While the hypothesis has since had to be appreciably modified its fundamental ideas have been brilliantly confirmed by subsequent investigations. Significant are the oceanic fossae that immediately front the convex sides of the arcs—foredeeps subsiding in *advance* of the outward moving geoanticlines and incidentally tracts of marked coastal instability (pp. 186–187).

How far did this outward movement, these advance folds proceed? Does Du Toit allow all the Pacific island chains to be linked up here? When the great WNW swing of Asia is replaced by an expansion toward the Pacific the system of rifts in the ocean floor over which the island chains as claimed by most geologists were formed, did not exist, because there was no tension to account for them, instead series of ripples were crumpled up on the floor. The transfor mation of the geanticline structures into rows of islands is explained by Du Toit as follows, their crest

could become deepened by crustal tension and broken into segments to form an island chain before vanishing. limbs were intermittently built up and destroyed during the Cretaceous-Tertiary through stretching in the direction of their length while they were still compressed by forces at right angles thereto (p. 293).

Trying to apply these ideas to South America which according to Du Toit as well as Wegener was pressing into the Pacific basin, the Juan Fernandez-Desventuradas-Merriam ridge could be compared to an advance fold. But it is not convex to the Pacific, nor fronted by a fossa—this is situated on the wrong side and may well stand in causal relation to the upheaval of the Cordillera. To think that the submarine ridge emerging in the Juan Fernandez and Desventuradas Islands is the easternmost advance wave from a western borderland seems too phantastic.

Du Toit's idea of the geological character of the ocean floor differs from Wegener's. Seismographic records, he says, scarcely bear out that the Pacific floor must be composed of basalt—the records could readily accord with a granitic layer up to about 10 km thick (p. 212). He was no believer in a more or less unlimited oversea migration of plants and animals, nor in land-bridges, and he criticises J. W. Gregory and the bridge constructing biogeographers they are wrong, and the displacement hypothesis interprets otherwise. But when he speaks of the extensive "march into the ocean of crustal waves thereby leaving their parent continents far in the rear" and of the "rhythmic intrusion culminating in the three migrations of the Cretaceo-Eocene, mid Tertiary and late Tertiary" (p. 214), these advance folds, when crumpled up from the ocean floor were absolutely devoid of every sign of terrestrial life and without a trace left of the sial cover I fail to see that they can solve any biogeographical problems—we have to fall back on oversea dispersal. Wegener's festoons were at least split off from the borders of a continent and left behind with their fauna and flora. With regard to Juan Fernandez we shall perhaps be able to find a less adventurous explanation of its history.

Two years after the appearance of his book, Du Toit summarized his theories in a paper which I think it is worth while to quote (82, 75-76). The basement of the Melanesian islands is, he says, for the most part continental, the ocean floor consists of a relatively thin structure of sial underlain by sima, but this does not allow us to regard the sial as continental, because it may be a product of magmatic differentiation from the sima. He points to the parallelism between the great Tertiary folding-zones, most evident along the west coast of the Americas, and the trend of the coast line, and he thinks that the "compressive phases" were contemporaneous all around from New Zealand across Antarctica to South America. Coming back on the advance-folds he remarks that some of Gregory's hypothetical bridges or land masses could well have been of this nature. The procedure is illustrated by a map showing the pressure direction and the formation of island arcs—except on the American side, where the sea is a blank.

Numerous biologists have found a solution of all or most of their difficulties to explain the present distribution of the organic world in the theory of continental drift, combined with large scale pole-wanderings. In view of this the opinions expressed by modern geologists and physiographers cannot be passed in silence. A symposium, arranged in 1950 (65) offers an opportunity to get acquainted with their attitude.

J. H. T. UMBGROVE, *The case for the crust substratum theory*, pp. 67–71

SUESS' terms sial and sima were petrographic. WEGENER attributed different physical properties to these types of rock: sial should be rigid but elastic, sima viscous. These statements lack foundation. Sima (basalt) has a higher melting-point, approximately 1300°C, sial (granites) approximately 700°C. The crystalline crust of the sima layer is at least as strong as the continental sial. Still the sial blocks were supposed to advance through the sima. UMBGROVE concludes that continental drift is impossible at present. This granted, was it perhaps possible in bygone times? The answer is fetched from the Atlantic and Indian oceans with the intervening African continent, if the floor of the oceans originated as thought WEGENER, the processes must have taken place during early Precambrian. UMBGROVE asks if not the thick blanket of sediments would have been squeezed and piled up in front when America ploughed westward. He calculates that considering the size of the westward drift, a plateau 200 km wide at sea level would have been formed in front, instead, "the continental slope is one of the steepest in the world and is fronted by deep-sea troughs —here we have, however, to consider the late upheaval of the Andes. And if, as WEGENER's theory requires, the Atlantic originated in comparatively recent times, how are we to explain the enormous thickness of its bottom sediments, according to HANS PETTERSSON a maximum of 10000 feet, "representing a time-span of 300 to 400 million years", which would bring us back to the Palaeozoic. If continental drift ever occurred, UMBGROVE asserts, it took place some 3000 million years ago and consequently loses every shade of interest to the biogeographer.

HAROLD JEFFREYS, *Mechanical aspects of continental drift and alternative theories*

JEFFREYS definitely rejects WEGENER's theory on geophysical grounds, WEGENER gave to the sima properties which the material has not, basic rocks are stronger than acidic, sima stronger than sial. The strength of the ocean floor must be overcome, if drift shall result. "I seriously suggest", he concludes, "that no more time be spent on discussion of this theory until a mechanism for it is produced, what it has done, and continues to do, is to distract attention from the serious problems of geophysics" (p. 80).

S. W. WOOLDRIDGE, *The bearing of Late-tertiary history on vertical and horizontal movements of the continents*

The nature of the mechanism of the "uplift" may remain in doubt, its reality can hardly be gainsaid ... in so far as such complementary foundering took place during Tertiary times, it is not directly relevant with the drift problem ... Vertical movements offer an alternative solution to some of the biological problems. Biological evidences of former facilities for exchange of biota are in themselves neutral in deciding which alternative should be preferred without paying attention to the ambiguity of much of the geological evidence and the grave geophysical difficulties (p. 81).

The progress of knowledge of geophysics certainly seems to point to thinking in terms of land bridges and their coastal margins.

The later findings of seismology, indicating three distinct rock-shells each probably capable of both vitreous and crystalline states, carry the possibility, as Jeffreys has clearly insisted, of vertical movements on a major scale. Such strong vertical movements are indeed not merely to be expected, they are widely and unarguably evidenced by the facts of geomorphology no less than those of stratigraphical geology (p. 82).

R. T. JOYCE. *The relation of the Scotia Arc to Pangaea*, pp. 82–88.

JOYCE made an attempt to reconstruct WEGENER's Pangaea in Lower Palaeozoic time. To him continental drift is a possibility only; he says that *if Pangaea did in fact exist*, his arrangement of the actual continents and islands—as usual, the Pacific island world is not involved—at the opening of the Palaeozoic era is more in accord with the known data than in Wegener's reconstruction (p. 87).

Two biogeographers took part in the symposium.

H. F. HINTON, *The Wegener-Du Toit theory of continental displacement and the distribution of animals*, pp. 74–79.

HINTON rejects the liberal construction of bridges to suit the demands of specialists. Beside the usual apprehensions he adds the following:

A further objection to the past existence of transoceanic bridges ... is the nearly complete absence of deep-sea deposits on the existing continents, since we would expect some of the latter to have been also elevated from the sea floor (p. 75).

This seems reasonable: nobody earnestly proposes to fill the surface of the globe with land, leaving no or little space for the water. Bridges of any considerable size cannot have been contemporaneous, and transgression on part of what is now land seems inevitable, if tracts of ocean floor were exposed. We have ample proofs that considerable transgressions occurred, but these ancient seas may have been too shallow to be of much importance as a support of the bridge hypothesis. HINTON thinks that we require relatively few inter-continental connections, the most important being Brazil–Africa and Australia–Antarctica, but not in the form of bridges—of such he admits isthmian and shelf bridges, nothing more. Thus, for those who insist on direct inter-continental contact the only hypothesis at their service is the drift theory, and he asserts that most of the modern biogeographers accept the broad outlines of this theory, unless it is claimed that sliding occurred long before the end of the Mesozoic. As we have seen, however, this is exactly what has been claimed. For his own part he puts much faith in chance dispersal across broad stretches of open water.

R. GOOD. *The distribution of the Flowering Plants in relation to theories of continental drift*.

After some remarks on the general distribution of plant families, grasses and Compositae taking the lead almost everywhere—which seems quite natural in view of the size and enormous climatic amplitude of these families—the preponderance, in nearly all floras of dicotyledons (2 $\frac{1}{2}$ to 4 times as many as the monocots), and the absence of any strongly marked South Pacific flora south of Hawaii and east of New Guinea, New Caledonia and New Zealand (which ought to show, I suppose, that the island swarms are not fragments of a larger land mass), GOOD continues p 74

A common expression of the theory of continental drift postulates that the sundering of various continental masses began in a relatively remote geological period and that it has continued without notable cessation ever since The distribution of Angiosperms does not seem to be in special accordance with any such particular course of events It suggests more strongly that sundering occurred after these plants as a group had become well diffused, let us say by the Eocene Similarly I know of nothing in the distribution of Angiosperms to show that drift is still going on Can it be that continental drift has in fact been, not a persistent process, but an intermittent feature of geological time, as for instance have the great glaciations? If so, and if it can further be shown that the most recent of these drift ages took place not earlier than the beginning of the Tertiary, then at last the plantgeographers will have to hand a master key to most of his perplexities

It will be difficult to shape a key that will fit a lock constructed in this fashion As the glacial periods were interrupted by interglacial periods, so the periods of sundering should have been interrupted by periods not of a standstill but of the land masses coming into contact again last time during the Jurassic-Cretaceous era, which saw the origin, evolution and dispersal over the globe of the Angiosperms to be followed by the last drift age

With regard to the relations and disjunctions between South America (with Juan Fernandez, etc) and Antarctica Australia and New Zealand, vertical movements seem to offer a less distant possibility

In a most cleverly written chapter GOOD (*109* 344-360) discussed landbridge versus continental drift If we cannot, he says, accept the former nor put our trust in dispersal, a changing position of the continents is the only way out of the difficulties This may be true, but we have seen that this theory does not help us to solve the problem concerning the oceanic islands GORDON (*113*) points out that the occurrence of a small but important subantarctic element in the Pacific, reaching north to the Hawaiian Islands where it is better displayed than in any of the Polynesian or Melanesian groups, makes it impossible to deny both land bridges and the efficiency of transoceanic dispersal without providing for migration with the help of shifting continents GOOD

has run into an impasse over the Pacific islands like Hawaii He has rejected the landbridge hypothesis in favour of continental drift But he excludes continental drift so far as the islands are concerned, for he accepts them as truly oceanic, not continental fragments Yet he will not accept overseas migration Well, I can't see what explanation remains, if all these three are excluded, but the plants are there (p 148)

WULFF (*291*) found that the biogeographers have good reason to support WEGNER's theory, much speaks against it, but he trusts that the difficulties will be overcome by and by He recognized that, with regard to the Pacific, they are very considerable and call for a modification of the theory

Chapter VI

Transoceanic migration

In some of my earlier papers I touched upon the great problem of long distance dispersal and the supposed efficiency of the transporting agents, see for instance *231* 20–30, where, however, only the flora was concerned. This time also the faunas are, to some extent at least, considered and I shall quote a number of authors, old and modern, who have expressed their opinion for or against overseas transport as the only possible means by which the isolated islands of the Pacific have received their indigenous flora and fauna.

Advocates of large-scale overseas migration

Among earlier authors ENGLER (*85*) and GRISEBACH exercised great influence on their contemporaries. They divided the world into flora domains, regions and districts, characterized by a combination of certain important elements and by a greater or lesser degree of endemism, but still they never doubted the facility with which plants travelled across the oceans, progressive endemism was the unavoidable corollary, but relict endemism was recognized as important. The attitude of this school is adequately expressed by GRISEBACH (*325* 469)

So merkwürdig es auch sein mag, dass sogar einzelne Holzgewächse sich hier über das Stille Meer verbreitet haben, so ist ihre Wanderung doch aus der antarktischen Meeresströmung, den herrschenden Westwinden, oder durch Mithilfe der Seevögel, vielleicht auch durch alte Verkehrswege wohl hinlänglich zu erklären, ohne dass die Annahme von Landverbindungen in der Vorwelt gerechtfertigt wäre, die durch keine geologische Tatsache gestützt wird

By some the case of Krakatau was quoted as a proof that plants and animals are able to travel across water barriers, it is mentioned by HAYEK (*304*), but with reservation

Wie die Besiedelung einer Insel erfolgt, haben die oben angeführten Beobachtungen bei der Wiederbesiedelung des Krakatau gelehrt. Aber die Entfernung des Krakatau von den nächst gelegenen Inseln ist keine allzugrosse, sie beträgt nur etwa 18–40 Km, also Entfernungen die auch durch die Flugtiere nicht allzuschwer überbrückt werden können (p 251)

When we have to deal with islands, separated by thousands of miles from all continents, the difficulties are of much greater magnitude and he continues

Und doch müssen wir annehmen, dass auch die weit entfernt gelegenen Inseln ihre Pflanzendecke von den zunächst gelegenen Festländern (und Inseln) erhalten haben, wenn auch vor undenklichen Zeiten und ganz allmählich. Dafür spricht auch der Umstand, dass die Flora dieser Inseln keineswegs von der übrigen Flora der Erde grundverschieden ist, sondern denselben Pflanzenfamilien angehört wie diese, demnach von derselben abstammen muss

The only exception known (at that time) was Juan Fernandez (Lactoridaceae) But he admits that there are grave difficulties

Selbst bei Inseln, die erst in relativ junger Zeit vom Festlande abgetrennt worden sind, ist ein weiterer Austausch der Florenelemente zum mindesten wesentlich erschwert und eine weitere Zuwanderung von Elementen der Festlandsflora wenig wahrscheinlich

If this be true, how was immigration over thousands of miles ever possible?

Several writers who have paid special attention to Pacific problems occupy, more or less dogmatically, the same standpoint as HAVEK SETCHELL, with whom I had the privilege to discuss this subject on various occasions was already quoted p 271, I shall add here what he says, in the same paper, about migration (*219* 300) He found that I was "too narrow" in my allowances for migration possibilities, he believed in "migration over very considerable breadth of barrier, whether of sea or land", and absence was not a result of failure to migrate successfully, but could be explained by obstacles to establishment He regarded the oceanic islands as Tertiary, but in his summary pp 307–309 admitted the possibility of their being considerably older, late Mesozoic or early to middle Tertiary, which would give time for extensive progressive evolution of endemic taxa and for the dying-out of their continental ancestors or they had developed in other directions, making the relationships difficult or impossible to recognize Geologists however, refuse to give even the Hawaiian Islands a greater age than late Tertiary or even Pleistocene It goes without saying that travel facilities are different in different cases, spore plants are supposed to spread more freely than seed plants, but even these are supposed to be quite capable Thus STEBBINS (*319* 537)

The seeds of plants may occasionally be transported over many hundreds of miles of ocean and may establish themselves on Oceanic islands like Hawaii, Juan Fernandez, St Helena and the Canary Islands

FLORIN has, he writes, shown that conifers of the south hemisphere have migrated freely from Australasia to South America and vice versa, whereas mammals are unable to pass and are absent from oceanic islands—but is it not customary to place them on a par? STEBBINS' Antarctic connection does not include land-bridges, for "it existed for plants, but not for vertebrates" (but what about birds?) He looks for assistance in lost islands between Antarctica and New Zealand, on the opposite side the width of open water is not so great, and seeds can still be carried from South America to Antarctica without much difficulty

As mentioned before, no botanist has greater confidence in long-distance dispersal than FOSBERG

transoceanic migration across at least 2500 miles without stepping stones is not only a possibility but a relatively common occurrence (*99* 867)

FOSBERG's subject was the American element in the Hawaiian flora, but in order to explain the presence of the dominant Australasian element we must count with still greater distances AXELROD (*14*) quoting FOSBERG takes a modified position In case of distances not exceeding some 200 or 300 miles there are no difficulties, "a complete flora can transgress such a barrier without the loss of any significant floristic units" A greater distance results in "waif assemblages", but many will find it impossible to regard e g the Hawaiian flora as a haphazard accumulation of waifs and their descendants. What AXELROD says about migration probabilities during different geological epochs is of greater interest.

> Since plants are controlled largely by climate, and since climate has been changing during geologic time, it follows that plants comprising different communities have had different possibilities at different times. ... probabilities for long-distance migration were much higher for tropical plants in the Eocene than they are to-day. Temperate forest species had a much higher probability from late Cretaceous to middle Tertiary, it is low now. Steppe plants had a higher probability during Pliocene than now. Desert species have a higher probability to-day than at any time before.

His conclusions are drawn from the size and area of populations shifting with the extension of climatic regions.

For my own part I have expressed my opinion on overseas migration in the Pacific on various occasions (231, 318, 248) and I am not going to repeat the discussion here. My general conclusion was that the effect of transoceanic migration has been largely overestimated.

GUPPY (121), who allowed birds, winds and currents to stock all oceanic islands with plants, arrived at the conclusion that this traffic was a thing of the past and that migration had practically ceased altogether. I expressed my doubts that it had ever been effective in any case with regard to seed-plants.

I have already remarked that SETCHELL laid stress upon what he called the CEB (climatic edaphic biotic) factor complex. The main difficulty for the vagabond plants was not to cover the distance, be it ever so great, but to become a successful member of a community already established in the place where it happened to alight, and this difficulty increased as time went by; most surfaces of the earth he says, are already stocked with closed vegetation, making it impossible for new arrivals to gain a foothold (219, 300). His ideas are clearly expressed in 318 (p. 874).

> As the islands have become more and more completely stocked each with its quota of plants and animals and have undergone various vicissitudes, particularly of elevation, erosion, etc. its hospitality to migrating germules necessarily has become less and less, the Biotic factor has become more complex and the Edaphic factor has also suffered change.

In my view the result could just as well be the opposite, for these 'vicissitudes', emergence, erosion, volcanic activity and so forth create new soil, a more varied topography, a multitude of different habitats, all of which ought to give newcomers increased opportunities to get established.

With SETCHELL, ANDREWS underlines the importance of CEB, genera expected to occur in Hawaii but absent "were not amenable to germination and survival after transport".

Long before SETCHELL, J. D. HOOKER, WALLACE and others had paid attention to the obstacles for the successful establishment of newcomers. WALLACE believed that St Helena had become stocked with plants during early Tertiary time, later there was no room left, and the flora had changed so completely that no plant was recognized as an insular form of a continental species.

We meet with SETCHELL's line of thinking in a recent paper by W. B. TAYLOR (263, 572). In recent volcanic islands are many unstocked habitats to begin with, but each new species would mean competition, and the entry of an additional species would be very difficult and consequently of rare occurrence. This may be so, but there are many communities of a more open character than the forest, and even a closed forest is not like a tin packed with cigarettes, young secondary forest associations, steppes and savannas ought to offer good housing grounds to an intruder, supposing that he likes climate and soil. Experience shows that numerous aggressive plants brought by man, not only herbs but also trees and shrubs, find suitable living conditions even in undisturbed natural communities. In Juan Fernandez I have had occasion to follow the invasion by *Aristotelia maqui* (chilensis) and to witness the fabulous ease with which it crowds out the native vegetation, and to observe *Ugni Molinae* springing up on the ridges where the plant cover was open and, from there, to enter the dense native brushwood. And they are only two of the many successful weeds, a third one, equally dangerous but of quite recent introduction, is *Rubus ulmifolius*. All three have fleshy fruits and are eaten by man and birds and propagate themselves rapidly. They are common on the opposite mainland (where of course, the brambleberry was introduced from Europe) but man, no bird carried them across to the islands. Similar examples are, I presume, offered by almost all oceanic islands. I just happened to read a book on Cape Verde Islands, where a naturalist tells us about *Lantana camara* spreading like wildfire and menacing the little there is left of natural savanna and steppe (*320*).

Most zoologists favour the theory of long distance dispersal. Mammals are, as a rule also bats, flying foxes and the like, excluded, but of birds some are able to cover very large distances, winged insects are carried off to distant places where they never wanted to go, and so forth. I shall quote some zoogeographers who, with reference to the Pacific have expressed their opinion on overseas transport.

PERKINS, in his introduction to Fauna Hawaiiensis (*193* XLVI), wrote

All the islands being volcanic and having been built up from a great depth of ocean at various periods, their entire fauna naturally originated from immigrants derived from other lands. These immigrants must have arrived either by flight, like the birds, or in drift like the flightless insects and probably the land Mollusca

Drifting logs were often regarded as an important kind of conveyance, but they come from North America and what they bring of animals, PERKINS says would serve no purpose because it is unlikely that the passengers would become acclimatized in Hawaii. The fauna must have come from the warmer parts of America, from Australia, Polynesia etc. "at rare intervals from the Eocene until now". If we have to believe the geologists, no Hawaii existed in the Eocene—and how did those, who arrive "now" manage to become endemic genera and species?—non-endemic flowering plants not brought by man are few.

In some instances GULICK (*119*) admits the possibility of land connections, but Hawaii, Juan Fernandez, Galapagos, St. Helena, etc. etc., have always been isolated. The question whether their fauna shows that "the ancestors possessed an almost inconceivable capacity for passing uninjured over vast stretches of ocean" is answered in the affirmative. It is significant that the Galápagos archipelago "was successfully reached by a giant tortoise", already WALLACE entertained the same idea—a strictly terrestrial animal crossing the ocean.

Some biogeographers prefer one dispersal agent, some another, most have confidence in all, but it goes without saying that different types of plants and animals have availed themselves of different kinds of transport. I shall quote GULICK (*119*, 414) first.

It is possible to go far toward a first diagnosis of the degree of a land's insularity by noting how exclusively it is peopled by types with a known capacity for colonizing across vast expanses of ocean. Our summary up to this point reveals very nearly which these forms may be. Quite a majority of them, both plants and animals, show characters that harmonize with wind-storm transportation. A respectable majority of the larger seeded palms and some tough-lived earth-inhabiting invertebrates, suggest transportation by water or on drift-wood. Such seeds and invertebrate eggs as can withstand the digestive tracts of a bird, have a very substantial travelling radius by that means, easy 500 miles in the routine seasonal migrations, and possibly stretching in the extremest cases to almost transoceanic distances. Dioecious plants and separate-sexed animals are statistically at a disadvantage, as compared to the reversed condition, because of their poorer chance of achieving fertilization. The ability to take a journey in a gravid condition helps the chances greatly.

"Types with a known capacity for colonizing"—GULICK proceeds from what should be proved, for their occurrence on isolated islands is in itself no proof of oceanity. Under his angle the great number of dioecious endemic phanerogams in Hawaii ought to have surprised him. It almost seems as if he believed that entire specimens with roots and all managed to reach a distant island and get established; surely, if only a male or an unfertilized female arrived, all was in vain until a mate of the opposite sex turned up, a pregnant female would of course do better (by the bye WALLACE tells a story of a pregnant boa constrictor arriving on a West Indian island with drift wood and in good condition). I guess we can leave these chances aside, for plants spread by means of seeds and whether wind-blown, epizoic or endozoic (provided they do not, as many assert, discharge their droppings soon after the departure), there is every chance that more than one seed of the same kind is brought, a single many-seeded berry is enough, and a bird picking drupes fills his stomach. A seed portion of a dioecious species gives under ordinary conditions, 50 % of each sex. In the Hawaiian flora we find, GULICK says (p. 418), 'a preponderance of plants spread by wind carried spores and minute seeds', species with drupes and berries are, however, numerous. As an example of a presumably definite case of bird rather than wind carriage he mentions the Hawaiian species of *Vaccinium*, which he derives from North America. Their presence is most interesting, "as the distances involved must be very close to the extreme physiological maximum that land birds can traverse and still carry fruit seeds in their droppings". To me it appears as a bad case of constipation. Besides, the Hawaiian Vaccinia are not related to North American groups but belong to a special section.

MAYR, an extreme "oceanist" who refuses to admit land connections for either Fiji or New Caledonia, in his paper on the Pacific bird fauna (*179*) includes a general survey of the dispersal chances for other animals and also for plants. The special instance cited (p. 197) is not very convincing.

Birds are excellent flyers and thus capable of rapid and active spreading, capable of crossing considerable stretches of open sea to settle in new territories. There is abundant evidence of this, such as the resettlement of Krakatau Island, the recent arrival of Australian birds in New Zealand, and the colonization of unquestionably oceanic islands.

Not even the arrival of Australian birds in New Zealand brings conviction, the colonization of "unquestionably oceanic islands" certainly does, if we can prove it. MAYR continues p. 198:

The possibility of transport by floats or in logs is not to be underestimated. Many tropical currents have a speed of at least 2 knots, that is, about 50 miles a day, or 1000 miles in three weeks. It is probably not a great task for a wood boring insect to survive 3 weeks in a drifting log. Air currents are, however, of uncomparably greater importance than sea currents. Even slight winds are of great influence on the distribution of floating and flying animals, as recent investigations have shown. It is astonishing how rich the "aerial plankton" is, even up to altitudes of 1000 meters and more. Normal winds would, of course, not account for the spreading of molluscs, flightless insects, and other small invertebrates. However, most of the islands, with which we are concerned, are situated within the zone of tropical hurricanes, the lifting force of which is quite extraordinary.

The fact that there are small molluscs and flightless insects on such typical oceanic islands as Easter Island, Juan Fernandez and Saint Helena is almost unassailable proof that such a method of dispersal is a reality. Tropical hurricanes carry for hundreds and even thousands of miles. The result of the recent surveys in the Hawaiian Islands, the Marquesas, and on Samoa indicate that there are indeed very few animals that cannot be transported across considerable stretches of the sea by winds, waves, other animals or man.

On p. 201 MAYR adds some general remarks:

The means of dispersal of most plants and animals are much more extensive than was formerly realized, and even rather irregular distributions can be explained without the help of land bridges. Dispersal across the sea is, of course, most obvious for birds, and ornithologists were among the first who accepted the ideas of the permanence of continents and oceans. Most entomologists are also beginning to realize that they can solve most of their distribution difficulties without land bridges. The conchologist, however, postulates even today continental connections between all or nearly all the islands where land shells exist.

As we shall see below (p. 350) MAYR declared himself unable to explain how land shells are dispersed.

It seems that, also with regard to the birds, MAYR contradicts himself, for in the same paper (p. 198) he asserts that most birds, particularly on tropical islands, precisely the islands we are discussing, are extraordinarily sedentary, and as an example he mentions that of 265 species known from that part of New Guinea which is opposite New Britain, a distance of 45 miles, only 80 occur on New Britain, and the situation in Western Papuan islands is even more conspicuous; he mentions two islands only 2 miles apart, with rather different fauna "Literally hundreds of similar instances could be listed all of them indicating the sedentary habits." One is likely to remember GUPPY's fruit eating pigeons which were thought to be responsible for the dissemination across the Pacific of seeds too large for other birds. The "pigeons" are, now at least, restricted in range and of very little use on longer distances. I cannot help drawing the conclusion from this that the sedentary habit was acquired after the great colonization had taken place.

Few phytogeographers have had greater faith in the capacity of wide ranging marine birds to carry diaspores than GRISEBACH. In his discussion of bipolar species found in the far north and the far south but not at all in intermediate zones he selected *Gentiana prostrata* Haenke as the best example. Its distribution is due, he says, to the wanderings of *Diomedea exulans* which,

abweichend von der Lebensweise der meisten anderen Zugvogel, uber beide Hemispharen, von Kap Horn bis zu den Kurilen und Kamtschatka, wandert und die Standorte jener Pflanze in der arktischen und antarktischen Flora in Verbindung setzt. Mit der Beute, die dieser Vogel verschlingt, kann er auch Samen von Pflanzen, welche, mit den Flussen ins Meer gespult, in den Magen der Fische ubergehen, in einzelnen Fallen ausstreuen, so dass sie an fernen Kusten aus seinem Dunger aufkeimen (325 469).

I have not come across any comments on this bold theory. It is difficult to take it seriously, but to GRISEBACH the only gap in his argumentation was that nobody had happened to witness such an event. If he is wrong, he asks, why is there no trace of this *Gentiana* in the Andes, where it would thrive just as well as in the Alps and in the mountains of Asia? To this should be remarked that *G. prostrata* is a polymorphous species of wide range and that it does occur in the Andes from Colombia to Chile, suggesting that it has migrated south along the mountains without the assistance of the albatross.

WALLACE (278 259) tells us, on the authority of MOSELEY, naturalist to the "Challenger" expedition, of the great albatross breeding on Marion Island in the midst of dense, low herbage. I can add that this bird also breeds on South Georgia and on some other southern islands, but as far as I know they do not shift breeding places, and even if they did, they do not go on shore between the breeding seasons. TAYLOR, in his important paper on Macquarie Island (263), tells us about a giant petrel which was captured, tagged and released on this island and shot on South Georgia, 8000 km away, four months later, but these birds are often seen on land where they attack the penguin chickens, this was at least the case on Paulet Island in the Antarctic. Whether they aid in the dispersal of diaspores is unknown.[1] TAYLOR quotes an observation made on Macquarie that seeds were found adhering to the feet of an albatross. These birds when building their nests regurgitate an oily fluid which makes seeds stick to their feet. Macquarie Island was ice-covered during the Glacial epoch and the plants, perhaps with the exception of some cryptogams, must have arrived since the retreat of the ice. The vascular flora consists of 35 species, all except 4 occurring in the New Zealand subantarctic area—the 3 species with a claim to be regarded as endemic should be reinvestigated—while those 4 species are found in subantarctic South America, from where they are derived. All Mac

---

[1] According to TAYLOR (p 570) the two truly Antarctic phanerogams *Deschampsia antarctica* and *Colobanthus crassifolius*, are very rare in the Antarctic and reproduce only vegetatively. I do not know where he obtained this information. They are scarce but have been reported from many localities along the coast and adjacent islands of Palmer Land between lat 62 and 68 and, in favourable situations at least, both of them flower and produce ripe seeds—see my paper in Botan Tidsskrift vol 51, 1954.

quarie plants have, TAYLOR states, propagules suited to bird transport. It is surprising that WERTH (317), who made a detailed study of the Kerguelen flora, asserts that not one of the flowering plants possesses any special dispersal mechanism for either wind, water or bird carriage. Still, the two islands have some 9 species in common (54). TAYLOR's conclusion that, "if long distance dispersal has occurred on Macquarie Island, then it could well have occurred elsewhere" is certainly correct; we know, for one thing, many wide-spread sea side plants and a number of widely dispersed aquatic species possibly transported by migratory birds. South Georgia is in much the same situation as Macquarie, but still rather heavily glaciated thanks to its great altitude, and the possibility that any higher plants survived the Glacial epoch is very small indeed, whereas indications that many mosses and lichens date from preglacial times are strong. The vascular flora is poorer than on Macquarie, and there are no endemic species. When TAYLOR accuses me of having argued against all overseas migration also in this case he must have misunderstood me. I expressly took this possibility into account in the paper he quotes (226).

WALLACE calls attention to sea birds breeding on islands in the tropics. *Phaeton* makes its nests on the Hawaiian Islands in 4000 ft. altitude and also in the highland of Tahiti, and such birds would account for the similarity of the mountain floras. In reality these floras have practically nothing in common. Miss GIBBS (321), discussing the origin of the montane flora of Fiji, refused to regard birds as capable agents; wind may have been more efficient.

No modern zoologist has tried to defend the theory of unlimited overseas migration with greater zeal than ZIMMERMAN. In his Introduction to "Insects of Hawaii" we read:

> There is no evidence whatsoever to support the contention that they (i e the Hawaiian Is) are of continental origin or character, or that they were ever joined together in an elongate subcontinental land-mass or even in a continuous subaerial mountain range (298 6)

And in opposition to certain other biologists he refuses to regard the islands as old; they are at most Pliocene and no part of them older than five million years, most of the lava is younger, the bulk of the land Pleistocene. He is opposed to my ideas but he thinks that the explanation offered by him will, partially at least, reconcile the differences between us. In an earlier paper (Amer Naturalist 76, 1942) to which he refers, he spoke of former high islands, other than those found on maps, which once existed; once more the "stepping-stones routes" are called to life. Atolls are the remnant of many of them, or reefs like among the Leeward Islands of Hawaii, and such preexisting islands would account for the immigration from all directions. He does not call for jumping of thousands of miles of open sea, but rather for series of shorter over water steps. I am afraid that we need some substantial refurnishing of the Pacific basin to supply a sufficient number of intermediate stations. Not all of these routes were, he says available at the same time, and this would explain the apparent difference in age of various sections of the biota (pp 51, 52). Most of the roads were cut off in Pliocene and early Pleistocene, some before Pliocene—when no land existed where stands the Hawaiian chain, if geologists are right. USINGER (273), describing the distribution of Heteroptera, also looks for convenient stepping stones.

Divergent opinions on the means of transport

The dispersal agents universally recognized as important are air currents, especially monsoon and trade winds, and cyclonic storms, ocean currents, birds and last not least man who with his domestic animals and goods has become more and more important, whether he brings plants, seeds and animals to extend their range—and many of them become naturalized—or carries diaspores on his body and his belongings unaware. It is as a rule not difficult to find out where we have to do with human action, but we shall limit ourselves here to a discussion of natural factors of distribution. This subject has been treated by innumerable writers in biology and a wealth of material was compiled by RIDLY (205), a firm believer in the great value of all kinds of dispersal mechanisms some of which are, of course, very wonderful. WULFF (291) in his chapter "Natural factors for distribution" is more critical. Of animals only the birds deserve to be mentioned, but the plumage is no good for carrying diaspores any considerable distance, especially over the sea, and the extreme marine birds, the strongest flyers, have no contact with land outside their own breeding-places. WULFF reduces the part taken by birds to almost nothing, but I believe that we have good reason to count with the migratory birds in certain cases. Water transport is responsible for the diffusion of litoral halophytes but rarely for migrations of inland species. Wind is important only on short distances, at least for seed plants, special devices do not help very much. Even RIDLY concluded that winged or plumed diaspores are not carried very far, spore-plants are more easily spread. WULFF remarks that according to BENTHAM Leguminosae and Labiatae hold their ground just as well if not better than Compositae. Altogether, if dispersal by natural factors had the significance ascribed to it, the vegetation of the globe within a certain climatic zone, would be homogeneous and the spore-plants at least ought to be cosmopolitan, but they are "localized in definite areas, their distribution paralleling that of flowering plants." (p. 128). GOOD observes (109) that we have no proofs that species equipped with special dispersal mechanisms are more widely distributed than others. That certain plants with such devices show very wide areas whereas others without them are rare and local means nothing, because the reverse is also true, climatic and edaphic factors should always be taken into account.

The relative value of the dispersal agents is put to the test when we deal with oceanic islands. SETCHELL (217) was inclined to give considerable credit to migratory birds. The occurrence of identical species of flowering plants in Arizona and Argentina and in California and Chile could be explained by bird transport and bipolarity had originated in the same way. Bird transport helped him to understand the remarkable disjunct areas of arborescent Compositae and Lobeliaceae, their birth place was in the Antarctic, and they had been carried by birds to New Zealand, Australia, Malaysia, Polynesia, Hawaii, South America and the high African mountains—we can add Saint Helena, Juan Fernandez and Desventuradas. In this case it is not the question of identical species and rarely of genera. It is not improbable that the secret of their origin and early history lies hidden in the far south, but this is all we can say. HEMSLEY (127: 66) when discussing the endemic Compositae of Saint Helena and Juan Fernandez said that "wind seems at first to be the most probable agent", still he doubted its efficiency. In STCHILL's view storms seem to offer more than a possibility in many instances, particularly tropical cyclones and vertical thrombs able to carry even heavy diaspores to a great altitude. In another paper (218) he points out that plant distribution in the Pacific has been from west to east against the prevailing winds and currents and, in the case of Hawaii, has given much better results than the expected east-west route, the "frequent cyclonic storms" are responsible for this anomaly together with adverse biotic factors, but I fail to see why they shouldn't offer the same difficulties for diaspores coming from the west.

ANDREWS (6: 615) paid special attention to the occurrence of scattered "Antarctic" genera and species in and around the Pacific and combines their distribution with the direction of ocean currents

> In the South Pacific the westerly current sweeps by Australia, New Zealand, Tahiti, and the whole of the west coast of South America, where it is joined by the cold uprising water along the South American coast. This gives rise to the north-moving Peruvian Current which sweeps by Juan Fernandez, Peru, Central America, and Mexico, whence there is a deflection westerly toward the Hawaiian Islands and the tropics. This knowledge of the general circulation within the Pacific appears to throw a flood of light on the occurrence of the Australian, New Zealand and western South American elements in the Hawaiian flora, such as ... (25 genera are enumerated). The influence of ocean currents is suggested particularly in the peculiar distribution of *Acaena*, *Gunnera*, *Nertera*, *Oreobolus*, *Santalum*, *Sophora*, and so on.

Juan Fernandez lies outside the Peruvian current, but also the outer island, Masafuera, is reached by drift wood. Its origin has not been investigated.

A look at a current-chart shows that ANDREWS reasoning has its weak points, besides, I cannot see that the genera he mentions are thalassochorous. I would recommend the reader to take a look at the many distribution maps published in a paper read on the same occasion when ANDREWS presented his argumentation (318).

With regard to the cyclonic storms several authors have, as we have seen, emphasized their prominent role in the violent dispersal of both plants and animals, they are, in fact considered to be the only imaginable force by which larger objects are transported and it is useless to deny that such events have taken place and still take place, even if it is difficult to find definite proofs that the transport did lead to the establishment of an immigrant from afar. Most authors who have taken refuge in cyclones have, however, expressed themselves in general terms without a clear idea of the extension of the cyclonic belts and the trend of the cyclones.

In two papers VISHER has summarized his studies on cyclonic storms in the Pacific. Three chief centres of origin are distinguished (322): (1) Western N. Pacific originating some distance east of the Philippines in lat. 8° to 25°, (2) Western

S Pacific, particularly between Australia and Samoa in lat 10° to 25°, (3) Eastern N Pacific off the west coast of Mexico and Central America Occasionally tropical storms develop near Hawaii and over Australia The normal course of (1) is WNW, recurring NE, and of (2) WSW, recurring SE To what extent plant distribution runs parallel to cyclone tracks has, as far as I am aware, not been investigated As VISHER says most of the cyclones originate over the sea "well out in the ocean" (p 87) They hit many of the Polynesian islands, and possibly collect diaspores on one and deliver them on another, but a frequent dispersal of species in this way does not appear very probable I wonder whether there is in Hawaii, with its 90% endemics, a single flowering plant likely to have been borne there by a cyclonic storm VISHER is, however, opposed to land connections in the Pacific, with one exception "it is known that Australia was formerly connected with Asia by way of the East Indies and New Caledonia" (323 77) With regard to Polynesia he points to the west–east hurricanes and their colonizing power Sea carriage also comes into the picture, violent cloudbursts may accompany the storm, brooks are transformed into swift rivers carrying plant material, tree trunks and soil, forming rafts which are washed out into the ocean

A recent paper by BERGERON (324) gives a somewhat different aspect His map shows the two areas in the Pacific north and south of the equator where hurricanes arise and how they move The Hawaiian islands lie, as a rule, outside the tracks The direction north of the equator is NW or WNW all through the hurricane belt, and there is no sign of an easterly direction enabling plants and animals to be carried all over Polynesia as far north and east as Hawaii, as VISHER supposed South of the equator the trend is S and SE, the east of the Pacific is not reached and Juan Fernandez lies, in longitude as well as in latitude, away from any cyclonic belt

It has often been stated that spore plants theoretically at least, have much greater facilities to colonize on long distances, but it has been shown that in reality their capacity is more limited than was formerly assumed

COPELAND (68 165-166) expressed his opinion on the diffusion of fern spores

> Fern spores are carried across water by the wind—ten miles of water is no barrier at all to their spread One hundred miles may be one hundred times as great a barrier, because the spores must hit a target, a suitable place to germinate and grow Still, ferns spread readily across seas this wide A thousand miles makes the obstacle again one hundred times as great the limited viability of the spores, the chance of falling or being washed out of the air, and the chance of very different climate at such distance, increase it materially Ferns rarely jump a thousand miles of ocean Still a number of species are believed to have crossed the south Atlantic, and I believe that three genera, *Plagiogyria*, *Coniogramme* and *Lomogramme*, have flown the north Pacific from Japan to Mexico, each in one single instance It is not exactly impossible that direct colonization has occurred between Chile, New Zealand, Tasmania, the Cape, and Tristan da Cunha

It should be mentioned that CHRIST (59), with his unique knowledge of the distribution of ferns, pointed to the insignificance of spore dispersal as an explanation of the origin of widely disjunct areas

The fact that IRMSCHER tried to prove that the distribution of plants strongly supports WEGENER's hypothesis does not lessen the value of what he says about the limited capacity of plants to migrate. It is small in the flowering plants (*143* 291)

> Dass bei den Blutenpflanzen die Beforderung der Samen und Fruchte durch Wind, Wasser und Tiere ganz wesentlich eingeschrankt werden muss und fur geschlossene Formationen auf grossen Entfernungen hin nicht in Frage kommt, ist heute von den Pflanzengeographen allgemein anerkannt.

IRMSCHER is too optimistic, we have seen that there are phytogeographers to whom overseas migration is not only possible and undoubtedly happens, on rare occasions at least, but rather of quite common occurrence. And with regard to spore plants their distribution should, if this be correct, show quite different distribution patterns than they actually do. The bryophytes are no exception to the rule. IRMSCHER remarks that already in 1903 STEPHANI denied that liverworts are able to make long and successful jumps. Attention should be paid to DOMIN's valuable paper (*76*) in which he brings together numerous facts illustrating the same definite distribution patterns in this as in other groups, and Miss FULFORD (e.g. *103*) has arrived at the same conclusion. We know that the spores, in many cases at least, are extremely sensitive to changed conditions and lose their viability very rapidly when exposed to the air—a promising field for experiments. Regarding mosses I refer to HERZOG's work (*129*) where he speaks against the belief in the importance and great range of dispersal through the air. We find, IRMSCHER says, the same disjunctions, the same part areas (Teilareale) in angiosperms, gymnosperms, ferns and bryophytes, and he continues p. 292

> Dass diese vier in ihren Verbreitungsmitteln so verschiedenen Pflanzengruppen dieselben Verbreitungszuge ihrer Disjunktelemente ergeben, zeigt wohl einwandfrei, dass hierfür der Wind ebenso wie andere aussere Krafte als Ursache abzulehnen sind. Waren sie in ausschlaggebender Weise an der Ausbreitung beteiligt, musste die Besiedelung entsprechend der Verschiedenheit der Fruchte, Samen und Sporen ebenso verschiedenartig ausgefallen sein, d.h. in den einzelnen Gruppen dieser biologischen Verschiedenheit entsprechende charakteristische Merkmale zeigen. Dies ist aber nicht der Fall. Der allen vier Gruppen gemeinsamen hochdisjunkten Ausbildung so vieler Areale muss vielmehr eine andere Ursache zu Grunde liegen.

This common cause was, in IRMSCHER's opinion, continental displacement in the sense of WEGENER. Those who disagree with him will have to look for vertical movements, emergence and submergence of land.

Lichens, fungi etc. were not included in IRMSCHER's discussion. A survey of their distribution patterns is something to be asked for. Lichens are said to depend on their vegetative reproduction bodies more than on spores.

It is maintained that, with certain exceptions, terrestrial animals spread less easily than plants. I have consulted a number of zoogeographers in order to learn their opinion on the mode of transport likely to be used by invertebrates in their supposed ocean voyages. Birds etc. are left aside here.

Numerous insects, butterflies, moths, flies, hymenoptera, grasshoppers, cockroaches, as well as spiders, myriapods, etc. follow man from land to land, from island to island. This is, I daresay, the only safe way for such animals to get abroad. For those, and they are in overwhelming majority, which are not anthropochorous the chance to cover large distances ought to be very small. However, ZIMMERMAN, in his admirable introduction to the Insects of Hawaii, surveys one order after the other and finds nothing that speaks against his belief in the permanent isolation of the Hawaiian as well as all other oceanic islands, and consequently concludes that, man-borne species excepted, all the ancestors of the Hawaiian insects were carried there by natural agents. Dispersal with the aid of birds is of slight importance, but he remarks that sea birds nest in forests on the islands; I do not think that this means very much, because they are stationary (comp. above, p. 337). Marine drift is probably the least successful of all methods, he thinks. Thus, the bulk of the insect fauna was and is wind-borne, a traffic going on without interruption. ZIMMERMAN refers to experiments clearly showing that both winged and unwinged insects are carried by air currents to great heights, 14,000—15,000 feet (p. 58). These are largely abnormal conditions and due to cyclonic storms, which account for the dispersal all over the mid-Pacific. The result is, as expected, a disharmonious fauna, where large groups common to all continents are lacking: "they have been eliminated by the selective agents of oversea dispersal." It would be interesting to know why all representatives of large and otherwise widely distributed insect groups are excluded from the passenger list. Besides, would not disharmony result even if land connections once existed?—the islands have remained isolated for a long time, perhaps millions of years, while migration, favoured by climatic and edaphic changes affecting the general character and composition of the vegetation has continued over land on the continents.

HINTON (65) who, as we have seen, was opposed against both continental drift and land bridges, believed that wind-borne and raft-borne transportation across the oceans must have been of common occurrence. If this be so, why did no snakes, frogs or gymnosperm cones ever get aboard the rafts and arrive at distant islands? Rafts formed by large uprooted trees are observed in big rivers like the Amazon or Orinoco, and I guess that an analysis of their composition would reveal the presence of a rather varied fauna. WALLACE'S Boa constrictor was referred to above (p. 335). Snakes and giant spiders are often found hidden in banana trunks imported to Europe from tropical America. On the other hand, the chances for the formation of substantial rafts are small within the tropical Pacific, where no big rivers empty.

What kind of invertebrates are likely to withstand transoceanic migration?

HINTON has an answer ready:

The chance of accidental dispersal varies according to the nature of the group. Colonization of the Hawaiian and other islands, always far removed from any continent, provides us with absolute proof of the kind of animals and plants that can withstand long distance wind or raft transportation across the oceans.

This sounds quite simple, but really is a very complicated problem, to which sufficient attention has not been paid. The possibilities vary according to size, flight capacity, habits, mode of reproduction, sensitiveness to changes of milieu, and so forth, and I am afraid that we have little knowledge, founded on facts, in most cases

Earthworms have been carried all over the world with the human traffic It is noteworthy that as a rule no truly indigenous species are found on oceanic islands, where, if land connections had existed, they could be expected, and even if the transport of eggs or living animals were effected only by means of rafts stocked with earth and plant material, as some believe, they ought to be present, but as far as I am aware, nobody has witnessed such a transport The presence of endemic *leeches* on Samoa and Juan Fernandez (Masafuera) can be understood only if the leeches are carried about on birds acting as hosts, otherwise I cannot see how they would be able to survive, they are very sensitive to exposure To these in particular I should like to apply what GULICK without referring to any special group of animals, wrote (*119* 405)

How is it possible at all for creatures that would die almost at touch of sea water to precede man by a million years on islands standing solitary in mid ocean? Are their remote homes really the left over fragments of ancient intercontinental land bridges, or are these creatures *prima facie* evidence that their ancestors possessed an almost inconceivable capacity for passing uninjured over vast stretches of open ocean? The extremes of hypothesis that have been proposed in response to this dilemma show us how difficult it has been to find a solution

Freshwater *crustaceans* occur on many islands, both traffic borne and indigenous species, only the raft theory would account for their spread

It is supposed that cocoons of *spiders* are transported by wind, webs are torn loose with cocoons attached and carried up into the air, where a storm takes care of them Theoretically this is not impossible but whether the contents stand a journey of thousands of miles is doubtful Adventitious species are found on Pacific islands, but the bulk of the spider faunas is indigenous and endemism is high BERLAND, pointing to the general distribution of genera and the high specific endemism, is in favour of former land connections (*23* 1052)

L isolation doit être assez ancien pour ce que cette faune ait pu acquérir les caracteres d endemisme qu elle presente Un botaniste a fixé vers le Pliocene cet isolement, mais je serais porte à croire qu il est plutôt plus ancien, en me basant sur la lenteur de l evolution des Araignées

MAYR, who rejects all land connections remarks (*179* 214)

Considering the haphazard manner by which these oceanic islands receive their populations it is rather astonishing how similar the faunas of the various islands are BERLAND, on the basis of the distribution of spiders, has come to the conclusion that the fauna of all Polynesia is so uniform as to suggest that these islands are but fragments of a single land mass This view is similar to Pilsbry s, founded on Mollusca Actually this paradox of the similarity of the faunas of oceanic islands is solved in quite different manner Of all the possible families, genera and species of the Papuan Region that are theoretically in a position to colonize, only a small fraction will eventually avail themselves of the opportunity

This is quite true, but will not the result become much the same with land connections? The main source of the fauna is the same, the similarity is a consequence, and local endemism is a result of isolation.

Acarids present the same problem. MUMFORD (*183*) remarks that is is very difficult to compile lists of species for the Pacific islands and that, at present, no safe conclusion can be drawn with regard to the distribution of genera. This is true, but we know that numerous indigenous species occur and that local endemism seems to be high. How these extremely delicate little animals would be able to stand long overseas voyages is difficult to imagine. They are plentiful in humid forest soils on Juan Fernandez and all the species except two adventitious ones are endemic. Little is known of their relationships. If washed down from the hill sides and carried out into the sea, they will die—only wind transport remains. *Pseudoscorpions* may be more resistant to both salt water and desiccation, but their pronounced endemism bears witness of long isolation. All the false scorpions recorded from Juan Fernandez are endemic, and there is one endemic genus. They were unknown when MUMFORD (l c 246) wrote

As Chamberlain points out, it is doubtful whether anything like true insular endemism occurs in most species of false scorpions because of the ease with which they are distributed

They are well adapted to be carried about by man. Among the *Myriapoda* are many local endemic species. These creatures are, according to my own experience, rather tough and might be able to spread by the same methods as earth-worms and land crustaceans. It is not very probable that they are blown from continents to distant islands. Cosmopolitan forms are probably adventitious. If this applies also to *Collembola* I do not know, very widespread species may be so ancient that they have attained their distribution when the map of the globe was quite different from the present one. It is unlikely that they are able to migrate overseas. LINDSAY (*167* 719) writes

The primitively wingless Collembola seem to constitute better material for distribution studies than any other insect order, because migration by flight is impossible and the delicate integument makes it very unlikely that the insect could be carried any appreciable distance by the sea

We can safely add that, if blown out over the ocean, they would soon perish. ZIMMERMAN suspects that none of the 32 species recorded for Hawaii is indigenous there thus, all are supposed to have been imported by the traffic. However 3 species are supposed to be endemic in Juan Fernandez. Two species of the Hawaiian *Thysanura* are "possibly endemic" (ZIMMERMAN) but perhaps adventitious. These creatures do not appear to be fit for long-distance dispersal, and the two species known from Juan Fernandez are endemic. One of them belongs to a monotypical genus with Australian affinities, a disjunction not easily bridged over without land connections

Getting to the true *insects*, their mode of dispersal certainly varies a great deal. Whereas butterflies, moths, flies, hymenoptera etc are known to be storm-driven and eventually carried far, heavy beetles, even if they be properly winged, are unfit for long journeys, whether they are transported by waves and currents and able to stand immersion in salt water during weeks and months I do not know. The endemic flightless insects have, just as the flightless birds, given cause to much speculation. They are supposed to descend from winged species, arrived, it is said, on an oceanic island; they had the choice of losing their wings or being blown off the island and lost altogether. ZIMMERMAN does not favour this view, for they may as well have lost their power of flight on the mother continent, which did not prevent them to be carried off by a hurricane. MAYR agrees with him, comp. quotation p. 336. Very well, but is it possible to imagine a flightless rail carried a thousand miles across an ocean?

There are numerous *Orthoptera* on Hawaii, most of them endemic species or even belonging to endemic genera. So far only 4 species have been reported from Juan Fernandez, two of them endemic. I presume that ZIMMERMAN regards these insects as normally wind-borne. The relations of the Hawaiian Gryllidae are with Indo-Pacific forms, so they have had a long way to go. The four species of *termites* found in Hawaii are adventitious, which should indicate that they are unable to reach oceanic islands without human assistance, but the single species discovered in Juan Fernandez (Masatierra) is endemic. Either did it, or its ancestor, arrive over land, or a colony was carried in a floating log, which may seem unlikely, or a storm brought a winged swarming couple which founded a new colony —even less probable. The termites are a very ancient order and date, it is said, back to the Mesozoic at least.

Mallophaga are spread with their bird hosts. All the endemic Hawaiian species live on the Drepanididae, and the marine birds here and on Juan Fernandez are infested with widespread forms. *Thysanoptera* seem to be easily spread with human traffic. Most of the 90 species found in Hawaii are adventitious, few indigenous. Two of the 4 species in Juan Fernandez are endemic. How these delicate insects manage to get about and to reach oceanic islands I cannot tell.

The Hawaiian islands have a rich and peculiar fauna of *Neuroptera* some 'among the most aberrant of all' (ZIMMERMAN p. 76). Of the five species recorded for Juan Fernandez 4 are endemic, one of them belonging to an endemic genus. Wind drift must be taken into account, but it cannot be very effective. The situation remains the same when we get to the *Lepidoptera*, about 1000 species in Hawaii of which 85 % have not been found elsewhere. Wind drift or immature stages (eggs, etc.) carried with plant material are the only possibilities, but they cannot be very great. So far only 26 indigenous species are known from Juan Fernandez, 70 % of them endemic; when the list of Dr KUSCHEL's collection, which contains over 50 species, has been published, the figures will undergo alteration. In his survey of the Pacific lepidoptera SWEZEY (262) includes the Galápagos Islands, but does not mention Juan Fernandez. The Pacific islands were, he says p. 319, populated from the Malayan and Oriental regions and the fauna arrived in the main by accident, winds, typhoons etc. or with plant material brought by currents. A comparable numerical development of species per genus has taken place in no other islands than the Hawaiian, and the author infers that they have a more ancient fauna, descended from ancestors that arrived at a more remote time. This does not accord with ZIMMERMAN's statement that no primitive family is represented in Hawaii. Probably the Hawaiian *Diptera* have been less collected. ZIMMERMAN, who is responsible for the figures quoted, indicates about 400 species, of which 60 % are endemic. In relation to their small size the Juan Fernandez Islands seem to be richer with about 150 indigenous species (64 % endemic). Our knowledge of the dipterous fauna is in the main due to Dr KUSCHEL's collections; the 25—30 species not yet reported on will raise the total number.

Over 1600 species of *Coleoptera* are reported from Hawaii, of which about 76 % are endemic, and there are numerous endemic genera. Numerous species found elsewhere are adventitious. In relation to its size, Juan Fernandez cannot be called poor (see above p. 307, etc.), and endemism is just as high here. I presume that ZIMMERMAN and others regard wind as the principal dispersal agent, though not for all kinds of beetles, because we have to do with many different types of animals and of habits and habitats. It is difficult to imagine how a flightless beetle would be able to keep afloat in the air for thousands of miles; he must have had a great need of the numerous 'stepping stones' postulated by ZIMMERMAN. It should perhaps be mentioned that GULICK (*119* 414) wrote that 'it can hardly be doubted that some carrion-feeding insects have been distributed by adhering to sea birds'. I doubt that this ever happened but as he had just discussed the transport of "invertebrate eggs" in the digestive tract of birds, I suppose that he means *eggs* of necrophilous flies or beetles which, brought across the sea, were deposited on another carrion and thus became established on an oceanic island.

The *weevils* a most important and interesting feature in isolated island faunas, are often dependent on definite host plants, and are thought to sail along on logs as stowaways. Evidently the Curculionidae have become something of a stumbling-block. USINGER (*273*) came to the conclusion that they must possess some unknown special means of dispersal. BRINCK, who discussed the coleopterous fauna of Tristan da Cunha (*316* 97—104) another isolated volcanic group of islands where geologists failed to discover any traces of land connections states that the fauna contains endemic elements and offers examples of remarkable disjunctions. It must have originated from extinct faunas of neighbouring continents if not of submerged lands. The only natural agent capable of transportation is the wind, but BRINCK is convinced that "at present no beetles are invading the islands by natural means" (p. 103), and the reason is not adverse conditions, for several species, introduced with the human traffic, have become naturalized. The unavoidable conclusion is that dispersal agents, man excepted are insufficient—and they were the same in the past. The original beetle fauna has survived from preglacial time, an hypothesis that nobody would feel inclined to reject, but it does not help us to understand by what means it was able ever to arrive. The weevils of Hawaii have had a long way to come, according to ZIMMERMAN the ancestors as a rule came from the south Pacific or Indo-Pacific regions. Generally he regards also the peculiar genera to have originated in Hawaii or, eventually, in one of the lost islands serving as intermediate stations, but among the weevils are some that defy all explanations.

Nesotocus is evidently a relict endemic genus of four closely allied species, and there appears to be nothing like it elsewhere. *Oodemus* with its 58 species is the largest genus of the Hawaiian Cossoninae, together with its close ally *Anotherus* (3 species) endemic, and I know of no genus or group of genera from any region from which is might have come. It is an anomaly.

Such cases bring us back to times long before the formation of the present Hawaiian chain, and similar cases are found also in Juan Fernandez, e.g. the endemic tribe *Juanorhini* of AURIVILLIUS. Other examples are offered by many other insect groups. And, leaving them aside for a moment, is not the endemic Hawaiian bird family Drepanididae another anomaly? Whereas BRYAN (*39* 188) finds a Malayan origin most acceptable, GULICK writes (*119* 420)

The history of Hawaiian land birds must have begun with the arrival of some form of tropical American honey creeper, which became in due time the progenitor of all 18 genera and 40 species of the Drepanididae.

He seems to have forgotten that the islands are claimed to have dived out of the ocean in late Pliocene and Pleistocene times.

Hymenoptera are plentiful in Hawaii, about 600 native species, among which endemics are numerous, and the ancestors are supposed to have come from the south and southwest Pacific, in exceptional cases from Asia and the Orient. This order is as yet little known in Juan Fernandez, see above p. 315. Wind drift seems to be the only possible mode of transport unless infected larvae of butterflies etc. arrived with drift wood, which does not seem very probable. Ants are easily spread with the traffic. Of the 3 species known in Juan Fernandez only one appears to have arrived without human assistance.

Among the *Heteroptera* in Hawaii, over 200 species and 80 % endemic, ZIMMERMAN pays special attention to the genus *Nysius*, which has its greatest known diversity in those islands. All are endemic and include the most divergent of all *Nysius* species. The ancestors are supposed to have come from the south and west Pacific. The genus is, according to USINGER (*273*) common in the Australian and Oriental regions extending through Melanesia to Fiji and Samoa without a single representative east of this line, but important in the Hawaiian chain, the author seems to have overlooked its occurrence in Juan Fernandez. *Nysius* is supposed to have reached Hawaii by a circuitous route over open water and the Leeward Hawaiian islands. This route is indicated by a submarine ridge of considerable depth and may once have been interrupted by island peaks such as Wake Island, thence it is followed to the Marianas and Caroline Islands and eventually to the rich Papuan and Australian regions. But in other cases it is less easy to construct a suitable route. "The presence of twenty very unique genera in Hawaii and their absence from old, high islands along the very route they are said to have traveled is inexplicable by present theories" (l.c. 315). Why not presume that all related genera have died out?, which is the easiest explanation.

Nysius is a widespread genus, well developed also in New Zealand, and the single Juan Fernandez species is claimed to be related to another from New Zealand. We know numerous examples of the same kind in other animal groups and particularly among the plants we have called Antarcto-tertiary.

The *Homoptera* present the same picture in Hawaii, about 350 native species, most of them endemic and suggesting a southwest Pacific ancestry. Of the species reported from Juan Fernandez only one third have been described, all endemic and as far as we know with their relatives in the south and central Pacific.

No order characteristic of insular faunas has aroused greater interest among biogeographers than the Pacific *land molluscs*, nowhere more wonderfully developed than in the Hawaiian chain. In the discussion of land connections they occupy a central position.

WALLACE found that the wide distribution of the land snails is "by no means so easy to explain as that of the insects", the chances have been "rare and exceptional", possibly eggs stuck to the feet of aquatic birds, or the animals themselves were storm carried, "attached to leaves and twigs"—this would be the only means by which viviparous forms could be transported.

GULICK (*119*) treats the land shell problem at some length. Speaking of Easter Island he asserts that "hurricanes spread gravid land snails as dust over almost as great distance as plant seeds can be blown", but he gives no facts to support this very positive statement. The land-shells of Juan Fernandez and Saint Helena are then remarked upon.

At least three elements can have derived their ancestry only from Polynesia, fully 3400 miles away, unless Easter Island served as a way station.

The archaic complexion of the snail fauna is not necessarily very significant, as younger continental forms do not for the most part yield minute, easily wind blown species.

Archaic—exactly, malacologists emphasize that more modern types do not occur on oceanic islands unless brought by man, and this has naturally enough, been used as an argument in favour of early land connections before the modern types existed. In GULICK's view the size, not the age, decides.

Large, softskinned creatures invariably make a poor showing. Large helices examplify this disability so excellently that their failure to arrive is a sort of negative criterium for insularity (p 414).

But neither are all continental species large, nor all insular ones small, and the oceanic snail fauna includes many forms that cannot spread like dust. GULICK remarks on the genus *Partula* that 'its 120 geographically restricted species mostly weigh too much and are too tender to fit easily into theories of transport by air or sea", and this makes him take into account the possibilities of "land ridges" to facilitate transport.

"It is evident", he says p 419, "that the vast diversification is a proof of the great local antiquity of these families, and hence of a considerable antiquity of their island habitat". This is not true of the islands as they appear now and as they have stood for probably millions of years.

Land snails, just as weevils, are dispersed by some unknown method, USINGER thinks (l c 315), while MAYR, as already quoted, regarded the presence of small molluscs on oceanic islands as a proof of the efficiency of hurricanes, but later on expressed himself as follows

It seems to me that the wide acceptance of land bridges by conchologists is chiefly due to three reasons (1) our almost complete ignorance of the means of dispersal of snails (2) our lack of knowledge of the speed of speciation in snails, and (3) faulty classification, particularly generic classification A Gulick has already directed attention to the presence of snails on most oceanic islands They were unquestionably carried there by some unknown means of transportation To me it seems incomparably simpler to assume a still unknown method of transportation than a land bridge that is unsupported by any other fact

Simple, no doubt, but we cannot get away from the problem by an ' ignoramus '

It is easy to understand that the presence of fairly large forms of land shells on distant islands has caused a good deal of trouble ZIMMERMAN tried to find a way out of the difficulties

It has been said that large snails such at the Hawaiian achatinellids and amastrids are particularly unsuited for overseas distribution However, if we approach the problem differently, different conclusions may be reached If, as I believe, the large Hawaiian snails have evolved from small or minute ancestors, then the argument based upon their large size loses its weight However, if small snails can be distributed overseas, then what is to prevent eggs or tiny, immature specimens of large species from being similarly transported? (l c 61)

In passing, ZIMMERMAN quotes H B BAKER, who thought that land-shells are carried along by migratory birds After these speculations it is refreshing to read BRYAN (40 9)

The presence of certain kinds of plants and animals found in Hawaii and related to species in the southwest Pacific is hard to explain by any known means of drift, either over the sea or through the air Land snails constitute one such group These mollusks, which breathe directly from the air, would drown in water, particularly salt water, yet they must have moisture They cannot stand long exposure to the sun, but live on the leaves and trunks of forest plants or beneath fallen leaves and trash on the ground How did their ancestors reach Hawaii if they could neither swim nor drift?

Opponents against the dogma of colonization across the oceans

Many biogeographers have arrived at the conclusion that the natural dispersal agents cannot be made responsible for the distribution of all kinds of biota across very wide expanses of open water Most of the authors are botanists, which is surprising because the chances should be greater for seeds and spores than for eggs or individuals of delicate creatures To ask for land bridges, or for extension of continental margins later submerged but leaving behind land fragments is to refuse to accept overseas migration as the only possible means of colonization Consequently, a number of authors have already been quoted in the chapter on the history of the Pacific basin, GOOD, IRMSCHER, WULFF, CAMPBELL, etc as well as my own contributions to the discussion, the latest in 1951 (248) I shall add here that I never disclaimed every possibility of migration over wide expanses of water, see 226 and 232 Various writers have compared isolated peaks on continents with oceanic islands and have stated that under present conditions an exchange of biota is improbable VAN STIENIS expressed his opinion when dealing with the Malaysian mountain flora in very plain terms (258), too many facts show the impossibility of attributing any importance worth mentioning to long distance dispersal, the theory is, when it comes to migrations of floras, "not worth a straw" and REICHE (203) referring to the history of the Chilean flora, called it "eine Kette von Unwahrscheinlichkeiten". GORDON (113) was strongly inclined do deny ist value and believed that plants, and more so plant associations, advance slowly over land and do not jump thousands of miles, he could not, however, help paying some attention to "Nature's great Krakatau experiment", of which enough has been said.

CAIN (42) thinks that "migration is usually not a random matter" (p 162) and that long distance dispersal rarely has resulted in migration and establishment, nor does it explain the discontinuous areas. In reality he belongs to the trustworthy opponents. One of the reasons advanced by him is, however not conclusive.

The phenomenon of local races (subspecific endemics) is entirely opposed to the idea of long-distance dispersal, for such variation depends upon isolation which would not exist if long distance dispersal were generally effective (p 161).

Those who are in favour of the theory emphasize the haphazard character of the procedure, success may follow once and never more. If the immigrant belongs to a polymorphous species, with intermediate forms between the subspecies or varieties, it may, isolated as it remains from the rest of the population, stand out as a separate insular taxon.

Among the zoologists few, mainly malacologists, are in favour of land connections, but some entomologists agree with them. BERLAND was already quoted. As a rule a connection South America–Antarctica–Australia (or New Zealand) is asked for, but to ENDERLEIN this bridge was not sufficient.

Die zahlreichen endemischen Gattungen (9) und Arten (2) zeigen, dass die Juan Fernandez-Inseln ein Refugium für die Reste der Faunen unfangreicherer untergegangener Gebiete darstellen, die nicht mit dem neotropischen Gebiet in Verbindung gestanden haben (ENDERLEIN 84 643).

Did ENDERLEIN dream of a submerged Pacific continent? Many of the island flies are also native of the mainland of Chile, others have their relations there, and if the islands were formerly connected with some other land, it was with South America. Besides, the majority of ENDERLEIN's new genera have been reduced to synonymy by later authors, his speculations have little weight, and WYGODZINSKY (294 81), referring to *Gigantodax kuscheli*, arrived at a different conclusion *Gigantodax* is an exclusively South American genus.

Chapter VII

Biological characteristics of isolated islands.

In his classical "Lecture on insular floras" (138) J D HOOKER formulated, in very lucid terms, the special features of island floras and his opinion on their evolution. As examples he chose Macaronesia, St Helena, Ascension and Kerguelen Island. Their peculiarities were stated under five items.

1 *In all cases considered floristic relations exist between the island and one mother continent*

2 *The floras of all the islands in question are more temperate in character than that of the mother continent on the same latitude*

This may be true in most cases, thanks to the influence of the surrounding ocean, it holds good for Juan Fernandez

3 *All these islands show many biological peculiarities by which they are distinguished*

The distinguishing characteristics are mainly expressed in endemism. HOOKER referred the endemics to two categories, such as do not show affinity to the plants on the mother continent, and such as, even if belonging to endemic genera, are related to continental ones

If we turn to the Pacific where, for obvious reasons, only the high volcanic, well watered islands are considered, we find that all of them are distinguished by numerous, in many cases also very remarkable endemics. Hawaii stand out above the others and so do Juan Fernandez and Desventuradas, the floras of Tahiti, Samoa, Marquesas etc, as well as of Micronesia, are less independent. The degree of spatial isolation is not conclusive, the flora of Juan Fernandez is more peculiar than that of Marquesas which are situated much farther away from any continent and this holds good not only for the angiosperms but also for the ferns. Endemism in angiosperms is 69 % in the former and 50 in the latter, of the ferns about 30 % in each, but only Juan Fernandez has an endemic genus

4 *The general rule is that the species also found in the mother continent are the most abundant, the peculiar species are rarer, the peculiar genera of continental affinity rarer still, but the plants with no affinity elsewhere are often very common*

This is, I suppose true of the islands examined by HOOKER, with the exception of St Helena before the arrival of man, but not of Hawaii, nor of Juan Fernandez. Some of the continental species—*Libertia* and a few grasses—are abundant, while others are rare, all according to the supply of suitable habitats, among the peculiar species of continental affinity are many quite common ones, e g the endemic species of *Acaena*, *Drimys*, *Dysopsis*, *Escallonia*, *Gunnera*, *Myrceugenia* (the leading forest tree on Masafuera), *Pernettya*, *Rhaphithamnus*, *Ugni*, *Erigeron fruticosus*, *Uncinia Douglasii*, and of the peculiar genera allied to South American ones. *Nothomyrcia* is the leading forest tree on Masatierra, where *Ochagavia* is also common. To these may be added such common endemics as *Boehmeria* and the species of *Fagara* and *Coprosma*, under the assumption that related species of *Boehmeria*, and representatives of *Coprosma* and *Fagara*, once belonged to the neotropical flora. The plants of no affinity in the mother country, that is the nearest continent, are as a rule very local, few are common and many extremely rare

Possibly I have misunderstood HOOKER here. When we say that a species is abundant in a country we mean that it is copious, if we call it common, it is widely spread, if we call it rare, it has been reported from a small number of localities only, and if we use "species" in plural we mean the same thing But what if HOOKER with "abundant" and "common" wanted to say that these species were the most numerous in the flora, and that the "rare" ones were few in number. If this was what HOOKER meant, the result will be: Species also found on the continent 46, endemic species allied to South American or other continental species 71, endemic genera, related to continental genera 5 (6 species), endemic genera not related to continental ones 12 (24 species). Still this is perhaps to give a wrong interpretation to HOOKER's words. There are very few native non endemics on St Helena, and they are of course not in the majority in the Canary Islands, nor are, in the latter place, the isolated endemic genera and species very many. In this case HOOKER says 'plants', not 'genera' and "species". If, to this group as represented in Juan Fernandez we add isolated endemic species, not related to any species in the mother continent, although the genera occur there, this group comprises 54 plants, or more than $1/3$ of the angiosperms, while group 2 is reduced from 71 to 40. The figures would be 46, 40, 6, 54, thus conforming much better to HOOKER's rule.

5 *Indigenous annual plants are extremely rare or altogether absent*

Here "rare" must mean few species, and Therophytes are very few in Juan Fernandez and some of the registered species perhaps not originally native.

How were plants transported to distant islands. HOOKER's answer is either across the sea or over submerged bridges and he adds "the naturalist who takes nothing for granted, finds insuperable obstacles to the ready acceptance of either". The situation is still the same 90 years after HOOKER.

HOOKER regarded the isolated island plants as "relics of a far more ancient vegetation than now prevails on the mother continent", but he most certainly never wanted to say that the continental flora was altogether younger than the insular, but that species now restricted to the island formerly occurred on the mother continent, having become replaced there by younger species. He based his opinion on the fact that Macaronesian relicts had been found as fossils in Tertiary deposits on the continent. Time has not permitted me to collect modern data and I can only suppose that some of the old determinations still hold good. The vegetation of Europe has undergone great changes within the lifetime of these Atlantic island species', they once grew in Europe, but were driven out from there to be preserved on the islands, which they had reached "when conditions may have been very different from what they are now".

The theory of a continental Macaronesia, including Madeira and the Azores, goes back to FORBES theory of the former connection between the British Islands and the mainland, definitely proved ages ago. FORBES went further and revived the old idea of a lost Atlantis, still favoured by many.

It is interesting to follow HOOKER's discussion with his friend DARWIN on island problems. DARWIN believed in the efficiency of dispersal agents to carry plants and animals across wide expanses of sea, and his arguments made such a deep impression on HOOKER that he became almost convinced. Still he hesitated, and certain serious difficulties prevented him from fully accepting DARWIN's ideas. The composition of the flora of the Azores was not what we had reason to expect from the direction of winds and currents. The Macaronesian Ornis is almost the same as in Europe and undoubtedly came from there, but the flora is considerably different, thus it may be argued that "the birds and plants do not come under the same category". DARWIN replied that

> the migration of birds is continuous and frequent, and the individuals surviving and breeding, they keep up the specific type, and do not give origin to local varieties whilst the transport of seeds is casual and rare, and very few surviving, these not being crossed by the original stock, in the process of time give rise to varieties, etc, and do not perpetuate the continental races (p 10)

This is the situation in a nut-shell, and DARWIN's arguments are repeated by scores of biogeographers to this very day.

Also St Helena, Ascension and Kerguelen made HOOKER hesitate

> They [St Helena and Ascension] have no land birds, but an African vegetation, and though nearly midway between Africa and America, they have scarcely a single American type of flowering plants and Kerguelen's Land has a flora of whose elements most have emigrated not from the nearest land, but from the most distant (p 10)

HEMSLEY (*127* 59) remarks that HOOKER seems to have forgotten the Compositae in St Helena, most of them showing American affinity

Kerguelen's nearest land is Antarctica, but not a single flowering plant is known from the coast south of Kerguelen Africa as a mother country—it goes without saying that subtropical or warm temperate plants cannot endure a subantarctic climate, and only the most distant lands, Tierra del Fuego and the Falkland Islands, were, thanks to the strong and constant west wind drift, regarded as a mother country Even if South Georgia served as an intermediate station, the distances are very great, besides, we do not look west for the ancestors of the peculiar endemics in the Kerguelen area Where the capacity of the dispersal agents appeared to be inadequate, HOOKER was strongly inclined to look for better land connections The existence of identical Macaronesian species on Madeira and the Canary Islands can, he says, hardly be explained without the help of

> intermediate masses of land, as the Salvages (supposing them to have been larger) the only conceivable means of interisland transport and if intermediate islands are granted (and Mr Darwin freely admits these), why not continents

He must have found that the distance between Madeira and the Canaries is too large to permit direct transport of diaspores under present wind and current conditions, in the Kerguelen case they are, at least, favourable Nevertheless, later on HOOKER's faith in transoceanic migration was not as steadfast as before, the case of Kerguelen troubled him (*339*)

> Turning to the natural agents of dispersion, winds are no doubt the most powerful, and sufficient to account for the transport of Cryptogamic spores, these, almost throughout the year, blow from Fuegia to Kerguelen Island, and in the opposite direction only for very short periods, but appear quite insufficient to transport seeds over 4000 miles (p 13)

> Various phenomenons common to Kerguelen, the Crozets and Marion, favour the supposition of these all having been peopled with land plants from South America by intermediate tracts of land that have now disappeared, in other words,

that those islands constitute the wrecks of either an ancient continent or an archipelago which formerly extended further westwards" (p. 15)

GULICK's paper "Biological peculiarities of oceanic islands" does not, contrary to its title, contain a review of the special characteristics of island biota, his object was to expound and defend the theory of permanent isolation of islands like the Hawaiian, Galapagos, Juan Fernandez, St Helena, etc., which are said to offer irrefutable proofs of true oceanity. Of this enough has been said already, I shall return to HOOKER's five points, to which others may be added

Endemism.—The occurrence of numerous genera and species restricted to oceanic islands has caused much discussion "Reichtum an Endemismen ist uberhaupt der hervorragendste Charakterzug der Inselfloren", HAYEK wrote (*304*) It is, however, equally pronounced in continental districts like the Cape region, southwestern Australia, western China, California or Chile, where local concentrations of endemics are found

If insular endemics show distant affinity only or, in extreme cases, no affinity at all, to continental taxa, they are looked upon as relicts, as the islands are geologically young, the endemics have not evolved there but must have immigrated from some mother country, where they have become extinct. They may, however, have undergone some change after their arrival to the island. There is also a possibility that the continental progenitor has, in its turn, changed in a different direction, making its descendants so unlike that their relations are obscured. Species only slightly different from continental ones are much more numerous than the relicts, they are supposed to have originated in the islands and give examples of so called progressive endemism. As CHRISTENSEN (*60* 149) pointed out, another alternative leading to the establishment of endemic species should be considered. On the continent, from where a plant found its way to an isolated island opportunities for crossing with other species often exist, eventually leading to the disappearance of the original taxon with its special characteristics. Its island offshoot does not share its fate but remains true to the original type. The island form did not originate through a genetic change of the continental species it represents the surviving species and is, as it were, a relict. This does not apply to the pteridophytes. Crosses are extremely rare, the fern species represent, in a high degree, pure lines, whence it follows that insular endemics are much rarer than among the phanerogams. This is true, but it is usually explained as a result of the enormous spore production and the facility with which they spread.

Opinions about the true nature of systematically isolated taxa vary GUPPY (*122*) regarded them as either highly specialized products of the islands, "the first of their race", or modified forms of allied continental genera, the majority of which had passed away, "the last of their race" and probably doomed, to him the islands appealed "more as registers of past floral conditions in the continents than as representing their present state"—this in accordance with HOOKER's views. The Age-and area theory of WILLIS (*286*) claims that wides are older than endemics, a rule with few exceptions, in another paper (*285*) he states that "insular endemic genera are as a rule young beginners, not relics" I have discussed his theories in an earlier paper (231) to which I refer. RIDLEY (205) called the island endemics 'newborn species', admitting that all did not fall within this category but were "epibiotics, relics at the end of their species life ... unable to reach another suitable spot for their growth". It is noteworthy that so many of the "epibiotics" are Composites, famous among diffusionists for their alleged effective dispersal mechanisms; in RIDLEY's eyes they are, perhaps, pseudo relicts. CAIN (42) takes more or less the same position: "the relic nature of an endemic should never be accepted without some form of positive evidence" (p. 227); proofs are hard to find, no island cases as clear as *Ginkgo* or *Metasequoia* are known. An endemic inhabiting a strikingly limited area may be a young species that had no time to spread, or it may be too stenotopic, but others are what CAIN (p. 230) calls "senescent", such species occupy a small area, are relatively constant, ecologically of narrow amplitude and show low competitive ability. They are unable to "penetrate the prevailing habitats that are dominated by the typical vegetation of the region" but behave just as stenotopic young beginners. If indeed old and senescent they ought to show some primitive characteristics. According to CAIN senescent species constitute "an anomalous element in the flora of a given region"; this may be true, for in many instances they survive from an earlier climatic period and are barely able to hold their ground under the changed conditions. Nevertheless there are cases when such anomalous species form the typical vegetation of a certain habitat and where nobody would dream of regarding them as young beginners; the "*Robinsonia* assemblage" in Masatierra offers a good example (see 251).

Number of species per genus. — We know that island floras contain a fair number of monotypical genera, many genera that are large elsewhere but represented on a given island by a single species, and few with many species, so that the numerical relation between species and genus approaches 1 and does not exceed 2 and this has been regarded as a good proof that the island is truly oceanic and has been peopled accidentally by waifs and strays. This rule is not without exceptions, among which the Hawaiian flora is the most striking. FOSBERG, who contributed a chapter on the higher flora to ZIMMERMAN's book (298), indicates 83 families, 216 genera and 1729 species of angiosperms. The figure for the genera may be a little too low. With regard to species all depends on the species concept. HILLEBRAND (307) was conservative; from his Flora DRUDE (305, 136) got the ratio 6.2 : 1 but scores of well marked species have been described since 1888, and in addition, particularly during the last two or three decades, a large number of taxa that are little more than microspecies; unfortunately no case of apomixis has been found as yet.[1] It is difficult to know which way to take out of this maze, neither the role played by hybridism nor the existence of modifications due to environment has been duly considered. Based on FOSBERG's figures, the relation species : genus is 8 : 1 and this is not at all what one expects to find in an oceanic flora. Nobody is, I think, likely to disclaim New

---

[1] Among taxonomists particularly responsible for this alarming increase F. F. SHERFF and H. ST. JOHN should be mentioned first, but some others have also contributed and the writer cannot plead innocent. SHERFF, in addition to numerous new species, has described an endless number of varieties.

Zealand's continentality. According to CHEESMAN the number of families is 97, of genera 382 and of species 1415, the relation in question is 3.7 : 1. I cannot attach much importance to such figures. If an island is a remnant of a submerged land-mass upon which during the process of sinking lava was ejected until the old foundation disappeared, only a small part of the flora and fauna will survive the catastrophe, and unless progressive endemism comes to play a rôle, the living world will present a picture of disharmony, with a reduced number of families and a low species genus ratio. Climatic changes will create a similar situation if a portion of a continental flora has lost its connection with the continent. The Falkland Islands rest on the continental shelf, they are formed by old sediments on a granitic foundation and are, universally I think, classified as continental islands, but their angiospermic flora is disharmonic and fragmentary: 38 families, 97 genera and 143 species, the ratio is 1.47 : 1. There is a single endemic genus and a small number of endemic species. The poverty is due to a severe climate and to losses suffered during the pleistocene period of solifluction, contemporaneous with the glaciation on the mainland. The constitution of a flora, continental or insular, depends on a combination of many factors, geological, historical, climatic, genetic and so forth.

Absence of large, widespread and "successful" families. — The lack of conifers in islands demonstrates, it is said, that such islands are not continental, for in all continents gymnosperms are plentiful, "cones do not float", and the seeds, winged or unwinged, have no chances to be carried very far, but it is surprising that also Taxads and many Podocarps, adapted, as it were to endozoochorous bird dispersal, are conspicuous by their absence. Consequently, islands where cone-bearing species exist are regarded as continental: New Zealand, Tasmania, Norfolk Island, New Caledonia, Fiji, etc.

Exceptions occur, islands looked upon as permanently isolated, Bermuda, the Azores, Madeira and the Canaries, have at least some species of *Juniperus*, perhaps junipers possess some kind of dispersal capacity and do not count, but we cannot get away from *Pinus canariensis*.

Other large and wide spread families very poorly represented on isolated islands are Leguminosae, Araceae and Orchidaceae. Peas are a staple food of many birds but few if any able to pass their digestive tract unharmed, they are too heavy to be carried any distance by wind and, notorious beach plants excepted, will sink in water. The dry pods would float but they do not fall off but open on the plant to discharge the seeds. Nevertheless *Sophora* sect. *Edwardsia* has a number of closely related species scattered over the south hemisphere on islands as remote as Diego Álvarez, Rapa, Easter and Marquesas, with one species, more well-marked than the rest, on Hawaii. This is a very puzzling case of disjunct distribution, but it is not expedient to draw any far-reaching conclusions from this unique case. The seeds are of the size of a small pea and not equipped with a capacity to travel greater than in hundreds of leguminous plants, which are within reach but never crossed any water barriers, nor used any land bridges. Did they not yet exist, were they not within reach when connection was established or have they all died out in the islands? Each alternative seems equally improbable. Araceae are plentiful in humid tropical climates, and some islands the Hawaiian for instance, ought to offer a suitable environment, still there is not a single native species. And it is strange that orchids, with their dust-like seeds, should be, if not altogether absent, so few, becoming fewer and fewer as we proceed east from Malaysia and Melanesia, cf. *318*, map 21. However, the seeds, even if carried far, rarely are able to retain their viability long enough to become established, should they happen to strike a spot where they can germinate. I believe that also where we find a very rich orchid flora most of the species occupy restricted areas, their advance over land is slow. A species introduced on purpose will, in rare instances, become naturalized, but I cannot remember ever having heard of an adventitious orchid. Taking all these circumstances into account, the poverty of distant islands, even if temporarily connected with other lands, is perhaps not altogether incomprehensible. Besides, the submerged links may, for all we know, have been poor in legumes, arum lilies and orchids. CAMPBELL, admitting that the total absence of *Araucaria*, *Agathis*, *Podocarpus*, *Ficus* and Araceae in oceanic islands of the Pacific is a valid objection not easy to explain, suggests that perchance they once did exist there but were destroyed by volcanic eruptions (*46*, 181).

The preponderance of woody plants in oceanic islands.—HEMSLEY (*127*, 31) emphasized the prominent part taken by arboreous and shrubby species in many islands and pointed out that in some cases they belong to otherwise herbaceous families. Many peculiar genera of Compositae are confined to islands such as Hawaii, Galapagos, and Juan Fernandez, and are scattered over Polynesia (see *318*, map 20) and in the Atlantic (Macaronesia, St Helena) and Indian oceans (Socotra, the Seychelles, Mascarene Islands) arboreous Compositae are, as HEMSLEY justly remarks, by no means restricted to island habitats but numerous in tropical regions of the continents, particularly in America. Both Hawaii and Juan Fernandez offer good examples of woody plants belonging to otherwise herbaceous families or genera, but HEMSLEY's statement p 31 about *Gunnera* in Juan Fernandez—"caulescent species unknown elsewhere"—is erroneous, for they are just as caulescent in Hawaii, besides, they are not woody but herbaceous.

Scarcity of herbaceous species, especially of therophytes.—Native annuals and biennials are rare in islands. They cannot have been less capable of migrating across the sea than trees or shrubs, nor could soil or climate prevent them from getting established, this is at once disproved by the countless herbaceous weeds brought by man which threaten to overrun so many islands. The reason must be historical. If it is true that life forms with a woody stem are the most ancient and if the original stock making up island floras dates back to before the rise of herbs, a period during which the distribution of land and sea was another than now, we can explain the high proportion of arborescent species in islands isolated since millions of years.

Evidence for a greater antiquity of lignified angiosperms.—The angiosperms originated in the Mesozoic and are traced back to the Lower Cretaceous. The tree form was the response to a warm and humid climate. These problems were subjected to a comprehensive analysis by SINNOTT and I W BAILEY (*224*) whom

I shall quote at some length. They state that evidence for a more recent origin of herbaceous plants is furnished by palaeontology, anatomy, phylogeny and phytogeography. Evidence from palaeobotany is, however, not conclusive, because herbs are much less fit to be preserved as fossils, but it is true that they increase in number in the younger formations. Evidence from anatomy and phylogeny are said to be positive; within a group including both ligneous and herbaceous species, the former show other primitive characters; of the Leguminosae the more primitive members are all woody (Mimosaceae, Caesalpiniaceae), the proportion of herbs being vastly greater among the Papilionaceae. The authors continue, p. 572

It is generally admitted that endemic species of a flora are for the most part more ancient than the non endemic element, for they must either have had their origin in the region — a process usually requiring a long time — or else they must be remnants of an older vegetation which has elsewhere become extinct. Endemic genera and finally endemic families are in this way regarded as progressively more ancient portions of the flora.

I doubt that this statement is of general application; we cannot argue that, in a given flora, all endemics are more ancient than the wides, because a widely distributed species may have remained unchanged for millions of years and be older than another which, for various reasons, happens to have become greatly restricted in range and endemic in a small area. WILLIS and his school are diametrically opposed to the opinion of SINNOTT and BAILEY and neither is in possession of the absolute truth.

Proceeding to an analysis of certain insular floras deserving special attention, the authors assume that, if woody types are more ancient than herbaceous, a flora which has been for a long time isolated ought to contain a large proportion of woody endemics, and this is what they do find. Their analysis of the Juan Fernandez flora was based on JOHOW's work, but this has long been out of date and the figures are incorrect (new ones will be found in Chapter IX) so I shall leave this subject aside here. The general conclusions in the chapter "Discussion of Isolated Insular Floras" deserve to be quoted in full (p. 579)

It is thus very clear that woody plants constitute a more conspicuous element in the flora of isolated oceanic islands than in the flora of adjacent continental areas from which their vegetation has possibly been derived, and also that the most ancient portion of the island floras, if endemism is to be regarded as a criterion of antiquity, is much more woody than the recently acquired elements. Annual herbs, which seem to be the last step in reduction, are almost entirely absent from insular floras, as has been noted by Darwin, Hooker, and others. Since the vegetation of these isolated oceanic islands is to be regarded as more ancient in its composition than that of larger land areas, it may be looked upon as a vestige of an earlier and much more uniform flora which flourished over the earth during the middle or latter part of the Tertiary, and before the great flood of herbaceous vegetation, developed chiefly in the north temperate lands, had spread over the globe. This conclusion is strengthened by the many similarities which these widely separated island floras bear to one another.

Some of the statements made by these authors are questionable, but in the main I agree, only I prefer to say "early to middle Tertiary". DARWIN, who was the first to note the predominance of trees on oceanic islands, tried to explain it as a result of natural selection. SINNOTT and BAILEY's criticism is absolutely convincing.

The authors also paid attention to The Ancient Flora of Antarctica, p. 592:

It seems to be a reasonably safe conclusion that all genera commonly designated as "Antarctic" from their confinement to the temperate region of the southern hemisphere, were inhabitants of the ancient Antarctic continent.

The authors made an attempt to reconstruct this flora and came to the conclusion that "two thirds of its endemic dicotyledons were woody plants" (p. 599).

In the authors opinion most of the herbaceous vegetation originated in the north; this may be so because in the latter part of the Tertiary period, with the increasing differentiation of climatic regions, the temperate and cold resistant flora is supposed to have taken possession of large areas, but these were concentrated in the north; except the Antarctic continent there was not much land in the far south.

Several authors have expressed the same opinion as SINNOTT and BAILEY. IRMSCHER (143) was convinced that most of the primitive angiosperms were trees and that the relation between tropical and temperate genera and species point in this direction; to take one example, it is generally acknowledged that the herbaceous, mainly temperate family Cruciferae descends from woody tropical Capparidaceae. (IRMSCHER might have called attention to the miniature *Lepidium* trees in Hawaii).

Auch sonst ist die Abstammung gemässigter Sippen von tropischen nachgewiesen worden. Diese Gegenüberstellung der gemässigten und tropischen Sippen lehrt aber auch ohne weiteres, dass mit der Anpassung von Formen an die extratropischen Zonen zugleich die Umprägung des Typus des Holzgewächses in den des Krautes vor sich ging, somit letztere als die jüngeren Formen die Abkömmlinge von Holzgewächsen sind (I, 209).

Dass die Theorie der Abstammung der übrigen Wuchsformen von der Gestalt des tropischen Baumes immer mehr an Boden gewinnt, geht zum Beispiel aus dem Buche von BEWS hervor: "The megatherm hygrophilous forest of the tropics is probably the most ancient type of habitat ... and most recent of all (life-forms) is the annual type" (II, 321).

The investigation of JEFFREY and TORREY (177) led to the conclusion that "the origin of the herbaceous type in Dicotyledons is from woody or arboreal forms", and STOCKWELL, in his monograph of *Chaenactis* (259, Compositae, 33 sp.), states that "within a family or genus, woody perennial species are more primitive than herbaceous annual species". An evolution in the reversed direction is, however, postulated by HUTCHINSON (140, I, 4) in the Polycarpicae. He regards the herbaceous Ranunculaceae as the most primitive, a woody structure is, in this order secondary. The current opinion is that the woody Magnoliaceae are among the oldest living angiosperms.

The rosette trees. — The common type of this interesting growth-form is characterized by a candelabrum-like mode of branching, the two or three (rarely more) innovations situated on practically the same level at the base of a terminal inflorescence, in some cases cauliflory is observed. A much more uncommon type is the unbranched stem terminated by a tuft of large leaves (if entire = GRISEBACH's *Clavija* form 325 I 11), either pollacanthic with lateral inflorescences or hapaxanthic when, after a number of years, a terminal inflorescence ends the life of the individual; this type is the most unusual of all. All kinds have in common the very short internodes and the short lived leaves, a self evident condition for the formation of a compact tuft. A reduction of the rosette tree to herbaceous state would result in a compact caudex multiceps or a single basal rosette; an hapaxanthic tree would become a therophyte.

These growth forms are by no means restricted to island habitats but are also found in all continents; they belong to many different genera and families and are characteristic of such dicotylous families as Araliaceae, Caricaceae, Theophrastaceae etc.; typical examples are found in Compositae (e.g. *Espeletia*, species of *Senecio*), Epacridaceae (*Dracophyllum*), Lecythidaceae (*Gtias*), Meliaceae (*Carapa*), Rutaceae (*Spathelia*), Sapindaceae, and so forth. Among the monocotyledons the vast majority of palms belong here; the Pandanaceae should of course be mentioned, and well-known examples are scattered through the Liliflorae (species of *Aloe*, *Cordyline*, species of *Yucca*, *Dracaena*, *Fourcroya* etc.), *Ravenala* in the Musaceae, and *Puya Raimondii* in Bromeliaceae. Hapaxanthic trees are few. KRAUSE (*162*) called attention to the interesting rutaceous *Sohnreya excelsa* Krause from Amazonas.

Thus, even if rosette trees are more or less widely distributed over the globe in warmer regions, it is a fact that they are a particularly conspicuous feature in island floras. In the Pacific they are very plentiful in the Hawaiian Islands, especially among the Compositae and Lobeliaceae, also the hapaxanthic type represented; they occur in the Galápagos Islands (GRISEBACH II 512), we find many in New Caledonia, they constitute a large proportion of the poor Juan Fernandez flora (see Chapter IX), and they are scattered over Oceania. In the Atlantic they are numerous in Macaronesia (e.g. *Campanula Vidalii* on the Azores, *Musschia* on Madeira, species of *Aeonium*, *Dracaena*, *Echium*, *Melanoselinum*, *Sonchus*, *Sinapidendrum*, etc.) I suppose that some are found also on the islands of the Indian Ocean, but I have no reliable information. I may be entirely wrong, but I have the idea that this is an old fashioned growth form, a relict element in island floras, and that the high volcanic islands of the Pacific and the Atlantic, which are so like each other in geology and topography, are, in their present shape, of approximately the same age and date back to a period of land submergence and great volcanic activity. Perhaps also the "inland islands", the high volcanic mountains of Africa deserve to be mentioned in this connection, famous as they are for their magnificent tree Lobelias and Senecios.

Rosette trees seem to favour open, sunny situations; this is certainly the case in Juan Fernandez, where they are definitely adapted to such habitats. Single specimens of a few species are sometimes found growing in the shade with the result that the internodes become much longer, the dense tuft dissolves and the formation of flowers is suppressed. SCHIMPER believed that they are adapted to a very windy climate and fit to withstand the pressure of strong winds better than trees of a more ordinary type but this theory has been refuted (227), and recent observations in the field have not made me alter my opinion

Absence of quadrupeds The only mammals regarded as possibly native in isolated islands are bats, but many islands do not have any Storm drift has been postulated, but if the distance be very great the animals might be without food too long unless Nature provides a fair supply of air-born insects To other land mammals wide stretches of open water are an absolute obstacle and their absence is regarded as one of the safest proofs of the permanent isolation of oceanic islands, just as the presence of endemic foxes in the Falkland Islands (now extinct) supports the theory of an earlier connection with South America

However, we cannot know that indigenous mammals never existed on islands gradually having become extinct when the submergence of land had proceeded and grazing grounds became smaller and smaller It would appear that this theory is contradicted by the fact that herbivorous mammals have been introduced by man to many islands and do make a living there also when not tended but if allowed to naturalize and multiply unrestrainedly in virgin surroundings, their ravages would perhaps prove catastrophal to the native vegetation and, as a consequence thereof to themselves They would die out and leave the flora to recover We must remember that the islands are small, most of them very small, that herbivorous animals need space and that pasture lands as they exist now are a result of cleared forest soil and introduction of innumerable alien weeds or cultigens Another explanation of the absence of mammals is that the islands were cut off so early that mammals had not yet taken possession of the earth or were not universally distributed and perhaps not within reach But these are mere wild speculations No fossil remains have been discovered, nor can they be expected on purely volcanic islands We cannot attack this problem with a hope of success as long as we know little or nothing of the geographical history of islands and archipelagoes But we had better remember that continental islands such as New Zealand, New Caledonia, etc are in the same precarious position with regard to mammals as the Hawaiian Islands

Native reptiles and amphibians are also absent CAMPBELL (46) mentions in passing that there are half a dozen lizards in Hawaii but all are species widespread in the South Pacific, most likely they were introduced with the early human immigrants or perhaps later That there are no frogs or toads would indicate, CAMPBELL thinks that the archipelago became isolated before the modern kinds of these animals had been developed But, as MUMFORD points out, many continental islands lack all lower vertebrates (183 248)

How can we explain all these peculiarities in oceanic islands HOOKER's answer was this

Thus, according to the hypothesis of trans-oceanic migration, and the theory of the derivative origin of species, we can understand why the ancient types should have survived on the islands to which but few of the superior race had penetrated —we can understand how it comes about, that so many continental species and genera are represented on the island by similar but not identical species and genera, and that there is such a representation of genera and species in the separate islands of a group,—we can understand why we find in the Atlantic island Floras of such a graduated series of forms, ascending from variety to genus, without those sharp lines of specific distinction that continental plants exhibit,—why whole tribes are absent in the Islands, why their Floras are limited, and species few in proportion to genera,—why so many peculiar genera tend to grotesque or picturesque arborescent forms (p. 11).

All this is, perhaps, not so easy to understand as HOOKER, impressed by DARWIN's theory, thought. Finally I shall quote the summary of WALLACE's General remark on Oceanic Islands (278 329–330), to bring this chapter to a close.

They all agree in the total absence of indigenous mammalia and amphibia, while their reptiles, when they possess any, do not exhibit indications of extreme isolation and antiquity (for the moment WALLACE seems to have forgotten the giant tortoises and the peculiar endemic lizards in the Galápagos, typically oceanic islands in his opinion). Their birds and insects present just the amount of specialisation and diversity from continental forms which may be well explained by the known means of dispersal acting through long periods, their land shells indicate greater isolation, owing to their admittedly less effective means of conveyance across the ocean, while their plants show most clearly the effects of those changes of conditions which we have reason to believe have occurred during the Tertiary epoch, and preserve to us in highly specialised and archaic forms some record of the primeval immigration by which islands were originally clothed with vegetation.

Chapter VIII

Evolution in Oceanic islands.

Ever since the high proportion of endemic organisms in oceanic islands and especially the occurrence of systematically isolated genera were first noticed, an explanation of this condition has been sought. Most authors have, as we have seen, assumed that the islands never had been connected with a continent and that, consequently, their entire living world had developed from a limited number of ancestors carried across the water. Even if the islands had emerged as late as during the Pliocene the time was thought to have been sufficient for immigrants to get transformed. It was a peculiar island world, the Galápagos Archipelago which gave birth to DARWIN's theory of origin of species through variation and natural selection, and HOOKER, when dealing with a number of islands, was convinced that DARWIN had given the solution to their problems and that their status strongly supported his theory.

And if many of the phenomena of oceanic island Flora are thus well explained by aid of the theory of the derivative origin of species, and not at all by any other theory, it surely is a strong corroboration of that theory. Depend upon it, the slow but steady struggle for existence is taking advantage of every change of form and every change of circumstance to which plants no less than animals are exposed, and, variation and change of form are the rules in organic life. By a wise ordinance it is ruled, that amongst the living beings like shall never produce its exact like, as no two circumstances in time or place are absolutely synchronous, or equal, or similar, so shall no two beings be born alike, that a variety in the environing conditions in which the progeny of a living being may be placed, shall be met by variety in the progeny itself. A wise ordinance it is, that ensures the succession of beings, not by multiplying absolutely identical forms, but by varying these, so that the right form may fill its right place in Nature's ever varying economy (258 11—12).

As we have seen already, HOOKER's first point when summarizing the characteristics of island floras was that also their most peculiar genera had their origin in a mother continent, that no oceanic island had been a centre for special creative forces. GRISEBACH (II 494) may have been the first to express another opinion. Referring to the systematically isolated endemics in St Helena, he argued that they never had had any allies elsewhere.

Nach diesen Thatsachen kann von einem Stammkontinent weder in dem Sinne die Rede sein, dass die Flora von daher durch natürliche Einwanderungen bereichert wurde, noch als ob die endemischen Arten aus Umbildungen von Pflanzen hervorgegangen wären, die in einer früheren Periode von auswärts dahin gelangten. Nur von gewissen klimatischen Analogien ist ihre Organisation der Ausdruck. S Helena verhält sich demnach ganz verschieden von den Kap Verden und liefert den vollgültigen Beweis, dass die Entstehung der Pflanzen auf Inseln, ebenso wohl wie auf Kontinenten, unabhängig von anderen Vegetationscentren möglich war. Warum sollte auch der geographische Umfang eines Gebiets auf die Kräfte, welche die Organisationen erzeugt haben, von Einfluss sein? In dem kleinsten Raume, wie im grössten, konnten sie in besonderer Weise sich entfalten nur werden sie im ersteren Falle weniger zahlreich sein müssen.

In his discussion of the Galápagos flora he admits that what he terms vicarious species, endemic in the islands, may have arisen through transformation of American species, but he doubts it.

Diejenigen, welche annehmen, dass die vikarnierenden Arten aus Umbildungen von eingewanderten hervorgegangen sind, können auch unter den endemischen Gewächsen der Galapagos Beispiele genug anführen, dass eine nahe Verwandtschaft dieselben mit Amerika, als ihrem vorausgesetzten Stammkontinent verbinde. Aber allgemein lässt sich dieser Gesichtspunkt nicht durchführen. Gerade unter den geselligen Holzgewächsen finden wir die eigentümlichsten Erzeugnisse, die Scalesien und andere Synanthereen, die nach ihrer systematischen Stellung dem Festlande ebenso fremdartig gegenüber stehen wie die Lobeliaceen des Sandwich-Archipels. Alle Beredsamkeit, womit die Abstammung der Vegetation ozeanischer Inseln von den Kontinenten vertheidigt zu werden pflegt, kann die Thatsache nicht verdunkeln, dass in solchen Fällen [the genus *Scalesia* etc. are mentioned] die Organisationen nicht anzugeben sind, aus deren Variation man sie hervorgegangen vorstellen möchte. Die nahe Verwandtschaft hingegen, welche zwischen vielen endemischen Erzeugnissen des Archipels und denen der amerikanischen Floren unleugbar besteht, kann aus dem Bildungsgesetz der räumlichen Analogien ebenso wohl, als aus einem genetischen Zusammenhang abgeleitet werden. Und warum sollte überhaupt das Festland vor den Inseln den Vorzug selbständig entstandener Organisationen gehabt haben, deren erste Erzeugung in den frühesten Perioden der Erdgeschichte jeder Möglichkeit einer Variation vorausging? warum sollte sich nicht später und an verschiedenen Orten sich wiederholt haben, was ursprünglich möglich war und wovon nur die Bedingungen ein noch ungelöstes Räthsel geblieben sind (II 512—513).

Such ideas have little more than historical interest. DRUDE, another leading authority on plant geography, was more in accordance with modern thought

dass die Flora der Inseln nicht nur als Transformationen der jetzt lebenden Kontinentalfloren erfasst werden darf, sondern dass auf vielen Inseln unzweifelhaft eine Weiter-entwickelung alter, vielleicht den Charakter einer älteren tertiären Periode repräsentieren der Stammfloren stattgefunden hat, welche sich hier im Schutze der Abgeschiedenheit fern von dem Einfluss kontinentaler Umwälzungserscheinungen sich erhalten konnten (305 128).

DRUDE agreed with HOOKER that extinct species, known as fossils in Europe, were the ancestors of species now endemic in Macaronesia.

With regard to the Pacific islands several authors have discussed the question to what extent endemism has been of a progressive kind and if not only species but also isolated genera have evolved on the islands from a limited number of unknown ancestors. Most of them, in spite of their firm belief that the islands are, geologically spoken, very recent, regard the insular biota as a local product; the first arrivals had had time to give rise to new genera, those that came a little later became new species, still more recent ones varieties of a continental species, and such as arrived in our era have not had time to change but are expected to do so, because isolation in a new and strange environment makes them adapt themselves by changing their genetic structure. HAYEK (304 252) expressed this very clearly.

Dass diese eingewanderten Elemente infolge ihrer Isolierung eigene Entwickelungsrichtungen einschlagen, die sich in einer oft auffallend grossen Zahl von Endemismen äussern, ist ja selbstverständlich.

Among botanists of the latest decennia ANDREWS (6) may be chosen as a representative of the school of "rapid adaptive radiation".

If a newcomer belongs to a primary form of a virile genus such as *Acacia*, *Coprosma*, etc. it may be expected rapidly to become differentiated into varieties and species. As Bentham pointed out long ago, the geographic station of a waif or colonist imposes variations upon it almost from the moment of its arrival. Eucalypts planted in New Zealand, California, and other places present marked differences from the forms the same species possess in Australia. In the second place, if the plant assemblage into which the waif or colonist arrives be a result of long continued struggle for existence such as occurs commonly in Holarctica and the cosmopolitan tropics, then the opportunity for the development of new forms is remote, unless the new arrival itself is a plastic form, and a grand example of the survival of the fittest. If, on the other hand, the newcomer belongs to an agressive species in its own continental setting, then it has, all other things being equal, an excellent chance of survival and of differentiating into new forms (p 617).

ANDREWS, himself an Australian, speaking on the Hawaiian flora, mentioned *Acacia*, *Coprosma* and other genera of Australian or southwest Pacific origin which developed new, endemic forms in Hawaii, where they take a prominent part in the vegetation. But when it comes to Eucalypts planted in California, nobody will, I suppose, consider this example as a proof of the origin of new taxa under the influence of new surroundings.

There is, he continues, a difference in the physical character of islands, some did not encourage the colonist to vary and evolve, others did.

If the island be very small and of negligible relief, it again has but little opportunity for differentiation, and, furthermore, if the island be even large and high, but the time be short the response will have been but slight (l c).

If, on the other hand, the island group lies in the tropics and is large in area, the islands of the group being close together, if the vertical relief be very great indeed if the precipitation be very variable it the soil be rich, but variable in porosity, if the plant assemblages into which the waifs or colonists entered are not the end result of severe plant competition, then the stage is set for the rapid differentiation of primary types of agressive genera

The evidence available suggests that these genera never existed as such on the land from where their immediate predecessors were derived, but that virile types, of the families concerned, arrived as waifs from Malaysia, Australia, New Zealand, Central and North America Once they found themselves removed from their former severe competition with other plants, they gave rise to the vigorous, endemic Hawaiian genera (p 618)

What ANDREWS depicts is an island which has reached maturity It has risen from the bottom of the ocean to an altitude where the moisture of the trade winds is condensed, where there are leeward and windward slopes, different habitats and a rich soil This island looks back on a very long history but life begins to arrive long before the island has come to rest Aerial plankton will bring microscopic green and bluegreen algae, bacteria spores of all kinds and also air borne seeds, and some drift may be washed up on the shores But to begin with there is little humidity and hardly anything we can call soil, we need water before even the most primitive organisms can exist, so that the island becomes fit to receive its first settlers, microscopic algae then mosses and lichens and mycelia of fungi, to form soil where the first seeds can germinate and start to form an incipient vegetation cover and an abode for a soil fauna and flora Lava cracks in cooling, some water may stand in the fissures which form the starting point for further development, a spectacle we have before our eyes where streams of lava are still formed Of higher plants, ferns are likely to be among the first to get established—GUPPY even spoke of the 'era of ferns", a halophytic *Asplenium* is the only living thing observed on the far flung reef Sala y Gomez between Easter Island and South America

An island in a comparatively recent stage, where there is plenty space for new settlers, let it be that little comfort is as yet offered would, we should think, offer good opportunities for "virile and agressive" immigrants to get a foothold and to become the ancestors of the most ancient element in the flora, but this is not what ANDREWS says In order to start an evolution of new species and genera a very great vertical relief, a variable precipitation and a rich soil are the conditions, but in order to get a rich soil cover we must have a closed vegetation cover also forest WALLACE (278 295), speaking of St Helena very rightly said that "no soil could be retained unless protected by the vegetation to which it in great part owed its origin", and the same is true everywhere If the change in environment, the new living conditions, are the cause of variation, why did they not act until the island was already more or less stocked with plants Were there no virile species among the earliest immigrants which took possession of the land and formed the oldest element of the flora? Was it lost among the later arrived aggressive newcomers It is calculated that about 90 % of the Hawaiian angiosperms are endemic, most of them belonging to endemic genera or to species very different from their continental congeners Do some of the most remarkable monotypical genera represent true relics, descendants from the earliest settlers, whereas the other are examples of progressive endemism? This is often said, but it is not, as far as I can see, what ANDREWS means.

In the opinion of zoologists still infected with Lamarckian ideas environment is the direct cause of new hereditary characters. Time after time we are told that as soon as a "germ" happens to land on an island, it gives rise to something new. However, this does not, MAYR says, imply that every little island is turned into a centre of evolution (179 216).

The small and usually rather isolated islands of Polynesia have not only not been new centres of evolution, like the Galapagos or Hawaiian Islands, but, on the contrary, there is good evidence that many of them are "traps". Species that reach these islands are doomed to extinction.

This is peculiar. There are many small islands stocked with both non endemic and endemic species, many of the latter stenotopic it is true, but quite able to hold their own as long the environment remains unchanged. It is a truism that, if a newcomer lands on an island where, for climatic or other reasons it cannot live, it is doomed to disappear pretty quickly, but there is no reason why, once established and able to reproduce itself, it would become extinct as long as the habitat does not undergo any change for the worse. It is generally known among ornithologists, MAYR says, that island birds are very vulnerable. He continues:

The recent considerations of Sewall Wright have given us a possible key to this curious phenomenon. Apparently in these isolated populations there is more gene loss than gene mutation. The species are therefore adjusted to an exceedingly narrow limit of environmental conditions. They are unable to respond to any major change of conditions and must die if such a change occurs, or are crowded out if competitors arrive.

We cannot be sure that mutations, should they be induced, would do them any good and we need not assume a "gene loss" to explain why organisms unable to escape to a more favourable habitat are bound to become exterminated as a result of "major changes of conditions".

ZIMMERMAN (298) is one of the prominent defenders of the idea that, in oceanic islands, as exemplified by the Hawaiian chain, a small number of immigrants has given rise to a comparatively rich fauna and flora, the proportion between genera and species attains figures expected under continental conditions but certainly not in oceanic islands. He admits that everything did not necessarily happen on the present islands as we behold them, for differentiation may have begun on some distant land and proceeded in the course of migration, with Hawaii as the terminus. He picked out, as an example, a large curculionid genus ranging from Australia to Micronesia and east to Marquesas, most islands or archipelagoes have their own endemic species, which have developed on their respective islands. He thinks that, if within a varying population, one pregnant female, not carrying the gene constitution of the entire population, gets isolated on an oceanic island, she may stand out as distinct from the average—and if this sequence of events "be accompanied by conditions conducive to isolation and survival, rapid and diversified speciation may follow" (p 125) This process is repeated on island after island, and "the intensity of divergence will be increased." It is not clear to me why the intensity would be increased. Now, if sufficient time has elapsed and the original sources have been eroded down and perhaps become sterile atolls, their faunas will have been exterminated and on the newer islands segregates without obvious ancestral relation will be left. This development explains why Hawaii has so many isolated endemic types. The living world in Hawaii is older than the rock—in a way, he says. Quite true, but it is not true that this possibility has, as he says, been entirely overlooked in previous discussions; I think that I have, on repeated occasions, expressed myself very clearly on this point, even if I do not agree with ZIMMERMAN when it comes to explain why and how it happened.

The biota as we know it today is in part the ultimate product of a progressional development which has moved and evolved along great insular archipelagos over periods of time much longer than the ages required for the development of the main Hawaiian Islands and their contemporary biota. Various genera and stem forms of groups of species may have evolved in islands—now atolls such as some of the leeward Hawaiian chain, the great Micronesian archipelagos, the Line Islands—which form the approach to Hawaii. However, some of the genera and the bulk of species known today have originated on our present main islands (p. 125). In contemporary Hawaii there are preserved remnants of a biota which has in part developed by unique methods and in which are preserved forms which are the end products of species chains that carry back, through archipelagos now worn away, to geological ages indeterminant (p. 126).

In few words, we have to do with relict as well as progressive endemism—nobody objects to that. A genus may be an ancient relic, while the actual species are the result of more recent, progressive differentiation. On the other hand, there is no reason why not a species could be immensely old without having undergone any perceptible change.

ZIMMERMAN does not hesitate to conjure up all the sunk archipelagos he needs, if only land connections are left out of the discussion. Once more he describes his vision on p. 127 which I shall permit myself to quote, with the obvious risk of tiring out the reader.

I believe that the great atoll chains of the Pacific may hold some of the now hidden clues to the stories of the magnificent biological development of Polynesia. Many of the peculiar endemic groups of the Hawaiian and southeastern Polynesian islands owe their existence, if not their very origin, to ancient high islands of the one time splendid archipelagos marked by clusters of coral reefs. Surviving lines of middle Tertiary and of perhaps even older continental faunas may have had their germ plasm filtered down through successively changing generations which have passed successfully through island maturity and degradation to atoll formation and have carried over to new high islands in different archipelagos. Thus, some supposedly old types such as certain land molluscs could have maintained themselves (but evolving) in insular isolation through long periods of time while their continental progenitors became extinct or restricted under continental conditions.

I cannot think of what kind of higher organisms would have passed successfully through island degradation down to atoll stage; they must have left for new high islands long before their abode became uninhabitable. Even if, as ZIMMERMAN thinks, much of the evolution took place during migration from island to island, specific segregation was mainly effected after arriving at the final station, in this case Hawaii This happened yesterday or the day before, geologically spoken "the rate of erosion is such that these main islands could not have stood here as they are longer than from a period late in the Tertiary" (p 121) "Explosive speciation" set in during late Pliocene and must have increased during "the great Pleistocene erosion which has left such a spectacular and rugged topography in its wake New land open to colonization is conducive to speciation" (p 122)

This late and rapid differentiation is illustrated by ZIMMERMAN for the land snails pp 98-101

Helicidae 59 species developed from one, or possibly two original immigrant stocks

Pupillidae Possibly 4 ancestral species gave rise to the 86 Hawaiian forms

Cochliocopidae-Cochliocopinae One immigrant of *Cochliocopa* stock could have given rise to the 142 forms

C Amastrinae 294 forms apparently developed from one basic stock

Tornatellinidae-Tornatellininae 117 forms derived from 4 or fewer ancestral forms

I Achatinellinae It appears certain that this subfamily had its origin and development in the Hawaiian area and all of the 215 forms may have been derived from a common tornatellinid ancestor

FOSBERG, in a chapter contributed to ZIMMERMAN's book, tried to fix the number of ancestors of the Hawaiian angiosperms His method is quite simple if the species, few or many, of a certain genus present the appearance of a more or less homogeneous group, only a single ancestor is made responsible for the segregation, if subgenera or sections are distinguished, we must count with the same number of ancestors as of taxonomic groups within the genus The method seems a little too easy, possibly we are confronted with a rather complicated question, the solution of which I am not going to attempt

SETCHELL (*218*) uttered some sensible words on migration and endemism

Where endemism of the degree of ordinal or family endemism occurs on oceanic islands, we may feel strongly inclined to believe that evolution of such degree took place on the continental area which was the source of the original migration and not on the island where now found, the original becoming later extinct, leaving the migrant as an endemic The same is true of generic endemism or even specific endemism of a strong type, that is when representing an isolated or aberrant species under the genus (p 874) To assume that insular conditions originate new forms is to overlook what has taken place on continents (p 875)

This is, however, what so many authors do They claim that oceanic islands follow their special laws, that a plant or an animal which happens to land far away, will, as it were, lose its balance, hidden factors, repressed as long as they lived on their fatherland under "severe competition", are set free and allow them to develop their inherent possibilities, they are not subjected to any struggle for existence in their new environment Says ZIMMERMAN "The environment, of course, plays an all-important part in the development of species   it is generally agreed that profound changes have been effected on organisms by environment" (p 187)

This is pure Lamarckian language. We may say, of course, that change of environment may cause mutations, but our experience tends to prove that only a fraction of 1% are valuable, the remainder, if not deleterious, at least indifferent. Mutations, gene losses, hybridization, polyploidy and so forth, all may have their share, but they are only ripples on the surface. No theory has been able to penetrate to the nucleus of the problem. Anyhow we have no reason to think that, in its production of species and genera, families and orders, Nature has followed other lines in islands than in continents. A prominent Swedish geneticist, after a life time's speculation on the causes generally accepted as responsible for the "origin of species", rejected all of them; unfortunately he threw the egg away with the shell and convinced himself that there had been no evolution at all. He did not, however, revert to an omnipotent creator but invented a new and entirely revolutionary theory; if there ever was a stillborn one, it was this (*186*).

I guess we can take it for granted that no peculiar outstanding types were created on young volcanic islands, whatever their present faunistic and floristic status may be like. Their basic stock is much older than the rocks and inseparably connected with the great continental faunas and floras. Wallace however, made a distinction between island and continental history. He emphasized that evolution has required an enormously long time to produce the present status, that from the Cretaceous until now nothing of a revolutionary character had happened; families, genera and in cases even species still living date from early Tertiary at least—but on islands the great period of creation was repeated during the last epochs.

Finally I shall quote some selected passages from STEBBINS' book on variation and evolution (*257*).

> The differentiation of orders and families of flowering plants through the action of natural selection under present conditions is well-nigh impossible. All the trends leading to the differentiation of families of flowering plants probably took place simultaneously and at a relatively early stage of angiosperm evolution. For instance, both distributional and paleontological evidence indicates that the Compositae, the most highly specialized family of dicotyledons, already existed in the latter part of the Cretaceous period, and distributional evidence indicates a similar age for the most advanced families of monocotyledons, the Orchidaceae and Gramineae. It is likely, therefore, that the major part of angiosperm evolution, involving the principal trends in the modification of the flowers, took place during the Mesozoic era (pp. 501–502).

The gymnosperms prove, he remarks, that neither great antiquity nor rigid stability necessarily leads to senescence, but here, as in other cases, a stenotopic character has resulted in restricted areas and also in extinction.

Isolated records excepted—the latest discovery is a palm from a Triassic stratum, if correctly determined—angiospermic fossils are found in greater quantity from younger Cretaceous and then in many surprisingly modern types. Evidence is strong, STEBBINS has found, that evolution was rapid during one period and slower during another. At the end of the Cretaceous and the beginning of the Eocene the number of modern types increased rapidly. In eocene deposits in North America and Eurasia "the majority of the species belonged to or closely approximated modern genera" (p. 520). This conclusion, mainly based on leaf impressions, is strengthened by the famous London clay from lower Eocene, where a wealth of fruits and seeds were found. The corresponding fossil floras of California include an increasing number of plants that cannot be distinguished from living genera, and abundant evidence shows that since late Pliocene "new species of woody plants have been added to the Californian flora only in such large and complex genera as *Eriogonum, Ceanothus, Arctostaphylos*, and various *Compositae*" (p. 521). The fossil floras of East Asia point in the same direction, the rate of evolution on woody plants has, since the middle of this period, been as slow or slower.

The most likely inference on the basis of all available evidence is that most of the woody species of to-day have existed for five million years or more, and that the evolution of the genetic isolation mechanism separating them took place largely during the early and middle parts of the Tertiary period (p. 522).

With regard to the herbaceous floras there is evidence for a rather rapid evolution during the later Tertiary. STEBBINS quotes the results obtained by ELIAS in fossil caryopses dating from lower Miocene to middle Pliocene and showing a distinct progression until the most recent ones cannot, to judge from the illustrations redrawn by STEBBINS, be distinguished from *Stipa* or *Piptochaetium*, an evidence from palaeontology which strengthens the theory of SINNOTT and BAILEY already referred to.

Isolation as a cause of evolution. — There is no reason why a species, which has migrated to an island, should change and give rise to new forms only because it is spatially isolated. A form of a varying population which gets isolated on an island, may possess characters making it stand out as a more or less well-marked form. As JORDAN (*151, 152*) says, isolation is not the direct cause of the origin. Spatial relation, STEBBINS remarks,

may persist over long periods of time without causing the isolated populations to diverge from each other enough to become recognizably distinct or even different .... the nature of many distributions strongly suggests that some of these disjunct segments of the same species have been isolated from each other for millions of years. There is some reason for believing, therefore, that geographic isolation alone does not result even in the formation of subspecies .... In small populations, which are particularly frequent on oceanic islands, spatial isolation is the usual precursor to divergence in non adaptive characters by means of genetic drift or random fixation (p. 197).

STEBBINS also points out that spatially isolated races or species usually are separated also by ecological barriers, because different areas also differ ecologically; distance may not be the original isolating factor, separation and differentiation may be due to the selective effect of ecological and climatic factors before geographical separation occurred. The Hawaiian Islands offer a wide field for a study of isolation and segregation resulting in local endemism (*242*). The continental flora inherited by a Great Hawaii included numerous populations gradually taking possession of the new soil, a process of very long duration, volcanic activity progressing from west to east, and when separation took place, different forms and species became isolated on different islands. The wonderful systems of valleys, effectively separated by high and very steep ridges, furthermore promoted segregation. Little has been done to examine the genotypical constitution of this astonishing assemblage of local forms, some may, for all we know, be ecotypes, but experimental studies have not been made. A limited number of hybrids have been described, but we know nothing of their behaviour. Anyhow, the floristic difference between the islands is very striking and hardly in favour of the theory of transoceanic migration, for the majority of organisms seem to have been unable to cross even the straits separating the islands, and biotic factors preventing establishment can hardly be made responsible in so many cases.

Chapter IX

Juan Fernandez—oceanic or continental?

To WALLACE as well as to the majority of biogeographers the Juan Fernandez Islands were typically oceanic in spite of their moderate distance from South America. They had the advantage of antiquity. WALLACE remarks, for the means of transmission had formerly been greater than now, their surface was varied, soil and climate favourable, "offering many chances for the preservation and increase of whatever plants and animals had chanced to reach them" (p. 287). Had the character of Masafuera been known to him he might have been less optimistic. The land shell fauna, entirely endemic, testified to the great age of the islands, for none had been introduced for so long a period that all which did come had given rise to new forms—or were the last of a fauna extinct on the continent.

JOHOW (150) based his opinion on WALLACE, when discussing the dispersal agencies and the morphology of the diaspores his starting point was *two* islands, Masatierra plus Santa Clara and Masafuera which has risen separately from the deep sea. It is strange that he never thought of another possibility, because the geologist who went with him and who wrote a chapter on the geology of Masatierra, claimed to have discovered, in one place, a fundament of rocks older than the omnipresent young basalt—JOHOW could not know that the interpretation of this stratum was false, as later shown by QUENSEL (302). After his visit to the Desventuradas JOHOW modified his opinion, the submarine ridge uniting these little islands with Juan Fernandez had then been discovered.

Die unter gleicher Breite mit dem Hafen Caldera und in derselben Entfernung vom Kontinent wie Juan Fernandez gelegene Inselgruppe ist vulkanischen Ursprungs und stellt, wie die von dem Mitglied der Expedition, Herrn Chaigneau, ausgeführten Lotungen ergaben, die über Wasser befindlichen höchsten Gipfel einer im Übrigen unterseeisch verlaufenden Bergkette dar, welcher auch die Inseln der Juan-Fernandez-Gruppe als südlichste Gipfel angehören. Aus dem Vergleiche der Floren und Faunen beider Archipele, welche trotz der grossen klimatischen Verschiedenheiten frappante Verwandtschaft aufweisen, ergiebt sich mit zwingender Notwendigkeit die Hypothese, dass die zwei Inselgruppen in der Vorzeit mit einander in Landverbindung gestanden haben und dass ihre Isolierung die Folge einer stattgehabten Senkung jener Bergkette ist (330 259).

In this assumption he may be quite right, but it finds, as already pointed out by REICHE (*203*, 269), little support in the flora for the two groups have only a single species in common (*241*), and the endemic genera and species are very different JOHOW's belief in their permanent isolation from the continent remained unchanged

In his tables, Contingente A and B, pp 218–220, is a column indicating (not always with sufficient accuracy) the nature of the fruits or seeds, and another stating the probable dispersal agent Of the 143 vascular plants known at that time, all the ferns and 34 phanerogams were supposed to have been wind-borne, 61 had been transported by birds, either inside or adhering to their feet or plumage, only one, *Sophora "tetraptera"*, with winged pods, had drifted with the current Five [*Eryngium bupleuroides* and *sarcophyllum*, *Apium fernandezianum Colletia spartioides* and *Fagara* (Zanthoxylum) *mayu*] offered too serious difficulties to make their presence in the islands explicable, but I cannot find that they are more "impossible" than many of the others In an earlier paper (*235*) I surveyed the nature of the diaspores, I shall not return to this question here but only repeat that almost one third of the flowering plants show no special adaptation to any particular mode of dispersal across the water, and I shall add a few remarks on some knotty cases Among the island Compositae, a family known to be well adapted to wind dispersal, are several species which lose their pappus when the achenes are still enclosed in the involucre, or where it is reduced to uselessness Only one species of *Sophora*, called *tetraptera*, was recognized by JOHOW and recorded from Chile Juan Fernandez, Easter Island and New Zealand Genuine *tetraptera* is restricted to New Zealand, but this is of less importance, the pods have narrow wings (poorly developed in some forms) which were supposed to help the pods to keep afloat, but as they open on the tree and drop their rather heavy seeds to the ground, the wings serve no purpose *Halorrhagis* is a somewhat similar case JOHOW, and others before and after him, identified the plant found on Masatierra with *H erecta* (alata), a New Zealand species with four narrow wings on the fruit, and he did not hesitate to regard it as wind-borne His *erecta* is, however, an endemic species, there are two more on Masafuera (see *229*, with illustrations), and their fruits are quite or almost unwinged There can be no question of an adaptation to wind carriage The same applies to *Selkirkia*, another of JOHOW's anemochorous plants Edible fruits, if not too big, will be swallowed by birds, but the indigestable stones and hard-coated seeds will be dropped before the islands are reached, and the diet of the wide-ranging and fast flying sea birds is another Epizoic transport is possible in a small number of cases, but otherwise the dispersal mechanisms, many of them quite wonderful, serve to maintain the population within its range and not to stock distant islands

Other advocates of the permanent isolation of Juan Fernandez are e g PLATE (*199*) GOURLAY (*301*), BURGER (*41*), and GOETSCH (*124*) PLATE drew his conclusions from a comparison between the littoral faunas of Juan Fernandez and the opposite coast

> Die Seichtwasser-Fauna weist deutlicher als die geologischen Verhältnisse darauf hin, dass Masatierra in der That als eine ozeanische Insel anzusehen ist, die nie in Zusammenhang mit dem Festland gestanden haben kann (p. 228),

but this did not prevent him from believing that Masatierra and Masatuera once formed a single large island, in spite of the distance (92 miles) and the deep water that separates them (p. 222). No more will be said here about a connection with the mainland, I have already discussed this question from an algologist's viewpoint, and with a different result (238).

The reason why GOLISCH rejected all land connections was his conviction of the easiness with which plants and animals are transported, the under title of his article reads "Plants make ocean voyages". He had little faith in the birds, wind and sea were the principal means of transportation, and as so many others he pointed to Krakatau as the classical example. The distance was very small, it is true, but winds and currents were favourable along the coast region of South America, and the flora was derived from southern Chile. Of the genera and species quite without relations not only in Chile, but in all America, he said nothing.

BÜRGER, who had visited the islands followed JOHOW, they were typically oceanic. After telling us about some of the most remarkable endemics, he exclaims

> Wer brachte diesen entlegenen Stätten solch köstliches Geschenk? Die Strömung, die Vögel und vor allem die Winde. Sie beluden sich mit Sporen und Samen selbst vom Feuerlande empfangenes gedieh. Doch aus viel weiteren Fernen kamen die Einwanderer, auch vom tropischen Amerika, Polynesien, ja sogar von Australien und Neuseeland und den Inseln des Indischen Ozeans (pp. 17–18).

The majority of the newcomers remained true to their stock in spite of the changed conditions, but others changed and some took such a fancy to the climate that from being herbs they became trees. I shall leave these speculations without comment, we have better reason to observe GOLISCH's paper which, in spite of being fairly recent, contains many amazing statements not supported by facts. Ignoring QUENSEL's report on the geology, he tells us that the islands rest "auf einem Sockel von grünlichem Andesit, der auch die Hauptmasse der Anden bildet". He had seen my writings on the flora, the use he made of them may be illustrated by a couple of examples. Among the plants introduced from Europe he mentions 'Aromo aus Castilien'—this is a local name for the endemic *Azara fernandeziana*! He rejects all land connections, the sandal-wood came from the East Indies, he had not observed that it belongs to a quite different section than *Santalum album*. The arborescent *Compositae* and *Plantago* had originated in the islands, "*Plantago fernandezia* und *Skottsbergii*, 1–2 m hoch mit 20 cm langen und 3 1/2 cm breiten an der Spitze des Stammes stehenden Blättern". He overlooked that the so called *P. Skottsbergii* is a modest annual and a form of the common Chilean *truncata*, a variable species. But GOLISCH knows what happened in the islands: "Dass der europäische Wegerich auf Juan Fernandez meterhohe Blütenähren und fusslange Blätter trägt, weist auf die Entwickelung hin, die seine Verwandten einstmal nahmen" (p. 29). This refers to *P. lanceolata*, which luxuriates in the islands, but cannot prove that the arborescent *P. fernandezia* evolved from one of the many Chilean species with which, from a systematic viewpoint, it has nothing to do.

GOETSCH was, perhaps, more familiar with zoology, but where he got the impression that the lower fauna was extremely poor, I cannot tell, unless JOHOW's meagre list was his only source. A considerable number of land shells and insects had been described, and everything tended to show that they represented but fragments of the fauna. The most efficient dispersal agent was, in this case, the current.

Wir wissen, dass die warmen Strömungen Ozeaniens bis an die Insel reichen und australische Pflanzen und Tiere verfrachten können. Aus diesem Grunde muss zwar die Insel auch ausserhalb des sog. Humboldtstroms liegen, der von der Antarctis bis zum Aequator und der südamerikanischen Westküste läuft. Wir wissen aber nun seit neueren Untersuchungen, dass dieser sog. Humboldtstrom keineswegs ein continuierliches Fliessen in nordlicher Richtung ist, sondern dass Oberflächen-Wasser vom Lande wegströmt und durch kaltes aus tieferen Schichten ersetzt wird. Der chilenische und patagonische Einfluss ist dadurch gesichert.

From what he just said we learn that the Humboldt current, whatever it is, and the upwelling cold water do not reach as far as Masatierra. On the other hand, it is not true that, as GOOD says (*109*, 220), Juan Fernandez lies entirely outside the Pacific beach drift. Drift-wood is found on the western side of Masafuera, but it shows very rough handling and must have been months or rather years under way, and if one has seen the place one feels convinced that not a single plant owes its presence in the island to this mode of conveyance, not to speak of the fauna. But GOETSCH believes that also the tropical element in the flora has arrived by sea, he continues.

Wir wissen endlich, dass vom Norden her dann dem Humboldtstrom eine warme Meeresströmung entgegenwirkt, der sogenannte Niño, der sich periodisch in einzelnen Jahren so geltend machen kann, dass seine Wirkung bis Valparaiso gespürt wird. Damit findet auch der tropische Einschlag in Fauna und Flora seine Erklärung (p. 38).

This cannot refer to the warm currents of Oceania mentioned before, because they came from Australia and did not bring the neotropical element. Does he think of the equatorial counter current which, occasionally, would extend its influence to the South American coast and become deflected south, thereby fetching new passengers? This current does not reach the coast.

Other authors have acted as spokesmen for the bridge-builders. W. A. BRYAN — not having access to his book I quote a newspaper article written by him (*500*) — believes that a prehistoric continent once embraced the Pacific islands, a theory based on the distribution of the land snails. Juan Fernandez belonged to the same geological period as Hawaii and their living world proves that at some time they were united. The general biological character is, he says, the same but there is a slight difference in the species. For details I refer the reader to *261* where I have reviewed his book. BRYAN was professor of zoology and geology in the University of Hawaii and had visited Juan Fernandez, but he does not appear to have profited very much by his visit.

Where BRANCHI (303) got his idea of the island flora I cannot tell, in any case not from facts in spite of having visited Masatierra.

Como curiosidad científica se puede decir que Masatierra no sería sino una de las tantas vetas del gran continente sumergido en el Océano Pacífico en épocas en que el continente sudamericano era un lecho de mar, y por consiguiente la isla sería más vieja que el suelo de la madre patria. Como comprobación está la ausencia de los volcanes, los escarpados farallones que muestran las capas geológicas, el deslizamiento de las rocas de la época glacial, y sobre todo la flora única, diversa del continente y que puede solo acercarse a la flora polinésica y australiana (p. 14).

I guess we can agree with him that this is all very curious, but it is not scientific.

To complete the picture we have better consult ARLDT's great work (8) in which the author draws his conclusions from the land fauna. ARLDT was one of the great bridge builders, but his Pacific bridges were of old date, and he thought that Juan Fernandez had been isolated since late Cretaceous times, so that only the most ancient element was supposed to have arrived over land (p. 322).

Wie Tristan da Cunha einen Rest des Sudatlantis darstellt, so die Juan Fernandez-Gruppe einen der Ozeanis der südpazifischen Landbrücke. Das beweisen nicht sicher die Vögel, auch nicht die Schmetterlinge, von denen die Nymphaliden durch die chilenische *Pyrameis carye* vertreten sind, die Pyraliden durch *Scoparia jagonoti*, neben denen noch weitere chilenische Formen genannt werden. Alle hatten auch transmarin die Inseln erreichen können. Wichtiger sind die Landschnecken, deren Gattungen fast alle auch in Chile vorkommen. Vertreten sind z. B. die Succineiden und Ferussaciden, sowie die Endodontiden. Diese sind hier mit *Amphidoxa* vertreten. Deren typische Untergattung ist auf Juan Fernandez endemisch. *Stephanoda* besitzt 6 endemische Arten auf den Inseln, andere auf Chiloe, in Chile, Patagonien, Feuerland, Argentinien, Paraguay, Brasilien und eine auch auf Kerguelen. Dagegen gehört die auf Juan Fernandez endemische *Fernandezia* zu den sonst hawaiischen Amastriden, die auf Hawaii auch ihre einzigen näheren Verwandten in den Achatinelliden besitzen. Hier kann nur eine Ausbreitung über Land angenommen werden. Von anderen Landtieren findet sich auf Juan Fernandez z. B. noch der Tausendfüssler *Geophilus laticollis*. Endlich sind sie auch von einem Oligochaeten erreicht worden, der Ocnerodrilinen *Kerria saltensis*, die auch in Chile vorkommt. Hier wäre eine jüngere überseeische Einwanderung denkbar. Aber *Kerria* ist auch alt genug, dass sie auf dem Landwege nach Juan Fernandez gekommen sein kann. Auch die Flora der Inseln zeigt interessante Beziehungen (pp. 324–325).

As could be expected, ARLDT's south Pacific bridge was supported mainly by the land molluscs, and they made him extend his bridge across the equator to Hawaii. There is in the Juan Fernandez flora some perplexing affinities with Hawaii that seem to defy all attempts to an explanation. The occurrence of two (not only one) endemic species of *Nesogeophilus* (formerly a subgenus of *Geophilus*) is interesting, *Kerria* is, perhaps, less important. Other striking cases of disjunction were already referred to in the lists of invertebrates above. It is a pity that ARLDT overlooked the leech *Nesophilaemon*, but also from what he says about the butterflies it is evident that the numerous zoological papers forming vol. II of "The Natural History of Juan Fernandez and Easter Island" had escaped his notice. The leech would, I suppose, have furnished him with one of the most eloquent evidences of former land connections. Nor did he know the botanical volume of this work, for he gives a summary of my 1914 paper (227) He agrees on the great age of the "Palaeopacific element", second comes the small neotropical, third the large Chilean group "hier liegt also wohl zum grossen Teil spate, uberseeische Einwanderung vor" This was, he found even more true of the subantarctic element, "das uberhaupt keine endemische Arten aufzuweisen hat"—very few were known then but later some endemic species were discovered

The question to which extent Juan Fernandez presents the biological peculiarities regarded as characteristic of oceanic islands—see Chapter VII—will now be answered We have seen that *endemism* is very high among the phanerogams and that the various kinds distinguished by HOOKER are represented, we have even a primitive endemic family, *Lactoridaceae*, we have a proportionately large number of peculiar genera, some of them quite isolated, particularly among the Compositae (*Centaurodendron, Dendroseris, Hesperoseris, Phoenicoseris, Rea, Rhetinodendron Robinsonia, Symphyochaeta, Yunquea*) but also in other families *Cuminia* (Labiatae), *Juania* (Palmae), *Megalachne* and *Podophorus* (Gramineae), further there are a few endemic genera closely related to South American ones, *Nothomyrcia* (Myrtaceae), *Ochagavia* (Bromeliaceae), and *Selkirkia* (Boraginaceae) As among the genera, so we find species of a strong character in *Chenopodium, Coprosma Eryngium, Euphrasia, Fagara, Peperomia, Plantago, Santalum, Urtica, Wahlenbergia*, well marked but not very aberrant species in *Berberis Boehmeria, Carex, Cladium, Colletia, Erigeron, Escallonia, Gunnera, Halorrhagis, Hesperogreigia, Ranunculus, Rhaphithamnus, Solanum* and *Ugni*, and many not very different from their continental congeners in *Abrotanella, Acaena, Apium, Azara Cardamine, Chusquea, Drimys, Dysopsis Galium, Luzula, Margyricarpus, Myriceugenia Pernettya, Phrygilanthus, Sophora, Spergularia* and *Urtica* Species undoubtedly native but also found elsewhere do not number more than 46, and in several cases their citizenship is open to question Endemism among the ferns is not so high, but there is one very aberrant genus (*Thyrsopteris*) and several peculiar species Bryophytes and lichens will not be considered, they were not included in HOOKER's paper and I have not had occasion to compare them with other island floras

There are no conifers, a single leguminous genus (*Sophora*) with two species, and no orchids The proportion genus species is 1 : 65 Mammals, batrachians, reptiles and fresh-water fishes are absent The earth worms are supposed to be adventitious with the possible exception of *Kerria saltensis* In all these respects Juan Fernandez agrees with the character attributed to oceanic islands

The high percentage of woody plants was emphasized by SINNOTT and BAILEY, but as the literature on which they based their figures is quite out of date, a new table was prepared

The object of SINNOTT and BAILEY was, as we have seen above, to show that the woody plants increase in number with the rising degree of endemism, and that the endemic genera were trees or shrubs and formed a more ancient element than the herbaceous plants which during former epochs were few in

Table VI

Percentage of woody and herbaceous species in Juan Fernandez

	Total	Woody	%	Herbaceous	%
Indigenous species	147	68	46 3	79	53 7
Not endemic	46	5	10 9	41*	89 1
Endemic, genus not endemic	71	37	52 1	34*	47 9
Also the genus endemic	30	27	90 0	3	10 0

* Four species suffruticose

comparison, and the Juan Fernandez Islands were regarded as supporting their hypothesis this, to judge from the table, they certainly do The five woody non endemic species are *Empetrum rubrum* and *Salicornia fruticosa* (low, erect shrubs), and *Myrteola nummularia*, *Rubus geoides* and *Calystegia tuguiorum* (trailing)

The rosette tree form is observed in 16 genera with together 31 species, belonging to six families, Boraginaceae, Bromeliaceae, Chenopodiaceae, Compositae, Plantaginaceae and Umbelliferae, the palm *Juania* is of course excluded As I have paid special attention to them in another paper (*251*), where they were well illustrated, no more will be said here

Annual and biennial herbs the therophytes of RAUNKIÆR, are not completely lacking, but they are very few *Cardamine chenopodifolia*, *Chaetotropis* (2 species), *Parietaria*, *Plantago truncata*, *Tetragonia* and *Urtica Masafuerae* In *251* I listed *Chaetotropis* among the hemicryptophytes, they give the impression of lasting more than one year and are found green at all seasons, and the same may be true of *Parietaria* I am not at all sure that *Plantago truncata* is native The *Cardamine* has been seen twice, last time in 1872, the *Urtica* not since 1854, when it was discovered It may be that it is an ephemerous plant and disappears in early spring, a season when very few botanists have visited the islands

Thus, the 'oceanic peculiarities' are all there, but possibly some of them can be explained otherwise Endemism of a very high degree within a small area is no monopoly of isolated islands, it will be sufficient to mention the Cape flora or southwestern Australia The large proportion of woody plants can be understood if the islands became isolated before the myriads of herbs, particularly the annuals of Central Chile, had evolved GRISEBACH'S 'Clavija' and related life forms are not confined to oceanic islands, if my interpretation of this morphological type as an evidence of antiquity is correct, we can understand why it takes such a prominent part in old island floras The reason why therophytes are almost wanting is not climatic This is amply proved by the innumerable annual weeds introduced with the traffic and thriving only too well The climate is of a modified Mediterranean type, and from a purely climatic viewpoint we should expect a large percentage of native annuals and biennials, this question was discussed at some length in *251* 827–830 Chile has hundreds of endemic therophytes, but they have not spread to the islands although many have special dispersal mechanisms, and they were not available at the time when the supposed connection with the mainland existed before the final uplift of the Andes.

The existence of many aberrant genera and species and, above all, the marked difference between the phanerogams of Masatierra and Masafuera shows that there is no exchange between the two islands in spite of the very moderate distance, even the 360 miles separating Masatierra from Chile should, in the eyes of the diffusionists, amount to little if sufficient time be granted. The Marquesas Islands, situated much farther away from the continent have a less peculiar angiospermous flora than Juan Fernandez, the very opposite ought to be expected if overseas migration had played the dominant rôle. The absence of the flora of Central Chile speaks against the efficiency of the natural dispersal agents. These circumstances are in favour of the opinion that the volcanic islands arose not from the depths of the ocean but on a piece of land formerly connected with South America and not sunk until the newborn islands, now reduced to ruins, had become a refuge for the ancient continental fauna and flora.

It is also true that several large and widespread families are lacking, such as leguminous plants (with one exception) and lilies, well developed in Chile, but they belong to the modern Chilean flora.

The plant world of oceanic islands is described as a haphazard collection of waifs and strays, and this is said to explain why so few genera contain more than a couple of species. But would not the result be the same if the actual islands originated through volcanic activity on a sinking land? Chance would decide what took possession of the new soil, and different sets find a refuge on Masatierra and Masafuera.

We know that of the mammals introduced by man the goat thrives and multiplies since 400 years and quickly became naturalized. There were no goats on the mainland when the land bridge existed, but there may of course have been some primitive mammals, if any of them reached the islands, they have disappeared long ago. The islands, as we see them, appear never to have offered great possibilities for the subsistence of a mammalian fauna. They are very small and as there was little open land there cannot have been any grazing grounds worth mentioning before man altered the landscape. Even after the ground has been cleared on all the lower slopes, pasture is miserable, and one valley after the other has been turned into a desert by the ravages of sheep and cattle. If left to run wild and multiply, the final result can be foreseen. Carnivorous animals need a prey, and there was none. The same is true of snakes which should thrive well now since the domestic rats and mice have been introduced.

Chile's mammalian fauna is poor and nobody knows if the huemul, the pudu, the Chilean rodents and small marsupials would be able to make a living on Juan Fernandez. Reptiles are poorly represented in Chile, there is not a single tortoise, very few snakes and a dozen lizards. Amphibians are few, but toads and frogs occur. Among the invertebrates are several orders, the chances of which successfully to get transported across the sea are very doubtful or, as far as we can see, none at all.

The insular peculiarities as displayed in Juan Fernandez (and in other similar cases) do not, I think, permit us to take a definite position against the hypothesis of former land connections

Chapter XI

The Chilean coast line and the history of the Andes.

From a look at the map we easily get the impression that the trend of the South American west coast is a product of the rise of the Andes because this enormous uplift must have been compensated by the submergence of old border lands and by the formation of a deep trench, and that these movements, which certainly were of very great magnitude, may have extended its effects west as far as to the region where we find the Juan Fernandez and Desventuradas Islands forming the exposed summits of a submarine ridge I shall call this ridge the Chaigneau Ridge after the Chilean navy officer who was the first to survey it

The Chaigneau Ridge. —The two archipelagoes lie within the 2000 m line, San Felix and San Ambrosio on a plateau rising above the 400 m curve and extending a long way toward Juan Fernandez, as seen from CHAIGNEAU's table (52) which is reproduced here with the soundings rearranged from N to S according to latitude and with the addition of some figures from the latest chart

The Merriam Ridge. —160 miles NW of San Felix–San Ambrosio another ridge, called the Merriam Ridge, was discovered during the U S "Carnegie" campaign 1928–29 (*11*) It extends between 25° 3′ 2 S, 82° 20′ W, and 24° 54′ S, 82° 13′ W the depths found were 1445 and 1260 m, respectively The bank rises 3000 m above the bottom and is only 10 miles wide Along the most elevated part 1186 1188 and 1168 m were found From the latter spot a series of soundings was taken SE of the ridge, showing the rapid increase of the depth 3 miles 1260 m, 9 miles 2751 m, 20 miles 3620 m, and 32 miles 4115 m the Merriam ridge is separated from the Chaigneau ridge by deep water Toward WNW the slope is more gradual until a depth of 3000 m is reached

North of the Merriam ridge, in 21° 40′ S 81° 40′ W, approximately a sudden rise, bounded by the 2000 m curve and surrounded by deep water, has been discovered (see map) Here the bottom rises to 972 m below the surface I do not know if this remarkable place has a name

The Carnegie Ridge. —During the cruise of the "Carnegie" two soundings about 100 miles off the coast of Ecuador lat 1° 32′ S, long 82° 16′, gave 1515 and 1454 m respectively, indicating a rise of 1800 m above the bottom, but before the entire distance along the coast has been surveyed we do not know if a series of ridges, probably much less well marked than the Chaigneau-Merriam ridge, can be traced all the way between lat 35° and the equator

Between these ridges and the coast is the deep trench (greatest depth 7635 m), and south of the latitude of Juan Fernandez depths exceeding 5000 m are still found, but farther south the 4000 m curve is soon reached and the trench disappears Older maps, two of which were reproduced in *227* 44, 45, show

Table VII

The Chaigneau Ridge

r = rock, s = sand

Depth in m	Bottom	S lat	W long	Remarks
38	—	26° 14'	79° 56'	14 km NE San Felix
80	—	26° 15'	80° 4'5	15 km N San Felix
69	—	26° 17'5	80° 8'5	4 km W San Felix
179	—	26° 18'5	80° 8'	5 km W San Felix
220	r	26° 18'5	79° 57'	Between San Felix and San Ambrosio
400	s	26° 18'5	79° 19'3	5 km NE San Ambrosio
250	s	26° 19'	79° 52'	3 km N San Ambrosio
150	s	26° 19'	79° 51'	3 km N San Ambrosio
215	s	26° 19'	79° 49'2	15 km NE San Ambrosio
182	--	26° 25'	79° 56'5	6 km S San Ambrosio
148	—	26° 20'	79° 52'	8 km S San Ambrosio
105	s	26° 30'	79° 49'	15 5 km S San Ambrosio
400	r	26° 36'5	80° 8'5	33 km S San Felix
550	r	27° 49'5	80° 14'	c 165 km S San Felix
675	r	28° 3'5	80° 16'	c 200 km S San Felix
660	r	28° 33'5	80° 11'	c 260 km S San Felix
660	r	29° 14'	80° 15'	c 310 km S San Felix
1300	r	30° 49'	80° 24'3	
1430	r	31° 26'	80° 10'	
1800	-	32° 45'5	80° 18'	Between Masatierra and Masafuera, about 1° N
1800	—	34° 34'	80° 36'	About 100 km SSE Masafuera

Juan Fernandez situated on a "lobe" with somewhat shallower water, less than 3000 m deep, extending NW from the coast and suggesting a possible former connection, but recent charts are less unambiguous. The 2000 m curve makes, however, a bulge around lat 38°, where a depth of only 1238 m is indicated while deeper water, 1400–1500 m, is met with near the coast. Soundings between the islands and the line where the trough stops are too few to be of much value, but in all probability the connection, if it did exist, should be looked for farther south. This is, as we shall see, also the opinion of the geologists. They do not hesitate to regard the banks just described as an extension from the continent. Nobody will, I suppose, argue that every marked rise of the ocean floor is a sign of sunken land, the majority of oceanographers prefer to call them independent products of volcanic action. Some, perhaps most of them, never reached the surface, some have done so, but were broken down, but many are still above the water and form the Pacific islands. But even the advocates of the permanence of this largest of basins admit that its margins are zones of considerable disturbance. If it can be proved, or at least be made probable, that the deep trench following the trend of the Andes is a consequence of the gigantic mountain building processes, the submarine ridges west of the trench cannot help to get implicated. This idea is by no means new, it has been expressed by many: "the width of South America may well be a good deal less now than before the Andes were uplifted", as GOOD says (*109*: 349), but some of these writers did not try to penetrate the complicated geographical-geological history of this region of great tectonic disturbance. This is true of myself, when I tried to describe what I imagined having occurred (*227*: 43), but it does not apply to IRMSCHER (*143*) who took pains to inform himself of the history of the Andes as told by geologists. That they arose in a geosyncline is proved by the Jurassic and Cretaceous beds now elevated thousands of meters and covering the older eruptives. To the east of the depression land had existed since the Permian, to the west was a Pacific land mass of hypothetical width, one opinion regarded the Coast Range as belonging to this land. IRMSCHER, who took WEGENER's side, did not ask for any large scale subsidence correlated with the uplift of the Andes, because the resistance of the sialic crust to the westward drift of South America was sufficient to account for uplift and folding. Consequently, he was unwilling to accept PENCK's intrusion theory: if, in the future, it should appear essential to accept a land mass, it could be nothing more than a narrow strip which, perhaps, had been connected with California (p. 45).

PENCK stellte die Ausbildung der ozeanischen Tiefen am Rande des sudamerikanischen Kontinentes, also das Versinken angrenzender Teile des Pazifiks, der aufwarts bewegten andinen Scholle gegenuber und schliesst, dass die nachstliegende Erklarung fur die Volumenanderungen unter der festen Kruste in dort stattfindenden Massenverschiebungen zu suchen ist. Wenn Massen aus der pazifischen Region in die andine ubertreten, so muss in ersterer die Kruste nachsinken (p. 51).

The cause of the uplift and folding was, according to PENCK, a result of the intrusion of the andesitic magma, which lifted the mountains but, IRMSCHER remarks, this could not be the only source of the tangential pressure.

Die mechanischen Ursachen des Faltenvorganges sind zweifellos anderer Natur, und die Magmaintrusion ist genau so eine Wirkung derselben wie die Faltung. Denn es steht fest, dass die Gebirgsbildung mit dem Empordringen des Magmas synchron ist und die Intrusion somit gleichzeitig mit der angenommenen allmahlichen Lostrennung Sudamerikas von Afrika.

Where does the Chaigneau-Merriam bank come in? WEGENER left it unexplained, according to DU TOIT it was an "advance fold".

BERRY and SINGEWALD (*29*), in their review of the tectonic history of South America, describe the development in the following terms:

Some students regard the Cordillera de la Costa in Chile as remnants of an ancient massif, the bulk of which has been downfaulted beneath the waters of the Pacific. It consists of crystalline rocks both igneous and metamorphic and these have commonly been assumed to be of great age—even Archean. This inference of antiquity rests, not upon their known relations, but upon the geosynclinal nature of the Andean seas which are clearly epicontinental and not shelf seas.

The sediments in this geosyncline are compressed between the Brazilian massif and another massif in the west, the vestiges of which should be looked for in the coast range. Anyhow, "that there was land to the west of the Western Andes cannot be doubted". These authors date the Concepción-Arauco series to the older Miocene and they do not regard the flora as a coast flora.

Let us now turn to BRÜGGEN, author of a modern handbook on the geology of Chile (33*I*). To begin with I shall allow myself to quote FLORIN's summary (95 4–6) of BRÜGGEN's earlier writings.

Until Middle Tertiary times the great Andes and the Coastal Range were a continuous upfolded mountain chain subjected to powerful denudation. The principal uplift of the Andes in Chile occurred in the Middle Cretaceous, and altered the palaeogeographical features of the Andean region considerably. The old geosynclinal had been turned into a continental area, at the western verge of which the border of the Pacific Ocean at the end of the Cretaceous occupied approximately the same line as to-day. Marine deposits of Danian as well as Palaeocene age are lacking, and at the beginning of the Tertiary period the continent probably extended further to the west.

In the Eocene and Oligocene, respectively, subsidences took place and the ocean encroached more and more on the land. The Concepción-Arauco coal measures are coastal deposits, which have been called the Concepción Series by BRÜGGEN. This series, about 400 m thick, rests unconformably on marine strata of Upper Cretaceous (Senonian) age. The shales containing fossil plants occur in conjunction with intercalated coal seems. The base of this section is of marine origin, and in addition marine layers are intercalated here and there in its middle part, which is otherwise generally built up of freshwater deposits. According to BRÜGGEN the Concepción Series is overlain by the deposits of the marine Navidad Series, which is upper Oligocene or Lower Miocene in age. BRÜGGEN came to the conclusion that the Concepción Series belongs to the Eocene, basing this on stratigraphical as well as on zoo-palaeontological evidence. The sediments of this series were according to him deposited on a broad, slowly sinking coastal plain, and subsequently subjected to considerable tilting and faulting, probably in the Miocene.

BERRY regarded both the Concepción and the Navidad series as belonging to the Lower Miocene or possibly Upper Oligocene, but according to BRÜGGEN this dating holds good for the latter only, while the former is much older, and whereas BRÜGGEN thinks that the Eocene coal flora was deposited in extensive coastal swamps, BERRY regarded it as neither limnic nor littoral but inhabiting a lowland area away from the coast. FLORIN found that the plant remains were laid down in the vicinity of the sea and that they are too well preserved to have been transported any great distance.

If it is true that the coast-line, at the end of the Cretaceous, occupied the same position as to-day, one is inclined to believe that the palaeogeography was different before the great uplift occurred in the Middle Cretaceous when a large scale subsidence ought to have taken place. The oscillations along the coast of central Chile during later times could hardly have involved the area where the submarine ridges are found, so that the possibility to link them to that part of the continent as late as that is small. Consequently attention has been directed farther south as already suggested. West Patagonia is a region of considerable and late subsidence, the longitudinal valley of central Chile disappeared under water to form the long series of the Patagonian channels, the Andean valleys became fiords and the broad dissected fringe of islands and skerries also give evidence to what has happened. The weight of the inland ice during the periods of glaciation must, however, also be taken into account.

The development of the coastal region, as told by BRUGGEN 1950, is explained by facts which if they have been correctly interpreted, open wide perspectives to the biologist even if serious difficulties still have to be overcome.

BRUGGEN begins by stating that "el mar del Eoceno" ended somewhere in the latitude of Arauco (38°), because a continental mass, "la Tierra de Juan Fernandez" still existed (p. 50) and pp. 56–59 he relates the history of this land. North of Rio Maullin (about 42°) is a zone of dislocations foreign to the structure of the Andes and this zone coincides with the direction of a broad submarine ridge which branches off from the continent; on this ridge are situated the Juan Fernandez Islands and, farther north, San Ambrosio and San Felix. Taking the 2000 m curve as a boundary, the ridge extends south to the Magellan Straits; we observe e.g. in the island Diego de Almagro the same northwest direction that we find in the Tertiary deposits of Paiga and other places in the zone north of Rio Maullin. To this must be remarked that the 2000 m line surrounds the Chaigneau ridge and that in order to unite it with West Patagonia the 3000 m curve has to be used. This is also seen from BRUGGEN's map, probably copied from SUPAN. The absence of marine sediments of Eocene age shows (p. 59) that the Juan Fernandez land was, at that time, united with the continent, but that, during the Oligocene, subsidence set in is evident from the extension of the marine Navidad series south to 45°, and this was, as we have heard, referred to Upper Oligocene or Lower Miocene. Also after the separation the Juan Fernandez land continued to exist until finally, presumably with the late Tertiary uplift of the Andes, the last rest disappeared but not before considerable magma ejections had given birth to the two archipelagoes. To judge from the degree of denudation and in view of the recent volcanic activity close to Masatierra and on San Felix[1] the islands are young, probably Pliocene,

cuando existia todavia un resto de la antigua Tierra de Juan Fernandez, *de la cual inmigro la flora del Eoceno*[2] Cuando mas tarde se hundio tambien este resto, sobresalian solamente las partes volcanicas, constituyendo las islas actuales de Juan Fernandez, que servian para refugio de la flora.

This is the process as I have described it (227 43) and BRUGGEN is of the same opinion from the geologist's viewpoint. And if we go back to HOOKER's lecture, we shall find that the same idea, applied to a different region, was familiar with him.

---

[1] This refers to the submarine eruption in 1835 near the coast of Masatierra, whether any signs are left I cannot tell, for the place has not been sounded. This eruption was simultaneous with an earthquake in Concepcion. Possibly there was a connection with the tsunami of Vallenar in 1922 and the eruption at San Felix three months later when gas was ejected on the island, killing a great number of sea birds.

[2] My italics

With regard to the objection that oceanic islands are volcanic, and hence probably not the mountain tops of sunk continents and that they contain no fossil mammals, we have in the Malay Archipelago, vast areas of land which if submerged (and they are exposed to constant subsidences and risings) would leave only isolated volcanic peaks, such as oceanic islands present. Were such an area to be submerged leaving exposed the volcanic peaks of Java and the Moluccas &c, &c, should we expect to find either recent or fossil terrestrial mammals upon them? Nor should it be overlooked that, as a general rule, islands diminish in size and numbers toward the centres of the great oceans, which, taken with the admission, that the great islands adjacent to the continents were previously united to them, would favour the hypothesis that all may have been so. And finally, we have instances of continental distribution presenting facts so analogous to oceanic, and hitherto so utterly unexplicable, on any hypothesis of migration that does not embrace immense geological changes, that we can scarcely avoid coupling the phenomena they present with those of oceanic islands (p. 11).

However, HOOKER did not stop here. When he threw the pros and cons into the balance, the scale of scruples sank.

On the other hand, to my mind, the great objection to the continental extension hypothesis is, that it may be said to account for everything, but to explain nothing; it proves too much, whilst the hypothesis of trans-oceanic migration, though it leaves a multitude of facts unexplained, offers a rational solution of many of the most puzzling phenomena that oceanic islands present: phenomena which, under the hypothesis of intermediate continents, are barren facts, literally of no scientific interest—are curiosities of science, no doubt, but are not scientific curiosities.

This was, I am afraid to say too much—but are not HOOKER'S words a good expression of the biogeographer's dilemma?

The latest brief outline of the history of the Andes is found in GOODSPEED'S monograph of *Nicotiana* (*112*), it was, partly at least, based on WEEKS paper (*279*). The sequence of events especially refers to the central Andes, with which the history of the southern Andes is said to agree. Four major periods of uplift are recognized, the final one during the Pliocene–Pleistocene, with an average elevation of 3500 m. Coincident with the uplift was a compensory coastal sinking. The troughing along the coast ceased with the foundering of the Pacific fore-lands at the close of the Miocene and early Pliocene. These lands are supposed to have extended an unknown distance westward (p. 31). It is possible that the border lands extended all the way north along Central America, Mexico and California, where are found islands in a position corresponding to that of the Galápagos and Juan Fernandez Islands.

From what has been said above I can only find that there is good geological evidence for a former extension west of the continent, uniting southern Chile with a "Juan Fernandez land". Before attempting to trace the sequence of immigration of the various floristic elements and of their fate we ought to know something of the fossil floras of Chile and, further, to devote a chapter to the supposed Antarctic migration routes.

Chapter XI

The Tertiary floras of Chile and Patagonia.

Tertiary plant fossils have been discovered in the coast region of south Chile, in Patagonia along the Andes south to the Magellan Straits, and in Tierra del Fuego. The richest localities are on the coast of the province of Arauco, 37°–37°30′ s. lat. in combination with the coal seams of Lota, Lebu etc. and east of Lake Nahuelhuapi on the Argentine side.

The Concepcion-Arauco series. —The fossil flora was examined by ENGELHARDT who described more than one hundred species of angiosperms, and later by BERRY (27). The determinations are, just as in all the other cases, based on leaf impressions, but although BERRY found that ENGELHARDT's determinations "are usually to be relied upon" (p. 75), very many of them are as well as his own, open to doubt. The species were as a rule referred to living genera, belonging to many more or less important tropical-subtropical families, Annonaceae, Apocynaceae, Bignoniaceae, Bombacaceae, Caesalpiniaceae, Combretaceae, Erythroxylaceae, Lauraceae, Lecythidaceae, Myrtaceae, Palmae, Sapindaceae, Styracaceae, Vochysiaceae, and so forth. In general character the flora approaches that of the Amazon basin, extended, the relief of the Andes being low at that time, to the west coast of the continent and reaching south at least to 40° s. lat. The flora contains ' no elements of the flora of Central Chile ' (p. 106)—*Cassia* is, however, one of the genera mentioned, another is *Myrceugenia*, represented by several species in central and south Chile (to know Myrtaceae without flower and fruit is well nigh impossible). BERRY referred the flora to the Lower Miocene, "it is surely not so old as Eocene", and also younger than the *Nothofagus* flora in the Magellanian zone (p. 115); this he considered to be of Lower Oligocene age.

There are two gymnosperm genera in BERRY's list which seem to disturb the impression of an otherwise homogeneous neotropical assemblage, *Araucaria* and *Sequoia*. The material was reexamined by FLORIN (95) who showed that *Araucaria araucoensis* Berry is a species of *Podocarpus* and *Sequoia chilensis* Engelhardt p. p. another. These together with a fern described by HALLE (*Lygodium 312*) are important additions to the Arauco flora. FLORIN, in accordance with BRIGGEN, refers it to the Eocene and characterizes it as follows:

> The composition of the fossil conifer vegetation, and the distributional aspects, of its constituents, indicate that it derives from a warm temperate or subtropical rain-forest, more particularly a lowland podocarp–evergreen dicotylous broad leaved tree forest, growing on the coastal plain or perhaps partly on low hills not far from the coast. The climate was probably characterized by great humidity and rather uniform temperature. It was frostless, and warmer than the present climate of the same district (p. 26).

The possibility that plant material from the uplands had been carried down and become mixed with material from the coastal plain is contradicted by the state of preservation which is the same in all cases (p. 26).

The Pichileufu flora. —The fossiliferous beds of Rio Pichileufu are situated in 41° s. lat. about 30 miles east of Lake Nahuelhuapi in a treeless steppe country

BERRY (28) distinguished more than 130 species, most of them referred to still living genera and belonging to 48 families and 21 orders. The general character is subtropical, and the following families may be mentioned: Anacardiaceae, Annonaceae, Apocynaceae, Asclepiadaceae, Bignoniaceae, Burseraceae, Caesalpiniaceae, Celastraceae, Cochlospermaceae, Erythroxylaceae, Euphorbiaceae, Flacourtiaceae, Icacinaceae, Lauraceae, Loganiaceae, Meliaceae, Mimosaceae, Monimiaceae, Moraceae, Myristicaceae, Myrtaceae, Nyctaginaceae, Rubiaceae, Rutaceae, Sapindaceae, Sapotaceae, Sterculiaceae, Styracaceae, Symplocaceae, Vitaceae. Of conifers we find *Araucaria pichileufuensis*, *Fitzroya tertiaria*, *Libocedrus pichilensis* and 2 *Podocarpus*, further, there is a species of *Zamia* and *Ginkgo patagonica*, and of ferns 3 species, one of them a *Dicksonia*. *Araucaria* and *Libocedrus* are, according to FLORIN, correctly named (95), *Ginkgo* should be called *Ginkgoites*, *Fitzroya* belongs to *Podocarpus*, and one of the *Podocarpus* sp. belongs to *Acmopyle* of PILGER.

There is no trace of Fagaceae and BERRY referred the flora to Lower Miocene and regarded it as contemporaneous with the Arauco flora, they have 20 species in common, the general character is the same and is said to bear witness of the same climate. The relief of the Andes was low, no rain shadow existed, prevailing westerly winds carried abundant moisture across the country, there was rain forest where now we have dry grass-land. Still, there is a difference between Arauco and Pichileufu. BERRY (27) pointed out that the present South Chilean rain forest flora is not represented in the Arauco flora whereas the Pichileufu beds contain such Chilean genera as *Azara*, *Berberis*, *Maytenus* and *Myrceugenia* and, in addition, the following Antarcto-tertiary genera: *Drimys*, *Embothrium*, *Eucryphia*, *Laurelia*, *Libocedrus* and *Lomatia*—provided that the determinations are correct. Nevertheless the age is supposed to be the same, Lower Miocene according to BERRY, Eocene according to FLORIN, thus older than the *Araucaria-Nothofagus* beds of Magallanes. It is surprising that, if the two floras are of exactly the same age, the advancing Antarctic flora had not found its way to the coast of Chile, Pichileufu ought to be younger, but perhaps still Eocene, a period of very great length.

The Chalia flora.—Of considerable interest was the discovery, in Santa Cruz Territory in the valley of Río Chalia about 51° S lat, of a fossil flora similar to the Arauco and Pichileufu floras and proving that the subtropical vegetation had extended far south. *Araucaria* and *Nothofagus* are absent, the only conifer found, *Fitzroya tertiaria*, is, as shown by FLORIN, a *Podocarpus*. Of angiosperm families Anacardiaceae, Annonaceae, Bignoniaceae, Lauraceae, Monimiaceae, Myrtaceae, Sterculiaceae etc. are represented, of Chilean genera *Laurelia* and *Peumus* may be mentioned. The age is early Miocene according to BERRY (334), Eocene according to FRENGUELLI (337), the climate warm temperate.

BERRY (315) regarded all the fossil floras containing an abundance of Fagaceae (*Nothofagus*, according to DUSÉN also *Fagus*, which is questionable) as of approximately the same age and older than the Concepción Arauco series.

The Ñirihuao flora.—Three localities close together on Ñirihuao river near Lake Nahuelhuapi. Some ferns, among them *Alsophila australis*, also known from Seymour Island, further *Zamia*, *Araucaria Nathorstii*, *Fagus* (?) and one species of *Nothofagus*. Age proposed by BERRY (*334*) Lowest Miocene or Upper Oligocene, then younger than the Magallanes flora.

The Magallanes flora.—DUSÉN (*79*) distinguished two plant bearing horizons, an upper *Araucaria* horizon and a lower *Nothofagus* horizon. Of the remaining dicotylous genera none were identified with living ones, DUSÉN preferred to call them *Escalloniphyllum*, *Hydrangeiphyllum* etc. There is no obviously tropical element, it is a temperate flora. DUSÉN regarded the two horizons as distinctly different in age, dating the upper to Lower Miocene, the lower to, perhaps, Oligocene. BERRY who doubted the correctness of this distinction, regarded them as older than the Concepcion-Arauco flora, which seems improbable.

The Seymour flora.—To judge from DUSÉN's description (*80*) the tropical element is not conspicuous, whereas the actual South Chilean forest flora is well represented *Araucaria* (nearly related to *A. araucana*), *Drimys*, *Nothofagus*, *Caldcluvia*, *Laurelia*, *Lomatia*, all supposed to be of Antarctic parentage, I can see little reason for BERRY's assertion that the Seymour flora contains "a large element of subtropical or warm temperate types like those found to day in southern Brazil" together with "another large element of forms suggestive of the existing temperate flora of Southern Chile and Patagonia", the former was subtropical and coastal, the latter temperate and montane, washed down DUSÉN thought, from the mountains and embedded together with the leaves of the lowland trees. The age was estimated to be Upper Eocene. FLORIN's discovery of a species of *Acmopyle* (*Phyllites* sp., DUSÉN) is of particular interest (*338*).

We have seen that BERRY considered the *Nothofagus* beds to be older than the Arauco Pichileufú deposits. All the local fossil floras of Patagonia are, he says (*335*), older than the marine Patagonian transgression and undoubtedly pre Miocene. FRENGUELLI distinguished three epochs (a) Late Cretaceous to early Eocene, with a tropical flora, known from the Chalia beds (b) an intermediate period with subtropical and temperate types (*Nothofagus*) mixed, to this he would I suppose, refer the Seymour flora, (c) the youngest epoch, Miocene-Pliocene, evidently extending into Pleistocene a temperate flora, now ranging along both sides of the southern Andes and characterized by the dominance of *Nothofagus* and of a number of conifers. The more or less corresponding development of the Andes was according to BERRY (*28*) (1) Eocene–early Miocene low relief no high continuous mountains, followed by (2) a period of great uplift, (3) late Miocene to early Pliocene mature erosion, low relief, (4) late Pliocene to Pleistocene extensive uplift, beginning of the formation of the Chilean and Peruvian deeps, where earlier there was land, (5) submergence of the coastal plain. Finally but not mentioned by BERRY, the series of glacial and interglacial periods, a most important factor of disturbance.

This is the background against which we have to discuss the history of the Juan Fernandez flora.

Chapter XII

Antarctica as a source of the present circumpolar floras.

Much has been written on this subject and it is not necessary to review the entire literature, which has been done already by several authors, but the Antarctic problems are so important when it comes to an analysis of Juan Fernandez that they cannot be passed in silence. J. D. HOOKER was the first to survey all the lands scattered around the Antarctic, Tierra del Fuego and the Falkland Islands, Kerguelen Island, Tasmania, New Zealand and its subantarctic dependencies; he was struck by the discontinuous distribution of many genera, families or even species—HEMSLEY, *127* (a), and the author (*228*) have given lists of such genera and species—he drew the consequences, although nothing was known then about the vanished flora of the large, ice covered continent, nor of the palaeogeography of the adjacent zone, and the idea that Antarctica had formerly extended farther north and that the sporadic southern islands eventually were remnants of larger land masses entered his mind. Since that, the various subantarctic and austral floras have become very well known, and the cases of remarkable disjunctions have multiplied. To those who adhere strictly to the hypothesis of long distance dispersal across the oceans this means nothing more than further proofs that they are right for the west-wind drift explains everything. Fortunately, the land bridge between South America and Antarctica rests on solid foundation, geographical as well as geological. In his important paper of 1929 (*137*) HOLTEDAHL has shown that the old idea of land connection between Tierra del Fuego and Graham land (Palmer peninsula) by way of the Burdwood Bank, Shag Rocks, South Georgia and the South Sandwich and South Orkney Islands which had been doubted by some holds good. We have to do with a mountain range, a continuation of the South American Andes, bordered by deep water which, on the Pacific side, has the character of an abysmal trench but which exhibits old sediments to such an extent that we are forced to postulate land where there is now deep sea. The South Sandwich Islands being entirely neovolcanic, have the appearance of an "oceanic" archipelago, but they were built up during late Tertiary times over an older foundation—a parallel to the history of Juan Fernandez and of many other islands.

It is quite evident that the South Shetland land mass has once had several times the width that it has to day. With their large amount of terrigenous, clastic sediments etc., the South Orkneys and also South Georgia agree with the folded ranges of the continent. In fact, in order to explain these masses of sediments we must necessarily assume land to have been present where there is now deep sea.

We need not assume that all the links of the Scotia or, as it is also called, South Antillean Arc were united at the same time; let it be that this is possible or even probable, if so, there was no communication by water between the Atlantic and the Pacific, which undoutedly must have had its consequences to the water circulation, a question I am quite unfit to discuss. To judge from the composition of the local subantarctic floras, rich in herbaceous plants belonging to many different families and orders, land communication must have persisted to middle or even late Tertiary times. That the connection goes far back is shown by the occurrence of a Gondwana flora on both sides of the Drake passage (Graham land Falkland Islands), and the Cretaceous rocks of South Georgia prove, as HOLTEDAHL says, the existence of a land mass of considerable size where there is now sea. JOYCE (65) remarks that "there is good evidence that the Scotia Arc with its extension into West Antarctica has persisted as a structural feature since Lower Palaeozoic times"

The Scotia passage offers one of the migration routes over land that we are in need of, but another passage, the Macquarie route between East Antarctica and Australia–New Zealand is required to make the transantarctic route complete. There are intermediate islands, Macquarie Auckland and Campbell Islands, with a subantarctic flora suggesting former connections, and there are tracts with shallower water between Tasmania and the continent but for want of geological evidence this bridge is hypothetical, and many authors prefer to speak of submerged intermediate islands sufficiently close to facilitate the spread of organisms able to cross moderate water barriers. As AXELROD says (14 183)

Archipelagoes of only slightly greater extent than those now present could account for the continuity of the Antarcto Tertiary Flora in all these regions during the early and middle Cenozoic

FLORIN, referring to the present and former distribution of conifers, expressed himself in similar terms

Antarctica has played an important rôle in the development and distribution of the southern group of conifers. The data related to its distributions considered in this paper seem most readily explained by assuming land connections, or at least much closer proximity between Antarctica and the adjacent southern ends of South America, Australia, New Zealand and South Africa (95 92),

and after the discovery of a Tertiary species of *Acmopyle* in Patagonia and a second fossil form in the Eocene of Seymour Island, he wrote (338 136)

Fur eine ehemalige Verknupfung der australischen Region mit der Antarktis spricht auch die Verbreitung der Gattung *Acmopyle* Dass also die Antarktis in diesem Falle als eine alte Vermittlerin zwischen der australischen Region und Sudamerika gedient hat, muss meines Erachtens angenommen werden

However one of the supposed links, Macquarie Island does not, it seems, possess any plants, perhaps not even mosses or lichens, dating back to the height of the Glacial Period, for this island was, at least during maximum glaciation, entirely ice-covered and must TAYLOR says, have received its present plant world, very poor it is true, in postglacial time from the north and across a considerable stretch of open sea (263) In Antarctica proper the situation is, with regard to lichens and mosses, different DAHL (72 231), basing his opinion on the discovery of numerous endemic lichens and of a few mosses not very far from the south pole, concludes that part of the flora survived the glaciations Here where high mountain ranges are found right along the coast, the inland ice, even during maximum glaciation cannot have covered everything. The flora may not have been as rich in species as it is now but perhaps a little more varied than one has been inclined to think. Many species are also found in the subantarctic zone, and further research work will, perhaps, reduce the number of endemic species.

FLORIN spoke, as we have seen, of a "proximity to South Africa". This is where most biogeographers hesitate, in spite of such eloquent facts as the distribution of Restionaceae, Proteaceae and other families, and the occurrence of a subgenus of *Gunnera* on African soil. HOOKER, it is true, had a vision of a larger Kerguelen land, but this was still a long way off from Africa. Perhaps GULICK (*119*) ought to be mentioned here; he opposed the continental nature of isolated islands, but he was tempted to exempt what he called "continental outsiders", "Kerguelen, Crozet, St Paul and two or three more"; the sea lacked the deepness of a typical ocean, and sediments occurred on Kerguelen; for these reasons he admitted a possible former existence of a 'northward lobe of the Antarctic continent.' The lichenologist C. W. DODGE has taken up this question; the lichen flora of "Kerguelia" presents features of great antiquity as well as of prolonged isolation (5 endemic genera), and the angiosperms include such aberrant types as *Pringlea* and *Lyallia*; it should be remembered that WERTH was opposed to overseas dispersal. Kerguelen is volcanic, but old: the oldest lavas dating from late Mesozoic or early Tertiary times, and on them fluviatile sediments and, on top of these, Oligocene strata rest. Erosion broke down the island during Miocene-Pliocene, but renewed volcanic activity followed from the end of Pliocene into Pleistocene. The Gaussberg Kerguelen ridge connects Antarctica with Kerguelen + Heard Island; an elevation of 400 fathoms would be sufficient to unite the two islands; a rise of 100 fathoms would transform the Crozet group into a single island; and DODGE supposes that there is a submarine connection between Kerguelen and the Crozet swell. Kerguelia in its prime would include all the islands, also Marion and Prince Edward. The great difficulty, the extension to South Africa, remains. So much seems to be certain that, if this bridge did exist, separation took place early; long before the other Antarctic connections were broken off.

I think that the majority of phytogeographers agree with MERRILL who, in his last work (*306*), wrote that

there is no reason whatever to doubt the validity of this ancient Antarctic route of migration of various families and genera of plants; certainly, no experienced phytogeographer would question the validity of this route, for it is as thoroughly established as its more evident equivalent by what is now the Arctic region (p. 178)

Most botanists have drawn their conclusions from the present distribution of the plants and this is, as a rule, all they can do, because few have left any traces of their distribution in earlier epochs. Nevertheless we have no good reason to doubt the important part taken by Antarctica in the history of the south hemisphere, but the proofs that such was the case, BERRY emphasizes (*28*, *34*), must rest on palaeobotanical evidence, and it happens that the fossil records are at variance with current ideas. The occurrence of *Araucaria*, *Drimys*, *Laurelia*, *Nothofagus* etc. in Tertiary deposits on Seymour Island would lead us to infer that they are of Antarctic origin and have radiated from there, but *Araucaria* once had a world-wide distribution, *Drimys* belongs to an order—Magnoliales—of Holarctic range, the same is true of Fagaceae, and even *Laurelia* is, BERRY points out, open to doubt, in spite of the fact that the Monimiaceae are a southern family. Many other genera, called Antarctic on the strength of their modern distribution, are known as fossils in the north temperate and Arctic zones. "*Araucaria* stands as a perpetual warning against forgetting that the past is the key to the present", BERRY wrote (l.c. 36). A Holarctic genus may have reached New Zealand or Australia as well as Patagonia from the north, never having used an Antarctic route, and without leaving a trace of its wanderings. On the other hand, the little we know about the preglacial vegetation of Antarctica is sufficient to prove that this large land mass, just as every other part of the globe, was inhabited by a rich and varied flora, that it may have been a primary centre of evolution, that, in other instances it served as a secondary centre and that it was a much trodden road between America and Australia-New Zealand.

Miss GIBBS appears to have been one of the very few experienced phytogeographers who refused to regard Antarctica either as a centre or as a migration route over land, it had always been surrounded on all sides by water and no other agents than "the wild west wind" (*106* 103) and a pole-ward north-west wind coming from Asia, were needed to explain every distribution pattern. The southern focus of development was not Antarctica but the mountains of New Guinea. The highland of Tasmania, the subject of her survey, had received nothing from the south, all the so called Antarctic plants genera like *Abrotanella*, *Astelia*, *Caipha*, *Colobanthus*, *Coprosma*, *Drimys* *Gaimardia*, *Gunnera*, *Lagenophora*, *Nothofagus* *Oreobolus* and so on, had come from New Guinea and from there they had radiated to Polynesia, Hawaii, Juan Fernandez Tierra del Fuego and, I presume, Antarctica. Had she lived to hear of the discovery of *Nothofagus* in New Guinea, where more species have been found than anywhere else, and in New Caledonia, and of the rich development of the Winteraceae in New Guinea, she would have regarded such finds as a forcible proof of the correctness of her opinion.

Many zoogeographers have looked with much suspicion at the Antarctic continent as a centre of radiation. SIMPSON, in his review of the theories involving Antarctica in the distribution of vertebrates (*223*), concluded that dispersal had been, in all cases, from north to south, not even the Scotia Arc had ever been used as a route of migration. His reasoning is logical and often conclusive. The invertebrates are, however, left aside. To quote part of his summary (p. 767)

There is no known biotic fact that demands an Antarctic land migration route for its explanation and there is none that it more simply explained by that hypothesis than by any other. The affinities of the southern faunas as a whole are what would be expected from the present northern connection known, or with considerable probability inferred, to have existed at appropriate times in the past. There are certain troublesome anomalies and exceptions in the evidence, but none of these can be adequately explained by postulating an Antarctic connection. The general weight of evidence is against such a connection.

In scientific theory the best supported and most nearly self-sufficient hypothesis should be preferred and unnecessary additional hypotheses should be rejected or held in abeyance. On this basis the Antarctic migration route hypothesis remains simply a hypothesis with no proper place in scientific thinking.

To this I shall make a few remarks. If SIMPSON had said "no fact involving the vertebrates" instead of "no biotic fact"—very well, let us assume that the routes across from and to either America or New Zealand were impassable to mammals, reptiles, amphibia and flightless land birds, birds with good flight capacity would have found little difficulty to cross, and many biotic facts are known that clearly speak in favour of an Antarctic migration route for invertebrates and plants. SIMPSON must have thought that either did the Antarctic continent never possess a fauna of land vertebrates or, if it did have one, it had evolved independently of all other faunas and disappeared without leaving a single trace. Only penguins are known in a fossil state in Antarctic Tertiary deposits. Until fossil land vertebrates are discovered, the question of the former existence of an Antarctic fauna of terrestrial vertebrates must be left open.

Among the invertebrates are many examples of a discontinuous distribution most readily understood if Antarctica is taken into account. Several were mentioned in the chapter devoted to the composition of the fauna of Juan Fernandez, a few more may be quoted here. BERLAND, dealing with the Pacific spider fauna (23)

> Nous avons tiré de notre étude cette notion importante que la liaison entre l'Australie et l'Amerique a eu lieu par une terre antarctique dont les temoins restent actuellement, mais ni par la Nouvelle Caledonie, ni par la Nouvelle Zelande, ni par le groupe Samoa-Tonga-Fiji, et, par voie de conséquence qu'elle n'a pas eu lieu par le centre du Pacifique (p. 1053)

BERLIOZ (24), with examples offered by the distribution and affinities of beetles, states that the group of Buprestidae, forming "le noyau essentiel in the Buprestid fauna of Australia, has mainly South American affinities (several genera), and that

> la faune des Lucanides d'Australie et de Papouasie présente avec celles de l'Amerique du Sud surtout de la region andine et patagonienne, des affinites aussi etroites que curieuses

Finally LINDSAY (167) calling attention to the Subantarctic Collembola, extremely delicate creatures "supposed not to be carried any appreciable distance either by wind or sea, thus being important proofs of former land connections", mentions a genus of 3 species of which one is Fuegian, one recorded from the Scotia Arc, and one found in New Zealand. And other similar examples may be found.

Chapter XIII

The history of Juan Fernandez—a tentative sketch.

In my first paper on the Botany of Juan Fernandez (227), where only the vascular plants as known at that time, were included, I expressed my view on the history of the flora in the following words

> Freilich haben wir keine Ahnung davon, wie schnell Arten oder Gattungen entstehen, aber wir können uns kaum denken, dass in der kurzen Zeit, die seit der Entstehung der jetzigen Inseln verflossen ist, sich Typen wie *Lactoris* oder *Robinsonia* aus "Keimen" entwickelten, die nach den Inseln gebracht wurden, um sich in ungestörter Isolierung umzuformen. Ich bin der Meinung, dass das alte Element nicht auf Masatierra oder Masafuera entstand sondern älter ist als die jetzigen Inseln, und dass es wenig wahrscheinlich ist, dass die alten endemischen (oder andere, eng verwandte) Gattungen und Arten von Juan Fernandez, noch nachdem die Inseln gebildet waren, die vielen vermeintlichen Ursprungsorte bewohnten, und dass Veränderungen in der Pflanzenwelt von Polynesien, Neuseeland Chile u. s. w. in quartärer Zeit die isolierte Stellung bewirkt haben. Ich glaube also, dass in vor- und frühtertiärer Zeit grössere Entwicklungszentra existierten, und dass ihre Flora nunmehr als ein altpazifischer Rest fortlebt. Auch eine Restflora wird sich aus vielen Familien und Gattungen aber verhältnismässig wenigen Arten zusammensetzen

At that time our knowledge of the flora was incomplete, much fresh and new material was added in 1916–17 I had fixed my attention on what I called the "Old Pacific element", but did not venture to look for an exact site of an evolution centre, though the possibility of Antarctica as an important source of genera and families had been pointed out before, the first sign of the presence of theretofore unknown, subantarctic flora in Masafuera had been observed, but I had no reason to link it with the Old Pacific types During the 1916–17 survey a rather strong Antarctic bicentric group took shape, and in my 1925 sketch of the history of the flora (231) not only was this, but also the Old Pacific plants claimed to have "reached Juan Fernandez over South America, where they have disappeared" (p 31) My object this time is to see if we can approach these problems in other than general terms

Our starting point is the "Tierra de Juan Fernandez" of BRUGGEN, forming a westward extension or lobe of South America, reaching the actual site of Juan Fernandez and Desventuradas Islands, as indicated by the bathymetrical conditions, something in keeping with the peninsula of Lower California and separated from the coast by a broad, toward the south gradually narrowed bay However, if we remember that the deep trough is supposed to have originated with the final uplift of the Andes, the present coast line ought to be recent all along, but this is not in accordance with the opinion that the Eocene Arauco flora was a coast flora The conclusion would be that the great depths were initiated already during Cretaceous times, getting deeper and deeper with the successive periods of uplift The Juan Fernandez land or peninsula formed part of the neotropical Eocene flora region which extended from Venezuela and Brazil to south Chile and east across the mountains, during this era of low relief, as shown by the fossiliferous beds of Pichileufu. As the Concepcion-Arauco flora it was a subtropical rain forest flora with podocarps, tree ferns, evergreen dicotyledonous trees and lianas, belonging to some 30 tropical families; the species were, with two exceptions, referred by BERRY to still existing genera—if the determinations are reliable. This is perhaps more than we can expect; all we can say is that BERRY was a man with a wide experience of both fossil and living tropical plants and that undoubtedly many of the families listed and perhaps also a fair number of the genera are correctly placed. Two are found in the present flora of Juan Fernandez. To *Azara celastrinifolmis* and *terraria*—and the fossil does suggest *Azara*—BERRY remarks (28 107):

As a recent form occurs on the island of Juan Fernandez one can predicate a considerable antiquity for the genus, which is more than verified by the present fossil forms

His *Berberis corymbosiflora* is of still greater interest

I have seen leaves of all the South American species and the most similar is *Berberis corymbosa* Hook. et Arn. of Juan Fernandez (16 75)

I have compared his illustrations with the island species and I am willing to testify to the striking similarity between them. A revision of these most important fossil floras, with application of modern technique, is eagerly longed for.

Anyhow, the neotropical character of the old flora has been safely established, and Arauco and Pichileufu agree in their general composition 20 species occur in both. If this flora extended to Juan Fernandez this land must have been sufficiently high to force the prevailing westerly winds to unload part of their moisture and to give rise to altitudinal belts. The flora most likely had its special distinctive marks. In view of the very large area it inhabits, it cannot have been uniform, and different floristic provinces showed special features and had their own endemics. If anything still survives in identical or very similar form can only be a subject of conjecture and is not demonstrated by leaf impressions. Two of the genera reported from the mainland, *Azara* and *Myrceugenia* still occur in Chile and Juan Fernandez, and I am inclined to believe that the endemic element in the insular forest flora dates back to early Tertiary times, genera like *Podophorus*, *Megalachne*, *Juania*, *Ochagavia*, *Nothomyrcia* and *Selkirkia*, and species of *Chusquea*, *Hesperogreigia*, *Urtica*, *Phrygilanthus*, *Chenopodium*, *Colletia*, *Drysopsis*, *Ugni*, *Eryngium*, *Rhaphithamnus*, *Solanum* and *Nicotiana*

Centaurodendron, *Yunquea* and the four endemic Cichoriaceous genera stand apart. They are montane and we have no clue at all to their history, but we can take it for granted that they are not 'new beginners', but old relicts, without any near relatives anywhere. Whether we assume that they arose in the islands and have left no marks in the continent, or derive the four dendroseroid genera, which form a natural group, from Antarctic ancestors, a possibility certainly not offered by *Centaurodendron* and *Yunquea*, we are victims of wild speculation

Few endemic ferns belong to the neotropical element, *Trichomanes Ingae*, *Dryopteris inaequalifolia*, *Asplenium macrosorum* and *stellatum Pellaea chilensis*,

Polypodium intermedium and *Ophioglossum fernandezianum*, but *Pellaea* and *Ophioglossum* do not grow in the forest, the former inhabiting the dry coast cliffs, the latter the open grass land, and they may have their own history.

How and when the non-endemic South American species reached Juan Fernandez is hard to tell. They are temperate and, with the exception of *Myrteola nummularia*, herbaceous. *Myrteola* is the only member of this group that extends south to the subantarctic zone. Of the others *Danthonia*, *Koeleria*, *Stipa*, *Piptochaetium*, *Eleocharis*, *Juncus procerus* (also *dombeyanus* and *imbricatus*?), *Libertia*, *Peperomia fernandeziana*, *Parietaria* and *Mimulus* show, in their mode of occurrence, every sign of being indigenous. Advocates of transoceanic dispersal would not hesitate to call them "late arrivals which have not had time to change", and a direct transport is not altogether impossible. It would be interesting to know if a grass land existed when Great Juan Fernandez was connected with the mainland, but unfortunately we do not even know the extension of the *Stipetum* when the early voyagers reported on the vegetation and already found the introduced *Avena barbata* in dominance in the treeless western part of Masatierra. A remark made by BRÜGGEN deserves to be quoted in this connection. A current coming from the south swept past the shore of Great Juan Fernandez. When, during the Navidad transgression, separation from Chile occurred,

el mar del polo sur entro en comunicación con el mar que bañaba las costas de Chile Central y el primer antecesor de la corriente de Humboldt llevo las aguas mas frescas hacia el norte, dando principio a la gran zona desertica

BRÜGGEN seems to have forgotten that at that time Antarctica was covered, not by an inland ice, but by luxuriant vegetation, and that the sea cannot have been cold, however, there must have been an upwelling of cold water, and the dry climate of the basal belt may have been as unfavourable for tree growth as it is now. Nevertheless I cannot believe that the present steppe-like communities date back to early or even middle Tertiary time. On the other hand it seems quite unlikely that the species of *Stipa*, *Piptochaetium*, *Danthonia*, etc. were introduced with the traffic while, in this respect, *Chaetotropis* (the endemic nature of *Ch. imberbis* questionable), the two *Cyperus*, *Juncus capillaceus*, *Paronychia*, *Centella*, *Hedyotis* and *Plantago truncata* are under suspicion.

Of the ferns found elsewhere *Polypodium lanceolatum* is pantropical and old enough to have belonged to the ancient flora, and this may be true also of *Trichomanes exsectum*, *Hymenophyllum* spp., *Adiantum chilense*, *Pteris chilensis* and *semiadnata*, and *Elaphoglossum*. I have suggested that the latter was carried directly to Masatierra by a northerly storm, and this could have been the case also with *Polypodium Masafuerae*, observed a single time 100 years ago and never again. *P. trichomanoides* remains doubtful in spite of the specimens still extant and labelled Juan Fernandez (249.766).

The presence of a large, presumably boreal element is not difficult to explain, for it extends all along the Andes to the far south. Many of the species are endemic, *Agrostis masafuerana*, 2 sp. of *Spergularia*, 2 *Berberis*, *Cardamine*, *Krues-*

schi, *Galium masafueranum* and 6 *Erigeron*. The Boreal character of these genera is recognized. This element extended south along the precursors of the late Tertiary mountains, the species of *Agrostis* (?), *Spergularia*, *Berberis*, *Cardamine* and *Galium* have their closest relatives either in the tropical Andes (*Berberis*) or in Chile. *Erigeron* deserves special attention on account of the large number of Andean species nearly related to each other but less so to the insular group, which shows a remarkable differentiation. *E. fruticosus* and its cognate *luteo-viridis*, the three herbaceous rosette herbs, and the peculiar *E. rupicola* of the coast rocks, of these *fruticosus* is found on both islands and the other species endemic on Masafuera.

Nine non endemic species, all found in Chile, also belong here, *Trisetum, Carex Banksii, Paronychia, Cardamine flaccida, Callitriche, Rubus, Empetrum, Calystegia* and *Gnaphalium*, and, among the ferns, perhaps *Cystopteris. Rubus geoides* forms together with *R. raduans* an isolated section but has a more southerly distribution, but all may have reached Juan Fernandez from South Chile.

Finally, *Cuminia* remains to be accounted for. Whether we link it with the palaeotropical Prasioideae, which seems to be the best way, or with *Bystropogon* it stands out as an isolated relict genus.

I have distinguished a large Antarcto-tertiary element, over 40 % of the angiosperms and 60 % of the ferns. Among the former there are three or, if *Lactoris* is kept aside, two groups, one of them (1) is still represented in South America, the other (2) not. In (1) two types can be distinguished, (a) not confined to subantarctic or alpine habitats and demanding a milder climate, to this lot I refer *Uncinia Douglasii* and *costata, Drimys, Phrygilanthus, Escallonia, Margyricarpus, Sophora, Gunnera, Apium, Pernettya* and possibly *Plantago fernandezia*. All have relatives in Chile. To these are added the species also occurring on the mainland *Danthonia, Koeleria, Juncus, Libertia, Acaena ovalifolia* (indigenous?), *Centella* and *Nertera*, the two grasses are however, only tentatively referred to this element.

The occurrence of an Antarctic element in the Eocene flora of the mainland has been demonstrated. BERRY lists *Araucaria, Libocedrus, Drimys, Embothrium, Lomatia* and *Eucryphia* from the Pichileufu beds, even if the "magnolia stock" is of Boreal origin this does not exclude the possibility that the Winteraceae radiated from Antarctica, a parallel case to Fagaceae and *Nothofagus*.

If we follow COPELAND many of the ferns also belong to 1 a *Hymenoglossum*, five species of *Hymenophyllum, Lophosoria, Polystichum, Blechnum, Hypolepis, Histiopteris, Gleichenia pedalis* (indigenous?) and *Lycopodium scariosum*.

Group 1 b includes the so called Subantarctic-Magellanian element inhabiting Fuegia, the Falkland Islands etc. ranging north along the Andes and belonging to a well known circumpolar assemblage of genera and species. Here we find *Oreobolus, Uncinia brevicaulis, phleoides* and *tenuis*, and *Lagenophora hirsuta* further three endemic species *Acaena masafuerana, Abrotanella crassipes*, both with near relatives in West Patagonia–Fuegia, finally *Agrostis masafuerana*, if its relation to the bicentric *A. magellanica* is confirmed after monographic treatment I brought it to the boreal group. The following pteridophytes are attached here *Serpyllopsis*, *Hymenophyllum falklandicum*, *Polypodium* (Grammitis) *magellanicum* *Gleichenia quadripartita*, and *Lycopodium magellanicum*.

Did this Antarctic element, mostly not endemic, extend to Great Juan Fernandez or did it arrive after the separation from the mainland took place, perhaps even after that the volcanic islands had been formed? The same question was raised when we discussed the non-endemic neotropical temperate *Stipa*, *Piptochaetium*, *Myrteola*, *Rubus*, and so forth; the Boreal group is, as we have seen, also involved. Is it probable that also this flora dates back to early or middle Tertiary times? This seems unlikely. The subantarctic species are, with the exception of *Grammitis*, restricted to the highland of Masafuera, but may have occurred also on Masatierra when the islands stood higher. Either we must assume that the land connection with the continent persisted much longer than is otherwise probable, or those species have immigrated across the water in late Pliocene or in postglacial time. I have suggested this on repeated occasions (*231, 232, 340*). However, we must not forget that we have to do not with stray colonists, but with plant communities composed by flowering plants, ferns, bryophytes and lichens. Unfortunately nobody beheld the vegetation before introduced species, *Anthoxanthum odoratum* and *Rumex acetosella*, had invaded the highland and changed the entire aspect beyond recognition.

To distinguish, among the bryophytes, the old element which undoubtedly must have formed an important part of the subtropical forest flora is more than I can undertake; we do not know if the many endemic species are relicts or not, in fact, we do not even know if they are endemic until the opposite mainland has been well explored. So much can be said that species with a pronounced tropical distribution are few, but if we add the Chilean species extending through the Valdivian and Magellanian forest zones, this South American group makes up about 40 % of the mosses and 30 % of the hepatics, endemic species of American affinity included. Perhaps half a dozen mosses, not counting the few that accompany man wherever he goes, and some liverworts, have a wide distribution outside America. The dominant element is Antarctic; this was emphasized by such authorities as CARDOT and HERZOG: 56 % of the mosses and 68 % of the hepatics were referred to the Antarcto-tertiary element.

When it comes to distinguishing corresponding groups among the lichens we move on very unsafe ground, but there are indications that, beside a large South American element, we also have an Antarctic group to which no less than 58 species were referred. They are austral or subantarctic bicentric or tricentric, but many of them range north into lower latitudes. A conspicuous part is formed by Stictaceae. The great bulk of the family is by no means southern, *Lobaria*, *Sticta* and *Pseudocyphellaria* are frequent in tropical, subtropical and temperate-oceanic climates throughout, but the austral-circumpolar species are so many that we cannot exclude Antarctica as a possible source.

We shall proceed to group 2. It comprises the genera or species which are foreign to the South American flora and have their relations in Australasia. JOHOW recognized very few, he had, just as several later authors, no other explanation to offer than that they had arrived across the Pacific from Australia, New Zealand, the East Indies, etc without reaching the coast of Chile. They are much more numerous than JOHOW thought, 28 species: *Cladium*, *Carex besteroniana*, *Peperomia besteroana*, *margaritifera* and *Skottsbergu*, *Bochmeria*, *Santalum*, *Ranunculus*, *Fagara* (2), *Halorrhagis* (3), *Euphrasia*, *Coprosma* (2), *Wahlenbergia* (5), *Robinsonia* (5), *Symphyochaeta* and *Rhetinodendron*, the three last genera endemic. Objections may be raised against including *Carex* and *Euphrasia*, the section to which *Carex besteroniana* was referred by KÜKENTHAL is almost confined to New Zealand and barely represented in Australia, Tasmania and Norfolk Island, but one little known Chilean species is included, and *Euphrasia formossisima* is distantly related to *E. perpusilla* of South Chile. The species of *Wahlenbergia* are puzzling, but I have given my reasons for bringing them here as representing an African sector. The most eloquent members are, perhaps, *Santalum*, *Ranunculus*, *Halorrhagis* and *Coprosma*.

This element is conspicuous also among the ferns: the extremely old *Thyrsopteris*, *Arthropteris*, entirely unfamiliar with the neotropical flora, *Dicksonia*, *Blechnum Schottu* and *Pteris berteroana*.

I never looked in earnest for a direct road across the south Pacific from Australasia to Juan Fernandez, a route which ought to have had South America as its terminus. I preferred to think that the group in question reached the islands over the Scotia bridge and South America where, however, it had become extinct. To prove this we must turn to palaeontological evidence. The Eocene beds on the mainland contain leaves of many different plants, and it is not impossible that a revision of the material will contribute to a solution of the problem. In the lists published by BERRY two items call for attention, *Cyatheoides thyrsopteroides* in the Arauco flora, and *Coprosma* from Pichileufu, but the material is sterile. It is true that, to judge from BERRY's illustrations, *Cyatheoides* suggests *Thyrsopteris*, but the author later (28, 57) compared it with his *Dicksonia patagonica*, which was found with sori and undoubtedly belongs to the Cyatheaceae. Thyrsopteris like fossils have been reported from various places in the north hemisphere. He described 2 species of *Coprosma*, based on leaf impressions which, as far as I can see, tell us little about their systematic position. To *C. spathulifolia* he remarks

> These tiny leaves have occasioned a good deal of trouble, as the South American representatives of the genus are not similar to the fossil. The Chilean species are not closely similar

and to *C. incerta*, a most appropriate name

> they are so much like the endemic species of Coprosma of the Juan Fernandez Islands and several forms from the Hawaiian Islands that I feel constrained so to identify them, at least tentatively

I cannot find that they agree better with *Coprosma* than with many other genera. When BERRY gives the distribution of the genus as "from the Malayan archipelago through the Pacific islands to Chile" he includes Juan Fernandez under Chile where, politically, the islands belong, for there are no species on the mainland

It is very easy to construct a hypothetical passage by which the '*Coprosma* group' reached Juan Fernandez without crossing the Antarctic or encroaching very much upon the surface of the Pacific Ocean. If we have reason to think that South America extended farther west I cannot see why this wasn't the case also with West Patagonia and Tierra del Fuego, a region which undoubtedly has undergone considerable submergence, we have to count with a wide Scotia bridge and an extension of Palmer (Graham) Land, where the geographical-geological situation is the same as in South America and where the uplift of the mighty "Antarctandes" ought to have been accompanied by submergence of the fore-land. Plants and animals could have travelled by a circuitous route from the New Zealand region over West Antarctica to Juan Fernandez without finding their way east to what is now Chile. This south Pacific path was suggested above when I tried to divide the angiosperms according to their supposed primary sources, the species involved are enumerated under I 3 forming a group "as far as known without continental American affinities either suggesting an ancient Antarcto-Pacific track east from Australasia without reaching America, or having arrived along the road over the Scotia Arc without leaving any traces in the present American flora." (p 269)

This idea of a South Pacific track is not new. It was postulated by ARLDT as a South Pacific bridge and it finds an expression in CROIZAT's South Pacific base-line, which, however, if it existed, hardly permits us to draw such far-reaching conclusions as he did. In the case of Juan Fernandez only 13 genera are concerned, belonging to 11 families, the ferns not included, but they make up 20 % of the angiosperms, and others may have existed that disappeared later.

It remains to see if, among the cryptogams, a '*Coprosma* group' can be recognized. In HERZOG's paper on the Hepaticae (*130*) a single species is indicated as restricted to New Zealand and Juan Fernandez, *Pallavicinia xiphoides*, and two endemic species are said to have their nearest allies not in South America but in New Zealand. No case equal to *Pallavicinia* is found among the mosses, but several endemic species are considered to be related, not to American ones, but to species inhabiting the south west Pacific region.

With regard to the *fauna* I shall confine myself to some general remarks.

The few land birds are of neotropical origin. Of the seven species, three, *Eustephanus galeritus*, the owl and the thrush, occur in identical forms on the mainland, the remainder are either endemic varieties or endemic species. The most divergent is *Eustephanus fernandensis*. GOETSCH's idea that it originated in the islands as a mutation of *E. galeritus* is contradicted by the fact that they are not at all closely related but even brought to different genera by some ornithologists. The former is a relict, the latter perhaps a late immigrant. Of the breeding sea birds the genus *Pterodroma* forms an austral circumpolar element and may, in preglacial time, have inhabited the coasts of Antarctica and adjacent islands.

Little can be said as yet about the invertebrates. The endemic leech, *Nesophilaemon*, is an important case of non-American ancestry, and the only terrestrial amphipod is bicentric. The spider fauna is an appendix to the fauna of South America, but with special features, there is no endemic genus, but specific endemism is high. In the fauna of the mainland Antarctic affinities have been stated to occur (BERLAND 23 1044).

The New Caledonia, New Zealand group has affinities with the Malaysian region and still more with Australia. But the small islands situated south of New Zealand, namely the Campbell, Auckland and Macquarie Islands, are different, they present, rather abundantly, a group of spiders, Cybaeinae, relatives of which are found in the extreme south of South America, these spiders are not present in New Zealand, but are allied to Australian and Tasmanian species.

This is an interesting observation, for it is known that connections between East Antarctica and lands to the north have been looked for both with New Zealand and over Tasmania with East Australia.

Among the millipedes *Aulacodesmus* and *Nesogeophilus* are austral genera and the species endemic, *Schizotaenia alata* is known from Chile, but the genus is eminently austral-bicentric. For the same reason the endemic genus of Thysanura merits to be noticed.

A very great number of insects have been reported from Juan Fernandez, most of them endemic, also many of the genera. The majority has been described only recently and very often nothing was said about their relations, where they were stated they are, as a rule, to be found in South America. Isolated forms are plentiful and bear witness of a long history. For the single termite an Antarctic ancestry is postulated. Most of the butterflies collected have not yet been described. Diptera are numerous and largely allied to American genera or species, and the non endemic forms mostly Chilean. I have not been able to get a proper insight into the distribution of the many genera found elsewhere. Little can be said about the beetles until Dr KUSCHEL's material has been described. Two presumably austral-bicentric cases are noticed, *Pycnomerodes* and *Eleusis*. As in so many oceanic islands there is in Juan Fernandez a remarkable display of endemic wingless Curculionids, living on the endemic plants of South American or Antarctic parentage, and examples of strict specialization are known. Host and lodger look back upon a long common history, but whether this implies a common original ancestral home or adaptation in the islands I cannot tell. Of Hymenoptera, *Haplogonatus*, *Prenolepis* and, perhaps, *Metcha* show Antarctic connections.

The antiquity of the endemic land shells cannot be disputed. The Tornatellids are an ancient Pacific group and their presence in Juan Fernandez as well as in other isolated islands and archipelagoes has been considered a proof of former land connections. Their display in Hawaii is unparalleled. GERMAIN summarized his opinion on the evolution of the Hawaiian fauna in the following terms which, mutatis mutandis, apply also to Juan Fernandez (*105* 995):

S'il est bien ainsi, cette famille primordiale [the ancestors of Achatinellidae, Amastridae, Leptachatinidae and Tornatellinidae] doit avoir une très ancienne origine et remonter au Paléozoïque ... le peuplement malacologique de l'archipel des Hawaii est fort ancien et doit remonter à des temps primaires. Il n'a pu se faire, comme le preuvent les développements précédents sur la répartition des genres et des espèces, que sur une aire continue, ce qui exclut la possibilité de considérer les îles Hawaii comme le résultat de l'activité des volcans sous-marins.

Finally, let us try to reconstruct the history of our islands, beginning with the time when there existed a "Tierra de Juan Fernandez" in BRÜGGEN's sense. It must have become isolated and reduced in size rather early. We do not know if the fauna included vertebrates other than birds; if it did they did not survive the long volcanic period. Unfortunately we know too little of their history in Chile, when they first appeared in modern forms, and so forth. The absence of all gymnosperms is difficult to explain. The Eocene flora of Chile contained several, *Araucaria*, *Libocedrus* and *Podocarpus*, all still living there and accompanied by *Fitzroya*, *Saxegothaea*, *Pilgerodendron* and *Dacrydium*, and even if no close land connection existed, some of them ought not to have had much greater difficulties to get transported across the water barrier than some of the angiosperms found on the islands. If, on the other hand, a land bridge existed, I can see no obvious reason why conifers did not use it or, if they did, why they didn't take possession of the new volcanic soil. Introduced araucarias, pines and cypresses do well on Masatierra. The only possibility, remote perhaps, could be that they had not been able to spread as far as to Juan Fernandez when the connection was cut. Their absence gives us no clue to the time when this happened.

Another element in the Chilean flora would seem to come to our rescue, the *Nothofagus* flora. In my sketch of 1925 (*231* 33) I expressed the idea that "the connections between the islands and the main land were severed before the south Chilean flora assumed its present composition, and also before the advancing *Nothofagus* flora reached these latitudes", and BRÜGGEN is of the same opinion. He states that tropical South America is the ancestral home of much of the Chilean forest flora, and adds

Pero, la actual flora de Chile central contiene, ademas, una mezcla con una flora de clima mas fresco, que despues de la separación de la Tierra de Juan Fernandez inmigró y que se caracteriza por los generos *Nothofagus*, *Araucaria*, etc

Araucaria was found in the Pichileutu beds which are supposed to be Eocene, whereas the southern beeches appear in this latitude considerably later. In the Magellanian region DUSÉN, as we have seen, distinguished two horizons, a lower, Oligocene, with *Nothofagus*, and an upper, Lower Miocene with *Araucaria*. According to BRÜGGEN the separation of Juan Fernandez from Chile took place during the Oligocene Navidad transgression. We would think that, if the bridge lasted longer, the *Nothofagus* flora ought to have invaded Juan Fernandez and to have found suitable stations in the montane belt, and that the rising volcanic islands offered acceptable habitats for a genus of such wide physiological amplitude.

Anyhow, during the final upheaval of the Andes when in any case, most of the land disappeared, leaving the submarine ridge with the rising volcanic masses standing, Central Chile definitely ceased to be a source of the island flora. This Chilean flora is, as REICHE pointed out, a product of the Andes with addition of an Antarctic element.

Submergence resulted in the displacement of the vegetation belts and in much loss of life when the volcanic eruptions began and lava flows and other ejected material covered part of the country. Long before that, important changes had taken place as a consequence of the cooling of the climate in post-Eocene time, and with the widening space of sea between the islands and the mainland the insular climate became more and more oceanic.

The rise of the Cordillera was an affair of great magnitude and long duration, and millions of years passed before the last remnant of the Juan Fernandez–Desventuradas ridge disappeared. Two eruption centres were formed, Masatierra + Santa Clara, and Masafuera. The first two form an arc, suggesting a remnant of a gigantic crater, but the place must be properly sounded in order to allow us to prove or disprove this hypothesis. I cannot even guess where the eruption centre of Masafuera should be looked for. Abrasion has, as could be expected, forced the coast escarpment back more on the west than on the east side, reducing the area of the island. A description of the topography of the islands is found in this volume, pp. 89–168. There is no sign of recent activity anywhere, no parasitic cones, no hot springs. When the map in "Der neue Brockhaus" (1938) marks Juan Fernandez as a seat of active volcanoes, this applies, I suppose, to the submarine eruption in 1835 near Masatierra and to the phenomena observed at San Felix some years ago in connection with an earthquake on the mainland, but otherwise nothing in the way of activity has been recorded after the tsunami in 1751, when also an earthquake occurred, and other earthquakes were registered in 1809, 1822 and 1835 (275).

As I said, I believe that Masatierra and Masafuera represent two separate centres, the distance between them is 92 nautical miles and the sea is deep. Whether they are of exactly the same age and became extinct at the same time is difficult to tell; to judge by the topography, Masafuera makes an impression of being much less eroded, and, as a consequence, younger, but the difference is, I think, mainly due to differences in the basalt, the petrographical structure is not quite the same. It is supposed that the eruptions began during Pliocene and lasted a very long time and that part of the submarine ridge was still above water when the main eruption centres became extinct. Otherwise the result would have been two lifeless islands without a sign of the old endemic biota. The flora and fauna were inherited from the sinking land. The process is easily observed in many volcanic islands and nowhere to greater advantage than in the island of Hawaii. As soon as the lava has cooled down, plants get established, microscopic algae, modest tufts of mosses and particularly lichens of the genus *Stereocaulon* (341), but a *conditio sine qua non* is that moisture is available, that erosion sets in and soil is formed. Even under very favourable conditions and with the sources for repopulation next door, it will take a long time before a closed vegetation cover gets established. With regard to Juan Fernandez, nothing much could happen until the islands had been built up to a considerable altitude, undoubtedly greater than now, when streams rushed down the mountain slopes and started to excavate valleys, for no plant cover, not to speak of forest growth, could get established until erosion and abrasion had done part of their work. This means that a good deal of the fundament, now hundreds of metres below the surface of the ocean, was still exposed and retained a portion of the original flora and fauna, which became the principal source of the flora and fauna of the volcanic soil. It goes without saying that chance played a dominant rôle and that the fragmentary character of the island world is easy to understand. It is also possible to understand why different species happened to become isolated on Masatierra and Masafuera. According to JOHOW Masafuera was populated through overseas transport from Masatierra and this explained why the former was so much poorer, but only 50% of the vascular plants found on Masafuera were known to him. Other reasons for the dissimilarities between the islands are differences in the topography, particularly in altitude; Masatierra is 915, Masafuera 1570 m high. If we could lower Masafuera 650 metres, the entire highland region with its special flora and fauna would disappear. The question of the origin of the alpine flora is, as we have seen, difficult to answer. Did it exist in the islands before the separation from Chile took place, and were there any habitats where it could thrive? Many of the species are of Antarctic origin and immigrated to the extreme south of America, with or perhaps after the *Nothofagus* flora, where they abound in the bogs of the rainy zone and in the mountains above the timberline. And if, as was explained above, the *Nothofagus* flora never had an opportunity to spread to Juan Fernandez over land, nor were those Magellanian plants able to come. There are several montane plants in Masafuera which undoubtedly date back to early times, but they are of different origin: the species of *Erigeron*, *Euphrasia formosissima*, *Megalachne masafuerana*, *Phoenicoseris regia*, *Ranunculus caprarum* and *Robinsonia Masafuerae*, all of them peculiar endemics, and of these *Ranunculus* and *Megalachne* are found only along the high ridge above 1300 m. Even if some of them are of Antarctic ancestry, their history is another. When it comes to the Magellanian group, *Oreobolus*, *Lagenophora*, *Gleichenia*, and so forth, it is difficult to exclude the possibility that they be glacial or postglacial immigrants. *Carex Banksii*, *Empetrum rubrum*—only a single plant seen—*Galium masafueranum*, *Gnaphalium spiciforme*, *Myrteola nummularia* and *Rubus geoides* are, as was already told, not of Antarctic origin, but may have extended far south after the recession of the ice and accompanied *Oreobolus*, etc. And we cannot refuse to admit that various Chilean ferns, bryophytes and lichens, belonging to the forest were transported across from South Chile, for even if the prevailing winds are westerly, storms from other directions occur, and there has been plenty time. Still, the floristic difference between the two islands is a warning not to put too much faith in the efficiency of the natural agents among which, in this case, the wind stands foremost.

The biological differences between Juan Fernandez and the mainland increased during the Ice Age. West Patagonia and Fuegia were covered by inland ice (*167*); if small, ice-free refuges occurred has not been definitely stated, but is not altogether improbable, their part taken in the repopulation of the country was, however, of minor importance. With the north–south trend of the Cordillera, the road toward north lay open, and the big island of Chiloe was not ice-covered, allowing the subantarctic flora and fauna to survive, perhaps also some of the hardy trees and shrubs. The high crests of the Andes in Central Chile were covered by glaciers descending into the valleys, squeezed between the mountains and the coast a migration back and forth went on during the successive interglacial and glacial periods. At times the subantarctic bog and heath must have occupied considerable areas north of their present range, but during all this shifting to and fro many species may have been lost, some of them surviving on Masafuera. The glaciers did not come down to the coast of Central Chile, but the climate was cold and numerous ancient stenotopic types, some of them surviving on Juan Fernandez, perished.

The influence of the glacial periods cannot have been very destructive on the islands. Some plant species reduced their range and became rare or extinct, several, apparently with a very narrow physiological amplitude, are on the verge of extinction today. In Masafuera, the timberline was lowered, I suppose, and the forest patches in the valleys came down toward the sea. Masatierra has no climatic upper timberline. In a depression on the summit of the highest peak, El Yunque, *Drimys Juania, Cuminia, Escallonia, Rhetinodendron, Dicksonia*, etc. etc., luxuriate more than anywhere else, thanks to the constant humidity.

Part 2

EASTER ISLAND

Chapter XIV

Composition, distribution and relationships of the Flora.

I Angiospermae

Gramineae

Paspalum L More than 200 trop to temp, most numerous in Amer
    forsterianum Fluegge N Caled
    scrobiculatum L var *orbiculare* (Forst) Domin N Guin, Austral, N Caled, Polyn

Axonopus Beauv About 75 the majority in N and S Amer
    paschalis Pilger Related, according to PILGER, to *A scoparius* (Fluegge) Pilger, a S American species

Stipa L [1]
    horridula Pilger Related species in S Amer and Austral

Sporobolus R Br Over 100, trop –subtrop most numerous in Amer
    elongatus R Br as *indicus* (L) R Br in 230] S As, Malays, Austral, N Zeal

Calamagrostis Adans About 150, mostly temp, north and south
    retrofracta (Willd) Link (*Agrostis* Willd, *A filiformis* (Forst) Spreng) Austral, Tasm, N Zeal, Polyn, Hawaii

Dichelachne Endl 2, Austral, N Zeal
    sciurea (R Br) Hook fil Austral, N Zeal

Danthonia DC
    paschalis Pilger Perhaps most nearly related to *D chilensis* Desv

Eragrostis Host Over 200, trop –subtrop
    elongata Jacq E Ind to Malays and Polyn

Cyperaceae

Cyperus L
    eragrostis Lam Very likely introduced, and this may be the case also with the other species

---

[1] The area of genera and species also found in Juan Fernandez was indicated in Pt I and is not repeated here

polystachius Rottb. Trop.-subtrop., wide spread
cylindrostachys Boeck. As the former
brevifolius (Rottb.) Hassk. Pantrop.
Scirpus L.
riparius Presl. N. Amer., Calif. to S. Amer., south to Fueg., Falkland I. I cannot find that var. *paschalis* Kuekenth. deserves to be distinguished.

Juncaceae

Juncus L.
plebeius R. Br. Colomb.-Urug., Austral., Tasm., N. Zeal.

Piperaceae

Peperomia Ruiz et Pav.
reflexa Dietr. Pantrop., very widespread north to Hawaii and south to N. Zeal., also on Rapa and possibly Pitcairn.

Chenopodiaceae

Chenopodium ambiguum R. Br. Austral., Tasm., N. Zeal.

Polygonaceae

Polygonum L. About 150, world-wide
acuminatum H. B. K. W. Ind., Centr. and S. Amer., Galáp. Is., trop. and S. Afr., Orient.

Nyctaginaceae

Boerhaavia L. About 20 Pantrop.
diffusa L. Widespread in the Pacific and a common weed in the Old and New World, probably of aboriginal introduction.

Aizoaceae

Tetragonia L.
expansa Murr.

Cruciferae

Nasturtium R. Br. About 50 Widespread, mostly temp.
sarmentosum (Sol.) O. E. Sch. Austral.-Polyn., Hawaii

Leguminosae

Caesalpinia L. At least 90–100, pantrop.
bonduc (L.) Roxb. Trop. As.-Polyn.
Sophora L.
toromiro (Phil.) Skottsb. Nearly related to the species from J. Fern.

Euphorbiaceae

Euphorbia L. 1500–1600, world-wide
hirta L. Indomal.-Polyn., often adventitious
serpens L. As the former, also common in trop. Amer.

Umbelliferae

Apium L.
   prostratum Labill. Austral. circump., incl. *A. australe* Thouars.

Primulaceae

Samolus L. 9 (12?), 1 cosmop., 2 (5?) N. Amer., 3 southern S. Amer., 1 S. Afr., 1 W. Austral., and the following
   repens (Forst.) Pers. Austral. circump.

Gentianaceae

Erythraea Neck. (Centaurium Hill.) 30–40, subtrop.–temp.
   australis R. Br. Austral., N. Caled., Fiji.

Convolvulaceae

Calystegia R. Br. 7–8 temp.–subtrop.
   sepium (L.) R. Br. forma. All continents, also reported from Australia, but possibly introduced in the S. hemisph.
Ipomaea L.
   pes caprae (L.) Roth. Pantrop.

Solanaceae

Lycium L. About 100, most numerous in S. Amer.
   carolinianum Walt. var. *sandvicense* (Gray) L. C. Hitchc. Rapa, Hawaii.

The flora is extremely poor, not much richer than in the low coral islands: 16 families, 26 genera and 31 species, and I am not at all sure that all of them are indigenous and did exist here before man appeared on the scene; some may have been accidentally or purposely introduced by the aborigines, by the American whalers and in modern times. With regard to the "endemic" *Solanum Insulae Paschalis* Bitter, see 249, it was used as medicine. Four species are endemic (13 %), but three of them belong to large grass genera needing monographic study. FORSTER mentions (377), beside some cultigens, only *Panicum filiforme* Jacq. (= Digitaria sanguinalis), a common weed, *Sheffieldia* (= Samolus) *repens*, *Avena filiformis* (= Calamagrostis retrotracta) and *Solanum nigrum*; in his journal (348) he refers to *Apium*, which he knew from New Zealand, to "*Mimosa*" (= Sophora), and also to the former occurrence of sandalwood. In regard to the distribution of *Santalum* in Southeastern Polynesia, where *S. insulare* Bert., including varieties, is known from Tahiti, Raiatea, Marquesas, and Austral Is., and *S. hendersonense* F. B. R. Brown (very close to the former) is found on Henderson Island in the extreme south east of the island swarm, it did not seem incredible that sandalwood once occurred on Easter Island, perhaps introduced by the aborigines not very long ago. *S. yasi* Seem. was introduced to Tonga and is well established there. The matter is sufficiently interesting to be discussed here.

Tradition tells that when Hotu Matua, the legendary hero of the Easter islanders, took possession of the island, he brought various useful trees and other plants, a story first told by FORSTER (348 583) MÉTRAUX (180 15–17) enumerates mahute (*Broussonetia papyrifera*) makoi (*Thespesia populnea*), hauhau (*Triumfetta semitriloba*), toromiro (*Sophora*), naunau (*Santalum*), and marikuru (*Sapindus saponaria*). None are of American origin, all point towards Malaysia-Polynesia.

In his description of a beautiful wooden hand presented to him by one of the natives and now in the British Museum, FORSTER says that "the wood of which it was made was the rare perfumed wood of Taheitee, with the chips of which they communicate fragrance to their oils", undoubtedly sandalwood, with which FORSTER was familiar. The natives were expert in the art of wood-carving, but the hand is very unlike all other objects, which were made of *Sophora* wood, called toromiro, while the name of the tree with the fragrant wood was *naunau*. COOKE (*343* 722) translated this word "bastard sandalwood". This is the name given to *Myoporum sandwicense* Gray in Hawaii, where the native name is *naio* (naeo, naico), *Santalum* is called *iliahi*, in Marquesas *puahi*, on Rapa *eahi*, in Tahiti and Tonga *ahi*. Whether or not the words *naunau* and *naio* have the same base I cannot tell; on Raivavae, Rapa and New Zealand the name of *Myoporum* is *ngaio*, whereas true sandalwood, in this case *Mida*, is called *maire*, the Hawaiian name for the fragrant *Alyxia olivaeformis* Gaud., transferred to *Mida* in New Zealand, where no *Alyxia* occurs.

Our main sources of Easter Island ethnology, ROGGEVEEN, LA PEROUSE, COOK, Mrs ROUTLEDGE, etc. do not mention sandalwood, while MÉTRAUX pays special attention to this subject, referring to FORSTER (*180* 17-18).

My informant gave "sandal" as the Spanish equivalent of the word *naunau*—the correct Spanish word is sandalo—and remarked that the tree had entirely disappeared since the time of SALMON (between 1880 and 1890). The last one on the island grew near Vai-mata, but died recently "because there were no more kings". From the distribution of the sandalwood it seems likely that the *naunau* was the true sandalwood and not the bastard. Sandalwood 'is found on the atolls of Elizabeth and Ducie, the nearest islands to Easter Island'.

Elizabeth I is another name for Henderson, a rocky coral island; Ducie is not quoted by BROWN (*35* III). To judge from the distribution, *naunau* could just as well refer to *Myoporum*, a genus represented by endemic species in Rapa —where, as we shall learn presently, *nau* means something quite different— and Austral Is but never reported from Easter Island. The wood, slightly fragrant, is said sometimes to have been used as a substitute for sandalwood in Hawaii. MÉTRAUX's informant seems to have been convinced of the earlier existence of real *Santalum* on his island. If so, and if it had been brought from Tahiti, it ought to have had the same name.

The story does not end here. One of my correspondents, Mr PAUL H STEELE of Sacramento, Cal, kindly called my attention to a book written by Padre SEBASTIAN ENGLERT, who has lived more than 15 years on Easter Island (*86*), a place in which Mr STEELE is particularly interested. As I had no opportunity to consult the book Mr STEELE copied and sent me the following remarkable passage

Nau o *Naunau* (Santalum) arbusto de la familia de las santalaceas, tambien llamado *nau opata*, porque crecia en los barrancos (opata) de la costa, entre rocas y piedras. Ahora ha desaparecido. Los ultimos ejemplares que algunos de los nativos actuales recuerdan haber visto todavia, se han secado hace unos 50 años. El *nau opata* daba como frutos, nueces del tamaño de castañas, los "mako i nau opata". Carl Friedrich Behrens nombra nueces entre los frutos que los isleños les regalaron en gran numero a el y a sus compañeros. Hotu Matua y su gente parecen haber traido gran cantidad de estas nueces, porque de ellas se alimentaron en los primeros meses despues de haber llegado a la isla. Al excavar la tierra en cuevas que estaban antiguamente habitadas se encuentran cascaras de estas nueces. Estas cascaras generalmente no estan quebradas, sino que han sido abiertas en forma de un pequeño circulo, para ser usadas por los niños en el juego del trompo. La madera del arbusto se utilizaba, por su exquisito aroma, para confeccionar un perfume, como lo veremos en otro capitulo.

This description does not at all fit either *Santalum* or *Myoporum*. The fruit of *Santalum* is an ellipsoid drupe with a thin fleshy mesocarp and a very hard endocarp, and I have never seen or heard of a kind the size of a castaña (chestnut), in the largest I have measured (*S. pyrularium* Gray) the drupe was 16–18 mm long and the stone 12–15 mm. According to HILLEBRAND (307, 390) the drupe measures up to 24 mm in length, but I have not seen any as large as that. Nor have I ever heard that the kernel is used as food, the idea that Hotu Matua's party could have maintained itself for months on nothing else is preposterous, and I fail to see how the stone could be used as a whipping top. The *naunau* which grew along the coast and produced the "cascaras" found in the caves cannot have been a species of *Santalum*. Fortunately this could be proved. Mr STEFEL had told me that Father ENGLERT had sent him two shells for his collection of Easter Island curios and had promised him more, of which he intended to send me samples. As time went by and no more came I asked him the favour of sending me one of his precious specimens as loan, and he willingly consented. It is a hard, brown and smooth, almost globular shell, 2.5 cm high, 3 cm wide, 2 mm thick, with a large irregular hole in the basal part. It has nothing whatever to do with *Santalum*. A passage in MÉTRAUX's book, p. 353, put me on the track. He quotes a song which the children used to sing when the tops were spinning, and it tells that the spinning-tops were made of *makoi* — *Thespesia populnea* capsules! A comparison with herbarium material showed that Mr STEFEL's specimen is a typical capsule of *Thespesia*, one of the "nuts" found in the caves. They made very poor food but good spinning tops. We did not see *Thespesia* on the island, but MÉTRAUX observed it growing on the cliffs at Poike (the eastern headland). Evidently the word *nau* or *naunau* has been altogether misplaced by the Easter islanders, although both MÉTRAUX and ENGLERT were told that it was the name of *Santalum*. We find the same word in Tahiti and the Tuamotu Islands for *Lepidium bidentatum* Montin, and this is called *naupata*, strikingly like ENGLERT's *nau opata* in Marquesas, in Tahiti *naupata* means *Scaevola frutescens*, which is called *naupaka* in Hawaii and *ngaungau* in Raiotonga, and on Rapa *nau* is used for *Sonchus oleraceus*. All these plants were used as medicine.

Geographical elements

In 1934 I made an attempt to arrange the vascular plants according to their distribution, with the following result (239 278–279, translated from French)

1 Australian-Polynesian element (12)
   a) Species found elsewhere Paspalum (2), Sporobolus, Calamagrostis, Dichelachne, Eragrostis, Juncus, Peperomia, Chenopodium, Nasturtium, Erythraea
   b) Endemic Stipa horridula
2 Palaeantarctic element (3)
   a) Species found elsewhere Apium, Samolus
   b) Endemic Sophora toromiro
3 American element (6)
   a) Species found elsewhere Cyperus vegetus, Scirpus, Polygonum, Lycium
   b) Endemic Axonopus paschalis, Danthonia paschalis
4 Wide spread tropical element (10) Cyperus (3), Boerhaavia, Tetragonia, Caesalpinia, Euphorbia (2), Calystegia, Ipomaea

Going into more detail, I have tried to rearrange the angiosperms in the following manner

I Palaeotropical element — 22 sp (70%)

1 *Pantropical* (6) Cyperus polystachyus, cylindrostachys and brevifolius, Peperomia reflexa, Boerhaavia diffusa, Ipomaea pes caprae
2 *Malaysian-Polynesian* (9) Paspalum forsterianum and scrobiculatum, Sporobolus elongatus, Calamagrostis retrofracta, Eragrostis elongata, Nasturtium sarmentosum, Caesalpinia bonduc, Euphorbia hirta and serpens
3 *Australian Polynesian* (7)
   a Endemic Stipa horridula (?)
   b Not endemic Dichelachne sciurea, Chenopodium ambiguum, Tetragonia expansa, Erythraea australis, Calystegia sepium (?)
   c Also in tropical America Juncus plebeius

II Austral-circumpolar element — 4 sp (12 9%)

a Endemic Danthonia paschalis, Sophora toromiro
b Not endemic Apium prostratum, Samolus repens

III Neotropical element — 5 sp (16 1%)

a Endemic Axonopus paschalis
b Not endemic Cyperus eragrostis, Scirpus riparius, Polygonum acuminatum, Lycium carolinianum var

I am strongly inclined to regard *Cyperus eragrostis* as a late immigrant from Chile *Lycium carolinianum* var *sandvicense* is a puzzling case, a form of a North American species but only found in Hawaii, Rapa and Easter Island It is a halophyte confined to the beach but one might expect it also to occur on the shores of California etc from where it has not been reported Beach plants are included in all the groups, in I *Ipomaea, Caesalpinia, Chenopodium* and *Tetragonia*, in II *Apium* and *Samolus*, in III *Lycium*, together they are 7, or 21% of the angiosperms.

If we want to trace an ancient Antarctic source, just as we did in Juan Fernandez, the Antarcto-tertiary group would consist of *Danthonia, Juncus, Sophora, Apium* and *Samolus*.

To judge by the geographical position of Easter Island the dominance of a Palaeotropical Pacific element was expected. The island certainly is remote from the large cluster of islands of South eastern Polynesia, but much more distant from South America. Consequently, the presence of a neotropical element is surprising. Future researches will perhaps show that *Stipa horridula* should be added, which makes little difference as long as the endemic *Axonopus* is claimed to be of neotropical parentage, and *Scirpus riparius* and *Polygonum acuminatum* remain American. Their mode of occurrence and ecology oblige us to regard them as truly indigenous unless they have been intentionally introduced in prehistoric time during one of the mythical cruises which according to HEYERDAHL, put Easter Island in contact with Peru. A direct transport of seeds across the ocean without man's assistance is difficult to imagine, and it is futile to speculate in land connections.

II Pteridophyta (63 · 2/9)

Polypodiaceae (in the old sense)

Asplenium L.
    adiantoides (L.) C. Chr. var. **squamulosum** C. Chr. et Skottsb. The species trop. As–Austral, N Zeal and Polyn, also E Afr and adjacent islands, the variety endemic.
    obliquum Forst. Austral circump. the only plant reported from Sala y Gomez.

Davallia Sm. About 40, wide-spread, mainly southern, As–Polyn, S Afr, Madag, a solitary species Ibero-Afr and Macaron.
    solida (Forst.) Sw. Indomal–Polyn–Austral.

Doodia R. Br. 12 "New Zealand and Juan Fernandez to Hawaii and Australia" (COPELAND 69 158), but "Juan Fernandez" is a mistake for Easter I.
    paschalis C. Chr. et Skottsb. Close to *D. blechnoides* A. Cunn (Austral).

Dryopteris Adans.
    Espinosai Hicken. Belongs to a neotropical group.
    gongylodes (Schk.) O. K. Pantrop.
    dentata (Forsk.) C. Chr. Pantrop.

Elaphoglossum Schott.
    Skottsbergii Krajina. Related to *E. tahitense* Brack.

Microlepia Presl 45–50, a pantrop. genus ranging north to Japan and south to Madag and N Zeal.
    strigosa (Thunb.) Presl Indomal–Polyn.

Polypodium L.
   scolopendria Burm. Palaeotrop., wide-spread.
Polystichum Roth
   Fuentesii Espinosa. Belongs to the *P. vestitum* assemblage.
Vittaria Sm. About 80, pantrop.-subtrop.
   elongata Sw. Indomal.-Polyn.-Austral.

Ophioglossaceae

Ophioglossum L.
   lusitanicum L. subsp. *coriaceum* (Cunn.) Clausen. Boliv.-Chile, Austral., Tasm., N. Caled., N. Zeal.
   reticulatum L. S.E. As., Philipp. N. Guin., Melan.-Polyn., east to Mangareva, Mascarene Is.

Psilotaceae

Psilotum Sw. 2 wide-spread sp.
   nudum (L.) Griseb. Pantrop.

Fifteen species are listed, 4 of them endemic (26.6%), the endemic variety of *Asplenium adiantoides* not counted.

Geographical elements

In my earlier subdivision (239) the following groups were distinguished:

1. Australian-Polynesian element (6)
   a) Species found elsewhere: Asplenium adiantoides, Elaphoglossum tahitense, Microlepia strigosa, Vittaria elongata, Ophioglossum coriaceum
   b) Endemic: Doodia paschalis
2. Palaeantarctic element (1)
   Found elsewhere: Asplenium obtusatum
3. American element (1)
   Endemic: Dryopteris Espinosai
4. Wide-spread tropical element (4): Dryopteris gongylodes and parasitica (=dentata), Polypodium phymatodes, Ophioglossum reticulatum

The list contains 12 species, two have been reported later and some nomenclatural changes have been made. A new geographical arrangement follows here.

I Palaeotropical element — 11 sp. (73.3%)

1. *Pantropical* (3) Dryopteris gongylodes and dentata, Psilotum nudum
2. *Palaeotropical* (1) Asplenium adiantoides (endemic variety)
3. *Malaysian-Polynesian* (6)
   a Endemic: Elaphoglossum Skottsbergii
   b Not endemic: Davallia solida, Microlepia strigosa, Polypodium scolopendria, Vittaria elongata, Ophioglossum reticulatum (also Mascarene Is.)
4. *Australian-Polynesian* (1)
   Endemic: Doodia paschalis

II. Austral-circumpolar element — 3 sp. (20%)

a. Endemic: *Polystichum Fuentesii*

b. Not endemic: *Asplenium obliquum*, *Ophioglossum lusitanicum* subsp. *coriaceum*

III. Neotropical element — 1 sp. (6.7%)

Endemic: *Dryopteris Espinosai*

We find the same dominance of a palaeotropical element as among the angiosperms. *Ophioglossum lusitanicum* is reported from Atlantic Europe, the Mediterranean and Macaronesia, whereas the subspecies is austral bicentric, an example of a remarkable discontinuous distribution. The American element is represented by a single endemic species and there is no fern corresponding to *Polygonum acuminatum* and *Scirpus riparius*. *Polystichum Fuentesii* and *Asplenium obliquum* are, perhaps, Antarctic and the latter was classified as such above (p. 282), but it is a seaside plant. If we follow COPELAND, *Asplenium Doodia* and *Davallia* are of Antarctic origin.

III. Musci (33, 265)

I have to thank Dr. HERMAN PERSSON for kind assistance in finding out about distribution.

Trematodon Michx. (Dicranaceae). About 70, mainly trop., south to N. Zeal.
 pascuanus Thér.

Campylopus Brid.
 introflexus (Hedw.) Mitt. See p. 227
 turficola Broth.
 hygrophilus Broth.
 dicranodontioides Broth.
 saxicola Broth.

Fissidens Hedw.
 pascuanus Broth.

Ptychomitrium (Bruch) Fuernr.
 subcylindricum Ther.

Hersia Hedw. (Trichostomaceae). About 30, widely distributed (Eur., N. Amer., E. As., N. Afr.)
 flavipes Hook. fil. et Wils. Java, Ceylon, E. Austral., Tasm., N. Zeal.

Bryum Dill.
 argenteum L. var. *lanatum* (Palis.) Bryol. eur. Widely spread in warmer countries, the species cosmop.

Philonotis Brid.
 laxissima (C. M.) Bryol. jav. F. Ind., Madag.

Papillaria C. M. (Meteoriaceae). About 70, a pantrop. genus.

paschalis Ther ex Broth. Related to *P. crocea* (Hpe) Jaeg. Ind., Ceylon, Java, Philipp., E. Austral., N. Zeal., Kermadec Is., Fiji)

Fabronia Raddi (Fabroniaceae) 90–100, half of them Amer., trop.–subtrop.

    macroblepharoides Broth. Related to *F. macroblepharis* Schwaegr. (Brazil), other related sp. in Afr. and Austral.

Rhacopilum Palis.

    cuspidigerum Schwaegr. Norfolk I., N. Caled., Samoa, Hawaii

Besides, BROTHERUS mentions *Weisia* sp. and *Macromitrium* sp.

Fourteen species are reported, 9 of them endemic (64.3 %), a high figure, but there can be no doubt that only a part of the mosses has been collected, and very likely the proportion of endemics will be reduced. Of greater interest are the endemic aquatic species of *Campylopus* of the crater lakes, possibly relicts from an era when the island was larger and higher than now and enjoyed a more humid climate. Probably many mosses and other cryptogams disappeared with the forest groves. Of the known species *Campylopus introflexus*, *Weisia flavipes* and *Rhacopilum cuspidigerum* have a southern distribution, *Philonotis laxissima* is palaeotropical and *Bryum argenteum* cosmopolitan and perhaps anthropochorous, the endemic species are supposed to have tropical relatives.

IV. Hepaticae (130)

Frullania Raddi

    lagenifera Schwaegr. Known before from the type locality only, said to be the Falkland Is., but this statement is subject to doubt, possibly Ins. Marianae is meant instead of Maclovianae.

Conditions are not favourable to hepatics but more species will be found. A *Lejeunea* was collected, but the material seems to have been lost (l.c. 699).

V. Lichenes (297)

My thanks are due to Dr. A. H. MAGNUSSON and Dr. R. SANTESSON, who helped with information on the distribution.

Arthonia Ach. About 500, the majority trop.–subtrop.

    fuscescens Fée Apparently only reported once before (trop. Amer.)

Opegrapha Humb. About 280, mostly warmer climates

    paschalis Zbr.

Graphis (Adans.) Ach.

    lineola Ach. Trop.–subtrop.

Diploschistes Norm. About 30, cold to temp. regions, trop. mountains

    anactinus Zbr. Described from Japan

    scruposus (L.) Norm. Wide-spread N. and S. temp.

Heppia Naeg. About 40, mostly warm and dry regions

    Guepini Nyl. N. Amer., Eur.

Lecidea (Ach.) Th. Fr.
: **paschalis** Zbr.

Cladonia (Hill.) Vainio
: *pityrea* (Flk.) Fr. Cosmop.

Acarospora Mass.
: **Skottsbergii** Zbr.

Parmelia (Ach.) De Not.
: *reticulata* Tayl. N. and S. Amer., W. and S. Eur., Afr., L. As., Austral.
: *conspersa* (Ehrh.) Ach. var. *lusitana* (Nyl.) S. Lur. the species cosmop.

Usnea Wigg.
: *subtortulosa* (Zbr.) Motyka (*344*) Masafuera. Described as *U. Stemerii* var. by ZAHLBRUCKNER who also distinguished var. *tincta* Zbr. and quoted it for Easter Island; this is called *U. tincta* by MOTYKA who records it for S. Amer. only.

Caloplaca Th. Fr.
: *rubina* Zbr. J. Fern.
: *lucens* (Nyl.) Zbr. Patag., Falkl., S. Georgia.

Buellia De Not.
: *stellulata* (Tayl.) Mudd. Cosmop.
: *fernandeziana* Zbr. J. Fern.
: *halophiloides* Zbr. var. The typical sp. J. Fern.
: **paschalis** Zbr.
: *glaziouana* M. Arg. Brazil.

Rinodina (S. Gray) Mass. About 300, very widely distributed.
: **Perousii** Zbr.

Pyxine (Fr.) Nyl.
: *enterozantha* Nyl. forma. S.W. Eur., Japan.

Physcia (Schreb.) Vainio
: *picta* (Sw.) Nyl. Wide-spread trop.–subtrop.

Anaptychia Koerb.
: *speciosa* (Wulf.) Mass. Widely distributed, in Amer. south to Fueg.

These 23 species, 5 regarded as endemic, represent, I am sure, only a minor part of the lichen flora and do not lend themselves to geographical speculations. There are several strange cases of disjunction serving, I daresay, to illustrate our insufficient knowledge of the distribution of lichens.

V. Fungi

Our collection contained a single species, *Bovistella pusilla* Lloyd, known before from Australia (*102*).

Chapter XV

Composition, distribution and relationships of the Fauna.

Indigenous vertebrates, birds excepted, lacking. The principal occupation in the island is farming; cattle and sheep are plentiful and roam over the island which, with the exception of outlying rocks, has lost its primitiveness. As a consequence of the changes in the plant cover, particularly the extermination of the indigenous trees, also the fauna was impoverished, while through the introduction of useful plants, numerous weeds and all kinds of goods many foreign insects and other invertebrates made their appearance, as the lists below will show. As little research work has been done hitherto, many more species will probably be found, indigenous as well as introduced.

Aves (175)

Sterna lunata Peale. Moluce., Polyn., Fiji, Hawaii.
Anous stolidus (L.) *unicolor* Nordmann. Sala y Gomez. The typical species trop.—subtrop., but not observed on the coast of America.
Procelsterna coerulea (Benn.) *skottsbergi* Loennb. Typical *coerulea* on Christmas I., 4 other subspecies scattered over the Pacific.
Gygis alba (Sparrm.) *royana* Matthews. With the typical species wide spread trop.
Pterodroma heraldica Salvin *paschae* Loennb. The typical species S. W. Pacific.
Sula cyanops (Sundev.) Trop. seas throughout the world.

According to the natives some other sea birds occur, but there are no land birds.

Oligochaeta (181)

Pheretima californica (Kbg.) Introduced. Reported from Calif., Mex., Madeira and Lower Egypt.

Araneida (22)

Scytodes lugubris Thorell. Burma, N. Caled., perhaps all over Oceania.
Pholcus phalangioides Fuessl. Eur., now spread over a large part of the globe.
Theridium tepidariorum C. Koch. Cosmop.
+ *Tetragnata Paschae* Berland. A large cosmop. genus.
Coriuna cetrata Simon. N. Caled.
Hasarius Adansoni Audouin. Cosmop.
Plexippus Paykulli Audouin. Cosmop.

Possibly all the spiders are adventitious (BERLAND l. c.). Two species were determined as to genus only.

Myriapoda (274)

Pachymerium ferrugineum Latz. Wide-spread in Eur., undoubtedly introduced, probably from Chile.

Orthomorpha gracilis Koch, Latz. Apparently wide spread, introduced.

A third species, belonging to *Iamyctes*, could not be named.

Collembola (216)

Entomobrya multifasciata (Tullb.) N. and S. Amer., Eur., N. As., N. Zeal., J. Fern. Introduced.

Embioptera (222)

Oligotoma Vosseleri (Krauss) Ceylon, Sumatra, Java.

Insecta

Odonata (225)

Pantala flavescens Fabr. Amer., Afr., As., Austral.

Orthoptera-Dermaptera (225, 201)

I am indebted to Dr. PRINCIS for information on the nomenclature and distribution.

Anisolabis Bormansi Scudd. Galáp. Is., Masatierra.

Onychostylus notulatus (Stål, Allaeta, 225, 297) Formosa, Malays., N. Guin., N. Caled., Samoa, Tahiti, Marquesas, Hawaii. Introduced from Tahiti.

Periplaneta Australasiae (Fabr.) Probably originally African, now cosmop., the genus Afr.–Orient.

Diploptera punctata (Eschtz. D. dytiscoides 225, 297) Ind., Ceylon, Burma, Malays., Austral., Samoa, Marquesas, Hawaii, the genus Oriental. Accidentally introduced.

Melanozosteria philpotti (Shaw) N. Zeal. An Australian genus, represented on some Pacific islands.

Blatella vaga Heb. N. Amer., Asia? The genus probably Oriental. Probably adventitious.

Orthoptera-Saltatoria (58)

Gryllus oceanicus Le Guillou. Malaysia and Japan to Polyn. CHOPARD regards its presence on Easter Island as a proof of the facility with which certain insects are transported large distances, nothing will prevent animals, he says, to be carried across the Pacific from Australia. In this case, however, I guess that man has been the agent.

Thysanoptera (3)

Haplothrips usitatus Bagn. var *inermis* Ahlb. The typical species in Hawaii

Neuroptera (92)

Chrysopa lanata Banks Widespread in S Amer and also found on Hawaii A wide-ranging genus of several hundred sp
+ *Chr Skottsbergi* Esben-Peters

Lepidoptera (13)

Agrotis ypsilon Rott Cosmop
Cuphis Loreyi Dup Widely distributed
Achaea melicerta Drury On all islands in the Pacific and Indian oceans
Phytometra chalcytes Esp Eur, As, most islands of the Pacific and Indian oceans

It is not probable that any of these Noctuidae are indigenous

Diptera (84)

Sarconesia chlorogaster (Wied) Chile, J Fern Introduced
+ ? *Lipsana insulae-paschalis* Enderl
Leptocera (Copiophila) *ferruginata* (Stenh) var *insulae-paschalis* Enderl The typical species, known from Eur, Ind and S Amer, lives in horse dung and was spread with the horse The variety was picked from the carcass of a sheep and has, ENDERLEIN remarks (l c 679) perhaps developed after the arrival in Easter Island where, however, there are many horses

Coleoptera

Curculionidae (12)
Aramigus Fullert Horn A noxious beetle, probably of N Amer origin, introduced into many countries and on some isolated islands
+ *Pentarthrum paschale* Auriv
Areocerus fasciculates Deg Cosmop introduced

Dytiscidae (299)
+ *Bidessus Skottsbergi* Zimmerm The occurrence of an endemic aquatic beetle in the crater lake of Rano Kao among the endemic hygrophilous mosses is of interest

Elateridae (308)
Simodactylus Delfini Fleut Chile- Austral, N Guin, N Brit, Solomon Is, Hawaii

Staphylinidae (25)
Philonthus longicornis Steph Cosmop

Hymenoptera

Formicidae (283)
Ponera trigona Mayr var *opacior* Forel N Amer, W Ind, Chile The typical species in Brazil, a subspecies in Austral
Cardiocondyla nuda Mayr subsp *minuta* Forel Hawaii The typical species Ind, Ceylon Austral, N Guin One subsp is Mediterranean

Tetramorium guineense Fabr. Probably of African origin, now pantrop. in hothouses in the temp. region.

T. simillimum F. Smith. As the former.

Plagiolepis maclavishi Wheeler. Formosa, Hawaii, Society Is.

Prenolepis bourbonica Forel subsp. *Skottsbergi* Wheeler. The typical species known from Chagos, Nicobar and Seychelle Is., and E. Afr., Pemba I. Other subspecies in Ind., Comoro Is., L. As., Philipp. Is. and Hawaii.

Ants are easily carried about by man, but it seems likely that Easter Island also has indigenous forms.

Vespidae (206).

Polistes hebraeus F. F. Afr., Madag., Ind., China, Tahiti?

Hemiptera (21)

Cicadula apricornis Sign. Wide spread, introduced.
Reduviolus capsiformis Germ. As the former.

Mollusca (189)

Limax arborum Bruch Chant. Cosmop., introduced.
Milax gagates Drap. As the former.
Melampus philippi Kuester. Perú.
+*M. pascus* Odhner. The genus distributed over the Pacific from Hawaii to N. Caled., S. Amer.

Tornatellinops impressa Mouss. (Syn. Pacificella variabilis Odhner l.c.) Distributed from Fiji to Easter Island. Perhaps introduced with living plant material.

The fauna, as known hitherto, presents the same picture of extreme poverty as the flora, and even if future researches will double the number of species and reveal the occurrence of groups not yet recorded, a considerable portion will consist of late immigrants. The known endemics are very few and one or two of them questionable, and our experience from the old list of Juan Fernandez Diptera (84) bodes no good for the single endemic genus. Altogether half a dozen endemic species and some endemic forms of lower category have been described, and of the species found elsewhere some are, perhaps, indigenous. An example of remarkable discontinuous distribution is offered by *Melanozosterra philpotti*, New Zealand and Easter Island, possibly it will be discovered in intermediate stations, but such stations are difficult to find in other cases where Easter Island is the terminus. *Ansolabus Bormansi*, Galápagos Islands + Juan Fernandez, *Chrysopa lanata*, South America and Hawaii, *Ponera trigona*, America, and *Haplothrips notatus*, Hawaii. A direct overseas transport is not very probable, and I cannot tell if these animals are likely to have been introduced with the traffic

Chapter XVI

The biogeographical history of Easter Island

The composition of the present fauna and flora does not help us to throw any light on the earlier history of Easter Island, and we do not know what they were like before the arrival of aboriginal man many centuries ago. We know that the island became densely populated, that the natural resources, evidently poor, were exploited, the soil cultivated wherever this was possible and a number of useful plants introduced from other parts of Polynesia, tradition tells that the first colonists arrived from Rapa, but other opinions have also been expressed. ROGGE-VEEN, the discoverer of the island in 1722, did not bring a naturalist, but to judge by his narrative the island must have looked much the same as when SPARRMAN and the FORSTERS, who came with COOK in 1774, made the first biological observations. FORSTER collected and cited a few species (346) and mentions, in his narrative (347), "Mimosa" (*Sophora toromiro*) and *Apium*, which he had observed before in New Zealand. If there had been other indigenous trees, they had disappeared, *Broussonetia papyrifera*, *Thespesia populnea* and very likely also *Triumfetta semitriloba* had been introduced but were scarce. For wood the natives depended on *Sophora*, and most of this was gone already. FORSTER found the place very barren, but on p. 578 he speaks of a hillock covered with toromiro, and later on another similar hill is mentioned (p. 592), but all the trees were low, not over 9 or 10 feet, the main trunk of the biggest as thick as a man's thigh. No wonder that the single canoe seen was a patchwork of pieces 2 or 3 feet long, and so was the paddle. The population did not exceed 700. When THOMPSON and COOKE (343) visited the island in 1886, groups of trees were observed in some places.

> In other parts of the island may be seen, in places in considerable numbers, a hardwood tree, more properly bush or brush, called by the natives toromiro. These must have flourished well at one time, but are now all, or nearly all, dead and decaying by reason of being stripped of their bark by the flocks of sheep which roam at will all over the island. None of the trees are, perhaps, over 10 feet in height, nor their trunks more than 2 or 3 inches in diameter (p. 705).

The last specimens of toromiro are restricted to the inside of the crater Rano Kao. Easter Island was made a national park in order to protect the unique stone monuments and is a bird sanctuary, but otherwise nature is not preserved but the land grazed over without restriction as far as I am aware.

Among the many isolated islands of the Pacific, Easter occupies a rather unique position. Oceanic islands belong to two main categories, high volcanic and low coralline, only the former are of greater biological interest and possess the standard set of "peculiarities" described by HOOKER, WALLACE and others. Easter Island seems to form a type by itself. It is volcanic and cannot be called low, for the highest mountain is 530 m high and some of the craters reach an altitude of 300—400 m, sufficient, one would think, to create a humid montane belt with fairly luxuriant arboreous vegetation, but of this there is nothing, in any case nothing left. Rains are frequent and the amount of precipitation is not small, but evaporation, favoured by high temperatures and the strong S E trade wind, is great and most of the water rapidly disappears underground. The climax vegetation is an oceanic steppe-like meadow or grass heath, as some would prefer to call it (342). The flora does not present many of the characteristics of oceanic islands. There are no endemic genera, no peculiar endemic species, no preponderance of woody plants, *Sophora* is the only tree and *Lycium* the only shrub, the flora is herbaceous, comprising few therophytes but many annual weeds. The ratio species : genus is 1.2 : 1. With the exception of *Gramineae*, which dominate, and *Cyperaceae* (some of these perhaps not indigenous) most large and world-wide families are absent, even Compositae, there are no conifers, no orchids but a fair number of ferns; in these respects the island conforms to typical oceanic islands.

On the other hand, Easter Island has little in common with the low islands, atolls or other coralline structures with no rock foundation exposed, where endemics are, as a rule, absent and the fragmentary flora consists of species easily transported by the natural agencies and by man.

The geographical position is unfavourable to immigration, the chances for the arrival of seeds from America small, the distance being 3700 km, and 1850 km separate Easter from Pitcairn, the nearest basaltic islet. On the other hand the chances for establishment ought to have been good, new surroundings, though perhaps not very varied, plenty of space, no competition, conditions furthering the evolution of new species and genera as many biogeographers believe, but nothing like that seems to have happened on Easter Island. The objection will be raised that we do not know, for the bulk of the original fauna and flora may have been destroyed by man and will remain unknown—but is it not surprising, if this be true, that no peculiar systematically isolated form was preserved to our days? After all, perhaps not. Truly, in many high and well populated Polynesian islands endemics are plentiful, growing on the elevated ridges, on the precipitous mountain sides, in the deep recesses of the gorges where cascades tumble down or even in less inaccessible, but uninhabited places, but the topography of Easter Island is different and I can see no reason why not man and his animals could have succeeded to exterminate practically everything of the original nature except the lichens and mosses covering the rocks and a few herbs and grasses.

Distance is not the only factor, time is another, the island is, somebody will say, perhaps too young. It has a youthful appearance, the craters are well preserved, but they are secondary and not responsible for the origin of the island, and their well preserved shape is no proof of youth. There is no sign of recent activity—FORSTER's idea that the decay during the 18th century of the old aboriginal culture was due to some volcanic catastrophe lacks foundation. As there are no permanent streams, erosion must be slight. The various *tanos* and other cones may be old enough and the foundation, on which they stand, very ancient. As BRÜGGEN says (331, 290)

A pesar de que los volcanes tienen sus formas muy bien conservadas, no existe en la tradición de los nativos ningún recuerdo de una erupción. La isla produce la impresión de tratarse del resto de un segmento de un enorme volcán central, en cuya superficie inclinada se han formado los cráteres actualmente visibles como conos adventicios superiores.

Easter Island is small, but not very small, 117 sq. km, and GULICK (*119*) called it "the wave-worn remnant of an island that could once have claimed about twice that area". Lack of time cannot have prevented the island to reach maturity and to acquire some internal harmony of the flora and fauna. Still, they are very disharmonious. The general situation of isolated islands is clearly set forth by GULICK (l.c. 413–414).

It is evident that mature groups of islands will attain an internal harmony from the standpoint of the systematist. But this harmony, instead of reflecting the pre-existent harmony of some continental source (as is the case for continental islands or land-bridge remnants), will be recognizably derivable by descent from a quite limited number of original importations, at the start distinctly miscellaneous and "disharmonic", as was observed to be the condition in Bermuda and St. Helena. Large series of related or previously associated forms will be found from the beginning in continental islands, but their counterpart must be brought into existence *de novo* if the group is truly oceanic. But this distinction, obvious in theory, is in practice very difficult to recognize, unless the oceanic condition is really extreme.

Easter Island complies with this condition and is often described as an example of a truly oceanic island, this is the general opinion, but it was told above (Chapter IV) that there is no lack of theories according to which Easter is a remnant of a land mass of continental size, a mid-Pacific continent or a land bridge uniting the Australian-New Zealandic area with South America and Hawaii, ARLDI, GERMAIN, GUILLEMIN, J. W. GREGORY, MEYRICK, PILSBRY etc. were quoted. It is not improbable that the island is the rest of a somewhat larger piece of land, but this is all we can say. The bathymetrical conditions—see map—hardly tempt us to construct bridges, even if not all signs of submergence are lacking. The 3000 m curve forms a large almost closed crescent, on the north extremity of which Easter Island rises. ENE is Sala y Gomez, extending SW–NE, 1200 m long, 150 m broad and 30 m high, and this tiny islet is the only visible part of a larger reef running in the direction NE ¼ N and called Scott Reef, where the smallest depth, 1950 m from the islet is 35 m only, between this place and the islet a series of soundings gave 55, 60, 49 and 46 m. The bank extends at least a couple of km west of the islet with depths of 42 to 68 m, and nowhere within this range a greater depth than 95 m was found (*172* 74). The scale of my map is too small to give these details. Proceeding east we find, in about the same distance from Sala y Gomez as this is from Easter Island another submarine ridge running N–S, bounded by the 1000 m curve and with depths as modest as 862 and 308 m. Further east again, in 97°30′ W. l., approximately, is another ridge trending W–E, where the smallest figure is 497 m. None of these shallow areas were, I believe, known to the bridge-builders. They must be welcome also to those who look, if not for sunken continents, at least for submerged islands used as way stations in the migrations. However, all this means a possible extension east, towards South America, but this is not where we ought to look for the vanished world that could have inhabited a greater and higher Easter Island, rather we have better look in the opposite direction.

It is FORREST BROWN's merit to have pointed to the large insular world known as Southeastern Polynesia as as important floristic—and, I presume, faunistic—centre, and from his Flora (35) and the reports published by members of other recent survey parties, sponsored by the Bishop Museum in Honolulu, the following data were compiled. The Society Islands are excluded and only the angiosperms considered. Included are the Marquesas, Tuamotu and Austral or Tubuai Islands, and the more isolated Rapa (Oparu), Mangareva (Gambier) Pitcairn and Henderson (Elizabeth) Island.

The Marquesas Islands are high, 800–1200 m, and belong, to judge from the geology and topography, to the same generation of Tertiary islands as Tahiti, Juan Fernandez, Macaronesia, etc. The Tuamotus proper are atolls. Of the Austral Islands the high basaltic are considered, Rimatara, 95 m, Rurutu, 410 m, Tubuai, 400 m, and Raivavae (Vavitao), 440 m, further, the following outlying islands are included: Rapa (Oparo), 640 m, Mangareva (Gambier), 400 m, Pitcairn, 350 m, and Henderson (Elizabeth), an islet of raised coral said to be only 25 m high (545) but nevertheless the home of an endemic *Santalum* (compare Laysan of the Leeward Hawaiian Islands with *S. ellipticum* var. *laysanense*). The Marquesas flora is considered to be well known and the same may be true of the flora of the other islands, even if no complete lists have been published, I suppose that all the novelties have been described, but my figures for wide spread species are, perhaps, too low. There is a difference between my figures and those given by BROWN, because varieties are counted by him as units equal to species, which explains why his figures for the endemics are so high.

The largest families are Rubiaceae (36), Cyperaceae (25), Compositae (19), Euphorbiaceae (16), Gramineae (13), Leguminosae (12), and Piperaceae (10). Other large and important families, such as Araliaceae, Cruciferae, Ericaceae, Malvaceae, Myrtaceae, Orchidaceae Sapindaceae, etc., are represented by fewer species. We have every reason to believe that the flora has suffered losses after man had taken possession of the soil.

The total number of presumably indigenous species—many of aboriginal introduction and not few later arrivals have become naturalized—is 282, of which 156 are endemic within the area. The genera are 145, of which only 3 are endemic according to BROWN. The ratio species genus is almost 2:1. No genus is very large, the largest is *Psychotria* with 12 species, and 10 have from 5 to 10 species each. The distribution of the species and the number of local endemics are indicated in Table XIII. The figures do not pretend to be exact.

A large proportion of endemics and of woody, arboreous or fruticose species —suffruticose excluded—are characteristic of oceanic floras of considerable antiquity. Of the 156 endemic species 113 (72.4 %) are woody, of the 126 found elsewhere 69 (54.8 %). The herbaceous species are, with very few exceptions, perennial. Systematically isolated types are few, and even the Marquesas Islands cannot in this respect, be compared with either Hawaii or Juan Fernandez.

Table VIII

Distribution of angiosperms in Southeastern Polynesia

	Number of species	Number of endemics	% endemics	Woody species Number	%
Marquesas	151	79	52.3	100	66.2
Tuamotu	44	3	7.0	23	52.3
Austral	80	12	15.0	53	66.7
Rapa	89	44	49.4	62	69.6
Mangareva	28	3	10.7	17	60.9
Pitcairn	26	2	7.7	19	73.1
Henderson	21	3	14.3	15	71.4
Total	282	156	55.3	182	64.5

BROWN (35) regards southeastern Polynesia, with the Tuamotus in the centre, as an old, submerged region.

Affinities point to the Tuamotuan region as one of the ancient mid-oceanic centers of origin for a large part of the dicotyledonous flora of southeastern Polynesia (III 6),

and, speaking of the distribution of *Fitchia*, he writes (l c 364)

The grouping and affinity of these allied species strongly suggest the Tuamotuan region as the center of origin at a rather remote period, possibly at the dawn of the Tertiary or somewhat earlier, when it may be assumed that high (pre-Tuamotuan) islands existed in place of the low (Tuamotuan) atolls of the present

Within the Marquesas archipelago the sea is shallow

Apparently, an emergence of 100 meters would cause land to appear in six places, an additional emergence of 300 meters would unite or bring into close contact all land areas of the archipelago. Botanical evidences, outlined in an earlier paper,[1] indicate that the islands were at one time 1000 to 2000 meters higher than at present (l c I 17)

The floristic affinities of this region is with Malaysia–Melanesia–Australia, there is no neotropical element in spite of the prevailing direction of winds and currents BROWN, who could be expected also to look toward America, remarks

The Cichorieae, to which *Fitchia* belongs, are best represented in Europe and America, pointing to a more remote American center of origin for the pre-Tuamotuan ancestral stock

This brings up the *Dendroseris-Thamnoseris* problem. The four dendroseroid genera form a very natural group, *Thamnoseris* of Desventuradas Islands stands apart, and so does *Fitchia*. If they are, at least distantly, related, and isolated from all other Cichoriaceous genera, then the possibility of an Antarcto-tertiary ancestry should be considered. I have, however, referred the *Dendroseris* assemblage to an ancient neotropical element, absent from the present continental flora,

---

[1] Proceed 2d Pan Pacif Sci Congr, Vol 2, 1923

and *Thamnoseris* finds no better place, but to derive *Fitchia* from an American source seems little inviting. Another solution is, perhaps, in sight. Professor GUNNAR ERDTMAN kindly told me that, to judge by the pollen morphology, *Fitchia* may have to be removed from the *Cichorium* subfamily where J. D. HOOKER placed it next to *Dendroseris* and where it has remained.

There is in the Pacific Ocean no island of the size, geology and altitude of Easter Island with such an extremely poor flora and with a subtropical climate favourable for plant growth, but nor is there an island as isolated as this, and the conclusion will be that poverty is a result of isolation—even if man is responsible for the disappearance of part of the flora, it cannot have been rich; the Marquesas Is. which have been inhabited longer, I believe, and formerly had a large native population, still preserve a fairly rich and varied angiospermic flora, half of which is endemic. The distances are too great to be overcome except on very rare occasions. The nearest land is to the west, the small most easterly islets of the Mangareva (Gambier) group, but winds (S.E. trade-wind) and currents are unfavourable for transport from W., and Easter Island appears to lie away from the cyclonic tracks. Beach drift is responsible for the arrival of several species, *Ipomaea Caesalpinia, Chenopodium Tetragonia Erythraea, Apium, Samolus Lycium* and perhaps some grasses and species of *Cyperus*, altogether about $^1/_4$ of the angiosperms. Storms bring light diaspores but it is noteworthy that *Compositae* are absent. I can find no special adaptations for bird carriage, but the possibility of rare cases of epizoic transport cannot be excluded. However that may be, Easter is a good example of an island peopled by "waifs and strays".

Affinities are, as we have seen, with Malaysia–Australia or pantropical, whereas the well marked east Polynesian flora has contributed nothing, not even its leading family Rubiaceae, rich in drupe-fruited forms. *Sophora toromiro* is allied to *S. "tetraptera"* of Raivavae and Rapa, I cannot tell if this is the true *tetraptera*, a native of New Zealand, but I do not think it is, and as BROWN's description (III 120) shows, it differs much from *toromiro*, which comes very close to *S. masafuerana*. Neither is of American ancestry, sect. *Edwardsia* is austral circumpolar and generally regarded to be of Antarctic origin or, at least, history.

With the exception of *Lycium carolinianum* var. *sandwicense* supposed to belong to the beach drift, there is, if *Fitchia* is definitely excluded, no American element in the flora of southeastern Polynesia, nor is it expected there. It is, as we have seen, found in Easter Island. Of the 3 endemic grasses, *Stipa* was tentatively brought to the palaeotropical element, *Axonopus* to the neotropical. *Danthonia* is an austral circumpolar tricentric genus. Three American, not endemic species *Cyperus eragrostis, Scirpus riparius* and *Polygonum acuminatum* remain to be accounted for.

If Easter Island once had a richer flora is an open question. According to newspaper reports a palynological survey of the swamp in the crater of Rano Kao was planned for HEYERDAHL's recent survey. The thickness of the loose, water soaked *Campylopus* peat was not measured by me, it is a somewhat dangerous quagmire which cannot be bored with the usual methods, but samples may be dug out from different depths and if pollen of species not growing on the island are found, some light will be thrown on the history of the flora.

The map accompanying this paper was prepared by the Oceanographical Institute in Goteborg. I am greatly indebted to the Director, Professor HANS PETTERSSON, and to Dr. BÖRJE KULLENBERG for valuable assistance.

May 1956.

Additions

P. 251

Usnea Gaudichaudii Motyka, known from the "espinal" of Central and North Chile is quoted for Juan Fernandez (Masatierra) by MOTYKA 344 600 as found by BERTERO 1830. As its occurrence there seems little probable—BERTERO collected also near Valparaiso, etc.—I have excluded the species from my list.

To Chapters IV and XVI

A recent paper by R. FURON, "Importance paléogéographique des mouvements de subsidence du Pacific Central" (Rev. gén. des Sciences 62, 1955), should be noted here. His object is expressed in the following terms:

> Constatant combien les biogéographes manquent de documentation geologique il nous a paru utile de regrouper les notions acquises au cours de ces dernières annees notions qui eclairent fort bien l'histoire du Pacifique depuis le Cretace p. 307

Whereas the Galapagos Islands show, he says, a purely oceanic type of rocks, andesitic basalt and tuff are found on Easter Island and andesite and trachyte on Pitcairn. Contrary to what was told above, corals of Cretaceous age were dredged in a depth of 2000 m on one of the Central Pacific guyots. The deep borings through atolls, the latest on Eniwetok in 1953, have penetrated through coral formations dating from Pleistocene to Eocene to the bedrock of basalt indicating a subsidence since the end of the Cretaceous of 2000 m. Perhaps other parts of the Pacific would give still greater figures.

To Chapter V

In the Proceedings of the Cottonwood Natur Field Club 31, 1955 T. A. SPRAGUE gives an account of the Drift Theory of DU TOIT and finds that, from a botanist's viewpoint this theory "offers the best explanation hitherto brought forward of the major problems of biogeography". With reference to the physical side of the drift process he quotes HOLMES' 'Principles of Physical Geography' (1944). In the case of Juan Fernandez which certainly is one of the *minor* problems, I cannot see that the drift theory offers an acceptable solution.

To Chapter VII, p. 360

An important paper by H. MOLHOLM HANSEN 'Life forms as age indicators", Ringkjobing 1956, confirms the opinions of SINNOTT & BAILEY and others

Bibliography

1. ABBAYES, H DES De speciebus generis lichenum Cladoniae ex Insulis Tristan da Cunha Results Norweg Exp to , no 4 1940
2. ADAMS, LE ROY The theory of isolation as applied to plants Science 22, 1905
3. AHLBERG, O Thysanoptera from Juan Fernandez and Easter Island Nat Hist Juan Fern III, 1922
4. ALEXANDER, C P Tipulidae (Diptera) (Insect J Fern 5) Rev Chil de Entomol 2, 1952
5. ANDREWES, H T Coleoptera Carabidae of the Juan Fernandez Islands Nat Hist Juan Fern III, 1931
6. ANDREWS, L C Origin of the Pacific Insular Floras Proceed 6th Pacif Sci Congr 1939, IV Berkeley 1940
7. —— The structure of the Pacific Basin Ibid VI
8. ARLDT, TH Die Entwickelung der Kontinente und ihrer Lebewelt Leipzig 1907 2d ed (vol I only), Berlin 1938
9. ARNELL, S List of Hepaticae collected in Marion Island by Mr R W Rand Svensk bot tidskr 47, 1953
10. —— Hepaticae of Chile and Argentina collected by R Santesson Ibid 49, 1955
11. AULT, J P Preliminary results of Ocean magnetic observations on the Carnegie October 1928 to January 1929 Terrestrial Magnetism and Atmospheric Electricity, March 1929
12. AURIVILLIUS, CHR Coleoptera Curculionidae von Juan Fernandez und der Oster Insel Nat Hist Juan Fern III, 1926
13. AURIVILLIUS, CHR, PROUT, L B & MEYRICK, E Lepidoptera von Juan Fernandez und der Oster-Insel Ibid 1922
14. AXELROD, D J Variables affecting the probabilities of dispersal Proceed of the Symposium on the South Atlantic Basin, 1949 Bull Amer Mus Nat Hist 99, 1952
15. —— A theory of Angiosperm evolution Evolution VI, 1952
16. BALFOUR-BROWNE, J Aquatic Coleoptera of Oceania Occ Pap B P Bishop Mus Honolulu XVIII 7, 1945
17. BARTRAM, F B Mosses of Chile and Argentina mainly collected by R Santesson Svensk bot tidskr 46, 1952
18. BECHYNE, J Alticidae (Coleoptera) (insect J Fern 11) Rev Chil de Entomol 2, 1952
19. BEIER, M Pseudoscorpione von Juan Fernandez Rev Chil de Entomol 4, 1955
20. BENTHAM, G Notes on the classification, history and geographical distribution of the Compositae Journ Linn Soc Bot 13, 1873
21. BERGROTH, E Hemiptera from Juan Fernandez and Easter Island Nat Hist Juan Fern III, 1924
22. BERLAND, L Araignées de l'île de Pâques et des îles Juan Fernandez Nat Hist Juan Fern III, 1924
23. —— Remarques sur la répartition et les affinités des Araignées du Pacifique Proceed 3d Pacif Sci Congr 1926 Tokyo 1928

24. BERLIOZ, J Quelques considerations entomologiques et conclusions sur le role biogeographique de la ligne de Wallace. Compte rendu Soc de Biogeogr 30ᵉ annee, no 258, 1953
25. BERNHAUER, M Coleoptera-Staphylinidae von den Juan Fernandez-Inseln und der Osterinsel Nat Hist Juan Fern III, 1921
26. BERRY, E W The origin and distribution of the family Myrtaceae Bot Gaz 59, 1915
27. —— The Flora of the Concepcion-Arauco coal measures of Chile Johns Hopkins Univ Stud, Geol 4 Baltimore 1922
28. —— Tertiary Flora from the Rio Pichileufu, Argentina Geol Soc of Amer Spec Pap No 12 Baltimore 1938
29. BERRY, E W & SINGEWALD, J J JR The tectonic history of Western South America Proceed 3d Pacif Sci Congr 1926 Tokyo 1928
30. BEWS, J W The World's Grasses London 1929
31. BITTER, G Die Gattung Acaena Bibl Botan 74, 1910–11
32. BOUL DE LESDAIN, M Lichens recueillis en 1930 dans les iles Kerguelen, Saint-Paul et Amsterdam Ann Crypt exot 4, 1931
33. BROTHERUS, V F Musci Insulae Paschalis Nat Hist Juan Fern II, 1924
34. —— The Musci of the Juan Fernandez Islands Ibid
35. BROWN, F B H Flora of Southeastern Polynesia I (1931), II (1931), III (1935) Bernice P Bishop Mus Bull 84, 89, 130 Honolulu
36. BRUCE, N Coleoptera-Cryptolagidae von Juan Fernandez Nat Hist Juan Ferr III, 1940
37. BRUES, C T A new species of parasitic Hymenoptera from Juan Fernandez Ibid 1924
38. BURTT, B L & HILL, A W The genera Gaultheria and Pernettya in New Zealand, Tasmania and Australia Linn Soc Journ Bot 49 611, 1935
39. BRYAN, F H JR A summary of the Hawaiian birds Proceed 6th Pacif Sci Congr 1939, IV Berkeley 1940
40. —— The Hawaiian Chain Honolulu 1954
41. BURGER, O Die Robinson-Insel Leipzig 1909
42. CAIN, S A Foundations of Plant Geography New York and London 1944
43. CAMP, W Distribution patterns of modern plants and the problems of ancient dispersals Ecol Monogr 17, 1947
44. CAMPBELL, D H The Derivation of the Flora of Hawaii Leland Stanford jr Univ Publ 1919
45. —— Australian element in the Hawaiian Flora Amer Journ of Bot 15, 1928
46. —— The Flora of the Hawaiian Islands Quarterly Rev Biol 8, 1933
47. —— Continental drift and plant distribution Science 95, 1942
48. CARDOT, J La Flore bryologique des Terres Magellaniques, de la Georgie du Sud et de l'Antarctide Wiss Ergebn schwed Sudpolar-Exp 1901–1903 IV 8, 1908
49. CARDOT, J & BROTHERUS, V F Les Mousses Bot Ergebn schwed Exp nach Patagonien und dem Feuerlande 1907–1909 K Sv Vet akad Handl 63 10, 1923
50. CARVALHO, J C M Miridae (Hemiptera) (Insect J Fern 3) Rev Chil de Entomol 2, 1952
51. Catalogue of Birds of the British Museum (Natural History) V (1881), XVI (1892)
52. CHAIGNEAU, J F Cordon submarino paralelo a las costas de Chile entre las islas Juan Fernandez y San Ambrosio Anuario hidrogr Marina de Chile 22, 1900
53. CHANEY, R W Tertiary centres and migration routes Ecol Monogr 17, 1947
54. CHEESEMAN, T F The vascular flora of Macquarie Island Scient Reports Australas Antarct Exp 1911–14, VII 1919
55. —— Manual of the New Zealand Flora 2d ed Wellington 1925
56. CHILTON, CH A small collection of Amphipoda from Juan Fernandez Nat Hist Juan Fern III 1921
57. CHINA, W L Homoptera-Cicadellidae Rev Chil de Entomol 4, 1955

58 CHOPARD, L Gryllides de Juan Fernandez et de l'île de l'âques Nat Hist Juan Fern III, 1924
59 CHRIST, H Geographie der Farne Jena 1910
60 CHRISTENSEN, C Demonstration of C Skottsberg's fern collection from Juan Fernandez Botan Tidsskr 37, 1920
61 —— The Pteridophytes of Tristan da Cunha Res Norweg Exp 1937–1938, no 6 Oslo 1940
62 CHRISTENSEN, C & SKOTTSBERG, C The Pteridophyta of the Juan Fernandez Islands Nat Hist Juan Fern II, 1920
63 —— The Ferns of Easter Island Ibid
64 CLAUSEN, R T A monograph of the Ophioglossaceae Mem Torrey Bot Club 10, 1938
65 Continental Drift A Symposium on the Theory of — The Advancement of Science VIII 29, 1951
66 COPELAND, E B Genera Hymenophyllacearum Philipp Journ Sci 67, 1938
67 —— Fern evolution in Antarctica Ibid 70, 1939
68 —— Antarctica as the source of existing ferns Proceed 6th Pacif Sci Congr 1939 IV Berkeley 1940
69 —— Genera Filicum Annal Crypt et Phytopath 5 Waltham, Mass 1947
70 CORTES, R Tachynidae (Diptera) (Insect J Fern 9) Rev Chil de Entomol 2, 1952
71 CROIZAT, L Manual of Phyto-Geography The Hague 1952
72 DAHL, E On different types of unglaciated areas during the ice ages and their significance to phytogeography New Phytologist 45, 1946
73 DARBISHIRE, O V The Lichens Wiss Ergebn schwed Sudpolar-Exp 1901–1903, IV 1 Stockholm 1912
74 DODGE, C W Lichens and Lichen Parasites Reports Brit Austral N Zeal Antarct Research Exp 1929–31 Ser B VII Adelaide 1948
75 DOMIN, K Monographische Ubersicht der Gattung Centella I Bot Jahrb fur System etc ed by A ENGLER, 41, 1908
76 —— Grundzuge der pflanzengeographischen Verbreitung und Gliederung der Lebermoose Mem Soc Roy de Sciences de Boheme 1923 Prague 1924
77 DU RIETZ, G E Two new species of Euphrasia from the Philippines and their phytogeographical significance Svensk bot tidskr 25, 1931
78 —— Problems of bipolar plant distribution Acta Phytogeogr Suec XIII, 1940
79 DUSEN, P Uber die tertiare Flora der Magellanslander Wiss Ergebn schwed Exp 1895–1897, I, 1907
80 —— Uber die tertiare Flora der Seymour-Insel Wiss Ergebn schwed Sudpolar-Exp 1901–1903, III, 1910
81 DU TOIT, L Our Wandering Continents Edinburgh and London 1937
82 —— Observations on the evolution of the Pacific Ocean Proceed 6th Pacif Sci Congr 1939, 1 Berkeley 1940
83 EMERSON, E A A new Termite from the Juan Fernandez Islands Nat Hist Juan Fern III, 1924
84 ENDERLEIN, G Die Dipterenfauna der Juan Fernandez-Inseln und der Oster-Insel Ibid 1938
85 ENGLER, A Versuch einer Entwickelungsgeschichte der Pflanzenwelt seit der Tertiarperiode II 1882
86 ENGLERT, S La Tierra de Hotu Matua Valparaiso 1948
87 EPLING, C Synopsis of the South American Labiatae Fedde, Repert Beih 85, 1935
88 —— The Labiatae of Chile Rev Universitaria 22, 1937
89 —— The distribution of the American Labiatae Proceed 6th Pacif Sci Congr 1939, IV Berkeley 1940
90 —— Distribución geográfica y parentesco de las Labiadas de la America del Sur Rev Universitaria 25, 1940

91 ERMIL, A Eine Reise nach der Robinson Insel Hamburg 1889
92 ESBEN-PETERSEN, P More Neuroptera from Juan Fernandez and Easter Island Nat Hist Juan Fern III, 1924
93 EVANS, A W The Thallose Hepaticae of the Juan Fernandez Islands Ibid II, 1930
94 FASSETT, N C Callitriche in the New World Rhodora 53, 1951
95 FLORIN, R The Tertiary fossil conifers of South Chile and their phytogeographical significance K Sv Vet akad Handl ser 3, 19, 1940
96 FLUKE, C L Syrphidae (Insect J Fern 18) Rev Chil de Entomol 4, 1955
97 FOSBERG, F R Derivation of the Flora of the Hawaiian Islands See ZIMMERMAN, E C
98 —— Lignes biogéographiques dans l'ouest du Pacifique Compte rendu Soc de Biogéogr 29 annee, no 256, 1952
99 —— The American element in the Hawaiian Flora Proceed 7th Intern Botan Congr 1950 Stockholm 1953
100 FREEMAN, P Mycetophilidae, Sciaridae, Cecidomyidae and Scatopsidae (Insect J Fern 13) Rev Chil de Entomol 3, 1953
101 FRIES, R E Die Myxomyceten der Juan Fernandez-Inseln Nat Hist Juan Fern II, 1920
102 FRIES, TH JR Die Gasteromyceten der Juan Fernandez und Osterinseln Ibid 1922
103 FULFORD, M Some distribution patterns of South American Leafy Hepaticae Proceed 7th Intern Botan Congr 1950 Stockholm 1953
104 GEBIEN, H Coleoptera-Tenebrionidae von Juan Fernandez Nat Hist Juan Fern III, 1921
105 GERMAIN, L L'origine et l'evolution de la faune de Hawaii Proceed 3d Pacif Sci Congr 1926 Tokyo 1928
106 GIBBS, L Notes on Phytogeography and Flora of the mountain summit plateau of Tasmania Journ of Ecology 8, 1920
107 GILIOGLY, L R Coleoptera-Nitidulidae (Insect J Fern 24) Rev Chil de Entomol 4, 1955
108 GOOD, R See Continental Drift
109 —— The Geography of the Flowering Plants 2d ed London 1953
110 GOODALL, J D, JOHNSON, A W, PHILIPPI, R A Las Aves de Chile I, 1946 II, 1951 Buenos Aires
111 GOODSPEED, T H Plant Hunters in the Andes New York 1941
112 —— The genus Nicotiana Waltham, Mass 1954
113 GORDON, H D The problem of sub-antarctic plant distribution Report Austral and New Zeal Ass Advancem Sci 27, 1949
114 GRANT, ADELE L A monograph of the genus Mimulus Ann Miss Botan Gard XI, 1924
115 GREGORY, H E Types of Pacific Islands Proceed 3d Pacif Sci Congr 1926, 2 Tokyo 1928
116 GREGORY, J W Theories of the origin of the Pacific Proceed Geol Soc London 86, 1930
117 GUIGNOT, F Dytiscidae (Coleoptera) (Insect J Fern 10) Rev Chil de Entomol 2, 1952
118 GUILLAUMIN, A Les regions floristiques du Pacific d'apres leur endemisme et la répartition de quelques plantes phanerogames Proceed 3d Pacif Sci Congr 1926 Tokyo 1928
119 GULICK, A Biological peculiarities of oceanic islands Quart Review Biol 7, 1932
120 GUNDERSEN, A Families of Dicotyledons Waltham, Mass 1950
121 GUPPY, H B Observations of a naturalist in the Pacific between 1896 and 1899 II London 1906
122 —— The island and the continent Journ of Ecol 7, 1919

123 GUTENBERG, B Geophysical and geological observations in the Pacific area and tectonic hypotheses Proceed 7th Pacif Sci Congr 1949, II Wellington 1953
124 GOETSCH, W Die Robinson-Insel Juan Fernandez und ihre biogeographischen Probleme Phoenix 19, 1933
125 HANDSCHIN, C Neuroptera (Insect J Fern 15) Rev Chil de Entomol 4, 1955
126 HARMSTON F C Dolichopodidae (Insect J Fern 17) Ibid
127 HEMSLEY, W B (a) Report on the Present State of Knowledge of Various Insular Floras (b) Report on the Botany of Juan Fernandez and Masafuera Rep Sci Res H M S Challenger Bot I, 1885
128 HENNIG, W Phryneidae, Helomyzidae, Lonchaeidae, Piophilidae, Anthomyzidae, Muscidae (Insect J Fern 16) Rev Chil de Entomol 4, 1955
129 HERZOG, TH Geographie der Moose Jena 1926
130 —— Die foliosen Lebermoose der Juan Fernandez-Inseln und der Oster-Insel Nat Hist Juan Fern II, 1942
131 —— Zur Bryophytenflora Chiles Revue Bryol et Lichenol XXIII, 1954
132 HESS, H H Drowned ancient islands of the Pacific Amer Journ Sci 244, 1946
133 HICKEN, C M Polypodiacearum argentinarum catalogus Rev Mus de La Plata 15, 1908
134 HILL, A W Antarctica and problems of geographical distribution Proceed 5th Intern Bot Congr 1926 Ithaca 1929
135 HINTON, H E See Continental Drift
136 HODGSON, E AMY & SAINSBURY, G O K Bryophytes collected by G E Du Rietz on the Antipodes Islands Svensk bot tidskr 42, 1948
137 HOLTEDAHL, O On the geology and physiography of some Antarctic and Sub-Antarctic islands Scient Res Norweg Antarct Exp No 3 Ed by Det norske videnskapsakademi Oslo 1929
138 HOOKER, J D Lecture on Insular Floras before the British Association at Nottingham, 1866 Also in Gard Chronicle, Jan 1867
139 HUE, A M Lichens Deuxieme Exped Antarct Française 1908–1910 Paris 1915
140 HUTCHINSON, J The Families of Flowering Plants I 1926 II 1934
141 HUXLEY, J Species formation and geographical isolation Proceed Linnean Soc Lond 1938
142 INSECTOS Los Insectos de las Islas Juan Fernandez Ed by Dr G Kuschel 1–12 Rev Chil de Entomol 2, 1951 — 13, 14, vol 3, 1953 — 15–27, vol 4, 1955
143 IRMSCHER, E Pflanzenverbreitung und Entwickelung der Kontinente I–II Mitteil Hamburg Inst allgem Botan 5, 1922 8, 1929
144 JEFFREY, E C & TORREY, R S Transitional Herbaceous Dicotyledons Annals of Botany 35, 1921
145 JEFFREYS, H See Continental Drift
146 JHERING, H Das neotropische Florengebiet und seine Geschichte Bot Jahrb fur System etc ed by A ENGLER 17, 1893, Beibl 42
147 JOHANSSON, L Ein neuer Landblutegel aus den Juan Fernandez-Inseln Nat Hist Juan Fern III, 1924
148 JOHNSTON, I M A revision of the South American Boraginoideae Contrib Gray Herb 78, 1927
149 —— Papers on the Flora of Northern Chile 1 The coastal Flora of the Departments of Chañaral and Taltal Ibid 85, 1929
150 JOHOW, F Estudios sobre la Flora de las Islas de Juan Fernandez Santiago 1896
151 JORDAN, D S The origin of species through isolation Science 22, 1905
152 —— Isolation with segregation as a factor in organic evolution Annual Rep Smithson Inst 1925 Washington 1926
153 JORDAN, K Coleoptera Anthribidae from Juan Fernandez Nat Hist Juan Fern III, 1931
154 JOYCE, J R T See Continental Drift

155 JUST, TH Geology and Plant Distribution Ecol Monogr 17, 1947
156 KAUSEL, E Contribución al Estudio de las Mirtáceas Chilenas I-II Rev Argent de Agron 9, 1942
157 ——— Notas Mirtológicas Lilloa 13, 1947
158 ——— Revisión del genero Escallonia Darwiniana 10, 1953
159 KEISSLER, K Ascomyceten, Fungi imperfecti und Uredineen von Juan Fernandez Nat Hist Juan Fern II, 1928
160 ——— Nachtrag zur Pilzflora von Juan Fernandez Ibid
161 KORMILEV, N A Tygicidae (Hemiptera) (Insect J Fern 1) Rev Chil de Entomol 2, 1952
162 KRAUSE, K Uber einen hapaxanthen Baum Mitteil deutsch dendrol Ges 1921
163 KRAUSEL, R Pflanzenwanderungen im Tertiar Proceed 7th Intern Botan Congr 1950 Stockholm 1953
164 KUKENTHAL, G Vorarbeiten zu einer Monographie der Rhynchosporoideae VIII Fedde, Repert 48, 1940 — XII Ibid 51, 1942
165 LAWRENCE, G H M Taxonomy of Vascular Plants New York 1951
166 LESNE, P Coleoptera-Bostrychidae et Cioidae de Juan Fernandez Nat Hist Juan Fern III, 1923
167 LINDSAY, A Biology and biogeography of the Antarctic and Subantarctic Pacific Proceed 6th Pacif Sci Congr 1939, II Berkeley 1940
168 LOOSER, G Nueva localidad cerca de Antofagasta del Helecho Polypodium Masafuerae Philippi Rev Universit 28 Santiago 1943
169 ——— Los Blechnum (Filices) de Chile Ibid 32, 1947
170 ——— Comparación de las Bromeliaceas de Chile con las de Argentina y Perú Rev Chil de Hist y Geogr n 110 (1947), 1948
171 ——— El genero Polypodium L y sus representantes en Chile Rev Universit 36 Santiago 1951
172 LOPEZ, J E Esploracion de las Islas esporadicas al occidente de la costa de Chile Anuario Hidrográf de la Marina de Chile II 1876
173 LOURTEIG, Alicia Ranunculaceas de Sudamerica templada Darwiniana 9, 1952
174 LONNBERG, E The Birds of the Juan Fernandez Islands Nat Hist Juan Fern III, 1920
175 ——— Notes on Birds from Easter Island Ibid 1921
176 MACKENZIE LAMB, I A monograph of the Lichen genus Placopsis Nyl Lilloa 13, 1947
177 MASSEE, G Lichenes The Subantarctic Islands of New Zealand Wellington 1909
178 MATTFELD, J Compositae Nova Guinea 14 4 Leiden 1932
179 MAYR, E The origin and history of the Bird Fauna of Polynesia Proceed 6th Pacif Sci Congr 1929 IV Berkeley 1940
180 METRAUX, A Ethnology of Easter Island Bull Bishop Mus Honolulu 1940
181 MICHAELSEN, W Oligochaeten von Juan Fernandez und der Oster-Insel Nat Hist Juan Fern III, 1921
182 MONTAGNE, C Liquenes, in GAY, Hist fis y polit de Chile Botánica 8 Paris 1852
183 MUMFORD, E P The present status of studies of faunal distribution with reference to Oceanic Islands Proceed 6th Pacif Sci Congr 1939, IV Berkeley 1940
184 MULLER, J Lichens Miss Scient du Cap Horn 1882-83 V Paris 1889
185 NAVÁS, L Neuropteres des Iles Juan Fernandez et de l'Ile de Pâques Nat Hist Juan Fern III, 1921
186 NILSSON, H Syntetische Artbildung Lund 1953
187 NIXON, G E J Hymenoptera-Braconidae (Insect J Fern 26) Rev Chil de Entomol 4, 1955
188 NYBELIN, O Nesophilaemon n g fur Philaemon skottsbergi I Johansson Zool Anzeiger 142, 1943

189 ODHNER, N HJ Mollusca from Juan Fernandez and Easter Island Nat Hist Juan Fern III, 1922 Addenda, ibid 1926
190 OGLOBIN, A Mymaridae (Hymenoptera) (Insect J Fern 12) Rev Chil de Entomol 2, 1952
191 —— Bethylidae v Dryinidae (Hymenoptera) (Insect J Fern 14) Ibid 3, 1953
192 OLIVER, W R B The genus Coprosma Bull Bishop Mus Honolulu 132, 1935
193 PERKINS, R C T Introduction, being a review of the land-fauna of Hawaii Fauna Hawaiiensis I Cambridge 1913
194 PFEIFFER, H Oreobolus R Br, eine merkwurdige Cyperaceengattung Fedde, Repert 23, 1927
195 PIC, M Coleoptera Anobiida de Juan Fernandez Nat Hist Juan Fern III, 1924
196 —— Coleoptera-Clavicornia et autres de Juan Fernandez Ibid
197 PILGER, R Uber einige Gramineae der Skottsbergschen Sammlung von Juan Fernandez Fedde, Repert 16, 1920
198 ——, Das System der Gramineae unter Ausschluss der Bambusoideae Bot Jahrb fur System etc ed by A ENGLER, 76, 1954
199 PLATE, L Zur Kenntnis der Insel Juan Fernandez Verhandl Ges fur Erdkunde Berlin XXIII, 1896
200 POPE, R D Coleoptera-Colydiidae (Insect J Fern 25) Rev Chil de Entomol 4, 1955
201 PRINCIS, K Uber einige neue bzw wenig bekannte Blattarien Arkiv f Zool 41, 1948
202 RAMBO, B Historia da flora do planalto riograndense Anais Bot Barbosa Rodriguez V, 1953
203 REICHE, K Grundzuge der Pflanzenverbreitung in Chile ENGLER & DRUDE, Vegetation der Erde 7 Leipzig 1907
204 RICHARDS, O W Sphaeroceridae (Insect J Fern 21) Rev Chil de Entomol 4, 1955
205 RIDLEY, H N The Dispersal of Plants throughout the World London 1930
206 ROMAN, A Ichneumoniden von Juan Fernandez Nat Hist Juan Fern III, 1924
207 ROMELL, L Basidiomycetes from Juan Fernandez Ibid II, 1928
208 SABROSKY, C W A new species of Ogcodes from the Juan Fernandez islands Rev Chil de Entomol 1, 1951
209 —— Chloropidae (Insect J Fern 19) Ibid 4, 1955
210 SAINSBURY, G O K A Handbook of the New Zealand Mosses Bull Roy Soc of N Zeal no 5, 1955
211 SANTIS, L DE Hymenoptera-Eulophidae, Entedontidae (Chalcidoidea I) (Insect J Fern 27) Rev Chil de Entomol 4, 1955
212 SATCHELL, G H Psychodidae (Diptera) (Insect J Fern 8) Rev Chil de Entomol 2, 1952
213 SCHENKLING, S Coleoptera Cleridae von Juan Fernandez Nat Hist Juan Fern III, 1931
214 SCHMID, F Trichoptera (Insect J Fern 4) Rev Chil de Entomol 2, 1952
215 SCHMIDT, A Coleoptera-Scarabaeidae von Juan Fernandez Nat Hist Juan Fern III, 1931
216 SCHOTT, H Collembola aus den Juan Fernandez Inseln und der Osterinsel Nat Hist Juan Fern III, 1921
217 SELCHELL, W A Les migrations des oiseaux et la dissemination des plantes Compte-rendu sommaire Soc de Biogeogr 22, 1926
218 —— Migration and endemism with reference to Pacific Insular floras Proceed 3d Pacif Sci Congr 1926 Tokyo 1928
219 —— Pacific Insular floras and Pacific paleogeography Amer Naturalist 69, 1935
220 SEWARD, A C A study in contrasts The present and past distribution of certain ferns Linn Soc Journ of Bot 46, 1922

221 SEWARD, A C & CONWAY, VERONA A phytogeographical problem fossil plants from the Kerguelen Archipelago Ann of Bot 48, 1934
222 SILVESTRI, F Thysanura and Embioptera Nat Hist Juan Fern III, 1924
223 SIMPSON, G G Antarctica as a faunal migration route Proceed 6th Pacif Sci Congr 1939 Berkeley 1940
224 SINNOTT, E W & BAILEY, I W The origin and dispersal of Herbaceous Angiosperms Ann of Bot 28, 1914
225 SJOSTEDT, Y Odonata Orthoptera Nat Hist Juan Fern III, 1924
226 SKOTTSBERG, C Die Gefasspflanzen Sudgeorgiens Wiss Ergebn Schwed Sudpolar-Exp IV Stockholm 1905
227 —— Studien uber die Vegetation der Juan Fernandez Inseln K Sv Vet-akad Handl 51, 1914
228 —— Notes on the relations between the floras of Subantarctic America and New Zealand Plant World 18, 1915
229 —— The Phanerogams of the Juan Fernandez Islands Nat Hist Juan Fern II, 1922
230 —— The Phanerogams of Easter Island Ibid
231 —— Juan Fernandez and Hawaii A phytogeographical discussion Bull Bishop Mus 16 Honolulu 1925
232 —— Einige Bemerkungen uber die alpinen Gefasspflanzen von Masafuera Veroff Geobot Inst Rubel 3 Zurich 1925
233 —— Einige Pflanzen von der Oster Insel Acta Horti Gotob 3, 1927
234 —— Remarks on the relative independency of Pacific Floras Proceed 3d Pacif Sci Congr 1926 Tokyo 1928
235 —— Pollinationsbiologie und Samenverbreitung auf den Juan Fernandez-Inseln Nat Hist Juan Fern II, 1928
236 —— The geographical distribution of the sandalwoods and its significance Proceed 4th Pacif Sci Congr 1929 III Batavia 1930
237 —— Notes on some recent collections made in the Island of Juan Fernandez Acta Horti Gotob 4, 1929
238 —— Marine algal Communities of the Juan Fernandez Islands Nat Hist Juan Fern II, 1941
239 —— Le peuplement des iles pacifiques du Chili Soc de Biogeogr IV, 1934
240 —— Greigia Berteroi Skottsb and its systematic position Acta Horti Gotob 11, 1936
241 —— Die Flora der Desventuradas-Inseln Goteb K Vet o Vitterh Samh Handl 5 e foljden, ser B, bd 5 6, 1937
242 —— Geographical isolation as a factor in species formation Proceed Linn Soc of Lond, Sess 150, 1938
243 —— On Mr C Bock's collection of plants from Masatierra (Juan Fernandez) with remarks on the flower of Centaurodendron Acta Horti Gotob 12, 1938
244 —— Hawaiian Vascular Plants Ibid 15, 1944
245 —— Peperomia berteroana Miq and P tristanensis Christoph, an interesting case of disjunction Ibid 16, 1947
246 —— Eine kleine Pflanzensammlung von San Ambrosio Ibid 17, 1947
247 —— The genus Peperomia in Chile Ibid
248 —— Biogeografiska Stillahavsproblem Statens naturv forskn -råd, årsbok 4 (1949-50) Stockholm 1951
249 —— A supplement to the Pteridophytes and Phanerogams of Juan Fernandez and Easter Island Nat Hist Juan Fern II, 1951
250 —— On the supposed occurrence of Blechnum longicauda C Chr in Brazil Svensk bot tidskr 48, 1954
251 —— The Vegetation of the Juan Fernandez Islands Nat Hist Juan Fern II, 1953

252 SLEUMER, H Revision der Gattung Pernettya Notizbl Botan Gartens Berlin 12, 1935
253 SMITH, A C Taxonomic notes on the old world species of Winteraceae Journ Arnold Arbor 24, 1943
254 —— The American species of Drimys Ibid
255 SOUZA LOPES, H & ALBUQUERQUE, D Calliphoridae, Sarcophagidae (Insect J Fern 22) Rev Chil de Entomol 4, 1955
256 SPARRE, B Review of CROIZAT, Manual of Phytogeography Rev Universitaria 38, 1953
257 STEBBINS, G L JR Additional evidence for a holarctic dispersal of flowering plants in the Mesozoic era Proceed 6th Pacif Sci Congr 1939, IV Berkeley 1941
258 STEENIS, C G G J VAN On the origin of the Malaysian mountain flora Bull Jard bot Buitenzorg, Ser 3, 13–14, 1935–36
259 STOCKWELL, P A revision of the genus Stenactis Contrib Dudley Herbar 1940
260 STRANEO, S L & JEANNEL, R Coleoptera-Carabidae (Insect J Fern 23) Rev Chil de Entomol 4, 1955
261 SVENSON, H Monographic studies in the genus Eleocharis V Rhodora 41, 1939
262 SWEZEY, O H Distribution of Lepidoptera in Pacific Island Groups Proceed 6th Pacif Sci Congr 1939, IV Berkeley 1940
263 TAYLOR, W B An example of long distance dispersal Ecology 35, 1954
264 THERIOT, J Mousses recoltees dans l'ile Mas a Tierra (Juan Fernandez) en 1927, par M Gualterio Looser Rev Chil de Hist Nat 31, 1927
265 —— Mousses de l'Ile de Pâques Revue bryol et lichenol Ser II 10, 1937
266 THOMPSON, G B Anoplura from Juan Fernandez Nat Hist Juan Fern III 1940
267 TONNOIR, A L Australian Mycetophilidae Proceed Linn Soc N S Wales 54, 1929
268 TRAGARDH, I Acarina from the Juan Fernandez Islands Nat Hist Juan Fern III, 1931
269 TURMEL, J M Répartition geographique des Eryngium II Bull Mus Nat d'Hist Nat Paris 1949
270 TUYAMA, T On Santalum boninense and the distribution of the species of Santalum Journ Japan Bot 15, 1939
271 —— On genus Haloragis and Micronesian species Ibid 16, 1940
272 UMBGROVE, J H T See Continental Drift
273 USINGER, R L Distribution of the Heteroptera from Oceania Proceed 6th Pacif Sci Congr 1939, IV Berkeley 1940
274 VERHOEFF, K Uber Myriapoden von Juan Fernandez und der Osterinsel Nat Hist Juan Fern III, 1924
275 VIDAL GORMAZ, F Geografia nautica de la Republica de Chile Anuario Hidrograf de la Marina de Chile 7, 1881
276 VIERHAPPER, F Uber echten und falschen Vikarismus Osterr botan Zeitschr 68, 1919
277 WAHRBERG, R Einige terrestre Isopoden von den Juan Fernandez-Inseln Nat Hist Juan Fern III, 1922
278 WALLACE, A R Island Life London 1880 3d ed 1911
279 WELLS, F G Paleogeography of South America Bull Geol Soc of Amer 59, 1948
280 WEGENER, A Die Entstehung der Kontinente und Ozeane Braunschweig 3d ed 1922, 5th ed 1936
281 WEIMARCK, H Studies in Juncaceae with special reference to the species in Ethiopia and the Cape Svensk bot tidskr 40, 1946
282 WEISE, J Coleoptera Chrysomelidae and Coccinellidae von Juan Fernandez Nat Hist Juan Fern III, 1924
283 WHEELER, W M Formicidae from Easter Island and Juan Fernandez Ibid

284 WILLIS, B Geotectonics of the Pacific Proceed 3d Pacif Sci Congr 1926 Tokyo 1928
285 WILLIS, J C Endemic genera of plants in their relation to others Annals of Bot 35, 1921
286 —— Age and Area A Study in the Origin and Distribution of Plants 1922
287 WINKLER, H Geographie, in Manual of Pteridology, ed by F Verdoorn The Hague 1938
288 WIRTH, W W Heleidae and Tendipedidae (Insect J Fern 7) Rev Chil de Entomol 2, 1952
289 —— Ephydridae (Insect J Fern 20) Rev Chil de Entomol 4, 1955
290 WOOLDRIDGE See Continental Drift
291 WULFF, L V An Introduction to Historical Plant Geography Waltham, Mass 1943
292 WYGODZINSKY, P Contribución al conocimiento del genero *Metapterus* Costa de las Americas y de Juan Fernandez Rev Chil de Entomol 1, 1951
293 —— Thysanura from Juan Fernandez Island Ibid
294 —— Simulidae (Diptera) (Insect J Fern 6) Rev Chil de Entomol 2, 1952
295 ZAHLBRUCKNER, A Die Flechten Bot Figebn schwed Exped nach Patagonien und dem Feuerlande VI K Sv Vet akad Handl 57 6 1917
296 —— Die Flechten der Juan Fernandez Inseln Nat Hist Juan Fern II, 1924
297 —— Die Flechten der Osterinsel, nebst einem Nachtrag zur Flechtenflora von Juan Fernandez Ibid 1926
298 ZIMMERMAN, F C Insects of Hawaii I Introduction Honolulu 1948
299 ZIMMERMANN, A Coleoptera-Dytiscidae von Juan Fernandez und der Osterinsel Nat Hist Juan Fern III, 1924
300 BRYAN, W A in "El Mercurio", Valparaiso, Apr 23, 1920
301 GOURLAY, W B in "The South Pacific Mail", Valparaiso, Feb 2, 1928
302 QUENSEL, P Die Geologie der Juan Fernandez-Inseln Bull Geol Inst Upsala 11, 1913
303 BRANCHI, F C La Isla de Robinson Valparaiso 1922
304 HAYEK, A Allgemeine Pflanzengeographie Berlin 1926
305 DRUDE, O Handbuch der Pflanzengeographie Stuttgart 1890
306 MERRILL, E D The Botany of Cook's Voyages Chronica Botanica 14 5/6 Waltham, Mass 1954
307 HILLEBRAND, W The Flora of the Hawaiian Islands Heidelberg 1888
308 FLEUTIAUX, L Coleoptera-Serricornia de Juan Fernandez et de l'Ile de Pâques Nat Hist Juan Fern III, 1924
309 SCHEDL, K E Chilenische Borkenkafer Rev Chil de Entomol 4, 1955
310 WYGODZINSKY, P Reduviidae y Cimicidae (Hemiptera) (Insect J Fern 2) Rev Chil de Entomol 2, 1952
311 ARWIDSSON, TH Einige parasitische Pilze aus Juan Fernandez und der Osterinsel Svensk bot tidskr 34, 1940
312 HALLE, T G A fossil fertile *Lygodium* from the Tertiary of South Chile Ibid
313 MALTA, N Die Gattung Zygodon Hook et Tayl Latv Univ Botan Dārza Darbi n 1 Riga 1926
314 FENNAH, R G Homoptera-Delphacidae Proceed Entomol Soc of London, Ser B 24, 1955
315 BERRY, E W Fossil plants from Chubut Territory collected by the Scarritt Patagonian Expedition Amer Mus Novit 536, 1932
316 BRINCK, P Coleoptera of Tristan da Cunha Results Norweg Scient Exped 1937–38 no 17 Oslo 1948
317 WIRTH, E Die Vegetation der subantarktischen Inseln Kerguelen, Possession und Heard-Eiland II Deutsche Sudpolar-Exped 1901–02 Bd VIII 1911
318 SKOTTSBERG, C The Flora of the Hawaiian Islands and the History of the Pacific Basin Proceed 6th Pacif Sci Congr 1939, IV Berkeley 1940

319 STEBBINS, G L Jr Variation and Evolution in Plants New York 1950
320 LINDBERG, H De bortglömda öarna Helsingfors 1955
321 GIBBS, LILIAN A Contribution to the Montane Flora of Fiji Journ Linn Soc Bot 39, 1909
322 VISHER, S S Tropical cyclones of the Pacific Bernice P Bishop Mus Bull 20, 1925
323 —— Tropical cyclones and the dispersal of life from island to island in the Pacific Amer Naturalist 59, 1925
324 BERGERON, T The problem of tropical hurricanes Journ R Meteor Soc 80 344 1950
325 GRISEBACH, A Die Vegetation der Erde 2d ed Leipzig I, 1872, II 1884
326 SKOTTSBERG, C On Scirpus nodosus Rottb Acta Soc pro Fauna et Flora Fenn 72, 1956
327 SANTESSON, R The South American Cladinae Arkiv for Bot 30, 1942
328 —— The South American Menegazziae Ibid
329 —— Contributions to the Lichen Flora of South America Ibid 31, 1944
330 JOHOW, F Ueber die Resultate der Expedition nach den Islas Desventuradas (San Ambrosio und San Felix) Verhandl d deutsch wissensch Vereins zu Santiago III Valparaiso 1898
331 BRÜGGEN, J Fundamentos de la Geologia de Chile Santiago 1950
332 MARTIN, C Landeskunde von Chile Hamburg 1909
333 STEPHANI F Bot Ergebn schwed Exped nach Patagonien und dem Feuerlande 2 Die Lebermoose K Sv Vet akad Handl 46, 1911
334 BERRY, E W Tertiary fossil plants from the Argentine Republic Proceed U S Nation Mus 73, 1928
335 —— A Miocene flora from Patagonia Johns Hopkins Univ Stud, Geol no 6, 1925 Not seen, only a preliminary notice in Proceed Nat Acad of Sci 11 7, 1925
336 FRENGUELLI, J Recientes progresos en el conocimiento de la geología y paleogeografía de Patagonia Rev Mus de Eva Perón (La Plata), N S IV, Geol, 1953
337 —— La Flora fósil de la región del alto Río Chalia en Santa Cruz (Argentina) Notas del Mus de Eva Perón (La Plata) XVI 98, 1953
338 FLORIN, R Die heutige und frühere Verbreitung der Gattung Acmopyle Pilger Svensk bot tidskr 34, 1940
339 HOOKER, J D Observations on the Botany of Kerguelen Island Philos Trans Roy Soc of London 168, 1879
340 SKOTTSBERG, C Antarctic Plants in Polynesia Essays in Geobotany in honor of W A Setchell Berkeley 1936
341 —— Plant succession on recent lava flows in the island of Hawaii Goteb K Vet o Vitterh Samh Handl, 6 e följden, ser B, bd 1 8, 1941
342 —— The Vegetation of Easter Island Nat Hist Juan Fern II, 1927
343 COOKE, G H Te pito te henua, known as Rapa Nui Rep Smithson Inst 1897 Rep U S National Mus Part I Washington 1899
344 MOTYKA, J Lichenum generis Usnea studium monographicum Lwów 1938
345 BRIGHAM, W T An index to the islands of the Pacific ocean Mem Bishop Museum Vol I 2 Honolulu 1900
346 FORSTER, G Florulae insularum australium Prodromus Goettingen 1776
347 —— A Voyage round the world commanded by Capt James Cook 1772, 3, 4 and 5 Vol I London 1777
348 —— De plantis esculentis insularum oceani australis Commentatio botanica Berlin 1786

Contents

Part 1 The Juan Fernandez Islands

Chapter I Composition, distribution and relationships of the Flora	193
Chapter II Sources of the island flora as judged by the total distribution of the geographical elements, with special reference to the composition of the Chilean flora	256
Chapter III Composition, distribution and relationships of the Fauna	292
Chapter IV Continental and Oceanic islands	317
Chapter V The Pacific Ocean and Continental Drift	325
Chapter VI Transoceanic migration	331
Chapter VII Biological characteristics of isolated islands	351
Chapter VIII Evolution in Oceanic islands	363
Chapter IX Juan Fernandez—oceanic or continental?	372
Chapter X The Chilean coast line and the history of the Andes	380
Chapter XI The Tertiary floras of Chile and Patagonia	386
Chapter XII Antarctica as a source of the present circumpolar floras	389
Chapter XIII The history of Juan Fernandez—a tentative sketch	394

Part 2 Easter Island

Chapter XIV Composition, distribution and relationships of the Flora	406
Chapter XV Composition, distribution and relationships of the Fauna	417
Chapter XVI The biogeographical history of Easter Island	421
Bibliography	428

Printed October 26th 1956

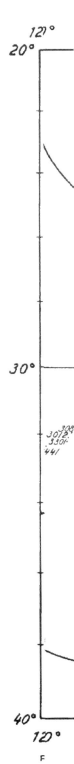

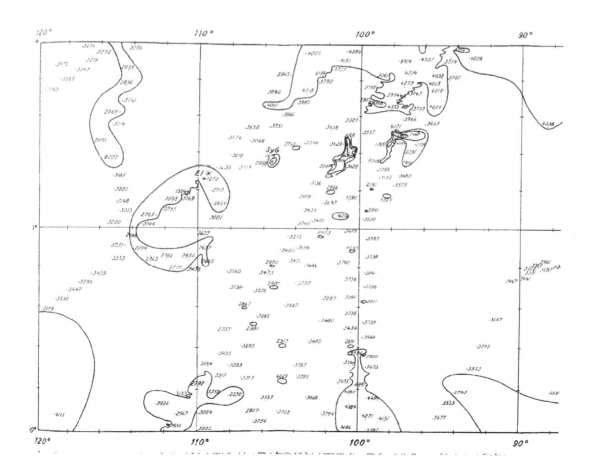

CPSIA information can be obtained at www.ICGtesting.com
Printed in the USA
LVOW01s0507260214

375208LV00006B/113/P